THE SOCIOLOGY OF KNOWLEDGE

The Sociology of Knowledge

A READER

EDITED BY
James E. Curtis and John W. Petras

PRAEGER PUBLISHERS

NEW YORK · WASHINGTON

BOOKS THAT MATTER

Published in the United States of America in 1970
by Praeger Publishers, Inc.
111 Fourth Avenue, New York, N.Y. 10003

Library of Congress Catalog Card Number: 69–12714

Printed in Great Britain

CONTENTS

PART THREE: THE SOCIOCULTURAL ENVIRONMENT AND IDEAS

PART FOUR: THE SOCIOLOGY OF KNOWLEDGE AND SOCIOLOGY

PART FIVE: CRITICISMS AND PROBLEMS

ACKNOWLEDGMENTS

WE SHOULD LIKE to express our appreciation to the following individuals for their critical reading of an early draft of the Introduction: James H. Barnett, University of Connecticut; Arthur Child, University of California at Davis; Lewis Coser, State University of New York at Stony Brook; Bernard N. Meltzer, Central Michigan University; and Joseph Zygmunt, University of Connecticut. We also wish to thank John Staude, of Washington University, and Kurt H. Wolff, of Brandeis University, for their suggestions regarding the content of this volume. Finally, we should like to thank Sharon Doleys for her valuable assistance in typing the manuscript.

INTRODUCTION

IN A SENSE, the sociology of knowledge in the field of sociology is analogous to the concept of attitude in social psychology. Although each concept occupies a central position in its respective field, both suffer from the lack of precise definition. This problem is not uncommon for concepts in these areas, but very few concepts have achieved such popularity in sociology.[1] Kurt H. Wolff, among others, has noted that the problem of definition has resulted in large part from the literal translation of the term *Wissenssoziologie* as "sociology of knowledge."[2] The effect of this translation has been to narrow the range of problems originally believed to be encompassed by the concept. Some of the studies included in this volume may seem to fall outside the traditional sociology of knowledge perspective. Our intent is to present representative studies within what we consider to be the major categories of interest, employing as our framework a broad conception of the sociology of knowledge. Thus, we have treated the sociology of knowledge as a particular frame of reference utilized with some consistency by sociologists. We have not treated it as a definite body of theory in its own right.

The sociology of knowledge has been restricted not only by the traditionally narrow approach but also by a concentration on the role of the social order in determining the mental perspectives of individual members. In fact, the formalization of this focus in the works of the German philosopher-sociologist Max Scheler was based on the *relationship* between the mind and the sociocultural environment. Becker and Dahlke have noted that Scheler, in contrast to contemporary writers, did not assign priority to either variable.[3] The popular conception of the sociology of knowledge as representing a one-sided determinism has been fostered through the close association of this field with such individuals as Mannheim and Durkheim. Indeed, most of the empirical studies in the area give evidence in support of this view.[4] The principal trend in the sociology of knowledge, especially within American sociology, however, has been toward emphasizing the functional relationship between the individual mind and the environment.[5]

There has also been a notable shift away from the concept of the group as a general membership category toward specifying those aspects of the particular group that have been most important in influencing the thoughts and ideas of social categories or individuals. The general trend of research in the sociology of knowledge has been toward specification of the forces involved in the functional relationship between the group and the individual.[6] This trend developed in large part out of the American social behaviorist tradition, as expressed in the writings of John Dewey, Charles Horton Cooley, William James, and George Herbert Mead.

The influence of John Dewey in the American tradition of the sociology of knowledge has remained for the most part unrecognized and consequently unappreciated, even though many of Dewey's works deal with problems of direct relevance to the sociology of knowledge. Dewey's definition of the relationship of individual and society is typified by the following statement, first published in 1915: "There are no such things as *pure ideas* and *pure reason*. Every living thought represents a gesture made toward the world, an attitude taken to some practical situation within which we are implicated."[7] As is characteristic of the works of the social behaviorists, Dewey's writings concentrate on the universality of the phenomenon of mutual dependence between a particular social order and the minds of the individuals who make up that social order. In Dewey's later works, the social group is conceived of as a collection of stimuli that will influence the behavior of the individual only to the degree that he interprets certain stimuli as significant within his particular psychological frame of reference.[8] In effect, the social behaviorists defined the social group as a network of forces whose impact on the individual is determined by the individual's interpretation of the stimuli he receives from his surroundings. The criteria that the individual utilizes in this mediating process have developed out of his previous interaction with stimuli.[9] A variation of this interpretation can be found in Piaget's emphasis on particular sequences in the cognitive development of the child. As Maier has noted, it is the "potential cognitive capacity" that plays the major role in the development of the ability to interpret the environment.[10]

Although our principal concern here is with developments in the sociology of knowledge after the translation of Mannheim's *Ideology and Utopia* was published in 1936, it should be recognized that the roots of this perspective go much further back in history.[11] Francis Bacon, in his *Advancement of Learning* and *Novum Organum*, was one of the first to demonstrate awareness of the sociology of knowledge perspective. His discussion of the various idols that rule the thoughts of men in different areas of social life is frequently cited as the earliest specific example of the approach itself.[12]

The development and specification of the approach in the twentieth century appear to have evolved out of three major movements of thought. The first and most often recognized source was the German philosophical-sociological tradition, with its sociocultural background, as manifested in the work of the nineteenth-century folk psychologists. Second was the influence that developed in France, especially through Durkheimian sociology and social psychology. The work of the nineteenth-century French crowd psychologists is important for an understanding of the background of this tradition. The third source derived from the movement of thought represented by the American social behaviorists, especially those who made up what is known as the "Chicago School" in sociology. (It is ironic that from a narrow perspective the works of these individuals are often considered to be the antithesis of a sociology of knowledge approach.) Not to be discounted in this connection was the role played by pragmatism in American philosophy in redirecting attention to the relationship between the individual and the social environment and away from a system of absolutism and determinism.[13]

Within the German branch of the sociology of knowledge two independent strands combined to become major influences. The folk psychologists helped to popularize the first strand, the idea that the material and cultural conditions of any society are related.[14] By insisting that the intellectual productions of society represent a "superstructure" erected on the material "substructure" of ethnicity, they were among the first social scientists to impute mental characteristics to a population on the basis of physical group membership.[15] Thus, they implied, as did Marx, that the various mental superstructures of the society do not exist independently.

In connection with the second strand, Raymond Aron has observed that the philosophical tradition in Germany created an idealism that pervaded the discipline of sociology and encouraged an effort on the part of German sociologists to grasp the uniqueness of the *Kulturwissenschaften* as opposed to the *Naturwissenschaften*. The two major influences in this respect were Wilhelm Dilthey and phenomenology in German philosophy.[16] This orientation, Aron reports, stands in sharp contrast to French sociology, which tends to be positivistic[17] and to deal with the psychological implications of the sociology of knowledge.[18]

Although those individuals most closely associated with the German branch—Ernst Grünwald, Karl Mannheim, Karl Marx, and Max Scheler—also concerned themselves with the behavior of individuals in particular social settings, behavior was treated primarily as existing within the vast network of ideas that enveloped the individual. Their attempts to explain this relationship emphasized that man occupies a particular position and role in history. As Aron and others have implied, their concern was primarily with the mind in relation to historical processes and development.[19] Their focus of interest, therefore, differed from that of, for example, Piaget, who is interested in the development of cognitive categories within the mind in relationship to a particular society. The German branch, on the other hand, focused on general categories within the social order that influence groups of men to move in a particular direction at a particular time and place in history.[20]

The sociology of knowledge approach in France is generally traced back no further than Durkheim, but the crowd psychologists who emerged in the last quarter of the nineteenth century can also be considered a significant influence. Gustav LeBon, for example, utilized his observations of political turmoil in France in formulating a general explanation for the behavior of individuals in a crowd. According to LeBon, an independent crowd mind seizes control of the individual mind. LeBon's contribution to the sociology of knowledge perspective was his analysis of the influence of the specific social situation on the thoughts and consequent behavior of the individuals in that situation, in the same way that Durkheim observed the processes through time within the social order as a whole.[21]

In Durkheim's works, the concept of the collective consciousness became the focal point for a sociology of knowledge. The minds of individuals in society were seen as extensions of the larger mind, the collective consciousness, from which they received their individual reality and which they reflected in the form of images and symbolic representations that had a shared source and meaning. These features of social life could never be reduced to the level of the individual mind.[22] The causal connections between the social milieu and the individual mind also provided the principal focus for the disciples of Durkheim—Lucien Levy–Bruhl, Charles Blondel, Maurice Halbwachs, and Marcel Mauss.[23]

The American branch of the sociology of knowledge, represented primarily by the social behaviorists, developed out of three principal influences at the turn of the century. First was the influence of American philosophy, particularly the works of the pragmatists. Secondly, the perspective of functional psychology, under the leadership of John Dewey, contributed to the idea of an interdependent *relationship* between the individual and the group. The social behaviorists themselves, several of whom worked simultaneously in the areas of philosophy, psychology, and sociology, provided a third major influence. Charles Horton Cooley, who worked strictly within the sociological tradition, was an exception to the multidisciplinary trend. Conversely, William James is a notable example of an individual active in more than one area—in this case, pragmatic philosophy and functional psychology. As Morton White has pointed out, the development of pragmatism can be seen as a revolt against the formalism that characterized American philosophy up to that time.[24] The revolt is best illustrated by James, whose monumental *Principles of Psychology* was a major step toward throwing off a psychology that had treated the individual as given and had represented society as a more or less tangential force operating upon human nature. This approach was antithetical to the sociology of knowledge approach, which claimed as a basic tenet that the principal role in the development of the individual was played by the sociocultural groups that provided the boundaries and content for mental constructions.[25]

The major impact of functional psychology on the sociology of knowledge tradition in America centered around its definition of the primary function of all human activity as the establishment of some sort of equilibrium between the individual and the environment.[26] More fundamental to the approach was its shift of emphasis in the search for a basis of human motivation—a question posed by most of social psychology at the time Dewey began his work on the nature of the mind and its relationship to behavior. The functional psychologists began with the proposition that goal-oriented activity can be taken as a given in man and that, consequently, the role of the behavioral scientist is to determine not the ultimate source but the direction of the behavior in any society. The sociocultural environment provides the individual with the appropriate categories of response for activity originally generated within the environment.

The frames of reference utilized by the three branches can be characterized briefly as follows. The German branch tended to combine a philosophical spiritualism with *Verstehende Soziologie* and a concern for the "universal processes of history." The French branch, epitomized in the works of Durkheim and the crowd psychologists, emphasized the relationship between individual minds and society, as well as the structuring influence of the particular sociocultural environment. Historical processes were de-emphasized in favor of the connection between the mind of the individual and a particular society at a particular time. The most prominent feature of the American tradition has been its emphasis on interdependence as the essential variable in understanding the relationship between the individual and the socio-cultural group.

One of our primary concerns in choosing and organizing the selections for this volume has been to illustrate these various trends and approaches. We make no attempt to define the sociology of knowledge; indeed, the selections we have chosen as representative of their respective areas will point to the near impossibility of doing so. We have combined what we regard as the most important classical statements in the sociology of knowledge with studies indicating trends and applications over the past thirty years. Our wish to represent all those who were influential in the development of the approach has led us to include translations of works by Ernst Grünwald and Max Scheler that have never before appeared in English.

EARLY STATEMENTS

Part I begins with a selection from Francis Bacon's discussion of the idols that rule the minds of men, which is considered by many to be the root of the sociology of knowledge perspective in modern social thought.[27] Using the analogy of a mirror, Bacon discusses the mind as reflecting particular conceptions of reality. In the words of Remmling, it is an "uneven mirror" that distorts the perceptions it receives in terms of its own peculiar construction.[28] Although Bacon claims that all knowledge is ultimately derived from observation, he is also aware that in observational experience the facts never speak for themselves. According to Bacon, the "raw data" taken in by observation are filtered through the psychological framework of the individual. This framework, in turn, is shaped by the various "idols" that are characteristic of the sociocultural environment. In elaborating upon the conditioning role played by the idols, Bacon has incorporated what he believed were the total range of variables, from those assumed to be inherent in the species, "idols of the tribe," to those that characterize the foundations of established philosophical systems, "idols of the theater." The importance of Bacon's work rests in his recognition of the relationship between the mind and the sociocultural environment. Their interdependence is the central focus of his discussion. Although the way in which the mind distorts social reality depends on its own peculiar structure, Bacon insists that the presence of distortion is due to man's existence in a sociocultural environment. In this sense, his discussion of the idols parallels the Mannheimian notion of total ideology (see below).[29]

Karl Marx's contribution to the sociology of knowledge was the emphasis on the economic factor as the most important of the existential bases of mental activity in any society. The selection from *The German Ideology* is a representative statement of the Marxian conception of ideology as a reflection of class interests. Although ideology arises out of the social conditions that characterize any historical period, the ideology itself can become a developing force, shaping the behavior of the individuals living under it. Especially interesting, Marx and Engels provide one of the earliest statements of a "vocabulary of motives" approach to behavior, at the same time recognizing the misunderstanding that such an approach may foster when applied from the outside:

> . . . if an epoch imagines itself to be actuated by purely "political" or "religious" motives, although "religion" and "politics" are only forms of its true motives, the historian accepts this opinion. The "idea," the "conception" of these conditioned men about their real practice, is transformed into the sole determining, active force, which controls and determines their practice.[30]

This failure to recognize the crucial role played by the economic factor in society is also the crux of their criticism of Feuerbach.

This selection also shows quite clearly why Marx is popularly regarded as representative of the sociology of knowledge perspective. His conception of the relationship between the mind and society leads him to the conclusion that the forces of production ultimately determine the mental structure of a particular epoch. Marx grants that the ideological structure can, in turn, influence social conditions, but this influence itself is always traceable to the underlying structure. Thus the ideological influence at any particular time is analogous to a sieve, which simply filters predetermined phenomena without affecting them appreciably.[31] It is within this conceptualization of the total society that Marx sees class differentiation developing, each class as an economic unit being stirred into being by its own position within the economic framework.[32]

Ideology develops as a function of a particular social class within a predetermined structure that also has a predetermined content. Extending this principle further, Marx believed that class position can also determine an "ideological advantage" for the power elite of any society. Thus, those who occupy positions of power in any society have an ideology that trickles down through the social structure and contaminates that of the proletarian classes. The ruinous effect of the ideology of the ruling class is heightened by the fact that economic and political power go hand in hand; to control the ideology in one realm is, by definition, to control it in the other. Objective superiority in the class system means subjective superiority, i.e., the power of ideological exploitation. As industrial society becomes more complex, therefore, one has the paradoxical combination of ideological exploitation of the masses and a diversifying ideological structure. As Dibble has pointed out:

> It is characteristic of Marx's thinking that he moves from . . . all-inclusive generalizations to very general propositions. That is, as we are using the terms "generalizations" and "propositions," he moves from statements which contend that something is always so to statements which contend that something varies concomitantly with something else. If it is the case, for example, that ideas are the conscious expression of the experiences men have in social relationships with each other, then it must also be the case that the greater the number of different kinds of social relationships one finds in a given society, the greater the number of different forms of consciousness one will also find in that society. The more complex and variegated the social structure, the greater the number of different constellations of ideas and belief systems, and the greater the difference between them.[33]

In summary, the Marxian perspective of the sociology of knowledge is best seen in Marx's view of ideology and the deterministic role played by the social order in its formation. The perspectives of the individuals within a society, however, are always dependent upon the distribution of those individuals within the total context. To paraphrase the final sentence in this selection, the illusions of men can easily be explained by their practical position in life, their job, and the division of labor.

Ever since publication of the translation of *Ideologie und Utopie* in 1936, Karl Mannheim has been the individual most frequently associated with the sociology of knowledge. Mannheim's theory revolves around three central concepts: ideology, utopia, and relationism. Defining the sociology of knowledge as the study of the relationship between knowledge and existence, Mannheim examines the genesis of ideas in terms of social processes characteristic of particular historical periods.[34] The manner in which the social and mental aspects of society are related can be seen in Mannheim's treatment of the two forms of ideology, the specific and the general.

In the specific, or particular, sense, ideology refers to a body of ideas used to mask the true interests of any individual or group. This usage of the term is synonymous with Marx's earlier usage, which emphasizes conscious concealment of the truth. It also corresponds to Pareto's description of the role of ideas and deception in maintaining positions of power in society. What Mannheim calls "total ideology" corresponds to the over-all phenomenon of the social determination of ideas as represented in the *Weltanschauungen* of different societies and social groups. The concept of total ideology, then, defines the perspective of the sociology of knowledge.[35]

Utopias are similar to ideologies in that they are systems of ideas that arise out of particular sociohistorical environments. But, instead of corresponding strictly to the environment, utopias arise in opposition to the prevailing belief structure and stress varying degrees of "wish-fulfillment."[36] The truth of a particular utopia is measured by its success in disturbing the existing social order of ideas and outlining a new way of life. Indeed, the only knowledge whose truthfulness is not related to conduct in a particular sociohistorical environment is that found in the natural and physical sciences. Very few individuals in society are able to escape mentally the boundaries established by their objective positions in the social order. There is a group of individuals, however, the intellectuals, who have the potentiality of possessing truth in any sociohistorical period because of their possible detachment from the social conditions that play a major role in determining thought.[37] Since perspectives gain validity through action and relevant actions are a function of particular sociohistorical processes, the intellectual must become aware of the relationship among the various levels of sociohistorical events if he is to be able to decipher truth.[38] For example, he must be able to distinguish between ideologies and utopias on the basis of their appropriateness and correspondence to the sociohistorical conditions in which they arise. The difficulty in discriminating between ideologies and utopias under actual circumstances has been the subject of several criticisms.[39]

As is shown in Part V of this volume, the philosophical problem of relativity is the source of most of the attacks on Mannheim's approach to the sociology of knowledge. In an attempt to move away from the notion of a sociohistorical determinism, Mannheim dropped the term "relativism" and substituted "relationism":

> Relationism does not signify that there are no criteria of rightness and wrongness in a discussion. It does insist, however, that it lies in the nature of certain assertions that they cannot be formulated absolutely, but only in terms of the perspective of a given situation.[40]

By using the term "relationism," Mannheim hoped to establish some boundaries of truth that would allow for a valid knowledge of sociohistorical processes. Mannheim believed that relationism provided him with the epistemological basis for a sociology of knowledge. Realistic thought is that which is fully adapted to an established social process during a particular historical period.[41] Others, however, disagree. For example, Mandelbaum writes:

> Mannheim's ideological doctrine is wholly relativistic; his attempts to substitute relationism for relativism by means of a sociology of

knowledge leads him to assume what had previously been denied: the possibility of objective historical knowledge. Along with Croce and Dilthey, Mannheim thus demonstrates the ultimate futility of any attempt to escape the consequences of historical relativism once the philosophic basis of that relativism is accepted.[42]

In summary, one finds few critics who disagree with W. Ziegenfuss' comment: "Mannheim's whole distinction between relationism and relativism is no more than a 'play on words'."[43]

After a period of relative disinterest, the works of Vilfredo Pareto have had a revival in American sociology during the past few years.[44] However, the lack of association between Pareto's writings and the sociology of knowledge has persisted even though, as Berger has noted, his entire output constitutes a contribution to the sociology of knowledge perspective.[45]

Pareto's conception of himself relative to the development of the field of sociology helps to explain the tone and emphases in his works. For example, he compared himself with the "father of sociology," Auguste Comte. Pareto believed that Comte had abandoned the role of the scientist in his quest for a humanistic religion that would become the "glue" of the social order. He perceived his own approach, rather, as an instrument for future sociologists to utilize in attempting to study society and its processes objectively. Pareto's methodology was based on the idea that the social system maintained itself in dynamic equilibrium through the functional interdependence of its various components. According to Pareto, once sociologists became aware of this fact, the methodology of the social sciences would change; studies of functional interdependence would take precedence over cause-and-effect approaches, which are of questionable applicability in a system characterized by mutually dependent elements.[46]

The dynamic equilibrium of society is affected by the balance among physical, external, and internal factors. The external conditions affecting the equilibrium of the social system arise primarily out of contacts with other societies. Physical factors are important in that they can play a directive role in social relationships. Pareto singles out the internal factors as the most important for understanding major shifts of equilibrium in the social system. Of the several internal factors, including race and ethnicity, he regards class-linked ideologies and their responses as especially important. These factors are best understood in the context of Pareto's theory of motivation.

The importance of Pareto's theory of motivation rests in its extension of the principle of mutual dependence to the realm of human behavior. The key concepts are "residues" and "derivations." Briefly, the residues in man are "manifestations of sentiments" that provide the basis for the type of equilibrium found in a society at a particular point in time. Although Pareto's usage is not entirely clear, the residues appear to be at least partly instinctive in origin, but they can be influenced by social conditions. Pareto lists more than fifty residues in man, grouped into six major categories.[47] The derivations are the ways in which man explains his conduct. They are verbal justifications that mask the true motives of behavior (residues) and, in combination with the latter, demonstrate that for the most part human behavior is nonlogical.[48] Pareto groups the derivations into four major categories.[49] The residues always underlie the dynamic equilibrium of the social system, whereas the derivations are part of the superstructure. Discussing the circulation of the elite, Pareto combines his conceptualizations of the social system, methodology, and motivation into a unified theory of human behavior. The circulation of the elite is the most enduring process of internal change and is therefore regarded as one of the most important influences on the social equilibrium in any society.

Pareto begins his discussion of stratification by introducing the idea of an objective ranking system. It is possible, he notes, to rank any individual in a society on a scale from 1 to 10, based on the objective factors surrounding his social position. (It is assumed that the ranking is completely value free and excludes such nonscientific aspects as individual potential.) Those who accumulate the highest scores are regarded as members of the elite, and their separation from the nonelites constitutes the basic division of the social structure. The elite group itself is then divided into two groupings, a governing and a nongoverning elite. It is the distribution of the residues and derivations throughout the governing and nongoverning populations that regulates the social equilibrium. The behavior of the ruling elites earns them the sobriquet "foxes" (clever and scheming). Those of the nonruling population who attempt to seize power are called "lions." The foxes are motivated by residues of combinations, manifested in behavior in the use of trickery and deception to maintain positions of power in society.[50] Lions, on the other hand, are motivated by residues of persistence of aggregates, and the behavioral manifestation is a persistent striving toward ideal goals coupled with a tendency to pursue objectives directly rather than by deception. Pareto's extension of the principle of mutual dependence to this level is as follows.

Residues predispose the individuals in whom they are found to behave in particular ways; therefore, those with similar residues are led to similar social situations. Residues are not randomly distributed throughout the social system, however. For example, residues of combinations are much more prevalent at the top of the hierarchy than at the lower levels. The position of the individual within the social structure greatly influences the types of residue that he acquires. For this reason, lions will eventually become foxes despite the revolutionary goals that they share at the time of their entrance into positions of power. Their eventual behavior serves to intensify the revolutionary zeal of each new group of lions, thereby heightening the effect of the already present residues of persistence of aggregates. Thus, history remains the "graveyard of aristocracies." The lions of history eventually become "routinized."

Pareto carries over from Marx the idea that class antagonisms are inherent in any social order. Although social conditions play a major role in the increase or decrease of conflict in a given period, the underlying antagonism between the classes remains. This antagonism, in combination with the residues characteristic of each class, helps to establish class ideologies. In summary, Pareto's theory of society and behavior presents a statement of the perceived relationship among man, the sociocultural environment, and the mental structures of society. In the words of Brigitte Berger:

The *Trattato* shows how a concept of social stratification may be developed in the perspective of a sociology of knowledge. Social strata are not primarily seen as determined by economic or other external factors, but as constellations of consciousness. Pareto also develops a comprehensive theory of social change based on his sociology of knowledge. Change in society means above all change in the consciousness of social groups.[51]

Émile Durkheim shared Pareto's concern for the development of a scientific sociology, but in Durkheim's theories of motivation the individual factor is negligible.[52] The sociologist must find his data regarding the genesis of behavior in society and its collective representations. The mind of the individual, according to Durkheim, is only one aspect of the collective mind of the social order. Durkheim emphasizes the concept of society as a system, but his analysis devotes much more space to the mental structure as the ultimate source of social organization.

The mental level of social organization in a society is manifested in the collective consciousness, which serves to bind the individual to the social group. The collective consciousness consists of the various symbols and shared representations that develop out of the group's perception of itself relative to the object that it utilizes. Collective representations can arise only through interaction and can never be explained in terms of the psychology of any one individual.[53] The selection reprinted here sets down Durkheim's ideas concerning the role of the sociocultural environment in developing the forms of mental activity within a society.

> . . . society is not at all the illogical or a-logical, incoherent and fantastic being which it has too often been considered. Quite on the contrary, the collective consciousness is the highest form of the psychic life, since it is the consciousness of the consciousnesses.[54]

As mentioned earlier, Durkheim's sociology is representative of the French approach to the sociology of knowledge and is also linked to the concern of the American social behaviorists. Max Scheler, however, developed an approach much closer to Pareto's and formulated many of his own contributions in critical response to Durkheim's theories.

Although Scheler is recognized as the father of the sociology of knowledge, his works have been known to most American sociologists only through secondary sources, as is also true of Ernst Grünwald's works. Through the inclusion of the present selections we hope to take a step toward the correction of this situation.[55]

Max Scheler's sociology of knowledge is only one aspect of his thought. Scheler regarded the sociology of knowledge as a necessary step in the formation of a philosophical anthropology. His attempt to develop an approach to behavior that would combine the biological, social, and cultural levels of man's existence is immediately apparent in his work. His discussion of the interaction of these levels in the development of the individual in society is very similar to the views of the American social behaviorists.[56] In its inclusiveness, his approach resembles Pareto's. In the weight he assigns to the metaphysical features of behavior, Scheler distinguishes himself from Durkheim and Marx and, in the first selection from his work, from Auguste Comte as well.

Scheler uses the term "codetermination" in explaining the relationship between the mind and social factors, in order to differentiate himself from Durkheim and Marx. Unlike Durkheim, Scheler separates the "object of selection" from the content and validity of ideas. For Scheler, the social determination of thought

> . . . refers *only* to the *selection* of objects of knowledge, which is determined by the controlling perspective of social interests. . . . Neither the content nor the validity of knowledge is sociologically determined, but the *forms* of the mental processes by means of which knowledge is acquired *are* always and necessarily codetermined sociologically—i.e., by the social structure.[57]

Staude states the implications of this view for the study of behavior as follows: "If the *actualization* of the *ideas* generated in a society was determined by the *prevailing material conditions*, the selection of the objects of knowledge was determined by the *prevailing interest perspectives* of the ruling social group."[58] That is, underlying the mutually dependent social and mental structure are the basic foundations of behavior—the drive structures of individuals. In this conception Scheler closely approximates Pareto's belief that there is a mutual dependence between the social and mental structures coupled with an underlying "drive structure" in the form of residues.[59] The mental structure of the society, however, exists as an independent variable, and Scheler criticizes Marx's refusal to recognize this fact. According to Scheler, Marx's error was not that he emphasized the economic factor in capitalistic societies but, rather, that he took the economic factor as an atemporal, independent variable, characteristic of all societies at all times and places. In Scheler's view, this factor is appropriate as an explanation only at particular times in history.[60]

The first selection touches upon Scheler's criticism of Comte for a different type of ethnocentrism. Comte's ideas are seen as little more than an expression of the ideology of the bourgeoisie, a group that Scheler singled out for criticism throughout his works. Scheler's distaste for this aspect of Comte's works is evident in his greater tolerance for the works of Marx, even though he believed Marx to be equally mistaken in his interpretation of the relationship between sociocultural conditions and mental activity in a society.

Scheler also criticized Comte's reworking of ideas originally advanced by Saint-Simon. Comte was especially influenced by Saint-Simon's ideas regarding rational social planning and social reform. Comte was convinced that social unity could be attained only through a new humanistic relationship based on a scientific theology that could withstand the secularization characteristic of social change. In his later life, Comte devoted more and more time to the development of such a religion. Also borrowed from Saint-Simon was the idea of a classifying scheme for the sciences, to facilitate the direction of rational control and planning in society. This, in turn, was based upon Comte's claim that the mind of man was characterized by three stages of knowledge: theological, metaphysical, and positivistic (scientific).

Scheler's criticisms of Comte (and Saint-Simon) center around two points. First, Scheler contends that the entire scheme of classifying the sciences rests on a fallacy—the belief that the various sciences can be measured against an ultimate test of "scientific truthfulness." But the several scientific disciplines have different objects of interest, which means that the questions they ask cannot be comparable. Secondly, Scheler takes Comte to task for his idea that society passes through three levels of knowledge, ultimately moving toward a scientific stage. In fact, all three stages coexist in some form in all societies. Elements of the first two stages always form an important part of any social structure, however advanced.[61] For Scheler, an understanding of man in relation to his sociocultural environment was to come about through the establishment of a philosophical anthropology. The sociology of knowledge perspective provided the philosophical framework for the study of human behavior.

The selections by Ernst Grünwald are taken from the posthumously edited work *Das Problem der Soziologie des Wissens, Versuch einer Kritischen Darstellung der Wissenssoziologischen Theorien.* In this book he systematically reviewed and analyzed earlier German writings bearing on the sociology of knowledge. The chapters reprinted here are generally regarded as the most representative of his thought.[62] Grünwald met an untimely death at the age of twenty-one, and it is difficult to suggest where his critique and refinement of the sociology of knowledge framework might have led in later writings. We have reproduced passages from his work because there are no finer attempts to analyze the German variants of the sociology of knowledge of his time.

The last two selections in Part I have been chosen as representative of the American branch of the sociology of knowledge tradition, which, as was pointed out earlier, concerned itself with the rise of mind and the mental aspects of society out of the interaction between the individual and the social group. The selection by John Dewey was formulated as a criticism of Herbert Spencer and the Spencerians. Here Dewey dismisses the notion that there is any difference in origin between the mental processes of civilized and primitive men. In both cases the process arises in interaction with a particular form of sociocultural environment. This selection also represents one of the earliest statements of Dewey's particular brand of pragmatism—instrumentalism.

Dewey's idea of an interactionist relationship between society and the mental structure extends into his philosophical views, in the notion that there can be no such thing as metaphysics, no knowledge of a reality that precedes the thinking individual, because all experience is interactional:

> When the individual is taken as something already given, anything that can be done to him or for him can only be by way of external impressions and belongings: sensations of pleasure and pain, comforts, securities. . . . Only in the physical sense of physical bodies that to the senses are separate is individuality an original dictum.[63]

Given Dewey's social conception of the mind, language was seen as the indispensable vehicle for human communication. The social development of the mind can take place only through communication "as a sharing whereby meanings are enhanced, deepened and solidified in the sense of communion."[64]

George Herbert Mead's theory of mind, self, and society is important to the sociology of knowledge for at least two reasons. First, it is one of the clearest statements on the interrelationship between the socio-cultural environment and the mental life of the individual and society. Second, the theory, if correct, provides an epistemological foundation for the sociology of knowledge. As Arthur Child has noted, if it is true that thought has a social basis and origin, then all mental activities are socially based.[65]

Mead sets forth a theory of mind that is, in all important respects, similar to Dewey's approach. The mind is defined in terms of functions. Its reality becomes apparent through behavioral manifestations. Mind, then, resides in a field of conduct that exists among individuals and not within them.[66] To Mead, as to Dewey, the mind is an instrument that functions to effect a stable relationship between the individual and his environment. The notion that the mind is selective, that it utilizes past experiences in evaluating the stimulus, closely follows the principles laid down by Dewey in his reflex-arc article and elaborates on the idea that consciousness, as it is organized within the individual, may be regarded from the point of view of its objects and their relation to conduct.[67]

Although Mead was greatly influenced by Wilhelm Wundt with regard to the concept of the gesture and its role in the social act, he criticized Wundt for postulating a social order that presupposed the existence of minds. This theory is faulty, according to Mead, because it leaves unanswered the question of the origin of minds. But the question can be answered:

> If . . . you regard the social process of experience as prior . . . to the existence of mind and explain the origin of minds in terms of the interaction among individuals among that process, then not only the origin of minds, but also the interaction among minds . . . cease to seem mysterious or miraculous. Mind arises through communication by a conversation of gestures in a social process or context of experience—not communication through mind.[68]

Mead also agreed with Dewey regarding the origin and function of language as a vehicle in individual development. "It arises . . . out of cooperative activities, such as those involved in sex, parenthood, fighting, herding, and the like, in which some phase of the act of one form . . . acts as a stimulus to others to carry on their parts of the social acts."[69] The laws of language are generalizations that do not have the slightest meaning if interpreted solely within the context of individual experience.[70] The relationship between the individual and the social order is always seen as one of interdependence, in which man is at the same time both determined and a determiner:

> I wish to emphasize . . . [that] the appearance of the self is antedated by the tendencies to take the attitudes of the others, so that the existence of others is not a reflection of his self-experience into other individuals. The others are not relative to his self, but his self and the others are relative to the perspective of his organism.[71]

In applying these principles to self-development, Mead identifies two stages: play and game. The game stage is reached when the child begins to internalize the roles of others. It is at this stage that mental life arises and the self becomes incorporated as an object within the individual "through his having assumed the generalized attitude of a member of the group to which that self belongs, a group that widens until it takes in all rational individuals, that is, all individuals who could indicate to one another universal characters and objects in cooperative activity."[72]

In summary, the works of Mead come to grips with the most crucial question confronting the sociology of knowledge: Is such an approach epistemologically possible? At the same time, Mead's works, like Dewey's, are linked to the French branch of the sociology of knowledge perspective through their concern with minds arising out of the social process. Although the emphases are decidedly different, the underlying principles are similar.

The remaining sections in this volume provide vivid illustrations of the multivariant directions taken by the sociology of knowledge in more recent years and show how these later approaches are tied to the early theoretical statements comprising Part I.

LATER PERSPECTIVES

Part II of this volume contains six selections representative of theoretical statements on the sociology of knowledge made during the past thirty years. For the most part, these statements lie in the German tradition of the sociology of knowledge, although the authors have tried to move beyond the basic premises that occupied Mannheim. These statements range from Hans Speier's early attempt to develop a sociology of knowledge that would avoid the pitfalls of sociological determinism to Peter Berger's "Identity as a Problem in the Sociology of Knowledge," which, by arguing (as does Child) that Mead's social behaviorism can provide an epistemological foundation for the sociology of knowledge, moves beyond the narrow definition of the sociology of knowledge.

Although his own approach is most heavily influenced by the German tradition, Speier departs from Mannheim on the possible existence of a social group comprised of "free-floating" intellectuals. According to Speier, there is no room in the sociology of knowledge for concepts analogous to Alfred Weber's "socially detached" individual: "The sociological question to be answered concretely in every concrete case is not whether a thinker is dependent, but in which specific interests—ecclesiastic, political, economic or otherwise—he is entangled."[73] Since the individual intellectual is never totally free of the influence of his social environment, the sociologist of knowledge must attempt to measure the *relative* detachment of the individual from his sociocultural environment at a particular time. That is:

> The philosophical task of a sociology of knowledge ... is to show to what extent philosophers have left immediate partisan interests behind them, and how by doing this they may have incidentally exerted a profounder influence upon the ethos of man than those who by being merely today's thinkers are already of the external yesterday.[74]

To avoid the sociological determinism implicit in this approach, Speier concentrates on explaining the concept of "needs," which underlies much of our thinking with regard to the social determination of ideas, and points out that this concept is not necessarily influential in the actual *determination* of ideas. That is, one cannot assume from the fact that a particular ideological system is used to explain a need that the system *arose* from that need. As we noted earlier, the analysis of Marx and Engels rests on this basic assumption.

The selection by Talcott Parsons represents an attempt to integrate a sociology of knowledge into a general theory of action. Although Parsons identifies the sociology of knowledge with the Mannheimian tradition, Max Weber also influenced his approach.[75] Parsons begins his analysis with the observation that, after Mannheim's works achieved recognition, the sociology of knowledge began to focus on the relationship between the social system and various empirical forms of knowledge. For example, a primary area of interest has always been scientific objectivity. Their focus on the social system has led sociologists of knowledge to neglect the cultural system, which, according to Parsons, is concerned primarily with underlying "grounds of meaning." The general theory of action, he believes, can provide a framework for the sociology of knowledge. Although he does not advocate the substitution of a general sociology of culture for the traditional concerns of the sociology of knowledge, Parsons believes that the most fruitful applications of the sociology of knowledge will come about when there is an understanding of how the underlying grounds of meaning interact with the social system in the formulation of particular mental productions at a particular time and place. Thus, as to the content of the sociology of knowledge—a matter of definition discussed earlier in this introduction—Parsons concludes:

> The term "knowledge" has seemed to me to refer to cognitively ordered orientations to objects, with reference both to empirical facts and to problems of meaning. The problem of ideology has been interpreted to concern the first context, especially when the social system itself is the empirical object; Weber's problem of the sociology of religious ideas concerns primarily the second context. It seems important to keep these two problem areas clearly distinct, but also to relate them as the two primary branches of the sociology of knowledge.[76]

The selection by Florian Znaniecki is one of the earliest statements on the sociology of occupations to utilize a sociology of knowledge framework. "In sociological studies of specialized persons, it is the connection between the individual and his social milieu which is the main object of interest; and his specialized activities are viewed with reference to the cultural setting in which they are performed."[77] In this selection, the influence of Znaniecki's general framework upon later studies, including several reprinted here, becomes apparent.

Examining the role played by the man of knowledge in all cultures, Znaniecki proposes a methodological stance similar to the one emphasized by Speier in "The Social Determination of Ideas." He asks: "Are the systems of knowledge which scientists build and their methods of building them influenced by the social patterns with which scientists are expected to conform as participants in a certain social order and by the ways in which they actually realize those patterns?"[78] In a certain sense, both Speier and Znaniecki are representative of the traditional perspective discussed by Parsons. The central theme for both men is scientific objectivity in relation to a particular sociocultural environment. Whereas Speier focuses on the nature of ideas relative to the position of the investigator and on "needs" as the link between the sociocultural environment and ideas, Znaniecki emphasizes the investigator's stance relative to "culture patterns" as the important variable for analysis. Znaniecki maintains that

> . . . uniformities of social systems, like those of all cultural systems, are chiefly the result of a reflective or unreflective use of the same *cultural patterns* in many particular cases. There is obviously a fundamental and universal, though unreflective, cultural pattern in accordance with which all kinds of lasting relationships between individuals and their social milieus are normatively organized and which we denote by the term "social role."[79]

Probably the best-known latter-day example of the sociology of knowledge perspective is Robert K. Merton's paradigm for the sociology of knowledge. The function of Merton's paradigm is to present a series of questions, the answers to which should provide the information necessary for a complete theory of the sociology of knowledge.[80] On the basis of the paradigm, Merton is able to criticize many of the traditional approaches to the sociology of knowledge. The paradigm provides the sociologist of knowledge with a tool for investigating relationships between the sociocultural environment and mental productions.[81] The work from which this selection is derived, Merton's *Social Theory and Social Structure*, can be seen as an attempt to demonstrate the many ways in which facets of social existence influence mental productions through their relationship to the existential bases. Thus, for example, whereas the bureaucrat develops his motivations and responses under the influence of a particular cultural pattern, the scientist may develop and pursue his interests under the influence of a different mental structure.[82]

The Kurt Wolff selection in Part II is an early attempt to establish empirically the validity of the concept of culture pattern and its utility as an indicator of social behavior. Although Wolff's works are firmly rooted in the German branch of the sociology of knowledge perspective, this selection is linked with the French tradition through its emphasis on mental representations in the form of culture patterns. Wolff's intention is to provide a groundwork for the establishment of the culture pattern at a level where it can be used in the prediction of behavior. In constructing this groundwork, Wolff urges a combination of observational and statistical data that would demonstrate the interrelatedness of the various patterns uncovered in a society. The interrelatedness pattern that has been demonstrated by the researcher is then tested pragmatically: does it allow the observer to anticipate the reaction of the culture's members to social change in various sectors of society? The manner in which Wolff followed this procedure through his own field notes is published in this volume for the first time.

Peter Berger's "Identity as a Problem in the Sociology of Know-ledge," the last selection in Part II, demonstrates that there is a definite relationship between Mead's social behaviorism and the traditional approach to the sociology of knowledge. Berger points to the neglect suffered by the American branch of the sociology of knowledge perspective, represented by the social behaviorists. He sees the concept of social identity as an excellent focal point for the study of relation-ships between the mental structures of individuals and the socio-cultural environment: *"Psychological 'knowledge' is always part of a general 'knowledge about the world'*—in this proposition lies the founda-tion of . . . the sociology of psychology."[83]

Earlier we mentioned that Mead's conception of how individual identities develop within a particular society provides a framework for the sociology of knowledge that enables it to move away from a deterministic position. Mead's theory of self-development takes into account the role of mental productions in constructing a social en-vironment through the individual's perception of the stimuli received from the outside world. Aside from the American tradition of the sociology of knowledge, the most outstanding use of interactionism as the link between mental productions and existential bases is to be found in the sociology of Max Weber.[84]

The statements presented in Part II illustrate the influence of the German tradition, which has come to be perceived as the mainstream of the sociology of knowledge. However, they also reveal interests parallel to those of the French branch, in the emphasis given to cultural systems and the nature of meaning as patterned by the society. Finally, the extension of the American branch of the sociology of knowledge tradition into the perspective can be seen in the selection by Berger. Parts III and IV demonstrate later applications made by proceeding within the general outlines of the framework without particular reference to the epistemological problems that concerned Mannheim in his attempts to develop the sociology of knowledge as a legitimate scientific method.

THE SOCIOCULTURAL ENVIRONMENT AND IDEAS

Writers who have used a sociological approach to the study of mental productions—whether or not they are sociologists—have typically been concerned with one or more of the five basic research questions posed by Merton in his paradigm. The investigations made in response to these questions, however, have been unsystematic, thereby compounding the difficulty of speaking of marked trends in the research literature.[85] Nevertheless, it is quite clear that study of the problems Merton raises has been a substantial part of sociological research from the beginnings of the sociology of knowledge. This remains true today, despite the proliferation of sociological subspecialities, the emergence of several "theories of the middle range,"[86] and a dominant theoretical orientation of "voluntaristic nominalism" in American sociology. All of these factors counteract the centrality of the traditional view. That sociologists publish comparatively little under the narrow "sociology of knowledge" label and that they are often dissatisfied with the vagueness of early theoretical formulations in this field are obvious from a review of the recent literature.[87] On the other hand, it is also obvious that the main preoccupation of sociologists and of scholars in other disciplines is to contribute more refined answers to broad questions in the sociology of knowledge: What are the existential bases of various types of mental production (beliefs, attitudes, motives, values, etc.)? How are mental productions related to the existential bases? Finally, what are the functions of these existentially conditioned mental productions?

Sociology of knowledge studies in both America and Europe have experienced a checkered career. In the eras of Durkheim, Mannheim, Marx, and Weber, such studies were explicitly viewed as central to the discipline of sociology. More recently studies labeled "sociology of knowledge" have often been seen as unfashionable and, therefore, have been evaluated unfavorably relative to works in other subdivisions of sociology. This appears to be especially true in American sociology, in which the narrow definition, in terms of a one-sided determinism, is popular. The negative appraisals of studies in the sociology of knowledge can also be attributed to the numerous grand and speculative formulations characteristic of many of these studies, and to their generally low quality by recent research standards.[88] Until recently, in the words of Adler, "The people best known as sociologists of knowledge have largely been engaged in interesting though unproductive philosophical speculation."[89] Coser and Rosenberg have pointed out that the early history of the sociology of knowledge was characterized by:

> . . . a tendency to set up grandiose hypothetical schemes which contributed a number of suggestive leads of the highest importance. Recently it has on occasion been caught in a tendency that should have been outgrown, toward eschewing speculation in favor of ever more trivial investigation. While this may be an antidote to the earlier types of premature generalization, it carries with it a danger of overlooking the significant on behalf of the provable. But such oscillation (Saint-Simon called it the law of alternativity between the generalizing and the particularizing approach to the sciences) is part of the development of any science.[90]

There are indications, however, that the American branch of the sociology of knowledge perspective is beginning to follow a course midway between the extremes of grand theory and limited research. Recent studies have manifested a lively interest in developing new ways of counting, classifying, analyzing, and operationalizing key variables. The analysis of large bodies of data from several substantive areas is beginning to yield empirical propositions and is bringing about a critical reformulation of several conceptual schemes. Our selections in Parts III and IV exemplify the use of these conceptual frameworks as well as several research methodologies. Included are examples of such techniques as historical research, observation, interviewing, and content analysis. Current uses of improved statistical and sampling procedures are also discussed.

Another trend in American studies has been the focus on social-psychological variables and, as previously mentioned, a concern with the forces involved in the relation between individual variables and components of the social structure. The Hinkles, as well as Kurt Wolff, have made the point that American sociology is characterized by an orientation of "voluntaristic nominalism," an orientation that rests upon "the assumption that the structure of all social groups is the consequence of the aggregate of its separate, component individuals and that social phenomena ultimately derive from the motivations of these knowing, feeling, and willing individuals."[91] As Wolff indicates, this perspective is clearly unsympathetic to the social-realistic view of the sociology of knowledge associated with Mannheim, Marx, and Durkheim. Its implication for American sociologists is that problems have often been pursued in the social-psychological tradition of social behaviorism, pragmatism, or social action theory.[92]

Using a comparative framework, Berger and Luckman have made a similar evaluation of the American branch of the sociology of knowledge tradition, noting that the social-psychological focus has not yet been related to a macrosociological perspective of knowledge. In Europe the total ignorance of Mead's work and the social behaviorist tradition is a severe theoretical defeat, especially in the neo-Marxist tradition:

> There is considerable irony in the fact that, of late, neo-Marxist theoreticians have been seeking a liaison with Freudian psychology (which is fundamentally incompatible with the anthropological presuppositions of Marxism), completely oblivious of the existence of a Meadian theory of the dialectic between society and the individual that would be immeasurably more congenial to their own approach.[93]

Merton has explored further differences between the European and American branches of the sociology of knowledge perspective, noting that, although they developed independently, both may be regarded as

"species of that genus of research which is concerned with the interplay between social structure and communications."[94] He goes on to
show that the sociology of public opinion and mass communication is
an important part of the sociology of knowledge in America. In fact,
the American perspective has been more concerned with the impact of
ideas on the public than with their structural determinants. Correspondingly, there has been less emphasis on studying the origin of ideas
and more concern with the social-psychological processes involved in
the acquisition or rejection of ideas. Whereas the American variant

> . . . is primarily concerned with public opinion, with mass beliefs,
> with what has come to be called "popular culture," the European
> version centers upon more esoteric doctrines, on those complex
> systems of knowledge which become reshaped and often distorted
> in their subsequent passage into popular culture.
>
> These differences in focus carry with them further differences:
> The European variant, being concerned with knowledge, comes to
> deal with the intellectual elite; the American variant, concerned
> with widely held opinion, deals with the masses. The one centers on
> the esoteric doctrines of the few, the other on the exoteric beliefs of
> the many. This divergence of interests has immediate bearing on
> every phase of research techniques.[95]

A final important development in this country is that several of the
ideas central to earlier theoretical formulations—including the basic
research focus on the reciprocal relationships between types of mental
productions and social structure—have become incorporated into a
latent frame of reference that underlies several empirically based theoretical perspectives in sociology and other social science disciplines.[96]
Coupled with this change is the great proliferation of subdivisions within sociology, each at least implicitly concerned with conceptions central
to the sociology of knowledge. As a result of these and other developments, investigators from different specialities and disciplines have been
studying sociocultural factors and types of mental productions, each in
terms of his own theoretical concerns. Important research in the
sociology of knowledge framework is currently being carried out in

psychology, anthropology, and history, as well as in various areas of concentration within sociology. Recent findings and promising developments in empirically based theory have come from research guided by role theory, reference group theory, symbolic interactionism, dissonance theory, and social exchange theory.[97] In the words of Coser and Rosenberg, "Many practitioners of what is in fact sociology of knowledge may at times be rather surprised when it is pointed out that, like Monsieur Jourdain they have been talking prose all along."[98]

The result of all this activity is that several "partial" sociologies of knowledge have emerged, each fostering a particular research interest and favored research technique. Several areas of study have drawn varying aspects of the sociology of knowledge into their own frameworks or orientations. However, these aspects of research and theory from the various fields have not as yet been brought together. Thus the circuit remains incomplete, precluding the development of a full sociology of knowledge. There is much more empirical and theoretical work in substantive areas than we are able to illustrate in this volume. Although much of this research has not been interpreted in a sociology of knowledge framework, it nevertheless provides an expanding empirical base against which key propositions can be tested.

Not to be neglected is the substantial research contribution being made by nonsociologists. Part III contains examples from linguistics and cultural anthropology. References throughout the text provide a guide to published literature that will allow the student to pursue other topics more intensively. We agree with Wolff that a broad inventory of relevant contributions to the sociology of knowledge, unrestricted by the space considerations that confine our choice here, would have to include works in at least the following areas:

In the *social sciences*, in addition to general sociological findings and to more specialized findings, . . . above all, social psychology in a very broad sense . . . cultural anthropology, particularly linguistics, with its various subdivisions, the study of "culture and personality," and the study of culture itself; in the *humanities*, social and cultural history, literary criticism, historical linguistics, and . . . methodological and empirical aspects of philosophy . . . and finally, in the *biological sciences*, whatever throws light upon the biological dimensions of intellectual behavior (that is, especially the field of human genetics). All these are sources of knowledge relevant to the problem of the relations between society and intellectual life.[99]

A challenging possibility that is yet to be realized is the systematic organization of relevant data from these areas into a viable sociology of mental productions.

In the various areas that contribute directly or indirectly to the sociology of knowledge perspective, important empirical findings are accumulating at such a pace as to preclude even a brief summary here. But before commenting on the illustrative selections chosen for Parts III and IV, we should like at least to list a few examples of notable substantive studies that we were unable to include.

Among the most conspicuous omissions are three studies written by Thorstein Veblen around the early 1900's that represent a major historical antecedent of the sociology of knowledge.[100] In these works Veblen concentrated for the most part on an analysis of the dependence of thought on existential bases, such as community social structure, institutional settings, and occupational roles. As Franz Adler has indicated, Veblen's *The Theory of the Leisure Class* could have been the point of departure for a systematic sociology of knowledge in America had it been followed immediately by detailed investigations of the research problems that it described. However, Veblen's study of the emergence and communication of ideas in the academy did anticipate a line of research in the sociology of education and science that has become a major contribution to the American branch of the sociology of knowledge perspective.

W. F. Ogburn's *Social Change* considers research problems in the sociology of education and science as well as several other substantive areas.[101] His work was guided by a modified Marxist theory—i.e., a technological theory of social and cultural change. Among the problems Ogburn studied were the importance of the cultural base, rather than "Great Men," as an explanation of the emergence of new ideas; the process and cumulative nature of technological development; and the influence of inventions on cultural and social systems.

Bernard Stern's work in approximately the same period is a pioneering study of the relationship between knowledge and organization in the medical profession. His analysis of the resistance to innovations in medical science is well documented, and it anticipates the findings and theoretical directions of more recent research in this field.[102]

S. C. Gilfillan specialized for the most part in the sociology of invention. In his book by that title, he presented an intensive analysis of recorded accounts of scientific discoveries. His intention was to develop a refined statement on the principles of social processes of invention.[103]

Robert K. Merton has written extensively on the sociology of science and academics. His "Science, Technology and Society in Seventeenth-Century England," first published abroad in 1938, is an established classic in the field.[104] This study considers Weber's earlier hypotheses regarding the relationship between religious ideas and the development of science. Through comprehensive historical research, Merton demonstrates connections between several cultural and social variables, on the one hand, and the emergence of systematic science, on the other. The Protestant ethic, cultural values, economic factors, the growth of population, and changes in military organization are all described as related to the development of science in England.

Between 1937 and 1941, Pitirim A. Sorokin published *Social and Cultural Dynamics*, a monumental four-volume work that is often overlooked as an early example of American sociology of knowledge.[105] In this and several later works, Sorokin maintained that forms of "cultural mentalities" should generally be seen as independent variables in the functional relationship between systems of ideas and social structure. Although his idealistic theoretical framework occasioned considerable criticism, Sorokin's imaginative works are essential reading in the sociology of culture. Especially noteworthy is his perceptive study on the concepts of causality, space, and time.[106]

In 1942, Logan Wilson published a study that remains an outstanding analysis of the role of American scholars.[107] He built explicitly on Znaniecki's earlier work in this area, part of which is reprinted below, in Part II. However, Wilson relied more heavily upon empirical data than Znaniecki did, and his work contains a systematic investigation of the structure and functioning of universities and their consequent effects upon academic productivity and thought styles.

For an appreciation of the richness of early American studies, we recommend, in addition to the works cited above, the concise historical reviews by Franz Adler, Bernard Barber, and Robert K. Merton.[108] More recent contributions to the sociology of knowledge, as we have frequently pointed out, include sociological research on all major social institutions. Directly or indirectly, studies of intra-institutional and inter-institutional relationships involve analyses of the relationship between components of social structure and forms of mental productions.[109] This is especially true of research in which the analytical definition of institutions is similar to the following: "*organized sets of obligatory norms* . . . defined in terms of the *primary focus of values or interests* around which these sets cluster."[110] We list here only a few relevant studies concerned primarily with the "points of intersection" of major institutions.

In the relationship between the family and other institutional orders, many of the problems outlined by Max Weber have been researched by sociologists, historians, economists, and psychologists.[111] The precise connections between religious beliefs, characteristics of the family, and aspects of the economic order have been the subject of sharply contradictory interpretations, and recent research has not settled the matter. But a direct outgrowth of Weber's analyses are the numerous outstanding studies on the relationship between family structure and children's achievement motivation and attitudes, particularly recent works by David McClelland, John W. Atkinson, and Bernard Rosen.[112] A similar line of research has centered around the interrelationship of family influence and educational and occupational aspirations.[113] Another pertinent area of research has been concerned with the changing social position of youth and the development of adolescent subcultures. Representative studies of the emergence of distinctive values and normative systems among adolescent and youth groups include recent publications by Bell, Coleman, Eisenstadt, Gottlieb *et al.*, and Rosenberg.[114]

Weber's work in the sociology of ideology also provided key insights into the processes of social and cultural change in several institutional spheres. Regardless of the validity of the arguments advanced by Weber's critics, his works clearly were the impetus for several studies of the relationship between religion and political and economic change in various cultures. Examples are Jonassen's study of Norway as a nineteenth-century case of religious influence on economic activity; Bellah's analysis of the role of religion and cultural variables in pre-industrial Japan; Israel's work on the influence of economic, political, and religious factors on the emergence of industrial society in England; Geertz's study of cultural and religious foundations of economic and political change in Indonesia; Hansen's study of the role of religion and medieval municipal institutions in northern Europe in impelling change from traditional constraints on economic activity to legal and economic rationality; and Marcuse's analysis of parallels to Weber's thesis in the impact of Marxist thought on Soviet development.[115] More recently, a few researchers have attempted to reappraise Weber's work in terms of empirical data from American society.[116] But many others who accept his basic thesis object to its application to contemporary societies. It is probably true that in our increasingly secular society the influence of religious culture on social behavior has been greatly attenuated. However, a more precise answer will require continued research and evidence that is more nearly conclusive than what is available at present.

Other valuable studies from the sociology of religion have a different emphasis and interest. Among those that deserve mention are H. Richard Niebuhr's investigation of the manner in which religious ideas are mediated by social structure and then, in turn, influence the social organization of religious groups and Marshall Sklare's attempt to isolate factors leading to a conservative orientation in Judaism.[117]

Numerous studies of social stratification and economic organization have also been related to the sociology of knowledge, although they have not been labelled as such by researchers. Studies of social class and occupational positions and their influence on styles of thought have become increasingly precise and have contributed valuable data. Through the years, several community studies, such as *Middletown*,

Yankee City, Democracy in Jonesville, Deep South, and *Small Town in Mass Society*, have shown how class and prestige structures are influential in the acquisition of various motives, values, and beliefs.[118] Gwynne Nettler has proposed a method of studying differences among the ways in which individuals in various occupational categories predict certain major events.[119] Richard Centers' work on the social psychology of classes is among the few American studies dealing with class consciousness in a manner similar to the German Marxist approach.[120] Knowledge and attitudes pertaining to the social-stratification system have been analyzed in several studies, such as those by A. W. Jones, Rogoff, Gross, and Manis and Meltzer.[121] Recently, both Barber and Kahl have reviewed research on social-class identification as part of larger studies of reference group behavior.[122] Still another area of study has focused on the influence of social-class variables in the communication of ideas and learning. Examples are studies by Warner, Hollingshead, Davis, Rogoff, Sewell, and others.[123]

In the study of economic institutions, one recent area of investigation has been the genesis and development of ideologies that become linked to concrete organizations in the economic sphere. Examples of this focus are Bendix's comparative study of ideologies of management in East Germany and the United States and Riley's *The Corporation and Its Publics: Essays on the Corporate Image*.[124] Studies in the sociology of occupations and professions by Hughes, Hall, Chinoy, Wilensky, Merton *et al.*, and Becker *et al.* have dealt with the processes involved in the development of group loyalties and the acquisition of occupational ideologies and vocabularies of motives.[125]

In political sociology, only two relevant research concerns will be mentioned. First, a vast amount of research on political socialization in America has demonstrated the importance of family-based experience and parental attitudes in determining political allegiances and attitudes. For example, Berelson *et al.* found that the traditional voting pattern of parents is a much better predictor of political persuasion than are social-class variables or religious background.[126] Herbert Hyman surveyed the literature in this area and found that party affiliation is apparently transmitted more readily than is ideology in the course of childhood socialization as a result of greater direct indoctrination, a narrower range of alternatives, and the greater simplicity of the symbols involved.[127] Broader political orientations seem to develop through adult socialization, but little research has been done on the social-psychological mechanisms involved at this level. Studies of the "radical right" by Hofstadter, Lipset, and others have led to a "status politics" explanation for this group. It is suggested that "extreme right" or "pseudo-conservative" political views in the United States tend to be held by members of status-threatened groups.[128]

In the second line of research in political sociology, several studies of mass communication and voting behavior have indicated that structures of interpersonal relationships intervene between mass-communication sources and the individual. These mediating networks selectively filter materials from the flow of information and thus influence the knowledge and political attitudes of those who later receive the communication. Studies of personal influence by Katz and Lazarsfeld and by Merton have added to the growing body of evidence in this area.[129]

In the sociology of education and science there has been a rapid increase in direct contributions to the sociology of knowledge. For example, the relationship of education and the political order has been studied in some detail in recent years. The effect of educational systems on the political attitudes of high-school and college students, including the revolutionary role of student political movements in developing countries, has been an area of inquiry.[130] Recent research has also pointed out determinants and effects of variations in skill, knowledge, and styles of thought in colleges and universities. Studies by Wallace, Goldsen *et al.*, and others on student and faculty subcultures have made contributions in this area.[131] Recent studies of science as a communication system, the social processes of scientific discovery and scientific productivity, and the social origins of sciences are too numerous to review here. Part of this task has been performed by Norman Storer and Bernard Barber in their attempt to determine the characteristics of science as a social system.[132]

Finally, the following areas are relevant to an understanding of the relationship between the sociocultural environment and ideas: national character studies; [133] experimental research on persuasion; [134] analyses of criticisms in scientific literature; [135] sociological studies of literature, rhetoric, art, and the processes of communication between a public and an author or artists; [136] and the social psychology of creativity. [137]

Part III of this volume opens with three articles reporting research in religion, language, and the structural dimensions of intellectual systems, respectively. The remaining four readings consider such diverse topics as occupational ideologies, the relationship between minority status and the "intellectual perspective," sources of bias in anthropological field research, and some sociocultural factors related to publishing in scientific journals.

The selections by Weber and Currie are concerned with research on the independent function of ideas and language. We have noted that the sociology of knowledge in the Marxian and Mannheimian tradition runs the risk of exaggerated social determinism, which often leads to a disregard for the interactional relationship between mental productions and social structure. But ideas can and do operate as independent variables in societal change. This was Weber's main contention in *The Protestant Ethic and the Spirit of Capitalism*—a cautious attempt to correct some of the one-sided, social-deterministic explanations of social change that had been proposed previously. [138] Any number of sections from this monumental study could have been included here, but the choice finally fell to Weber's concluding statements on the ethos of Protestantism.

Weber notes that the rise of Protestantism in Germany, Switzerland, England, and the Netherlands coincided historically with the rise of "modern" capitalism in these countries and attempts to demonstrate how the Puritan branch of Calvinism and emerging capitalism reinforced each other in influencing large-scale changes in the social structure of these countries. [139] He supports his thesis by utilizing comparative data on the role of religious ideologies in Ancient China, India, and Palestine. [140] His dominant concern in several works was to determine what general social and cultural conditions favored the emergence of economic rationality. Briefly stated, Weber's thesis was that the values and beliefs of the Puritanical tradition—asceticism, sobriety, industriousness, and perseverance—facilitated the development of modern capitalism by inadvertently encouraging adherents of this religious group to pursue worldly success as a mark of grace. Here is Weber's vivid statement of the behavioral consequences of these values:

> The religious life of the saints, as distinguished from the natural life, was . . . no longer lived outside the world in monastic communities, but within the world and its institutions. This rationalization of conduct within this world, but for the sake of the world beyond, was the consequence of the concept of the calling of ascetic Protestantism. Christian asceticism, at first fleeing from the world into solitude, had already ruled the world which it renounced from the monastery and through the church. But it had on the whole left the naturally spontaneous character of daily life in the world untouched. Now it strode into the marketplace of life, slammed the door of the monastery behind it, and undertook to penetrate just that daily routine of life with its methodicalness, to fashion it into a life in the world, but neither of nor for this world.[141]

Weber contended that the Protestant concepts of salvation and the "calling" had the unanticipated consequence of motivating a large segment of the population to work diligently, to innovate in the world of work, to save money, and to reinvest it in business enterprises. Birnbaum summarizes this process as follows:

> Calvin posed an absolutely transcendental God, decreeing salvation or damnation at will. This created a terrible inner isolation for the believer, an intolerable burden of anxiety to know whether he was one of the elect. This anxiety forced the development of Calvinism (after Calvin) in a Puritan direction. One could know one was saved by works, which could not, however, insure one's salvation. Deprived of the relief of the confessional, deprived of the inward conception of grace possessed by Lutheranism . . . Puritanism turned outward. A modification of Luther's conception of the calling developed. One had a duty to work in the world, not because God had sanctified one's position, but because that position was an

opportunity to honour the glory of God. The absolute transcendence of God resulted in a rejection of the notion that God dwelt in the world—the world was, rather, an impersonal sphere, a setting for the labours of those who were, not vessels of the Divine, but its instruments.[142]

The Calvinist, never certain of his election, looked for signs of salvation in earthly prosperity. Moreover, he was not permitted to use his accumulating wealth in the pursuit of luxury or frivolous pleasure; he could demonstrate his election only by success in suppressing the natural man, by regular and rationalized work, and by systematic planning of his life—qualities that proved most fruitful in the world of work and business.

Weber agreed with Marx and his followers that Protestantism was not wholly responsible for the emergence of capitalism; certain economic conditions were necessary. But, given these preconditions, the Protestant constellation of religious ideas provided the "necessary" motivation and style of thought for the development of a new form of economic order.[143] In the selection reprinted below, Weber emphasizes that he does not argue for a monocausal view of the relation between religion and economic activity. This point is also stressed in his later studies of the world religions, in which he demonstrates the importance of technology, rational price systems, free markets, and other economic factors in explaining general economic development. Moreover, in several instances he explains the emergence and acceptance of ideologies in terms of characteristics of social-class structure before analyzing the subsequent independent role of these belief systems.

Weber's work is extremely important in that it shows the fruitfulness of a blend of historical and sociological analyses. Of even greater significance are his main theoretical points on the psychological function of belief systems and his contention that an appropriate ideology does not automatically emerge from a given social institution but may evolve from different institutional spheres of the society.

Several of the selections in Part III emphasize that motives, attitudes, values, and opinions are acquired through symbolic communication.

Thus, the manner and extent to which symbolic systems affect mental productions are most pertinent to the sociology of knowledge. Recently, intense research interest and activity have developed among linguistic anthropologists and psychologists regarding this question.[144] The selection by Ian D. Currie discusses a focal point of this research— the Sapir-Whorf linguistic-relativity hypothesis. This notion is one extreme facet of cultural relativism: the view that an individual's behavior, thought, and experiences can be understood only in terms of his cultural context. Linguistic-relativity propositions can be traced back to the German philosophical tradition of the eighteenth century. Friedrick Trendelenberg, among others, suggested that Aristotle's logic was greatly dependent upon certain features of the Greek language and would have been vastly different if he had lived in another culture. Similarly, linguistic *Weltanschauung* hypotheses, positing that a particular language structure implies a unique world view and perception of reality, were advanced by Wilhelm von Humboldt and, more recently, Ernst Cassirer.[145] Edward Sapir (an anthropologist) and Benjamin Whorf (a lay student of linguistics) formulated a similar thesis in America.

In his essay on "The Status of Linguistics as a Science," Sapir made the following statement, which is characteristic of his views on language as a partial "guide to social reality":

Though language is not ordinarily thought of as of essential interest to the students of social science, it powerfully conditions all our thinking about social problems and processes. Human beings do not live in the objective world alone, nor alone in the world of social activity as ordinarily understood, but are very much at the mercy of the particular language which has become the medium of expression for their society. It is quite an illusion to imagine that one adjusts to reality essentially without the use of language and that language is merely an incidental means of solving specific problems of communication or repletion. The fact of the matter is that the "real world" is to a large extent unconsciously built up on the language habits of the group. No two languages are ever sufficiently similar to be considered as representing the same social reality. The worlds in which different societies live are distinct worlds, not merely the same worlds with different labels attached.[146]

Whorf developed his corresponding argument in a series of brilliant papers on the American Indian languages. In one of the finest statements of his point of view, Whorf wrote:

> The background linguistic system (in other words, the grammar) of each language is not merely a reproducing instrument for voicing ideas but rather is itself the shaper of ideas, the program and guide for the individual's mental activity, for his analysis of impressions, for his synthesis of his mental stock in trade. Formulation of ideas is not an independent process, strictly rational in the old sense, but is part of a particular grammar and differs, from slightly to greatly, as between different grammars. We dissect nature along lines laid down by our native language. The categories and types that we isolate from the world of phenomena we do not find there because they stare every observer in the face; on the contrary, the world is presented in a kaleidoscopic flux of impressions which has to be organized by our minds—and this means largely by the linguistic systems in our minds. We cut nature up, organize it into concepts, and ascribe significance as we do, largely because we are parties to an agreement to organize it in this way—an agreement that holds through our speech community and is codified in the patterns of our language. The agreement is, of course, an implicit and unstable one, BUT ITS TERMS ARE ABSOLUTELY OBLIGATORY; we cannot talk at all except by subscribing to the organization and classification of data which the agreement decrees.[147]

Although the works of Sapir and Whorf were sometimes inconsistent and often not sufficiently precise for empirical tests, their central thesis remained the notion "that language functions not simply as a device for reporting experience but also, and more significantly, as a way of defining experience for its speakers."[148] In other words, language not only expresses ideas but also shapes them. Even basic concepts, such as those dealing with time, space, and matter, are linguistically relative and hence variable. Currie reviews this perspective in some detail and also surveys the types of evidence that Whorf and others cite in support of their thesis. As Currie asserts, conclusive evidence has not yet emerged from the research; however, several investigations have suggested that the main contentions of the formulation differ widely in validity. Still others have called into question the limits, interpretations, and verifiability of the thesis.

Many analyses in the sociology of knowledge takes as a point of departure a substantive property of some mode of thought; the selection by Jules J. Wanderer pursues a somewhat different strategy. Wanderer asks us to consider the possibility of supplementing this substantive approach with structural data that can be empirically generated. He emphasizes that the structural properties of particular intellectual systems can be uncovered as new subject matter for the sociology of knowledge. Furthermore, he believes that a useful method of doing so would be Guttman-scale analysis. In a unique application, Wanderer applies this technique to materials from the intellectual systems of Euclid and Spinoza in an attempt to show common features in the manner in which they structured their respective demonstrations of proof. Wanderer recognizes limitations on the applicability of this technique, but his relatively unassuming study is important as a reminder of the need to develop both new sources of data and imaginative research approaches in this area.

From studies of social status and social roles that may be related to the sociology of knowledge, we have chosen works by Vernon Dibble, Melvin Seeman, and Dennison Nash. Dibble's selection poses several problems that are relevant for an understanding of the flow of ideas in a complex society. In looking at the relationship between occupational ideologies and other systems of beliefs, he considers one aspect of the Durkheimian problem: What are the factors contributing to cultural consensus in a highly differentiated society? Rather than analyze the manner in which systems of beliefs become linked to an over-all system, he approaches the problem obliquely by asking: What are "the conditions under which consensus will or will not ensue from acceptance by some group of beliefs that had emerged out of conditions peculiar to other groups"? Specifically, he focuses on conditions under which occupational belief systems are diffused beyond the groups in which they first developed. Drawing upon data and propositions that have emerged from studies of stratification, attitude change, and mass communication, Dibble tentatively indicates that this diffusion is determined by such factors as the rank of an occupation, its internal organization, the parochialism of its ideology, the intended audience, relationships between practitioners and laymen, and the social position of laymen. In this essay, he both raises and clarifies a number of important questions that preoccupy researchers who adopt the sociology of knowledge perspective in studies of occupations and of mass communication.

Several theorists have noted that conditions producing social marginality are ubiquitous in complex societies. Marginality is virtually correlative with diversity in social characteristics and social change, and nearly every member of a complex society will experience marginality to some degree. The negative as well as the positive consequences of more "enduring" or ideal-typical forms of marginality have been discussed by many writers. For example, Veblen's essay on "the intellectual pre-eminence of the Jew," Simmel's analysis of the objective perspective of "the stranger," and works by Park, Stonequist, and Riesman have all suggested that a marginal social position may become a catalyst for creative thought.[149] Melvin Seeman uses the insights made possible by the role analyses of Simmel and Veblen and by psychological learning theory to analyze empirically the relationship between occupancy of a marginal position and intellectual "creativity."[150] His working hypothesis is that successful experience in a marginal situation will increase the likelihood of "high" intellectual perspective, since "the individual whose attempt to accommodate to the conflict in values that marginality imposes is reinforced by success will . . . learn the value of (and techniques for) questioning 'givens' and seeking new solutions." Although Seeman's limited data cannot conclusively verify this relation, he does present evidence pointing to the plausibility of the thesis. In addition, he suggests several similar lines of research for consideration by psychologists and sociologists.[151] Further research will no doubt yield other refined measures and definitions, but Seeman's study clearly shows that it is possible, at the present time, to submit hypotheses in this area to rigorous empirical testing.

Dennison Nash's "The Ethnologist as Stranger" applies the theoretical perspectives of Schütz and Simmel in analyzing the social role of the anthropological field worker as a "source of bias." Drawing on the published accounts of anthropologists as well as on his own experience in the field, Nash hypothesizes that the ethnologist in his data-gathering capacity has a role like that of the stranger. The objectivity of the ethnologist's final field report will reflect his perception of this role and his cognitive adaptations to it in a particular social situation. Social-psychological research has yielded tentative inventories of possible adaptation mechanisms and the perceptual, cognitive, and personality changes that may occur in such a role. Nash's paper raises a number of crucial points regarding the nature of social science research, several of which are taken up more directly by articles in Part IV.

The final selection in Part III is an example of recent empirical studies of the social organization of science. Although it has been suggested that scientific achievements should be judged without reference to the scholar's social characteristics, Diana Crane's study of the evaluation of articles by scientific journals reveals a significantly different pattern. Other recent studies have pointed out that a scholar's present position in the social structure of science may affect his future career and his scientific productivity.[152] Diana Crane takes these findings as the point of departure for an analysis of the academic characteristics of contributors to three professional journals in the social sciences. Her data tend to substantiate the appraisal that journal editors operate as "gate-keepers" of science by selectively screening the information that is permitted to circulate through these journals in the scientific community. The evaluation of scientific papers in her sample was apparently affected by nonscientific factors. The author concludes that "as a result of academic training, editorial readers respond to certain aspects of methodology, theoretical orientation, and modes of expression in the writings of those who have received similar training." In Part IV, John Walton offers further evidence on the effects of academic discipline and training in his study of conflicting findings in community power research.

In Part IV, we depart from a more traditional exposition of the sociology of knowledge to illustrate a recent tack taken by several American scholars in this field. The ten selections included bring together many of the conceptualizations discussed in the first three sections and apply them to the discipline of sociology itself. All these works take steps in the direction of a sociology of sociology by emphasizing the significant role of sociocultural variables and the "human factor."

Although sociologists have long been aware of the relationship between sociocultural variables and the development of types of scientific knowledge, the importance of this relationship for knowledge in the social sciences has been more or less overlooked until recently. To be sure, there was speculation about the impact of social and cultural factors upon the works of intellectuals in early studies by Mannheim, Weber, and Veblen, and in later works by Wilson, Znaniecki, Myrdal, and Lynd.[153] But sociologists have been reluctant to test empirically the relevance of many hypotheses suggested in these works for the development of knowledge in sociology. Studies on the impact of the social organization of the discipline, the prevailing climate of opinion, and the social background and personal values of researchers have been out of fashion, the assumption being, perhaps, that improvements in research techniques rule out significant influence by such factors. This assumption is clearly called into question by the works included in Part IV.

No major American or European scholar has yet specialized in research in the sociology of sociology,[154] and only occasionally are students introduced, in graduate courses, to some of the scattered findings in this area. There have been no large-scale studies of sociology as a research or teaching enterprise. The paucity of studies in this area is interesting in view of the rapid development of research interest in the sociologies of professions, education, and science, and in view of the great practical and scientific value that studies of sociology itself would certainly provide in these fields. This relative neglect is itself an interesting problem deserving of study from a sociology of knowledge perspective.

Fortunately, this selective inattention is being remedied, albeit slowly. Studies of sociology within a sociology of knowledge framework have increased in number of late and the growing interest in this area has been reflected in several symposia focusing on "sociological self-analysis." The essays collected under such titles as *Politics, Ethics, and Social Research; Reflections on Community Studies; Sociologists at Work: Essays on the Craft of Social Research;* and *Sociology on Trial* are examples of this emphasis.[155] Certain prominent scholars have made repeated appeals for more research in the sociology of sociology.[156] These appeals in themselves are "proof that the sociology of knowledge is with us, if not in all desirable clarity of subject matter, at least as a perspective."[157] Chronic controversies in the literature on the scientific and professional nature of the discipline, problems of theoretical and methodological unification in sociology, and the problem of values and valuations in sociological theory and research have provided additional impetus for study.

The research literature has tended to focus on aspects of a central question: What is the role of sociocultural variables—particularly socially imposed values, ideologies, and belief systems—in theoretical and research activity in the social sciences? Sociologists currently offer varied answers to this question. The central variables discussed most frequently are the political values and individual choices involved in research activity that may affect the objectivity and scientific validity of the results.

Most of the issues involved were spelled out much earlier in Max Weber's essays on methodology in the social sciences.[158] Although most current interpretations disagree with or refine Weber's orientation, he must nevertheless be acknowledged as one of the first to discuss problems in the sociology of sociology systematically. Throughout his work, Weber expressed deep concern for the nature of scientific inquiry in the social sciences, and his studies offer broad theoretical insights into the interdependence of scientific knowledge and values in society. In his essays on "Science as a Vocation" and "The Meaning of 'Ethical Neutrality' in Sociology and Economics," he stressed a major distinction between facts and values and emphasized that it is the job of science to discover and analyze the latter. He discussed differences between the natural and social sciences, recognizing that social influences and values are involved to a greater extent in the social sciences. It was his contention that values and valuations are essential subject matter in studies by social scientists. Moreover, a researcher's choice of problems for investigation may be influenced by personal and cultural values.

In all other respects, however, Weber maintained that the social sciences must be free of the influence of implicit subjective factors. The collection, analysis, and interpretation of data must be *Wertfrei*— value-free. Although he recognized that difficult moral problems arise when one tries to separate one's personal life from one's role as scientist, he insisted that the social scientist must strive to accomplish this separation. This point is clearly made in his spirited and perceptive essay on the vocation of science:

> It is said, and I agree, that politics is out of place in the lecture room. It does not belong there on the part of the students. . . . Neither does politics, however, belong in the lecture room on the part of the docents, and when the docent is scientifically concerned with politics, it belongs there least of all.
>
> To take a practical political stand is one thing, and to analyze political structure and party positions is another. When speaking in a political meeting about democracy, one does not hide one's personal standpoint; indeed, to come out clearly and take a stand is one's damned duty. The words one uses in such a meeting are not means of scientific analysis but means of canvassing votes and winning over others. They are not plowshares to loosen the soil of contemplative thought; they are swords against the enemies: such words are weapons. It would be an outrage, however, to use words in this fashion in a lecture or in the lecture room.[159]

Thus Weber presents the dilemma faced by a scientist who, as researcher and teacher, must deal in the realm of facts—with "what is"

—but who, as a citizen, is duty-bound to consider "what ought to be." Expressions of values are mandatory in certain situations, but, when acting as a scientist, one must refrain from making value judgments pertaining to facts.

Although most contemporary American sociologists may aspire to an ethically neutral form of sociology, as developed in Weber's works,[160] a number of leading scholars, arguing essentially from a sociology of knowledge perspective, have seriously challenged this position. Through the years, proponents of various views have debated a number of issues, including the degree to which the social sciences are themselves rooted in values, the manner in which values should be studied, and the degree to which the sociologist can be, or should be, value-free.[161] An American challenge to the "separation of values" viewpoint on these questions was made by Wirth and Shils in their introduction to the English translation of Mannheim's *Ideology and Utopia*. These men were among the first to call attention to the implications of the sociology of knowledge perspective for the social sciences as developed in Europe. They argued, as did Mannheim, that a sociologist's perceptions and thoughts are deeply influenced by his social situation and by the dominant values of his culture and that these influences necessarily affect his scientific work. They cannot be eliminated by refinements in research techniques, but they can be studied and taken into account by others in the interpretation of scientific findings.

In 1938, Robert S. Lynd echoed these views in his Stanford Little Lectures at Princeton. The following year, Lynd's lectures were published in the widely read *Knowledge for What?* Lynd noted that early American sociology had been concerned with social reform and had been engaged in research directed toward the solution of societal problems. By the late 1920's and 1930's, increased interest had developed in the scientific state of the discipline, leading to a greater concern with objectivity, developments in methodology, and the investigation of less value-laden empirical problems. There was a gradual shift toward empirical positivism and a value-free interpretation of sociology. Lynd believed that this reaction was most unfortunate, and he made a

spirited appeal for more involved and pragmatic research. He emphasized that sociologists are members of the society that they attempt to
study. Social ties give them perspectives, values, biases, and opinions
that *must* influence their research, whether they choose to recognize it
or not. However, these social ties also sensitize the social scientist to
major societal problems and stresses, and it is his responsibility to involve
himself in attempts to find solutions for these problems. Lynd contended that the sciences had been widely accepted only because they
paid off in practical terms. He appealed to sociologists to recognize this
fact and to remove themselves from their "sheltered tradition of 'scientific' objectivity."

More recently, C. Wright Mills espoused many of the same viewpoints in several works, particularly *The Sociological Imagination*. Mills
argued that contemporary sociologists often use the notion of scientific
objectivity as a rationale for accepting a particular theoretical perspective on society. He attacked the "separation of values" orientation,
contending that

> whether he is aware of it or not, anyone who spends his life studying
> society and publishing the results is acting morally and usually
> politically as well. The question is whether he faces this condition
> and makes up his own mind, or whether he conceals it from himself
> and from others and drifts morally. Many, I should say most, social
> scientists in America today are easily or uneasily liberal. They con-
> form to the prevailing fear of any passionate commitment. This,
> and not scientific objectivity, is what is really wanted by such men
> when they complain about making value judgments.[162]

This view has found general support in a series of works by the noted
economist Gunnar Myrdal, particularly in the methodological appen-
dices to *An American Dilemma*. Myrdal argues that a disinterested
sociology is impractical, if not impossible, since the social sciences in
any country are part of a cultural system and cannot transcend the
values and assumptions of this system.[163] All research in the social
sciences involves viewpoints at various stages of the investigation, and
these viewpoints presume valuations. Myrdal also notes that a researcher

can begin with any set of value premises he chooses, but that his work is more likely to be financed and accepted if his value premises are in accord with the dominant viewpoints in his own and other disciplines. Myrdal emphasizes that, given the obvious influences of cultural values and personal choices in research activity, the researcher should specify his assumptions and choices so that other scholars can bear them in mind in considering his findings and conclusions.

Through the years, the writings of these and other challengers to the concept of scientific objectivity have attracted considerable attention.[164] Several hypotheses have grown out of these works that point to sociological self-analysis as a potentially fruitful direction of study. Part IV opens with two valuable papers that span a range of these suggested research directions. Taken together, Merton's "Social Conflict over Styles of Sociological Work" and McKee's "Some Observations on the Self-Consciousness of Sociologists" provide an introduction to the sociology of sociology.

Merton's paper serves several other important functions. It notes the tentative and hazardous nature of many current interpretations in the sociology of sociology; it calls for comparative historical analysis of the development of sociology in various countries and suggests an informal agenda of research orientations; it provides a concise review of three broad phases of development in sociology, drawing on reports given at the Fourth World Congress of Sociology. A cogent portion of the paper is concerned with processes of interaction among sociologists and, in particular, with certain social conflicts and their consequences for the development of sociology as a discipline. Contrary to the assertions of many others, Merton argues that the controversy among sociologists has less to do with intellectual bases of disagreement than with competing views on the appropriate role of the sociologist and the proper allocation of intellectual resources. Finally, the paper considers the possible role played by heterodoxies among the sociologists of each nation in the development of a world sociology.

McKee's paper complements Merton's by discussing significant research problems, not the least of which is the tension between the two "images" of sociological work mentioned above: sociology as "concerned" and as "value-free." Whereas Merton's concern is with the role of social processes internal to sociology, McKee's paper focuses on the ways in which sociology may be affected by societal conditions. McKee takes a suggestive step in the direction of a sociology of sociology by pointing out several major developments—all related to the progressive rationalization of life—that appear to be changing the nature of sociology. He chides sociologists for their failure to appreciate and study the sweeping impact on social science made by professionalization, modernization, and national policies.

It is perhaps too soon to review trends in the literature in response to such calls for research as those by Merton and McKee. It is certainly too early to suggest which parts of the emerging literature will prove most fruitful in the long run. Here we can merely indicate some of the tentative steps in the direction of a sociology of sociology in America that have been taken recently. There have been at least four lines of inquiry. First, through the years, scholars have utilized an implicit sociology of knowledge framework in several fine studies of trends and movements in the history of social thought. This type of research has been greatly extended in the past few years. Second, and more recently, there have been indications that comparative studies of sociology in various countries are beginning to receive more attention. Third, limited research has developed on certain values and interests of sociologists—e.g., studies of their voting behavior, styles of work, and publication productivity. Finally, there has been continued interest in the possible effects of implicit ideologies and value premises in certain areas of contemporary American theory and research. These lines of inquiry are hardly distinct from one another, but they do illustrate certain foci of research contributing to a sociology of sociology. We could not hope to review all the relevant studies from each line of inquiry, much less to reproduce them here. We must be content to mention a few valuable contributions to each line of inquiry and to include some of the most provocative studies reflecting these interests.

Studies of the History of Sociology. Notable examples of studies utilizing the sociology of knowledge perspective in analyses of the history of American sociology are works by Coser on conflict theory and by the Hinkles on general developments in sociological theory and research, particularly their excellent treatment of the emergence of major assumptions and divisions in the discipline.[165] Robert Nisbet, in a brilliant work, has traced the development of sociological ideas in Europe as responses to major events and processes of history.[166] Among many other valuable contributions in a similar vein, the works of Heinz Maus and Harry E. Barnes deserve mention for their discussions of the intellectual and sociohistorical roots of ideological components of early European and American social thought.[167] Studies on the relationship between prevailing climates of opinions and the work styles and social thought of various founding fathers of the discipline have been conducted by several scholars, especially Notestein on William G. Sumner, Rosenberg on Thorstein Veblen, and Coser on Georg Simmel.[168]

Most previous studies on the history of social theory have offered qualitative descriptions of the ideas and value premises of the individual or groups studied, roughly correlated with their social position and the dominant values or climate of opinion of the times. Rarely have such studies employed refined techniques of content and logical analysis. Their conclusions must therefore be viewed as tentative.

Examples of the techniques often employed in such studies are provided in the selection by Bend and Vogelfanger, as well as in the point of origin of their analysis: the classic study by C. W. Mills on "The Professional Ideology of Social Pathologists." Through analysis of the content of early textbooks on social problems, Mills suggested ways in which value orientations were operative in early American sociology. He discovered that the authors of these texts tended to have similar social backgrounds and group memberships, which might explain the consensus on evaluations and interpretations of social problems that is evident in their works. Mills maintained that the type and scope of the analyses conducted by these early sociologists implied a particular perspective and attitude. For example, he found that these authors had defined social problems as deviations from selected norms of a rural society—norms that they implicitly sanctioned—without considering the consequences of social change or shifts in standards. Bend and Vogelfanger review Mills' thesis and then report on their replication of his study with a selection of widely used texts on contemporary social problems. They demonstrate that a number of his observations must be qualified, since the study of social pathology has been affected by advances in sociology over the past twenty-five years. Some of the standards and conceptualizations noted in the earlier study have disappeared from the literature; others remain. Bend and Vogelfanger cite other shortcomings, as well, in current research on social problems.

Studies of Sociology in Different Countries. A systematic comparison of theoretical and substantive emphases in contemporary sociology in a number of countries is not available at the present time. However, the recent growth of interest in international sociology has yielded a number of descriptive studies of the discipline in other countries. Most of these relate the state of the discipline in a particular nation to its language, unique cultural values, and historical developments in social institutions. The comparative evidence from such studies clearly suggests that sociology as it is taught and practiced in a particular society is largely a product of the complex sociocultural system. Variant developments in sociology from a cross-cultural perspective are illustrated and explained in several anthologies on sociological theory, notably those by Roucek, Becker and Barnes, and Gurvitch and Moore.[169] Until recently, most of this literature had focused on countries from which American sociology derived much of its intellectual heritage—Germany, France, Britain, and Italy. However, recently there have appeared discussions of develoments in sociology in Russia and Eastern Europe, as well as in Asia, Africa, and South America.

The thoughtful and penetrating comparative analyses of American and European variants of the sociology of knowledge by Merton and Wolff also deserve careful study.[170] Merton contends, as did Mannheim earlier, that the European sociology of knowledge perspective on the social roots of knowledge tends to take on special pertinence under certain sociocultural conditions.

With increased social conflict, differences in the values, attitudes and modes of thought of groups develop to the point where the orientation which these groups previously had in common is overshadowed by incompatible differences. Not only do there develop distinct universes of discourse, but the existence of any one universe challenges the validity and legitimacy of the others. The co-existence of these conflicting perspectives and interpretations within the same society leads to an active and reciprocal *distrust* between groups. Within a context of distrust, one no longer inquires into the content of beliefs and assertions to determine whether they are valid or not, one no longer confronts the relevant evidence, but introduces an entirely new question: how does it happen that these views are maintained? Thought becomes functionalized; it is interpreted in terms of its psychological or economic or social or racial sources and functions.[171]

It is clear that these social conditions were present in Europe when the sociology of knowledge developed there, but America has never experienced them to the same extent. This fact perhaps helps to explain why the sociology of knowledge developed by German and French scholars took on a very different character after being introduced to American sociology.

Both Merton and Wolff show in some detail that the European and American variants of the sociology of knowledge differ in their conceptions of subject matter, appropriate research techniques and procedures, the data necessary to certify facts, and the place of facts in the development of the social sciences. The excerpt from Wolff's work offers a brief but cogent description of the dominant metaphysical premises of the two variants. Here Wolff emphasizes that sociology, in not being greatly self-critical, does not "wholly reject its own metaphysical inclinations." He asserts that the American and European variants have tended to bestow reality on different aspects of social phenomena. Viewed generally, American sociology is characterized by a concern with individual-psychological realism, social-historical nominalism, and scientific truth. European sociology is characterized more by a concern with social-historical realism, individual-psycholological nominalism, and existential truth. Another important point in Wolff's paper is his contention that "methodological problems, on the one hand, and volitional and metaphysical problems, on the other, have different criteria of confirmation of truth." He suggests that the sociology of knowledge, being "applied theory," is not consistent with the formalism of current American sociology.

Studies of American Sociologists. We noted earlier that sociologists are notorious for studying everything except their own discipline and its institutional patterns. What critiques of sociological theory and research exist generally focus on the past or on other countries. There have been no systematic empirical studies of American sociologists, although we have some data on the voting behavior, styles of work, and professional orientations of small samples. Lazarsfeld and Thielens, for example, report a study based on 2,451 interviews with social scientists. Analysis of their data on the voting behavior and political orientations of 405 sociologists in the sample shows that this group was somewhat more liberal and more inclined to the Democratic Party than were members of other social science disciplines.[172] Turner obtained similar findings for a sample of 298 sociologists.[173] These studies suggest that this particular voting pattern is probably related to experience and professional training rather than to such factors as religious background, ethnicity, place of residence, or parental political-party preference. The relationship between class origins and the political ideologies of sociologists has been considered in a secondary analysis of the Lazarsfeld and Thielens data.[174]

Several studies have been conducted on factors in the work style and publication productivity of sociologists.[175] Although all these studies base their conclusions on data derived from a few variables in limited samples, available findings do tend to indicate consistently that occupational and institutional social conditions are reflected in the prolificacy and merit of publications. It has been found, for example, that publication prolificacy tends to be related to the rate of educational progress, early publication activity, academic origin, sex, and religion. The merit of publications appears to be influenced in greater measure by situational pressures, the researcher's area of academic interest, and his orientation toward the community of disciplinary specialists (as opposed to the community of college teachers).

Logan Wilson has made several suggestions for further directions of study in his discussion of the function of social pressures, role conflicts, and reference group behavior in academia. In a more recent volume, *The Academic Marketplace*, Caplow and McGee touch upon similar aspects of teaching and research in situations of higher learning. Lewis Coser, in his tentative discussion of the functions of small group research in the current organization of American sociology, is among the few who have considered the importance of further studies of these phenomena in the discipline of sociology itself.[176]

The periodic debates in the literature on the nature of sociology as a research and teaching enterprise may be regarded as harbingers of such studies. A few discussions of the social organization of sociology and sociologists' roles, styles of work, and dilemmas of professional orientation have emerged from these debates. For example, complementing our selections by Merton and McKee are essays by Mills, Hughes, Goode, and Parsons, among others.[177] Unfortunately, as Merton indicates, discussions in these areas have often become attacks and polemical defenses of various viewpoints on sociological work. It would seem desirable to have, in the future, systematic studies of the values, interests, and opinions of various social scientists as compared with those of other groups. If it is found that social scientists do have characteristic values, it would be important to study both the precise causes of these distinctive attitudes and their consequences for research activity. Some hypotheses and important data bearing on this general question are supplied in the other selections in Part IV, which analyze various "choices" forced upon the social scientist.

The Role of Implicit Value Premises and "Choices" in Theory and Research. For some time, scholars have sought to demonstrate that ideologies and value premises play an important role in sociological theorizing and research. More than twenty years ago, Kurt H. Wolff described a general conservative orientation in American sociology, citing the selective inattention to certain areas of study and particular usages of such concepts as caste, folkways, and mores.[178] He attempted a socio-cultural interpretation of this orientation, taking into account power distributions in society, social backgrounds of individuals, attitudes, beliefs, values, opinions, etc. In a similar vein, Maurice Stein has recently argued that some of the other concepts utilized by contemporary sociologists—norms, roles, and social system—imply a conservative political bias.[179] These views also find support in studies that point to the pervasive influence of personal choices made by researchers.

Several distinct problems of values and choices come to the fore in Part IV. Some of the authors argue that values are invariably embedded in the concepts and theories used in the social sciences. Others contend that values, as reflected in the choices made in the gathering, analysis, and interpretation of data, play a significant role in the scientific investigation of a problem. Cutting across these questions is the question of the role of certain liberal and conservative tendencies among sociologists. These issues are considered from different perspectives by the various authors. Their findings and conclusions are basically in accord, although they differ in their suggestions for the use of the sociology of knowledge perspective and other measures to minimize the influence of the human factor in research activity. Each author asks us to consider the importance in the research enterprise of certain demands and values imposed upon researchers by primary groups, their social backgrounds, and the wider society. After applying this perspective to various aspects of sociology, each author concludes that the sociocultural system has a significant impact upon the investigator, his methodologies, and his modes of analysis.

Their data suggest that there are several relatively "open" choice points in the scientific method and that decisions made at these points will selectively distort "reality" for the investigator. They present evidence that socially influenced choices of research problems, theoretical perspectives, models of society, hypotheses, concepts, and research techniques, for example, help to determine the nature of the data that the researcher will analyze and interpret. These decisions, along with reportorial styles, selectively determine the nature of the findings that will reach the scientific public. The selections in Part IV suggest the importance of developing the sociology of knowledge perspective not as a process of determining truth per se, but as a method of sensitizing researchers to the effects of value premises and individual choices upon research operations and the measures that might be used to counteract these effects.[180]

The selection by Leonard Lieberman provides both a brief historical background and a contemporary judgment on the basic ideological schism between what he terms the "lumpers" and the "splitters" in the anthropological study of race. Lieberman regards the chronic controversies between these groups of scholars as an illustration of how knowledge in the social sciences may be influenced by changing social and cultural structures. He finds (as does John Walton in the last study in Part IV) that the use of refined and varied research techniques in gathering data has not necessarily reduced disagreements among scholars; the same research findings have been interpreted as consistent with opposing theoretical perspectives.

The first selection by John Horton is a spirited attack on current attempts at objectification and reification in certain areas of the social sciences. Horton focuses for the most part on ideological perspectives and implicit value premises in contemporary uses of the concepts of alienation and anomie. It is his contention that, despite many arguments to the contrary, contemporary studies of these phenomena are far from objective. Horton briefly reviews previous uses of these concepts, noting particularly that Marx and Durkheim used them in an evaluative sense for radical attacks upon the dominant values of developing industrial societies. Horton then maintains that these concepts have been redefined by contemporary researchers in accord with a conservative and conformist ideology, under the guise of value-free sociology. He suggests that further study may yield an explanation in terms of changes in social structure and in the class position of sociologists.

The second selection by Horton and those by Adams, Williams, and Walton offer insights and empirical data bearing on a current debate in the literature regarding the impact of prevailing images of societal organization on research. Horton surveys the ramifications of theoretical perspectives in the study of social problems, with specific examples from research on the problem of the American Negro. Theories of social problems are discussed as normative perspectives that interpret social facts on the basis of particular images of man and society. Horton offers an ideal-typical classification of elements in what he interprets as the polar theoretical frameworks in contemporary sociology—the "order" and the "conflict" perspectives. Some of the underlying value premises of these perspectives are discussed, and their implications for research are outlined.

The views presented in the selection by Bert N. Adams are in essential accord with those of Horton. Adams outlines a number of other issues involved in the debate between the "order" and "conflict" perspectives, pointing to the great need for theoretical synthesis in this area. Such a synthesis, he suggests, would result in the dominance of a coercion (conflict) framework. Adams further suggests that coercion, conflict, and change are "more basic societal attributes" than are equilibrium and consensus.

Robin M. Williams, Jr., takes exception to this view in a brief commentary on the papers by Horton and Adams. He acknowledges a need for theoretical synthesis but asserts that such a synthesis should not result from attempts to delineate more "basic" or fundamental societal attributes.[181] According to Williams, research results make it evident that social groups are characterized by a number of societal processes— consensus, sociability interdependence, and conflict. "The real job is to show how actual social structure operating in these ways can be predicted and explained." Williams discusses other issues involved in this controversy and indicates some of the methodological disadvantages of studying ideological components of social theory as artificially polarized positions. He points out the need for more refined studies to consider internal variations in theoretical perspectives and emphasizes that several overlapping debates have often become tied together in the literature. This has had the effect of blurring the distinctions between key concepts.

The research reported by Walton represents a significant attempt to place hypotheses and conclusions from previous qualitative studies on a firmer empirical basis. Walton discusses a concrete example of the influence of certain perspectives and choices in the recent prolific but contradictory interdisciplinary research on community power. He finds that the disciplinary background of researchers (political science or sociology) tends to determine the research techniques utilized. These, in turn, are related to the type of community power structures found in research. Walton echoes an opinion expressed by Robin Williams, namely, that to demonstrate the influence of value premises or social factors on findings is not to show any inherent unreliability in the scientific method. But Walton's findings clearly indicate that we should look at the product of research from a sociology of knowledge perspective if we want to understand the process of research fully. It is becoming more and more apparent that this is a prime necessity in many areas of "chronic controversy" in the social sciences.

CRITICISMS AND PROBLEMS

The four selections in Part V complement several of the selections in Parts II, III and IV and afford a sampling of the criticisms directed against the sociology of knowledge approach since the translation of Mannheim's works. In essence, most criticisms have singled out the epistemological problem, ending with some form of the following question: If all ideas are socially determined and at the same time are relative to a particular sociocultural environment, then is not the sociology of knowledge itself the product of the particular sociocultural forces operative at a particular time and, therefore, lacking in validity except in terms of the immediate situation?[182] For the most part, later developments in the sociology of knowledge have ignored this problem. Instead they have utilized the perspective in attempts to understand the relationship between ideas and the sociocultural environment. Thus, almost all of the later studies reprinted here begin with the basic premise that ideas are influenced by a definable sociocultural environment, and that this connection underlies the relationship among ideas, behavior, and the existential bases of behavior. As we have stated, we believe that many of the problems in the sociology of knowledge stem from the difficulty in distinguishing this perspective from the basic "sociological approach" to behavior.

Beyond the general area of epistemological validity, the criticisms have concentrated on the grounds on which ideas and ideologies are assigned to particular social categories in order to understand the mental productions arising out of their social relationships and, further, on whether or not the sociology of knowledge can be reconciled with a view of scientific truth as relatively unaffected by the particular sociocultural environment. The latter point is the focus of the criticisms offered by Sir Karl Popper in the first selection of Part V. This question takes the following form: Is scientific objectivity on the part of the observer the source or the result of the objectively institutionalized framework of science?

Popper takes the sociologist of knowledge to task for the claim that awareness of the sociocultural determinants of behavior will free intellectuals from the influence of these determinants and allow them to step outside the "total ideology." What is needed, according to Popper, is the realization that many of the nonscientific features of the social sciences are due to the lack of a universe of discourse within which results can be weighed against universal scientific truth. As far as Popper is concerned, the social sciences have not yet acquired a "publicity of method." Thus, the future of the social sciences depends not so much on the acquisition of a sociology of knowledge perspective, but on engagement in piecemeal social research, the results of which can be tested in terms of researchable hypotheses and measured against universal scientific criteria. The scientist's critical inspection of his own perspective is no guaranteee that he will rid himself of subjectivity. In fact, practicality in the sense of application of findings means that a certain amount of involvement is necessary for the social scientist.[183]

In our next selection, Gerard De Gré follows dissatisfaction with the term "sociology of knowledge" to its logical conclusion, urging substitition of the term "gnosio-sociology." De Gré's study is important not only because it attempts to clarify the perspective of the sociology of knowledge, but also because it is one of the earliest pleas by a sociologist that the sociologist of knowledge (gnosio-sociologist) divest himself of concern for epistemological problems. The term "gnosio-sociology," therefore, turns out to be something more than a semantic device. In the past, many sociologists of knowledge stepped beyond a particular perspective for understanding mental processes in the environment and moved toward the establishment of certain propositions regarding a theory of knowledge. This forced the theorist to deal with the epistemological problem. The inability to do so in a satisfactory fashion was the major flaw in the works of Durkheim, for example. "The sociological *theory of knowledge*, as contrasted with the *sociology* of knowledge, . . . is an epistemological position which attempts to infer from the findings of gnosio-sociology certain hypotheses concerning the relationship between propositions and *that which* the propositions are about."[184]

It appears that this distinction, if adopted by the sociologist of knowledge, would meet several of Popper's major objections to the approach. In proposing three elements as necessary for a sociology of knowledge, De Gré makes a determined effort to avoid the epistemological problems surrounding the area.

The selection by Arthur Child attempts to come to grips with a series of related methodological and theoretical questions that he posed in an earlier study on "The Problem of Imputation in the Sociology of Knowledge."[185] He had concluded that article with

a criticism which strikes at the very heart of Lukács's theory: How is one to know which thoughts, feelings, etc., are, in point of fact, the ones rationally suited for a given class position? For this, after all, is Lukács's criterion of imputation. And the standard can only be the "ideology of the proletariat" itself. But thereby we enter a vicious circle, for it is rational suitability that determines the ideology of the proletariat, and it is the ideology of the proletariat that determines rational suitability. . . .

Imputations have been made and will continue to be made. While we have refuted the attempts to justify them, the question therefore remains, do they have any justification? Can they be justified? If so, in what sense? A consideration of this problem, we feel, would prove long and difficult. And whether the answer, in the end, should turn out to be positive or should prove merely negative, it would require an examination of the more fundamental assumptions implicit in the process of imputation.[186]

In developing an approach to this general problem of imputation, Child emphasizes the psychological relatedness among the members of particular classes.[187] The ability of the observer to impute ideologies depends to a great extent on the distinction between class as a membership category and class as an affiliational category. The affiliational categories include not only socio-economic groupings but also groups that are ideologically organized. In groups of the latter type the problem of imputation diminishes because the observer need be aware of only the major feature upon which the appeal of the ideology is based. In the final analysis, Child concludes, it is with respect to affiliational groups that the observer can validly engage in the imputation of ideas.

The final selection, by Frank Hartung, deals with most of the criticisms directed against the sociology of knowledge approach since it became popular. Hartung begins by discussing the ramifications of what he regards as the two major problems in the sociology of knowledge. The first problem involves the locus of the existential basis of thought. In essence, this problem is analogous to the first question posed by Merton in his paradigm. The second involves the way in which thought is related to the imputed existential base. This problem corresponds to the third question in Merton's paradigm. Missing is Merton's second question, which further specifies the steps between one and three—"What mental productions are being sociologically analyzed?" The main body of Hartung's analysis is devoted to a critique of the Mannheimian approach to the sociology of knowledge. Hartung is one of several writers who go beyond the traditional critique of the epistemological question and look into the *intent* behind Mannheim's analysis. He finds that much of Mannheim's interest and concern can be understood as an attempt to solidify the social basis of his own social group, the intellectuals. In conclusion, Hartung writes, "Mannheim has completely failed to show how the validity of a proposition is even partially dependent upon the social situation of the one who asserted it."[188]

The selections included in this volume raise more questions than they answer. Studies guided by a sociology of knowledge perspective may continue to oscillate between the generalizing and the particularizing approach to science illustrated here, but it seems more likely that the current trend toward a *rapprochement* of theory and methods will continue in American research. Several years ago, Merton commented as follows on general developments in American sociology:

> The stereotype of the social scientist high in the empyrean of pure ideas uncontaminated by mundane facts is fast becoming no less out-moded than the stereotype of the social researcher equipped with questionnaire and pencil, hot on the chase of the isolated and meaning-less statistic. For in building the mansion of sociology during the last decade, theorist and empiricist have learned to work together. What is more, they have learned to talk to one another in the process. At times, this means only that a sociologist has learned to talk to himself, since increasingly the same man has taken up both theory and research. Specialization and integration have developed hand in hand.[189]

In these introductory remarks, we have touched upon several areas within which we believe that such a synthesis has taken place. Our endeavor will have been successful if this volume has sharpened the reader's appetite for the vast body of literature that comes under the heading "sociology of knowledge."

NOTES

1 The articles concerned with attitude cited in Richard Dewey and W. J. Humber, *An Introduction to Social Psychology* (New York: The Macmillan Co., 1966), p. 222, provide examples of the haziness of the concept. For a statement on the varying uses of the term "sociology of knowledge", see Peter Berger and Thomas Luckman, *The Social Construction of Reality* (Garden City, N.Y.: Doubleday & Co., 1966), pp. 1–17. The

definition proposed by these authors represents the most inclusive one to date, i.e.: "The sociology of knowledge must concern itself with everything that passes for 'knowledge' in society" (p. 13).

2 Kurt H. Wolff, "The Sociology of Knowledge and Sociological Theory", in L. Gross (ed.), *Symposium on Sociological Theory* (New York: Harper and Row, 1959), p. 568. Berger and Luckman (in *The Social Construction of Reality*) have broken out of the traditionally narrow approach by generalizing the concept of knowledge. In lectures to his students, Robin M. Williams, Jr., has stated that a more appropriate label for the field would be "sociology of culture." The use of this term, he believes, would sensitize researchers to look for the relationships that exist between any unit of culture and any unit of society. He notes that self theory, reference group theory, consistency theory, etc., have not been seen as fitting the sociology of knowledge perspective in its traditional conceptualization because of the limiting definition of "knowledge."

3 Howard Becker and Helmut Otto Dahlke, "Max Scheler's Sociology of Knowledge," *Philosophy and Phenomenological Review*, II (1942), 310–31. Berger and Luckman (in *The Social Construction of Reality*) also point out that the stated concern of the sociology of knowledge has been with the relationship between the individual and society; however, they fail to note that almost all of the empirical and theoretical work in this area has focused on the social *determination* of the mental system of society. Examples of the stated concern with the relationship can be seen in the following definitions of sociology of knowledge, which are typical: "the branch that studies relationships between thoughts and society"—Lewis Coser and Bernard Rosenberg, *Sociological Theory* (New York: The Macmillan Co., 1964), p. 667; "concern with relations between knowledge and other existential factors in society"—Robert K. Merton, *Social Theory and Social Structure* (Glencoe, Ill.: The Free Press, 1957), p. 456; "seeks to analyze the relationship between knowledge and existence"—Karl Mannheim, p. 109, below.

4 This conception could perhaps be termed the "sociological bias" in the sociology of knowledge approach. Although claiming to be aware of the functional relationship between individual thoughts and the environment, sociologists have continued to operate primarily on the basis of "groups influencing behavior." It is interesting to note that, although Max Scheler emphasized the relational aspect, he formulated the sociology of knowledge to demonstrate how social reality determined the existence of ideas but not necessarily their content. Today sociologists tend to take the former as given and concentrate on how the content of ideas is determined by the sociocultural environment. The studies on time as a sociocultural product, the studies surrounding the Sapir-Whorf hypothesis, and the studies in the area of achievement motivation, several of which we discuss in this introduction, illustrate this tendency.

5 This is not to disagree with Kurt Wolff's comment that the sociology of knowledge perspective never became influential in American sociology because of the nominalism characteristic of sociology in this country. Wolff's remark refers specifically to the Mannheim approach to the sociology of knowledge, and he is therefore correct in his observation. See Wolff, "The Sociology of Knowledge and Sociological Theory," pp. 580–92. For a similar characterization of American sociology, see Roscoe C. Hinkle and Gisela J. Hinkle, *The Development of Modern Sociology* (New York: Random House, 1954).

6 That is, more and more emphasis is being given to those aspects of the groups that are seen as influencing specific units of knowledge: e.g., attitudes, beliefs, values. This trend is simply a specific form of a more general trend in sociology as a whole, especially in

America. See John W. Petras, "The Genesis and Development of Symbolic Interactionism in American Sociology" (unpublished Ph.D. dissertation, University of Connecticut, 1966); and Melvin Seeman, "Review of the International Encyclopedia of the Social Sciences," *American Sociological Review*, XXXIII (1968), 805–8.

7 In the preface to John Dewey, *German Philosophy and Politics* (New York: G. P. Putnam's Sons, 1915). This statement contains the essence of the pragmatic approach to reality and knowledge.

8 See, especially, John Dewey, *Human Nature and Conduct* (New York: Henry Holt & Co., 1922).

9 This notion is best illustrated by the concept of habit as developed by Dewey. See John W. Petras, "John Dewey and the Rise of Interactionism in American Social Theory," *Journal of the History of the Behavioral Sciences*, IV (1968), 18–29. For a similar interpretation of the works of George Herbert Mead, see Herbert Blumer, "Society as Symbolic Interaction," in A. Rose (ed.), *Human Behavior and Social Processes* (Boston: Houghton Mifflin Co., 1962), pp. 179–92.

10 Henry W. Maier, *Three Theories of Child Development* (New York: Harper and Row, 1965). Space limitations prevent us from including a selection by Piaget. His studies are important for the sociology of knowledge in that they demonstrate empirically the interdependent relationship between the child's mental abilities and the sociocultural environment. For an appreciation of this contribution we recommend all of Piaget's translated works, particularly Jean Piaget, *Six Psychological Studies* (New York: Random House, 1967). Also see Millie Almy, with Edward Chittenden and Paula Miller, *Young Children's Thinking* (New York: Columbia Teachers College, 1966).

11 An excellent unpublished source on the historical development of the sociology of knowledge perspective, which traces it back to the Skeptics of ancient Greece, is Louis Wirth's lectures in the Sociology of Knowledge course at the University of Chicago. collected by his students. We have been afforded the use of a copy by Bernard N. Meltzer.

12 Francis Bacon, pp. 89–96, below.

13 These are the same three sources suggested by Coser and Rosenberg, *Sociological Theory*, pp. 667–84. On the role played by pragmatism in this regard, see C. Wright Mills, *Sociology and Pragmatism* (New York: Oxford University Press, 1966); and Morton White, *Social Thought in America* (Boston: Beacon Press, 1963). See also Henry D. Aiken, "Pragmatism and America's Philosophical Coming of Age," in William Barrett and Henry D. Aiken (eds.), *Philosophy in the Twentieth Century* (New York: Random House, 1962), pp. 47–81; Thelma Herman, "Pragmatism: A Study in Middle-Class Ideology," *Social Forces*, XXII (1943–44), 405–10; and John W. Petras, "Psychological Antecedents of Sociological Theory in America: James Mark Baldwin and William James," *Journal of the History of the Behavioral Sciences*, IV (1968), 132–42. For a brief discussion of the sociologists who made up the Chicago School, see R. E. L. Faris, *Chicago Sociology* (San Francisco: Chandler Publishing Co., 1967).

14 For an excellent discussion of the role of the folk psychologists in this regard, see Fay Berger Karpf, *American Social Psychology* (New York: McGraw-Hill Book Co., 1932), p. 41–65. For a shorter discussion with a different focus, see E. K. Francis, "The Nature of the Ethnic Group," *American Journal of Sociology*, LII (1947), 393–400.

15 As will be seen in selections throughout this volume, the problem of imputation has long been considered the central epistemological issue in the sociology of knowledge.

16 Raymond Aron, *German Sociology* (New York: The Free Press of Glencoe, 1964). p. 108. For an example of Wilhelm Dilthey's work in this area, see his *Pattern and Meaning in History: Thoughts on History and Society* (New York: Harper Torchbooks, 1962). For further discussion of Dilthey's influence on German sociologists, specifically Max Weber, see Don Martindale, *The Nature and Types of Sociological Theory* (Boston: Houghton Mifflin Co., 1962), pp. 277–383. On the role of phenomenology in the development of German social thought, see Quentin Lauer, *Phenomenology: Its Genesis and Prospect* (New York: Harper Torchbooks, 1965); and Anna-Teresa Tymieniecka, *Phenomenology and Science in Contemporary European Thought* (New York: Noonday Press, 1962). The works of Alfred Schütz are among the finest statements of the relationship between phenomenology and the problem of the sociology of knowledge, although they are largely unappreciated in American sociology because they have only recently become available in English translation. Berger and Luckman explicitly use many of Schütz's ideas in *The Social Construction of Reality*. Other selections in this volume also utilize his theoretical framework. The primary focus of Schütz's theories can be found in his *Collected Papers*, Vol. I: *The Problem of Social Reality*, ed. by Maurice Natanson (The Hague: Martinus Nijhoff, 1962).

17 Aron, *German Sociology*, p. 109.

18 An example would be Durkheim's concern with the influence of society in establishing categories of thought within the mind of the individual. This particular approach to the relationship between the mind and society has no counterpart in German sociology, in large part because the orientation of German sociologists was derived primarily from philosophical rather than psychological concerns. Durkheim was interested in how the social order affected individual psychologies (not to be confused with psychologism). German sociology was concerned with group behavior, not group development.

19 Aron, *German Sociology*, p. 117. For Mannheim, this relationship became a validity test for the sociology of knowledge perspective—an aspect of his work discussed later in this introduction. Furthermore, Aron notes, Max Weber and others manifested a concern with this relationship in their focus on the "unique historical event." This orientation was epitomized in the works of Marx and Weber by their treatment of capitalism as a unique event in the total range of systems of production. For similar analyses of sociology in Germany, see Jurgen Herbst, *The German Historical School in American Scholarship* (Ithaca, N.Y.: Cornell University Press, 1965), pp. 151–59; and Heinz Maus, *A Short History of Sociology* (London: Routledge and Kegan Paul, 1962), pp. 68–78. For a detailed analysis of the intellectual conditions that gave rise to the varying orientations in German and French sociology, see Robert Nisbet, *The Sociological Tradition* (New York: Basic Books, 1966).

20 This statement suggests one area in which French sociology was closer to American than to German sociology. For the most part, American sociology has been social-psychological rather than historical in orientation. For example, if one disregards the more manifest aspects of Durkheim's sociology—i.e., the notion of a collective consciousness and the idea that society is *sui generis*—there are many parallels between his social psychology and the works of American social behaviorists. For an analysis of this aspect of Durkheim's sociology, see Gregory P. Stone and Harvey A. Farberman, "On the Edge of *Rapprochement*: Was Durkheim Moving Toward the Perspective of Symbolic Interaction?," *Sociological Quarterly*, VIII (1968), 149–64.

21 See Gustav LeBon, *The Crowd* (New York: Viking Press, 1960). For a comparison of

Durkheim and LeBon, see Karpf, *American Social Psychology*, pp. 134–44. Also see George Simpson (ed.), *Emile Durkheim: Selections from His Work* (New York: Thomas Y. Crowell Co., 1963), pp. 1–7; and Harry J. Kienzle, "The Philosophy and Sociology of Emile Durkheim: A Study of the Philosophical Presuppositions of a Science" (unpublished Ph.D. dissertation, University of Connecticut, 1966). For Karl Mannheim's criticism of LeBon, see *Man and Society* (London: Routledge and Kegan Paul, 1940), pp. 61–63. In a series of works on the French Revolution and the history of English literature, the French historian Hippolyte Taine developed a similar perspective, emphasizing race, the social milieu, and the historical situation as important codeterminants of human thought and culture. See, for example, Hippolyte Taine, *Introduction to the History of English Literature* (Paris: Hachette, 1863).

22 For a good example of this point of view in the works of Durkheim, see the preface to his *Rules of Sociological Method* (2d ed.; New York: The Free Press of Glencoe, 1964), in which he answers critics of the earlier edition.

23 Lucien Levy-Bruhl, *How Natives Think* (London: Allen & Unwin, 1926), *Primitive Mentality* (New York: The Macmillan Co., 1923), *The Soul of the Primitive* (New York: The Macmillan Co., 1928); Charles Blondel, *La conscience morbide* (Paris: F. Alcan, 1914); Maurice Halbwachs, *Les causes du suicide* (Paris: Libraire Alcan, 1930); Emile Durkheim and Marcel Mauss, "De quelques formes primitives de classification," *L'année sociologique*, VI (1901–2). For a later influential work in this same tradition, see Marcel Granet, *La pensée chinoise* (Paris: La Renaissance du Livre, 1934).

24 White, *Social Thought in America*.

25 William James, *Principles of Psychology* (2 vols.; New York: Henry Holt & Co., 1890). On the influence of James in the redirection of psychology, see James Mark Baldwin, *Fragments in Philosophy and Science* (New York: Charles Scribner's Sons, 1902), p. 371; Harry E. Barnes, "Some Contributions of American Psychology to Social and Political Thought," *Sociological Review*, XIII (1921), 157; Richard Hofstadter, *Social Darwinism in American Thought* (Boston: Beacon Press, 1962), p. 159; Floyd N. House, *The Development of Sociology* (New York: McGraw-Hill Book Co., 1936), p. 314; William McDougall, "The Late William James as Psychologist," *Sociological Review*, III (1910), 314; and M. J. Vincent, "Current Trends in Sociology," *Sociology and Social Research*, XXIII (1938–39), 40.

26 Floyd House (in *The Development of Sociology*, p. 319) has listed the following major characteristics of functional psychology, as compared to the older psychology: (1) Functional psychology emphasizes the integrated activity of the whole organism; (2) the function of this activity is to effect some sort of equilibrium between the organism and the environment; and (3) Such activity always involves the environment as well as the organism. See also George Herbert Mead, *Movements of Thought in the Nineteenth Century* (Chicago: University of Chicago Press, 1936), pp. 386–404.

27 Theodor W. Adorno, "Discussion," *Transactions of the Fourth World Congress of Sociology*, IV (1959), 104. Also see Hans Speier, p. 278, below.

28 Gunter W. Remmling, *Road to Suspicion* (New York: Appleton-Century-Crofts, 1967), p. 122.

29 For a more extended discussion of Bacon's theory of the idols in relation to other aspects of his philosophy, see W. T. Jones, *A History of Western Philosophy*, II (New York: Harcourt, Brace and Co., 1952), 601–13.

30 Karl Marx and Friedrich Engels, p. 99, below.

31 The gradual de-emphasis of this deterministic position was the subject of a letter from Engels to Joseph Block in 1890, cited by Benjamin Walter, "The Sociology of Knowledge and the Problem of Objectivity," in L. Gross (ed.), *Sociological Theory: Inquiries and Paradigms* (New York: Harper and Row, 1967), p. 342. Engels emphatically denied that the economic element was the sole determining factor. Bottomore and Rubel point out that many of Marx's criticisms regarding the problem of ideology and false consciousness were formulated with the vision of a rigorous social science that would allow the scientist to transcend the immediate social situation in a manner analogous to Mannheim's free-floating intellectual. See T. B. Bottomore and M. Rubel, "Marx's Sociology and Social Philosophy," in Bottomore and Rubel (eds.), *Karl Marx: Selected Writings in Sociology and Social Philosophy* (London: C. A. Watts, 1956), p. 24. The same point is made by Tucker, who states, "Hegelianism becomes the prototype of all ideological thinking since history began. And the transition of Marx from Hegelianism to inverted Hegelianism, now called the Materialistic Conception of History, becomes the transition of mankind from the philosophical stage of mystified ideological thought to the stage of positive science." See Robert C. Tucker, *Philosophy and Myth in Karl Marx* (New York: Cambridge University Press, 1961), p. 181.

32 Lewis A. Coser, *Continuities in the Study of Social Conflict* (New York: The Free Press, 1967), pp. 140–41. For an excellent discussion of the Marxian position in comparison with Auguste Comte's, see Charles Madge, *Society in the Mind: Elements of Social Eidos* (New York: The Free Press of Glencoe, 1964), pp. 60–74, esp. p. 67.

33 Vernon K. Dibble, "The Diffusion of the Bureaucratic Outlook: Some Lessons from the *Verein für Sozial Politik*" (unpublished Ph.D. dissertation, Columbia University, 1961), p. 6.

34 Mannheim's later works show a decreasing emphasis upon the historical frame of reference as essential for an understanding of the relationship between ideas and the social environment. See Nicholas S. Timasheff, *Sociological Theory: Its Nature and Growth* (New York: Random House, 1967), p. 307; and Ernest Manheim, *Essays on the Sociology of Culture* (London: Routledge and Kegan Paul, 1962), pp. 5–6.

35 Maurice Mandelbaum has summarized the two usages as emphasizing "falsity" and "understanding," respectively. See *The Problem of Historical Knowledge* (New York: Liveright, 1938), pp. 69–70. For a comparison of the views of Marx and Mannheim, see T. B. Bottomore, "Some Reflections on the Sociology of Knowledge," *British Journal of Sociology*, VII (1956), 52–58.

36 For example, the followers of Thomas Münzer, representing one form of the utopian mentality, were further removed from the objective social situation than the liberal humanitarians, who represented still another form.

37 For a sociology of knowledge interpretation of why Mannheim singled out intellectuals as the potential bearers of truth, see Frank E. Hartung, pp. 686–705, below.

38 See Toyomasa Fusé, "The Sociology of Knowledge Revisited: Some Remaining Problems and Prospects," *Sociological Inquiry*, XXXVII (1967), 246. See also Franz Adler, "The Range of the Sociology of Knowledge," in Howard Becker and Alvin Boskoff (eds.), *Modern Sociological Theory in Continuity and Change* (New York: Holt, Rinehart, and Winston, 1957), p. 410. For statements on the similarity between Mannheim's approach to the sociology of knowledge and pragmatism, see Werner Stark, *The Sociology of Knowledge* (London: Routledge and Kegan Paul, 1958), pp. 326–28; Merton, *Social Theory and Social Structure*, pp. 489–508; and especially C. Wright Mills,

"Methodological Consequences of the Sociology of Knowledge," *American Journal of Sociology*, XLVI (1940), 316–30.

39 See, e.g., Merton, *Social Theory and Social Structure*, pp. 503–4; Alexander von Schelting, "Review of *Ideologie und Utopie*," *American Journal of Sociology*, I (1936), 664–74.

40 Karl Mannheim, p. 124, below.

41 Stark, *The Sociology of Knowledge*, p. 325.

42 Mandelbaum, *The Problem of Historical Knowledge*, p. 82.

43 Quoted in Stark, *The Sociology of Knowledge*, p. 338.

44 See, for example, S. F. Finer, *Vilfredo Pareto: Sociological Writings* (New York: Frederick A. Praeger, 1966); and Joseph Lopreato, *Vilfredo Pareto* (New York: Thomas Y. Crowell Co., 1965).

45 Brigitte Berger, "Vilfredo Pareto and the Sociology of Knowledge," *Social Research*, XXXIV (1966), 265–1. This article also contains a systematic comparison of the views of Durkheim, Marx, and Weber with those of Pareto on the perceived role of ideology in society.

46 We suggest that one reason for the lack of appreciation of Pareto in a sociology of knowledge perspective might be the "strain" in his works toward explanations of mutual interdependence and away from those of cause and effect. His emphasis is quite different from that of Durkheim, for example, who perceived a search for cause-and-effect relationships as most valuable for an understanding of man in society. This perception clearly places Durkheim in the popular conception of the sociology of knowledge.

47 The six groupings are: (1) Residues of Combinations, (2) Residues of Persistence of Aggregates, (3) Residues of Manifestations of Sentiments Through External Acts, (4) Residues of Sociability, (5) Residues of Individual Integrity, and (6) Sex Residues.

48 The fundamental distinction among social acts is between logical and nonlogical types of behavior. Since most behavior in society is ultimately motivated by forces that are not subject to rational control, the scientist must constantly question his own objectivity.

49 The four groupings are: (1) Simple Affirmation (2) Authority (3) Accord with Sentiments or Principles, and (4) Verbal Proofs.

50 See, for example, Lopreato, *Vilfredo Pareto*, pp. 23–25.

51 Berger, "Vilfredo Pareto and the Sociology of Knowledge," pp. 280–81.

52 Again, this position identifies Durkheim with the traditional sociology of knowledge approach.

53 The particular form of the collective representations, in turn, can be traced to the nature of internal differentiation in any society. In Durkheim's theory of social organization, this provides the basis for the movement of a society from a mechanical to an organic base.

54 Émile Durkheim, p. 157, below.

55 We should like to call attention to two valuable secondary sources on the works of Scheler and Grünwald. John Staude's *Max Scheler* (New York: The Free Press, 1967) provides excellent insight into the relationship between Scheler's sociology of knowledge and his over-all philosophy. For an appreciation of the role played by Ernst Grünwald in the sociology of knowledge, see Kurt H. Wolff, "Ernst Grünwald and the Sociology of Knowledge: A Collective Venture in Interpretation," *Journal of the History of the Behavioral Sciences*, I (1965), 152–64.

56 Staude, *Max Scheler*, pp. 172–73.

57 *Ibid.*, p. 165.

58 *Ibid.*, p. 176.

59 For Scheler's own statement on the role of emotions in motives and social relationships, see *Beitrage zur Feststellung der Beziehungen zwischen den Logischen und ethischen Prinzipien* (1899) cited in Staude, *Max Scheler*, p. 14.

60 See also Howard Becker and Helmut Otto Dahlke, "Max Scheler's Sociology of Knowledge," *Philosophy and Phenomenological Review*, II (1942), 317.

61 For Scheler's statement on the different levels of existence in the world, see *Die Stellung des Menschen in Kosmos* (Darmstadt, 1928). Werner Stark (*The Sociology of Knowledge*, p. 34) notes that Scheler utilized the same three categories to explain the types of knowledge in society, each with a representative individual role and a corresponding type of social cooperation. For an excellent critique of Scheler's view of man and his ideas concerning the nature of social bonds, see Schütz, *The Problem of Social Reality*, pp. 150–79.

62 Personal communication from Kurt H. Wolff, October 4, 1967. For a critique of the Marxian position on the sociology of knowledge, which is based upon earlier criticisms by Grünwald, see Adler, "The Range of the Sociology of Knowledge," esp. pp. 399–406.

63 John Dewey, *Reconstruction in Philosophy* (New York: Henry Holt & Co., 1920), p. 144.

64 John Dewey, *Experience and Nature* (New York: W. W. Norton & Co., 1925), p. 204.

65 Arthur Child, "The Theoretical Possibility of the Sociology of Knowledge," *Ethics*, LI (1941), 416. For an interpretation that places more emphasis on the interactional side of the mind-and-society relationship in Mead, see John C. McKinney, "The Contributions of George Herbert Mead to the Sociology of Knowledge," *Social Forces*, XXXIV (1955), 144–49.

66 George Herbert Mead, p. 260, below.

67 See John Dewey, "The Reflex Arc Concept in Psychology," *Psychological Review* (1896), pp. 357–70.

68 George Herbert Mead, *Mind, Self, and Society* (Chicago: University of Chicago Press, 1934), p. 50.

69 George Herbert Mead, *Philosophy of the Present* (Chicago: Open Court, 1932), p. 167.

70 See George Herbert Mead, "The Relations of Psychology and Philology," *Psychological Bulletin*, I (1904), 377.

71 George Herbert Mead, *Philosophy of the Act* (Chicago: University of Chicago Press, 1938), p. 153.

72 *Ibid.*, p. 375.

73 Hans Speier, p. 276, below.

74 *Ibid.*, p. 277.

75 According to Parsons, it was Weber who made the most significant contribution toward solving the problem of the relationship between the *Idealfaktoren* and *Realfaktoren*. See Talcott Parsons *et al.* (eds.), *Theories of Society* (New York: The Free Press of Glencoe, 1961), p. 989.

76 Talcott Parsons, p. 304, below.

77 Florian Znaniecki, p. 313, below.

78 *Ibid.*, p. 318.

79 *Ibid.*, p. 316.

80 Adler singles out the first question, "Where is the existential basis of mental production

located?," as an example of how Merton's scheme ignores the possibility that the relationship can work in the other direction and therefore relegates the sociology of knowledge to an attempt to locate the sources of one-sided causal relationships. See Franz Adler, "The Range of the Sociology of Knowledge," p. 415, and "The Sociology of Knowledge Since 1918," *Midwest Sociologist*, VII (1955), 11. Merton's scheme, if Adler's criticism is valid, reflects what we have called the "sociological bias" inherent in the sociology of knowledge.

81 For a more recent example of a paradigm that attempts to operationalize the central theoretical concepts in the sociology of knowledge with a view toward empirical testing, see Irving L. Horowitz, "A Formalization of the Sociology of Knowledge," *Behavioral Science*, IX (1964), 45–55.

82 See also Werner Stark, *The Sociology of Knowledge*, pp. 24–25.

83 Peter L. Berger, p. 380, below.

84 For an excellent and concise evaluation of Weber's contributions in this area, see Julien Freund, *The Sociology of Max Weber* (New York: Pantheon, 1968), pp. 87–131.

85 For selected reviews of the research literature in America, see Leo P. Chall, "The Sociology of Knowledge," in Joseph S. Roucek (ed.), *Contemporary Sociology* (New York: Philosophical Library, 1958), pp. 286–303; Kurt H. Wolff, "The Sociology of Knowledge and Sociological Theory," and "The Sociology of Knowledge in the United States of America," *Current Sociology*, XV (1967), 1–52; Merton, *Social Theory and Social Structure*, esp. chaps. xii–xiv; Adler, "The Range of the Sociology of Knowledge," and "The Sociology of Knowledge Since 1918"; Coser and Rosenberg, *Sociological Theory*; Bernard Barber, "Sociology of Knowledge and Science," in H. L. Zetterberg (ed.), *Sociology in the United States of America: A Trend Report* (Paris: UNESCO, 1956), pp. 68–70, and "Sociology of Science: A Trend Report and Bibliography," *Current Sociology*, V (1956), 91–153.

86 Merton, for example, notes: "Our main task *today* is to develop special theories applicable to limited ranges of data . . . rather than to seek at once the 'integrated' conceptual structure adequate to derive all these and other theories" (in *Social Theory and Social Structure*, p. 9).

87 In addition to the articles included in Parts III and IV, the following are noteworthy examples of attempts by American sociologists at methodological and theoretical clarification. C. Wright Mills, "Methodological Consequences of the Sociology of Knowledge," "Language, Logic, and Culture," *American Sociological Review*, IV (1939), 670–80, and "Situated Actions and Vocabularies of Motive," *American Sociological Review*, V (1940), 904–13; Franz Adler, "A Quantitive Study in the Sociology of Knowledge," *American Sociological Review*, XIX (1954), 42–48; Gwynne Nettler, "A Test for the Sociology of Knowledge," *American Sociological Review*, X (1945), 393–99; Arthur Child, "The Theoretical Possibility of the Sociology of Knowledge," pp. 392–418, "The Existential Determination of Thought," *Ethics*, LII (1942), 153–85, "The Problem of Imputation in the Sociology of Knowledge," "The Problem of Truth in the Sociology of Knowledge," *Ethics*, LVIII (1947), 18–34, and "On the Theory of the Categories," *Philosophy and Phenomenological Research*, VII (1946), 316–35; Frank Hartung "The Sociology of Positivism," *Science and Society*, VIII (1944), 328–41; Gerard De Gré, *Society and Ideology: An Inquiry into the Sociology of Science* (Garden City, N.Y.: Doubleday & Co., 1955); Joseph Roucek and Charles Hodge, "Ideology as the Implement of Purposive Thinking in the Social Sciences," *Social Science*, XI (1936), 25–34;

Kurt H. Wolff, "The Sociology of Knowledge: Emphasis on an Empirical Attitude," *Philosophy of Science*, X (1943), 104–23; Virgil Hinshaw, Jr., "Epistemological Relativism and the Sociology of Knowledge," *Philosophy of Science*, XV (1948), 4–10; Thelma Lavine, "Sociological Analysis of Cognitive Norms," *Journal of Philosophy*, XXXIX (1942), 342–56; I. L. Horowitz, *Philosophy, Science, and the Sociology of Knowledge* (Springfield, Ill.: Charles C. Thomas, 1961); and B. Walter, "The Sociology of Knowledge and the Problem of Objectivity."

88 Although these are general criticisms that can be and are leveled at the literature in any developing area, they appear to be especially applicable to the sociology of knowledge.

89 Adler, "The Sociology of Knowledge Since 1918," p. 3.

90 Coser and Rosenberg, *Sociological Theory*, p. 682.

91 Hinkle and Hinkle, *The Development of Modern Sociology*, p. v.

92 Wolff, "The Sociology of Knowledge and Sociological Theory." The intellectual antecedents of social action theory can be traced back to the German idealistic tradition in social science, especially to the later "interactionist" works of Max Weber.

93 Berger and Luckman, *The Social Construction of Reality*, p. 178.

94 Merton, *Social Theory and Social Structure*, p. 439.

95 *Ibid.*, p. 441. For further comparisons, the reader is again referred to Kurt H. Wolff, "The Sociology of Knowledge and Sociological Theory," only part of which is reprinted in this volume (see pp. 320–41, below). For other reviews of the European literature, see the periodic trend reports on the sociologies of ideology, science, politics, and religion in *Current Sociology* (UNESCO). Also important are the critical reviews in G. Gurvitch, "Sociologie de la connaissance et psychologie collective," *L'année sociologique*, I (1948), 463–86; and Joachim Lieber, *Wissen und Gesellschaft, die Probleme der Wissenssoziologie* (Tübingen: Max Niemeyer, 1952).

96 For a more extensive statement on this point, see Chall, "The Sociology of Knowledge."

97 For a general overview of these perspectives, see B. Biddle and E. Thomas (eds.), *Role Theory: Concepts and Research* (New York: John Wiley and Sons, 1966); J. C. Manis and B. N. Meltzer (eds.), *Symbolic Interaction: A Reader in Social Psychology* (Boston: Allyn and Bacon, 1967); J. B. Carroll (ed.), *Language, Thought, and Reality: Selected Writings of Benjamin Lee Wolff* (Cambridge, Mass.: The M.I.T. Press, 1958); J. W. Brehm and A. R. Cohen, *Explorations in Cognitive Dissonance* (New York: John Wiley and Sons, 1962); Peter M. Blau, *Exchange and Social Power in Social Life* (New York: John Wiley and Sons, 1964).

98 Coser and Rosenberg, *Sociological Theory*, p. 680.

99 Kurt H. Wolff, "A Preliminary Inquiry into the Sociology of Knowledge from the Standpoint of the Study of Man," *Scritti di Sociologia e Politica in Onore di Luigi Sturzo*, III (Bologna: Zanichelli, 1953), 587.

100 Especially *The Theory of the Leisure Class* (New York: The Macmillan Co., 1899), *The Place of Science in Modern Civilization* (New York: Huebsch, 1919), and *The Higher Learning in America* (New York: Huebsch, 1918).

101 W. F. Ogburn, *Social Change* (New York: Huebsch, 1922). See also his *The Social Effect of Aviation* (Boston: Houghton Mifflin Co., 1946), and *Technology and International Relations* (Chicago: University of Chicago Press, 1949).

102 Bernard Stern, *Social Factors in Medical Progress* (New York: Columbia University Press, 1927). A recent study that considers the same problem is reported in James Coleman *et al.*, *Medical Innovation: A Diffusion Study* (Indianapolis, Ind.: Bobbs-Merrill Co., 1966).

103 S. G. Gilfillan, *The Sociology of Invention* (Chicago: Follett, 1935). See also his *Inventing the Ship* (Chicago: Follett, 1935). Also important are articles on the social process of scientific discovery by Robert K. Merton: "Priorities in Scientific Discovery: A Chapter in the Sociology of Science," *American Sociological Review*, XXII (1957), 635–59; "Singletons and Multiples in Scientific Discovery: A Chapter in the Sociology of Science," *Proceedings of the American Philosophical Society*, CV (1961), 470–86; and "Resistance to the Systematic Study of Multiple Discoveries in Science," *European Journal of Sociology*, IV (1963), 237–82.

104 Robert K. Merton, "Science, Technology and Society in Seventeenth-Century England," *Osiris*, IV (Belgium, 1938), 360–632.

105 Pitirim A. Sorokin, *Social and Cultural Dynamics* (4 vols.; London: Allen & Unwin, 1937–41).

106 Pitirim A. Sorokin, *Sociocultural Causality, Space, and Time* (Durham, N.C.: Duke University Press, 1943).

107 Logan Wilson, *The Academic Man* (New York: Oxford University Press, 1942).

108 Adler, "The Range of the Sociology of Knowledge"; Barber, "Sociology of Science: A Trend Report and Bibliography"; and Merton, *Social Theory and Social Structure*, chap. xii.

109 Scholars have often expressed strong preferences for particular levels of research analysis—e.g., a concern with interpersonal exchanges or with more large-scale social structures. Cf., for example, George C. Homans, "Bringing Men Back In," *American Sociological Review*, XXIX (1964), 809–18; Berger and Luckman, *The Social Construction of Reality*; Walter Buckley, *Sociology and Modern Systems Theory* (Englewood Cliffs, N.J.: Prentice Hall, 1967); and Stanley Taylor, *Conceptions of Institutions and the Theory of Knowledge* (New York: Bookman Associates, 1956).

110 Robin M. Williams, Jr., "Recent Development in Research on Social Institutions," *Annals of the American Academy of Political and Social Science*, CCCLXXIV (1967), 172.

111 For example, C. H. George and Katherine George, *The Protestant Mind in the English Reformation* (Princeton: Princeton University Press, 1961); E. E. Hagen, *On the Theory of Social Change* (Homewood, Ill.: Dorsey Press, 1962), chap. xiii; G. Lenski, *The Religious Factor* (Garden City, N.Y.: Doubleday & Co., 1961); S. M. Lipset and R. Bendix, *Social Mobility in Industrial Society* (Berkeley, Calif.: University of California Press, 1959); David C. McClelland, *The Achieving Society* (Princeton: Princeton University Press, 1961); and Benjamin Nelson, *The Idea of Usury* (Princeton: Princeton University Press, 1949).

112 McClelland, a pioneer in this area, acknowledges his debt to Weber in *The Achieving Society*, p. 391. See also David C. McClelland *et al.*, *The Achievement Motive* (New York: Appleton-Century-Crofts, 1953); J. W. Atkinson, *An Introduction to Motivation* (Princeton: D. Van Nostrand Co., 1964), chap. ix; and J. W. Atkinson (ed.), *Motives in Fantasy, Action and Society* (Princeton: D. Van Nostrand Co., 1958). In addition, see the following works by B. C. Rosen *et al.*: "Family Structure and Achievement Motivation," *American Sociological Review*, XXVI (1961), 574–85; "The Achievement Syndrome and Economic Growth in Brazil," *Social Forces*, XLII (1964), 341–54; "The Psychological Origins of Achievement Motivation," *Sociometry*, XXII (1959), 185–218; B. C. Rosen *et al.* (eds.), *Achievement in American Society* (Cambridge, Mass.: Schenkman Publishing Co., 1968). Fine comparative reviews of the sociological and psychological research can be found in Roger Brown, *Social Psychology* (New York: The Free Press

of Glencoe, 1965), chap. ix; and Heinz Heckhausen, *The Anatomy of Achievement Motivation*, trans. by D. C. McClelland *et al.* (New York: Academic Press, 1967).

113 See Glen H. Elder, Jr., "Family Structure and Educational Attainment: A Cross-National Analysis," *American Sociological Review*, XXX (1965), 81–96. A review of further research is contained in Joseph A. Kahl, *The American Class Structure* (New York: Holt, Rinehart and Winston, 1964), chap. x. For a review of the literature concerning Negro families, see T. F. Pettigrew, *A Profile of the American Negro* (Princeton: D. Van Nostrand Co., 1964), especially chap. v.

114 R. R. Bell, "The Adolescent Subcultures," in R. R. Bell (ed.), *The Sociology of Education* (Homewood, Ill.: Dorsey Press, 1962); J. S. Coleman, *The Adolescent Society* (New York: The Free Press of Glencoe, 1962); S. N. Eisenstadt, *From Generation to Generation* (Glencoe, Ill.: The Free Press, 1956); David Gottlieb *et al.*, *The Emergence of Youth Societies: A Cross-Cultural Approach* (New York: The Free Press, 1966); and M. Rosenberg, *Society and the Adolescent Self-Image* (Princeton: Princeton University Press, 1965). See also the research-trend report by David Matza, "Position and Behavior Patterns of Youth," in R. E. L. Faris (ed.), *Handbook of Modern Sociology* (Chicago: Rand McNally & Co., 1964), chap. vi; and F. Elkin and W. A. Westley, "The Myth of Adolescent Culture," *American Sociological Review*, XX (1955), 680–84. The last-mentioned article is a critique of earlier research, in which youth subcultures are discussed as adaptations of adult outlooks and sentiments regarding the special social position of youth.

115 C. T. Jonassen, "The Protestant Ethic and the Spirit of Capitalism in Norway," *American Sociological Review*, XII (1947), 676–86; R. N. Bellah, *Tokugawa Religion* (Glencoe, Ill.: The Free Press, 1957); H. Israel, "Some Religious Factors in the Emergence of Industrial Society in England," *American Sociological Review*, XXI (1966), 589–99; C. Geertz, "Social Change and Economic Modernization in Two Indonesian Towns: A Case in Point," in Hagen, *On the Theory of Social Change*; N. W. Hansen, "Early Flemish Capitalism: The Medieval City, The Protestant Ethic and the Emergence of Economic Rationality," *Social Research*, XXXIV (1967), 226–48; and Herbert Marcuse, *Soviet Marxism* (New York: Columbia University Press, 1958).

116 See the conflicting findings and interpretations in the following American studies, which relate various measures of religious background to occupational and educational aspirations, achievement, and social mobility: R. W. Mack *et al.*, "The Protestant Ethic, Level of Aspiration, and Social Mobility: An Empirical Test," *American Sociological Review*, XXI (1956), 295–300; Lenski, *The Religious Factor*; J. Veroff *et al.*, "Achievement Motivation and Religious Background," *American Sociological Review*, XXVII (1962), 205–17; A. J. Mayer and H. Sharp, "Religious Preference and Worldly Success," *American Sociological Review*, XXVII (1962), 218–27; A. M. Greeley, "Influence of the 'Religious Factor' on the Career Plans and Occupational Values of College Graduates," *American Journal of Sociology*, LXVIII (1963), 658–71; M. Bressler and C. F. Westoff, "Catholic Education, Economic Values and Achievement," *American Journal of Sociology*, LXIX (1965), 225–33; A. M. Greeley, "The Protestant Ethic: Time for a Moratorium," *Sociological Analysis*, XXV (1964), 20–33; Seymour Warkov and A. M. Greeley, "Parochial School Origins and Educational Achievement," *American Sociological Review*, XXXI (1966), 406–14; and N. D. Glenn and R. Hyland, "Religious Preference and Worldly Success: Some Evidence from National Samples," *American Sociological Review*, XXXII (1967), 73–85.

117 H. Richard Niebuhr, *The Social Sources of Denominationalism* (New York: Henry Holt & Co., 1929); and Marshall Sklare, *Conservative Judaism* (Glencoe, Ill.: The Free Press, 1955).

118 Robert S. Lynd and Helen M. Lynd, *Middletown* (New York: Harcourt, Brace, 1929), and *Middletown in Transition* (New York: Harcourt, Brace, 1937); W. Lloyd Warner and Paul S. Lunt, *The Social Life of a Modern Community* (New Haven, Conn.: Yale University Press, 1941), and *The Status System of a Modern Community* (New Haven, Conn.: Yale University Press, 1942); W. Lloyd Warner *et al.*, *Democracy in Jonesville* (New York: Harper and Row, 1949); W. Lloyd Warner (ed.), *Yankee City* (New Haven, Conn.: Yale University Press, 1963); Allison Davis, Burleigh Gardner, and Mary Gardner, *Deep South* (Chicago: University of Chicago Press, 1941); and Arthur J. Vidich and Joseph Bensman, *Small Town in Mass Society* (Princeton: Princeton University Press, 1958).

119 Nettler, "A Test for the Sociology of Knowledge."

120 Richard Centers, *The Psychology of the Social Classes, A Study of Class Consciousness* (Princeton: Princeton University Press, 1949). The approach of an earlier study was also similar to the German branch of the sociology of knowledge perspective; see Max Lerner, *Ideas Are Weapons: The History and Uses of Ideas* (New York: Viking Press, 1939).

121 A. W. Jones, *Life, Liberty and Property* (Philadelphia: J. B. Lippincott, 1941); Natalie Rogoff, "Social Stratification in France and the United States," *American Journal of Sociology*, LVIII (1953), 347–57; Neal Gross, "Social Class Identification in the Urban Community," *American Sociological Review*, XVIII (1953), 398–404; Jerome G. Manis and Bernard N. Meltzer, "Attitudes of Textile Workers to Class Structure," *American Journal of Sociology*, LX (1954), 30–35.

122 Bernard Barber, *Social Stratification* (New York: Harcourt, Brace, 1957), chap. ix; and Kahl, *The American Class Structure*, chap. vi.

123 W. Lloyd Warner *et al.*, *Who Shall Be Educated?* (New York: Harper & Bros., 1944); August B. Hollingshead, *Elmstown's Youth* (New York: John Wiley and Sons, 1949); W. Allison Davis, *Social Class Influences upon Learning* (Cambridge, Mass.: Harvard University Press, 1948); Natalie Rogoff, "Local Social Structure and Educational Selection," in A. H. Halsey *et al.* (eds.), *Education, Economy and Society* (New York: The Free Press of Glencoe, 1961), pp. 241–51; and W. H. Sewell *et al.*, "Social Status and Educational and Occupational Aspiration," *American Sociological Review*, XXII (1957), 67–73. In England, Basil Berstein has conducted a good deal of research on the relationship of social class, learning, and linguistic development. See, for example, his "Social Class and Linguistic Development: A Theory of Social Learning," in Halsey *et al.*, *Education, Economy and Society*. Good overviews of the American literature on the subject can be found in R. J. Havighurst and B. J. Neugarten, *Society and Education* (Boston: Allyn and Bacon, 1967); and S. S. Boocock, "Toward a Sociology of Learning: A Selective Review of Existing Research," *Sociology of Education*, XXXIX (1966), 1–45.

124 Reinhard Bendix, *Work and Authority in Industry: Ideologies of Management in the Course of Industrialization* (New York: John Wiley and Sons, 1956); and John W. Riley (ed.) *The Corporation and Its Publics: Essays on the Corporate Image* (New York: John Wiley and Sons, 1963).

125 E. C. Hughes, "Institutional Office and the Person," *American Journal of Sociology*, XLIII (1937), 404–13; Oswald Hall, "The Stages of a Medical Career," *American Journal of Sociology*, LXIII (1948), 327–36; Ely Chinoy, *Automobile Workers and the*

American Dream (Garden City, N.Y.: Doubleday & Co., 1955); H. L. Wilensky, *Intellectuals in Labor Unions: Organizational Pressures on Professional Roles* (Glencoe, Ill.: The Free Press, 1956); Robert K. Merton *et al.*, *The Student Physician* (Cambridge, Mass.: Harvard University Press, 1957); and H. S. Becker *et al.*, *Boys in White* (Chicago: University of Chicago Press, 1961). Relevant theoretical perspectives are contained in C. W. Mills, "Situated Actions and Vocabularies of Motives"; and Talcott Parsons, *Essays in Sociological Theory* (Glencoe, Ill.: The Free Press, 1949), chap. viii.

126 B. R. Berelson *et al.*, *Voting* (Chicago: University of Chicago Press, 1954). For other studies showing this type of family influence, see H. Shepard and A. Kornhauser, *When Labor Votes* (New York: University Books, 1956); and David L. Westby and R. G. Braungart, "Class and Politics in the Family Backgrounds of Political Activities," *American Sociological Review*, XXXI (1966), 690–92.

127 Herbert H. Hyman, *Political Socialization* (Glencoe, Ill.: The Free Press, 1959).

128 Richard Hofstadter, "The Pseudo-Conservative Revolt—1955," in Daniel Bell (ed.), *The Radical Right* (Garden City, N.Y.: Doubleday & Co., 1962), pp. 63–80; and S. M. Lipset, "The Sources of the 'Radical Right'" and "Three Decades of the Radical Right: Coughlinites, McCarthyites, and Birchers," in *ibid.*, pp. 259–377.

129 Merton, *Social Theory and Social Structure*, chaps. x and xiv; E. Katz and Paul F. Lazarsfeld, *Personal Influence* (Glencoe, Ill.: The Free Press, 1955); and E. Katz, "The Two-Step Flow of Communication," *Public Opinion Quarterly*, XXI (1957), 61–78. Robert Park was one of the first to relate the study of mass communication to the sociology of knowledge; see his "News as a Form of Knowledge: A Chapter in the Sociology of Knowledge," *American Journal of Sociology*, XLV (1940), 669–86. Alfred Schütz's early work on the differential evaluation of information sources by the expert, the well-informed citizen, and the man on the street is also relevant in this context; see his "The Well-Informed Citizen: An Essay on the Social Distribution of Knowledge," *Social Research*, XIII (1946), 463–78.

130 Seymour M. Lipset (ed.), "Student Politics," *Comparative Educational Review*, X (1966); V. O. Key, Jr., *Public Opinion and American Democracy* (New York: Alfred A. Knopf, 1961); and E. Litt, "Education, Community, Norms and Political Indoctrination," *American Sociological Review*, XXVIII (1963), 69–75. For a statement on the relevance of Mannheim's sociology of knowledge, especially his concept of the "political generation," see Fusé, "The Sociology of Knowledge Revisited," pp. 252–53.

131 W. L. Wallace, *Student Culture: Social Structure and Continuity in a Liberal Arts College* (Chicago: Aldine, 1966); R. K. Goldsen *et al.*, *What College Students Think* (Princeton: D. Van Nostrand Co., 1960); and T. N. Newcomb and E. K. Wilson (eds.), *College Peer Groups: Problems and Prospects for Research* (Chicago: Aldine, 1966).

132 Bernard Barber, *Science and the Social Order* (New York: The Free Press of Glencoe, 1952); and Norman Storer, *The Social System of Science* (New York: Holt, Rinehart and Winston, 1966). Several earlier studies are reprinted in B. Barber and W. Hirsch (eds.), *The Sociology of Science* (New York: The Free Press of Glencoe, 1962); and Norman Kaplan (ed.), *Science and Society* (Chicago: Rand McNally & Co., 1965). Works by Machlup and Etzioni illustrate a recent research interest in the macrosociology of science and knowledge. These works focus upon the societal conditions under which information and knowledge can be made available for societal planning and guidance. See Fritz Machlup, *The Production and Distribution of Knowledge in the United States* (Princeton: Princeton University Press, 1962); and Amitai Etzioni, "Toward a Theory of

Societal Guidance," *American Journal of Sociology*, LXXIII (1967), 173–87, and *The Active Society: A Theory of Societal and Political Processes* (New York: The Free Press, 1968).

133 "National Character in the Perspective of the Social Sciences," *Annals of the American Academy of Political and Social Science*, CCCLXX (1967).

134 Ralph L. Rosnow and Edward J. Robinson (eds.), *Experiments in Persuasion* (New York: Academic Press, 1967).

135 For a statement on this research development see Chall, "The Sociology of Knowledge," pp. 295–300.

136 In the sociology of literature, Duncan's analysis and lengthy bibliography are unsurpassed; see Hugh D. Duncan, *Language and Literature in Society* (Chicago: University of Chicago Press, 1953). A good idea of research in the sociologies of literature and art can be formed from Leo Lowenthal, *Literature and the Image of Man* (Boston: Beacon Press, 1957); Hugh D. Duncan, *Modern Sociological Theory*, pp. 482–97; and Robert N. Wilson (ed.), *The Arts in Society* (Englewood Cliffs, N.J.: Prentice-Hall, 1964).

137 See Frank Barron, "The Psychology of Creativity," in F. Barron *et al.* (eds.), *New Directions in Psychology*, II (New York: Holt, Rinehart and Winston, 1965); Storer, *The Social System of Science*, chap. iv; Calvin W. Taylor and Frank Barron (eds.), *Scientific Creativity: Its Recognition and Development* (New York: John Wiley and Sons, 1963); and Manis I. Stein and S. J. Heinze, *Creativity and the Individual* (Glencoe, Ill.: The Free Press, 1960).

138 This argument originally appeared in "Die protestantische Ethik und der Geist des Kapitalismus," *Archiv Sozialwissenschaft und Sozialpolitik Statistik*, XX, XXI (1904–5). In 1920, these articles were reprinted as the first study in Weber's unfinished comparative analysis of the world religions, *Gesammelte Aufsätze zur Religionssoziologie* (3 vols.; Tübingen: J. C. B. Mohr, 1920–21). The first English translation by Talcott Parsons appeared in 1930 (New York: Charles Scribner's Sons). Of the many critiques and attempts to refine Weber's analysis, the following are especially good sources of historical data on the development of capitalism: Lugo Bretano, *Die Anfange des Modernen Kapirolismus* (Munchen: K. B. Akademie des Wissenschaten, 1910); Richard H. Tawney, *Religion and the Rise of Capitalism* (London: John Murray, 1926); Kurt Samuelsson, *Religion and Economic Action: A Critique of Max Weber*, trans. by E. G. French (New York: Basic Books, 1961). A. Fanfani's *Catholicism, Protestantism, and Capitalism* (London: Sheed and Ward, 1935) contains several mistaken criticisms of Weber but is a good source on the role of Catholicism and on "premodern" forms of capitalism. The most comprehensive and lucid introductions to Max Weber's general sociology are Freund, *The Sociology of Max Weber*, and Reinhard Bendix, *Max Weber: An Intellectual Portrait* (Garden City, N.Y.; Doubleday & Co., 1960).

139 Many criticisms of Weber's analysis are based on conflicting conceptions of capitalism. Weber did not use the entire historical phenomenon of developing capitalism as a focal point in his research but selected certain features that seemed peculiar to the Western variant: namely, factors in the systematic and rational organization of production. The ideal typical characteristics of this form of capitalism are the emergence and enlargement of a specific production establishment "at the expense of precapitalist production units. This production establishment . . . is based on the organization of formally free labor and the fixed plant. The owner of the plant operates at his own risk and produces commodities for anonymous and competitive markets. His operations are usually controlled rationally by a constant balancing of costs and returns. All elements, including

his own entrepreneurial services, are brought to book as items in the balancing of his accounts." See H. H. Gerth and C. W. Mills (trans. and eds.), *From Max Weber* (New York: Oxford University Press, 1958), pp. 67–68.

140 These other societies, he pointed out, had economic, legal, and political bases not dissimilar to those of precapitalist Europe; yet modern capitalism did not develop there, according to Weber, because the major religions in these countries were obstacles to the development of capitalism. In China, for example, he demonstrated that Confucianism, by espousing moderation and traditionalism, impeded capitalistic forms of economic activity. See Weber, *The Sociology of Religion*, trans. by E. Fischoff (Boston: Beacon Press, 1963); *The Religion of China* (Glencoe, Ill.: The Free Press, 1951); *Ancient Judaism* (Glencoe, Ill.: The Free Press, 1952); and *The Religions of India* (Glencoe, Ill.: The Free Press, 1958), the last three trans. by H. H. Gerth and D. Martindale.

141 Weber, *The Protestant Ethic*, pp. 153–54.

142 Norman Birnbaum, "Conflicting Interpretations of the Rise of Capitalism: Marx and Weber," *British Journal of Sociology*, IV (1953), 138.

143 On the differences between Marx and Weber regarding the rise of capitalism, see *ibid.*; also see E. Fischoff, "The Protestant Ethic and the Spirit of Capitalism," *Social Research*, II (1944), 53–77. For Weber's view on the economic determinants of social change, see his *General Economic History*, trans. by Frank Knight (New York: Harper and Row, 1961), esp. pp. 224–70.

144 Although sociologists have acknowledged the importance of language in social behavior, the interrelations of language, thought, and society have been more or less neglected. With the exception of the symbolic interactionists in America, few sociologists have contributed to the sociology of language, with the notable exception of Heinz Kloss in Germany, Basil Berstein in England, and Joshua Fishman and Joyce O. Hertzler in the United States. The scope and nature of the interdisciplinary literature bearing on the sociology of language are suggested by W. Bright (ed.), *Sociolinguistics* (The Hague: Moüton, 1966) ; J. J. Gumperz and D. Hymes (eds.), "The Ethnography of Communication," *American Anthropology*, LXVI (1964); Joyce O. Hertzler, *A Sociology of Language* (New York: Random House, 1965); H. Hoijer (ed.), *Language in Culture* (Berkeley, Calif.: University of California Press, 1954); D. Hymes (ed.), *Language, Culture and Society* (New York: Harper and Row, 1964); and S. Lieberson (ed.), "Explorations in Sociolinguistics," *Sociological Inquiry*, XXXVI (1966).

145 See Wilhelm von Humboldt, *Über die Kawisprache*, Part I: *Über die Verschiedenheir des Menschlichen Sprachbaues und Ihren Einfluss auf die geistige Entwickelung des Menschengeschlechts* (Berlin: Abhandlungen der akademic der Wissenschafton zu Berlin, 1936); Ernst Cassirer, *Philosophie der Symbolischen Formen: Die Sprache* (Berlin: Bruno Cassirer, 1923), trans. by Ralph Mannheim as *The Philosophy of Symbolic Forms* (2 vols.; New Haven, Conn.: Yale University Press, 1953); "Le langage et la construction du monde des objets," in Pierre Janet and George Dumas (eds.), *Psychologie du langage* (Paris: Alcan, 1933), pp. 18–44; and "The Influence of Language upon the Development of Scientific Thought," *Journal of Philosophy*, XXXIX (1942), 309–27. For the early influential contributions of Franz Boas, an anthropologist, to the discussions of linguistic relativity, see his *Race, Language and Culture* (New York: The Macmillan Co., 1940). The history of related research in American anthropology has been outlined by Dell Hymes, "On a Typology of Cognitive Styles in Language," *Anthropological Linguistics*, III (1961), 22–54. General contributions in French linguistic sociology have been traced

by Émile Durkheim, *The Elementary Forms of Religious Life*, trans. by J. W. Swain (Glencoe, Ill.: The Free Press, 1915), pp. 75–76, 435–38; and Marcel Cohen, *Pour une sociologie de langage* (Paris: Albin Michel, 1956), and "Social and Linguistic Structure," *Diogenes*, XV (1956), 38–47. For a systematic review of Marcel Granet's extensive work on the influence of Chinese language structure, see C. W. Mills, "The Language and Ideas of Ancient China," in I. L. Horowitz (ed.), *Power, Politics and People* (New York: Ballantine Books, 1963), pp. 423–38.

146 Edward Sapir, "The Status of Linguistics as a Science," *Language*, V (1929), 209; reprinted in D. B. Mandelbaum (ed.), *Selected Works of Edward Sapir in Language, Culture and Personality* (Berkeley, Calif.: University of California Press, 1949), pp. 160–68.

147 John B. Carroll (ed.), *Language, Thought and Society: Selected Writings of Benjamin Lee Whorf* (New York: John Wiley and Sons, 1956), pp. 212–13.

148 Hoijer, *Language in Culture*, p. 94. Cf. also the recent works of Marshall McLuhan, which adopt, with modification, several arguments advanced by the Sapir-Whorf hypothesis. McLuhan develops an unorthodox characterization of the grammar of language and extends grammatical analysis to include several modes of social communication—e.g., newsprint, radio, and television. See especially his *Understanding Media: The Extension of Man* (New York: McGraw-Hill Book Co., 1964), and the discussion of his work in sociolinguistics in James W. Carey, "Harold Adams Innis and Marshall McLuhan," *Antioch Review*, XXVII (1967), 5–39.

149 Thorstein Veblen, "The Intellectual Pre-eminence of Jews in Modern Europe," *Political Science Quarterly*, XXXIV (1919), reprinted in Bernard Rosenberg (ed.), *Thorstein Veblen* (New York: Thomas Y. Crowell, 1963), pp. 91–100; Georg Simmel, "The Stranger," in *The Sociology of Georg Simmel*, trans. and ed. by Kurt Wolff (Glencoe, Ill.: The Free Press, 1950), pp. 402–8; Robert E. Park, *Race and Culture*, (Glencoe, Ill.: The Free Press, 1950), pp. 345–66; Everett V. Stonequist, *The Marginal Man: A Study in Personality and Culture Conflict* (New York: Charles Scribner's Sons, 1937); and David Riesman, *Individualism Reconsidered* (Glencoe, Ill.: Free Press, 1954). Other studies and essays in a similar vein are: Milton M. Goldberg, "A Qualification of the Marginal Man Theory," *American Sociological Review*, VI (1941), 52–58; Alfred Schütz, "The Stranger: An Essay in Social Psychology," *American Journal of Sociology*, XLIX (1944), 499–507, and "The Homecomer," *American Journal of Sociology*, L (1945), 369–76; E. C. Hughes, "Social Change and Status Protest: An Essay on the Marginal Man," *Phylon*, X (1949), 58–65; and D. Nash and A. Wolfe, "The Stranger in Laboratory Culture," *American Sociological Review*, XXII (1957), 400–05.

150 Although we have not included a theoretical selection by Simmel, his important contribution to the study of ideas and social structure should not be overlooked. Many developments in role and reference group theory were anticipated by Simmel's work in Germany. In several essays, he made systematic use of the concept of social role. Later, this concept entered American social theory through the works of Robert Park and others in the Chicago School. Finally, a clear and succinct definition of role emerged in Ralph Linton's *Study of Man* (New York: Appleton-Century-Crofts, 1936), chap. viii. Merton acknowledges Simmel's influence in his development of a theory of reference group behavior and social structure (*Social Theory and Social Structure*, p. 310). For a concise statement on Simmel's influence in America, see Lewis A. Coser (ed.), *Georg Simmel* (Englewood Cliffs, N.J.: Prentice-Hall, 1965), pp. 1–26.

151 For another valuable study by Seeman along these same lines, see "The Intellectual and the Language of Minorities," *American Journal of Sociology*, LXIV (1958), 25–35.

152 For a popular account of the same phenomenon, see Theodore J. Gordon, "Bucking the Scientific Establishment," *Playboy*, XV (1968), 127–34, 150–55.

153 Mannheim, *op. cit.*; Max Weber, *The Methodology of the Social Sciences*, trans. by E. A. Shils and H. A. Finch (Glencoe, Ill.: The Free Press, 1949); Veblen, *The Higher Learning in America*; Logan Wilson, *The Academic Man*; Florian Znaniecki, *The Social Role of the Man of Knowledge* (New York: Columbia University Press, 1940); Gunnar Myrdal, *Values in Social Theory* (New York: Harper and Row, 1959); and Robert S. Lynd, *Knowledge for What?* (Princeton: Princeton University Press, 1939).

154 In addition to his work in other areas, Irving Louis Horowitz has produced a series of stimulating essays on the state of American sociological research, in "an ongoing effort … to develop a sociology of sociology." See his "Mainliners and Marginals: The Human Shape of Sociological Theory," in L. Gross, *Sociological Theory: Inquiries and Paradigms*, p. 377; "Social Science Objectivity and Value Neutrality: Historical Problems and Projections," *Diogene*, XXXIX (1962), 17–44; "Consensus, Conflict, and Cooperation: A Sociological Inventory," *Social Forces*, XLI (1962), 177–88; "Anthropology for Sociologists: Cross-Disciplinary Research as Scientific Humanism," *Social Problems*, II (1963), 201–6; "Establishment Sociology: The Value of Being Value-Free," *Inquiry: An Interdisciplinary Journal of Philosophy and Social Science*, XI (1963), 129–40; "Professionalism and Disciplinarianism: Two Styles of Sociological Performance," *Philosophy of Science*, XXXII (1964), 275–81; and "Max Weber and the Spirit of American Sociology," *Sociological Quarterly*, V (1964), 344–54. Charles H. Page has outlined a number of issues that should be raised in any systematic study of sociologists as teachers. See his "Sociology as a Teaching Enterprise," in Robert K. Merton *et al.* (eds.), *Sociology Today* (New York: Harper and Row, 1965), pp. 579–99; and *Sociology and Contemporary Education* (New York: Random House, 1963). Willard Waller had collected a great deal of material on sociology teachers as part of a projected comprehensive study before his death in 1945. Unfortunately his materials on this subject are not available. His early book on *The Teaching of Sociology* (New York: John Wiley and Sons, 1932) focused mainly on public-school education, but its insights on the informal structure of teaching situations have not been surpassed in more recent literature.

155 Gideon Sjoberg (ed.), *Politics, Ethics, and Social Research* (Cambridge, Mass.: Schenkman Publishing Co., 1967); Arthur J. Vidich, Joseph Bensman, and Maurice Stein (eds.), *Reflections on Community Studies* (New York: John Wiley and Sons, 1964); Philip E. Hammond (ed.), *Sociologists at Work: Essays on the Craft of Social Research* (New York: Basic Books, 1964); and Maurice Stein and Arthur Vidich (eds.), *Sociology on Trial* (Englewood Cliffs, N.J.: Prentice-Hall, 1963). See also I. L. Horowitz (ed.), *The Rise and Fall of Project Camelot* (Cambridge, Mass.: The M.I.T. Press, 1967); and John Seeley's essays on the social psychology of sociology in his *The Americanization of the Unconscious* (New York: International Science Press, 1967).

156 See, for example, Page, "Sociology as a Teaching Enterprise," and the introductory essays by Raymond Aron and Robert K. Merton in Volumes II and III, respectively, of *Transactions of the Fourth World Congress of Sociology* (1959). Among others, Coser and Moore have insisted on the importance of developing a systematically critical sociology; Lewis Coser, *Men of Ideas* (New York: The Free Press of Glencoe, 1965); and Barrington Moore, Jr., "Tolerance and the Scientific Outlook," in Robert P. Wolff, Barrington

Moore, Jr., and Herbert Marcuse, *A Critique of Pure Tolerance* (Boston: Beacon Press, 1965).

157 Kurt H. Wolff, "Editorial Note," *Transactions of the Fourth World Congress of Sociology*, IV (1959), v.

158 See, especially, "The Meaning of 'Ethical Neutrality' in Sociology and Economics" and "The Objectivity of the Social Sciences," in Weber, *The Methodology of the Social Sciences*; also Weber, "Science as a Vocation," in Gerth and Mills, *From Max Weber*.

159 Weber, "Science as a Vocation," p. 145.

160 Alvin Gouldner has recently argued that contemporary sociologists have misinterpreted Weber's works and are building up a "myth" around the notion of a value-free science. He argues that Weber's writings on objectification and ethical neutrality in science can be viewed as a "proposal for academic truce," given the conditions in higher education in Weber's time. See his "Anti-Minotaur: The Myth of a Value-Free Sociology," *Social Problems*, IX (1962), 199–213.

161 For a concise statement of three "leading points of views" on these questions—the value separation position, the legitimacy of value espousal, and "the extreme behaviorist position"—see George Simpson, *Man in Society* (Garden City, N.Y.: Doubleday & Co., 1954), pp. 78–81. George Lundberg has argued for the behaviorist position, especially in "Sociologists and the Peace," *American Sociological Review*, IX (1944), 1–13, and *Can Science Save Us?* (New York: Longmans, Green, 1947). On values as subject matter in the social sciences, see Clyde Kluckhohn, "Values and Value-Orientations in the Theory of Action: An Exploration in Definition and Classification," in Talcott Parsons and Edward Shils (eds.), *Toward a General Theory of Action* (Cambridge, Mass.: Harvard University Press, 1952); Paul Kecskemeti, *Meaning Communication and Value* (Chicago: University of Chicago Press, 1952), chap. xi; and a recent review of definitions, measures, and data on the role of values in behavior, in Robin M. Williams, Jr., "Individual and Group Values," *Annals of the American Academy of Political and Social Science*, CCCLXXI (1967), 20–37. On the issue of whether a social scientist can be or should be "value-free," see Read Bain, "The Scientist and His Values," *Social Forces*, XXXI (1952), 106–9; Howard Becker, "Supreme Values and the Sociologist," *American Sociological Review*, VI (1941), 155–72; N. N. Foote, "Anachronism and Synchronism in Sociology," *Sociometry*, XXI (1958), 17–29; Warren G. Bennis, "Values and Organization in a University Social Research Group," *American Sociological Review*, XXI (1956), 555–63; Svend Riemer, "Values and Standards in Research," *American Journal of Sociology*, LV (1949), 131–36; Arnold M. Rose, "The Relation of Theory and Method," in L. Gross, *Sociological Theory: Inquiries and Paradigms*, pp. 207–19; Florian Znaniecki, "Should Sociologists Be Also Philosophers of Values?" *Sociology and Social Research*, XXXVII (1952), 79–84; and H. A. Shepard, "The Value System of a University Research Group," *American Sociological Review*, XIX (1954), 456–62.

162 C. Wright Mills, *The Sociological Imagination* (New York: Grove Press, 1961), p. 79.

163 Gunnar Myrdal, *An American Dilemma* (rev. ed.; New York: Harper and Row, 1962), pp. 103–64. See also Myrdal's collected essays on methodology in social science, *Values in Social Theory*.

164 Cf. Arnold M. Rose, "The Relation of Theory and Method," "Sociology and the Study of Values," *British Journal of Sociology*, XII (1956), 1–17, and "The Selection of Problems for Research," *American Journal of Sociology*, LIV (1948), 219–27; Gouldner, "Anti-Minotaur: The Myth of a Value-Free Sociology"; Foote, "Anachronism and Syn-

chronism in Sociology"; papers by W. H. Werkmeister, P. H. Furfey, L. Gross, and G. Sjoberg in L. Gross, *Symposium on Sociological Theory*; and Maurice Stein, *Eclipse of the Community* (New York: Harper and Row, 1960), pp. 304–37.

165 Lewis A. Coser, *The Functions of Social Conflict* (Glencoe, Ill.: The Free Press, 1956), esp. chap. i, and *Continuities in the Study of Social Conflict*; and Hinkle and Hinkle, *The Development of Modern Sociology*.

166 Nisbet, *The Sociological Tradition*.

167 Maus, *A Short History of Sociology*; and Harry E. Barnes *et al.*, *An Introduction to the History of Sociology* (Chicago: University of Chicago Press, 1948).

168 Robert B. Notestein, "William Graham Sumner: An Essay in the Sociology of Knowledge," *American Journal of Economics and Sociology*, XVIII (1959), 397–413, and "William Graham Sumner" (unpublished Ph.D. dissertation, University of Wisconsin, 1954); Bernard Rosenberg, *The Values of Veblen: A Critical Appraisal* (Washington, D.C.: Public Affairs Press, 1956); and Lewis A. Coser, "George Simmel's Style of Work: A Contribution to the Sociology of the Sociologist," *American Journal of Sociology*, LXIII (1958), 635–41, reprinted with other appraisals of Simmel's work in Coser, *Georg Simmel*.

169 Roucek, *Contemporary Sociology*; Howard Becker and Harry E. Barnes, *Social Thought from Lore to Science* (New York: Dover Publications, 1961); and Georges Gurvitch and W. E. Moore (eds.), *Twentieth Century Sociology* (New York: Philosophical Library, 1946). Several other scattered reviews of sociology in various nations have appeared. See, for example, Volume I of *Transactions of the Fourth World Congress of Sociology* (1959), Becker and Boskoff, *Modern Sociological Theory in Continuity and Change*; D. Peter Mazur, "National Boundaries and the Development of Sociology," *Sociological Inquiry*, II (1963), 99–113; A. Simirenko (ed.), *Soviet Sociology* (Chicago: Quadrangle Books, 1966); George Fischer, *Science and Politics, The New Sociology in the Soviet Union* (Ithaca, N.Y.: Cornell University Center for International Studies, 1964), and "Current Soviet Work in Sociology: A Note on the Sociology of Knowledge," *American Sociologist*, I (1966), 127–32; Talcott Parsons, "An American Impression of Sociology in the Soviet Union," *American Sociological Review*, XXX (1965), 121–25; Robert K. Merton and H. W. Riechman, "Notes on Sociology in the U.S.S.R.," *Current Problems in Social-Behavioral Research* ("Symposium Studies Series, No. 10", [Washington, D.C.: National Institute of Social and Behavioral Science, 1962]); Theodore Abel, "Sociology in Postwar Poland," *American Sociological Review*, XV (1950), 104–6; Florian Znaniecki, "European and American Sociology After Two World Wars," *American Journal of Sociology*, LVI (1950), 217–21; L. Rosenmayr, *Sociology in Austria* (Frankgasse, Austria: Hermann Bohlass Nachf, 1966); N. L. Whetten, "Sociology in Latin America," *Sociology and Social Research*, XLII (1957), 87–91; R. C. Williamson, "Sociology in Latin America," *Sociology and Social Research*, XL (1955), 24–30; R. N. Saksena (ed.), *Sociology, Social Research and Social Problems in India* (New York: Asia Publishing House, 1961); M. B. Clinard and J. W. Elder, "Sociology in India: A Study in the Sociology of Knowledge," *American Sociological Review*, XXX (1965), 501–7; J. F. Steiner and K. K. Morioka, "Present Trends in Japanese Sociology," *Sociology and Social Research*, XLI (1956), 87–91; R. Lewis, "Sociology in Korea," *Phylon*, XX (1964), 164–74; Albert R. O'Hara, "The Recent Developments of Sociology in China," *American Sociological Review*, XXVI (1961), 928–29; and C. C. Moskos and W. Bell, "Emerging Nations and Ideologies of American Social Scientists," *American Sociologists*, II (1967), 67–72.

170 Merton, *Social Theory and Social Structure*, esp. pp. 439–55; and Wolff, "The Sociology of Knowledge and Sociological Theory."
171 Merton, *Social Theory and Social Structure*, p. 457.
172 Paul Lazarsfeld and Wagner Thielens, Jr., *The Academic Mind: Social Scientists in a Time of Crisis* (Glencoe, Ill.: The Free Press, 1958).
173 H. A. Turner *et al.*, "Political Orientations of Academically Affiliated Sociologists," *Sociology and Social Research*, XLVII (1963), 273–89.
174 Erdman Palmore, "Sociologists' Class Origins and Political Ideologies," *Sociology and Social Research*, XLVII (1962), 45–50.
175 See, especially, Bernard N. Meltzer, "The Productivity of Social Scientists," *American Journal of Sociology*, LV (1949), 25–29; Jerome G. Manis, "Some Academic Influences upon Publication Productivity," *Social Forces*, XXIX (1951), 267–72; Nicholas Babchuk and Alan P. Bates, "Professor or Producer: The Two Faces of Academic Man," *Social Forces*, XL (1962), 241–48; Lewis A. Coser, "The Functions of Small Group Research," *Social Problems*, III (1955), 1–6; Jules J. Wanderer, "Academic Origins of Contributors to *The American Sociological Review*, 1955–65," *American Sociologist*, I (1966), 241–43; Elbridge Sibley, *The Education of Sociologists in the United States* (New York: Russell Sage Foundation, 1963); and Sylvia R. Fava, "The Status of Women in Professional Sociology," *American Sociological Review*, XXV (1960), 271–76. Other related materials include Leland J. Axelson, "Graduate Schools and the Productivity of Their Graduates," *American Journal of Sociology*, LXVI (1960), 171–75; Diana Crane, "Scientists at Major and Minor Universities: A Study of Productivity and Recognition," *American Sociological Review*, XXX (1965), 699–714; Bernard Berelson, *Graduate Education in the United States* (New York: McGraw-Hill Book Co., 1960); Joseph Ben-David, "Scientific Productivity and Academic Organization in Nineteenth Century Medicine," in Barber and Hirsh, *The Sociology of Science*, pp. 305–38; Donald C. Palz, "Some Factors Related to Performance in a Research Organization," in *ibid.*, pp. 356–69; S. Cole and J. R. Cole, "Scientific Output and Recognition: A Study in the Operation of the Reward Systems of Science," *American Sociological Review*, XXXII (1967), 377–90; and Harriet Zuckerman, "Nobel Laureates in Science: Patterns of Productivity, Collaboration and Authorship," *American Sociological Review*, XXXII (1967), 391–403.
176 Logan Wilson, *The Academic Man*; Theodore Caplow and Reece J. McGee, *The Academic Marketplace* (New York: Basic Books, 1958); and Coser, "The Functions of Small Group Research."
177 C. Wright Mills, "Two Styles of Research in Current Social Studies," *Philosophy of Science*, XX (1953), 266–75; Everett C. Hughes, *Men and Their Work* (Glencoe, Ill.: The Free Press, 1958), pp. 157–68; William J. Goode, "Community Within a Community: The Professions," *American Sociological Review*, XXII (1957), 194–200; Talcott Parsons, "Some Problems Confronting Sociology as a Profession," *American Sociological Review*, XXIV (1959), 547–59, and "The Professions and the Social Structure," *Social Forces*, XVII (1939), 457–67; Robert K. Merton, "The Role of the Intellectual in Public Bureaucracy," *Social Forces*, XXIII (1945), 405–15; Robert M. Habenstein, "A Critique of 'Profession' as a Sociological Category," *Sociological Quarterly*, IV (1963), 291–300; David J. Gray, "Sociology as a Science: A Dysfunctional Element," *Journal of Economics and Sociology*, XXI (1962), 337–46; Horowitz, "Mainliners and Marginals"; Bernard Barber, "American Sociology in Its Social Context," *Transactions of the Fourth World Congress of Sociology*, I (1959), 181 ff.; Samuel Stouffer, "Some Observations in Study

Design," *American Journal of Sociology*, LV (1950), 355–61; Paul F. Lazarsfeld and Sydney S. Spivak, "Observations on the Organization of Empirical Social Research in the United States," *Information Bulletin of the International Social Science Council* (1961); and Marshall B. Clinard, "The Sociologist's Quest for Respectability," *Sociological Quarterly*, VII (1966), 399–412.

178 Kurt H. Wolff, "Notes Toward a Sociocultural Interpretation of American Sociology," *American Sociological Review*, XI (1946), 545–53.

179 Maurice Stein, "The Poetic Metaphors of Sociology," in Stein and Vidich, *Sociology on Trial*, pp. 173–82.

180 See James E. Curtis and John W. Petras, "Community Power, Power Studies, and the Sociology of Knowledge," *Human Organization*, forthcoming.

181 Demerath and Peterson point out that there are at least three main positions on these views of societal organization. "One line of cleavage is between those who assert that 'consensus' and 'conflict' theory are two sides of one scheme soon to be merged and those who insist that conflict theory is distinct and incompatible with consensus theory. Between these two viewpoints is yet a third, that conflict and consensus are incompatible *but mutually fruitful* views of society, both of which must be taken into account for the fullest development of social theory." See D. J. Demerath III and R. A. Peterson (eds.), *System Change and Conflict* (New York: The Free Press, 1967), p. 263.

182 For one of the earliest statements of this criticism, see von Schelting, "Review of *Ideologie und Utopie*," pp. 664–74.

183 C. Wright Mills's "Methodological Consequences of the Sociology of Knowledge" embodies many of the critical points made by Popper. In response to Speier's position, Mills writes: "Those who contend that sociological investigations of thinking have no consequences for the truth or validity of that thinking misunderstand the source and character of the criteria upon which truth and validity are at any time dependent. They also overlook the fact that these criteria themselves and the selective acceptances and rejections of one or another of them by various elites are open to cultural influence and sociological investigation. Apparently they assume, without surveying the possibilities, that whatever validity depends upon, it cannot be examined empirically and sociologically. This view is underpinned by a blurred theory of knowledge and mind that prohibits analysis of those aspects or junctures in knowledge processes at which extra-logical factors may enter and be relevant to the truthfulness of the results. For their attack is often against the view that the validity of a judgment depends upon its genesis, and they are inclined to interpret 'genesis' in terms of an individual's motivation for thought" (p. 320).

184 Gerard de Gré, pp. 666–67, below.

185 Arthur Child, "The Problem of Imputation in the Sociology of Knowledge."

186 *Ibid.*, pp. 218–19.

187 For a critique of Child's position on the problem of imputation, see Kurt H. Wolff, "On the Scientific Relevance of 'Imputation,'" *Ethics*, LII (1950), 69–73.

188 Frank E. Hartung, p. 701, below.

189 Merton, *Social Theory and Social Structure*, p. 102.

Part One: Early Statements

Part One: Early Education.

FRANCIS BACON

On the Interpretation of Nature and the Empire of Man

39. Four species of idols beset the human mind, to which (for distinction's sake) we have assigned names, calling the first Idols of the Tribe, the second Idols of the Den, the third Idols of the Market, the fourth Idols of the Theater.

40. The formation of notions and axioms on the foundation of true induction is the only fitting remedy by which we can ward off and expel these idols. It is, however, of great service to point them out, for the doctrine of idols bears the same relation to the interpretation of nature as the confutation of sophisms does to common logic.

41. The idols of the tribe are inherent in human nature and in the very tribe or race of man, for man's sense is falsely asserted to be the standard of things; on the contrary, all the perceptions both of the senses and the mind bear reference to man and not to the universe, and the human mind resembles those uneven mirrors that impart their own properties to different objects, from which rays are emitted and distort and disfigure them.

42. The idols of the den are those of each individual, for everybody (in addition to the errors common to the race of man) has his own individual den or cavern, which intercepts and corrupts the light of nature, either from his own peculiar and singular disposition or from his education and intercourse with others, or from his reading, and the authority acquired by those whom he reverences and admires, or from the different impressions produced on the mind, as it happens to be preoccupied and predisposed, or equable and tranquil, and the like; so that the spirit of man (according to its several dispositions) is variable, confused, and, as it were, actuated by chance;

Novum Organum (New York: Colonial Press, 1900), pp. 319–27.

and Heraclitus said well that men search for knowledge in lesser worlds, and not in the greater or common world.

43. There are also idols formed by the reciprocal intercourse and society of man with man, which we call idols of the market, from the commerce and association of men with each other; for men converse by means of language, but words are formed at the will of the generality, and there arises from a bad and unapt formation of words a wonderful obstruction to the mind. Nor can the definitions and explanations with which learned men are wont to guard and protect themselves in some instances afford a complete remedy—words still manifestly force the understanding, throw everything into confusion, and lead mankind into vain and innumerable controversies and fallacies.

44. Lastly, there are idols that have crept into men's minds from the various dogmas of peculiar systems of philosophy and also from the perverted rules of demonstration. These we denominate idols of the theater, for we regard all the systems of philosophy hitherto received or imagined as so many plays brought out and performed, creating fictitious and theatrical worlds. Nor do we speak only of the present systems, or of the philosophy and sects of the ancients, since numerous other plays of a similar nature can still be composed and made to agree with each other, the causes of the most opposite errors being generally the same. Nor, again, do we allude merely to general systems, but also to many elements and axioms of sciences that have become inveterate by tradition, implicit credence, and neglect. We must, however, discuss each species of idols more fully and distinctly in order to guard the human understanding against them.

45. The human understanding, from its peculiar nature, easily supposes a greater degree of order and equality in things than it really finds; and, although many things in nature be *sui generis* and most irregular, it will yet invent parallels and conjugates and relatives, where no such thing is. Hence the fiction that all celestial bodies move in perfect circles, thus rejecting entirely spiral and serpentine lines (except as explanatory terms). Hence also the element of fire is introduced, with its peculiar orbit, to keep square with those other three that are objects of our senses. The relative rarity of the elements (as they are called) is arbitrarily made to vary in tenfold progression with many other dreams of like nature. Nor is this folly confined to theories, but it is to be met with even in simple notions.

46. The human understanding, when any proposition has been once laid down (either from general admission and belief, or from the pleasure it affords), forces everything else to add fresh support and confirmation; and, although most cogent and abundant instances may exist to the contrary,

yet it either does not observe or despises them, or gets rid of and rejects them by some distinction, with violent and injurious prejudice, rather than sacrifice the authority of its first conclusions. It was well answered by him who was shown in a temple the votive tablets suspended by such as had escaped the peril of shipwreck and was pressed as to whether he would then recognize the power of the gods, by an inquiry, "But where are the portraits of those who have perished in spite of their vows?" All superstition is much the same, whether it be that of astrology, dreams, omens, retributive judgment, or the like, in all of which the deluded believers observe events that are fulfilled, but neglect and pass over their failure, though it be much more common. But this evil insinuates itself still more craftily in philosophy and the sciences, in which a settled maxim vitiates and governs every other circumstance, though the latter be much more worthy of confidence. Besides, even in the absence of that eagerness and want of thought (which we have mentioned), it is the peculiar and perpetual error of the human understanding to be more moved and excited by affirmatives than negatives, whereas it ought duly and regularly to be impartial; nay, in establishing any true axiom the negative instance is the most powerful.

47. The human understanding is most excited by that which strikes and enters the mind at once and suddenly, and by which the imagination is immediately filled and inflated. It then begins almost imperceptibly to conceive and suppose that everything is similar to the few objects that have taken possession of the mind, whilst it is very slow and unfit for the transition to the remote and heterogeneous instances by which axioms are tried as by fire, unless the office be imposed upon it by severe regulations and a powerful authority.

48. The human understanding is active and cannot halt or rest, but even, though without effect, still presses forward. Thus, we cannot conceive of any end or external boundary of the world, and it seems necessarily to occur to us that there must be something beyond. Nor can we imagine how eternity has flowed on down to the present day, since the usually received distinction of an infinity, *a parte ante* and *a parte post*, cannot hold good; for it would thence follow that one infinity is greater than another and also that infinity is wasting away and tending toward an end. There is the same difficulty in considering the infinite divisibility of lines arising from the weakness of our minds, which weakness interferes to still greater disadvantage with the discovery of causes; for, although the greatest generalities in nature must be positive, just as they are found, and in fact not causable, yet the human understanding, incapable of resting, seeks for something more intelligible. Thus, however, whilst aiming at further progress, it falls back to what is

actually less advanced, namely, final causes; for they are clearly more allied to man's own nature than to the system of the universe, and from this source they have wonderfully corrupted philosophy. But he would be an unskillful and shallow philosopher who should seek for causes in the greatest generalities and not be anxious to discover them in subordinate objects.

49. The human understanding resembles not a dry light, but admits a tincture of the will and passions, which generate their own system accordingly; for man always believes more readily that which he prefers. He, therefore, rejects difficulties for want of patience in investigation; sobriety, because it limits his hope; the depths of nature, from superstition; the light of experiment, from arrogance and pride, lest his mind should appear to be occupied with common and varying objects; paradoxes, from a fear of the opinion of the vulgar; in short, his feelings imbue and corrupt his understanding in innumerable and sometimes imperceptible ways.

50. But by far the greatest impediment and aberration of the human understanding proceeds from the dullness, incompetency, and errors of the senses, since whatever strikes the senses preponderates over everything, however superior, that does not immediately strike them. Hence, contemplation mostly ceases with sight, and a very scanty regard, or perhaps none, is paid to invisible objects. The entire operation, therefore, of spirits enclosed in tangible bodies is concealed and escapes us. All of that more delicate change of formation in the parts of coarser substances (vulgarly called alteration, but in fact a change of position in the smallest particles) is equally unknown; and, yet, unless the two matters we have mentioned be explored and brought to light, no great effect can be produced in nature. Again, the very nature of common air, and all bodies of less density (of which there are many), is almost unknown; for the senses are weak and erring; nor can instruments be of great use in extending their sphere or acuteness—all the better interpretations of nature are worked out by instances, and fit and apt experiments, where the senses only judge of the experiment, the experiment of nature and the thing itself.

51. The human understanding is, by its own nature, prone to abstraction and supposes that which is fluctuating to be fixed. But it is better to dissect than to abstract nature; such was the method employed by the school of Democritus, which made greater progress in penetrating nature than did the rest. It is best to consider matter, its conformation and the changes of that conformation, its own action and the law of this action or motion; for forms are a mere fiction of the human mind, unless you will call the laws of action by that name.

52. Such are the idols of the tribe, which arise either from the uniformity

of the constitution of man's spirit, or its prejudices, or its limited faculties, or restless agitation, or from the interference of the passions, or the incompetency of the senses, or the mode of their impressions.

53. The idols of the den derive their origin from the peculiar nature of each individual's mind and body, and also from education, habit, and accident; and, although they be various and manifold, yet we will treat some that require the greatest caution and exert the greatest power in polluting the understanding.

54. Some men become attached to particular sciences and contemplations, either from supposing themselves the authors and inventors of them, or from having bestowed the greatest pains upon such subjects, and thus become most habituated to them. If men of this description apply themselves to philosophy and contemplations of a universal nature, they wrest and corrupt them by their preconceived fancies. Aristotle affords us a signal instance, for he made his natural philosophy completely subservient to his logic and thus rendered it little more than useless and disputatious. The chemists, again, have formed a fanciful philosophy with the most confined views from a few experiments of the furnace. [William] Gilbert, too, having employed himself most assiduously in the consideration of the magnet, immediately established a system of philosophy to coincide with his favourite pursuit.

55. The greatest and, perhaps, radical distinction between different men's dispositions for philosophy and the sciences is this, that some are more vigorous and active in observing the differences of things, others in observing their resemblances; for a steady and acute disposition can fix its thoughts and dwell upon and adhere to a point through all the refinements of differences, but those that are sublime and discursive recognize and compare even the most delicate and general resemblances. Each of them readily falls into excess, by catching either at nice distinctions or at shadows of resemblance.

56. Some dispositions evince an unbounded admiration of antiquity, others eagerly embrace novelty, but few can preserve the just medium so as neither to tear up what the ancients have correctly laid down nor to despise the just innovations of the moderns. But this is very prejudicial to the sciences and philosophy and, instead of a correct judgment, we have but the factions of the ancients and the moderns. Truth is not to be sought in the good fortune of any particular conjuncture of time, which is uncertain, but in the light of nature and experience, which is eternal. Such factions, therefore, are to be abjured, and the understanding must not allow them to hurry it on to assent.

57. The contemplation of nature and of bodies in their individual form distracts and weakens the understanding; but the contemplation of nature and of bodies in their general composition and formation stupefies and

relaxes it. We have a good instance of this in the school of Leucippus and Democritus, as compared with others, for they applied themselves so much to particulars as almost to neglect the general structure of things, whilst the others were so astounded whilst gazing on the structure that they did not penetrate the simplicity of nature. These two species of contemplation must, therefore, be interchanged, and each employed in its turn, in order to render the understanding at once penetrating and capacious and to avoid the inconveniences we have mentioned and the idols that result from them.

58. Let such, therefore, be our precautions in contemplation, that we may ward off and expel the idols of the den, which mostly owe their birth either to some predominant pursuit or, secondly, to an excess in synthesis and analysis or, thirdly, to a party zeal in favor of certain ages or, fourthly, to the extent or narrowness of the subject. In general, he who contemplates nature should suspect whatever particularly takes and fixes his understanding and should use that much more caution to preserve it equably and in an unprejudiced manner.

59. The idols of the market are the most troublesome of all, those namely that have entwined themselves round the understanding from the associations of words and names. For men imagine that their reason governs words, whilst, in fact, words react upon the understanding; and this has rendered philosophy and the sciences sophistical and inactive. Words are generally formed in a popular sense and define things by those broad lines that are most obvious to the vulgar mind; but, when a more acute understanding or more diligent observation is anxious to vary those lines and to adapt them more accurately to nature, words oppose it. Hence, the great and solemn disputes of learned men often terminate in controversies about words and names, in regard to which it would be better (imitating the caution of mathematicians) to proceed more advisedly in the first instance and to bring such disputes to a regular issue by definitions. Such definitions, however, cannot remedy the evil in natural and material objects, because they consist themselves of words, and these words produce others; so that we must necessarily have recourse to particular instances and their regular series and arrangement, as we shall mention when we come to the mode and scheme of determining notions and axioms.

60. The idols imposed upon the understanding by words are of two kinds. They are either the names of things that have no existence (for as some objects are from inattention left without a name, so names are formed by fanciful imaginations that are without an object) or the names of actual objects, but confused, badly defined, and hastily and irregularly abstracted from things. Fortune, the *primum mobile*, the planetary orbits, the element of fire, and like

fictions, which owe their birth to futile and false theories, are instances of the first kind. And this species of idols is removed with greater facility, because it can be exterminated by the constant refutation or the desuetude of the theories themselves. The others, which are created by vicious and unskillful abstraction, are intricate and deeply rooted. Take some word for instance, such as "moist," and let us examine how far the different significations of this word are consistent. It will be found that the word "moist" is nothing but a confused sign of different actions admitted of no settled and defined uniformity. For it means that which easily diffuses itself over another body; that which is indeterminable and cannot be brought to a consistency; that which yields easily in every direction; that which is easily divided and dispersed; that which is easily united and collected; that which easily flows and is put in motion; that which easily adheres to and wets another body; and that which is easily reduced to a liquid state, though previously solid. When, therefore, you come to predicate or impose this name, in one sense flame is moist; in another, air is not moist; in another, fine powder is moist; in another, glass is moist; so that it is quite clear that this notion is hastily abstracted from water only, and common ordinary liquors, without any due verification of it.

There are, however, different degrees of distortion and mistakes in words. One of the least faulty classes is that of the names of substances, particularly of the less abstract and more defined species (those then of "chalk" and "mud" are good, those of "earth" are bad); words signifying actions are more faulty, as "to generate," "to corrupt," "to change"; but the most faulty are those denoting qualities (except the immediate objects of sense), as "heavy," "light," "rare," "dense." Yet, in all of these, there must be some notions a little better than others, in proportion as a greater or lesser number of things come before the senses.

61. The idols of the theater are not innate, nor do they introduce themselves secretly into the understanding, but they are manifestly instilled and cherished by the fictions of theories and depraved rules of demonstration. To attempt, however, or to undertake their confutation would not be consistent with our declarations. For, since we agree neither in our principles nor in our demonstrations, all argument is out of the question. And it is fortunate that the ancients are left in possession of their honors. We detract nothing from them, seeing that our whole doctrine relates only to the path to be pursued. The lame (as they say) in the path outstrip the swift who wander from it, and it is clear that the very skill and swiftness of him who runs not in the right direction must increase his aberration.

Our method of discovering the sciences is such as to leave little to the acuteness and strength of wit and, indeed, rather to level wit and intellect. For, as in the drawing of a straight line or an accurate circle by hand, much depends on its steadiness and practice, but, if a ruler or compass be employed, there is little occasion for either; so it is with our method. Although, however, we enter into no individual confutations, yet a little must be said, first, of the sects and general divisions of these species of theories; secondly, something further to show that there are external signs of their weakness; and, lastly, we must consider the causes of so great a misfortune and so long and general a unanimity in error, that we may thus render the access to truth less difficult and that the human understanding may more readily be purified and brought to dismiss its idols.

62. The idols of the theater, or of theories, are numerous and may, and perhaps will, be still more so. For, unless men's minds had been now occupied for many ages in religious and theological considerations, and civil governments (especially monarchies) had been averse to novelties of that nature even in theory (so that men must apply to them with some risk and injury to their own fortunes, and not only without reward, but subject to contumely and envy), there is no doubt that many other sects of philosophers and theorists would have been introduced, like those that formerly flourished in such diversified abundance amongst the Greeks, For as many imaginary theories of the heavens can be deduced from the phenomena of the sky, so it is even easier to found many dogmas upon the phenomena of philosophy—and the plot of this our theater resembles those of the poetical, where the plots that are invented for the stage are more consistent, elegant, and pleasurable than those taken from real history.

In general, men take for the groundwork of their philosophy either too much from a few topics, or too little from many; in either case, their philosophy is founded on too narrow a basis of experiment and natural history and decides on too scanty grounds. For the theoretic philosopher seizes various common circumstances by experiment, without reducing them to certainty or examining and frequently considering them, and relies for the rest upon meditation and the activity of his wit.

There are other philosophers who have diligently and accurately attended to a few experiments and have thence presumed to deduce and invent systems of philosophy, forming everything to conformity with them.

A third set, from their faith and religious veneration, introduce theology and traditions, the absurdity of some among them having proceeded so far as to seek and derive the sciences from spirits and genii. There are, therefore, three sources of error and three species of false philosophy; the sophistic, the empiric, and the superstitious.

2

KARL MARX AND
FRIEDRICH ENGELS

Concerning the Production of Consciousness

IN HISTORY UP to the present, it is certainly an empirical fact that separate individuals have, with the broadening of their activity into world-historical activity, become more and more enslaved under a power alien to them (a pressure that they have conceived of as a dirty trick on the part of the so-called universal spirit), a power that has become more and more enormous and, in the last instance, turns out to be the *world market*. But it is just as empirically established that, by the overthrow of the existing state of society by the Communist revolution and the abolition of private property that is identical with it, this power, which so baffles the German theoreticians, will be dissolved; and that then the liberation of each single individual will be accomplished in the measure in which history becomes transformed into world history. From the above it is clear that the real intellectual wealth of the individual depends entirely on the wealth of his real connections. Only then will the separate individuals be liberated from the various national and local barriers, be brought into practical connection with the material and intellectual production of the whole world, and be put in a position to acquire the capacity to enjoy this all-sided production of the whole earth (the creations of man). Universal dependence, this natural form of the world-historical cooperation of individuals, will be transformed by this Communist revolution into the control and conscious mastery of these powers, which, born of the action of men on one another, have till now overawed and

---

German Ideology, edited by R. Pascal (New York: International Publishers Co., Inc., 1963), pp. 27–43. Reprinted by permission of International Publishers Co., Inc. Copyright © 1947 International Publishers Co.. Inc.

governed men as powers completely alien to them. Now this view can be expressed again in speculative-idealistic, i.e., fantastic, terms as "spontaneous generation of the species" ("society as the subject"), and thereby the series of interrelated individuals can be conceived as a single individual that accomplishes the mystery of generating itself. It is clear here that individuals certainly make one another, physically and mentally, but do not make themselves either in the non-sense of Saint Bruno or in the sense of the "unique," of the "made" man.[1]

Our conception of history depends on our ability to expound the real process of production, starting out from the simple material production of life, and to comprehend the form of intercourse connected with this and created by this (i.e., civil society in its various stages) as the basis of all history; further, to show it in its action as state and so, from this starting point, to explain the whole mass of different theoretical products and forms of consciousness, religion, philosophy, ethics, etc., etc., and to trace their origins and growth, by which means, of course, the whole thing can be shown in its totality (and therefore, too, the reciprocal action of these various sides on one another). It has not, like the idealistic view of history, in every period to look for a category, but remains constantly on the real ground of history; it does not explain practice from the idea but explains the formation of ideas from material practice; and, accordingly, it comes to the conclusion that all forms and products of consciousness cannot be dissolved by mental criticism, by resolution into "self-consciousness" or transformation into "apparitions," "specters," "fancies," etc., but only by the practical overthrow of the actual social relations which gave rise to this idealistic humbug; that not criticism but revolution is the driving force of history, also of religion, of philosophy and all other types of theory. It shows that history does not end by being resolved into "self-consciousness" as "spirit of the spirit," but that in it at each stage there is found a material result: a sum of productive forces, a historically created relation of individuals to nature and to one another, which is handed down to each generation from its predecessor; a mass of productive forces, different forms of capital, and conditions, which, indeed, is modified by the new generation on the one hand, but also on the other prescribes for it its conditions of life and gives it a definite development, a special character. It shows that circumstances make men just as much as men make circumstances.

This sum of productive forces, forms of capital, and social forms of intercourse, which every individual and generation finds in existence as something given, is the real basis of what the philosophers have conceived as "substance" and "essence of man" and what they have deified and attacked: a real basis that is not in the least disturbed in its effect and influence on the development of men by the fact that these philosophers revolt against it as "self-consciousness" and "the unique." These conditions of life that different generations find in existence decide also whether or not the periodically recurring revolutionary convulsion will be strong enough to overthrow the basis of all existing forms. And if these material elements of a complete revolution are not present (namely, on the one hand the existence of productive forces, on the other the formation of a revolutionary mass that revolts not only against separate conditions of society up till then but against the very "production of life" till then, the "total activity" on which it was based), then, as far as practical development is concerned, it is absolutely immaterial whether the "idea" of this revolution has been expressed a hundred times already; as the history of Communism proves.

In the whole conception of history up to the present, this real basis of history has either been totally neglected or else considered as a minor matter quite irrelevant to the course of history. History must therefore always be written according to an extraneous standard; the real production of life seems to be beyond history, while the truly historical appears to be separated from ordinary life, something extra-superterrestrial. With this the relation of man to nature is excluded from history and hence the antithesis of nature and history is created. The exponents of this conception of history have consequently only been able to see in history the political actions of princes and states, religious and all sorts of theoretical struggles, and in particular in each historical epoch have had to share the *illusion of that epoch*. For instance, if an epoch imagines itself to be actuated by purely "political" or "religious" motives, although "religion" and "politics" are only forms of its true motives, the historian accepts this opinion. The "idea," the "conception" of these conditioned men about their real practice, is transformed into the sole determining, active force, which controls and determines their practice. When the crude form in which the division of labor appears with the Indians and Egyptians calls forth the caste system in their state and religion, the historian believes that the caste system is the power that has produced this crude social form. While the French and the English at least hold by the political illusion, which is moderately close to reality, the Germans move in the realm of the "pure spirit" and make religious illusion the driving force of history.

The Hegelian philosophy of history is the last consequence, reduced to its "finest expression," of all this German historiography, for which it is not a question of real, nor even of political, interests, but of pure thoughts, which inevitably appear, even to Saint Bruno, as a series of "thoughts" that devour one another and are finally swallowed up in "self-consciousness." And equally inevitably, and more logically, the course of history appears to the Blessed Max Stirner, who knows not a thing about real history, as a mere tale of "knights," robbers and ghosts, from whose visions he can, of course, only save himself by "unholiness." This conception is truly religious: it postulates religious man as the primitive man and, in its imagination, puts the religious production of fancies in the place of the real production of the means of subsistence and of life itself. This whole conception of history, together with its dissolution and the scruples and qualms resulting from it, is a purely *national* affair of the Germans and has only *local* interest for the Germans, as, for instance, the important question treated several times of late: how really we "pass from the realm of God to the realm of man"—as if this "realm of God" had ever existed anywhere save in the imagination, and the learned gentlemen, without being aware of it, were not constantly living in the "realm of man" to which they are now seeking the way; and as if the learned pastime (for it is nothing more) of explaining the mystery of this theoretical bubble-blowing did not on the contrary lie in demonstrating its origin in actual earthly conditions.

Always, for these Germans, it is simply a matter of resolving the non-sense of earlier writers into some other freak, i.e., of presupposing that all this nonsense has a special meaning that can be discovered; while really it is only a question of explaining this theoretical talk from the actual existing conditions. The real, practical dissolution of these phrases, the removal of these notions from the consciousness of men, will, as we have already said, be effected by altered circumstances, not by theoretical deductions. For the mass of men, i.e., the proletariat, these theoretical notions do not exist and hence do not require to be dissolved, and if this mass ever had any theoretical notions, e.g., religion, etc., these have now long been dissolved by circumstances. The purely national character of these questions and solutions is shown again in the way these theorists believe in all seriousness that chimeras like "the God-Man," "Man," etc., have presided over individual epochs of history (Saint Bruno even goes so far as to assert that "only criticism and critics have made history") and, when they themselves construct historical systems, they skip over all earlier periods in the greatest haste and pass immediately from Mongolism to history "with meaningful content," that is to say, to the history of the Halle and German Annals[2] and the dissolution of the Young-Hegelian school into a general squabble. They forget all other nations, all real events, and the *theatrum mundi*[3] is confined to the Leipzig Book Fair and the mutual quarrels of "criticism," "man," and "the unique."

If these theorists treat really historical subjects, as, for instance, the eighteenth century, they merely give a history of the ideas of the times, torn away from the facts and the practical development fundamental to them; and even then they only give these ideas in order to represent them as an imperfect preliminary stage, the as yet limited predecessor of the real historical age, i.e., the period of the German philosophic struggle from 1840 to 1844. As might be expected when the history of an earlier period is written with the aim of accentuating the brilliance of an unhistoric person and his fantasies, all the really historic events, even the really historic invasions of politics into history, receive no mention. Instead we get a narrative based on systematic constructions and literary gossip, such as Saint Bruno provided in his now forgotten history of the eighteenth century.[4] These highfalutin, bombastic hucksters of ideas, who imagine themselves infinitely exalted above all national prejudices, are thus in practice far more national than the beer-quaffing German philistines who dream of a united Germany. They do not recognize the deeds of other nations as historical: they live in Germany, to Germany, and for Germany; they turn the Rhine-song into a religious hymn and conquer Alsace-Lorraine by robbing French philosophy instead of the French state, by Germanizing French ideas instead of French provinces. Herr Venedey is a cosmopolitan compared with the Saints Bruno and Max,[5] who, in the universal dominance of theory, proclaim the universal dominance of Germany.

It is also clear from these arguments how grossly Feuerbach is deceiving himself, when (*Wigand's Quarterly*, II [1845]) by virtue of the qualification "common man" he declares himself a Communist, transforms the latter into a predicate of "*man*," and thereby thinks it possible to change the word "Communist," which in the real world means the follower of a definite revolutionary party, into a mere category. Feuerbach's whole deduction with regard to the relation of men to one another goes only so far as to prove that men need and always have needed each other. He wants to establish consciousness of this fact, that is to say, like the other theorists, merely to produce a correct consciousness about an existing fact; whereas for the real Communist it is a question of overthrowing the existing state of things. We thoroughly appreciate, moreover, that Feuerbach, in endeavoring to produce consciousness of just *this* fact, is going as far as a theorist possibly can, without ceasing to be a theorist and philosopher. It is characteristic, however, that Saint Bruno and Saint Max seize on Feuerbach's conception of the Communist and put it in place of the real Communist—which occurs, partly, merely in order that they can combat Communism too as "spirit of the spirit," as a philosophical category, as an equal opponent, and, in the case of Saint Bruno, partly also for pragmatic reasons.

Like our opponents, Feuerbach still accepts and at the same time misunderstands existing reality. We recall the passage in the *Philosophy of the Future*[6] where he develops the view that the existence of a thing or a man is at the same time its or his essence, that the conditions of existence, the mode of life and particular activity of an animal or human individual are those in which its "essence" feels itself satisfied. Here every exception is expressly conceived as an unhappy chance, as an abnormality that cannot be altered. Thus, if millions of proletarians feel themselves by no means contented in their conditions of life, if their existence [is in contradiction with their "essence," then it is certainly an abnormality, but not an unhappy chance; an historical fact based on quite definite social relationships. Feuerbach is content to affirm this fact; he only interprets the existing sensuous world, has only the relation of a theorist to it],[7] while in reality for the practical materialist, i.e., the Communist, it is a question of revolutionizing the existing world, of practically attacking and changing existing things. When occasionally we find such views with Feuerbach, they are never more than isolated surmises and have much too little influence on his general outlook to be considered here as anything else than embryos capable of development.

Feuerbach's "interpretation" of the sensuous world is confined, on the one hand, to mere contemplation of it and, on the other, to mere feeling; he says "man" instead of "real, historical men." "Man" is really "the German." In the first case, the contemplation of the sensuous world, he necessarily lights on things that contradict his consciousness and feeling, that upset the harmony of all parts of the sensuous world and especially of man and nature, a harmony he presupposes.* To push these on one side, he must take refuge in a double perception, a profane one that only perceives the "flatly obvious" and a higher more philosophical one that perceives the "true essence" of things. He does not see how the sensuous world around him is, not a thing given direct from all eternity, ever the same, but the product of industry and of the state of society; and, indeed, in the sense that it is an historical product, the result of the activity of a whole succession of generations, each standing on the shoulders of the preceding one, developing its industry and its intercourse, modifying its social organization according to the changed needs. Even the objects of the simplest "sensuous certainty" are only given him through social development, industry, and commercial inter-

---

*Feuerbach's failing is not that he subordinates the flatly obvious, the sensuous appearance, to the sensuous reality established by more accurate investigation of the sensuous facts, but that he cannot in the last resort cope with the sensuous world except by looking at it with the "eyes," i.e., through the "spectacles," of the *philosopher*.

course. The cherry tree, like almost all fruit trees, was, as is well known, only a few centuries ago transplanted by commerce into our zone, and therefore only by this action of a definite society in a definite age provided for the evidence of Feuerbach's "senses." Actually, when we conceive things thus, as they really are and happened, every profound philosophical problem is resolved, as will be seen even more clearly later, quite simply into an empirical fact.

For instance, the important question of the relation of man to nature (Bruno goes so far as to speak of "the antitheses in nature and history," as though these were two separate "things" and man did not always have before him an historical nature and a natural history) out of which all the "unfathomably lofty works" on "substance" and "self-consciousness" were born, crumbles of itself when we understand that the celebrated "unity of man with nature" has always existed in industry and has existed in varying forms in every epoch according to the lesser or greater development of industry, just like the "struggle" of man with nature, right up to the development of his productive powers on a corresponding basis. Industry and commerce, production and the exchange of the necessities of life themselves determine distribution, the structure of the different social classes, and are, in turn, determined by these as to the mode in which they are carried on; and so it happens that in Manchester, for instance, Feuerbach sees only factories and machines where 100 years ago only spinning-wheels and weaving-looms were to be seen, or in the Campagna of Rome he finds only pasture lands and swamps, where in the time of Augustus he could have found nothing but the vineyards and villas of Roman capitalists. Feuerbach speaks in particular of the perception of natural science; he mentions secrets that are disclosed only to the eye of the physicist and chemist: but where would natural science be without industry and commerce? Even this "pure" natural science is provided with an aim, as with its material, only through trade and industry, through the sensuous activity of men. So much is this activity, this unceasing sensuous labor and creation, this production, the basis of the whole sensuous world as it now exists, that, were it interrupted for only a year, Feuerbach would not only find an enormous change in the natural world, but would very soon find that the whole world of men and his own perceptive faculty, nay his own existence, were missing.

Of course, in all this the priority of external nature remains unassailed, and all this has no application to the original men produced by "generatio æquivoca" (spontaneous generation); but this differentiation has meaning only in so far as man is considered to be distinct from nature. For that matter, nature, the nature that preceded human history, is not by any means the nature in which Feuerbach lives, nor the nature that today no longer exists anywhere (except perhaps on a few Australian coral islands of recent origin) and that, therefore, does not exist for Feuerbach. . . .

Certainly Feuerbach has a great advantage over the "pure" materialists in that he realizes how man too is an "object of the senses." But apart from the fact that he only conceives him as a "sensuous object," not as "sensuous activity," because he still remains in the realm of theory and conceives of men not in their given social connection, not under their existing conditions of life, which have made them what they are, he never arrives at the really existing active men, but stops at the abstraction "man," and gets no further than recognizing "the true, individual, corporeal man" emotionally, i.e., he knows no other "human relationships" "of man to man" than love and friendship, and even then idealized. He gives no criticism of the present conditions of life. Thus, he never manages to conceive the sensuous world as the total living sensuous activity of the individuals composing it; and therefore when, for example, he sees instead of healthy men a crowd of scrofulous, overworked, and consumptive starvelings, he is compelled to take refuge in the "higher perception" and in the ideal "compensation in the species," and thus to relapse into idealism at the very point where the Communist materialist sees the necessity, and at the same time the condition, of a transformation both of industry and of the social structure.

As far as Feuerbach is a materialist he does not deal with history, and as far as he considers history he is not a materialist. With him materialism and history diverge completely, a fact that explains itself from what has been said.[8]

History is nothing but the succession of the separate generations, each of which exploits the materials, the forms of capital, the productive forces handed down to it by all preceding ones, and thus, on the one hand, continues the traditional activity in completely changed circumstances and, on the other, modifies the old circumstances with a completely changed activity. This can be speculatively distorted so that later history is made the goal of earlier history, e.g., the goal ascribed to the discovery of America is to further the eruption of the French Revolution. Thereby history receives its own special aims and becomes "a person ranking with other persons" (to wit: "self-consciousness, criticism, the unique," etc.), while what is designated with the words "destiny," "goal," "germ," or "idea" of earlier history is nothing more than an abstraction formed from later history, from the active influence that earlier history exercises on later history. The further the separate spheres, which interact on one another, extend in the course of this development, the more the original isolation of the separate nationalities is destroyed by the developed mode of production and intercourse and the division of labor naturally brought forth by these, the more history becomes the world history. Thus, for instance, if in England a machine is invented that in India or China deprives countless workers of bread and overturns the whole form of existence of these empires, this invention becomes a world-historical fact. Or again, take the case of sugar and coffee, which have proved their world-historical importance in the nineteenth century by the fact that the lack of these products, occasioned by the Napoleonic Continental system, caused the Germans to rise against Napoleon and thus became the real basis of the glorious Wars of Liberation of 1813. From this it follows that this transformation of history into world history is not indeed a mere abstract act on the part of the "self-consciousness," the world spirit, or of any other metaphysical specter, but a quite material, empirically verifiable act, an act the proof of which every individual furnishes as he comes and goes, eats, drinks, and clothes himself.

The ideas of the ruling class are in every epoch the ruling ideas: i.e., the class, which is the ruling material force of society, is at the same time its ruling intellectual force. The class that has the means of material production at its disposal has control at the same time over the means of mental production, so that thereby, generally speaking, the ideas of those who lack the means of mental production are subject to it. The ruling ideas are nothing more than the ideal expression of the dominant material relationships, the dominant material relationships grasped as ideas; hence, of the relationships that make the one class the ruling one, therefore the ideas of its dominance. The individuals composing the ruling class possess, among other things, consciousness, and therefore think. In so far, therefore, as they rule as a class and determine the extent and compass of an epoch, it is self-evident that they do this in their whole range, hence, among other things, rule also as thinkers, as producers of ideas, and regulate the production and distribution of the ideas of their age: thus, their ideas are the ruling ideas of the epoch. For instance, in an age and in a country where royal power, aristocracy, and bourgeoisie are contending for mastery and where, therefore, mastery is shared, the doctrine of the separation of powers proves to be the dominant idea and is expressed as an "eternal law." The division of labor, which we saw above as one of the chief forces of history up till now, manifests itself also in the ruling class as the division of mental and material labor, so that inside this class one part appears as the thinkers of the class (its active, conceptive ideologists, who make the perfecting of the illusion of the class about itself their chief source of livelihood), while the others' attitude to these ideas and illusions is more passive and receptive, because they are in reality the active members of this class and have less time to make up illusions and ideas about themselves. Within this class this cleavage can even develop into a certain opposition and hostility between the two parts, which, however, in the case of a practical collision, in which the class itself is endangered, automatically comes to nothing, in which case there also vanishes the semblance that the ruling ideas were not the ideas of the ruling class and had a power distinct from the power of this class. The existence of revolutionary ideas in a particular period presupposes the existence of a revolutionary class; about the premises for the latter sufficient has already been said above.

If now in considering the course of history we detach the ideas of the ruling class from the ruling class itself and attribute to them an independent existence, if we confine ourselves to saying that these or those ideas were dominant, without bothering ourselves about the conditions of production and the producers of these ideas, if we then ignore the individuals and world conditions that are the source of the ideas, we can say, for instance, that, during the time that the aristocracy was dominant, the concepts honor, loyalty, etc., were dominant; during the dominance of the bourgeoisie, the concepts freedom, equality, etc. The ruling class itself on the whole imagines this to be so. This conception of history, which is common to all historians, particularly since the eighteenth century, will necessarily come up against the phenomenon that increasingly abstract ideas hold sway, i.e., ideas that increasingly take on the form of universality. For each new class that puts itself in the place of one ruling before it is compelled, merely in order to carry through its aim, to represent its interest as the common interest of all the members of society, put in an ideal form; it will give its ideas the form of universality and represent them as the only rational, universally valid ones. The class making a revolution appears from the very start, merely because it is opposed to a *class*, not as a class but as the representative of the whole of society; it appears as the whole mass of society confronting the one ruling class. It can do this because, to start with, its interest really is more connected with the common interest of all other non-ruling classes, because under the pressure of conditions its interest has not yet been able to develop as the particular interest of a particular class. Its victory, therefore, benefits also many individuals of the other classes that are not winning a dominant position, but only in so far as it now puts these individuals in a position to raise themselves into the ruling class. When the French bourgeoisie over-threw the power of the aristocracy, it thereby made it possible for many proletarians to raise themselves above the proletariat, but only in so far as they became bourgeois. Every new class, therefore, achieves its hegemony only on a broader basis than that of the class ruling previously, in return for which the opposition of the non-ruling class against the new ruling class later develops all the more sharply and profoundly. Both these things determine the fact that the struggle to be waged against this new ruling class, in its turn, aims at a more decided and radical negation of the previous conditions of society than could all previous classes that sought to rule.

This whole semblance, that the rule of a certain class is only the rule of certain ideas, comes to a natural end, of course, as soon as society ceases at last to be organized in the form of class rule; that is to say, as soon as it is no longer necessary to represent a particular interest as general or "the general interest" as ruling.

Once the ruling ideas have been separated from the ruling individuals and, above all, from the relationships that result from a given stage of the mode of production, and in this way the conclusion has been reached that history is always under the sway of ideas, it is very easy to abstract from these various ideas "the idea," "die Idee," etc., as the dominant force in history and thus to understand all these separate ideas and concepts as "forms of self-determination" on the part of *the* concept developing in history. It follows then naturally, too, that all the relationships of men can be derived from the concept of man, man as conceived, the essence of man, *man*. This has been done by the speculative philosophers. Hegel himself confesses at the end of *The Philosophy of History* that he "has considered the progress of *the concept* only" and has represented in history "the true theodicy."[9] Now one can go back again to the "producers of the concept," to the theoreticians, ideologists, and philosophers, and one comes then to the conclusion that the philosophers, the thinkers as such, have at all times been dominant in history: a conclusion, as we see, already expressed by Hegel. The whole trick of proving the hegemony of the spirit in history ("hierarchy," Stirner calls it) is thus confined to the following three tricks.

1. One must separate the ideas of those ruling for empirical reasons, under empirical conditions and as empirical individuals, from these actual rulers, and thus recognize the rule of ideas or illusions in history.

2. One must bring an order into this rule of ideas, prove a mystical connection among the successive ruling ideas, which is managed by understanding them as "acts of self-determination on the part of the concept" (this is possible because by virtue of their empirical basis these ideas are really connected with one another and because, conceived as *mere* ideas, they become self-distinctions, distinctions made by thought).

3. To remove the mystical appearance of this "self-determining concept" it is changed into a person—"self-consciousness"—or, to appear thoroughly materialistic, into a series of persons, who represent the "concept" in history,

into the "thinkers," the "philosophers," the ideologists, who again are understood as the manufacturers of history, as "the council of guardians," as the rulers. Thus, the whole body of materialistic elements has been removed from history and now full rein can be given to the speculative steed.

Whilst in ordinary life every shopkeeper is very well able to distinguish between what somebody professes to be and what he really is, our historians have not yet won even this trivial insight. They take every epoch at its word and believe that everything it says and imagines about itself is true.

This historical method that reigned in Germany (and especially the reason why) must be understood from its connection with the illusion of ideologists in general, e.g., the illusions of the jurists, politicians (of the practical statesmen among them, too), from the dogmatic dreamings and distortions of these fellows; this illusion is explained perfectly easily from their practical position in life, their job, and the division of labor.

NOTES

1 See note 5, below.

2 *Die Hallischen Jahrbücher für deutsche Wissenschaft und Kunst* (Leipzig, 1841–42). These were the chief organs of the Young-Hegelians; both were edited by Arnold Ruge.

3 "Theater of the World."

4 Bruno Bauer, *Geschichte der Politik, Cultur und Aufklärung des 18ten Jahrhunderts* (Charlottenburg, 1843 and 1845).

5 Bruno Bauer and Max Stirner. [Marx nicknames these individuals "Saint Bruno" and "Saint Max" because they interpret the material relationships as spiritual.—ED.]

6 Ludwig Feuerbach, *Grundsätze der Philosophie der Zukunft* (1843).

7 The words in brackets are suggested by the editor of the *Gesamtausgabe* to fill in a gap in the MS.

8 Marx sums up his criticism of Feuerbach in the famous *Theses on Feuerbach*. See pp. 195–99.

9 By "theodicy" is meant a proof of the justice and goodness of God. Cf. Leibniz's *Theodicy* (Indianapolis, Ind. Bobbs-Merrill Co., 1966).

3

KARL MANNHEIM

The Sociology of Knowledge

I. THE NATURE AND SCOPE OF THE SOCIOLOGY OF KNOWLEDGE

(a) Definition and Subdivisions of the Sociology of Knowledge

THE SOCIOLOGY OF knowledge is one of the youngest branches of sociology; as theory it seeks to analyze the relationship between knowledge and
existence; as historical-sociological research it seeks to trace the forms that
this relationship has taken in the intellectual development of mankind.

It arose in the effort to develop as its own proper field of search those
multiple interconnections that had become apparent in the crisis of modern
thought, and especially the social ties between theories and modes of
thought. On the one hand, it aims at discovering workable criteria for
determining the interrelations between thought and action. On the other
hand, by thinking this problem out from beginning to end in a radical,
unprejudiced manner, it hopes to develop a theory, appropriate to the
contemporary situation, concerning the significance of the non-theoretical
conditioning factors in knowledge.

Only in this way can we hope to overcome the vague, ill-considered, and
sterile form of relativism with regard to scientific knowledge which is
increasingly prevalent today. This discouraging condition will continue to
exist as long as science does not adequately deal with the factors conditioning
every product of thought that its most recent developments have made
clearly visible. In view of this, the sociology of knowledge has set itself the

Ideology and Utopia, translated by Louis Wirth and Edward Shils (New York: Harvest
Books, 1936), pp. 264–90. Reprinted by permission of Harcourt, Brace & World, Inc.,
and Routledge & Kegan Paul, Ltd.

task of solving the problem of the social conditioning of knowledge by boldly recognizing these relations and drawing them into the horizon of science itself and using them as checks on the conclusions of our research. In so far as the anticipations concerning the influence of the social background have remained vague, inexact, and exaggerated, the sociology of knowledge aims at reducing the conclusions derived to their most tenable truths and thereby to come closer to methodological mastery over the problems involved.

(b) The Sociology of Knowledge and the Theory of Ideology

The sociology of knowledge is closely related to, but increasingly distinguishable from, the theory of ideology, which has also emerged and developed in our time. The study of ideologies has made it its task to unmask the more or less conscious deceptions and disguises of human interest groups, particularly those of political parties. The sociology of knowledge is concerned not so much with distortions due to a deliberate effort to deceive as with the varying ways in which objects present themselves to the subject according to the differences in social settings. Thus, mental structures are inevitably differently formed in different social and historical settings.

In accordance with this distinction we will leave to the theory of ideology only the first forms of the "incorrect" and the untrue, while one-sidedness of observation, which is not due to more or less conscious intent, will be separated from the theory of ideology and treated as the proper subject matter of the sociology of knowledge. In the older theory of ideology, no distinction was made between these two types of false observation and statement. Today, however, it is advisable to separate more sharply these two types, both of which were formerly described as ideologies. Hence we speak of a *particular* and of a *total* conception of ideology. Under the first we include all those utterances the "falsity" of which is due to an intentional or unintentional, conscious, semi-conscious, or unconscious, deluding of one's self or of others, taking place on a psychological level and structurally resembling lies.

We speak of this conception of ideology as *particular* because it always refers only to specific assertions which may be regarded as concealments, falsifications, or lies without attacking the integrity of the *total mental structure* of the asserting subject. The sociology of knowledge, on the other hand, takes as its problem precisely this mental structure *in its totality*, as it appears in different currents of thought and historical-social groups. The sociology of knowledge does not criticize thought on the level of the assertions themselves, which may involve deceptions and disguises, but examines them on the structural or noological level, which it views as not necessarily being the same for all men, but rather as allowing the same object to take on different forms and aspects in the course of social development. Since suspicion of falsification is not included in the total conception of ideology, the use of the term "ideology" in the sociology of knowledge has no moral or denunciatory intent. It points rather to a research interest which leads to the raising of the question of when and where social structures come to express themselves in the structure of assertions, and in what sense the former concretely determine the latter. In the realm of the sociology of knowledge, we shall then, as far as possible, avoid the use of the term "ideology," because of its moral connotation, and shall instead speak of the "perspective" of a thinker. By this term we mean the subject's whole mode of conceiving things as determined by his historical and social setting.

2. THE TWO DIVISIONS OF THE SOCIOLOGY OF KNOWLEDGE

(a) The Theory of the Social Determination of Knowledge

The sociology of knowledge is on the one hand a theory, and on the other hand an historical-sociological method of research. As theory it may take two forms. In the first place it is a purely empirical investigation through description and structural analysis of the ways in which social relationships, in fact, influence thought. This may pass, in the second place, into an epistemological inquiry concerned with the bearing of this interrelationship upon the problem of validity. It is important to notice that these two types of inquiry are not necessarily connected and one can accept the empirical results without drawing the epistemological conclusions.

The Purely Empirical Aspect of the Investigation of the Social Determination of Knowledge. In accord with this classification and disregarding the epistemological implications as far as possible, we will present the sociology of knowledge as a theory of the social or existential determination of actual thinking. It would be well to begin by explaining what is meant by the wider term "existential determination of knowledge" (*Seinsverbundenheit*[1] *des Wissens*). As a concrete fact, it may be best approached by means of an illustration. The existential determination of thought may be regarded as a demonstrated fact in those realms of thought in which we can show (*a*) that the process of knowing does not actually develop historically in accordance with immanent laws, that it does not follow only from the "nature of things" or from "pure logical possibilities," and that it is not driven by an "inner dialectic." On the contrary, the emergence and the crystallization of actual thought is influenced in many decisive points by extra-theoretical factors of the most diverse sort. These may be called, in contradistinction to purely theoretical factors, existential factors. This existential determination of thought will also have to be regarded as a fact; (b) if the influence of these existential factors on the concrete content of knowledge is of more than mere peripheral importance, if they are relevant not only to the genesis of ideas, but penetrate into their forms and content, and if, furthermore, they decisively determine the scope and the intensity of our experience and observation, i.e., that which we formerly referred to as the "perspective" of the subject.

Social Processes Influencing the Process of Knowledge. Considering now the first set of criteria for determining the existential connections of knowledge, i.e., the role actually played by extra-theoretical factors in the history of thought, we find that the more recent investigations undertaken in the spirit of the sociologically oriented history of thought supply an increasing amount of corroborative evidence. For even today the fact seems to be perfectly clear that the older method of intellectual history, which was oriented towards the a priori conception that changes in ideas were to be understood on the level of ideas (immanent intellectual history), blocked recognition of the penetration of the social process into the intellectual sphere. With the growing evidence of the flaws in this a priori assumption, an increasing number of concrete cases makes it evident that (a) every formulation of a problem is made possible only by a previous actual human experience which involves such a problem; (b) in selection from the multiplicity of data there is involved an act of will on the part of the knower; and (c) forces arising out of living experience are significant in the direction which the treatment of the problem follows.

In connection with these investigations, it will become more and more clear that the living forces and actual attitudes which underlie the theoretical ones are by no means merely of an individual nature, i.e., they do not have their origin in the first place in the individual's becoming aware of his interests in the course of his thinking. Rather, they arise out of the collective purposes of a group which underlie the thought of the individual, and in the prescribed outlook of which he merely participates. In this connection, it becomes more clear that a large part of thinking and knowing cannot be correctly understood, as long as its connection with existence or with the social implications of human life are not taken into account.

It would be impossible to list all the manifold social processes that, in the above sense, condition and shape our theories, and we shall, therefore, confine ourselves to a few examples . . .

We may regard competition as such a representative case in which extra-theoretical processes affect the emergence and the direction of the development of knowledge. Competition[2] controls not merely economic activity through the mechanism of the market, not merely the course of political and social events, but furnishes also the motor impulse behind diverse interpretations of the world that, when their social background is uncovered, reveal themselves as the intellectual expressions of conflicting groups struggling for power.

As we see these social backgrounds emerge and become recognizable as the invisible forces underlying knowledge, we realize that thoughts and ideas are not the result of the isolated inspiration of great geniuses. Underlying even the profound insight of the genius are the collective historical experiences of a group that the individual takes for granted but that should under no conditions be hypostatized as "group mind." On closer inspection it is to be seen that there is not merely one complex of collective experience with one exclusive tendency, as the theory of the folk-spirit maintained. The world is known through many different orientations because there are many simultaneous and mutually contradictory trends of thought (by no means of equal value) struggling against one another with their different interpretations of "common" experience. The clue to this conflict, therefore, is not to be found in the "object in itself" (if it were, it would be impossible to understand why the object should appear in so many different refractions), but in the very different expectations, purposes, and impulses arising out of experience. If, then, for our explanation we are thrown back upon the play and counterplay of different impulses within the social sphere, a more exact analysis will show that the cause of this conflict between concrete impulses is not to be looked for in theory itself, but in these varied opposing impulses, which in turn are rooted in the whole matrix of collective interests. These seemingly "pure theoretical" cleavages may, in the light of a sociological analysis (that uncovers the hidden intermediate steps between the original impulses to observe and the purely theoretical conclusion), be reduced, for the most part, to more fundamental philosophical differences. But the latter, in turn, are invisibly guided by the antagonism and competition between concrete, conflicting groups.

To mention only one of the many other possible bases of collective existence, out of which different interpretations of the world and different forms of knowledge may arise, we may point to the role played by the relationship between differently situated generations. This factor influences in very many cases the principles of selection, organization, and polarization of theories and points of view prevailing in a given society at a given moment. (This is given more detailed attention in the author's essay entitled "Das Problem der Generationen."[3]) From the knowledge derived from our studies on competition and generations, we have concluded that what, from the point of view of immanent intellectual history, appears to be the "inner dialectic" in the development of ideas, becomes, from the standpoint of the sociology of knowledge, the rhythmic movement in the history of ideas as affected by competition and the succession of generations.

In considering the relationship between forms of thought and forms of society, we shall recall Max Weber's[4] observation that the interest in systematization is in large part attributable to a scholastic background, that the interest in "systematic" thought is the correlate of juristic and scientific schools of thought, and that the origin of this organizing form of thought lies in the continuity of pedagogical institutions. We should also mention at this point Max Scheler's[5] significant attempt to establish the relationship between various forms of thought and certain types of groups in which alone they can arise and be elaborated.

This must suffice to indicate what is meant by the correlation between types of knowledge and of ideas, on the one hand, and the social groups and processes of which they are characteristic.

The Essential Penetration of the Social Process into the "Perspective" of Thought. Are the existential factors in the social process merely of peripheral significance, are they to be regarded merely as conditioning the origin or factual development of ideas (i.e., are they of merely genetic relevance), or do they penetrate into the "perspective" of concrete particular assertions? This is the next question we shall try to answer. The historical and social genesis of an idea would only be irrelevant to its ultimate validity if the temporal and social conditions of its emergence had no effect on its content and form. If this were the case, any two periods in the history of human knowledge would be distinguished from one another by the fact that in the earlier period certain things were still unknown and certain errors still existed which, through later knowledge, were completely corrected. This simple relationship between an earlier incomplete and a later complete period of knowledge may to a large extent be appropriate for the exact sciences (although indeed today the notion of the stability of the categorical structure of the exact sciences is, compared with the logic of classical physics, considerably shaken). For the history of the cultural sciences, however, the earlier stages are not quite so simply superseded by the later stages, and it is not so easily demonstrable that early errors have subsequently been corrected. Every epoch has its fundamentally new approach and its characteristic point of view, and consequently sees the "same" object from a new perspective.

Hence the thesis that the historico-social process is of essential significance for most of the domains of knowledge receives support from the fact that we can see from most of the concrete assertions of human beings when and where they arose, when and where they were formulated. The history of art has fairly conclusively shown that art forms may be definitely dated according to their style, since each form is possible only under given historical conditions and reveals the characteristics of that epoch. What is true of art also holds *mutatis mutandis* good for knowledge. Just as in art we can date particular forms on the ground of their definite association with a particular period of history, so in the case of knowledge we can detect with increasing exactness the perspective due to a particular historical setting. Further, by the use of pure analysis of thought structure, we can determine when and where the world presented itself in such, and only in such a light to the subject that made the assertion, and the analysis may frequently be carried to the point where the more inclusive question may be answered, *why* the world presented itself in precisely such a manner.

Whereas the assertion (to cite the simplest case) that twice two equals four gives no clue as to when, where, and by whom it was formulated, it is always possible in the case of a work in the social sciences to say whether it was inspired by the "historical school," or "positivism," or "Marxism," and from what stage in the development of each of these it dates. In assertions of this sort, we may speak of an "infiltration of the social position" of the investigator into the results of his study and of the "situational-relativity" (*Situations-gebundenheit*), or the relationship of these assertions to the underlying reality.

"Perspective" in this sense signifies the manner in which one views an object, what one perceives in it, and how one construes it in his thinking. Perspective, therefore, is something more than a merely formal determination of thinking. It refers also to qualitative elements in the structure of thought, elements that must necessarily be overlooked by a purely formal logic. It is precisely these factors that are responsible for the fact that two persons, even if they apply the same formal-logical rules, e.g., the law of contradiction or the formula of the syllogism, in an identical manner, may judge the same object very differently.

Of the traits by which the perspective of an assertion may be characterized, and of the criteria that aid us to attribute it to a given epoch or situation, we will adduce only a few examples: analysis of the meaning of the concepts being used; the phenomenon of the counter-concept; the absence of certain concepts; the structure of the categorical apparatus; dominant models of thought; level of abstraction; and the ontology that is presupposed. In what follows, we intend to show, by means of a few examples, the applicability of these identifying traits and criteria in the analysis of perspective. At the same time, it will be shown how far the social position of the observer affects his outlook.

We will begin with the fact that the same word, or the same concept in most cases, means very different things when used by differently situated persons.

When, in the early years of the nineteenth century, an old-style German conservative spoke of "freedom" he meant thereby the right of each estate to live according to its privileges (liberties). If he belonged to the romantic-conservative and Protestant movement he understood by it "inner freedom," i.e., the right of each individual to live according to his own individual personality. Both of these groups thought in terms of the *qualitative conception of freedom* because they understood freedom to mean the right to maintain either their historical or their inner, individual distinctiveness.

When a liberal of the same period used the term "freedom," he was thinking of freedom *from* precisely those privileges that to the old-style conservative appeared to be the very basis of all freedom. The liberal conception was, then, an *equalitarian conception of freedom*, in the case of which "being free" meant that all men have the same fundamental rights at their disposal. The liberal conception of freedom was that of a group which sought to overthrow the external, legal, non-equalitarian social order. The conservative idea of freedom, on the other hand, was that of a constratum which did not wish to see any changes in the external order of things, hoping that events would continue in their traditional uniqueness; in order to support things as they were, they also had to divert the issues concerning freedom from the external political realm to the inner non-political realm. That the liberal saw only one, and the conservative only another side of the concept and of the problem was clearly and demonstrably connected with their respective positions in the social and political structure.[6] In brief, even in the formulation of concepts, the angle of vision is guided by the observer's interests. Thought, namely, is directed in accordance with what a particular social group expects. Thus, out of the possible data of experience, every concept combines within itself only that which, in the light of the investigators' interests, it is essential to grasp and to incorporate. Hence, for example, the conservative concept of *Volksgeist* was most probably formulated as a counter-concept in opposition to the progressive concept of "the spirit of the age" (*Zeitgeist*). The analysis of the concepts in a given conceptual scheme itself provides the most direct approach to the perspective of distinctively situated strata.

The absence of certain concepts indicates very often not only the absence of certain points of view, but also the absence of a definite drive to come to grips with certain life-problems. Thus, for example, the relatively late appearance in history of the concept "social" is evidence for the fact that the questions implied in the concept "social" had never been posited before, and likewise that a definite mode of experience signified by the concept "social" did not exist before.

But not only do the concepts in their concrete contents diverge from one another in accordance with differing social positions, but the basic categories of thought may likewise differ.

So, for example, early nineteenth-century German conservatism (we draw most of our illustrations from this epoch because it has been studied more thoroughly from a sociological point of view than any other), and contemporary conservatism too, for that matter, tend to use morphological categories which do not break up the concrete totality of the data of experience, but seek rather to preserve it in all its uniqueness. As opposed to the morphological approach, the analytical approach characteristic of the parties of the left broke down every concrete totality in order to arrive at smaller, more general units that might then be recombined through the category of causality or functional integration. Here it becomes our task not only to indicate the fact that people in different social positions think differently, but to make intelligible the causes for their different ordering of the material of experiences by different categories. The groups oriented to the left intend to make something new out of the world as it is given, and therefore they divert their glance from things as they are, they become abstract and atomize the given situation into its component elements in order to recombine them anew. Only that appears configuratively or morphologically which we are prepared to accept without further ado, and which, fundamentally, we do not wish to change. Still further, by means of the configurative conception, it is intended to stabilize precisely those elements which are still in flux, and at the same time to invoke sanction for what exists because it is as it is. All this makes it quite clear to what extent even abstract categories and principles of organization, which are seemingly far removed from the political struggle, have their origin in the metatheoretical pragmatic nature of the human mind, and in the more profound depths of the psyche and of consciousness. Hence to speak here of conscious deception in the sense of creating ideologies is out of the question.

The next factor which may serve to characterize the perspective of thought is the so-called thought-model; i.e., the model that is implicitly in the mind of a person when he proceeds to reflect about an object.

It is well known, for instance, that once the typology of objects in the natural sciences was formulated, and the categories and methods of thought derived from these types became models, it was thenceforth hoped to solve all the problems in the other realms of existence, including the social, by that method. (This tendency is represented by the mechanistic-atomistic conception of social phenomena.)

It is significant to observe that when this happened, as in all similar cases, not all the strata of society oriented themselves primarily to this single model of thought. The landed nobility, the displaced classes, and the peasantry were not heard from during this historical period. The new character of cultural development and the ascendant forms of orientation toward the world belonged to a mode of life other than their own. The forms of the ascendant world-perspective, modeled on the principles of natural science, came upon these classes as if from the outside. As the interplay of social forces brought other groups, representing the above-mentioned classes and expressing their life-situation, into the forefront of history, the opposing models of thought, as, for instance, the "organismic" and the "personalistic" were played off against the "functional-mechanistic" type of thought. Thus Stahl, for instance, who stood at the apex of this development, was already able to establish connections between thought-models and political currents.[7]

Behind every definite question and answer is implicitly or explicitly to be found a model of how fruitful thinking can be carried on. If one were to trace in detail, in each individual case, the origin and the radius of diffusion of a certain thought-model, one would discover the peculiar affinity it has to the social position of given groups and their manner of interpreting the world. By these groups we mean not merely classes, as a dogmatic type of Marxism would have it, but also generations, status groups, sects, occupational groups, schools, etc. Unless careful attention is paid to highly differentiated social groupings of this sort and to the corresponding differentiations in concepts, categories, and thought-models, i.e., unless the problem of the relation between super- and substructure is refined, it would be impossible to demonstrate that corresponding to the wealth of types of knowledge and perspectives which have appeared in the course of history there are similar differentiations in the substructure of society. Of course, we do not intend to deny that of all the above-mentioned social groupings and units class stratification is the most significant, since in the final analysis all the other social groups arise from and are transformed as parts of the more basic conditions of production and domination. None the less the investigator who, in the face of the variety of types of thought, attempts to place them correctly can no longer be content with the undifferentiated class concept, but must reckon with the existing social units and factors that condition social position, aside from those of class.

Another characteristic of the perspective is to be found by investigating the level of abstraction beyond which a given theory does not progress, or the degree to which it resists theoretical, systematic formulation.

It is never an accident when a certain theory, wholly or in part, fails to develop beyond a given stage of relative abstractness and offers resistance to further tendencies toward becoming more concrete, either by frowning upon this tendency toward concreteness or declaring it to be irrelevant. Here, too, the social position of the thinker is significant.

Precisely in the case of Marxism and the relation it bears to the findings of the sociology of knowledge can it be shown how an interrelationship can often be formulated only in that form of concreteness which is peculiar to that particular standpoint. It can be shown in the case of Marxism that an observer whose view is bound up with a given social position will by himself never succeed in singling out the more general and theoretical aspects which are implicit in the concrete observations that he makes. It might have been expected, for instance, that long ago Marxism would have formulated in a more theoretical way the fundamental findings of the sociology of knowledge concerning the relationship between human thought and the conditions of existence *in general*, especially since its discovery of the theory of ideology also implied at least the beginnings of the sociology of knowledge. That this implication could never be brought out and theoretically elaborated, and at best only came partially into view, was due, however, to the fact that, in the concrete instance, this relationship was perceived only in the thought of the opponent. It was probably due, furthermore, to a subconscious reluctance to think out the implications of a concretely formulated insight to a point where the theoretical formulations latent in it would be clear enough to have a disquieting effect on one's own position. Thus we see how the narrowed focus which a given position imposes and the driving impulses which govern its insights tend to obstruct the general and theoretical formulation of these views and to restrict the capacity for abstraction. There is a tendency to abide by the particular view that is immediately obtainable, and to prevent the question from being raised as to whether the fact that knowledge is bound up with existence is not inherent in the human thought-structure as such. In addition to this, the tendency in Marxism to shy away from a general, sociological formulation may frequently be traced to a similar limitation which a given point of view imposes on a method of thinking. For instance, one is not even allowed to raise the question whether "impersonalization" (*Verdinglichung*), as elaborated by Marx and Lukács, is a more or less general phenomenon of consciousness, or whether capitalistic impersonalization is merely one particular form of it. Whereas this overemphasis on concreteness and historicism arises out of a particular social location, the opposite tendency, namely the immediate flight into the highest realms of abstraction and formalization, may, as Marxism has rightly emphasized, lead to an obscuring of the concrete situation and its unique character. This could be demonstrated once more in the case of "formal sociology."

We do not wish in any way to call into question the legitimacy of formal sociology as one possible type of sociology. When, however, in the face of the tendency to introduce further concreteness into the formulation of sociological problems, it sets itself up as the only sociology, it is unconsciously guided by motives similar to those which prevented its historical forerunner, the bourgeois-liberal mode of thought, from ever getting beyond an abstract and generalizing mode of observation in its theory. It shies away from dealing historically, concretely, and individually with the problems of society for fear that its own inner antagonisms, for instance, the antagonisms of capitalism itself, might become visible. In this it resembles the crucial bourgeois discussion of the problem of freedom, in which the problem usually was and is posited only theoretically and abstractly. And even when it is so posited, the question of freedom is always one of political, rather than of social, rights, since, if the latter sphere were considered, the factors of property and class position in their relation to freedom and equality would inevitably come to light.

To summarize: the approach to a problem, the level on which the problem happens to be formulated, the stage of abstraction and the stage of concreteness that one hopes to attain, are all and in the same way bound up with social existence.

It would be appropriate finally to deal with the underlying substratum in all modes of thought, with their presupposed ontologies and their social differentiations. It is precisely because the ontological substratum is fundamentally significant for thinking and perceiving that we cannot deal adequately in limited space with the problems raised thereby, and we refer, therefore, to more elaborate treatments to be found elsewhere.[8] At this point, let it suffice to say that, however justified the desire of modern philosophy may be to work out a "basic ontology," it is dangerous to approach these problems naïvely, without first taking into account the results suggested by the sociology of knowledge. For if we approached this problem naïvely, the almost inevitable result would be that instead of obtaining a genuine basic ontology, we would become the victims of an arbitrary accidental ontology which the historical process happens to make available to us.

These reflections must suffice in this connection to clarify the notion that the conditions of existence affect not merely the historical genesis of ideas, but constitute an essential part of the products of thought and make themselves felt in their content and form. The examples we have just cited should serve to clarify the peculiar structure and the functions of the sociology of knowledge.

The Special Approach Characteristic of the Sociology of Knowledge. Two persons, carrying on a discussion in the same universe of discourse—corresponding to the same historical-social conditions—can and must do so quite differently from two persons identified with different social positions. These two types of discussion, i.e., between socially and intellectually homogeneous participants and between socially and intellectually heterogeneous participants, are to be clearly distinguished. It is no accident that the distinction between these two types of discussion is explicitly recognized as a problem in an age like ours. Max Scheler called our contemporary period the "epoch of equalization" (*Zeitalter des Ausgleichs*), which, if applied to our problems, means that ours is a world in which social groupings that had hitherto lived more or less isolated from one another, each making itself and its own world of thought absolute, are now, in one form or another, merging into one another. Not only Orient and Occident, not only the various nations of the west, but also the various social strata of these nations, which previously had been more or less self-contained, and, finally, the different occupational groups within these strata and the intellectual groups in this most highly differentiated world—all these are now thrown out of the self-sufficient, complacent state of taking themselves for granted, and are forced to maintain themselves and their ideas in the face of the onslaught of these heterogeneous groups.

But how do they carry on this struggle? As far as intellectual antagonisms are concerned, they usually do so with but few exceptions by "talking past one another"; i.e., although they are more or less aware that the person with whom they are discussing the matter represents another group, and that it is likely that his mental structure as a whole is often quite different when a concrete thing is being discussed, they speak as if their differences were confined to the specific question at issue around which their present disagreement crystallized. They overlook the fact that their antagonist differs from them in his whole outlook, and not merely in his opinion about the point under discussion.

This indicates that there are also types of intellectual intercourse between heterogeneous persons. In the first, the differences in the total mental structure remain obscurely in the background in so far as the contact between the participants is concerned. Consciousness for both is crystallized about the concrete issue. For each of the participants the "object" has a more or less different meaning because it grows out of the whole of their respective frames of reference, as a result of which the meaning of the object in the perspective of the other person remains, at least in part, obscure. Hence "talking past one another" is an inevitable phenomenon of the "age of equalization."

On the other hand, the divergent participants may also be approached with the intention of using each theoretical point of contact as an occasion for removing misunderstandings by ascertaining the source of the differences. This will bring out the varying presuppositions that are implied in the two respective perspectives as consequences of the two different social situations. In such cases, the sociologist of knowledge does not face his antagonist in the usual manner, according to which the other's arguments are dealt with directly. He seeks rather to understand him by defining the total perspective and seeing it as a function of a certain social position.

The sociologist of knowledge has been accused, because of this procedure, of avoiding the real argument, of not concerning himself with the actual subject matter under discussion, but, instead, of going behind the immediate subject of debate to the total basis of thought of the asserter in order to reveal it as merely one basis of thought among many and as no more than a partial perspective. Going behind the assertions of the opponents and disregarding the actual arguments is legitimate in certain cases, namely, wherever, because of the absence of a common basis of thought, there is no common problem. The sociology of knowledge seeks to overcome the "talking past one another" of the various antagonists by taking as its explicit theme of investigation the uncovering of the sources of the partial disagreements which would never come to the attention of the disputants because of their preoccupation with the subject matter that is the immediate issue of the debate. It is superfluous to remark that the sociologist of knowledge is justified in tracing the arguments to the very basis of thought and the position of disputants only if and in so far as an actual disparity exists between the perspectives of the discussion resulting in a fundamental misunderstanding. As long as discussion proceeds from the same basis of thought, and within the same universe of discourse, it is unnecessary. Needlessly applied, it may become a means for sidestepping the discussion.

The Acquisition of Perspective as a Precondition for the Sociology of Knowledge. For the son of a peasant who has grown up within the narrow confines of his village and spends his whole life in the place of his birth, the mode of thinking and speaking characteristic of that village is something that he takes entirely for granted. But for the country lad who goes to the city and adapts himself gradually to city life, the rural mode of living and thinking ceases to be something to be taken for granted. He has won a certain detachment from it, and he distinguishes now, perhaps quite consciously, between "rural" and "urban" modes of thought and ideas. In this distinction lie the first beginnings of that approach which the sociology of knowledge seeks to develop in full detail. That which within a given group is accepted as absolute appears to the outsider conditioned by the group situation and recognized as partial (in this case, as "rural"). This type of knowledge presupposes a more detached perspective.

This detached perspective can be gained in the following ways: (*a*) a member of a group leaves his social position (by ascending to a higher class, emigration, etc.); (*b*) the basis of existence of a whole group shifts in relation to its traditional norms and institutions;[9] (*c*) within the same society two or more socially determined modes of interpretation come into conflict and, in criticizing one another, render one another transparent and establish perspectives with reference to each other. As a result, a detached perspective, through which the outlines of the contrasting modes of thought are discovered, comes within the range of possibility for all the different positions, and later gets to be the recognized mode of thinking. We have already indicated that the social genesis of the sociology of knowledge rests primarily upon the last mentioned possibility.

Relationism. What has already been said should hardly leave any doubt as to what is meant when the procedure of the sociology of knowledge is designated as "relational." When the urbanized peasant boy, who characterizes certain political, philosophical, or social opinions to be found among his relatives as "rustic," he no longer discusses these opinions as a homogeneous participant, that is, by dealing directly with the specific content of what is said. Rather he relates them to a certain mode of interpreting the world which, in turn, is ultimately related to a certain social structure which constitutes its situation. This is an instance of the "relational" procedure. We shall deal later with the fact that when assertions are treated in this way it is not implied that they are false. The sociology of knowledge goes beyond what, in some such crude way as this, people frequently do today, only in so far as it consciously and systematically subjects all intellectual phenomena without exception to the question: In connection with what social structure did they arise, and are they valid? Relating individual ideas to the total structure of a given historico-social subject should not be confused with a philosophical relativism which denies the validity of any standards and of the existence of order in the world. Just as the fact that every measurement in space hinges upon the nature of light does not mean that our measurements are arbitrary, but merely that they are only valid in relation to the nature of light, so in the same way not relativism in the sense of arbitrariness but *relationism* applies to our discussions. Relationism does not signify that there are no criteria of rightness and wrongness in a discussion. It does insist, however, that it lies in the nature of certain assertions that they cannot be formulated absolutely, but only in terms of the perspective of a given situation.

Particularization. Having described the relational process, as conceived by the sociology of knowledge, the question will inevitably be raised: what can it tell us about the validity of an assertion that we would not know if we had not been able to relate it to the standpoint of the asserter? Have we said anything about the truth or falsity of a statement when we have shown that it is to be imputed to liberalism or to Marxism?

Three answers may be made to this question:

(a) It may be said that the absolute validity of an assertion is denied when its structural relationship to a given social situation has been shown. In this sense there is indeed a current in the sociology of knowledge and in the theory of ideology which accepts the demonstration of this sort of relationship as a refutation of the opponents' assertion, and which would use this method as a device for annihilating the validity of all assertions.

(b) In opposition to this, there may be another answer, namely that the imputations that the sociology of knowledge establishes between a statement and its asserter tells us nothing concerning the truth-value of the assertion, since the manner in which a statement originates does not affect its validity. Whether an assertion is liberal or conservative in and of itself gives no indication of its correctness.

(c) There is a third possible way of judging the value of the assertions that the sociologist of knowledge makes that represents our own point of view. It differs from the first view in that it shows that the mere factual demonstration and identification of the social position of the asserter as yet tells us nothing about the truth-value of his assertion. It implies only the suspicion that this assertion might represent merely a partial view. As over against the second alternative, it maintains that it would be incorrect to regard the sociology of knowledge as giving no more than a description of the actual conditions under which an assertion arises (factual genesis). Every complete and thorough sociological analysis of knowledge delimits, in content as well as structure, the view to be analyzed. In other words, it attempts not merely to establish the existence of the relationship, but at the same time to particularize its scope and the extent of its validity. The implications of this will be set forth in greater detail.

What the sociology of knowledge intends to do by its analysis was fairly clearly brought out in the example we cited of the peasant boy. The discovery and identification of his earlier mode of thought as rural, as contrasted with "urban," already involves the insight that the different perspectives are not merely particular in that they presuppose different ranges of vision and different sectors of the total reality, but also in that the interests and the powers of perception of the different perspectives are conditioned by the social situations in which they arose and to which they are relevant.

Already upon this level the relational process tends to become a particularizing process, for one does not merely relate the assertion to a standpoint but, in doing so, restricts its claim to validity which at first was absolute to a narrower scope.

A fully developed sociology of knowledge follows the same approach which we have illustrated above in the case of the peasant boy, except that it follows a deliberate method. With the aid of a consistently elaborated analysis of the perspective, particularization acquires a guiding instrument and a set of criteria for treating problems of imputation. The range and degree of comprehension of each of these several points of view becomes measurable and delimitable through their categorical apparatus and the variety of meanings which each presents. The orientation toward certain meanings and values which inheres in a given social position (the outlook and attitude conditioned by the collective purposes of a group), and the concrete reasons for the different perspectives which the same situation presents to the different positions in it thus become even more determinable, intelligible, and subject to methical study through the perfection of the sociology of knowledge.[10]

With the growing methodological refinements in the sociology of knowledge, the determination of the particularity of a perspective becomes a cultural and intellectual index of the position of the group in question. By particularizing, the sociology of knowledge goes a step further than the original determination of the facts to which mere relationism limits itself. Every analytical step undertaken in the spirit of the sociology of knowledge arrives at a point where the sociology of knowledge becomes more than a sociological description of the facts which tell us how certain views have been derived from a certain milieu. Rather it reaches a point where it also becomes a critique by redefining the scope and the limits of the perspective implicit in given assertions. The analyses characteristic of the sociology of knowledge are, in this sense, by no means irrelevant for the determination of the truth of a statement; but these analyses, on the other hand, do not by themselves fully reveal the truth because the mere delimitation of the perspectives is by no means a substitute for the immediate and direct discussion between the divergent points of view or for the direct examination of the facts. The function of the findings of the sociology of knowledge lies somewhere in a fashion hitherto not clearly understood, between irrelevance to the establishment of truth on the one hand, and entire adequacy for determining truth on the other. This can be shown by a careful analysis of the original intention of the single statements of sociology of knowledge and by the nature of its findings. An analysis based on the sociology of knowledge is a first preparatory step leading to direct discussion, in an age which is aware of the heterogeneity of its interests and the disunity of its basis of thought, and which seeks to attain this unity on a higher level.

(b) *The Epistemological Consequences of the Sociology of Knowledge*

In the opening paragraph of this chapter we maintained that it was possible to present the sociology of knowledge as an empirical theory of the actual relations of knowledge to the social situation without raising any epistemological problems. On this assumption, all epistemological problems have been avoided or put into the background. This reserve on our part is possible, and this artificial isolation of a purely abstracted set of problems is even desirable as long as our goal is merely the disinterested analysis of given concrete relationships, without distortion through theoretical preconceptions. But once the fundamental relationships between social situations and corresponding aspects are reliably established, one cannot but devote oneself to the frank disclosure of the valuations following from them. Anyone who has a sense for the interconnection of problems which inevitably arise out of the interpretation of empirical data, and who at the same time is not blinded by the intricacy of specialization in modern learning, which very often prevents a direct attack on problems, must have noticed that the facts presented under the section of "Particularization" are in their very nature hard to accept as mere facts. They transcend bare fact, and call for further epistemological reflection. On the one hand, we have the mere fact that when, through the sociology of knowledge, a relationship is pointed out between an assertion and a situation, there is contained in the very intent of this procedure the tendency to "particularize" its validity. Phenomenologically, one may take cognizance of this fact without disputing the claim to validity implied in it. But, on the other hand, the further fact that the position of the observer does influence the results of thought, and the fact (intentionally dealt with by us in great detail) that the partial validity of a given perspective is fairly exactly determinable, must sooner or later lead us to raise the question as to the significance of this problem for epistemology.

Our point is not, therefore, that the sociology of knowledge will, by its very nature, supplant epistemological and noological inquiry, but rather that it has made certain discoveries that have more than a mere factual relevance, and that cannot be adequately dealt with until some of the conceptions and prejudices of contemporary epistemology have been revised. In the fact, then, that we always attribute only partial validity to particular assertions, we find that new element which compels us to revise the fundamental presuppositions of present-day epistemology. We are dealing here with a case in which the pure determination of a fact (the fact of the partiality of a perspective which is demonstrable in concrete assertions) may become relevant for determining the validity of a proposition and in which the nature of the genesis of an assertion may become relevant to its truth (*wo eine Genesis Sinngenesis zu sein vermag*). This, to say the least, furnishes an obstacle to the construction of a sphere of validity in which the criteria of truth are independent of origins.

Under the dominant presuppositions of present-day philosophy it will be impossible to utilize this new insight for epistemology, because modern theory of knowledge is based on the supposition that bare fact-finding has no relevance to validity. Under the sanctions of this article of faith, every enrichment of knowledge arising out of concrete research that—seen from a wider point of view—dares to open up more fundamental considerations, is stigmatized with the phrase "sociologism." Once it is decided and elevated into the realm of the a priori that nothing can come out of the world of empirical facts which has relevance for the validity of assertions, we become blind to the observation that this a priori itself originally was a premature hypostatization of a factual interrelationship which was derived from a particular type of assertion and was formulated overhastily into an epistemological axiom. With the peace of mind that comes from the a priori premise that epistemology is independent of the "empirical" special sciences, the mind is once and for all closed to the insight which a broadened empiricism might bring. The result is that one fails to see that this theory of self-sufficiency, this gesture of self-preservation, serves no other purpose than that of bulwark for a certain type of academic epistemology which, in its last stages, is attempting to preserve itself from the collapse which might result from a more developed empiricism. The holders of the older view overlook the fact that they are thereby perpetuating not epistemology as such and preserving it from revision at the hands of the individual sciences, but rather merely one specific kind of epistemology, the uniqueness of which consists only in the fact that it once was at war with an earlier stage of a more narrowly conceived empiricism. It then stabilized the conception of knowledge which was derived from merely one particular segment of reality and represented merely one of the many possible varieties of knowledge.

In order to discover where the sociology of knowledge may lead us, we must once more go into the problem of the alleged primacy of epistemology over the special sciences. Having opened the problem by a critical examination, we shall be in a position to formulate, at least sketchily, a positive presentation of the epistemology already implicit in the very problem of the sociology of knowledge. First we must adduce those arguments which undermine or at least call into question the absolute autonomy and primacy of epistemology as over against the special sciences.

Epistemology and the Special Sciences. There is a twofold relationship between epistemology and the special sciences. The former, according to its constructive claims, is fundamental to all the special sciences, since it supplies the basic justifications for the types of knowledge and the conceptions of truth and correctness which these other rely upon in their concrete methods of procedure, and affects their findings. This, however, does not alter the fact that every theory of knowledge is itself influenced by the form which science takes at the time and from which alone it can obtain its conception of the nature of knowledge. In principle, no doubt, it claims to be the basis of all science but in fact it is determined by the condition of science at any given time. The problem is thus made the more difficult by the fact that the very principles, in the light of which knowledge is to be criticized, are themselves found to be socially and historically conditioned. Hence their application appears to be limited to given historical periods and the particular types of knowledge then prevalent.

Once these interrelationships are clearly recognized, then the belief is no longer tenable that epistemology and noology, because of their justifiable claim to foundational functions, must develop autonomously and independently of the progress of the special sciences, and are not subject to basic modifications by these. Consequently, we are forced to recognize that a wholesome development of epistemology and noology is possible only if we conceive of their relationship to the special sciences in the following sense:

New forms of knowledge, in the last analysis, grow out of the conditions of collective life and do not depend for their emergence upon the prior demonstration by a theory of knowledge that they are possible; they do not therefore need to be first legitimized by an epistemology. The relationship is actually quite the reverse: the development of theories of scientific knowledge takes place in the preoccupation with empirical data and the fortunes of the former vary with those of the latter. The revolutions in methodology and epistemology are always sequels and repercussions of the revolutions in the immediate empirical procedures for getting knowledge. Only through constant recourse to the procedure of the special empirical sciences can the epistemological foundations be made sufficiently flexible and extended so that they will not only sanction the claims of the older forms of knowledge (their original purpose) but will also support the newer forms. This peculiar situation is characteristic of all theoretical, philosophic disciplines. Its structure is most clearly perceivable in the philosophy of law that presumes to be the judge and critic of positive law, but that is actually, in most cases, no more than an ex post facto formulation and justification of the principles of positive law.

In saying this, no denial is made of the importance of epistemology or philosophy as such. The basic inquiries which they undertake are indispensable, and indeed, if one attacked epistemology and philosophy on theoretical grounds, one could not avoid dealing with theoretical principles oneself. Such a theoretical attack would, of course, precisely to the extent that it penetrates into fundamental issues, be in itself a philosophical concern. To every factual form of knowledge belongs a theoretical foundation. This basic function of theory, which is to be understood in a structural sense, must never be misapplied by using its character to give a priori certainty to particular findings. If misused in this manner it would frustrate the progress of science and would lead to the displacement, by a priori certainties, of views deriving from empirical observations. The errors and the partiality in the theoretical bases of science must continually be revised in the light of the new developments in the immediate scientific activities themselves. The light that is thrown by new factual knowledge upon the theoretical foundation must not be allowed to be obscured by the obstacles to thought which theory may possibly erect. Through the particularizing procedure of the sociology of knowledge, we discover that the older epistemology is a correlate of a particular mode of thought. This is one example of the possibility of extending our field of vision by allowing newly discovered empirical evidence to throw new light upon our theoretical foundations. We are thus implicitly called upon to find an epistemological foundation appropriate to these more varied modes of thought. Moreover, we are required to find if possible a theoretical basis under which can be subsumed all the modes of thought which, in the course of history, we have succeeded in establishing. We can now examine how far it is true that the hitherto dominant epistemologies and noologies furnish only one particular foundation for a single type of knowledge.

NOTES

1 Here we do not mean by "determination" a mechanical cause-effect sequence: we leave the meaning of "determination" open, and only empirical investigation will show us how strict is the correlation between life-situation and thought-process, or what scope exists for variations in the correlation. [The German expression *Seinsverbundenes Wissen* conveys a meaning which leaves the exact nature of the determinism open.]

2 For concrete examples, cf. the author's paper "Die Bedeutung der Konkurrenz im Gebiete des Geistigen," *Verhandlungen desgten deutschen Soziologen Tages in Zürich* (Tübingen, 1929), pp. 35–83.

3 *Kölner Vierteljahrshefte für Soziologie*, VIII (1928).

4 Cf. Max Weber, *Wirtschaft und Gesellschaft* (Tübingen, 1925), particularly the section on the sociology of law.

5 Cf., especially, his works *Die Wissensformen und die Gesellschaft* (Leipzig, 1926) and *Die Formen des Wissens und der Bildung*, I (Bonn, 1925).

6 Cf. the author's "Das konservative Denken," in *Archiv für Sozialwissenschaft und Sozialpolitik*, LVII, 90 ff.

7 The history of theories of the state, especially as viewed by F. Oppenheimer in his *System der Soziologie*, Vol. II: *Der Staatt*, is a treasure of illustrative material.

8 Cf. the author's "Das konservative Denken," pp. 489 ff. and especially p. 494; and his *Ideology and Utopia* (New York: Harvest Books, 1936), pp. 88 ff., 98 ff., and 193 ff.

9 A good example is furnished by Karl Renner, in *Die Rechtsinstitute des Privatrechts* (Tübingen: J. C. B. Mohr, 1929).

10 For further details, cf. the treatment of the relationship of theory and practice, in the author's *Ideology and Utopia*, Part III, where we have endeavored to carry out such a sociological analysis of the perspective.

4

VILFREDO PARETO

Selections from "The Mind and Society"

149. Every social phenomenon may be considered under two aspects: as it is in reality, and as it presents itself to the mind of this or that human being. The first aspect we shall call *objective*, the second *subjective*. Such a division is necessary, for we cannot put in one same class the operations performed by a chemist in his laboratory and the operations performed by a person practicing magic; the conduct of Greek sailors in plying their oars to drive their ship over the water and the sacrifices they offered to Poseidon to make sure of a safe and rapid voyage. In Rome the Laws of the XII Tables punished anyone casting a spell on a harvest. We choose to distinguish such an act from the act of burning a field of grain.

We must not be misled by the names we give to the two classes. In reality both are subjective, for all human knowledge is subjective. They are to be distinguished not so much by any difference in nature as in view of the greater or lesser fund of factual knowledge that we ourselves have. We know, or think we know, that sacrifices to Poseidon have no effect whatsoever upon a voyage. We therefore distinguish them from other acts that (to our best knowledge, at least) are capable of having such effect. If at some future time we were to discover that we have been mistaken, that sacrifices to Poseidon are very influential in securing a favorable voyage, we should have to reclassify them with actions capable of such influence. All that of course is pleonastic. It amounts to saying that when a person makes a classification, he does so according to the knowledge he has. One cannot imagine how things could be otherwise.

The Mind and Society, translated by Andrew Bongiorno, edited by Arthur Livingstone (New York: Harcourt, Brace, and Co., 1935), pp. 76–79, 889–91, 894–98, 905–8, 1423–32. Reprinted by permission of The Pareto Fund.

150. There are actions that use means appropriate to ends and which logically link means with ends. There are other actions in which those traits are missing. The two sorts of conduct are very different according as they are considered under their objective or their subjective aspect. From the subjective point of view nearly all human actions belong to the logical class. In the eyes of the Greek mariners sacrifices to Poseidon and rowing with oars were equally logical means of navigation. To avoid verbosities which could only prove annoying, we had better give names to these types of conduct.[1] Suppose we apply the term *logical actions* to actions that logically conjoin means to ends not only from the standpoint of the subject performing them, but from the standpoint of other persons who have a more extensive knowledge—in other words, to actions that are logical both subjectively and objectively in the sense just explained. Other actions we shall call *non-logical* (by no means the same as "illogical"). This latter class we shall subdivide into a number of varieties.

151. A synoptic picture of the classification will prove useful:

GENERA AND SPECIES	HAVE THE ACTIONS LOGICAL ENDS AND PURPOSES:	
	Objectively?	*Subjectively?*

CLASS I: LOGICAL ACTIONS
(The objective end and the subjective purpose are identical.)

	Yes	Yes

CLASS II: NON-LOGICAL ACTIONS
(The objective end differs from the subjective purpose.)

Genus 1	No	No
Genus 2	No	Yes
Genus 3	Yes	No
Genus 4	Yes	Yes

SPECIES OF THE GENERA 3 AND 4

3α, 4α	The objective end would be accepted by the subject if he knew it.
3β, 4β	The objective end would be rejected by the subject if he knew it.

The ends and purposes here in question are immediate ends and purposes. We choose to disregard the indirect. The objective end is a real one, located within the field of observation and experience, and not an imaginary end, located outside that field. An imaginary end may, on the other hand, constitute a subjective purpose.

152. Logical actions are very numerous among civilized peoples. Actions connected with the arts and sciences belong to that class, at least for artists

and scientists. For those who physically perform them in mere execution of orders from superiors, there may be among them non-logical actions of our II–4 type. The actions dealt with in political economy also belong in very great part in the class of logical actions. In the same class must be located, further, a certain number of actions connected with military, political, legal, and similar activities.

153. So at the very first glance induction leads to the discovery that non-logical actions play an important part in society. Let us therefore proceed with our examination of them.

154. First of all, in order to get better acquainted with these non-logical actions, suppose we look at a few examples. Many others will find their proper places in chapters to follow. Here are some illustrations of actions of Class II:

Genera 1 and 3, which have no subjective purpose, are of scant importance to the human race. Human beings have a very conspicuous tendency to paint a varnish of logic over their conduct. Nearly all human actions therefore work their way into genera 2 and 4. Many actions performed in deference to courtesy and custom might be put in genus 1. But very, very often people give some reason or other to justify such conduct, and that transfers it to genus 2. Ignoring the indirect motive involved in the fact that a person violating common usages incurs criticism and dislike, we might find a certain number of actions to place in genera 1 and 3.

Says Hesiod: "Do not make water at the mouth of a river emptying into the sea, nor into a spring. You must avoid that. Do not lighten your bowels there, for it is not good to do so." The precept not to befoul rivers at their mouths belongs to genus 1. No objective or subjective end or purpose is apparent in the avoidance of such pollution. The precept not to befoul drinking water belongs to genus 3. It has an objective purpose that Hesiod may not have known, but which is familiar to moderns: to prevent contagion from certain diseases.

It is probable that not a few actions of genera 1 and 3 are common among savages and primitive peoples. But travelers are bent on learning at all costs the reasons for the conduct they observe. So in one way or another they finally obtain answers that transfer the conduct to genera 2 and 4.

★   ★   ★

799. There is, for example, a principle, or if you prefer, a sentiment, in virtue of which certain numbers are deemed worthy of veneration. It is the chief element, *a* . . . But the human being is not satisfied with merely associating sentiments of veneration with numbers; he also wants to "explain"

how that comes about, to "demonstrate" that in doing what he does he is prompted by force of logic. So the element *b* enters in, and we get various "explanations," various "demonstrations," as to why certain numbers are sacred. There is in the human being a sentiment that restrains him from discarding old beliefs all at once. That is the element *a* . . . But he feels called upon to justify, explain, demonstrate his attitude, and an element *b* enters in, which in one way or another saves the letter of his beliefs while altering them in substance.

★   ★   ★

1401. Suppose we go back for a moment and translate into the terminology of residues and derivations the matter . . . where we used letters of the alphabet in place of words. Concrete theories in social connections are made up of residues and derivations. The residues are manifestations of sentiments. The derivations comprise logical reasonings, unsound reasonings, and manifestations of sentiments used for purposes of derivation: they are manifestations of the human being's hunger for thinking. If that hunger were satisfied by logico-experimental reasonings only, there would be no derivations; instead of them we should get logico-experimental theories. But the human hunger for thinking is satisfied in any number of ways; by pseudo-experimental reasonings, by words that stir the sentiments, by fatuous, inconclusive "talk." So derivations come into being. They do not figure at the two extreme ends of the line, that is to say, in conduct that is purely instinctive, and in strictly logico-experimental science. They figure in the intermediate cases.

1402. Now the only things of which we have any direct knowledge are the concrete reasonings that correspond to these cases. So we analyzed many of them, distinguishing an element that is virtually constant, *a*, from an element that is more variable, *b*. Those elements we have named, respectively, *residues* and *derivations*, and we have seen that the more important element as regards the social equilibrium is the residues. But in that we go counter to common opinion, which is controlled by the notion that all conduct is logical, and is inclined to invert the relation and ascribe the greater importance to derivations (§1415). The person who is influenced by a derivation imagines that he accepts or rejects it on logical experimental grounds. He does not notice that he ordinarily makes up his mind in deference to sentiments and that the accord (or conflict) of two derivations is an accord (or conflict) of residues. When, then, a person sets out to study social phenomena, he halts at manifestations of social activity, that is to say, at derivations, and does not carry his inquiry into the causes of the activity, that is to say, into residues. So it has come about that the history of social institutions has been a history of derivations, and oftentimes the history of mere patter. The history of theologies has been offered as the history of religions; the history of ethical theories, as the history of morals; the history of political theories, as the history of political institutions. Metaphysics, moreover, has supplied all such theories with absolute elements, from which it was thought that conclusions no less absolute could be drawn by pure logic. So the history of the theories has become the history of the deviations observable in the concrete from certain ideal types existing in the mind of this or that thinker. Not so long ago, some few scholars sensed that that procedure was taking them far afield from realities, and to get back to the real, they replaced such abstract "thinking" with a search for "origins," but without noticing that in so doing they were merely replacing one metaphysics with another, explaining the better known by the less known, and facts susceptible of direct observation by fancies which, for the simple reason that they related to times very remote, could not be proved; and meantime adding on their own account principles, such as unitary evolution, that altogether transcended experience.

1403. Derivations, in a word, are things that everybody uses. But the writers of whom we are thinking ascribe an intrinsic value to derivations and regard them as functioning directly as determinants of the social equilibrium. For us, in these volumes, they figure only as manifestations, as indications, of other forces that are the forces which really determine the social equilibrium. Very, very often, hitherto, the social sciences have been theories made up of residues and derivations and furthermore holding in view the practical purpose of persuading people to act in this or that manner deemed beneficial to society. These present volumes aim instead at bringing the social sciences wholly within the logico-experimental field, quite apart from any purpose of immediate practical utility, and in the sole intent of discovering the uniformities that prevail among social phenomena. If one is writing a book with a view to inducing people to act in a given way, one must necessarily resort to derivations, for they are the only language that reaches the human being in his sentiments and is therefore calculated to modify his behavior. But the person who aims at logico-experimental knowledge and nothing else must take the greatest pains not to fall into derivations. They are objects for this study, never tools of persuasion.

★　　　★　　　★

1411. When the logician has discovered the error in a reasoning, when he can put his finger on the fallacy in it, his work is done. But that is where the work of the sociologist begins, for he must find out why the false argument is accepted, why the sophistry persuades. Tricks of sophistry that are mere finesses in logic are of little or no interest to him, for they elicit no very wide response among men. But the fallacious, or for that matter the sound, theories that enjoy wide acceptance are of the greatest concern to him. It is the province of logic to tell why a reasoning is false. It is the business of sociology to explain its wide acceptance.

1412. According to Mill there are, in the main, two sources of ethical error: first, indifference to knowledge of the truth; and then, bias, the most common case being "that in which we are biased by our wishes," though after all we may accept agreeable and disagreeable conclusions alike provided they manage to arouse some strong emotion. Mill's "indifference" and "bias" would be what we mean by sentiments corresponding to residues. But Mill handles them very badly, being led astray by his preconception that only logical behavior is good, beneficial, praiseworthy, whereas non-logical conduct is necessarily evil, harmful, blameworthy. He is not in the least aware that he himself does most of his thinking under the influence of just such a "bias."

1413. A person who is trying to prove something is almost always conscious of the purpose of his derivation. Not so, oftentimes, the person assenting to the conclusion that the derivation reaches. When the purpose is to justify some rule of conduct, the effort is to associate the norm with certain residues by more or less logical arguments if the primary aim is to satisfy the hankering for logic in the individuals who are to be influenced; by heaping up residues if the primary appeal is to sentiment.

1414. Arranging these procedures in order of importance, they may be represented as follows: 1. The purpose. 2. The residues with which we start. 3. The derivation. A graph will make the situation clearer. Let B stand for the purpose that is to be attained, starting with the residues R' R'' R''' ... and working up to the derivations $R'rB$, $R'tB$, $R'vB$. ... In the case of a moral theory, the purpose, let us say, is to establish the precept forbidding homicide. That objective can be reached by a very simple derivation, namely, the blood-taboo. One can also start with the residue of a personal god, and attain the objective by way of many different derivations. One may

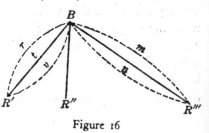

Figure 16

start with a metaphysical residue, a residue of social utility, a residue of personal utility, or some other residue, and get to the point desired by way of a literally huge number of derivations.

1415. Theologians, metaphysicists, philosophers, theorists of politics, law, and ethics . . . are inclined to assign first place to derivations. What we call residues are in their eyes axioms or dogmas, and the purpose is just the conclusion of a logical reasoning. But since they are not as a rule in any agreement on the derivation, they argue about it till they are blue in the face and think that they can change social conditions by proving a derivation fallacious. That is all an illusion on their part. They fail to realize that their hagglings never reach the majority of men, who could not make head or tail of them anyhow, and who in fact disregard them save as articles of faith to which they assent in deference to certain residues.[2]

1416. What we have just been saying leads to very important conclusions with reference to the "logic of sentiments."

1. If the basic residue from which a derivation develops disappears and is not replaced by another, the purpose also disappears.[3] That is the usual case in logical reasonings based on experimental premises: that is to say, a scientific theory is discarded in the light of new facts. However, even in such a case it is often possible for a conclusion to hold its ground if the erroneous premises can be replaced by new ones. But in non-scientific reasonings what usually happens is that abandoned premises are replaced by new ones— one residue gives way to other residues. Only in the exceptional case does such substitution fail to occur. Between the two extremes come intermediate cases. The disappearance of the residue from which a derivation has been evolved does not eradicate the purpose entirely, but merely weakens it, saps its vitality. The ideal remains but is accepted with less fervor. It has been observed in India that native converts lose the morality of their old religion without acquiring the morality of their new customs and beliefs.

2. In the case of a scientific argument, if it can be shown that the conclusion does not follow logically from the premises, the argument falls. But in an unscientific reasoning, if one form of derivation is demolished, another immediately is brought forward. If it is shown that the reasoning which connects a given conclusion (the purpose) is unsound, the only result as a rule is that a new derivation takes the place of the old one which has been overthrown. That comes about because the residue and the purpose are the basic elements in such reasonings. The derivation is secondary—often very, very secondary. The various Christian sects have doctrines as to good works and predestination that, from any logical standpoint, are altogether different and sometimes even antithetical or contradictory. Yet there is no difference between them as regards practical morals. A Chinese, a Moslem, a Calvinist, a Catholic, a Kantian, a Hegelian, a Materialist, all refrain from stealing; but each gives a different explanation for his conduct. In other words, it is a case of a number of derivations connecting one residue that is operative in all of

them with one conclusion which they all accept. And if someone chances to invent a new derivation or refute one of the existing ones, his achievement has no practical consequences and the conclusion remains the same.

3. In scientific thinking the most stable conclusions are obtained by drawing strictly logical inferences from premises that have experimental verifications which are as nearly perfect as possible. In unscientific thinking the strongest conclusions are those which rest on powerful residues without any derivations. Next come conclusions that are obtained from strong residues supported, in the form of derivations, by residues which are themselves relatively powerful. In proportion as the distance between residue and conclusion lengthens, in proportion as residues are replaced by logical reasonings, the security of the conclusion lessens, except for some few scholars. The plain man is convinced by the plain Christian catechism, never by fine-spun theological disquisitions. The latter exert but an indirect influence at the most. The plain man, to be sure, admires them without understanding them, and that admiration serves to endow them with a prestige that is carried over to the conclusions. That was the case in our day with Marx's *Capital*. Some few Socialists in Germany may have read it, but those who can possibly have understood it must have been as rare as white blackbirds. But the devious and obscure disquisitions in the book were admired at long range and so conferred prestige upon it. That admiration helped to determine the form of Socialist derivations, but not the residues or the conclusions, which existed before the book was written and will continue to be there after the book has been forgotten, and which are common both to Marxians and non-Marxians.

4. From the logical standpoint two contradictory propositions cannot hold side by side. From the standpoint of non-specific derivations two apparently contradictory propositions can very well stand together in one individual, one mind. The following propositions seem to be contradictory: "It is wrong to kill," "It is right to kill"; "It is wrong to appropriate other people's property," "It is right to appropriate other people's property"; "Wrongs must be forgiven," "Wrongs must not be forgiven." And yet they can be accepted at one and the same time by one and the same person in virtue of interpretations and distinctions that serve to explain the contradiction away. So, from the logical standpoint, if $A=B$, it follows inexorably that $B=A$; but no such consequence is necessary in a reasoning by derivations.

★   ★   ★

1435. II–*a*: *Authority of One Individual or of a Number of Individuals.* An extreme case would be the derivation that is strictly logical. It is evident that in a given connection the opinion of an expert has a greater probability of being verified by experience than the opinion of a person who is ignorant of the matters in hand or but slightly acquainted with them. That is a purely logico-experimental situation and we need not linger on it. But there are other kinds of derivations in which the individual's competence is not experimental. It may be assumed to exist from misleading evidence or be altogether fictitious. In the case least remote from the logico-experimental situation the authority is presumed on grounds that may or may not be sound, it being a question of a greater or lesser degree of probability. Next to that would come the case where the competence is stretched, through sentiments of group persistence, beyond the limits within which it is experimentally valid. The situation dealt with in the familiar maxim, "Cobbler, stick to your last"—*Sutor, ne ultra crepidam*—is of all times and places.[4]

1436. Because he is a first-class politician, Theodore Roosevelt is sure that he also knows history; and he makes bold to deliver a lecture in Berlin in which he makes brilliant display of his perfect ignorance of Greek and Roman history. The university that once listened to the lectures of Mommsen confers on him the title of Doctor *honoris causa*. He makes the discovery—and it is a feat indeed—that the apothegm, *Si vis pacem, para bellum*, is George Washington's—and he becomes a corresponding member of the French Institute of Moral and Political Sciences.[5] Now indubitably Roosevelt is a past master in the art of manipulating elections. He knows all the ins and outs of publicity. He is not a bad hunter of the white rhinoceros. But how can all that make him competent to advise the English on how to govern Egypt, or the French on the number of children they should have? Undoubtedly political considerations and considerations of rather undignified adulation figured in the honors that were conferred upon Roosevelt by the French Institute and the universities of Berlin and Cambridge, to say nothing of the flattery which he received from influential statesmen in the course of his rapid flight through Europe. But even where those considerations were not operative there was plenty of admiration for Roosevelt's fatuous chatter. The feeling was that there was a man who was man enough to get himself elected to the Presidency of the United States and to make a terrible noise in that office, and that therefore he must surely be competent in any matter relating to the historical and social sciences. It was the feeling also that a man who is competent in one thing is competent in everything; along with a sentiment of generic admiration that prevents people from distinguishing the respects in which a man is competent from the respects in which he is not.[6]

In a day gone by the prestige of the poet intruded upon every field of human activity, in many cases with some slight logico-experimental justification, since the poet was often a scholar. That consideration no longer applies to the poets and *literati* of our time. Yet in many cases such men are reputed authorities in matters altogether strange to them. Here is a Brieux, who "solves" some "social question" for us in every one of his dramatic productions. He "discovers" a thesis that has been a commonplace from times most ancient and in the footsteps of Plutarch and Rousseau solemnly tells mothers that they ought to suckle their children. That wins him loud applause from hosts of men and women of no great brains. Anatole France is a novelist of the very first rank, a great stylist, and a master of literary form. He has written in marvelous language novels distinguished for a keen psychological insight and sagacious irony. In all such connections his authority is not to be disputed. And then, one fine day, he takes it into his head to extend that authority to matters about which he knows much less. He sets out to solve questions of politics, economics, religion, history; he becomes Dreyfusard, Socialist, theologian, historian; and people flock in throngs to him in all of those varied metamorphoses. The sentiment of authority re-enforced by political passions was so strong in his case that it resisted all proofs to a contrary in itself more plausible. Andrew Lang, in his time, called attention to the serious and astonishingly numerous errors that France's *Jeanne d'Arc* contains, some childish some unintentional, and some that cannot, unfortunately, be called unintentional. In spite of everything the book still has hosts of admirers and enjoys a not little prestige.[7]

★   ★   ★

2029. There are people who worship Napoleon Bonaparte as a god. There are people who hate him as the lowest of criminals. Which are right? We do not choose to solve that question in connection with a quite different matter. Whether Napoleon was a good man or a bad man, he was certainly not an idiot, nor a man of little account, as millions of others are. He had exceptional qualities, and that is enough for us to give him a high ranking, though without prejudice of any sort to questions that might be raised as to the ethics of his qualities or their social utility.

2030. In short, we are here as usual resorting to scientific analysis, which distinguishes one problem from another and studies each one separately. As usual, again, we are replacing imperceptible variations in absolutely exact numbers with the sharp variations corresponding to groupings by class, just as in examinations those who are passed are sharply and arbitrarily distinguished from those who are "failed," and just as in the matter of physical age we distinguish children from young people, the young from the aged.

2031. So let us make a class of the people who have the highest indices in their branch of activity, and to that class give the name "elite."

2032. For the particular investigation with which we are engaged, a study of the social equilibrium, it will help if we further divide that class into two classes: a *governing elite*, comprising individuals who directly or indirectly play some considerable part in government, and a *non-governing elite*, comprising the rest.[8]

2033. A chess champion is certainly a member of the elite, but it is no less certain that his merits as a chess-player do not open the doors to political influence for him; and hence, unless he has other qualities to win him that distinction, he is not a member of the governing elite. Mistresses of absolute monarchs have oftentimes been members of the elite, either because of their beauty or because of their intellectual endowments; but only a few of them, who have had, in addition, the particular talents required by politics, have played any part in government.

2034. So we get two strata in a population: (1) A lower stratum, the *non-elite*, with whose possible influence on government we are not just here concerned; then (2) a higher stratum, *the elite*, which is divided into two: (*a*) a governing elite; (*b*) a non-governing elite.

★   ★   ★

2041. The manner in which the various groups in a population intermix has to be considered. In moving from one group to another an individual generally brings with him certain inclinations, sentiments, attitudes, that he has acquired in the group from which he comes, and that circumstance cannot be ignored.

2042. To this mixing, in the particular case in which only two groups, the elite and the non-elite, are envisaged, the term "circulation of elites" has been applied[9]—in French, *circulation des elites* (or in more general terms, "class-circulation").

2043. In conclusion we must pay special attention (1) in the case of one single group, to the proportions between the total of the group and the number of individuals who are nominally members of it but do not possess the qualities requisite for effective membership; and then (2) in the case of various groups, to the ways in which transitions from one group to the other occur, and to the intensity of that movement—that is to say, to the velocity of the circulation.

2044. Velocity in circulation has to be considered not only absolutely but also in relation to the supply of and the demand for certain social elements. A country that is always at peace does not require many soldiers in its governing class, and the production of generals may be overexuberant as compared with the demand. But, when a country is in a state of continuous warfare, many soldiers are necessary and, though production remains at the same level, it may not meet the demand. That, we might note in passing, has been one of the causes for the collapse of many aristocracies.[10]

2045. Another example. In a country where there is little industry and little commerce, the supply of individuals possessing in high degree the qualities requisite for those types of activity exceeds the demand. Then industry and commerce develop and the supply, though remaining the same, no longer meets the demand.

2046. We must not confuse the state of law with the state of fact. The latter alone, or almost alone, has a bearing on the social equilibrium. There are many examples of castes that are legally closed, but into which, in point of fact, newcomers make their way, and often in large numbers. On the other hand, what difference does it make if a caste is legally open, but conditions *de facto* prevent new accessions to it? If a person who acquires wealth thereby becomes a member of the governing class, but no one gets rich, it is as if the class were closed; and if only a few get rich, it is as if the law erected serious barriers against access to the caste. Something of that sort was observable toward the end of the Roman Empire. People who acquired wealth entered the order of the curials. But only a few individuals made any money. Theoretically, we might examine any number of groups. Practically, we have to confine ourselves to the more important. We shall proceed by successive approximations, starting with the simple and going on to the complex.

2047. *Higher Class and Lower Class in General.* The least we can do is to divide society into two strata: a higher stratum, which usually contains the rulers, and a lower stratum, which usually contains the ruled. The fact is so obvious that it has always forced itself even upon the most casual observation, and so for the circulation of individuals between the two strata. Even Plato had an inkling of class-circulation and tried to regulate it artificially. The "new man," the upstart, the *parvenu*, has always been a subject of interest, and literature has analyzed him unendingly. Here, then, we are merely giving a more exact form to things that have long been perceived more or less vaguely. Formerly, we noted a varying distribution of residues in the various social groupings, and chiefly in the higher and the lower class. Such heterogeneousness is a fact perceived by the most superficial glance.

2048. Changes in Class I and Class II residues occurring within the two social strata have an important influence in determining the social equilibrium. They have been commonly observed by laymen under a special form, as changes in "religious" sentiments, so called, in the higher stratum of society. It has often been noted that there were times when religious sentiments seemed to lose ground, others when they seemed to gain in strength, and that such undulations corresponded to social movements of very considerable scope. The uniformity might be more exactly described by saying that in the higher stratum of society Class II residues gradually lose in strength, until now and again they are reinforced by tides upwelling from the lower stratum.[11]

2049. Religious sentiments were very feeble in the higher classes in Rome toward the end of the Republic; but they gained notably in strength thereafter, through the rise to the higher classes of men from the lower, of foreigners that is, freedmen, and others, whom the Roman Empire raised in station. They gained still further in intensity in the days of the decadent Roman Empire, when the government passed into the hands of a military plebs and a bureaucracy originating in the lower classes. That was a time when a predominance of Class II residues made itself manifest in a decadence in literature and in the arts and sciences, and in invasions by Oriental religions and especially Christianity.

2050. The Protestant Reformation in the sixteenth century, the Puritan Revolution in Cromwell's day in England, the French Revolution of 1789, are examples of great religious tides originating in the lower classes and rising to engulf the skeptical higher classes. An instance in our day would be the United States of America, where this upward thrust of members of lower classes strong in Class II residues is very intense; and in that country one witnesses the rise of no end of strange and wholly unscientific religions— such as Christian Science—that are utterly at war with any sort of scientific thinking, and a mass of hypocritical laws for the enforcement of morality that are replicas of laws of the European Middle Ages.

2051. The upper stratum of society, the elite, nominally contains certain groups of people, not always very sharply defined, that are called aristocracies. There are cases in which the majority of individuals belonging to such aristocracies actually possess the qualities requisite for remaining there; and then again there are cases where considerable numbers of the individuals making up the class do not possess those requisites. Such people may occupy more or less important places in the governing elite or they may be barred from it.

2052. In the beginning, military, religious, and commercial aristocracies and plutocracies—with a few exceptions not worth considering—must have constituted parts of the governing elite and sometimes have made up the whole of it. The victorious warrior, the prosperous merchant, the opulent plutocrat, were men of such parts, each in his own field, as to be superior to the average individual. Under those circumstances the label corresponded to an actual capacity. But as time goes by, considerable, sometimes very considerable, differences arise between the capacity and the label; while, on the other hand, certain aristocracies originally figuring prominently in the rising elite end by constituting an insignificant element in it. That has happened especially to military aristocracies.

2053. Aristocracies do not last. Whatever the causes, it is an incontestable fact that after a certain length of time they pass away. History is a graveyard of aristocracies. The Athenian "people" was an aristocracy as compared with the remainder of a population of resident aliens and slaves. It vanished without leaving any descent. The various aristocracies of Rome vanished in their time. So did the aristocracies of the Barbarians. Where, in France, are the descendants of the Frankish conquerors? The genealogies of the English nobility have been very exactly kept; and they show that very few families still remain to claim descent from the comrades of William the Conqueror. The rest have vanished. In Germany the aristocracy of the present day is very largely made up of descendants of vassals of the lords of old. The populations of European countries have increased enormously during the past few centuries. It is as certain as certain can be that the aristocracies have not increased in proportion.

2054. They decay not in numbers only. They decay also in quality, in the sense that they lose their vigor, that there is a decline in the proportions of the residues which enabled them to win their power and hold it. The governing class is restored not only in numbers, but—and that is the more important thing—in quality, by families rising from the lower classes and bringing with them the vigor and the proportions of residues necessary for keeping themselves in power. It is also restored by the loss of its more degenerate members.

2055. If one of those movements comes to an end, or worse still, if they both come to an end, the governing class crashes to ruin and often sweeps the whole of a nation along with it. Potent cause of disturbance in the equilibrium is the accumulation of superior elements in the lower classes and, conversely, of inferior elements in the higher classes. If human aristocracies were like thoroughbreds among animals, which reproduce themselves over long periods of time with approximately the same traits, the history of the human race would be something altogether different from the history we know.

2056. In virtue of class-circulation, the governing elite is always in a state of slow and continuous transformation. It flows on like a river, never being today what it was yesterday. From time to time sudden and violent disturbances occur. There is a flood—the river overflows its banks. Afterwards, the new governing elite again resumes its slow transformation. The flood has subsided, the river is again flowing normally in its wonted bed.

2057. Revolutions come about through accumulations in the higher strata of society—either because of a slowing-down in class-circulation, or from other causes—of decadent elements no longer possessing the residues suitable for keeping them in power, and shrinking from the use of force; while meantime in the lower strata of society elements of superior quality are coming to the fore, possessing residues suitable for exercising the functions of government and willing enough to use force.

2058. In general, in revolutions the members of the lower strata are captained by leaders from the higher strata, because the latter possess the intellectual qualities required for outlining a tactic, while lacking the combative residues supplied by the individuals from the lower strata.

2059. Violent movements take place by fits and starts, and effects therefore do not follow immediately on their causes. After a governing class, or a nation, has maintained itself for long periods of time on force and acquired great wealth, it may subsist for some time still without using force, buying off its adversaries and paying not only in gold, but also in terms of the dignity and respect that it had formerly enjoyed and which constitute, as it were, a capital. In the first stages of decline, power is maintained by bargainings and concessions, and people are so deceived into thinking that that policy can be carried on indefinitely. So the decadent Roman Empire bought peace of the Barbarians with money and honors. So Louis XVI, in France, squandering in a very short time an ancestral inheritance of love, respect, and almost religious reverence for the monarchy, managed, by making repeated concessions, to be the King of the Revolution. So the English aristocracy managed to prolong its term of power in the second half of the nineteenth century down to the dawn of its decadence, which was heralded by the "Parliament Bill" in the first years of the twentieth.

NOTES

1 It would perhaps be better to use designations that have no meanings in themselves, such as letters of the alphabet. On the other hand, such a system would impair the clarity of our argument. We must therefore resign ourselves to using terms of ordinary speech; but the reader must bear in mind that such words, or their etymologies, in no way serve to describe the things they stand for. Things have to be examined directly. Names are just labels to help us keep track of them.

2 Political economy has been and largely continues to be a branch of literature, and as

such falls under anything that may be said of derivations. It stands as a matter of plain fact that economic practice and economic theory have followed altogether divergent paths.

Pierre Bayle, *Dictionnaire historique, s.v. Augustin:* "To anyone examining the question without prejudice and with the necessary competence, it is so evident that the doctrines of St. Augustine and Jansenius, Bishop of Ypres, are one and the same, that one can hardly keep one's temper at the thought that the Court of Rome could boast of condemning Jansenius and meantime keep the Saint secure in all his glory. The two things are altogether incompatible. Not only that: in condemning Calvin's doctrine of free-will, the Council of Trent necessarily condemned the doctrine of St. Augustine. . . . There are people who regard it as a very happy circumstance that the masses at large take such little interest in the vicissitudes of doctrine, are in fact incapable of doing so. If they did, they would be rising more often against theologians than against usurers. 'If you do not know,' they might say to them, 'that you are deceiving us, your stupidity deserves your being sent to till the soil. If you do know what you are doing, you deserve prison on bread and water for your wickedness.' . . . [In that, Bayle is mistaken. A person may be as intelligent as one could wish and yet assent to contradictory derivations in the best faith. That happens every day, and especially on such matters as "free will." Bayle is right in what follows:] But there is little to fear. All the masses ask is to be led along the beaten paths; and even if they wanted more than that, they would not be capable of mastering the subject. Their daily occupations have not permitted them to acquire sufficient competence for that."

3 That is a particular case of the general theory of the reciprocal influence of residues and derivations upon each other.

4 Jeremy Bentham, *Tactique des assemblées législatives,* II, 23–24, expresses an altogether erroneous opinion: "Authority has been the support over countless centuries of the most discordant systems, the most monstrous opinions. [Such opinions are supported by residues and explained by derivations, among which the derivation of authority.] The religions of the Brahma, of Foh, of Mohammed, rest on nothing else. [Not at all! Authority is only one of many derivations that are called in to logicalize the various group persistences.] If authority is a thing that cannot be questioned, the human race that people those vast territories has no hope ever of escaping from darkness." In that we get, first of all, the usual error of assuming that all conduct is logical and that beliefs are products of reasoning. The fact is—they are dictated by sentiment. Implicit, secondly, is a conflict between the Religion of Progress in which Bentham believes and the "super-stition" of authority that he combats. To adopt the superstition would be tantamount to renouncing every hope of progress for the peoples of Asia; and since such a thing is inconceivable, the superstition has to be rejected. That is one of the usual confusions between the question of the utility of a doctrine and its accord with experimental facts.

5 [And yet why not George Washington, as well as some other modern? For the phrase has no classical authority. Vegetius, *De re militari,* III, *proemium,* said, "*Qui desiderat pacem, præparet bellum*"; and Cicero, *Philippicæ,* VII, 6, 19, "*Si pace frui volumus bellum gerendum est.*"—A.L.]

6 The public attentions showered on Roosevelt were to a certain extent logical actions. It was believed at the time in Europe that Roosevelt would again be President of the United States, and the idea was to work for favors from him. Those calculations went amiss, however: Roosevelt was not re-elected. To counterbalance such fawning, the

Pope refused to receive Roosevelt, a Genoese nobleman denied him entrance to his palace, and Maximilian Harden wrote an article lampooning German adulators of Roosevelt.

7 Andrew Lang, *La Jeanne d'Arc de M. Anatole France*, chap ix, "The Forest of Errors," pp. 95–102 [Lang's review was written in French and seems never to have appeared, as such, in English. It contained material that Lang had already put forward against Anatole France in *The Maid of France, Being the Story of the Life and Death of Jeanne d'Arc* (London, 1908)—A.L.]: France states that "the tax imposed . . . upon the population of Domremy amounted to not less than £220 in gold." Lang informed France before the definitive publication of the *Jeanne d'Arc* that "for the tax to have reached such a sum, we should have to assume that Domremy had as large a population as Orléans. . . . I had already called M. France's attention to this error, but it has not been corrected in the revised edition. . . . M. France obstinately maintains that a certain young woman whose son was godson to Jeanne 'ridiculed her because of her devoutness,' mentioning the testimony of the woman as proof. Now there is not a suggestion of any such thing in the woman's testimony; and I am not alone in having called M. France's attention to that fact. That is how he bases his work on 'the most reliable sources,' to use the words of his new preface, and 'interpreting them with all the insight of a real scholar,' to believe his good-natured critic, M. Gabriel Monad!" Lang notes other errors of minor importance but which go to show that France took the writing of his book not overseriously: "In a short passage from the celebrated letter of [Jean de] Gerson, every sentence as translated by M. France becomes nonsense. A versified proverb of Dionysius Cato, '*Arbitrii nostri non est quod quisque loquatur*,' becomes in the book of M. France, 'Our arbiters are not what each one says.' Of the false rumors current regarding Jeanne, Gerson says, '*Si multi multa loquantur pro garrulitate sua et levitate aut dolositate aut alio sinistro favore vel odio. . . .*' M. France translates that as follows: 'If several witnesses have testified to Jeanne's garrulousness, and to her frivolousness and shrewdness . . .'! In the sentence next following Gerson alludes to the words of the Apostle, '*Non oportet servum Dei litigare*,' and M. France translates, 'It is not meet to involve the servant of God in this question.'" Noting another important error on France's part, Lang comments: "While M. France was finding in Dunois's testimony things that were not there, it was quite natural that he should fail to observe that D'Aulon was a member of the Royal Council and had been summoned by the King along with the other Councillors to pass on Jeanne's first petition—a thing that must surely strike us as altogether natural. But it is very regrettable that after his attention had been called to these points by the 'praiseworthy conscientiousness of Mr. Andrew Lang,' he should have allowed his fabrication to stand in his revised edition." Though Salomon Reinach shows himself very kindly disposed toward Anatole France, he is forced to admit the latter's errors (in *Cultes, mythes et religions*, IV, 311–12): "I am going to say at the outset that M. Lang is often right in his criticisms of M. France, that he is inclined to attach a great deal of importance to small matters." But he concedes (p. 320) that France did not rectify errors that had been called to his attention: "In spite of the improvements M. France has made, his book is still very inaccurate. Perhaps we ought to assume that M. France shared his labors with others, using what we call a '*nègre*,' and not a very trustworthy '*nègre*.'" As regards the Cato proverb in dispute between Lang and France, France should have remembered that in the *Distica Catonis*, a work well known and greatly admired in centuries past, the proverb reads, III, 2: "*Cum recte*

vivas ne cures verba malorum: arbitrii non est nostri quid quisque loquatur." ("So long as you live rightly, give no thought to the words of the malicious. It is not within our power to control what people say.")

8 Marie Kolabinska, *La Circulation des élites en France* (Lausanne, 1912), p. 6: "We have just enumerated different categories of individuals comprising the elite. They may also be classified in many other ways. For the purpose I have in view in this study it is better to divide the elite into two parts: one, which I will call *M*, will contain those individuals in the elite who share in the government of the state, who make up what may be more or less vaguely called 'the governing class.' The other part, *N*, will be made up of the remainder of the elite when the part *M* has been set off from it."

9 [And most inappropriately, for, in this sense, the phrase never meant more than circulation within the elite. Furthermore, the elite is not the only class to be considered, and the principles that apply to circulation with the elite apply to circulation within such lower classes as one may choose for one purpose or another to consider.—A.L.]

10 Kolabinska, *La Circulation des élites en France*, p. 10: "Inadequate recruiting in the elite does not result from a mere numerical proportion between new members and old. Account has to be taken of the number of persons who possess the qualities required for membership in the governing elite but are refused admittance; or else, in an opposite direction, the number of new members the elite might require but does not get. In the first case, the production of persons possessing unusual qualities as regards education may far surpass the number of such persons that the elite can accommodate, and then we get what has been called an 'intellectual proletariat.' "

11 Many writers who are not equipped with this general conception fall into contradictions. Sometimes the clarity of the facts forces itself upon them; then again preconceptions will blur their view of things. Taine is an example. In the *Ancien régime* he well notes (chap. iii) that the mind of the masses at large is steeped in prejudices (is, in our terms, under the sway of Class II residues). On that basis he should go on and conclude that the French Revolution was a particular case of the religious revolution, where popular faith overwhelms the scepticism of the higher classes. But, consciously or otherwise, he succumbs to the influence of the preconception that the higher classes are educators of the masses, and views unbelief and impiety in the nobility, the Third Estate, and the higher clergy as among the main causes of the Revolution. He notes the difference between France and England in that regard and seems on the verge of ascribing to that circumstance the fact that the revolution which occurred in France did not occur in England. Says he, Bk. IV, chap ii, sec. 1 (Vol. II, p. 118): "In England [the higher class] speedily perceived the danger. Philosophy was precocious in England, native to England. That does not matter. It never got acclimated there. Montesquieu wrote in his travel note-book in 1729 (*Notes sur l'Angleterre*, p. 352): 'No religion in England. . . . If anyone brings up the subject of religion, he is laughed at.' Fifty years later the public mind has about-faced: 'all those who have a tight roof over their heads and a good coat on their backs' [The expression is Macaulay's.] have seen what these new doctrines mean. In any event they feel that speculations in the library must not become preachings on the streets. [They and Taine therefore believe in the efficacy of such preachings.] Impiety seems to them bad manners. They regard religion as the cement that holds public order together. That is because they are themselves public men, interested in doing things, participating in the government and well taught by daily personal experience. . . . [Yet a few lines before that Taine had refuted himself:]

When you talk religion or politics with people, you find their minds almost always made up. Their preconceptions, their interests, their situation in life, have convinced them already, and they will listen to you only if you tell them aloud things they have been thinking in silence." If that is so, the "preachings in the street" to which Taine alludes ought not to be very effective, and if they are, it cannot be that people "will listen to you only if you tell them aloud things they have been thinking in silence." As a matter of fact, it is these latter hypotheses that more closely approximate experience. The mental state of the French people toward the end of the eighteenth century had been but little affected by the impiety of the higher classes, any more than the mental state of the Romans had been affected by the impiety of the contemporaries of Lucretius, Cicero, and Caesar, or the mental state of the European masses by the impiety of the nobility and higher clergy at the time of the Reformation. Belin, *Le Commerce des livres prohibés à Paris de 1750 à 1789*, pp. 104-5: "One may assert that the works of the philosophers did not directly reach the masses or the lower bourgeoisie. The working-men, the tradesmen, did not know Voltaire and Rousseau until the time of the Revolution, when their tribunes began to gloss them in inflammatory harangues or to translate their maxims into legislation. When they stepped into the limelight they had certainly not read the great books of the century, though they could not have missed entirely the more celebrated of the literary quarrels. The true disciples of the *philosophes*, the faithful patrons of the peddlers of forbidden literature, were the nobles, the abbés, the members of the privileged classes, idlers about the parlors of society who were on the lookout for some distraction from their relentless tedium and threw themselves head-long into philosophical discussions and soon let themselves be vanquished by the new spirit [That is all borne out by experience; the following less so.], without foreseeing the remoter consequences of the premises that they were adopting so gaily.... [Belin makes a further point:] The privileged for that matter were the only ones who could afford the exorbitant prices that any lover of forbidden books had to pay."

5

ÉMILE DURKHEIM

Elementary Forms of Religious Life

WE ARE NOW able to see what the part of society in the genesis of logical thought is. This is possible only from the moment when, above the fugitive conceptions which they owe to sensuous experience, men have succeeded in conceiving a whole world of stable ideas, the common ground of all intelligences. In fact, logical thinking is always impersonal thinking, and is also thought *sub specie æternitatis*—as though for all time. Impersonality and stability are the two characteristics of truth. Now logical life evidently presupposes that men know, at least confusedly, that there is such a thing as truth, distinct from sensuous appearances. But how have they been able to arrive at this conception? We generally talk as though it should have spontaneously presented itself to them from the moment they opened their eyes upon the world. However, there is nothing in immediate experience which could suggest it; everything even contradicts it. Thus the child and the animal have no suspicion of it. History shows that it has taken centuries for it to disengage and establish itself. In our Western world, it was with the great thinkers of Greece that it first became clearly conscious of itself and of the consequences which it implies; when the discovery was made, it caused an amazement which Plato has translated into magnificent language. But if it is only at this epoch that the idea is expressed in philosophic formulæ, it was necessarily pre-existent in the stage of an obscure sentiment. Philosophers have sought to elucidate this sentiment, but they have not succeeded. In order that they might reflect upon it and analyze it, it was necessary that it be given them, and that they seek to know whence it came, that is to say, in what experience it was founded. This is in collective experience. It is under the form of collective thought that impersonal thought is for the first time revealed to humanity; we cannot see by what other way this revelation could have been made. From the mere fact that society exists, there is also, outside of the individual sensations and images, a whole system of representations which enjoy marvelous properties. By means of them, men understand each other and intelligences grasp each other. They have within them a sort of force or moral ascendancy, in virtue of which they impose themselves upon individual minds. Hence the individual at least obscurely takes account of the fact that above his private ideas, there is a world of absolute ideas according to which he must shape his own; he catches a glimpse of a whole intellectual kingdom in which he participates, but which is greater than he. This is the first intuition of the realm of truth. From the moment when he first becomes conscious of these higher ideas, he sets himself to scrutinizing their nature; he asks whence these pre-eminent representations hold their prerogatives and, in so far as he believes that he has discovered their causes, he undertakes to put these causes into action for himself, in order that he may draw from them by his own force the effects which they produce; that is to say, he attributes to himself the right of making concepts. Thus the faculty of conception has individualized itself. But to understand its origins and function, it must be attached to the social conditions upon which it depends.

It may be objected that we show the concept in one of its aspects only, and that its unique role is not the assuring of a harmony among minds, but also, and to a greater extent, their harmony with the nature of things. It seems as though it had a reason for existence only on condition of being true, that is to say, objective, and as though its impersonality were only a consequence of its objectivity. It is in regard to things, thought of as adequately as possible, that minds ought to communicate. Nor do we deny that the evolution of concepts has been partially in this direction. The concept which was first held as true because it was collective tends to be no longer collective except on condition of being held as true: we demand its credentials of it before according it our confidence. But we must not lose sight of the fact that even today the great majority of the concepts which we use are not methodically constituted; we get them from language, that is to say, from common experience, without submitting them to any criticism. The scientifically elaborated and criticized concepts are always in the very slight minority. Also, between them and those which draw all their authority from the fact that they are collective, there are only differences of degree. A collective representation presents guarantees of objectivity by the fact that it is collective: for it is not without sufficient reason that it has been able to generalize and maintain itself with persistence. If it were out of accord with the nature of things, it would never have been able to acquire an extended and prolonged empire over intellects. At bottom, the confidence inspired by scientific concepts is due to the fact that they can be methodically controlled. But a collective representation is necessarily submitted to a control that is repeated indefinitely; the men who accept it verify it by their own experience. Therefore, it could not be wholly inadequate for its subject. It is true that it may express this by means of imperfect symbols; but scientific symbols themselves are never more than approximative. It is precisely this principle which is at the basis of the method which we follow in the study of religious phenomena: we take it as an axiom that religious beliefs, howsoever strange their appearance may be at times, contain a truth which must be discovered.[1]

On the other hand, it is not at all true that concepts, even when constructed according to the rules of science, get their authority uniquely from their objective value. It is not enough that they be true to be believed. If they are not in harmony with the other beliefs and opinions, or, in a word, with the mass of the other collective representations, they will be denied; minds will be closed to them; consequently it will be as though they did not exist. Today it is generally sufficient that they bear the stamp of science to receive a sort of privileged credit, because we have faith in science. But this faith does not differ essentially from religious faith. In the last resort, the value which we attribute to science depends upon the idea which we collectively form of its nature and role in life; that is as much as to say that it expresses a state of public opinion. In all social life, in fact, science rests upon opinion. It is undoubtedly true that this opinion can be taken as the object of a study and a science made of it; this is what sociology principally consists in. But the science of opinion does not make opinions; it can only observe them and make them more conscious of themselves. It is true that by this means it can lead them to change, but science continues to be dependent upon opinion at the very moment when it seems to be making its laws; for, as we have already shown, it is from opinion that it holds the force necessary to act upon opinion.[2]

Saying that concepts express the manner in which society represents things is also saying that conceptual thought is coeval with humanity itself. We refuse to see in it the product of a more or less retarded culture. A man who did not think with concepts would not be a man, for he would not be a social being. If reduced to having only individual perceptions, he would be indistinguishable from the beasts. If it has been possible to sustain the contrary thesis, it is because concepts have been defined by characteristics which are not essential to them. They have been identified with general ideas[3] and with clearly limited and circumscribed general ideas.[4] In these conditions it has possibly seemed as though the inferior societies had no concepts properly so called; for they have only rudimentary processes of generalization and the ideas which they use are not generally very well defined. But the greater part of our concepts are equally indetermined; we force ourselves to define them only in discussions or when doing careful work. We have also seen that conceiving is not generalizing. Thinking conceptually is not simply isolating and grouping together the common characteristics of a certain number of objects; it is relating the variable to the permanent, the individual to the social. And, since logical thought commences with the concept, it follows that it has always existed; there is no period in history when men have lived in chronic confusion and contradiction. To be sure, we cannot insist too much upon the different characteristics which logic presents at different periods in history; it develops like the societies themselves. But howsoever real these differences may be, they should not cause us to neglect the similarities, which are no less essential.

We are now in a position to take up a final question which has already been raised in our introduction[5] and which has been taken as understood in the remainder of this work. We have seen that at least some of the categories are social things. The question is where they got this character.

Undoubtedly it will be easily understood that since they are themselves concepts, they are the work of the group. It can even be said that there are no other concepts which present to an equal degree the signs by which a collective representation is recognized. In fact, their stability and impersonality are such that they have often passed as being absolutely universal and immutable. Also, as they express the fundamental conditions for an agreement between minds, it seems evident that they have been elaborated by society.

But the problem concerning them is more complex, for they are social in another sense and, as it were, in the second degree. They not only come from society, but the things which they express are of a social nature. Not only is it society which has founded them, but their contents are the different aspects of the social being: the category of class was at first indistinct from the concept of the human group; it is the rhythm of social life which is at the basis of the category of time; the territory occupied by the society furnished the material for the category of space; it is the collective force which was the prototype of the concept of efficient force, an essential element in the category of causality. However, the categories are not made to be applied only to the social realm; they reach out to all reality. Then how is it that they have taken from society the models upon which they have been constructed?

It is because they are the pre-eminent concepts, which have a preponderating part in our knowledge. In fact, the function of the categories is to dominate and envelop all the other concepts: they are permanent molds for the mental life. Now, for them to embrace such an object, they must be founded upon a reality of equal amplitude.

Undoubtedly the relations which they express exist in an implicit way in individual consciousnesses. The individual lives in time, and, as we have said, he has a certain sense of temporal orientation. He is situated at a determined point in space, and it has even been held, and sustained with good reasons, that all sensations have something special about them.[6] He has a feeling of resemblances; similar representations are brought together and the new representation formed by their union has a sort of generic character. We also have the sensation of a certain regularity in the order of the succession of phenomena; even an animal is not incapable of this. However, all these relations are strictly personal for the individual who recognizes them, and consequently the notion of them which he may have can in no case go beyond his own narrow horizon. The generic images which are formed in my consciousness by the fusion of similar images represent only the objects which I have perceived directly; there is nothing there which could give me the idea of a class, that is to say, of a mold including the *whole* group of all possible objects which satisfy the same condition. Also, it would be necessary to have the idea of group in the first place, and the mere observations of our interior life could never awaken that in us. But, above all, there is no individual experience, howsoever extended and prolonged it may be, which could give a suspicion of the existence of a whole class which would embrace every single being, and to which other classes are only coordinated or subordinated species. This idea of *all*, which is at the basis of the classifications which we have just cited, could not have come from the individual himself, who is only a part in relation to the whole and who never attains more than an infinitesimal fraction of reality. And yet there is perhaps no other category of greater importance; for as the role of the categories is to envelop all the other concepts, the category par excellence would seem to be this very concept of *totality*. The theorists of knowledge ordinarily postulate it as if it came of itself, while it really surpasses the contents of each individual consciousness taken alone to an infinite degree.

For the same reasons, the space which I know by my senses, of which I am the center and where everything is disposed in relation to me, could not be space in general, which contains all extensions and where these are co-ordinated by personal guidelines which are common to everybody. In the same way, the concrete duration which I feel passing within me and with me could not give me the idea of time in general: the first expresses only the rhythm of my individual life; the second should correspond to the rhythm of a life which is not that of any individual in particular, but in which all participate.[7] In the same way, finally, the regularities which I am able to conceive in the manner in which my sensations succeed one another may well have a value for me; they explain how it comes about that when I am given the first of two phenomena whose concurrence I have observed, I tend to expect the other. But this personal state of expectation could not be confounded with the conception of a universal order of succession which imposes itself upon all minds and all events.

Since the world expressed by the entire system of concepts is the one that society regards, society alone can furnish the most general notions with which it should be represented. Such an object can be embraced only by a subject which contains all the individual subjects within it. Since the universe does not exist except in so far as it is thought of, and since it is not completely thought of except by society, it takes a place in this latter; it becomes a part of society's interior life, while this is the totality, outside of which nothing exists. The concept of totality is only the abstract form of the concept of society: it is the whole which includes all things, the supreme class which embraces all other classes. Such is the final principle upon which repose all these primitive classifications where beings from every realm are placed and classified in social forms, exactly like men.[8] But if the world is inside of society, the space which this latter occupies becomes confounded with space in general. In fact, we have seen how each thing has its assigned place in social space, and the degree to which this space in general differs from the concrete expanses which we perceive is well shown by the fact that this localization is wholly ideal and in no way resembles what it would have been if it had been dictated to us by sensuous experience alone.[9] For the same reason, the rhythm of collective life dominates and embraces the varied rhythms of all the elementary lives from which it results; consequently the time which it expresses dominates and embraces all particular durations. It is time in general. For a long time the history of the world has been only another aspect of the history of society. The one commences with the other; the periods of the first are determined by the periods of the second. This impersonal and total duration is measured, and the guidelines in relation to which it is divided and organized are fixed by the movements of concentration or dispersion of society; or, more generally, the periodical necessities for a collective renewal. If these critical instants are generally attached to some material phenomenon, such as the regular recurrence of such and such a star or the alternation of the seasons, it is because objective signs are necessary to make this essentially social organization intelligible to all. In the same way, finally, the causal relation, from the moment when it is collectively stated by the group, becomes independent of every individual consciousness; it rises above all particular minds and events. It is a law whose value depends upon no person. We have already shown how it is clearly thus that it seems to have originated.

Another reason explains why the constituent elements of the categories should have been taken from social life: it is because the relations that they express could not have been learned except in and through society. If they are in a sense immanent in the life of an individual, he has neither a reason nor the means for learning them, reflecting upon them, and forming them into distinct ideas. In order to orient himself personally in space and to know at what moments he should satisfy his various organic needs, he has no need of making, once and for all, a conceptual representation of time and space. Many animals are able to find the road which leads to places with which they are familiar; they come back at a proper moment without knowing any of the categories; sensations are enough to direct them automatically. They would also be enough for men, if their sensations had to satisfy only individual needs. To recognize the fact that one thing resembles another which we have already experienced, it is in no way necessary that we arrange them all in groups and species: the way in which similar images call up each other and unite is enough to give the feeling of resemblance. The impression that a certain thing has already been seen or experienced implies no classification. To recognize the things that we should seek or from which we should flee, it would not be necessary to attach the effects of the two to their causes by a logical bond, if individual conveniences were the only ones in question. Purely empirical sequences and strong connections between the concrete representations would be as sure guides for the will. Not only is it true that the animal has no others, but also our own personal conduct frequently supposes nothing more. The prudent man is the one who has a very clear sensation of what must be done, but which he would ordinarily be quite incapable of stating as a general law.

It is a different matter with society. This is possible only when the individuals and things which compose it are divided into certain groups, that is to say, classified, and when these groups are classified in relation to each other. Society supposes a self-conscious organization, which is nothing other than a classification. This organization of society naturally extends itself to the place that this occupies. To avoid all collisions, it is necessary that each particular group have a determined portion of space assigned to it: in other terms, it is necessary that space in general be divided, differentiated, arranged, and that these divisions and arrangements be known to everybody. On the other hand, every summons to a celebration, a hunt, or a military expedition implies fixed and established dates and, consequently, that a common time be agreed upon, which everybody conceives in the same fashion. Finally, the cooperation of many persons with the same end in view is possible only when they are in agreement as to the relation which exists between this end and the means of attaining it, that is to say, when the same causal relation is admitted by all the cooperators in the enterprise. It is not surprising, therefore, that social time, social space, social classes, and causality should be the basis of the corresponding categories, since it is under their social forms that these different relations were first grasped with a certain clarity by the human intellect.

In summing up, then, we must say that society is not at all the illogical or a-logical, incoherent and fantastic being which it has too often been considered. Quite the contrary, the collective consciousness is the highest form of the psychic life, since it is the consciousness of the consciousnesses. Being placed outside of and above individual and local contingencies, it sees things only in their permanent and essential aspects, which it crystallizes into communicable ideas. At the same time that it sees from above, it sees farther; at every moment of time, it embraces all known reality; that is why it alone can furnish the mind with the molds which are applicable to the totality of things and which make it possible to think of them. It does not create these molds artificially; it finds them within itself; it does nothing but become conscious of them. They translate the ways of being which are found in all the stages of reality but which appear in their full clarity only at the summit, because the extreme complexity of the psychic life which passes there necessitates a greater development of consciousness. Attributing social origins to logical thought is not debasing it or diminishing its value or reducing it to nothing more than a system of artificial combinations; on the contrary, it is relating it to a cause which implies it naturally. But this is not saying that the ideas elaborated in this way are at once adequate for their object. If society is something universal in relation to the individual, it is none the less an individuality itself, which has its own personal physiognomy and its idiosyncrasies; it is a particular subject and consequently particularizes whatever it thinks of. Therefore collective representations also contain subjective elements, and these must be progressively rooted out if we are to approach reality more closely. But howsoever crude these may have been at the beginning, the fact remains that with them the germ of a new mentality was given, to which the individual could never have raised himself by his own efforts: by them the way was opened to a stable, impersonal, and organized thought which then had nothing to do except to develop its nature.

Also, the causes which have determined this development do not seem to be specifically different from those which gave it its initial impulse. If logical thought tends to rid itself more and more of the subjective and personal elements which it still retains from its origin, it is not because extra-social factors have intervened; it is much rather because a social life of a new sort is developing. It is this international life which has already resulted in universalizing religious beliefs. As it extends, the collective horizon enlarges; the society ceases to appear as the only whole, to become a part of a much vaster one, with indetermined frontiers, which is susceptible of advancing indefinitely. Consequently things can no longer be contained in the social molds according to which they were primitively classified; they must be organized according to principles which are their own, so logical organization differentiates itself from the social organization and becomes autonomous. Really and truly human thought is not a primitive fact; it is the product of history; it is the ideal limit toward which we are constantly approaching, but which in all probability we shall never succeed in reaching.

Thus it is not at all true that between science on the one hand, and morals and religion on the other, there exists that sort of antinomy which has so frequently been admitted, for the two forms of human activity really come from one and the same source. Kant understood this very well, and therefore he made the speculative reason and the practical reason two different aspects of the same faculty. According to him, what makes their unity is the fact that the two are directed toward the universal. Rational thinking is thinking according to the laws which are imposed upon all reasonable beings; acting morally is conducting oneself according to those maxims which can be extended without contradiction to all wills. In other words, science and morals imply that the individual is capable of raising himself above his own peculiar point of view and of living an impersonal life. In fact, it cannot be doubted that this is a trait common to all the higher forms of thought and action. What Kant's system does not explain, however, is the origin of this sort of contradiction that is realized in man. Why is he forced to do violence to himself by leaving his individuality, and, inversely, why is the impersonal law obliged to be dissipated by incarnating itself in individuals? Is it answered that there are two antagonistic worlds in which we participate equally, the world of matter and sense on the one hand, and the world of pure and impersonal reason on the other? That is merely repeating the question in slightly different terms, for what we are trying to find out is why we must lead these two existences at the same time. Why do these two worlds, which seem to contradict each other, not remain outside of each other, and why must they mutually penetrate one another in spite of their antagonism? The only explanation which has ever been given of this singular necessity is the hypothesis of the Fall, with all the difficulties which it implies, and which need not be repeated here. On the other hand, all mystery disappears the moment that it is recognized that impersonal reason is only another name given to collective thought. For this is possible only through a group of individuals; it supposes them, and in their turn, they suppose it, for they can continue to exist only by grouping themselves together. The kingdom of ends and impersonal truths can realize itself only by the cooperation of particular wills, and the reasons for which these participate in it are the same as those for which they cooperate. In a word, there is something impersonal in us because there is something social in all of us, and since social life embraces at once both representations and practices, this impersonality naturally extends to ideas as well as to acts.

Perhaps some will be surprised to see us connect the most elevated forms of thought with society: the cause appears quite humble, in consideration of the value which we attribute to the effect. Between the world of the senses and appetites on the one hand, and that of reason and morals on the other, the distance is so considerable that the second would seem to have been able to add itself to the first only by a creative act. But attributing to society this preponderating role in the genesis of our nature is not denying this creation; for society has a creative power which no other observable being can equal. In fact, all creation, if not a mystical operation which escapes science and knowledge, is the product of a synthesis. Now if the synthesis of particular conceptions which take place in each individual consciousness are already and of themselves productive of novelties, how much more efficacious these vast syntheses of complete consciousnesses which make society must be! A society is the most powerful combination of physical and moral forces of which nature offers us an example. Nowhere else is an equal richness of different materials, carried to such a degree of concentration, to be found. Then it is not surprising that a higher life disengages itself which, by reacting upon the elements of which it is the product, raises them to a higher plane of existence and transforms them.

Thus sociology appears destined to open a new way to the science of man. Up to the present, thinkers were placed before this double alternative: either explain the superior and specific faculties of men by connecting them to the inferior forms of his being, the reason to the senses, or the mind to matter, which is equivalent to denying their uniqueness; or else attach them to some superexperimental reality which was postulated, but whose existence could be established by no observation. What put them in this difficulty was the fact that the individual passed as being the *finis naturæ*—the ultimate creation of nature; it seemed that there was nothing beyond him, or at least nothing that science could touch. But from the moment when it is recognized that above the individual there is society, and that this is not a nominal being created by reason, but a system of active forces, a new manner of explaining men becomes possible. To conserve his distinctive traits it is no longer necessary to put them outside experience. At least, before going to this last extremity, it would be well to see if that which surpasses the individual, though it is within him, does not come from this superindividual reality which we experience in society. To be sure, it cannot be said at present to what point these explanations may be able to reach, and whether or not they are of a nature to resolve all the problems. But it is equally impossible to mark in advance a limit beyond which they cannot go. What must be done is to try the hypothesis and submit it as methodically as possible to the control of facts. This is what we have tried to do.

NOTES

1 Thus, we see how far it is from being true that a conception lacks objective value merely because it has a social origin.
2 See also Émile Durkheim, *Elementary Forms of Religious Life* (New York: Collier Books, 1961), p. 239.
3 Lucien Lévy-Bruhl, *Les Fonctions mentales dans les sociétés inférieures*, pp. 131–38.
4 *Ibid.*, p. 446.
5 See Durkheim, *Elementary Forms of Religious Life*, p. 30.
6 William James, *Principles of Psychology* (New York: Dover Publications, 1890), I, 134.
7 Men frequently speak of space and time as if they were only concrete extent and duration, such as the individual consciousness can feel, but enfeebled by abstraction. In reality, they are representations of a wholly different sort, made out of other elements, according to a different plan, and with equally different ends in view.
8 At bottom, the concept of totality, that of society and that of divinity are very probably only different aspects of the same notion.
9 See Durkheim, *Classifications primitives*, pp. 40ff.

6

MAX SCHELER

On the Positivistic Philosophy of the History of
Knowledge and Its Law of Three Stages*

Translated by Rainer Koehne

THE PROBLEMS OF a sociology of knowledge and cognition, in their variety, scope, articulation, and intrinsic interrelatedness, have hitherto hardly been perceived or correctly posed, to say nothing of being solved. While the sociological approach has long been accepted, for example, in the theory and history of art,[1] and the sociology of religious communities was greatly advanced by E. Troeltsch, M. Weber, W. Dilthey, and others, there are only sporadic observations in the works of German scholars on the connection of social cooperation, division of labor, ethos and spirit of leading groups with the structure of philosophy, the structure of science, their objects, their aims and methods, their organization in schools, in knowledge societies (e.g., the Platonic Academy, Peripatetic School, modern and medieval organization of the estate of the scientists and scholars, etc.).[2]

* In the translation of this essay and the next, by Scheler, and of the two selections by Grünwald, the phrasing and construction of the German originals were followed as closely as possible. Whenever translation into more idiomatic English would have impaired the accurate reproduction of the author's argument and concrete meaning, the verbatim rendering was preferred, even where the author's German phrasing seemed awkward, a case not infrequent with Scheler. Such departures from idiomatic or graceful wording, which usually indicate undercurrents of meaning, were not corrected but, according to the translator's best ability, faithfully reproduced. Furthermore, Scheler's use of quotes and emphasis is so idiosyncratic that it was retained in the translation of his work exactly as in the German original, except as used for literary references in footnotes.

Translated from *Schriften zur Soziologie und Weltanschauungslehre* (Bern: Francke Verlag, 1963), pp. 27–35.

Thus, by G. Simmel, F. Toennies, W. Sombart, W. Dilthey, and H. Bergson much that is valuable was said on the necessary connection of the dominance of a quantitative, chiefly mechanical view of nature and soul which deprives the bodies of qualities with the rise of industry and technology, whose representatives at the top of society do not want to meditate again and again on the great miracle of nature (as do the Brahmans, the leading caste of the Indian social structure) or to contemplate it in wonder and fathom its essence by rational thought (as did the Greek thinkers, free men with a slave economy as their underlying basis) but want to control and direct it for human purposes ("knowledge is power"—Bacon); and they also wrote on the connection of this quantifying world view with the monetary and acquisitive economy which turns goods into dequalified commodities. As Sombart writes, though with some exaggeration, "The spirit of modern natural science (Galileo, Ubaldis, Huygens, Newton) was born of the spirit of double entry and the ledger."

In all these cases we have valuable aperçus, but a deeper grounding of these as well as other intuitively perceived relationships is still completely lacking. It could be achieved only by the fruitful connection of a deepened epistemology of the mechanistic natural science with the science of the ethos of human groups (since it is the dominant ethos which imparts to any science the aim of its studies and researches, on which, in turn, its logical forms and methods depend) as well as with an accurate history of the rise of this type of world concept as opposed to the medieval-scholastic way of thinking, which apprehended nature as a hierarchy of form activities in the same manner as it apprehended society as a hierarchy of estates. Furthermore, there are subtle observations on the French, English, and German national spirit in mathematics and theoretical physics in P. Duhem,[3] who very subtly compares these sciences with contemporaneous art (drama, novel), the structure of the state and economy, and the customs and values of the country in question, so that from French, English, German exact science, we see the face of the particular national genius shine forth. Later Oswald Spengler, in a rather dilettante fashion, exaggerated this method of tracing science to the particular "culture soul" to grotesque proportions, ascribing to it a fatelike operation in certain predetermined phases. He carried this so far that it becomes impossible to understand the international historical *rational* nexus of the advances of knowledge which factually exists, which is never totally interrupted by the rise, maturity, and decline of national cultures (or cultures otherwise defined, by unity of language, religion, political conception or race as the primary defining factor).

Thus, there arise, among others, these basic questions which, to be answered, require a *pure sociology of knowledge* which is part of the philosophic discipline of epistemology: (1) To what degree are the different sciences bound by the culture souls (e.g. nationally)? No doubt this is the case far more with philosophy and metaphysics than with the positive sciences; with the *Geisteswissenschaften* far more than with mathematics and the natural sciences; with biology[4] far more than with physics; etc. (2) Which elements of the sciences—e.g., of Indian, Greek, and modern mathematics—are bound in this manner, and which are as "true results" *detachable* from the particular forms of envisioning their respective worlds of objects and from the nationally and culturally conditioned methods or forms of thinking? (3) Which tasks of research and study permit in principle free substitution, and thus unlimited cooperation, of the talented of all nations and cultures, and which essentially preclude such cooperation by the very nature of their subject matter, so that cooperation of the nations themselves, as collective intellectual entities and individualities (and not of any members of them), and the mutual complementing of their particular dispositions and forms of vision and thought will be required for reaching the most adequate knowledge of the object? (4) Which elements of knowledge, and the sciences of which objects, can in such a way survive the decline of an entire national culture that they may enter into a continuous connection of meaning with the science of a new or different culture soul, and thus enter into a continuous progress, and which elements of knowledge and the sciences of which objects cannot?

To my knowledge, such specifications and refinements of the questions to be posed have hardly been made so far, and in particular a connection between the sociological questions and epistemology is still lacking. Only the positivistic philosophy of Auguste Comte, Herbert Spencer, and others has brought epistemology into closer connection with sociological statics and dynamics.

Comte's famous division of the sciences is closely related to his law of the three stages through which each part of knowledge is thought to develop; for a given science is assumed to pass the earlier from the theological to the metaphysical stage, and from the metaphysical to the positive stage, the simpler and more abstract (according to the order of Comte's table) is its object. The positivistic ideal of knowledge by which this whole line of development is ultimately measured (and which also is the starting point for its construction) consists, however, in an enormous restriction of the aim of knowledge: (1) to *voir pour prévoir*, or reception into the burning consciousness of only those world contents and relationships which are fit for foreseeing the direction of future things; and (2) to the discovery of mere laws (quantitatively determinable relationships) of sensuous phenomena, leaving aside all questions concerning the "essence" of things or "substances" and "forces."

It is deplorable and a great flaw that that philosophy which regards positivistic-sensualist epistemology in every form as erroneous—and that is most of German philosophy—has not yet achieved a sociological and philosophy of history doctrine of the forms of cognitive cooperation and the laws of development of the various elements and kinds of knowledge that could effectively counter the positivist doctrines.[5]

The positivistic doctrine of the three stages of knowledge is basically mistaken in both its forms, that given to it by Comte, Mill, and Spencer, as well as that given to it by Mach and Avenarius. Religious, metaphysical, and positive thinking and knowing are not historical stages of the development of knowledge but permanent attitudes of mind and forms of knowledge given with the human mind as essential features of it. None of them can ever substitute for or represent any other. The tasks of understanding the world from personal causes, of making intelligible to intuitive reason the essence relations and the eternal relations of ideas realized in the world of the accidentally real (and to construct a metaphysics from that basis), and of unambiguously ordering and classifying the phenomena in a mathematical symbolism as well as determining their interrelationships in that manner, these are tasks of equal originality and right which also were equally original in differentiating themselves from undifferentiated mythical thought.

Today it is no longer necessary to elucidate Comte's profound error in considering religion a primitive explanation of nature by which the group adjusted to nature, so that the progress of science would cause its gradual disintegration and eventual extinction. Comte does not correctly perceive the *essence* of religion, as the community of the person and the supra-individual whole of the group with a holy power envisioned as the source of all things. Nor is religion a metaphysics secondarily turned into images, a "metaphysics for the people," as Fichte, Hegel, Schelling, Schopenhauer, and E. v. Hartmann thought. In this case of making theological thought precede metaphysical thought and considering the former a condition of the latter, Comte saw things in one respect more correctly than German idealism. All the systems of metaphysical thinking we know, the Indian, the Greek, the Christian and the modern one, all bear the mark of their religious environment. Yet, metaphysics is not a stage in the development of religion but differentiates itself from religion as genuinely as it does from the positive sciences. W. Dilthey's attempt[6] to regard religion, but not metaphysics, as grounded in a lasting disposition of the human mind and to consider metaphysics as merely a historical category of the mind[6] must also be considered erroneous.

Religion, metaphysics, and positive science rest on three different motives, on three entirely different groups of acts of the knowing mind, three different aims, three different personality types, and three different social groups. Also the historical forms of movement of these three mental powers are essentially different.

As for the *motive*, religion rests on the person's irresistible urge for mental self-preservation by salvaging, rescuing the core of personality into a holy power which is personal itself and governs the world. Metaphysics rests on the motive of an ever-renewed wonder that there is anything instead of nothing. Positive science rests on the need of a direction of nature according to values and purposes which became differentiated as "arbitrary" from the particular purposes with which man is entwined so far as vocationally working. Positive science therefore arose only where a working class slowly interpenetrated with a higher class that had freedom and leisure, as happened, on the greatest scale, with the European urban bourgeoisie.

Religion is grounded in particular receptive *acts* of the mind (hoping, fearing, loving, willing, knowing, etc.), the common trait of which is that the finite experience of the world cannot give them fulfillment if offered to them as object and aim, and that they have as object something thought of as "holy," "divine."[7] Metaphysics, on the other hand, attains its goal, which is knowledge of essences, by essence-visioning reason, not by observation and inference; while science does by observation, experiment, induction, deduction.[8] Again, the *aim* of religion is the salvation of the person and group; that of metaphysics, the highest forming of the person by wisdom; and that of positive science, the representation of the world in mathematical symbols, which intentionally neglects everything that is in the world "essence-like" and admits only the *relationships* of the phenomena, in order to direct and control nature by these relationships.

Religion has its *leading type* in the *homo religiosus*, or saint—that is, a human type who is believed, followed, trusted exclusively because of his charismatic qualities. He does not substantiate his words by objective norms existing outside of him, but demands faith merely because *he*, as *person*, speaks and acts in this particular way, and because of his uniquely experienced relationship to God. Besides the saint, there is the priest, as cult technician and ecclesiastic official; his authority is always a derived one, and rests on the charismatic quality of the founder of the religion, church, or sect. In metaphysics, in contrast to the religion, leader is the sage, a peculiar, intellectual personal type, quite different from the *homo religiosus*. He gives some system or other of the essence structure of the world—i.e., its primal constants—which is to say of a *whole* world—it is not a specialized departmental or vocational knowledge or anything of the sort. But what he asserts he proves by ultimate intuitive insights which he asks to be performed. In positive science, the leader type is the scientist, who never attempts to give something that is whole and completed, a system, but merely wants to continue, at some point, the essentially infinite progress called science. To the *homo religiosus* correspond as social sphere churches, sects, congregations; to the sage, schools in the ancient sense; to the scientist, the republic of science with its various organizations (e.g., universities, technical and other specialized schools, academies, learned societies), which always strives to be international.

No less fundamentally different—although this was never recognized by positivism—are the forms of historical movement of the three basic types of cognition. Since religion always rests on faith, free acceptance of the charismatic person's teaching of God, himself and salvation, it is always a whole, something absolutely perfect and complete. The leader is always the "one and only" and does not tolerate anyone else beside him as "mediator." Every great founder of a religion says in some form of other: "He who is not for me is against me." And there is in the case of religion nothing which may be called development or progress, merely deeper intrusion into the substance of the original revelation—i.e., that which the original *homo religiosus* envisioned and taught of God. Besides, there is only the possibility of replacing the one "one and only" by another "one and only"; there cannot be recognition of a number of equally genuine leaders as in philosophy, art, science. A further essential feature of religion is that a movement, revival, conversion never occurs with a forward but always with a retrospective view, as a "back to the sources," a recovery of something lost, a reformation. The intention, at least, of the *homo religiosus* is never to teach something new, but always to teach something old.

Positivism fell into its deep errors concerning the sociological dynamics of knowledge because its orientation was Europistic in the narrowest sense. The enormous fallacy of its doctrine of progress was to mistake the West European form of movement of knowledge during the last three centuries, which is a very small and narrowly localized piece of the curve of the intellectual development of mankind, and that piece described in a one-sided aspect for a law of the whole development of mankind. What in fact was a period of religious and metaphysical decadence in the history of a small group of mankind, the negative counterpart of its progress in positive science—i.e., the decadence of the bourgeois-capitalist age—it took for a normal process of a "withering away" of the religious and metaphysical spirit.

Positivism was for that reason also unable to perceive a most fundamental fact of the development of knowledge in universal history, namely, the varied distribution among the great cultures of mankind of ability of the three kinds of knowledge essential to the human mind and the diverse social structures which correspond to their varied effects. The intellectual condition of the Indian and East Asian culture is characterized by the predominance of the metaphysical attitude over the religious and the positive-scientific one. In these cultures there is therefore no progress of knowledge as an infinite process, no rational, specialized science based on division of labor which serves a vocationally differentiated social body and a trained body of department officials, and seeks to produce a world concept which makes technical control of the world possible. Instead, there is something quite different: in the first place, an ever-renewed exercising of mental attitudes by which one is made wise, with fixed materials for these exercises which do not substantially change or grow. These materials are the ancient written monuments of the exemplary sages (e.g., the Vedic texts, the traditions of Buddha, of Confucius, Lao-tse, etc.). They are not learning matter, but matter for exercising mental functions: materials of meditation. They are read not once or twice to learn their content, but read again and again, to practice them as exemplary patterns, and in combination with a particular psychological technique, new and ever higher attitudes of consciousness which then may be applied at every moment of life toward the whole accidental world experience. Hence, the aim of this science in India and China is the forming of man, not knowledge of rules by which nature can be directed. In contrast to European science, which ascends from the inanimate over the animate world to the soul and God, it starts at the soul and from there descends to the order of the inanimate world. The highest classes of India and China thus as one-sidedly aim at the forming of man as those of Europe aim at achievement and control. To each kind of science belongs a kind of technics: to the Asian ideal of knowledge, the bio- and psychotechnics of self-salvation (objectification of all wishing and willing, of all passions and affects before a purely contemplative mind); to the European ideal, the inorganic technics of the control of nature.[9]

The error of positivism did not consist in its assumption that the religious sense of man, as an organ of knowledge, is in the course of history, more decreasing than increasing, but in asserting the same for the religious needs, the urge for religion, and in taking the decrease of the psychic and intellectual dispositions for getting in immediate touch with the transcendent as evidence that what is given to the religious sense does not possess objective reality. It did so because of a mistaken doctrine of progress which is also a

European prejudice. The correct conclusion to be drawn from the decrease of the religious sense of man is merely the insight that, in matters of religion, the later mankind always has merely to preserve what an earlier mankind perceived—unless new voluntary self-revelations of God to man take place and are believed.[10]

Metaphysics, too, does not progress as positive science does. The possible metaphysics are a number of limited types (W. Dilthey), which always recur and again and again enter into struggles and disputes with one another, on very different levels of methodical development and grounding. This is in the nature of the metaphysical form of knowledge, the basic means of which is the vision of essences. Essences and essence relations, after all, are world constants; knowledge of them is evident, complete, and a priori to the quantity of inductive experience. Therefore metaphysical knowledge is in principle possible at any historical stage of positive science that may be forming the given quantity of human experience. It necessarily lacks the character of an infinite process which is found wherever there is observation, induction, and deduction. And lacking the cumulative "progress" which belongs to the essence of positive science, metaphysics also lacks the phenomenon accompanying "progress"—namely, the devaluation of the state of science which is at each given time the earlier one. The systems of Plato and Aristotle, Augustine, Descartes, Leibniz, Kant, etc., are not obsolete today, as are Lavoisier's chemistry and Newton's mechanics, and they can never become obsolete. Metaphysics, with its several basic types, grows, and in growing perfects itself, but it does not progress.[11] Furthermore, since it is the work of the sage, system metaphysics is not capable of being run by division of labor, as is positive science. It remains personally bound to the intellectual physiognomy of its originator, of which his "world" is the reflection. The great metaphysicians are therefore irreplaceable, whereas the great discoveries in the positive sciences—e.g., principle of inertia, theorem of the conservation of energy, second law of thermodynamics—were made by many scientists simultaneously.[12] The state of problems at a given time and the automatism of method seem to produce by themselves the results of of the positive sciences. Often the scientists appear as mere servants, mouthpieces of the method and the continuous scientific, objective-logical process. The works of Plato and Kant, on the other hand, are always unique, and it is inconceivable that another could have found what they found.

Furthermore, the metaphysical systems remain bound to nation and culture. Indian metaphysics could originate only in India, and could not have originated in Greece, even as Greek metaphysics could not have originated in India. Positive science, on the other hand, moves by division of labor, impersonally, continuously, internationally, and by a cumulative progress connected with a devaluation of each earlier state.

Hence religion, metaphysics, and positive science are different from one another by essence in all these directions and, as tasks and problems, are all genuine basic properties of the human mind.

As a practical demand concerning constructions of the organizations of education in the various nations, it follows that in such a construction there should not be one-sided training in the direction of any one of these forms of knowledge but a harmonious training in all of them.[13]

NOTES

1 A recent example is W. Hausenstein, *Die Kunst und die Gesellschaft* (Munich, 1917).

2 Cf. G. Simmel, *Philosophie des Geldes* (Leipzig, 1900); F. Toennies, *Philosophische Terminologie* (Berlin, 1921) and *Gemeinschaft und Gesellschaft* (2d ed.; 1912); W. Sombart, *Der moderne Kapitalismus* (2d ed.; Munich and Leipzig, 1916); W. Dilthey, *Einleitung in die Geisteswissenschaften* (Leipzig, 1883), and especially "Das natuerliche System der Geisteswissenschaften," in W. Dilthey, *Gesammelte Schriften*, II (Leipzig, 1914), and H. Bergson, *Matière et mémoire* and *L'évolution créatice*.

3 Cf. P. Duhem, *Ziel und Struktur der physikalischen Theorien*, trans. by F. Mach (Leipzig, 1908).

4 Cf. the concluding sections of the profound work by E. Rádl, *Geschichte der biologischen Theorien* (2d ed.; 1913), II.

5 In the *Forschungsinstitut für Sozialwissenschaften* of the University of Cologne, Sociological Division, I have therefore among other things made it my task to pay special attention, in close connection with the system of philosophy which I have been developing for years, also to the sociology of knowledge. In the present context, space would not permit even an indication of the detailed program of these tasks. See, however, the large collective volume, which Scheler edited for the Institute, *Versuche zu einer Soziologie des Wissens*, (Munich, 1924).

6 Cf. Dilthey, *Einleitung in die Geisteswissenschaften*.

7 Something more specific on these matters is to be found in the study "Probleme der Religion" in my book *Vom Ewigen im Menschen* (Leipzig, 1921).

8 See for this the study "Vom Wesen den Philosophie" in *ibid*.

9 Cf. my study "Vom Sinn des Leides," in *Schriften zur Soziologie und Weltanschauungslehre* (Leipzig, 1923–24).

10 Cf. my study "Probleme der Religion."

11 Hegel's error was to attribute the same form of movement to religion as is found with metaphysics. This is his erroneous Gnosticism.

12 Cf. A. Vierkandt, *Die Stetigkeit im Kulturwandel* (Leipzig, 1908).

13 For conclusions to be drawn from this fundamental demand for the shaping of the German educational institutions my treatise "Universitat und Volkshochschule" in the volume on *Soziologie des Volksbildungswesens*, ed. by L. v. Wiese (Munich, 1921).

7

MAX SCHELER

The Sociology of Knowledge: Formal Problems
Translated by Rainer Koehne

A NUMBER OF formal problems closely link the sociology of knowledge, on the one hand, to epistemology and logic and, on the other, to developmental psychology. All these problems together rest on three possible basic relations of knowledge to society. First, knowledge of members of a group of each other and the possibility of their "understanding" of each other is not an element which is added to a social group, but co-constitutes the object "human society." Anything that is objectively collected only by our thought (for example, classifying races by objective traits: color of skin, shape of skull; or statistical concepts: the Cologne dead of 1914) is *not* a sociological object. Furthermore, there belongs to any "group" a knowledge, however vague, of its own existence, as well as commonly recognized values and aims. (Therefore, no class without class consciousness, etc.) In some way or other, any knowledge, and especially all common knowledge of identical objects, determines in many ways the specification (*Sosein*) of the society. But all knowledge is ultimately also conversely determined by the society and its structure.[1]

THE PRINCIPAL AXIOMS OF THE SOCIOLOGY OF KNOWLEDGE
The chief axioms of the sociology of knowledge are still little recognized in their full significance. They are:

(1) The knowledge which each man has of being a *member of a society* in general is not empirical but a priori knowledge. It genetically precedes

---

Translated from *Die Wissensformen und die Gesellschaft* (Bern: Francke Verlag, 1960), pp. 52–69.

the stages of his self and self-value consciousness: no *I* without a *We*; and genetically, the *We* always has content before the I.[2]

(2) The empirical relations of a man's participation in the experiences of his fellow men materialize in various ways, which depend on the essence structure of the group. These can be apprehended by ideal types. The one pole is identification, as found, for instance, in primitive men, the masses, hypnosis, certain morbid states, and the relation of mother and child.[3] At the other pole is inference by analogy from the bodily gesture to the specification of the experience. In this type the life of the "other" is grasped by the "one" only in the individualistic "societal" form; therefore always in relation to a "stranger." On the other hand, a conscious contract is also first concluded with the "stranger." Where contract binds wills in law, the form of inference obtains with regard to knowledge.

Between these two forms of transference many others are situated which I will merely enumerate. In the first place, co-experiencing, by contagion, without knowledge of the fact of the co-experiencing; next, the forms of the involuntary *imitation* of actions, expressive movements (a later stage), and, in the case of purposive movements, the so-called copying, which in the case of the relationship of whole generations of a group is called "tradition." This is a process fundamentally different from all historical knowledge; it constitutes not the knowledge of history but the very possibility of history, the historicity of life. All these forms of transference are found in the higher animals. In sharp contrast to them is the immediate subjective *understanding* of the experiences and feelings of others according to qualitative laws of the processes of motivated experience, and the objective understanding of meanings either residing in material things (works of art, monuments, tools, inscriptions, etc.) or connected with repeatable acts in the form of an objective "meaning" or "calling." An example of the latter would be language as seen in contrast to the ability to express mere inner states, however rich, specialized, and differentiated that ability may be. In the higher apes, twenty-two distinct forms of expressing affects were observed, but even if 1,000 could be observed this would not mean the presence of even a trace of language or significative function. But representation, e.g., self-representation in singing or dance or the representation of meaning in objective materials as with pictography and art, also mores, customs, rites, cults, ceremonies, and signal codes, are objectified forms of behavior related to understanding which are common to the group. The different types of understanding, as well as all types of sympathy as distinct from contagion, belong specifically to human society—the animals don't have them.

So far we have only very imperfect knowledge regarding whether or not there are besides these forms of transference—which also include teaching and instruction, making known and taking notice, disclosing and not disclosing, commanding and obeying, suffering and forgiving, etc., which is to say, all acts of the *mind* which involve meaning and are specifically social—any others which occur outside of any consciousness, and are realized by heredity. What seems certain is that there is no inborn knowledge of particular objects, but only inborn functions, more general or more specific, for the acquiring of certain types of knowledge. It seems certain also that inherited "talent", both of individuals and of genealogical hereditary races, basically also differs for the acquisition of knowledge—and the chief ground of the specification of the estate and vocational differentiation within the various nations lies in these differences of original talent, not in differences of class disposition, demands of society, or any milieu influences whatever. But if *talent* is to be regarded as cumulated by heredity, even if there is no transmission of acquired functions by heredity, as is according to the present state of the science of heredity likely also for the psychic factors of talent, it seems to be different with *genius*.[4] A genius enters existence, not by the laws of heredity, but "meteorlike" and strangely independent of the accumulation of talents, the inheritance of which seems to be governed by Mendel's laws. Genius, wherever it appears, is not specified for particular skills, as talent, but is largely separable from these special skills. Only by combining with special talents (musical talent, technical-constructive talent, etc.) does genius also assume a special direction in which it operates. Its marks everywhere are *love of a cause* to the degree of ecstatic dedication to ideas and values —that is, an *excess* of the mind over the biologically important—and originality of the work, which is created according to no rule (Kant).

Now, whatever their genetic origin, it is the joint willing, joint loving, joint hating, etc., from which derive two categories which are also essential for the sociology of knowledge: the *group soul* and the *group mind*. These are for us not metaphysical entities, substances that precede the joint living and experiencing. They are merely the subjects of the psychic or intellectual content which produces itself ever anew in the togetherness[5]—never the mere sum of the knowledge of the individuals "plus" a subsequent mere communication of that knowledge. Only for the individual's knowledge of himself and of his specification, the joint knowing is also a barrier; the more so the more primitive and less developed the group. We call "group soul" only those mental activities which are "performed," as spontaneous acts, but merely "happen," such as expressive reactions and other automatic and semi-automatic functions; while we call "mind" of a group the subject that constitutes itself in the joint performance of fully conscious, spontaneous acts with an objective-intentional direction. Thus, myths and fairy tales which artistically are not individually formed, the "natural" folk language, folk songs, folk religion, folkways, customs and costumes, are based on the group soul; while the state and law, the educated language, philosophy, art, science and public opinion of a group rest largely on the group mind. The group soul, "lives and grows," as it were, in everyone, even when all are asleep; only its activity, not that of the group mind, may be called "organic" in the Romantic sense. The group soul is in its origins *impersonal*, anonymous. The group mind, on the other hand, appears only in *personal representatives*. Always determined in its content, values, aims, and direction by personal leaders and examples, at any rate by a "small number" (v. Wiese), an "elite" (Pareto), it "bears" its objects and goods by acts which are *spontaneously* performed. These objects and goods, therefore, will fall into nothingness if the acts are not *spontaneously performed*. Thus, every cultural possession related to the group mind is a continuous re-acquisition which at the same time is original acquisition, is *creatio continua*. The group soul acts in the group from "below" to "above", the group mind from "above" to "below."

The sociology of knowledge, which must trace the laws and rhythms of the downward flow of knowledge from the top of society (i.e., the intellectual elites) and determine the manner of its distribution over the various groups and strata with time as well as the ways in which this distribution is organized by society—partly by institutions for the dissemination of knowledge such as schools and newspapers, and partly by barriers to it, such as mysteries, indexes, censorship, and the prohibition of certain kinds of knowledge for some castes,[6] estates, or classes—deals chiefly with the group mind.

(3) A third principle of the sociology of knowledge, which at the same time is a theorem of epistemology, says that there is in the order of origin of our knowledge of reality—i.e., anything potent to act—a fixed structure, and likewise in the filling of the spheres of knowledge, which are constants of the human mind, as well as of the spheres of objects correlated to them with content.[7]

Before stating this law, let us enumerate the spheres of being and object spheres which are not reducible to each other. They are: (*a*) the absolute sphere, of the real and valuable, of the sacred; (*b*) the sphere of a co-world, ante-world, and post-world in general—i.e., the sphere of society and history, or of "the others"; (*c*) the spheres of the outer world and the inner world, and the sphere of one's own body and its environment; (*d*) the sphere of that which is "meant" as "alive"; (*e*) the sphere of the corporeal, inanimate world which is dead and appears as "dead." The posited content of these spheres is of course subject to continuous historical change. To this day, epistemology has never ceased in its attempts (not to be described here) to reduce these spheres to one another. Sometimes the attempt was made to reduce the inner to the outer world (Condillac, Mach, Avenarius, materialism); sometimes the outer to the inner world (Descartes, Berkeley, Fichte); sometimes the sphere of the absolute to the others (e.g., by trying to infer causally the essence and existence of something divine in general); sometimes the vital world to the pregivenness of the dead corporeal world (as in the empathy theory of life, espoused among others, by Descartes and Th. Lipps); sometimes the assumption of a co-world to a pregivenness of the own inner world of the assuming subject combined with that of an outer corporeal world (philosophic theory of analogy inference and empathy theory of the consciousness of others); sometimes the general differentiation of subject and object to pregivenness of the co- or "fellow man," to whom an environmental element—as, for instance, "this tree"—is supposed to be introjected, followed by subsequent introjection by the observer to himself (Avenarius); sometimes one's own body to a merely associative coordination of the self-perception of the own self and organ sensations with the own body as perceived from outside. All these attempts are fundamentally fallacious. These spheres are irreducible; and all are as spheres equally genuinely given with every human consciousness. On the other hand, it is demonstrable that there is an order in the givenness and pregivenness of these spheres which is a matter of essence and remains constant in every possible development of man. This is to say that in each stage of development one of these spheres is already filled with content while another is not yet filled with content—and is already filled with concrete content while another is not yet filled with concrete content. Also, there can still be doubts in one of these spheres as to the reality of an object defined as to its specification when there is no longer a possibility of doubt as to the reality of an object of another sphere defined as to its specification.

If we leave aside the place of the sphere of the absolute in this order, the following proposition which is basic for the purposes of sociology of knowledge will stand. In the sense just indicated, the social sphere of the co-world and historical sphere of the ante-world is pregiven to all subsequent spheres with respect to (*a*) reality, (*b*) content and concreteness of content. "Youness" is the most fundamental existence category of human thinking. That is why primitive men apply it indiscriminately to all phenomena of nature, which is to them primarily an expressive field and a language of ghosts and demons dwelling behind the phenomena. I will add a few other laws of pregivenness which are also relevant in this context: (1) The sphere of the outer world is always pregiven to that of the inner world. (2) The world meant as "live" is always pregiven to the world meant as "dead" or inanimate

—which means simply: *not* animate. (3) The outer world of the co-subjects in the co-world is always pregiven to anything that I as an individual happen to have and know of the outer world. Also, the outer world of my co-world is always pregiven to the inner world of my co-world. (4) The inner world of the co-, ante-, and post-world (as a perspective of expectation) is, as a sphere, always pregiven to my own inner world as a sphere. Or, as Th. Hobbes clearly recognized, all self-observation is a behaving toward myself as if I were another: it is not a condition but the result and imitation of the observation of others. (5) My own and every other body is, as a field of expression (not as corporeal object), pregiven to any distinction of corporeal body and body soul (i.e., the "inner world").

Thus, the assumption of the reality and specification of the society and history in which a man is placed is not, as is still believed by so many, founded on the assumption of the reality and particular shape of the so-called "corporeal world" or that of a content of inner self-perception. It is not accidental that there have been numerous philosophers who denied the existence of a real, inanimate, extended world (Plato and Aristotle, Berkeley and Fichte, Leibniz and Kant, etc.), but very few who denied the existence of an animal or even a plant. Even Berkeley, with his radical idealism already has doubts with plants if he might carry through with them his "*esse—percipi.*" But never and nowhere was there ever a solipsist! That too—apart from the abundance of proofs for our law furnished from all parts of genetic psychology, although they cannot be mentioned here—shows clearly how much more deeply the conviction of the *reality of society* is rooted in us than the conviction of any other object of any other sphere of knowledge or being. Every other reality can still be doubted or left in abeyance when we cannot any more doubt *this* reality or leave it in abeyance.

What follows from these laws for the sociology of knowledge? First, that the sociological character of all knowledge, of all the forms of thinking, perception, cognition, is indubitable: not, of course, the content of all knowledge and still less its objective validity, but the *selection* of its objects according to the *ruling social-interest perspective*; and furthermore that the "forms" of the mental acts by which knowledge is won are always and *necessarily sociologically* co-conditioned, i.e., by the structure of society.[8] Now, since explaining consists in reducing the relatively new to something already known and since, according to the principle stated above, society is always "better known" than anything else, we may expect what a plethora of sociological studies have actually shown: that the subjective forms of thinking and perception as well as the classification of the world by categories—i.e., the categorization of knowable things in general—are co-conditioned by the division and classification of the groups (e.g., clans) making up the society.[9]

In this connection not only do the curious facts on the collective world views of primitive men discovered by Lévy-Bruhl, Graebner, Thurnwald, as well as many other ethnological studies, become fully understandable, but also the deep-reaching structural analogies which exist between the structure of the content of the knowledge of nature and the soul[10] as well as the structure of metaphysical and religious "knowledge" on the one hand, and on the other hand the structure and organization of society and, in the political age, the hierarchy of the social parts. To trace these structural identities of the view of the world, the view of the soul, and the view of God for all the principal knowledge types (religious, metaphysical, and positive knowledge) and on all evolutionary stages of society with stages of social organization is a particularly enticing object of the sociology of knowledge. A systematic exposition of these structural identities is still lacking,[11] and so is an attempt to express the identities found in some *simple laws*. All these attempts find their ultimate justification in our formal principle of the laws of pregivenness of the spheres. But also in the development of knowledge some biomorphic world view always genetically precedes that which acknowledges the distinctive character and the distinctive laws of the inanimate and dead, or even tries to reduce the living to something in-animate and dead (as does modern mechanistic biology), and furthermore the fallacy of the theory of projective empathy, which is equally untrue for the sociology of primitive men and child psychology,[12] are fully explained only by this structural law.

THE CHIEF TYPES OF KNOWLEDGE

Further formal problems of the sociology of knowledge are the identification of the *chief types of knowledge* which must be subjected to sociological investigation, the problem of their *social origin*, and their *forms of movement*.

The epistemologists usually consider as the basis of all knowledge, whether it be artificial and higher historical-positive knowledge, redemptive educative or positive-pragmatic knowledge, religious or metaphysical knowledge, theoretical or value knowledge, that knowledge which they call "the natural world view." What they have in mind seems to be a way of seeing the world supposed to be the minimum constant element found at any time and any place where "men" happen to live. They are wont to take this "natural world view" as their "starting point," and they may give it attributes such as "naturally grown," "practical," and the like. But this concept harbors the same snares (Tücken) as the famous "state of nature" of the old ecclesiastic or anti-ecclesiastic doctrine of natural law. The ecclesiastic natural law equated this state with "Paradise," making the "*status naturæ*" sometimes more similar, sometimes more dissimilar, to the sinful state, depending on the dogmatic significance attributed to the "Fall." Hobbes, in a deliberate counter-doctrine to that of the Church, equated it with the "bellum omnium contra omnes"; Rousseau equated it with the idyllic state without private property; and the Marxists with "the free and equal" men who "originally" lived in a state of communal property and promiscuity. In fact we know nothing of any "state of nature," and the content of the natural state assumed in each of these cases is just a foil and background to the politics of future interests which each of these typical ideologies seeks to justify. Is the "natural world view" of the epistemologists anything better? I think not. Berkeley, for instance, believes that natural man is an idealist in his sense and says that "matter" was an "invention" of crotchety "scholars." Others make the natural world view realistic and ascribe to it just one particular categorical structure—e.g., a multitude of dead things in space and time, uniformity of happenings, interaction, etc. Kant, Avenarius, Bergson, and now N. Hartmann—all of them give entirely different versions of the natural world view. Unfortunately, each is exactly what it should be to be a fit "starting point" for the preconceived theory of knowledge which each of these philosophers wants to prove.

Therefore, the traditional concept of natural world view, which is absolutely constant, has to be roundly rejected by the sociology of knowledge. But it must introduce instead the concept of a "relatively natural world view", which is defined by the following statement: to the relatively natural world view of a group subject belongs everything that is in that group accepted as "given" *without question*, as well as every object and content of meaning in the structural forms of that "given" without special spontaneous acts, which is in the group generally held and felt as something *that cannot and need not be justified*. But exactly that can be fundamentally different for different groups, or for one group in different stages of its development.[13] One of the most certain insights we owe to the sociology of knowledge of the so-called primitives, of the biomorphic world view of the child, and of the whole West up to the beginning of the modern age, which is also demonstrated by comparing the relatively natural (by the above criterion) world views of the largest cultures, is that *there is no* one, constant natural world view of "man" and that the diversity of world views reaches into the *categorical structures of the given itself*, To primitive man, demons and ghosts are given in the act of perception just as "naturally" and without question as they are *not* given to us. The absolutely one natural world view is therefore

not more than a limit concept for assessing developmental stages of the relatively natural world view.

The absolutely constant natural world view, that idol of epistemology
that has existed so far, must be replaced by an attempt to discover *laws of
transformation* among relatively natural world-view structures.[14] O. Spengler
is absolutely right in writing in the first volume of his work, *The Decline
of the West*, the very words I wrote in 1914:[15] "Kant's table of categories is
just a table of the categories of the European mind." But the attempt to
formulate a transformation theory of the relatively natural world view can
have any prospect of success only if the sociology of knowledge establishes
close relations with *genetic psychology*, to use for its own purposes the *parallel
coordinations of developmental stages* already discovered in that field. Such
parallel coordinations exist between a great variety of different series.[16]
Each of these parallel coordinations of psychic stages, investigated by a large
literature, could assume great significance for the sociology of knowledge
of the relatively natural world views and their transformations into one
another In many respects they already have, as is shown by the studies of
Edinger, McDougall, Thorndike, Köhler, Koffka, Bühler, Stern, Jaensch,
the psychiatrists and neurologists Childer, Birnbaum, Storch, Freud, and
the ethnologists and sociologists Preuss, Graebner, Lévy-Bruhl, Durkheim,
Niceforo, etc. After all, the sociology of knowledge has for its subject not
only the sociology of knowledge of truth but also the sociology of social
delusion, of superstition, of the sociologically conditioned errors and forms
of deception.

The relatively natural world views are natural growths which *advance
only in very great dimensions of time.* They are utterly touchable by percepts;
they can probably be changed in a more than superficial sense only by racial
mixing, and perhaps mixing of languages and cultures. At any rate, they
belong to the lowest centers of the automatically functioning group "soul";
they certainly do not belong to the group "mind."

It is only on the great massifs of the relatively natural world views that
the knowledge forms of the *relatively artificial* or *"educated" world views*
rest. If we order these by degree of artificiality, starting with the least artificial,
we must mention: (1) *myth and legend,* as the undifferentiated predecessors
of religious knowledge, metaphysical knowledge, and knowledge of nature
and history; (2) that knowledge which is implicitly given with the *natural
folk language* (in contrast to the educated language, elevated poetic language
or terminology), which was studied already by Wilhelm von Humboldt in
his investigations of the relationship of inner linguistic forms and world
view,[17] and recently by Finck and Vossler; (3) *religious knowledge,* in its

various states of aggregation from the devout, warmly emotional, vague intuition to the firmly fixed dogma of a priest church; (4) the basic forms of *mystic knowledge*; (5) *philosophic-metaphysical knowledge*; (6) the *positive knowledge* of mathematics, the natural sciences, and the *Geisteswissenschaften*; and (7) *technological knowledge*

If the slowest and clumsiest form of historical movement is that of the relatively natural world views, it seems to become accelerated with the increasing artificiality of knowledge. Obviously the positive religions move essentially far more slowly than do metaphysical systems, which fall into larger families within the latitudes prescribed by the great world religions. Within a given culture, the chief types of metaphysics are relatively few in number, and in recognition and acceptance they outlast much longer periods than the positive sciences, the results of which change hourly.

Each type of knowledge develops its own language and its own style for the expression of the knowledge, and in this respect religion and metaphysics necessarily remain tied to the natural folk languages in a higher degree than the sciences, which, especially in the case of mathematics and the natural sciences, develop purely artificial terminologies.[18] As every publisher knows, mathematics and the natural sciences are incomparably more internationalized than the *Geisteswissenschaften*; this is, besides intrinsic reasons of the objects of these sciences, a result of that linguistic fact. Only the mystic type of knowledge is, so to speak, the born adversary of language or any formulated expression. For this reason alone it must have a strong individualizing, isolating tendency, which, however, combines with a cosmopolitan tendency. For mystic knowledge, as we know, is supposed to be fundamentally "ineffable." This applies both to the "light" intellectual mysticism of ideas and the "dark" vitalistic mysticism of one-feeling into the primeval ground of creative nature (*natura naturans*)—a contrast found in the history of mysticism in all cultures, which probably has its origin in the contrast and tension between matriarchal and patriarchal cultures. From Plotinus to Bergson, mysticism looks upon language not merely as an inadequate means for expressing thought and that which is experienced and visioned in the mystic *unio* and *extasis*, but its representatives are, beyond that, inclined to see as the most profound and most unconquerable *source of deception and error* for that "knowledge" which they, as mystics, strive for. This is true for both religious and metaphysical mysticism. All mystics believe what Schiller says, "*Spricht die Seele, so spricht schon die Seele nicht mehr.*" ["When the soul speaks, the soul speaks no longer."] Therefore we find the concept of "*sanctum silentium*", which is basic to the sociology of knowledge, in all mystic orders, sects and communities of every kind and in all cultures, and both in the dark, orgiastic, vital mysticism which artificially eliminates the "mind," and in the mind-like, light, idea mysticism which eliminates sensation and the vital urges, existing also quite independently of the positive content of the given religious and metaphysical systems (without whose presence no mysticism can appear). Silence on the "mysteries" is not only a rule directed at outsiders, as in the case of state, trade, and other secrets, but part of the very method by which this knowledge is found. In the Quaker sect, for instance, the union of minds and wills is expected to be brought about by silent prayer, until one member, seized by the "Holy Ghost Himself," finds the word of the hour and so states the true objective of the community and of God.[19]

A problem of the first order in the sociology of knowledge is that of the *origin* of the more or less *artificial* types of knowledge. In the following only the chief types of knowledge will be examined in that respect.

In all these types, the striving for knowledge grows out of the impulse of an inborn vital urge which man has in common with the higher vertebrates, especially the apes. The apes already show an uncommon curiosity in investigating objects and facts which seem to have no biological utility or harmfulness for them either as individuals or as a species. Everything unusual, everything that disrupts an immediate expectation context, touches off this impulse, which no doubt belongs to the large family of power urges and is closely connected with the constructive and the playful urge. But from this impulsive affect of stupor and curiosity, some new emotional factors branch off. A form somewhat higher than curiosity is desire for knowledge, which may be directed not only at new things but also at things already known. From it alone originate the affects and urges connected with the higher knowledge types which represent an intellectual transformation of these urges:

There is, first, the uncheckable urge, first of the *group* and only secondarily of the individual, to "rescue," to "save," their existence, fate, and welfare, and to get into a knowledge connection with a reality seen as "overpowering and holy" and believed to be the highest good and the ground of existence of "everything." This is the abiding root of all *search for religious knowledge.*

Secondly, there is the far more intellectual feeling of *wonder* (θαυμάζειν), to found a new type of knowledge. It is profoundly different from all stupor affects such as stupefaction, puzzlement, amazement, etc., and from all impulses for rescue, security, salvation. This wonder may be evoked suddenly by any object, even the most familiar and usual—but by every object only under one essential condition: that it is understood as an *example* which represents an ideal type, an *essence*; that it is not, in other words, related to its surroundings in time and space, immediate and mediate to what philosophy calls the "secondary causes," but stands before the mind in the posture of the question: why, how, what for, does "something of the sort" *exist at all,* and *not not exist?* If this question is directed at the existence and the essence structure of a whole world in general, the purely "metaphysical" wonder is reached. This act of wonder and the feelings accompanying it are the abiding source of all searching for *metaphysical knowledge,* as Aristotle already clearly recognized. It is—and remains—essential for this cognitive attitude that the object which is placed "in idea" is not examined for its accidental here-and-now existence and here-and-now specification or for the reasons of this accidental existence and specification—i.e., why it is now exactly here and not there, and why it is now and not then—with no attention paid to its positional value in the time-and-space order (an order which primitive men, according to recent studies by Lévy-Bruhl,[20] probably do not possess in pure form, detached from matter shaped into objects)—but that it is instead *immediately and directly related to some prima causa,* as a representative of *its* ideal essence type.[21]

The third emotion which produces a new type of desire for knowledge grew from the search—which only became intentional secondarily—for experiences that first merely occurred accidentally in *acting* and *working* at the world, and only secondarily become intentional. This is the emotion of the *striving for power and rule* over the course of nature, over the men and events of society, over psychic and organic processes, and, in the magic technics, even the attempt to direct and *rule* supernatural forces or forces which so appear to us, and for that purpose to *"foresee"* the phenomena.

This urge has a deeper basis in the constructive and playful, the tinkering and experimenting urges which originally are free of purpose. They are *simultaneously* the root of all positive sciences and of all technics, which, if their emotional basis is considered, are closely related in their origin. Precisely correlated with this intellectualized urge for power and rule is the ability, no doubt already found in the highest vertebrates, to adjust apparently by insight, without a need to try, and beyond mere instinctive action or self-training by trial and error, to new, *atypical* environmental situations, in such a way that biologically useful behavior results; i.e., practical-technical intelligence (the psychic definition of which[22] we cannot yet give very adequately). It is essential for the origin of this practical intelligence that, in view of the conditioning of even the simplest sensation by attention and urges, which today is scientifically continued, our natural world of sense perception already is of such a kind that relatively constant and regular features of the factual occurrences of nature in time have essentially a greater chance and prospect to be registered by sensations and perceptions than those features which are relatively inconstant or unique in time. And that therefore the thresholds of noticeability, which always accompany the so-called thresholds of stimulation, always favor the constant and regular and everything which offers a spatio-temporal pattern of a unified meaning—e.g., everything that is ordered symmetrically. Furthermore, that as E. Jaensch made probable this tendency to select the constant and regular is not transferred from the perceptual to the imaginative images but accrues equally originally to both these series, since both develop from an original form of visional images, which are far less proportionate to the stimulus than the perceptions of adults.[23] Thus, neither so-called pure reason (rationalism, Kant) nor (as the empiricists thought) sensual experience—which takes shape after and according to this selective tendency of possible attention—is the ultimate basis of the conviction, guiding all the research of the positive sciences, of the existence of a specificational spatio-temporal natural law. The basis is rather that *entirely biological*—and not at all rational or "intellectual"—*drive for power and rule*, which determines both intellectual behavior toward the world in perception, imagination, and thought, and practical behavior in acting upon the world and for moving environmental objects, and determining both of these equally originally. Unity of theoretical and active or practical behavior toward the world is secured by that, as are common structural forms in both types of behavior.

The need to discover "secondary" causes operating according to certain laws, which arises in this manner, is as distinct from the religious need for welfare, rescue and salvation as it is from the metaphysical need for causality which drives toward the cause of the existence of a thing that represents an "idea" in "the," or some, *causa prima*. In sharpest contrast to the need for metaphysical knowledge, the object of the question asked by positive science is not the highest existence ground of an object raised "in idea," the existence of which causes "wonder" (why death? why pain? why love? why man? etc.), but just the *positional value* of an object in the spatio-temporal nexus is to be foreseen, for the purpose of control over nature. (*Voir pour prevoir, Wissen ist Macht*, etc.) What positive science asks is: "Why is such and such a thing here and not there?" And this also is the basic question for every sort of technics; for technics wants to divide things up in order to recombine them in a more desired spatio-temporal pattern and therefore also wants to foresee the outcome of such interventions in the course of nature.

Since the positivism of Comte and Spencer—which is no philosophy but just a specifically West European ideology of late occidental industrialism—acknowledged only the third of the roots of man's desire for knowledge, without however clearly perceiving its biological origin, it had to mis-apprehend not only the essence of religion and metaphysics but also their history, and to make what in fact are three entirely constant forms of knowledge, utterly irreplaceable by one another, into historical antecedent forms and temporal "stages" of knowledge development. And only the emotions and cognitive methods of religion and metaphysics are *monopolies of "homo sapiens,"* while the root of technics and positive science (notwith-standing their co-conditioning by the mind) is just a gradual growth from the faculty of practical-technical intelligence which animals already have. The later positivists had for this reason alone to deny the psychic-mental *difference of essence between man and animal.*[24]

Only he who has understood the three distinct roots of the three different types of knowledge can clearly perceive also: (1) the distinct ideal-typical leader qualities in these three fields of knowledge (*homo religiosus*, sage, and scientist and technician), (2) the distinct sources and methods of their ac-quisition of knowledge (God contact of the charismatic leader, idea-thinking, inductive and deductive inference), (3) the distinct forms of movement of their development, (4) the distinct basic social forms expressing the acquisi-tion and conservation of knowledge, (5) their distinct functions in human society, and (6) their distinct social origins (classes, vocations, estates).

NOTES

1 The Age of Enlightenment saw, very one-sidedly, only the conditioning of society by knowledge. It was the great discovery of the nineteenth century and the part of the twentieth century which has elapsed to perceive also that knowledge is conditioned by society.

2 The full epistemological foundation of this proposition is given in Part C of my book *Wesen und Formen der Sympathie* (1923).

3 Cf. *ibid.*, Part A II, where all these formal problems were fully clarified.

4 Cf. *ibid.*, p. 143.

5 That the togetherness is productive is, understood correctly, an important insight of O. Spann; cf. *System der Gesellschaftslehre* (Berlin, 1914).

6 A radical example is the withholding of the sacred scriptures of Hindu religion and meta-physics from the lowest caste, the Sudras. Also think of the withholding of free reading of the Holy Scriptures from laymen in the medieval Church, although this was not complete; likewise, secret diplomacy, etc.

7 For the full proof of this structure law I must refer to the first volume of my *Metaphysik*, to be published soon.

8 I say: *co*-conditioned. To be rejected is sociologism, which, as a parallel to psychologism,

neither differentiates the forms of thinking and perception from the forms of being, nor the successive reflexive cognition of these forms from the forms themselves, and which with Kant reduces the forms of being to the forms of thinking and perception, but in contrast to him then reduces these subjective forms to the forms of work and speech of "society." In logic and epistemology there corresponds to this doctrine of origin a conventionalism of the kind first taught by Th. Hobbes ("Truth and Falsehood are attributes of Speech, not of Things"), and recently affirmed by H. Poincaré. According to the sociologistic doctrine, not only history but also the scientific world view in general is a *fable convenu*. Already De Bonald was on the wrong track in wanting to make social consensus the criterion of truth and in placing all knowledge in the "tradition of language" while regarding language itself as derived from a primal revelation. His doctrine is just the ecclesiastic-orthodox parallel to positivistic sociologism, as exemplified by Durkheim. Such deviate paths of sociology are avoided if all functional forms of thinking are regarded as derived from a *functionalization of a grasping of essences* at *things themselves*, seeing only the particular *selection* to which this functionalization is subject as the work of *society* and its *interest perspective* as against the "pure" realm of essences. That there may be then, and particularly then, a prelogical stage of human society, as assumed, correctly in my opinion, by Lévy-Bruhl, I have shown briefly in my "Bermerkungen" on W. Jerusalem's paper in *Kolner Vierteljahreshefte für Sozialwissenschaften*, I(1922), 3.

9 On such divisions, as occurring on the basis of patriarchal totemistic cultures, cf. Graebner, *Die Weltanschauung der Primitiven*; also L. Lévy-Bruhl, *Das Denken der Naturvölker*(Vienna, 1921).

10 Cf. the end of my study "Die Idole der Selbsterkenntnis" (1911), in *Vom Umsturz der Werte*. Thus the faculties of the soul assumed by Plato correspond exactly—in accordance with his proposition that the state is the "great man"—to the natural estates assumed by him as parts of the state.

11 In Germany, M. Weber, C. Schmitt in his notable book *Politische Theologie* (1922), O. Spengler in some deep perceptions of his well-known work, have started to advance these problems for the better-known, well-lit areas of society. On the structural identity of the political monarchy of the high cultures and their monotheism, cf. Graebner, "Gottesglaube und Staatsgedanke," in *Die Weltanschauung der Primitiven*, pp. 109 ff.

I have pointed out such structural identities for the city particularism and polytheism of the Greeks (as well as for Plato's pluralistic conception of his "ideas"); for the Stoicist doctrine, to which the world becomes one big community (cosmopolity), a large-scale empire in which increasing universalism and individualism are interdependent; for the conception of the world as a hierarchy of teleological form activities, and the feudal estate structure of contemporary society; for the conception of world and soul by Cartesianism and its following (Malebranche), and the state of the absolute monarchy, likewise, for Calvinism and the new concept of sovereignty (in both cases the intermediary forces and *causae secundae* are eliminated in favor of the *causa prima*); for the essential relationship of deism (engineers and machinist's God), free-trade doctrine, political liberalism, associational psychology, and the doctrine of balance of power in foreign policy; for the social individualism of the Age of Enlightenment and the monadological system of Leibniz; for the conception of organic nature as "struggle of life" and practical-ethical utilism, the economic system of competition, and the class-struggle attitude (Karl Marx, Malthus, Darwin); for Kant's doctrine that the intellect must produce an order of nature and of the moral world from a chaos of sensations and affects, and the becoming of the Prussian state (see my book *Die Ursachen des Deutschenhasses*); for the connection of the sociological bases of Tsarism with the intellectual content of the Orthodox religion. Cf. also my discussion of structural affinities of the systems of theism, materialism, and monism with certain constitutional forms of the state in *Wesen und Formen der Sympathie*. Cf. also Schmitt, *Politische Theologie*.

12 Cf. my book *Wesen und Formen der Sympathie*, pp. 277 ff.; also Graebner, *Die Weltanschauung der Primitiven*, p. 132; "In primitive thought the attributes have a much greater role, the substances a much lesser role than with us; most substance-like still is the conception of the animal and human organism." Also cf. L. Lévy-Bruhl, *Das Denken der Naturvölker*, translated by Jerusalem, and his basic, new book *La Mentalité primitive* (Paris, 1922) and Jerusalem's article in the volume edited by me, *Versuche zu einer Soziologie des Wissens* (Munich, 1924). To regard these analogies as just primitive anthropomorphisms would be very much mistaken; they exist in the very highest cultures.

13 Cf. my example in my paper "Weltanschauungslehre, Soziologie und Weltanschauungssetzung," in *Schriften zur Soziologie und Weltanschauungslehre* (Bern, 1963).

14 Probably the greatest categorical difference is that between matriarchal and patriarchal cultures. For this see Graebner, *Die Weltanschauung der Primitiven*.

15 "Die geistinge Einheit Europas," in *Der Genius der Krieges* etc. (1915).

16 Here I will mention only the most important ones, as I will examine such parallel coordinations in greater detail in my *Philosophische Anthropologie*:

1 between the stages of development of the psychic functions of man up to the end of his second year, i.e., the actual "becoming man", and the psychic functions and aptitudes of adult higher vertebrates (Edinger);

2 between the picture of the human soul altered by pathological deficiencies and those animal psyches in which the deficient function is not yet developed (e.g., lack of frontal brain functions in apes);

3 between the normal psychic behaviour of primitive groups and the pathological (or at least abnormal) psychic behaviour of adults on a higher level of civilization (see Schilder, Storch, and others);

4 between the psyche of the primitives and that of the child (see W. Stern, E. Jaensch, Buhler, Koffka, Lévy-Bruhl);

5 between the elimination of the higher psychic centers in the constitution of the mass psyche with men of higher civilization and the animal soul or animal societies (see Scheler, *Wesen und Formen der Sympathie*);

6 between the ephemerous formation of the mass psyche within civilization and the lasting psychic direction of the primitive horde (see also S. Freud's *Massenpsychologie und Ichanalyse*);

7 between the mass soul and the pathological or abnormal consciousness (hysteria, depersonalization, hypnosis; cf. Freud, *Massenpsychologie und Ichanalyse*, and P. Schilder, *Über das Wesen der Hypnose*);

8 between the behaviour of masses and that of children;

9 between the normal behaviour of children and the pathological abnormal behaviour of adults (inhibitions of development and infantilisms);

10 between the growth and decay of psychic functions at the various ages of individuals and the parallel stages of aging peoples and civilizations (compare my paper

"Altern der Kulturen," which appears in *Kölner Vierteljahresschrift für Sozialwissen-schaften*);

11 between the psychic life of children and that of women ("constitutional infan-tility" of the female psychophysical organism); furthermore, between the differen-tial psychology of the sexes and patriarchal and matriarchal cultures;

12 between the mentality and educational condition of the lower classes of a society and the educational condition of the elites of two, three, or more generations earlier ("stratification theory" of knowledge and class structure).

17 Cf. Graebner, *Die Weltanschauung der Primitiven*, chap iv, "Weltanschauungen und Sprachen."

18 Cf. F. Toennies's penetrating attempt to write a history of philosophic terminology (1906).

19 The groups, techniques, authorities with which the "speaking of the Holy Ghost" is connected within the various religious communities of the Christian culture—e.g., papacy, council, community, "*spiritus sanctis internus*" with Luther—perhaps constitute a feature of these communities which is the most important for the sociology of religion.

20 Cf. *La Mentalité primitive*, p. 520; "L'espace y est plutot senti que conçu; ses directions sont lourdes de qualités, et chacune des ses regions . . . participe de tous ce qui s'y trouve habituellement."

21 On the lacking sense of primitive men for the *causae secundae* cf. Lévy-Bruhl, *Des Denken der Naturvölker*, especially at the end.

22 Concerning the dispute on "insight" in animals, cf. W. Köhler, *Intelligenzprüfungen bei Menschenaffen* (2d ed.; Berlin, 1922); and the partly critical, partly confirming discussions in K. Bühler, *Die geistige Entwicklung des Kindes* (3d ed.; 1923); K. Koffka, *Die Grund-lagen der psychischen Entwicklung* (1921); O. Selz, *Über die Gesetze des geordneten Denk-verlaufs* (1913–22); and G. Kafka, "Tierpsychologie," in *Handbuch der vergleichenden Psychologie* (1922), I.

23 Cf. E. Jaensch, *Der Aufbau der Wahrnehmungswelt* (1924).

24 On this difference of essence between man and animal in general, which is something quite separate from the empirical—i.e., anatomical, physiological, psychological—species difference of primitive men and apes, cf. my published *Philosophische Anthro-pologie* and my study "Zur Idee des Menschen."

8

ERNST GRÜNWALD

Systematic Analyses
Translated by Rainer Koehne

THE FIRST CHAPTER of this treatise tried to give an account of the antecedents of the sociology of knowledge, the gradual development of its
proper themes, the articulation of its relevant problems. It described the
development of the sociology of knowledge up to the moment when the
problems which had appeared under other titles and as part of larger disciplines gain so much urgency[1] that a special science must be established to
deal with them. This raises the question of the logical place of the sociology
of knowledge in the system of the sciences.

The *locatio*—to use the term of scholastic logic—of the sociology of knowledge leads to still another question: it is not sufficient to ascertain the *genus
proximum* of the sociology of knowledge; to get at last a somewhat more
precise definition, its *differentia specifica* must also be ascertained as clearly as
possible. So far, "sociology of knowledge" was defined as "the theory of the
connectedness of knowledge and social being." This definition may be
convenient for the history of the antecedents of the sociology of knowledge,
because in that earlier period the problems were not yet sharply defined,
but it is unfit for any work that actually pretends to scientific standing.
Ambiguities which exist in almost every term of this definition must be
clarified, especially the central concept of the sociology of knowledge,
connectedness with being, must be subjected to lengthy analyses, around
which further investigations dealing with the basic concepts of the sociology
of knowledge will be grouped.

By directing our analysis to the concept of connectedness with being,

---

"Systematische Analysen," in Walther Eckstein (ed.), *Das Problem der Soziologie des
Wissens* (Wien-Leipzig: Wilhelm Braumüller, 1934), pp. 52–106.

access to deeper layers of the problems, possible in principle today, will undeniably be barred from the outset. . . . Thus, we cannot even consider the question of the specific features of the human essence and of the basic features of cognition in which the possibility of a connectedness with being is *founded*, although a discussion of these features is a necessary condition for any developed theory of connectedness with being. For example, the question would have to be raised how cognition grows out of the specific character of human existence; to what extent the possibility in principle of any connectedness with being is preformed in the fact that cognition can be understood as an ontological relationship; how the expression "connectedness with being" as used in the sociology of knowledge might rest on an essential possibility that cognition be connected with being; etc. The problem in other words, would be to make explicit the metaphysics of cognition which would be the necessary precondition for making the expression of "connectedness of cognition with being" meaningful which in turn is a necessary precondition of a sociology of knowledge. The metaphysical premises which form the latent basis of any sociology of knowledge would have to be uncovered with utmost clarity, but, of course, with no possibility of a scientific decision on their material correctness. It would merely have to be shown what metaphysical position would have to be taken by anyone who asserts the possibility of a sociology of knowledge.

A historical survey of the ontology of cognition since antiquity would have to show furthermore what positions the various philosophic systems take with respect to the essential possibility of a sociology of knowledge, or to what extent it is possible, from the position of each system, to conceive a corresponding system of sociology of knowledge.[2]

It is particularly regrettable that we are also unable to discuss the relationship of the being of man to "its" consciousness, which is self-consciousness; or the question of the extent to which there may to every becoming reflected of existence correspond a change of that existence itself, so that in order not to miss a changed being, reflection would have to change too, which is the problem of Hegel's *Phenomenology*; or, finally, the theories which were advanced, before and after Hegel, for this group of problems. Not even the most superficial treatment can be given to these fundamental questions, which would have to be taken up in detail by any theory of sociology of knowledge wishing to become clear on its own tasks and on its limits.

But since the present treatise looks at the problems of the sociology of knowledge not *modo recto*, but only indirectly, this shortcoming must be taken into the bargain. It is a treatise that seeks to report on the treatment of these problems till now. Therefore the problems themselves are given attention only for the purpose of getting the tools to grasp the theories of sociology of knowledge more precisely. . . . The analyses which follow do not seek to advance to "the things themselves" but will be content to interpret the theories which do advance to the "things themselves," allegedly or in fact. . . . To say the same thing differently, the subject of this treatise is not the problems of the sociology of knowledge but the theories on these problems. Therefore we renounce a *limine* the purpose of vindicating to its results an absolute truth borne out by the empirical facts. It mainly seeks to show what premises must be accepted by the existing theories of the sociology of knowledge, if they be true. The analyses to be presented should therefore not be understood as asserting, for instance, that there is in fact a metaphysical entity "class," to which a particular way of thinking corresponds; they seek to show merely that the theory of the sociology of knowledge necessarily assumes the existence of such an entity and of a way of thinking in conformity to it; but no judgment shall be attempted as to whether these assumptions of the sociology of knowledge have material truth, or whether the entities the existence of which it affirms are empirically demonstrable.

It further follows from this that the systems of sociology of knowledge to be reviewed will not be examined for their material truth, that there will be nowhere any investigation of how far they are capable of proving themselves when applied to the empirical objects. In this treatise the primary object is to discuss the possibility of a sociology of knowledge and the premises by which it is made possible.

That this attempt to reflect about the essence of the basic concepts which pass from one study in the sociology of knowledge to the next, burdened with ambiguities, cannot and will not lead to any definite results is the plainer since it quite intentionally advances only to a certain layer of the problems, carefully avoiding the deeper ones. Should it be possible also to interpret the following analyses as prolegomena to future investigations which will dig more deeply, this result would have to be considered as a byproduct, besides their real purpose.

As the subject of the first analysis, the position of the sociology of knowledge in the system of the sciences was chosen.

To begin with, it is undisputed and probably undisputable that the sociology of knowledge means to be a science. Also not to be disputed is its character as a *Geisteswissenschaft*, which is to say that its object is meaning or sense, and therefore its appropriate method is understanding, since this is the specific mode of the apperception of meaning or sense. This fact, that the object is meaning and the appropriate method understanding, appears here as the most essential feature of the *Geisteswissenschaften*. Against this feature, the problems of the specific forms of conceptualization (Rickert) move to the background, especially since in Rickert's system[3] neither the position of sociology nor that of the sociology of knowledge—which is, of course, not even explicitly mentioned—is entirely clear.

Hence, the sociology of knowledge—this can be considered demonstrated without further proof—is a *Geisteswissenschaft* whose subject has something to do with knowledge, cognition, and thought.

But here the difficulties begin. There are, after all, several older, generally recognized disciplines which have knowledge, cognition, and thought for their subject: epistemology especially, then logic, psychology, etc.[4] What is the relation of the sociology of knowledge to these firmly established disciplines? Does it supersede them? How does it bear on their results? Do they leave any room for it at all? Are not all the possible ways of approaching cognition already taken up by epistemology, psychology, logic, etc.? Is there still another way of approaching the phenomenon of cognition that could be claimed by the sociology of knowledge? What does the sociology of knowledge really want from cognition and thought? One might think that the answer to these and similar questions could be found by reflecting on the term "sociology of knowledge" and what it denotes. The sociology of knowledge, it might be argued, is a part of sociology—namely, sociology of knowledge—just as the sociology of law is sociology of law, and the sociology of religion is sociology of religion. Therefore one might think that the subject of the sociology of knowledge is to be determined by reflecting upon the tasks and problems of sociology.

However, if, in this definition of the sociology of knowledge as "sociology" of "knowledge," the usual definition of sociology is inserted in this definition of the sociology of knowledge, an absurdity results. For example, if Wilhelm Jerusalem's definition of sociology as the science of "the social group in its organized unity" and its relationship to the individual is used,[5] it will be impossible to speak of a "sociology of knowledge." As "the science of the social group," sociology is clearly defined; its subject is the human group itself. If "sociology" is the "science of society," the concept of a sociology of some cultural phenomenon such as law, religion, language, or knowledge does not seem to make sense. Thus, Jerusalem's definition of sociology gives no access to the concept of the sociology of knowledge.

That this paradox is not the result of Jerusalem's particular definition of sociology is shown by the fact that the "sociology of knowledge" remains just as elusive when other definitions are used—for example, M. Weber's, now generally accepted as at least a starting point for further analyses: "Sociology is a science conerning itself with the interpretative understanding of social action and thereby with a causal explanation of its course and consequences."[6]

It takes little reflection to show that this definition of sociology, however it may be interpreted, also permits no access to a sociology of knowledge. For M. Weber, too, sociology is defined as science of social action; and therefore knowledge and cognition cannot be its object.

But there seems to be a way out of the difficulty: the sociology of knowledge might be interpreted as applied sociology, as the science of that social action which is carried out in the sphere of knowledge and thought, just as the other forms of applied sociology—the sociology of religion, of law—have as their theme social action carried out in the area of the cultural phenomena of religion or law. . . .

But this argument does not withstand closer analysis. The attempt to make the sociology of knowledge a part of "sociology"[7] by defining it as the science of that social action which is performed in relation to the acquisition and dissemination of knowledge is bound to fail. For if there is consensus on any point in the discipline which today claims the name "sociology of knowledge," it is on the fact that the definition given above, "science of the connectedness of knowledge with social being," applies to it. This definition is the *fundamentum inconcussum* of all systems which see the sociology of knowledge as a genuine discipline in its own right.

It is obvious even at this point, before the necessary clarification of ambiguities, that this definition, however it may be understood, does not define the discipline which the other definition attempts to specify. The science which has for its subject the connectedness of knowledge with social being cannot be identical with the science of that social action which is performed in relation to the acquisition and dissemination of knowledge.

Thus the last attempt to interpret the sociology of knowledge as part of "sociology" is demonstrated to be a failure. The sociologies of religion, law, art, music, etc., cannot be established as parts of "sociology," regardless of whether the latter is interpreted as the science of the human group existing independent from the individual man (Jerusalem) or as the science of social action, of the societalness of man. No doubt there is an "applied sociology" dealing with those acts of social action which are realized in the sphere of the acquisition and dissemination of knowledge, and in this sense there can be a "sociology" of education, of the press, of the community of science. This discipline may be a part of "special sociology" in Spranger's sense,[8] which is defined by the fact "that for an assumed substantive area of culture (which as a rule is derived from one particular structuring value direction), the specific correlated forms of association are sought out and analyzed."[9] But the point is that discipline is not sociology of knowledge in the usual sense of the word "sociology."[10] The central problem of the sociology of knowledge does not enter into the "sociological" analysis of scientific activities conceived as a part of "sociology."

Before we attempt to resolve the paradox that the sociology of knowledge is no "sociology," a simplification of the terminology should be introduced. The "sociologies" of the various areas of culture will be referred to by one term, "sociology of culture." This is to say that "sociology of culture" will not be used to mean the "historico-sociological" discipline for which A. Weber uses this term[11] and which deals with a heterogeneous set of problems, nor the partial level of "sociology" which Scheler contrasted to the "sociology of the real,"[12] or Kantorowicz' "sociology of culture," which is defined as "the branch [of "sociology"] directed at civil society as a whole" (which is "sociology");[13] rather, "sociology of culture" will here be used to mean the whole of the "sociologies" of the several cultural areas, the several "manifestations of historico-social reality" (Dilthey). The sociology of culture in this sense is therefore not a uniform concrete discipline but the sum of several such disciplines, unified not only by the fact that these various cultural areas, after all, constitute "culture,"[14] but also by a specific method, yet to be discussed, and specific basic concepts. Just as the sociology of knowledge has been tentatively defined as "the science of the connectedness of knowledge with social being," so the sociology of culture can be defined as the discipline (or, more correctly, the whole of the several disciplines) which takes as its theme the connectedness of the several cultural objectifications with social being.

Thus, the specific set of problems of the sociology of culture remains excluded from "sociology" as science of social action—i.e., from that "sociology" which will be called, although the term is stylistically intolerable, the "sociology of society" or "social sociology" (Vierkandt).

But a more incisive analysis will find that the fundamental difference between the two "sociologies" is even deeper. Not only can cultural sociology not be interpreted as a part of social sociology, but it must beyond that be said that the two disciplines have nothing whatever in common except the name, "sociology." ...

In order to understand the common name of these two disciplines, which cannot be comprehended by looking at their present state, one must go back to the situation from which the theme of "sociology" grew. It would have to be recalled—and this is not the proper place to do so—that "sociology" arises chiefly as an "oppositional science" of the rising bourgeoisie,[15] that this bourgeoisie, in a characteristic antithesis, set the phenomena of human existence which are relevant to itself—i.e., the socio-economic nexuses—against the un- and antibourgeois "state," as "civil society," and made these phenomena the theme of a particular science, namely "sociology"; and that in the course of development this original theme split in two.[16] On the one hand, the science of civil society became by radical dehistoricalization of its questions the science of "society" and later, when "society" was recognized as a hypostatization of the social acts, which alone are given to sober description, as a metaphysical substance,[17] the science of societalness as a constant property of human nature, the science of social action as such (M. Weber). On the other hand, it would have to be shown how the other discipline which grew out of "sociology" kept the original questions inasmuch as it intended to analyze the several cultural phenomena in their connectedness with that which constitutes civil or bourgeois society—viz., social being. To the latter, civil society turned out to be primarily an economic structure, a level—the fundamental one—of human existence. Marx gives the concept of "social being" that accent of absoluteness which in Hegel's system is the feature of the absolute mind. The civil or bourgeois society which to Hegel is just a step in the evolution of the absolute mind, has the same relevance to Marx that reason has to Hegel. It is the *ens realissimum*, while all other levels of human existence are just its manifestation, its "expression."

Later this concept of "social being" is dehistoricalized in the same way as the concept of "society" of social sociology: the unique historical entity of bourgeois society becomes the logical and systematic category of the "productive relations" which bring forth the superstructure in all periods of history. Thus there grow from "sociology as a science of reality" two disciplines, neither of which will be a science of a concrete reality and both of which try to apply their basic concepts generally to all historical periods. In any case, the rift between the sociology of society and the sociology of culture is now so deep that nothing common to them is to be found.

But perhaps the objection could be raised that there must be something common to the sociology of society and the sociology of culture, since both, as seems to be shown by their name, "sociology," are sciences of the social. Therefore it might be said that "science of the social" is the genus encompassing them both.

But this objection to the complete separation of the sociologies of society and of culture also turns out to be mistaken on closer analysis. The very concept of the "social" which is expected to establish the sociological character of the two disciplines means something different in both cases.

As was expounded above, the central concept of social sociology is "social action" as understood by M. Weber, who defines action as "social" "insofar as its subjective meaning takes account of the behavior of others and is thereby oriented in its course."[18] Thus, the concept of the "social" here, denotes: (1) a specific meaning connected with the action by the actor, (2) which meaning consists in somehow—the *how* is not relevant here—being related to a *You*.

But this concept of the "social" does not appear at all in cultural sociology; and what would be the sense of having it there, especially in the sociology of knowledge? Cultural sociology is "sociology," rather, because its central concept is social being. In this concept, "social" does not mean a specific quality of the subjectively intended meaning of any psychic acts; it means: belonging to civil society, proceeding from it, related to it. Therefore "social" is for cultural sociology the constituting feature of the objectively existent civil or bourgeois society, from which—as a modified form of the absolute mind—emanate the phenomena of culture. Yet it must at once be admitted that neither the concept of "civil society" nor that of "social being"— which are equipollent—can be defined quite unambiguously. For usually they do not mean the purely economic structure only but are used to indicate all, or almost all, the cultural phenomena thought to "condition" a given intellectual creation. The concept of "civil" or "bourgeois" society assumes various shades of meaning depending upon the particular basic concept to which it is contrasted, but in the center of these peripheral meanings there remains, as a hard core, the economic structure, or the social being in the narrowest sense.[19]

While social sociology is restricted in principle to analyses of psychic acts, cultural sociology—and that is another fundamental difference between these two "sociologies"—is of an essentially antipsychological disposition. To cultural sociology, the subjective meaning an individual associates with a cultural product realized by him is on principle irrelevant. It seeks, rather, to interpret a product of the mind as a manifestation of social being, and this character need not in any way be conscious to the subject who realizes the product of mind.[20]

Thus, while social sociology operates with soul (or motivational) understanding, cultural sociology rejects this method on principle. Yet, since it proved to be a *Geisteswissenschaft*, it must try to grasp its object by understanding. What, then, is its specific mode of understanding?

Three forms of understanding[21] can be distinguished: soul understanding (motivational understanding), mind understanding, and manifestational understanding. The first of these is the understanding of any psychic processes;[22] mind understanding understands objectifications of the mind, cultural phenomena, ideal objectivities: propositions, works of art, etc. Finally, there is manifestational understanding. Its immediate *occasio* is an intellectual content, as in the case of mind understanding, but this content is not understood with respect to its immanent sense but as a manifestation of some absolute which emanates it from itself. For example, Kantianism is understood not as a system of philosophy but as a manifestation of the rising bourgeoisie; the works of Phidias are not interrogated for their artistic content but interpreted as manifestations of "Hellenic man."

Soul understanding is to be understood, with a grain of salt, to mean the method of psychology; mind understanding is practised by the *Geisteswissenschaften* in the narrower sense, i.e., the sciences which question the intellectual objectifications for their immanent meaning; and one of the disciplines that employ manifestational understanding—all of which come under the concept of "external view," which is yet to be discussed—is cultural sociology.

Thus the sociology of knowledge does not interpret a proposition according to its immanent sense but looks at it as a "symbol," a vehicle of another meaning which in principle is unknown to the subject positing the proposition. And the specific trait of the sociology of knowledge is to be found in the fact that it looks at social being as the "most real" sphere, to which all thinking is thought to be tied and which is believed to manifest itself in every proposition. In principle it is possible to assume some other sphere as the absolute, as the emanation of which the proposition is to be considered. The reversal of Hegel's philosophy of history—which is the root in intellectual history of all such forms of treatment—does not need to be in the direction of social being. . . . In any case, the thesis that social being really is the absolute level and that all cultural phenomena are really its emanations is not empirical; it is in no way included in the propositions themselves that I must interpret every proposition as a manifestation of, specifically, social being. The thesis that social being is objectively the *ens reallissimum* is no more capable of proof by discursive reasoning than that history is the realization of a divine plan of salvation. Every other level of human existence, race, character type, ethnic type, some depth layers of the soul, etc., might just as well be assumed to be the "most real" sphere manifesting itself in all the others. We have with that arrived at the *genus proximum* of cultural sociology, and thereby at a further generic concept of the sociology of knowledge. Knowledge, law, art—in short, culture—can be interpreted by manifestational understanding as emanations of various layers, posited, in each case, as absolute. If all these possible functionalizations of the various cultural phenomena to various absolute layers are now called "external views,"[23] it is possible to establish the sequence: sociology of knowledge, cultural sociology, external view.[24]

This means—to formulate the result of the foregoing analysis in another direction—that it is erroneous to identify connectedness with social being and "connectedness with being." Cultural sociology, the science of the connectedness of the cultural phenomena with social being, is not identical with external view, as science of connectedness with being in general. Rather, it is one of several possible types of interpretation.

Important conclusions follow from this pluralism of possible external views. Several possible external views exist;[25] each claiming to be the only true view, and saying that it alone exposes the true origin of the cultural phenomena. Just dig deep enough, it says, and you will hit the layer which is affirmed to be absolute; only by reaching this layer, subordinating all other spheres to its expressions, will you be pursuing true science.

Now, is it possible to resolve the apparent antinomy that each external view maintains it is the only true one, while only one of them can be true? Is it possible to ascertain which one of the several external views is the true one, which uncovers real nexuses? It is possible to answer unambiguously, by scientific means, which level of human existence it is that manifests itself in thinking and judging?[26] The question is, in other words, how to delimit the sociology of knowledge against other possible external views of knowledge.

The essence of the external view, as was said, is that a proposition is interpreted as a manifestation of some sphere assumed as absolute, or ultimate, reality. The question now can be re-formulated as the question whether a scientific, generally binding proof is possible that this or that level of human existence is the *ens realissimum*. Can it be proved by scientific means—others cannot be considered if sociology of knowledge is to be analyzed as a strict science—that only social being is possessed of full ontic reality and that the existence of all others is merely derived?

To this question there is only one answer: it is utterly impossible to furnish a generally binding, stringent proof by discursive reasoning that social being alone possesses full reality and that the other levels exist only insofar as they are in a relation of methexis to this absolute. I may believe or may furnish some metaphysical proof that social being is the absolute, but, as long as I am pursuing science, I am confronting a pluralism of possible absolutes among which a choice is impossible. Science cannot show any way out of this polytheism of absolute layers. All possible external views stand on one level with equal right, all are equally valid; but none is absolutely valid. Each external view is valid only if I perform an act of metaphysical positing by which it will be founded—that is, if I believe that the sphere it raises into the absolute really is the absolute. Thus I may hold only the statements of cultural sociology to be true if I faithfully accept the premise that all cultural phenomena are a manifestation of social being, that the objectifications of culture must be interpreted as emanations of social being. Only by this "basic thesis" do the statements of cultural sociology receive validity. But the thesis is scientifically undemonstrable, therefore also scientifically irrefutable; it is valid for me if I posit it as valid by what is scientifically regarded as an act of pure arbitrariness. Hence, each of the possible external views is founded by an arbitrary act and is "decernism."[27] Objectively, the possible external views are entirely non-obligatory. They have validity only for one who accepts their metaphysical premise: hence the external views have only hypothetical character, possessing no *fundamentum in re*.

But this means, further, that the claim of the sociology of knowledge of being capable of uncovering real nexuses, of being capable of showing how a proposition is in fact a manifestation or causal product of social being of such or such type, is untrue. For an identical claim is made, with equal right, by each of the possible external views of knowledge and cognition: each pretends that it and it alone is capable of uncovering relations that really exist. The sociology of knowledge does not have the possibility of ascertaining real manifestational, real causal relations; it can only affirm possible causal nexuses, a possible relationship of "expression." It is quite incapable of definite proof that, say, Kantianism is actually a causal product of the interests of the rising bourgeoisie (or a manifestation of its economico-social condition). All it can affirm is: assuming the basic thesis that every proposition and every system of propositions is a causal product of the interests (a manifestation of the social being) of a particular class, Kantianism may be interpreted as the causal product of the interests (the manifestation of the social being) of the German bourgeoisie at the end of the eighteenth century. Only if I accept the undemonstrable basic thesis may I attribute validity to a proposition of the sociology of knowledge based on that thesis. Hence, the sociology of knowledge is not a science the statements of which are unconditionally valid for each thinking individual, but a possible scheme of interpretation.[28]

The specific feature of the method of cultural sociology now is more evident: cultural sociology is that discipline which, assuming a particular basic thesis, interprets the cultural phenomena which are primarily the object of other sciences as manifestations of social being. . . .[29]

It has been apparent so far that this mode of interpretation is not confined to the immanent sense of a work of art, proposition, legal institution, or religious dogma but wants to interpret them as manifestations of the economic situation of the proletariat, the feudal style of life, the yellow race, the post-war generation, the Swabian stock, the German mind, Hellenic man, late capitalism, or Renaissance man. Thus, a new concept emerges, the meaning of which has not yet been accurately determined—namely, the concept of manifestation, of "expression", as it is usually called. In the case of the external view, it will have to be determined more accurately which meaning is attached to this very ambiguous term.

It is customary to oppose the mode of the understanding of the external view, or "expressional understanding," to the understanding of the immanent sense, or the internal view. (In the present analyses, the term "expressional understanding"—which is incorrect as will be shown presently—has from the outset been replaced by "manifestational understanding.") Each proposition, it is said, has, as a meaningful form, an immanent sense. (For the sake of simplicity we will mention only the possible external views of cognition, which most distinctly present the problems discussed.) We may here ignore the fact that this immanent sense extends in three dimensions—declaring a psychic act, signifying a content, naming an object—as well as the fact that each proposition made with communicative intent also is meant to fulfill a steering function.[30]

It is in the essence of a proposition to want to be understood by its immanent sense and, in addition, to raise a claim of validity, wanting not merely to be understood but also to be considered true. But since it does not always see the intention of being recognized as true, it reduces that demand to asking the understanding observer at least to consider the claim of validity. In a less personifying manner this may be described by saying that a proposition must be considered in some doxic modality.[31]

Now, to the internal view which should grasp this immanent sense is usually opposed the external view. A proposition, it is said,[32] is "expression" in two ways: on the one hand, it expresses its immanent sense; on the other hand, it expresses the level of being which is posited as the absolute one. Therefore it should be possible to interpret a proposition either in the internal view, as expression of its immanent sense, or—this being the task of the external view—as expression of the absolute layer, for its functional meaning. From this position arise most complex problems; e.g., if the immanent sense can be confronted with the functional sense, etc.

This whole "dual aspect theory," which seems so plausible is wrong from beginning to end. The faulty premises on which it is based can be stated as three theses: (1) The relation between the absolute and the proposition is an expressional relation of the same character as that between the proposition and its immanent sense. (2) The vehicle of the (alleged) expressional meaning is the proposition. (3) The vehicle of the (alleged) expressional meaning "has" that meaning in identically the same way as the proposition "has" its immanent sense. These three theses, which are the basis of the "dual aspect" theory, should now be subjected one by one to critical analysis. The investigations which have been carried out on the nature of the internal view will stand that analysis in good stead—while at the same time their whole relevance will finally be revealed.

First, in which sense can the proposition be called the "expression" of some level of being of the subject who pronounces it?

Recently in philosophy the concept of "expression" has been very much in the foreground. Attempts are made to bring a number of the most difficult problems of philosophy closer to solution. It is believed that by introducing the symbol relation a more accurate comprehension of the psychophysical problem will become possible;[33] and Cassirer believes he has found in the symbol the phenomenon which characterizes the grasping of the world by the mind, in its three forms—language, myth, and science. The concept of symbol is said to

> . . . encompass the totality of those phenomena in which the sensuous is in any way filled with meaning, in which a sensuous content, while preserving the mode of its existence and facticity, represents a particularization and embodiment, a manifestation and incarnation of a meaning. . . .

> It is the pure fact of expression—the fact that a certain phenomenon in its simple "givenness" and visibility makes itself known to be inwardly animated—which first and most immediately tells us how consciousness, while remaining purely within itself, can at the same time apprehend another reality. Here we can no longer inquire into the origin of this fact itself and seek to explain it, for any attempted solution is bound to move in a circle. How can the sheer phenomenon of expression be understood by and *derived* from something else which transcends it when expression is itself the vehicle which *leads* us to every kind of transcendence, to all consciousness of reality? [Emphasis as in the original.][34]

The characteristic of this irreducible phenomenon therefore is that something immediately given in actual sensuousness at the same time has a function of representation and is the expression of something non-sensual, a sense or meaning. The representative function is not added onto the datum but belongs to it and cannot in any simple way be separated from it.

> The reality of the phenomenon cannot be separated from its representative function; it ceases to be the same as soon as it signifies something different,

as soon as it points to another total complex as its background. It is mere abstraction to attempt to detach the phenomenon from this involvement, to apprehend it as an independent something outside of and preceding any function of indication.[35]

If in a given case our attention is first directed at the present datum as such—as when we don't "understand" "what it means"—and we then grasp the representative function, our mode of viewing undergoes an "essential phenomenal modification."[36]

If it is now considered whether the relation between the *ens realissimum* and the vehicle of the functional meaning is grasped by this concept of expression, it appears at once that it is no expressional relation. For "expression" means that an unsensual sense manifests itself in something senseless which is given sensually. But in the case of the external view there is no question of such a relation. Here the vehicle of meaning in which the meaning is thought to "express" itself is itself an unsensual sense. While in the case of the expressional relation a complex of physical data, the "expression" in its physical side (the sensuous sign, the articulated complex of sounds, the written character on paper, and the like),[37] expresses a meaning which is an ideal whole, the external view considers as vehicle of the manifestational meaning something itself unsensual—namely, the proposition content. That which is expressed in the expressional relation proper is for the manifestational understanding that which expresses. But by thus being, as it were, lifted up one step, the relation loses the character of an expressional relation, in the exact sense which was fixed above, following Cassirer: for now that which expresses is no longer something sensually given but is itself a meaning, and thus an ideal object.

It is true that everyday language uses the term "expression" for this relation also; but it does so with a specific turn which clearly shows the true nature of this relation: it is not said that the absolute "is expressed" but that it "expresses itself" or "reveals" or "manifests" "itself" in the proposition. This form is so symptomatic for the relation between the absolute layer and the vehicle of the functional meaning that this relation may be called, as we have done, "manifestational relation."

But is the difference between expressional relation and manifestational relation sufficiently characterized by saying that the latter is "one step above" the former? Would the manifestational relation become identical with the expressional relation if this difference could be removed? Is the absolute, then, the "meaning" or "sense" of the layer of the propositions? That it is not so is easy to see. For not only is the proposition something unsensual, but at the same time that which manifests itself, the *ens realissimum*, is not an ideal object but something existing factually. To say that the absolute is the "meaning" of the proposition is meaningless because the *ens realissimum* has no ideal being but is intended by the external view as a really existent entity, even though that entity may be accessible only to metaphysical vision;[38] and something really existent cannot have the character of "sense," of "meaning."

But only from the fact that the absolute is really existent follows the difference between the expressional and manifestational relation which really is fundamental: that the expressional relation denotes a purely logical relation, while the manifestational relation denotes a real relation. Of course, the manifestational relation can also be used for purposes of cognition, as one can infer from the directly given proposition the absolute layer which manifests itself in that proposition. But primarily this manifestational relation remains a real relation; the cognitional relation is only founded on this relation, which has the logical priority. Because *realiter* the absolute emits the proposition, the proposition can be interpreted as manifestation of the absolute.

A more accurate analysis shows that the external view interprets the relation between the *ens realissimum* and the cultural phenomenon as an emanatist one. The absolute emits from itself the other layers, which are ontically less real, and the proposition, too, is an entirely passive emanation of the ὄντως ὄν, which alone possesses full existence. This emanatist character of the manifestational relation is clearly expressed by the forms of speech which were quoted—for instance, that the absolute layer "expresses itself"— and by the active role thereby attributed to it.[39]

These brief remarks conclude the analysis of the manifestational relation between absolute layer and proposition, except that one important difference between the emanatistic manifestational relation and the expressional relation between a proposition and its immanent sense remains to be pointed out. In the internal view, expression and that which is expressed are in an indissoluble correlation. A proposition is proposition only by having a sense, and the sense can be grasped only if it is expressed. Proposition, sense, and the relation of the two form an indissoluble unity for the internal view.[40]

On the other hand, the manifestational relation between the emanating layer and the vehicle of the functional meaning does not even enter into the scope of the internal view. This means that the manifestational relation is not visible for the primary mode of viewing propositions, for which the proposition exists purely in its expressional relation, without being bound *a tergo*, without being connected with being. Hence, that approach which alone does justice to the proposition (for which see below) and can say something about its claim of validity does not grasp the connectedness with being which appears in the manifestational relation.

Thus, the relation between the absolute and the vehicle of the functional meaning is much looser than that between the proposition and its immanent sense. Whereas the latter relation belongs to the essence of a proposition, the former is non-essential, accidental, to the proposition itself.

We see that a quick reflection on the essence of the relation between the particular absolute layer and the proposition has shown that to speak of an "expressional relation" is entirely mistaken. Instead, a relation *toto coelo* different from it can be pointed out; namely, the manifestational relation.

Now, according to the plan indicated above, the second point which needs clarification must be analyzed: is the proposition really the vehicle of the manifestational meaning and the object of the specific mode of understanding of the external view?

A glance at the most widely accepted theories of propositions as well as an attempt of our own reflection on what is meant by the word "proposition" show clearly that the object of the external view cannot be the proposition itself. To the essence of a proposition—that is, the general doctrine—belongs its claim of validity. A proposition is therefore fully understood only if its claim of validity is taken into consideration. A view that abstracts from this constituent characteristic of a proposition cannot be said to consider the *proposition*. Although the proposition "prefers" to be affirmed, to be accepted as valid, it is not important in which doxic modality the proposition is viewed, but it is necessary that I take some position on the proposition and its claim of validity.

But this can be done only as long as I am looking at the significatory or representative aspect[41] of a proposition, since the concept of validity, or truth, is meaningful only in that dimension. Even in the declaratory aspect, the standard of truth must already be replaced by that of truthfulness or honesty.

Now there is only one mode of viewing a proposition which looks at the immanent sense, and thus, a fortiori, its representative function. The psychological view, or soul understanding, has for its object the realization (this term here being interpreted as denoting the act, not the result of the act) of the proposition; the external view does not grasp the immanent sense itself but interprets it as manifestation of the absolute; it is therefore only the mind understanding, which is to say, the internal view, that has the immanent sense itself for its object. Grasping the immanent sense is the exclusive "privilege" of the internal view. This view alone is able to perceive the representative function of the proposition, which, as we know, is an aspect of the immanent sense; therefore it alone can say anything about the validity, the manner in which the proposition fulfills its representative function; and therefore it alone has for its object the proposition itself.

On the other hand, the external view, which *per definitionem* does not do justice to the immanent sense of the proposition but on principle goes behind it, *a limine* does not get the representative function and thus the claim of validity into sight. It cannot affirm, deny, doubt, question, or consider it likely, but necessarily remains in the 'Ἐποχή'[42] regarding the claim of validity of the proposition.

To this statement that the external view can *a limine* say nothing about validity we will have to return again and again. In particular it will have a role when the question will be investigated whether "sociologism" is justified. Within the current analysis, however, it has no function but that of one member of a larger chain of reasoning. It serves only to arrive at a definite answer to the question, raised above, if the object of the external view is in fact the proposition. Since validity is a constituent of the proposition, and the external view cannot say anything about its validity, it is impossible that the proposition should be the object of the external view. The dual-aspect theory of the sociology of knowledge, the thesis that there is a twofold mode of viewing propositions, internal and external, thus proves incorrect in still another respect. The question is not of one object that may be considered in two aspects. Rather, the proposition is exclusively the object of the internal view; the object of the external view, the vehicle of the manifestational meaning, is not the proposition but the proposition without its essential constituent, without that property which makes it a proposition; or, if you like, the mere "proposition material." The manifestational meaning attaches to this proposition material, this something not quite accurately describable by words that remains when the proposition is deprived of its claim of validity.

Now there remains to be analyzed the third problem, whether the proposition material, the "vehicle" of the manifestational meaning, "has" that meaning directly, in the sense in which the proposition itself "has" the immanent sense. Does the proposition material manifest the existential layer of the proposing subject raised to the absolute in the same sense as the proposition itself expresses its immanent sense?

To answer this important question, we must hark back to the earlier definition of the external view. The external view of a "proposition" consists in interpreting the proposition material as an emanation of some existential layer of the proposing subject which was raised to be the absolute, the ὄντως ὄν. The proposition material is construed as a manifestation of the bourgeois walk of life, the inferiority complex, Catholicism, the yellow race, a desert tribe, the late medieval style. The sociology of knowledge, so it was characterized above, is that particular form of external view that would understand the proposition material as a manifestation of the social being; it could be paralleled by an equally justified geographic external view of knowledge to which geographic and climatic conditions are the ultimate agent, or by a psychoanalysis of knowledge, of which there are beginnings, which would interpret such proposition as manifestation of some depth layer of the soul; and thus the number of possible external views could be extended still further—theoretically to infinity.

It was already shown that all possible external views are of equal value, that they can all claim but hypothetical validity. The insight of the "decernistic" character of the external views yields the answer to the question here discussed: whether the proposition material "has" the manifestational meaning in the same way in which the proposition itself has its immanent sense; in other words, whether the manifestational meaning is connected with the proposition material in an indissoluble unity. The answer can only be negative. Since every external view is only hypothetically valid, through assuming the basic thesis of that external view, the proposition material also "has" the manifestational meaning asserted by the particular external view only hypothetically. The proposition material has no manifestational meaning at all, but this is only "imparted" to it by the external view. But since the particular external view is not an "understood" mode of consideration but rather, is only constituted by the basic thesis, and since, furthermore, the manifestational meaning is "imparted" by the particular external view, the proposition material "has" the manifestational meaning only "by grace of"[43] the particular thesis.

Thus it turns out that the proposition material in itself does not have any manifestational meaning. It depends entirely upon the pleasure, the "decision," of the observer if he wants to interpret the given proposition material as a manifestation at all. This can be expressed by saying that the manifestational understanding is only facultative: no one can be forced to interpret a proposition for its manifestational meaning. To be grasped as expression belongs to the proposition itself: the expressive understanding is obligatory. Without internal view I cannot, after all, even decide whether a given datum is a proposition.

Likewise, it depends upon the observer's pleasure which sphere he wants to see manifested in the proposition material. The thesis that the categorical imperative—or, more precisely, the material of the proposition: the categorical imperative—is in itself a manifestation of the social being of some stratum is essentially undemonstrable. In itself, the categorical imperative is not a manifestation of the social being of some class, or of Protestant rigorism, or of the climate of Königsberg. Rather, all these possible forms of manifestational meaning are "imparted" to the material by the observer.

This expression, "imparting," needs further clarification. It is not intended to mean that I will read any arbitrary concrete manifestational meaning into the given concrete proposition material. It means, rather, that I enter the proposition material into the scheme of interpretation of the particular external view, as constituted by the basic thesis which was arbitrarily chosen. Within this purely "subjective" scheme of interpretation, the proposition material "automatically" assumes special manifestational meaning, which is not conditioned by the basic thesis. To put it differently: whether I read any manifestational meaning at all in the proposition depends upon my pleasure, and likewise it is entirely in my discretion which sphere I wish to see manifested in the proposition. But the concrete form of the absolute to which I impute the given concrete proposition no longer depends on my pleasure but is potentially—to be sure, only potentially—implied in the proposition material. It is not implied in the categorical imperative itself or its material that I must interpret it as manifestation of an *ens realissimum*. And if I make the purely arbitrary decision to understand it as a manifestation, I must make the further subjective decision of which sphere I wish to see manifested in it. This second decision I make by assuming a basic thesis which is in no way implied in the object, the categorical imperative. But if I have decided for a certain basic thesis, wishing, for example, to interpret the categorical imperative, in the manner of the sociology of knowledge, as an emanation of social being, then it no longer depends upon my pleasure whether I will see the feudal, bourgeois, or proletarian social being manifested in it, but I must impute it to bourgeois thinking, that thinking which is "adequate" to the social being of the bourgeoisie. The problems connected with imputation, the question of the way in which a given proposition is imputed to a concrete form of an absolute, can only later be discussed in another context.

Thus, all possible manifestational "meanings" which a proposition material can ever assume in the possible external views are implied in it in *potentia*. One of these is actualized, and thus realized, only when the proposition material is subjected to the corresponding type of external view. Whether the proposition is subjected to a given view depends on whether I consider this type of external view correct; and it will appear correct to me if I accept the basic thesis which founds it, which is itself purely metaphysical. Therefore, whether or not a concrete manifestational meaning assumed by a

given concrete proposition material is realized depends ultimately upon my
subjective conviction. The use of the expression that the external view
"imparts" its manifestational meaning to the proposition material means
nothing but this.

The complete contrast of the internal and the external view, between
immanent and manifestational meaning, becomes particularly clear at this
point. The immanent sense exists as such, independently of whether I do or
do not realize the proposition *hic et nunc*. But the manifestational meaning
exists only hypothetically, conditionally. Only if I place the proposition
material, the vehicle of every possible manifestational meaning, into an
arbitrary context, which is not preformed in the proposition itself, will it
assume a corresponding manifestational meaning.

From the insight that each external view is merely hypothetical it also
becomes clear how the several external views are related to one another.
The claim by each external view of being the only true one turns out to be
untenable. All external views are equally true—and each is true only if its
basic thesis is assumed. None of the external views has the character of
absolute, unconditional truth—each is only hypothetically valid. Their basic
theses are mutually contradictory, but since I can never accept more than
one basic thesis, the external views are never actually in contradiction. Just
as I cannot acknowledge that there are two omnipotent deities, or, as jurist,
allow two sovereign states to exist side by side, I am also unable simultaneously to declare two different layers the absolute.[44]

The collision of possible external views therefore turns out to be only an
apparent problem. For each external view is founded by an act of metaphysical assumption, and therefore the different external views can no more be
confronted than the dispute among metaphysical systems can be settled by
scientific means.

If the hypothetical character of every possible external view is recognized,
the limits of the sociology of knowledge, which is one form of external
view, are also seen more clearly. The external view does not represent real
relations of manifestation but establishes possible ones. A proposition is not
realiter a manifestation of some absolute, but—once the absolute is posited
by an act not supportable by any scientific grounds—it may be understood
as a manifestation of that sphere. And since I cannot convince anyone by
scientific methods that the basic thesis which founds a particular form of
external view is true, and since a truthfulness of the sociology of knowledge above the merely hypothetical is therefore not demonstrable, the
results of that discipline cannot be forced on anyone. All propositions of the
sociology of knowledge are true only if I posit the basic thesis, which is to

say, accept a metaphysical—i.e., not scientifically demonstrable—premise. Thus the sociology of knowledge does not and cannot ascertain as a manifestation of which stratum a proposition originated, but it investigates as manifestation of which stratum it may be understood.

With that, the doctrine of connectedness with being changes into its opposite. Precisely from the pluralism of possible external views and the competition resulting from that pluralism the insight develops that thought itself cannot simply be said to be connected with being (this expression here being interpreted in the sense of the sociology of knowledge). It follows precisely from the fact that several spheres claim the proposition as their manifestation that the proposition is in itself not the emanation of any absolute, but is itself an absolute.

But if every external view is merely an indication of possible manifestations, then the connectedness of knowledge with social being which is affirmed by the sociology of knowledge is also only conditional—i.e., hypothetical. It, too, can be established only by means of the basic thesis of the sociology of knowledge. That the connectedness with social being exists factually is just as much a purely metaphysical thesis as every proposition raising a layer of human existence to absoluteness. That thought is in itself a manifestation of social being is possible in principle, but, for our knowledge, at any rate, undemonstrable. What can be said scientifically is only that a given concrete proposition appears as a manifestation of a concrete form of social being—such as the proletarian existence of the postwar period or the bourgeois existence of the pre-March years—if the scientifically undemonstrable thesis that all thought and knowledge are to be interpreted as manifestations of social being is assumed. Only that and nothing else can be meant by the sociology of knowledge, if it understands itself. And if the analysis of the external view presented here is correct, this is all that can in fairness be expected of the sociology of knowledge. Whether or not this restriction of its capacity will be thought to call its character as a science into question depends on the demands one makes of a strict science.

The frequently advanced thesis that a proposition is the expression of two layers or has a dual meaning or can be interpreted in two ways has thus proved wrong in three ways: (1) The proposition is "expression" only of its immanent sense; "it" is connected with the absolute by a relation of manifestation; (2) The proposition itself has but *one* sense, the immanent sense; the vehicle of the manifestational sense is not the proposition but the proposition material; (3) The propositional material does not "have" the manifestational meaning in the same way in which it has its immanent sense; the manifestational meaning must be "imparted" to it.

If the question is now raised whether the internal and external views are two interpretations of equal right, the answer must be, according to what has been said, in the negative. Absolute primacy is to be attributed to the internal view, which alone has the cultural phenomenon itself for a theme; the external view, by remaining in the 'Εποχή', renounces from the outset any grasp of the intellectual substance and contents itself with the "material" of that substance. Only the internal view comprehends the immanent sense of its object in its actuality, in contrast to the external view, which by-passes it, trying to find the "true" sense only behind it, and therefore considers as unnecessary any investigation of the claim to validity of the immanent sense. Only the internal view grasps something that hovers free and is valid without any presuppositions, which must be brought in from without—namely, the immanent sense. The external view has only hypothetical validity; its object, the manifestational meaning, exists only for one who accepts its basic thesis; and that basic thesis, as must be stressed again and again, is not a part of the intellectual substance but a metaphysical assumption that no one can be forced to accept.

The primacy of the internal view, which already becomes apparent from these reiterations of earlier arguments, is definitely established by still another fact. So far the analyses which were presented have used the concepts of "cognition" and "knowledge" in their everyday sense. But assuming that it should be necessary to define the subject of the sociology of knowledge with somewhat greater precision, to which discipline should one turn for a definition? Is, perhaps, the sociology of knowledge itself capable of giving a definition of its subject, "cognition and knowledge"? Can it say what knowledge and cognition really is?

This question of the province of the external view may not have much urgency with regard to the several external views of knowledge, since a general consensus on what knowledge is can usually be assumed on this level of investigation, but it takes on the greatest relevance for those external views whose subject cannot be accepted as so firmly and undisputedly established. Every sociology of law, for example, would have to face at the outset the question of what it meant by the concept "law" [*Recht*]. And, apart from that, this problem is of general significance because it is suitable for determining the capacity of the external view in an important respect.

To state the question in the most general terms, can an external view furnish a definition of the cultural phenomenon which it takes for its theme? The reasons for the negative answer that must be given result from the previously mentioned features of the external view. Assuming, for example, that the sociology of law itself could develop a definition of law, there would be two definitions of law, since the theory of law, as the internal view of law, cannot be denied the right to define law, and there is nothing to guarantee the congruence of these two definitions. It is already very probable at this point of the analysis that the definition by the internal view deserves preference; for it alone sees the juridical proposition itself, while the external view can grasp only the "material" of that proposition. In addition, as we know, the external view does not have absolute validity as the internal view does but is merely hypothetical. But how can a mode which is of only conditional validity establish a generally binding definition? That the external view cannot give a definition of the cultural phenomenon which is its theme becomes more likely.

This likelihood grows into certainty if it is remembered that there are in relation to the internal view, not one external view, but many equally possible modi of functionalizing interpretation. Now, which one of the several external views of law can give the definition of law? Why should the definition of law by the sociology of law be more correct than that by the external view which approaches law from the viewpoints of psychoanalysis?

It turns out that, even when defining its subject, the external view already cannot do without the immanent interpretation. Only from the immanent interpretation will it learn what it should deal with. There is only *one* possible authority that can provide the definition of a cultural phenomenon, and that authority is the internal view. Every external view that realizes its own limits must *a limine* refrain from trying to give a definition of the cultural phenomenon which forms its material.[45]

Still another point needs clarification. The thesis that the material of the propositions can be interpreted as a manifestation of the *ens realissimum* must be analyzed in some detail. What can be actually meant by the thesis— the basic thesis, as we know, of the sociology of knowledge—that in the material of the proposition manifests itself, for instance, the social being of some stratum?

Although no manifestational meaning is included in the essence of a proposition, the proposition material, and thus the proposition, nevertheless offers certain indications which show to which class—if the basic thesis of the sociology of knowledge is to be assumed—it is to be imputed. Otherwise the concept of imputation would be meaningless. But what do these indications consist in?

In order to make the matter clearer and better to survey, the concept of the material of a proposition must be examined a bit more closely. It was defined above in a purely negative way, as the "residue" left when the essential feature of the proposition, its claim to validity, is taken away. . . .

What, then, is this mysterious residue which we call the material? It is the proposition viewed in the Ἐποχή, and it therefore is, like the proposition, the expression of an immanent sense. The material of the proposition also expresses the immanent sense, but it has this expressive function only *in potentia*; it becomes actual only when the proposition material assumes a character of validity—i.e., becomes a proposition. It is the characteristic property of the material of the proposition that it includes all possible relations—expressive as well as manifestational—only latently, potentially. It must be awakened by influences from without to actualize the sense dormant in it. In the external view, this actualization takes place by the insertion of the material of the proposition into a scheme of interpretation in which it unveils its correlated manifestational meaning. The internal view, on the other hand, obtains the—immanent—meaning of the proposition material by imparting a character of validity to it, making it a proposition.

The proposition material thus turns out to be the vehicle—if only potentially—of the immanent sense. If this definition of the proposition material—which is sufficiently precise for the present problem—is inserted in the question raised above, the problem can be expressed as follows: what does it mean to say that the proposition material, which is potentially expression of the immanent sense, can be interpreted as a manifestation of the absolute layer?

Primo loco the proposition, and hence the proposition material, is the vehicle of the immanent sense. But the immanent sense is in some form oriented by the object intended by the proposition and determined by that object.[46] How, then, can the proposition "in addition" be interpreted as the manifestation of some layer of being? How is it possible, one is tempted to formulate this question, that the proposition material can be potentially expression and at the same time manifestation? How can the proposition material—potentially, that is—be both object-adequate and site-adequate? Does it make sense to demand from a proposition connected with being, and thus fully determined, that it should be oriented by its object?

If the question is put in this form, a satisfactory answer seems to be difficult if not impossible. But in fact the situation is not that the proposition material has two distinct meanings. It is precisely by the specific mode in which it is expression that it can be interpreted as manifestation. Precisely by the way in which the proposition grasps its intended object can it be interpreted as an emanation of the absolute. The "connectedness with being" becomes apparent precisely in the way in which the mind grips a factual situation.

For a more exact understanding of this statement it is necessary to touch briefly on the theory of propositions, which—usually quite latently—is the basis of every system of sociology of knowledge. Almost all theories of sociologies of knowledge are driven by the "logic of things themselves"— often in complete contrast to their own epistemological premises—toward a very specific view of the role of thought in the cognition of reality—a view which strongly leans on the epistemology developed by the Southwest German school.

In this view, the proposition does not appear as the faithful image of "reality." The extensive and intensive infinity of the "reality" given to me must first be conquered by the process by thought. And it is here, in this necessary process of transformation by thought which forms the objects of knowledge out of the prescientific givenness, that the sociology of knowledge perceives the effect of connectedness with being. The reality "given" to pre-scientific experience can in no way be influenced by the connectedness with being but is pregiven, identically and never to be fully grasped, to all standpoints. On the other hand, the object of knowledge of which scientific statements are made can manifest a connectedness with being. From this it follows that the "influence" of the absolute sphere must operate in the space between the object of experience and the object of knowledge—that is, in the formation process itself. From every part of given reality, from every object of experience, an infinite number of objects of knowledge may be formed, because of its intensive infinity. All these objects of knowledge stand side by side with equal right; however different among themselves, they are all simplifying, abbreviating representations of the same section of reality. They all revolve around the infinite wealth of the material of experience which is not given to thought but only accessible in living.

Now, one can, if one so wishes, see manifested in the concrete mode of each "aspect" the existential layer of the subject forming the object of knowledge which was made the absolute. The object of knowledge is the "product" of two "factors": on the one hand, of the object of experience, where it is the simplified representation; on the other hand, of the standpoint from which the simplification is made. Since the standpoint therefore constitutes the object of knowledge as much as the object of experience does and may be looked at as "conditioned" by the *ens realissimum*, connectedness with being is of constitutive relevance for the object of knowledge.

The role of "connectedness with being"[47] can therefore be defined as having a selecting relevance for the object of experience but as constituting relevance for the object of knowledge.[48]

From this position, which every fully thought-out theory of sociology of knowledge must take, the much discussed problem of whether the effect of "connectedness with being" is selecting or constituting turns out to be merely apparent. The "connectedness with being" "has" not only the effect that a proposition is realized earlier or later: it has not only a "sluice-opening" function[49] to the proposition. For it is essentially impossible to realize all the possible propositions on a factual condition, since their number is infinite. Just as only a limited number of objects of knowledge can in practice be formed from a factual condition, only some of the possible propositions are realized. Thus, it is not only the *hic et nunc* of a realization which would take place in any case that is "conditioned" by "connectedness with being," but also the decision as to which of the infinite number of possible propositions are actualized, are really performed.

On the other hand—to indicate now only the position at the other extreme; the concrete forms the problem takes in the different systems of sociology of knowledge will have to be mentioned in connection with the analysis of each of these systems—the absolute does not "constitute" a proposition quite independently, for in that case it would be quite impossible to understand that the proposition can be called a proposition on some object, fact, or factual condition. The object of knowledge, and thus also the proposition directed at it—since the object of knowledge "exists" only in the propositions —is constituted by the joint operation of the object of experience and the absolute layer. Both determine the object of knowledge; precisely because the latter is a processed form of the object of experience, it is possible to interpret it as a manifestation of the absolute.

Hence the whole proposition material cannot be described as the vehicle of the manifestational meaning, but only a part, which in connection with a second factor, no less important for constituting the object, "produces" the object of knowledge, the proposition, and consequently the proposition material. The proposition material is not in its totality manifestation of social being, race, religion; but only by the standpoint "betrayed" by it can one advance through it to the absolute.

So far, the question of how the proposition material can potentially manifest a layer of being has been postponed. A brief analysis must now be devoted to an attempt to bring this question closer to solution. . . . How can a proposition have a manifestational value in addition to its immanent sense, with the three dimensions mentioned?

The sociology of knowledge answers this question, too, by pointing out that each proposition is the "product" of two components, the material of experience, which is empirically found and is accessible only in experience, and meta-empirical elements which form the objects of knowledge from this material. These meta-empirical elements, if subjected to a closer analysis, separate into several layers. First there are the ultimate formal concepts which are given with the essence of human cognition, and without which no cognition would be possible: the categories[50] superimposed on this fundamental stratum of the "primitive concepts of reason" are those metaphysically rooted convictions, ideals, and norms to which A. Weber vindicates the form of movement specific to "culture."[51] Their characteristic, although forming the *conditio sine qua non* of all science, is that they are not accessible to discursive reasoning, to science, and therefore are neither provable nor disprovable scientifically. Here the "arbitrary" component of cognition and thought is to be sought—i.e., that component which is not determined by the object but rather precedes the object, determining it. The actual cognition, which entirely follows the laws of formal logic, is fully "bound by the object." Likewise the categories given with the essence of cognition are without any "arbitrariness." But in this intermediate space between the categories and that knowledge which follows the form of movement "civilization,"[52] the "arbitrariness" of knowledge unfolds. Among other things, all metaphysical assumptions belong here. They pervade the universe of knowledge founded on them in such a way that they can be discovered more or less distinctly in every proposition. That these metaphysical assumptions are variable in the highest measure is shown by a glance at the history of metaphysical beliefs.[53] To confuse them with the categories and therefore believe that their variability proves that of the categories is the πρῶτον ψεῦσος of all theories which deny the constancy of the categories.

Besides these metaphysical assumptions, the universe of subcategorical meta-empirical concepts includes ultimate decisions on values. They, too, enter into the proposition and can be discovered in it. Like those assumptions, they are not accessible to discursive reasoning and therefore are above any scientific proof or disproof. The insight that they are in the greatest measure subject to change is owed not only to the advent of the sociology of knowledge.

Now this subcategorical meta-empirical sphere, the elements of which we have sketched very inaccurately and superficially, co-constitutes many propositions. Every object of knowledge is co-constituted by the categories, but with most of them this noncategorical layer is also operative. And in this layer of "cultural" knowledge which extends below the level of the categories one finds the starting point for the recognizability of the connectedness with being. That knowledge whose objects are co-constituted by these meta-empirical elements below the categories is called "knowledge connected with being." This definition seems to succeed in pinpointing somewhat more accurately this important concept, which is not sharply defined by the sociology of knowledge.

But on closer scrutiny it appears that an unproved assertion is implied if this phenomenon is called "knowledge connected with being": namely, the assumption that the selection of the meta-empirical elements employed in the particular case is the work of some "being," some absolute. In fact it can be shown only that atheoretical forces enter into the formation of concepts; it is not correct that the concepts can be proved to be the "product" of some layer of human existence assumed as absolute, or even of the social being, as the sociology of knowledge would claim. Atheoretical forces cannot simply be equated with the influence of an existential sphere, although the likelihood may be great that some layer of human being is operative—without any visible way of scientifically ascertaining these influences.

That the sociology of knowledge has illuminated this meta-empirical sphere is a merit that cannot and should not be denied. It has shown how deeply thought is conditioned by antecedent atheoretical decisions and value judgments, to what great extent it rests on meta-empirical, ideological premises, and how little it is above proof of its "arbitrariness," its "subjectivity" (in the "bad" sense). At the same time the sociology of knowledge has made it likely that thought is not free in this seemingly "arbitrary" sphere either, but that an influence of forces must be assumed which are not conscious to the naïve mind. But beyond this point a sociology of knowledge that understands its tasks and its limits may not go; as soon as it simply equates "atheoretical influences" with "influencing by an absolute layer" and the latter with "influencing by social being," it obstructs for itself the road to a level of problem discussion which it might otherwise well be able to reach.[54]

It is apparent, then, that "being"—which is not necessarily "social being" —is considered by the external view as a determinant of the meta-empirical layer below that of the categories—i.e., a determinant of the sphere of culture in A. Weber's sense. From this sphere the "connectedness with being" enters into the proposition and the object of knowledge.

At this point a thesis is proved which was advanced above without demonstration. It was said above that, although placing the material of a proposition into a scheme constituted by a particular basic thesis is a matter of "subjective" arbitrariness, the proposition material, once entered into the scheme, reveals a manifestational meaning which is potentially included in it. It clearly proves to be the manifestation of a definite concrete form of the absolute; hence, for the interpretation of the sociology of knowledge, of a particular class. If the basic thesis of the sociology of knowledge is assumed, the categorical imperative definitely appears as the manifestation of bourgeois and not of feudal or proletarian being. This statement, which was taken for granted, should now be examined. By what criterion is it decided whether a given proposition is to be interpreted as a manifestation of bourgeois or of proletarian being? In the view of the sociology of knowledge, is every proposition of a proletarian—to stay with proletarian thinking as an example—to be imputed to the proletariat?

This introduces into this discussion its decisive concept, which is that of imputation. The essence of the external view, *sub specie* of this concept, is the fact that it imputes an intellectual product posited by an individual, not to that individual, but to a concrete form of the layer of being which was made absolute behind the individual subject.

The correctness of the thesis advanced above, that all possible external views have equal right, also becomes evident. The subject who actually thinks the proposition—i.e., the individual—stands in many existential layers which may be posited as absolute. It is a member of a class, a nation, an age, a generation, a character type, etc. The individual thinking subject can be envisaged as the "exponent" or "agent" of all these layers. Each of these layers may be posited as the absolute; to each of them the individual's proposition may be imputed.[55] The essential necessity of a pluralism of external views therefore results also from the fact that the individual stands in a plurality of spheres that can be posited as absolute.[56]

In the view of the sociology of knowledge, which proposition, then, is to be imputed to the proletariat? Does it suffice for interpreting it as a manifestation of proletarian being that it is a proposition of a proletarian, a member of the stratum called the proletariat?

After all, the result of pure description, from which we have to start, is just this: there is given a number of judging subjects who see an intended object in different "aspects"; this difference of aspects can be traced to the fact that the several subjects start from different metaphysical premises, employ the same concepts with differing meanings, etc. Only that is result of the sober description of the given facts from which any theory of connectedness with being, any external view, will have to start out. The reason the several subjects have differing meta-empirical axioms, take a given concept in this or that particular meaning, is not visible to pure description.

Now, do all members of a class have identical axioms? Do, for instance, all proletarians have the same axioms, so that the thinking of all of them can be imputed to the proletariat?

As is found *prima vista*, it is not possible to impute factually every proposition of a proletarian to the proletariat itself.[57] Several proletarians, indusputably belonging to the proletariat, utter views so strongly divergent—even in the field of politics, where the connectedness with being is said to be especially evident[58]—that the thinking of all of them cannot possibly be imputed to the proletariat—otherwise the paradox would result that the proletariat "emanates" mutually contradictory propositions. It follows from this that there must be proletarians whose thinking cannot be imputed to the proletariat. On the other hand, there are no proletarians whose thinking is described as "proletarian."

But if not all propositions of proletarians can be imputed to the proletariat, and on the other hand thoughts coming from non-proletarians can be called specifically proletarian, where, then, in the view of the sociology of knowledge, is the criterion of true proletarian thinking? What are the requirements that a proposition must meet in order to be imputed to the proletariat?

In jurisprudence, from which the concept of imputation is taken, the problem is much simpler, for the law determines when the actions of an individual are to be imputed to a "juristic person" whose "agent" or "organ" the acting individual is considered to be.[59] But—apart from other differences between cultural sociological and juristic imputation not relevant here— the external view lacks an authority that sets definite rules which designate the actions and propositions to be imputed and the subject to whom the imputation is to be made. The answer often heard, that the thinking to be imputed to the proletariat is that which is "adequate" to the proletarian being, introduces a new concept, which, however, does not solve the problem but merely shifts it. For now it must be asked, which thinking is adequate to the proletarian being, and therefore imputable to it?

Equally unsatisfactory is the thesis that the thinking which serves the interest of the proletariat is proletarian thinking.[60] Aside from the fact that the concept of the "true proletarian interest," one would think, should be as difficult to determine as that of "adequate consciousness," to maintain that the thinking which corresponds to the interest of a class is to be imputed to it is to lapse back into the theories of the Enlightenment, into the psychological theory of knowledge.

Since the search for a criterion of the thinking to be imputed to the proletariat is unsuccessful, the question should be asked: are the social-sociological concepts of "class" and "proletariat," from which all attempts at imputation started, really adequate to the themes of the sociology of culture which are here discussed? Does not any attempt to impute some thinking to the "proletariat" as defined by the conceptual apparatus of the sociology of society constitute a hopeless undertaking from the outset? Must not the problem of imputation seem impossible to solve so long as it is based on the social-sociological definition of class as "all persons in the same class situation?"[61] Does it make any sense to try to impute to a group thus defined the propositions of the individuals constituting it? Is it really meaningful to speak of the thinking of a class which is so defined?

An analysis just slightly more accurate shows indeed that all these objections are fully justified. The analyses carried out so far have, after all, also used a quite specific concept of class. It is not identical with that of social sociology—this much can be said even before closer investigation.

It turns out that the difference between social and cultural sociology reaches into the very formation of concepts. The social-sociological concept of "class" is quite unknown to cultural sociology; it would simply not know what to do with that concept. Cultural sociology has at its disposal a specific class concept which is fully understood only if its origin is remembered. Like the central concept of cultural sociology, that of the social being, the cultural-sociological concept of "class," grew out of religious and metaphysical notions. No more than the concept of "race" is a datum of nature for the "biological" external view is class to the sociology of culture the social phenomenon which forms the object of social sociology. Rather, "class" is to cultural sociology a metaphysical entity possessing its own thought which may manifest itself in the thinking and actions of the partaking (i.e., not composing) individuals. As for Hegel, the national spirits are emanations, concrete forms, of the world spirit, not groups of individuals belonging together by virtue of some social-sociological criterion, so class is for cultural sociology not "all persons in the same class situation," but a metaphysical entity. Perhaps one might say, schematically and roughly: as social being is to the world, the class, as interpreted by cultural sociology is to Hegel's national spirit. It is the "general substantial" in which every individual must stand and from which he cannot break out. Like every nation, every class has its own principle which it is called to realize. Even more clearly than the national spirits, the classes are "links in the process that the spirit come to free recognition of itself."[62] One by one, they are the vehicles of the world spirit which emanates from itself to them. The sequence of the classes antithetically opposed to one another forms the content of world history. "Religion, science, art, the destinies of men, events"[63] are but an unfolding of class. The individuals do not think and act independently but are ontically less real parts, members of the whole.

These analogies of class (as interpreted by cultural sociology) and national spirit are not just external. Not only logically but also historically, the class concept of the sociology of culture is a modified form of Hegel's concept of the national spirit.

The specific form of the class concept with which the sociology of culture, and hence also the sociology of knowledge, operates is purely metaphysical.

The entity "class" is no more demonstrable to discursive thought than that of the Nordic race, Gothic man, the "Greek soul," etc., from which the several cultural phenomena are thought to emanate. Genetically considered, all these concepts are variants of Hegel's "principle": as with Hegel, there stands behind the particular cultural phenomena the "principle" as emanations of which they are to be interpreted.[64] Purely scientific thought is readily inclined to interpret the statement that these entities operate as real forces, and that they emanate from them the particular cultural phenomena, as a positing of a *qualitas occulta*, a constructing from the given particular mind products, a reality that is behind these products and not given empirically, which it then elevates into the *causa efficiens* of these very products.[65] The only answer to this objection that the various external views which operate with such concepts could give would be that they did not invent these entities, but that they had resulted to them as results of an immediate metaphysical vision.

One who believes that to base an important fundamental concept of a pretended science on metaphysical vision is to pass beyond the inevitable metaphysical minimum, and therefore to be burdened by a one-sided metaphysical construction, will be tempted to try to avoid the positing of a *qualitas occulta* by interpreting the proletariat (as interpreted by cultural sociology), or Faustian man, or the "Hellenic soul," etc., as a mere scheme of interpretation: the proletariat, he might say, as interpreted by cultural sociology is not an empirically demonstrable reality, but nevertheless can be construed as a conception of "objectively understandable possibilities."[66] In other words, all phenomena which are not fully intelligible to the thinking which contemplates them are reduced, as it were, to a common denominator from which, however unintelligible it may be, all cultural phenomena are then deduced. The unintelligible in the given data is concentrated in one point, not empirically given, from which all particular phenomena appear intelligible.[67] In this manner the objection of positing a *qualitas occulta* is avoided without the need of recourse to the metaphysical.

But this attempt of re-interpretation would overlook the fact that the relation between the individual (or the intellectual content realized by the individual) and the *ens realissimum* is for the external view not only a logical but also—and primarily—a real relation (see above, pp. 200–201), so that no justice is done to the nature of the manifestational relation—which claims to be a primarily real one—if one interprets as a mere figment the entity which objectifies itself in the individuals and in the intellectual contents realized by them.[68]

Now that the class concept employed in cultural sociology has been explicated a little more clearly it will perhaps be easier to solve the problem of imputation. Class[69] is for cultural sociology not the sum of the individuals but a whole, a principle, which emanates from the individuals. For cultural sociology a proletarian is not one who has a low income or a certain position in the productive process, or who lives by selling his labor power; he is a proletarian who ontically partakes of the metaphysical entity proletariat. Here the proletariat is before its members, who have existence only through it,[70] and the thinking and action of the partaking individuals are also conditioned by this $Μέθεξις$. To each particular concrete situation of the proletariat, each step of its self-realization, there corresponds a particular consciousness, not of the individual proletarians, but of the proletariat as such; namely, the consciousness which is being-adequate, or—since the concept of being-adequacy is ambiguous[71]—site-adequate; i.e., the class consciousness.[72]

And just as the individuals partake in the proletariat ontically, they partake in its consciousness, and do so even if—because of their lesser ontic reality—they never fully comprehend it. From the standpoint of the individual proletarian, class consciousness, therefore, is the ideal type of site-adequate consciousness.[73]

If, thus, not the individual proletarian but the proletariat in its totality appears as the subject of imputation, there is, on the other hand, no total anarchy among the metaphysical assumptions and valuations. Here also the object of imputation is not some isolated assumption or valuation but a whole or a system of meta-empirical concepts. In the view of the external view, it is not so that, for instance, any metaphysical assumption is compatible with any valuation in the ethical field, but groups of such belief unite into a structural unity, held together by affinity of meaning. The several axioms condition one another not—or not only—purely logically. For reasons which are meaningful, i.e., understandable, though not always explainable, propositions which are somehow "akin" combine into a unified, self-contained system, a set of axioms, a *Weltanschauung*. Such totalities of meaning, though not further explainable, are demonstrable to any plain description.[74]

Now what is imputed to particular classes are these *Weltanschauungen*, not isolated meta-empirical propositions. Therefore in cultural sociology a concrete content of consciousness is not imputed via the individual thinking subject, to the class to which the individual belongs through his class situation as established by the mean of social sociology, but, eliminating the subject, the class itself appears as the direct point of reference. As a metaphysical entity, the class possesses a form of being and a consciousness adequate to that being, a *Weltanschauung* which is adequate to it. The individual partakes of the proletariat only ontically and ontologically. Its being is a "part" of the being of the proletariat, its consciousness, its *Weltanschauung*; "part" of the consciousness, the *Weltanschauung* of the proletariat.

The sociology of knowledge—which here exemplifies all of cultural sociology, even every external view—therefore does not make the imputation in such a way that a concrete proposition—or, more exactly, proposition material—is first imputed to the individual subject positing it (as would be the "understood" naïve mode of imputation, which imputes a statement to him who makes it), and then, because that individual subject belongs by his class position to a specific class, is imputed to that class. Rather, the imputation is not made via the individual subject at all. In the view of the sociology of knowledge the proposition manifests by its set of axioms the total *Weltanschauung* standing behind it and "back-grounding" it, and this structural whole of the *Weltanschauung* is in relation of full site-adequacy to a meta-empirical entity, "proletariat" or "bourgeoisie." Thus the proposition is without mediation by the "actual" subject, directly imputed to the class by way of the total *Weltanschauung*.

But when dwelling upon this specific mode of imputation of the external view, another important fact must not be neglected. As was shown above, pp. 200–201 and 218, the sociology of knowledge thinks of the connection of proposition and class not just as a logically constructed but as an objectively existent, real connection. The proposition is not only imputed to the proletariat but also factually "produced" by it. There is, therefore, apart from the imputation relation, the real relation. This factual nexus runs so that the proletariat produces, on the one hand, the individual, and on the other hand, a specific set of ideological axioms. The proposition, which is πρότερον πρὸς ἡμᾶς, proves to be ὕστερον τῇ φύδει.

Only from this specific interpretation of the class concept by cultural sociology can the problems of imputation be solved; as long as one tries to overcome them by means of the conceptual apparatus of social sociology, they get entangled in difficulties which increase with the effort. The problems from which the present analysis started are caused only by the fact that the social-sociological concept of class is used in addition to the specifically cultural-sociological interpretation of what it is to belong to a class. This leads to the problem of how an individual who, according to social sociology, belongs to the proletariat can in his thinking determine on non-proletarian propositions, and how, conversely, a subject who in his class situation, interpreted in the way of social sociology, is not a proletarian can think in a proletarian fashion. The problem dissolves only when it is seen that two different concepts were employed *promiscue.*

With that, the problem of adequacy has not indeed been solved but nevertheless has been shifted in such a way that it is much simplified. The question no longer is whether a given proposition is directly adequate to the social being of the individual thinking subject, a question to which no answer can be found because an individual consciousness may also be site-inadequate and, in the view of the sociology of knowledge, approaches adequacy only in an infinite progression. The question is now shifted from the adequacy of the sub- and superstructure of the individual to the adequacy of the being and the consciousness of the whole class, and here the situation is simplified by the fact that the class in its totality always has a site-adequate consciousness, in the view of the sociology of knowledge.[75]

The question how the class consciousness of the proletariat as distinguished from the psychologically accessible consciousness of the individual proletarians can be definitely established does not offer any difficulty to the sociology of knowledge. The typical answer has been well known since Marx: for the group in which the particular thinker partakes with regard to being and consciousness, ontically and ontologically, site-adequation and object-adequation become one thing. The genuine, i.e., site-adequate thinking of the group, must therefore also be true, i.e., object-adequate. And since—which is the other required premise—the thinker wholly belongs to his group and is thus ontically as real as that group itself which manifests itself in him, full site-adequacy and therefore—according to the first assumption—also full object adequacy, full truth is guaranteed to his thinking. Therefore, he—i.e., the thinker confronted with this question in the individual instance—is capable of establishing the consciousness of the particular classes definitely and correctly, without difficulty.

The circularity of this argument is evident: because truth is guaranteed to all my propositions, my proposition that the knowledge of truth is guaranteed to my group is true; and truth is guaranteed to all my propositions because truth is guaranteed to the group to which I existentially belong. This is the circle on which every argument refuting the suspicion of false consciousness is based.

But without such circles the sociology of knowledge could not exist.

★   ★   ★

The analysis of some of the important basic concepts of the sociology of knowledge should be broken off at this point since this is primarily a historical treatise which should not be unnecessarily burdened by systematic investigations. Its result—to stress once more what is most relevant—has been the following:

The sociology of knowledge is a part of the sociology of culture, which in turn is a form of external view. Each discipline dealing with the connectedness with being of a culture phenomenon is to be called external view; the sociology of culture is that form of external view which has for a theme the connectedness of the phenomena of culture with social being; and that part of the sociology of culture which has for a theme the connectedness of knowledge and cognition with social being is to be called sociology of knowledge.

The specific subject of the sociology of knowledge, by which that discipline is distinguished from other parts of the sociology of culture, can here not be led toward further clarification but must be presupposed in its everyday sense. "Connected" with the social being "are" the contents of the judgments performed by which knowledge is acquired or transmitted. On the other hand, the concept by which the sociology of culture is distinguished from other forms of external view—i.e., that of social being—turns out to be a civil society, given the accent of absoluteness: as a secularized form of the world spirit, as the primarily economic structure of human existence raised to the rank of a metaphysical entity. From the fact that this concept has nothing to do with the concept of social action, which is the basic concept of the "sociology of society," there follows the nonexistence of a generic concept of "sociology" which includes both cultural sociology and social sociology.

The subsequent analysis dealt with the essence of the external view, especially the basic concepts of the several possible external views of propositions and judgments. Every external view is established by a scientifically undemonstrable and metaphysically rooted basic thesis which makes one particular stratum of being the absolute and seeks to interpret all other strata of human existence, all other culture phenomena, as ontically less real emanations of that *ens realissimum*. It follows from this pluralism of possible external views that none of them represents real relations between the absolute stratum and the emanation but that only hypothetical relations, valid if the basic thesis is assumed, are constructed. The specific relation between the absolute stratum and the culture phenomenon is not a relation of expression but a relation of manifestation, to be seen in emanative terms, a relation which is both a real and a logical relation. This manifestational meaning attaches, not to the judgment or proposition itself but to the proposition without its defining feature, the claim of validity, accessible only to the internal view, which considers the immanent meaning. It attaches, in other words, to the proposition material. Since every external view has only hypothetical character, the proposition material does not have the manifestational meaning immediately, but the latter is bestowed on it "by grace of" the basic thesis. The proposition material includes its manifestational meaning only virtually, as realized only by an intervening external view.

Further, the proposition has this potential manifestational meaning, not in addition to, but in and through its proper meaning, which also is immanent in it only latently. The objectivity intended by the proposition, the object of cognition, is in the view of the sociology of knowledge not identical with the material of experience immediately given in experience but is a selection from the infinite wealth of given data. The material is formed into the object of cognition partly by the categories which are part of the essence of cognition, and partly by meta-empirical concepts, valuations, and norms, which are established metaphysically. One particular complex of such meta-empirical convictions, held together by affinities of meaning, appears as the consciousness adequate to the situation of a group interpreted as a metaphysical entity. If some thinking subject shows by the manner in which he forms his objects of cognition that he possesses the set of metaphysical axioms which is adequate to such a group and its social being, his thinking is imputed to that group—i.e., is interpreted as an emanation of that group.

The sociology of knowledge, in conclusion, is that discipline which, assuming its specific basic thesis, seeks to interpret the contents of all propositions factually performed as a manifestation of social being.[76]

The fact that the analyses produced here start almost exclusively from the concepts developed by the historical theory, leaving in the background those resting on a positivistic basis, may be justified in a number of ways.

For one thing, the need for a greater consideration of the historical theory follows from the intention of these analyses, which, as must be stressed again and again, is primarily to make explicit the latent premises of the sociology of knowledge and to lift the set of axioms on which it rests into consciousness. Now, since most of the systems of the sociology of knowledge which exist today start from premises very close to the historical theory, there is less need to indicate the positivistic axioms distinctly.

Beyond that, however, a conception of the sociology of knowledge free of contradictions cannot be worked out on the basis of the psychological theory of the Enlightenment. For the theory which historically issued from the Enlightenment becomes, before even entering into the concrete problems of the sociology of knowledge, entangled in the basic antinomy of positivism: that by its belief that it does not believe anything, it deprives itself *a limine* of the possibility of becoming conscious of its meta-empirical premises. The result of this basic attitude is that the positivistic sociology of knowledge too cannot essentially become clear on its own prejudices and its assumptions in the meta-empirical area, and that it must remain with its delusion of being nothing but pure science. It therefore seems very doubtful whether the psychological theory is capable of exposing the metaphysical premises of the propositions it examines and of interpreting them with a view to their manifestational meaning.

But also its concrete assertions in the sociology of knowledge fail vis-à-vis the empirical experience which the naturalistic-positivistic theory acknowledges as the only criterion of truth. It is not at all demonstrable empirically that every man is induced by his economic interests to hide from his fellow man and himself the pure truth he knows. That thesis has to face other assertions which have a more solid empirical foundation, namely, "Economic interests are not alone decisive," "Man is also guided by ideals," etc. To dispute on every proposition its immanent claim to be interpreted according to its intended meaning, anti-metaphysical positivism would probably need more concrete investigations instead of the general "prejudice," carried to the material from without, that every proposition claims validity unjustly and in fact serves only the concealment of interests. An empirical theory may not start from such assumptions, which are in no way derived from experience.

Furthermore, the naturalistic thesis ventures out to the very uncertain field of motivational understanding, in which it will hardly be possible, one should think, to establish a scientific theory. Psychic understanding works —whether for essential reasons, or only today, may be left undecided—with such "unscientific" means that it is easy to dispute the scientific validity of its results as well, no matter how evident these may seem in everyday life. In addition, psychic understanding rests to such an extent on deliberate— chiefly verbal—utterances of the You that a mode of consideration which *a limine* declares all these utterances as spurious, as derivatives or cloaks, does not have much prospect of success.[77] If from the outset I bar myself from access to the You—over verbal statement—which is, after all, that which can be best controlled scientifically, I will be unable to vindicate the strictly scientific validity of my propositions about the You. And if I cannot claim this scientific character for them, it is out of the question to base the whole sociology of knowledge on them.

In other words, the psychological theory gets entangled into the difficulty, apparently insurmountable, that on the one hand it undertakes to ascertain motives which activate men in their actions, while on the other it deliberately neglects, and even declares erroneous, the statements which the individuals make about these motives, and which are the only way by which these motives are accessible to me.

Furthermore: in the psychic field into which the positivistic sociology of knowledge ventures, without having to do so, it assumes a specific hierarchy which is not at all to be taken for granted. Interests seem to it truer, more real, than "ideologies." Although both proceed from the same personality core, interest is thought to be closer to it than ideology and therefore is thought to have more "truth." Consciousness thus separates into two different spheres, that of the interests, which alone has full ontic reality, and the "derived," less real, up-in-the-clouds sphere of ideology, which is thought to be definitely determined by the former and therefore to raise its claim of validity without justification. Whether this dualism of consciousness and the distribution of the reality accent connected with it is really obtained in a purely empirical way must appear doubtful. But in addition the psychological theory removes the basis on which it stands by positing the ideology as unreal. It is led to an infinite regression: if thinking raises its claim of validity without justification, if it never can hit its intended object, how, then, can the proposition that thinking can never hit its intended object itself be true? To the extent that the psychological theory wants to reflect on the validity of a proposition by showing its conditioning by interests—and that, so far as its intention is concerned, it always does—it necessarily falls prey to the absurdity of sociologism and relativism and thereby cancels itself. The Enlightenment theory cannot show convincingly that it is not itself a cloak of economic interest and therefore raises its claim of validity with justification. This regression, from which the historical theory—if it does not forgo sociologism—can save itself by a jump into the metaphysical—a *salto mortale* if you wish—the positivistic theory cannot escape because it has totally overcome metaphysics.

To mention only one more thing, it would seem that Mannheim's thesis[78] that to stay with the partial-ideology concept in a period in which the total-ideology suspicion has arisen means to lag behind the level of problems already reached can rightly be invoked against the positivistic sociology of knowledge.

These are the main reasons that every attempt to establish a system of sociology of knowledge on a positivistic-naturalistic basis appears hopeless.

The intentions which have grown out of the concrete investigations in the field of the sociology of knowledge itself correspond to the interpretation developed here of the basic concepts of the sociology of knowledge, which by all appearances seems the only possible one. The sociology of knowledge largely operates with this conceptual apparatus, even though it may not lift it into the full clarity of reflection. Yet there are directions which reject the interpretation given here and believe that they must formulate their basic concepts differently. The last task of the present chapter is therefore to sketch a typology of the various interpretations of the basic concepts of the sociology of knowledge. To avoid burdening our presentation by tiresome, all-too-subtle casuistry, going to the finest details, only the very roughest features of such a catalogue of the possible (and factually worked out) interpretations of the basic concepts of the sociology of knowledge will be indicated.

The starting point for such a typology, in which every factually used concept of the sociology of knowledge has its logical place, is necessarily the difference, developed above, between psychological and historical theory, which reaches down into fundamental concepts. For the former theory, *consciousness is the causal product of the interests, which are determined by the socio-economic position*, while the latter describes the *superstructure as the site-adequate manifestation of social being*. Now the concept of manifestation is quite multifarious. A casuistry probing deeply enough would find that either the existence or the specification of consciousness is interpreted as manifestation of social being. In the first case the sphere of consciousness as such in its totality does not really exist ontically, but in its existence only represents a "reflection" of the absolute social being; in the second, the stratum of consciousness has its own existence, but is determined by social being in its concrete shape.

Another criterion for categorizing the theories of sociology of knowledge is provided by the fact that consciousness is either interpreted as a concrete image of the social being or is declared merely "adequate" to it, in a way not precisely described. As examples of the first—which might be called a copy theory in the sociology of knowledge—may be mentioned the assertion that the Hellenic pantheon is a "copy" or "image" of Greek particularism, or Durkheim's thesis that the categories are "images" of the social structure of the group, *"faites à l'image des chose sociales."*[79]

These examples illustrate still another difference: it is possible to maintain a connectedness with being either of the content or of the form of thinking. Either *what* is thought appears as a "product" of the social being or the *how* of thinking—"by means of which conceptual forms" or "which" apparatus of the thinking concerned—is described as "connected with being."[80] It is not possible to enter here into the details of this distinction or to clarify by examples each of the possible interpretations which are shown here only schematically.

Deeper problem layers are reached by another criterion, which divides the theories of sociology of knowledge into three groups. For there are in principle three answers to the question to which level of thinking connectedness with being extends and what relevance it therefore has for judgments and propositions. First, it may be said that "being" determines only the chance for a proposition of being accepted or being rejected. According to this view, the connectedness with being is irrelevant for the content of the proposition and for its realization; the operation of connectedness with being is dsicovered only *post festum*, in the *reception* the proposition finds after it is pronounced. This effect of connectedness with being was not discovered by the sociology of knowledge. It is part of common knowledge, expressed for a long time in poignant adages.

A greater relevance is indicated to connectedness with being by the second possible view: being is assumed to have a *selecting* relevance for the proposition. In this view, that a proposition which in itself is possible at all times is factually thought, realized, here and today, is to be interpreted as an effect of social being. But the content of the proposition is still thought of as quite independent of atheoretical influences: not the judgment but the judging is thought to be conditioned by social being, which therefore has a purely genetic relevance.

Against both of these views is a third interpretation, that social being constitutes the proposition itself, its content. The standpoint of the subject, it is said, determines, via the "aspect structure," the axioms, form, and content of the concrete proposition. As proof of this statement it is cited "that from most concrete propositions of men it can be told when and where they originated, when and where they were formulated."[81] Judging here does not mean the realizing of a free-hovering sphere of truth prexistent to any cognition but perspectivic grasp of a partial truth necessarily conditioned by the standpoint of the subject.

The contrast between the second and third views is sometimes expressed by saying that for the former view the act of thinking, for the latter the content (this term here being taken in contrast to the act, not—as above—to form), appears connected with being.

Finally, the theories of sociology of knowledge may be classified from the viewpoint of whether or not they vindicate to connectedness with being any relevance for the validity of the knowledge that is connected with being. In this respect, only two mutually contradictory positions are possible.[82] For connectedness with being either does concern the validity—the view of this school may be called sociologism[83]—or the validity of the proposition is not touched in any way by the connectedness with being. . . .

NOTES

1 The reasons are not to be analyzed here. Some hints will be found in K. Mannheim, in *Archiv für Sozialwissenschaft*, LIII.
2 Cf. P. Landsberg, "Zur Soziologie der Erkenntnistheorie," in *Schmollers Jahrbuch*, LV; and the radical adoption of the "aristocratic epistemology" in E. Landmann,

"Wissen und Werten," in *Schmollers Jahrbuch*, LIV, esp. 292ff. The concluding chapter of Freyer, *Soziologie als Wirklichkeitswissenschaft*, should also be considered in this context. Here all the problems associated with the catchwords "knowledge" and "will" would have to be tackled both historically and systematically. As hints for a historical investigation see Empedocles (γνῶσις τοῦ δμοίου τῷ δμοίῳ); Plato (e.g., *Timæus*, 37A ff.; *7th Letter*, 343E ff.); then, for example, Augustine, "non intratur in veritatem nisi per caritatem," Pascal's "logique du cœur"; in our day especially Scheler, etc.

3 Cf. the development of Rickert's system, especially with respect to the field of sociology, in H. Oppenheimer, *Die Logik der soziologischen Begriffsbildung*; and, as a criticism of that study, v. Schelting, in *Archiv für Sozialwissenschaft*, LVIII.

4 At this level of our analysis the well-known equivocations in the concept of "cognition" can be disregarded. They will be considered later, in connection with the typology of the sociology of knowledge.

5 *Einleitung in die Philosophie*, p. 218 [translated by C. F. Sanders as *Introduction to Philosophy* (New York: The Macmillan Co.), p. 276]; *Einführing in die Soziologie*, p. 18; and, in a similar sense, *Gedanken und Denker*, N.F., p. 140.

6 M. Weber, *Wirtschaft and Gesellschaft* (Tübingen, 1922), p. 1. [Translation quoted from Max Weber, *Economy and Society*, ed. by G. Roth and C. Wittich (New York: Bedminster Press, 1968), I, 4.] The problems posed by this definition, and especially by the concept of social action, need not be discussed in this context, nor does the question how "causal explanation" could be compatible with "understanding." Examples of attempts to work out an unambiguous and noncontradictory concept of sociology from M. Weber's definition are: F. Sander, "Der Gegenstand der reinen Gesellschaftslehre," in *Archiv für Sozialwissenschaft*, LIV; and A. Schütz, *Der sinnhafte Aufbau der sozialen Welt* (1932). Also Th. Geiger's article "Soziologie," in *Handwörterbuch der Soziologie*, ed. by Alfred Vierkandt (Stuttgart, 1931), which may be considered as rather representative of contemporary German sociology, maintains a view which follows M. Weber on the concept of "empirical sociology as a special science," as the sociology of society is called.

7 Even at this stage of investigation the concept of "sociology" is already so problematic that we enclose the term in quotes.

8 E. Spranger, "Die Soziologie in der Errinnerungsgabe für M. Weber," in *Schmollers Jahrbuch*, XLIX (1925), 1386.

9 Similarly Troeltsch, *Historismus*, p. 64; v. Wiese, in *Verhandlungen des 7. Deutschen Soziologentages*, p. 121. As important studies in this field cf. R. Müller-Freienfels, "Zur Soziologie und Sozialpsychologie der Wissenschaft," *Sociologus*, VII (1931), and "Zur Soziologie der Gruppenbildung in den Wissenschaften," *Sociologus*, VIII (1932), 62–70.

10 It is probably unnecessary to refute expressly a possible stricture to the effect that the present analyses assume an arbitrary and overly narrow definition in approaching their object. Their sole aim is to explicate the research intentions which guide the discipline known today as sociology of knowledge. Only the view latently underlying the sociology of knowledge itself is to be shown.

11 See especially A. Weber, "Prinzipielles zur Kultursoziologie," in *Archiv für Sozialwissenschaft*, XLVII; *Ideen zur Staats- und Kultursoziologie* (Karlsruhe, 1927); and "Kultursoziologie," in *Handwörterbuch der Soziologie*.

12 See M. Scheler, "Weltanschauungslehre, Soziologie und Weltanschauungssetzung,"

in *Kölner Vierteljahreshefte für Soziologie*, II; the "Einleitung," in *Versuche zu einer Soziologie des Wissens*, ed. by M. Scheler (Munich, 1924); and *Die Wissensformen und die Gesellschaft* (Leipzig, 1926).

13 *Hauptprobleme der Soziologie, Erinnerungsgabe für M. Weber*, I, 85.

14 A more precise definition of "culture" may perhaps be forgone in the present context. It will be sufficient to state that "culture" encompasses the several objectifications of historico-social reality—i.e. what is generally called the cultural phenomena or areas.

15 Cf. for instance C. Brinkman, *Versuch einer Gesellschaftswissenschaft* (1919).

16 On this departure of sociology from its original research intention cf. Landshut, *Kritik der Soziologie*.

17 This insight, too, is owed to Marx, who was the first to perceive the undemonstrated character of the entity "society." Cf. for instance, the "Manuscripts of 1844" (in *Marx-Engels-Gesamtausgabe*, Vol. 1/3, p. 117): "To be avoided above all is establishing 'society' once again as an abstraction over against the individual. The individual *is the social being*. The expression of his life—even if it does not appear immediately in the form of a *communal* expression carried out together with others—is therefore an expression and assertion of *social life*." [Translated and edited by Lloyd D. Easton and Kurt H. Guddat as *Writings of the Young Marx on Philosophy and Society* (Garden City, N.Y.: Anchor Books, 1967), p. 306. Emphasis is the translator's.]

18 M. Weber, *Wirtschaft und Gesellschaft*, p. 1. [Quoted from Weber, *Economy and Society*, I, 4.]

19 As not quite opportune appears the attempt to call "sociological method" a "dialectic totality view" which relates to each other as junctions the "political, social, economic, ideological levels" (H. v. Borch, "Zur Soziologie der chinesischen Revolution," in *Archiv für Sozialwissenschaft*, LXIII, 625). The reasoning given for this use of the term "sociological"—"the unity within which this functionalization takes place is society" does not seem to be entirely valid. For one thing, it neglects the fundamental difference between social sociology, which alone knows the concept of society, or better, societalness, and cultural sociology. And then it is probably not particularly suitable to derive the term for this method from "society," which is no more than the frame of all these functionalizations; with equal right it could be called "psychological," because all these connections exist in the consciousness of the individual. The same objection must be made for the distinction, proposed by E. Rothacker, between a "cultural sociology in the wider sense," as the science of connectedness with being in general, and a "cultural sociology in the narrower sense," as functionalization of the cultural phenomena to "forms of social life" (in *Verhandlungen des 7. Deutschen Soziologentages*, p. 136). One does not quite see why a discipline investigating the connectedness of the cultural phenomena with "historical being in general" should be given the name "cultural" sociology.

20 The fact that the relations which form the subject of cultural sociology would in principle not become conscious to the individuals who posit the intellectual products with seeming spontaneity is used by Scheler as an argument against M. Weber's definition of sociology: "If someone has a particular conviction concerning the divine, the history of his people, or the architecture of the heavens 'because' he belongs to the privileged estates or to the suppressed strata, because he is a Prussian official or a Chinese coolie, because he represents with respect to blood this or that mixture of races, neither he nor any other man needs to 'know' or even to 'sense' this fact" in *Die Wissensformen und die Gesellschaft*, p. 2A). This reasoning, which is quite correct as far as it goes, leads Scheler to

reject M. Weber's "restriction" of the subject of sociology to the "subjectively intended meaning." But actually such statements—which concern features of cultural sociology, not, as Scheler says, of "sociology"—do not constitute an argument against M. Weber's definition—which encompasses only social sociology, not, as M. Weber says, "sociology."

21 The analyses of which we here offer the results in condensed form cannot be reproduced even sketchily in this context; nor is it possible to examine the concept of "understanding" itself, which must be presupposed in this context.

22 The problems developing from this point—the whole problem of the You would here have to be opened up—cannot be entered into in this context. Also, the widening and transformation which the concept of motivational understanding undergoes in Freyer's concept of "physiognomic interpretation" in *Theorie des objektiven Geistes*, pp. 30 ff.) can only be mentioned but not discussed in detail.

23 The term is from Mannheim, "Ideologische und soziologische Interpretation geistiger Gebilde," in *Jahrbuch für Soziologie*, II, 424 ff.

24 "External view" as such of course does not exist any more than "cultural sociology" does; it, too, is just a formal, generic concept for the several possible external views.

25 That in fact there is hardly any other sociology than cultural sociology—and that only in very modest beginnings—is of course no objection to the following analysis. It still needs to be taken seriously, because as in every systematic investigation, the point is possibility, not reality.

26 For the sake of simplicity, only the possible external views of knowledge and cognition are referred to here; but results for the external view of the other cultural phenomena are not essentially different.

27 Cf. H. Dingler, *Der Zusammenbruch der Wissenschaften und der Primat der Philosophie*, pp. 72 ff.

28 Cf. K. Jaspers, *Die geistige Situation unserer Zeit*, p. 140: "Expressionist vision does not become cogent knowledge but remains a possibility merely, and is once more itself an expression for the essence of him who thus contemplates things." [Translated by Eden Paul and Cedar Paul as *Man in the Modern Age* (London: George Routledge & Sons, 1933), p. 180.] Jaspers, however, does not develop the consequences which follow from this for the "sciences of man"—the sociological, psychological, and anthropological external views. The thesis advanced by E. R. Curtius (in *Deutscher Geist in Gefahr* [1932], pp. 96 ff.) that, although no general statement can be made on the truth of the external views, the determinants of thought can be uncovered for each individual separately, since they depend on the "psychic structure" of the subject, seems not quite acceptable. For however conflicting the several external views may be, in one respect they are fully agreed: the "psychic structure" cannot be accepted as ultimate but is itself a "product," of whatever power, is raised to being the *ens realissimum*. But this means that the problem of the pluralism of external views arises again, since it must be asked which level should be considered the "cause" of the given "psychic structure." Thus, Curtius does not successfully dispute the need to make a choice.

29 A critique of the cultural-sociological analyses attempted hitherto would have to start chiefly from these points. The claim that cultural sociology is capable of uncovering real relations between the various cultural phenomena would have to be examined. For example, is a discipline possible that uncovers the real relationship of religion to all contemporaneous cultural phenomena—which M. Weber, among others, would

inaugurate? (It is not quite appropriate to call such a discipline "sociology of religion."—
Cf. n. 19. Of course, M. Weber sees clearly that an attempt to discover all the determinants of an economic ethics, for instance, would be a "limitless venture" in *Gesammelte Aufsätze zur Religionssoziologie*, I, 239.) The purely "spiritualistic causal interpretation of culture and of history," he says, is as "one-sided" as the "materialistic" one.
(I, 205). "Each is equally possible, but each, if it serves not as the preparation, but as the
conclusion of an investigation, accomplishes equally little in the interest of historical
truth" (I, 205 ff.). [The last two translations are quoted from Max Weber, *The Protestant
Ethic and the Spirit of Capitalism*, trans. by Talcott Parsons (New York: Charles Scribner's Sons, 1958), p. 183.] But factually it appears rather doubtful, from what has been
expounded so far, whether a "synthesis" of the "one-sidedly" "materialistic" and the
"one-sidedly" "spiritualistic" interpretations is at all possible. Since every causal chain
in principle runs into infinity, it is hard to see how any picture could be given, however
superficial, of all the determinants of even a single isolated event. Further discussion of
this view is not part of the intention of this study, as it belongs not to cultural sociology
but to cultural history.

30 E. Husserl, *Logische Untersuchungen*; K. Buhler, *Die Krise der Psychologie*.

31 On the concept of doxic modality and that of doxic modification, see Husserl, *Ideen zu
einer reinen Phänomenologie und phänomenologischen Philosophie*; Halle a.d.s., 1913, pp.
214 ff. On the thesis that the claim of validity is immanent to the proposition see,
however, Husserl, *Formale und transzendentale Logik* (1929), p. 174. A discussion of this
point is not possible in the present context.

32 As the most consistent statement of this "dual aspect theory" of propositions see Mannheim, in *Jahrbuch für Soziologie*, II, 424 ff.

33 Klages.

34 E. Cassirer, *Philosophie der symbolischen Formen*, III (Berlin, 1929), pp. 109, 108. [Trans-
lated by Ralph Manheim as *The Philosophy of Symbolic Forms* (New Haven: Yale University Press, 1957), pp. 93, 92.]

35 *Ibid.*, p. 163.

36 Husserl, *Logische Untersuchungen*, II/1 (4th ed.; Halle a.d.s., 1928), p. 41.

37 *Ibid.*, p. 31.

38 It should be kept in mind that the main purpose of these analyses is to lay bare the
intentions of the sociology of knowledge and to exhibit the logical premises and implications of that position. In this context, the question whether the meta-empirical entity
which is hypostatized into an absolute by the external view is factually existent or is a
mere construct of the external view is entirely irrelevant.

39 But it must be remembered that linguistic custom—here as in other cases—is not
entirely unambiguous and should be only employed with greatest caution.

40 Cf. the succinct formulations of the more general relation "sign-sense" in Freyer,
Theorie des objektiven Geistes, pp. 15 ff., 51.

41 Husserl, *Logische Untersuchungen*, II/1; Bühler, *Die Krise der Psychologie*.

42 It is obvious that the concept of 'Ἐποχή in this context does not have the same pregnant
meaning as Husserl's "phenomenological 'Ἐποχή" (cf. his *Ideen zu einer reinen Phänomenologie und phänomenologischen Philosophie*, pp. 55 ff.), since not only the general thesis
which belongs to the essence of the natural attitude is bracketed but in fact the validity
claim of any proposition. Here 'Ἐποχή means inability to determine anything concerning the validity claim of a proposition.

43 This pregnant phrasing is borrowed from A. Pfänder's *Logik*, where, however, it is used in a very different context.

44 From the fact that the several external views cannot be confronted there follows the need to reject the thesis advanced by M. Weber that each "interpretation of history from a particular point of view"—a concept to some extent similar to that of the external view—forms merely "a partial picture, a piece of preliminary work for full historical knowledge of a culture" (in *Gesammelte Aufsätze zur Wissenschaftslehre* [Tübingen, 1922 , p. 164). For, first, the several external views represent not real nexuses but possible relations; and secondly, neither a piecing together of these different interpretations to form one total view representing the totality of the culture nor a synthesis of their meta-empirical basic theses is possible. M. Weber himself must admit: "There is no plainly 'objective' scientific analysis of cultural life or . . . of the 'social phenomena' independently from 'one-sided' viewpoints according to which they are—expressly or tacitly, consciously or unconsciously—selected as objects of study, analyzed, and articulated for presentation" (p. 170).

45 The internal view, or "substantive hermeneutics" (Freyer), therefore has the same primacy against the external view as against historical interpretation; as immanent understanding precedes manifestational understanding, so also "the theoretical view of the object logically precedes its historical study" (H. Jecht, *Wirtschaftsgeschichte und Wirtschaftstheorie* [1928], pp. 34 ff.). Also cf. Mises, "Geschichte und Soziologie," in *Archiv für Sozialwissenschaft*, LXI.

46 This definition of the relation of the meaning of a proposition and the intended object is purposely unclear and meaningless because it wishes to be limited to the common *fundamentum inconcussum* of all directions of epistemology; the definition is an attempt to mark the common denominator of all gnosiological theories.

47 After the foregoing analyses it probably hardly needs mentioning that the expressions, for instance, that the connectedness with being "exists," "operates," "has significance," or "exerts effects" must not be taken literally but are merely abbreviations for saying, which would be awkwardly circumstantial: "One can—assuming the particular basic thesis—interpret—if one so wishes—this or that intellectual product as a manifestation of the layer of being made the absolute," etc.

48 That this interpretation actually grasps the intention of the presently existing systems of sociology of knowledge becomes particularly evident from Mannheim, "Das Problem einer Soziologie des Wissens," in *Archiv für Sozialwissenschaft*, LIII. First Mannheim energetically attacks (pp. 616 ff.) Scheler's conception of a universe of ideas existing before cognition, but finally (pp. 623 ff.) is himself forced into the position taken by Scheler: that is, the position taken by the analyses given here. It is also symptomatic that Rothacker, who starts from metaphysical premises quite different from Scheler's or Mannheim's, arrives at exactly the same conception as they (in *Verhandlungen des 7. Deutschen Soziologentages*, p. 147). Historicism, which faces a similar problem, also finally arrives at the view here sketched; cf., for instance, Troeltsch, *Historismus*, p. 43; and Mannheim, "Historismus," in *Archiv für Sozialwissenschaft*, LII, 26.

49 Scheler, *Die Wissensformen und die Gesellschaft*, p. 32.

50 It is not true that it was the sociology of knowledge which showed the variability of the categories to be an undeniable empirical fact. Jerusalem and Cosentini (in *Verhandlungen des 7. Deutschen Soziologentages*, p. 238) and Scheler and Mannheim agree in maintaining that the "belief in a timeless, absolutely unchangeable structure of our reason was shown

to be erroneous" (Jersualem, "Die soziologische Bedingtheit des Denkens und der Denkformen," in *Versuche zu einer Soziologie des Wissens*, p. 183), that Kant's table of categories is the table of categories of the European mind (Scheler, *passim*, e.g., in *Die Wissensformen und die Gesellschaft*, p. 60), etc. No attempt to prove these important theses by purely empirical studies can be undertaken with success. On the contrary, all ethnological studies said to support them prove—often against their intention—that the variability of the categories cannot be established empirically either. Only the variability of the subcategorical meta-empirical elements, which will have to be discussed and which must be admitted as a matter of course, could be shown in a relatively unambiguous manner.

Something else must be added to this. If it were assumed that the categories undergo changes, then it would not be possible for the sociology of knowledge to demonstrate these changes. For since it is a *Geisteswissenschaft* (see above, pp. 189–90 ff.), its means of cognition is understanding. But to understand a You and its utterances, however much they may have become detached from it, your form of thinking and perceiving must have at least a minimum of similarity with mine. Without this "common denominator" understanding is out of the question. Cf. for this the observation made by W. Dilthey, *Gesammelte Schriften*, V (Leipzig and Berlin, 1921–   ), 329 ff.; and also Freyer, *Theorie des objektiven Geistes*, p. 1: "A commonness of the essential structure of human nature . . . is a necessary condition of apperception in the manner of the *Geisteswissenschaften*." A kind of thinking with categories different from ours would be entirely incomprehensible to us and therefore outside the grasp of the sociology of knowledge.

Cf. further the hints in the analysis of Mannheim's system (pp. 125 ff., above) on the direction which would have to be taken by a discussion of this point, and the discussions in Mises, "Geschichte und Soziologie," pp. 493 ff., and Schelting, in *Archiv für Sozialwissenschaft*, LXII, 31 ff., aptly formulating something which, properly speaking, is a matter of course.

51 See A. Weber, *Ideen zur Staats- und Kultursoziologie*, pp. 2–3; and his article "Kultursoziologie," pp. 287A–289A.

52 See n. 51.

53 For instance, cf. Dilthey's *Weltanschauungslehre*, in *Gesammelte Schriften*, VIII (Leipzig and Berlin, 1931), which seeks access to the historical problems from this constant flux of the philosophic systems.

54 Thus, virtually all theories of *Weltanschauung* are agreed that the connection of the parts of a *Weltanschauung* is to be understood as intersystematic, and that even for explaining the change of *Weltanschauungen* a basis underlying the sphere of thought does not necessarily have to be assumed. See, for instance, Rothacker, *Logik und Systematik der Geisteswissenschaften* (1927), *passim*, and explicitly, for instance, p. 143; F. Kröner, *Die Anarchie der philosophischen Systeme* (1929), *passim*; etc.

55 However, as soon as all these concepts are employed in the external view, they assume a very specific coloring and shading, at variance with their usual one.

56 This is called, though not from the particular viewpoint of a theory of external views, "multiplicity of types" by R. Müller-Freienfels, *Allgemeine Sozial- und Kulturpsychologie*, pp. 63 ff. Also cf. Jonas, in *Verhandlungen des 6. Deutschen Soziologentages*, p. 112.

57 Since this analysis is only to serve as an example, let it be assumed that the concepts "class," "proletariat," etc., can be clearly and precisely defined by the sociology of

society. The fact that such definitions which fully satisfy scientific standards are today quite lacking does not change the essential tenets here to be proved.

58 Cf. Mannheim, *Ideologie und Utopie* (1929).

59 Note, by the way, that in the external view also—as, in fact, in every "emanatistic" theory—the individuals are called "agents" or "exponents" of the absolute who, against their wills, perform the "business of the world spirit."

60 See, for example, E. Zilsel, *Der Kampf* (1930), IV.

61 M. Weber, *Wirtschaft und Gesellschaft*, p. 177.

62 G. Hegel, *Die Vernunft in der Geschichte*, ed. by Georg Lassen (Leipzig, 1920), p. 41.

63 *Ibid.*, p. 42.

64 Cf. Hegel, *Vorlesungen über die Geschichte der Philosophie*, I, in *Werke*, XIII (Berlin, 1833), 68 ff.; and *Die Vernunft in der Geschichte, passim.*

65 Cf. Singer, in *Verhandlungen des 6. Deutschen Soziologentages*, p. 105.

66 M. Weber, *Gesammelte Aufsätze zur Wissenschaftslehre, passim.*

67 Cf. also Nietzsche: "Where our ignorance begins, where we cannot see farther, we place a word. . . . These are . . . horizon lines of our knowledge . . . (in *Werke*, *Pocket Edition*, IX, 368).

68 Rothacker's subtle analysis of "manifestational understanding" (in *Logik und Systematik der Geisteswissenschaften*, pp. 124 ff.) does not do full justice to this dual character of the manifestational relation; for it is characteristic of this relation that it is not a mere "relation of expression" (p. 124), not *only* an object of "physiognomic understanding," but also—and primarily—a real relation; as in Rothacker himself (pp. 27 ff., esp. p. 28). The same duality of real and cognitive relation is demonstrated for psychic understanding by G. Ichheiser, "Eindruck und Ausdruck," in *Kölner Vierteljahreshefte für Soziologie*, XI.

69 The concept "class" here has only the function of exemplification and stands for all units of imputation occurring in the difference external views.

70 It is not accidental that all terms of the most radical realism of universals occur in this context; for of the two roots of the sociology of knowledge, naturalism and objective idealism, the latter is by far the stronger. Marxism, too, which in its combination of Hegel and Enlightenment is a small-scale reproduction of the field of possible sociology of knowledge, takes on, even in its otherwise most radically positivistic form, a Hegelian tune whenever it turns to the question of imputation; and on the other hand the Hegel renaissance within Marxism starts from exactly this point of class consciousness. Cf. G. Lukacs, *Geschichte und Klassenbewusstsein* (Berlin, 1923), and *Archiv für die Geschichte des Sozialismus und der Arbeiterbewegung*, II, 222.

71 Since it is also employed for the *adæquatio rei et intellectus.*

72 This cultural-sociological concept of class was first developed by Lukács, *Geschichte und Klassenbewusstsein.*

73 This too, was first established by Lukács.

74 Here also belongs the structural connection of "individualism" and cosmopolitanism which was so clearly pointed out by Jerusalem. This is the reason that every sociology of knowledge presupposes a developed theory of *Weltanschauungen*. Hints at such a theory are found, for instance, in J. Fichte's contrasting of "dogmatism" and "idealism": see "Erste Einleitung in die Wissenschaftslehre," in *Werke*, ed. Medicus, III, 1–33. The real founder of the theory of *Weltanschauungen* was Dilthey: see *Werke, passim*, esp. VIII; also K. Jaspers, *Psychologie der Weltanschauungen* (3d ed.; 1925), and *Philosophie*, esp. I,

213 ff.; Müller-Freienfels; Scheler; A. Grünbaum, *Herrschen und Lieben* (1925); H. Nohl, *Die Weltanschauungen in der Malerei* (1908), and *Stil und Weltanschauung* (1920); Mannheim, esp. "Beiträge zur Theorie der Weltanschauungsinterpretation," in *Jahrbuch für Kunstgeschichte*, I; P. R. Rohden, "Die weltanschaulichen Grundlagen der politischen Theorien," in "Deutscher Staat und deutsche Parteien," *Meinecke-Festschrift*, pp. 1–35; particularly important is Rothacker, *Logik und Systematik der Geisteswissenschaften*. Also to be mentioned is Kröner's "systematology," for which see *Die Anarchie der philosophischen Systeme*; etc.

75 For site-adequacy, as we know, is not only a logical but also a real relation. The consciousness is not accidentally adequate to the being, having adjusted to it but: the consciousness is an emanation from the being and therefore conforming to it from the beginning. From the fact that the site-adequation is founded on the emanatistic relation which constitutes the existence of the superstructure it follows that the superstructure is either site-adequate or does not exist.

76 It is believed that this interpretation, which of course attains full distinctness only through the results of the analyses here carried out, grasps with some precision the intentions of the discipline which today calls itself sociology of knowledge. There can be no full critical discussion of other definitions—so far as such definitions are in fact attempted. Only that by G. Lehmann (in *Lehrbuch der Soziologie und Sozialphilosophie*, ed. by Dunkmann [1932]) will be discussed very briefly. Lehmann defines the sociology of knowledge as "science of the knowledge of the social (society as nexus of meaning and as imparting meaning), in so far as that knowledge is knowledge of culture and an expression of culture" (p. 284). A need to restrict, especially, the subject of the sociology of knowledge, i.e., knowledge, by allowing only "knowledge of the social" to become the theme of the sociology of knowledge, is not quite evident. Of course the definition given by Lehmann is, as a nominal definition, not "wrong"; but it bypasses the discipline which today calls itself sociology of knowledge and which would interpret all knowledge, not only that of the social, as "expression of culture"—as Lehmann rather imprecisely puts it. But entirely incomprehensible is his addition: "in so far as that knowledge is knowledge of culture"; for he himself says: "All knowledge . . . is, by its habit and inner structure, knowledge of culture and consciousness of culture" (p. 275). Thus there remains only the definition of the sociology of knowledge as science of the knowledge of the social in so far as it is "an expression of culture"—a definition which in no way is precise.

77 "If somebody firmly says that a certain motive is actuating him, he is right. Nobody can dispute against him the evidence of this inner connection. For where would be the platform from which this could be done?" (H. W. Gruhle, "Die Selbstbiographie als Quelle historischer Erkenntnis," in *Hauptprobleme der Soziologie, Erinnerungsgabe für M. Weber*, I, 163). For historiography, in the widest sense, the problem of motivational understanding is expecially significant; cf. for instance, G. Simmel, *Probleme der Geschichtsphilosophie* (2nd ed.; 1905), etc.

78 Mannheim, *Ideologie und Utopie*, p. 23 ff.

79 E. Durkheim, in *Année sociologique*, XII, 36 ff.

80 This differentiation is especially significant in the sociology of art, where either the subject or the style of the work of art can be interpreted as manifestation of the social being of the artist. The first is done—to give only trivial examples—by the assertion that the fact that Renaissance painting takes scenes from the mythology of antiquity as subjects

must be interpreted sociologically. For the other view, differences among various renderings of "one and the same" subject—e.g., the Crucifixion—become the object of cultural-sociological analysis. . . . But there, too, site correspondence must not be confused with object correspondence. That a work of art takes its own time as a subject and "copies" it as adequately as possible is in itself no proof that this work is a particularly correct "expression" of its time. On the other hand, from the fact the art of a stratum does not make the present its theme it cannot be concluded that that direction in art is not site-adequate. . . . The thesis that a painting, *Iron Rolling Mill*, is possible only when the fact, iron rolling mill, exists, the appearance of which is in turn socio-economically determined—this thesis is indisputable, so much so that it almost seems trivial, but it does not constitute cultural sociology. To build a sociology of art on it would make as little sense as an attempt to deduce the need for a "zoology of art" from the fact that animals can be made the subject of artistic representation. The sociology of art begins only when the question is raised why the artist chose the iron rolling mill among all things as the subject to be treated artistically—a way of posing the problem found in W. Hausenstein, in *Archiv für Sozialwissenschaft*, XXXVI, 750 ff.—and the further question of how the artistic treatment of the subject can be interpreted sociologically.

81 Mannheim, "Wissensoziologie," in *Handwörterbuch der Soziologie*, p. 662A.

82 The third possibility asserted by Mannheim, which he calls "relationism," is in fact relativism.

83 The term "sociologism," so much used, is almost nowhere fully clarified. It is true that the study by J. Schmidt-Hartefeld, *Das Erziehungsideal als Ausdruck des sozialen Lebens* (1931), attempts a clear definition. It defines "as sociologistic the overestimation of the influence of social causality on the forming of a cultural phenomenon within the social structure or on the forming of the cultural content" (p. 6). This introduces a quantitative element into the definition, which is always awkward and gives room for arbitrariness. Since this definition of sociologism is furthermore *ex professo* exclusively guided by the concept of social sociology, and therefore also conceives of "sociologism"—in the two variants of "descriptive" and "normative" sociologism—as social sociology going beyond its proper scope, it does not even touch the specific problems of the sociology of knowledge. To be sure, Schmidt-Hartefeld is *in praxi* forced to accept the problems and the conceptual apparatus of the sociology of culture to such an extent that he finally calls Marx's statement that social being determines consciousness the most succinct expression of sociologism (p. 19), but he does not realize that this blatantly contradicts his own official formulation. It cannot be said that the discussion of the concept sociologism gains any clarity by this surreptitious adoption of the problems of the sociology of culture. Thus, Schmidt-Hartefeld defines in a "summary" as the "principle of explanation and valuation" of sociologism "that of social causality upon all contents found within the social structure, the formal and material conditioning of all knowledge, culture, and values by natural causalities of the social structural laws and laws of evolution. By extending this principle of social causality to include the historical genesis of all cultural phenomena, this universalistic and positivistic theory comes to include the philosophy of history" (p. 39; cf. p. 156). The question whether this definition brings the concept of sociologism closer to clarification may here be left in *suspenso*.

Somewhat too general but not to be rejected *a limine* is the definition given by Curtius: "Sociologism is the utopian ideology of the interests of sociology in the guise of theory" (in *Deutscher Geist in Gefahr*, p. 81).

9

ERNST GRÜNWALD

The Sociology of Knowledge and Epistemology
Translated by Rainer Koehne

As "SOCIOLOGY" OF "knowledge," the sociology of knowledge reaches into the sphere of two sciences: it is sociology, and it is the science of knowledge. How its sociological character is to be interpreted was shown above [in the preceding selection]. There remains the task of analyzing its relationship to other disciplines which address themselves to knowledge and cognition. This investigation will have to be on the problems of sociologism; that is, the question of whether the sociology of knowledge can say anything about the validity of the propositions it takes for a manifestation of social being.

Were this analysis to begin by asking if sociologism is true—if it is true that the interpretation of a proposition as a manifestation of social being destroys its claim to validity—it would miss the issue. What has to be examined critically is not the material truth of sociologism but its formal lack of inner contradictions. It must not be asked whether sociologism be true—for that would already imply recognition of its possibility in principle. It must be asked, rather, whether sociologism is at all meaningful, whether the possibility exists of designing a sociologistic system free of inner contradictions.

Sociologism is comprehended in two theses: first, that all thought and knowledge are linked to the subject's being; and, secondly, that this connectedness with being bears on the validity of propositions. The latter thesis can be defined to mean that the connectedness with being destroys validity

Translated from "Wissenssoziologie und Erkenntniskritik," in Walther Eckstein (ed.), *Das Problem der Soziologie des Wissens* (Wien-Leipzig: Wilhelm Braumüller, 1934), pp. 228–35.

completely, so that every proposition so connected is wrong; which would be tantamount to saying that every proposition which exists is wrong, that there is no true proposition.

There is no need for lengthy discussion to prove that this variant of sociologism is a form of skepticism that cancels itself out and is therefore absurd. For the thesis that all thought is connected with being and therefore cannot claim truth is itself claiming truth. The content of the proposition, which asserts the impossibility of a true proposition, contradicts the form of that proposition, which implies the possibility and reality of a true proposition. This means that the proposition is paradoxical in a specific sense.[1] If all propositions are wrong, then the proposition that all propositions are wrong is wrong, and hence it is untrue that all propositions are wrong, etc.[2]

This—if you will—absolute sociologism has today largely been replaced by a more modest variant which limits the relevance to validity of connectedness with being to merely saying that the proposition, although it lacks general validity, is true "for" certain groups of men; in other words, that it has a relative, limited validity. The proposition has truth, it is said, only for the "social *lebensraum*" from which it originated; it is a "partial aspect," and that means that its area of validity is also particularized. This is often visualized by the simile of a landscape: just as a spatial object can by its essence be given only in aspects, it is of the essence of the given in general, and especially of historical and social reality, that it can be grasped only in perspectives. In this manner an attempt is made to establish a moderate sociologism, so-called relationism, supposed to lie between relativism and absolutism, "on a middle ground not discovered hitherto."[3] "Relationism" declares war on every epistemology that has existed so far as well as on every absolutism, but, on the other hand, it still somehow wants to escape the incongruities of relativism.

However strongly relationism may try to resist refutation—i.e., by the proposition that to speak of a truth *for* this one or that one is an absurdity to start with,[4] which is called "the idealistic epistemology prevailing today"[5] —by disparaging that proposition and the thinking from which it originates as the absolutizing of a partial aspect (namely, the view of the natural sciences): it remains itself an infallible proof of the correctness of this allegedly obsolete and untenable standpoint; for it claims absolute validity for this same proposition, that all thought is only relatively valid. Relationism asserts the view that everything given—this word being taken in the widest possible sense—can be grasped only in perspectives; but this proposition itself is supposed to be valid absolutely, not just for one perspective. In each proposition it advances, relationism is thus obliged to contradict its own thesis. One could say: if sociologism is true, then sociologism is wrong; if its thesis is correct, that all thought wrongly claims absolute validity, then sociologism cannot correctly raise its claim to truth either. And should relationism object, as it has not done so far, that it does not claim absolute validity for its propositions, that its whole system is only relatively true—then it would be claiming absolute validity for its propositions.

It is, after all—as relationism itself thus experiences at its "own body"— part of the very concept of a proposition to claim general validity. Even if I say that a proposition is only relatively valid, and, further, that the first assertion, that proposition A is only relatively valid, is itself only relatively valid, and so on, I must in the end arrive at a proposition that is generally and absolutely valid; if only to that, that all my former propositions claimed only relative validity. This trivial fact can perhaps be stated thus: even if a proposition claims merely relative validity, it claims that relative validity absolutely; even if the object of its claim is limited, the claim itself is absolute. If I posit a proposition, I posit its absolute, timeless validity. True, I could limit the proposition artificially, but I could do so only by asserting a fresh proposition, which again raises an absolute claim to validity, and so on *ad infinitum*.

The infinite regression which opens up behind every proposition, the absurdity which arises for every relativism from its iterability *in infinitum*, cannot pass undetected by relationism itself. But the way in which relationism tries to evade this threatening relativism is logically questionable. Relationism sees a way out of the infinite regression in the

> ... possibility of positing thought in the system of the world totality as an appearance of a greater factor and to devaluate the sphere of theoretical expression in which this inner contradiction arises. Therefore, if . . . thought (the sphere of concepts, propositions, inference, etc.) is regarded not as the sphere of the ultimate constitution of objects but as expression only, this otherwise unbridgeable contradiction is devalued. But no doubt this way of overcoming the purely theoretical contradiction is not an immanently theoretical one, and he who . . . thinks . . . from the standpoint of thought will never be able to go along with it.[6]

This argument, it must be admitted, is in contradiction to any logic known so far; for such an argument relationism must indeed create a new, "dynamic" concept of truth. So far it has not occurred to anyone to declare the devaluation of a contradiction its "overcoming." In any logic known so far, a contradiction is not overcome if I disparage its importance. In addition, the question arises, and must be taken seriously, who it actually is that posits thought as a partial appearance and by whom the sphere of theoretical expression is "devalued." Is it not thought that performs this positing, this devaluation? Is not thought, the sphere of theoretical expression, by that fact still more acknowledged as the ultimate, highest authority? Even he who does not "think from the standpoint of thought" still thinks; for him too, then, thought is the highest authority.

With regard to the infinity of the regression, the comparison to the landscape that is visible only in perspectives also proves to be incorrect. For the perspectivity of the spatial object is of only one level; for above the perspectives, each of which is valid for only one standpoint, there is the level of the generally valid propositions about this perspectivity, and all the following levels are likewise absolutely valid: the propositions about the propositions about the perspectivity, etc. But with relationism the perspectivity goes on to infinity. Not only is every proposition about an object only relatively valid; but also this proposition, that every proposition is only relatively valid, is only relatively valid; and this proposition, that the proposition that every proposition on the object is only relatively valid is only relatively valid, is again only relatively valid; and so on *in infinitum*. In other words, while in the case of a landscape a view is unambiguously related to a standpoint, and to a standpoint A unambiguously corresponds a view M, no such unambiguous coordination is possible here. For the coordinating proposition that the view M corresponds to the standpoint A and is relative to it is not generally valid but is valid only relatively to a standpoint B; and the proposition that this proposition is relative to the standpoint B is itself relative to a standpoint C; and so on in an infinite regression.[7]

The "middle ground" between relativism and absolutism on which relationism pretends to stand thus turns out to be an illusion. Relativism and absolutism are contradictory opposites with no more "middle ground" between them than exists between true and false, yes and no.

Quite apart from the fact that relationism gets entangled in all the absurdities of skepticism and relativism, it can be proved positively wrong (if such proof should still be needed). For it fails to recognize two fundamentally important facts: first, that the object of any consideration from without, and hence the object of the sociology of knowledge, is not the proposition itself but its material, and that the sociology of knowledge therefore does not deal in that area consisting of the claim to validity and cannot say anything about it; secondly, it overlooks the merely hypothetical character of the sociology of knowledge. It does not state real relationships but merely indicates possible relationships.[8]

It was shown above that I can take a stand on the claim to validity which every proposition raises only if I address myself to the significative function of the proposition concerned, since the dual concept true-false is meaningful only in that dimension. Since any consideration from without "parenthesizes" the whole immanent meaning, it cannot observe the significative function as such and therefore must remain in the ʿΕποχή vis-à-vis the claim to validity. Only if one starts from the view that the total proposition is the object of the sociology of knowledge, a view which to every sober description proves wrong *prima vista*, can one lapse into sociologism.

But the definite fallacy of the thesis of sociologism is shown still more clearly by the fact mentioned above. The connectedness with social being could have "relevance to meaning" (Mannheim) only if it existed in fact, as a probable phenomenon. But, as was shown, this is not the case: the connectedness with social being is not an existent fact but "exists" only hypothetically, conditionally, "by the grace of" the arbitrarily chosen basic thesis. It is I by whose "granting" the connectedness with social being is "founded." The descriptive finding merely yields the conclusion that different propositions start from different metaphysical axioms and that this ideologically conditioned background "betrays itself" in the particular proposition. But, beyond this undoubtable descriptive result, sociologism claims to be able to find a connectedness of the proposition with the social being of the subject. But since such a connectedness—which is what sociologism means by the misleading term "connectedness with being"—is actually not demonstrable, the incorrectness of the conclusions sociologism draws from it and its alleged "relevance to meaning" follows.

No doubt every epistemology will have difficulty in solving in a completely satisfactory manner the problem of how an objectively valid proposition can grow out of psychic acts which are in the causal nexus of the course of nature and fully determined by it. But the problem of the methexis is not just an internal affair of the sociology of knowledge but an eminently philosophic question. To demand that the sociology of knowledge solve this problem is not only to give it a task not appropriate to it, which it therefore cannot possibly solve, but also implies recognition of sociologism, the unwarranted pretension of the sociology of knowledge to be in the position of having a say on questions of epistemology and philosophy. In any case, it is to be denied that the insights of the sociology of knowledge compel "a revision of the basic assumptions of the now-prevailing epistemology."[9] In fact, the sociology of knowledge has in no way either enriched or changed the general philosophic problem of the methexis.

Thus, sociologism proves to be not only a skeptical relativism and therefore absurd, contradicting its own presuppositions, but also positively wrong, since—as a consequence of its inadequate description of the given facts—it starts from materially wrong premises. Each attempt to form a sociologism overstates the demands which can be made of the sociology of knowledge in such a way that it can only lead to a complete breakdown and thus a discrediting of the sociology of knowledge. Only if it gives up its pretension to be sociologism can the sociology of knowledge become a science.

NOTES

1 It appears rather doubtful that the "theory of logical types" developed by recent mathematical logic (Russell) can resolve this paradox, even aside from the fact that the paradox is in no way settled within mathematical logic itself. The "axiom of reducibility" by which Russell is obliged to restrict the theory of types meets strong opposition from others. (Cf., for example, Weyl, "Philosophie der Mathematik," in *Handbuch der Philosophie*, II, 40.) Let it here be assumed—in order to meet sociologism as far as possible—that the theory of types in its present form is an undisputable truth. But this theory also does not save skepticism from its vicious circle. According to that theory, the proposition "All propositions are false" is not absurd because the statement is restricted to propositions of the first level, whereas it is itself a proposition of the second level. But now total skepticism takes another step and says: "All propositions of the second level are false"—which proposition is again not absurd according to the theory of types since it is itself a proposition of the third level. But even if it is not absurd, it is nonetheless materially false since of the two propositions of the second level: "All propositions of the first level are false" and "Not all propositions of the first level are false," one must be true according to the views of the excluded third; therefore, the proposition of the third level: "All propositions of the second level are false" is itself false. (On this argument cf. O. Becker, "Mathematische Existenz," in E. Husserl's *Jahrbuch*, VIII.

An additional difficulty arises especially for sociologism. A sociologism operating with the total ideology concept would repay the theory of types for its help by "exposing" even this concept as "connected with being" and "therefore" false. Furthermore, sociologism would be shown false precisely by assumption of the theory of types because, ignoring that theory, it affirms the falseness of all propositions of all levels. Thus, the theory of types also cannot save sociologism from the reproach of absurdity.

2 This age-old argument of the peritrope is given a very succinct phrasing in K. Mannheim's early study, "Die Strukturanalyse der Erkenntnistheorie," in *Kant-Studien*, Ergänzungsheft 57 (1922), pp. 20 ff.

3 Mannheim, *Handwörterbuch*, p. 667B.

4 Husserl, *Logische Untersuchungen*, I, 117.

5 Mannheim, *Handwörterbuch*, p. 670B.

6 Mannheim, "Soziologie des Wissens," *Archiv für Sozialwissenschaft*, LIII, 581 ff.

7 K. Jaspers does not detect the faultiness of the simile of the perspectives any more than Mannheim does. He, too, fails to pay attention to the infinite regression necessarily resulting from "perspectivism." See, for example, the following noteworthy passage from *Psychologie der Weltanschauungen* (3d ed.; 1925), p. 22: "We want ... to get out of ourselves, to jump over ourselves, to discover, as it were, an Archimedean point outside of all subject-object relations to make an object of the totality of these. It is evident that this is not possible absolutely and therefore not possible at all, but the maximal mobility which we give to our subject standpoint gives us a substitute. The totality of these subject standpoints, which correct, restrict, and relativize one another, and none of which we take, must be our substitute for the Archimedean point that we ... cannot reach ... from our prison." The danger of the regression, which is clearly recognized, is to be avoided by a "sliding of standpoints" which anticipates the dynamic synthesis of Mannheim. Whether such sliding really is a "substitute" for a fixed Archimedean point beyond perspectivity is very doubtful. See also p. 144 in Jaspers.

8 See above, pp. 72 ff. and 65 ff.

9 Mannheim, *Handwörterbuch*, p. 668A.

10

JOHN DEWEY

Interpretation of the Savage Mind

THE PSYCHICAL ATTITUDES and traits of the savage are more than stages through which mind has passed, leaving them behind. They are outgrowths which have entered decisively into further evolution, and as such form an integral part of the framework of present mental organization. Such positive significance is commonly attributed, in theory at least, to animal mind; but the mental structure of the savage, which presumably has an even greater relevancy for genetic psychology, is strangely neglected.

The cause of this neglect I believe lies in the scant results so far secured, because of the abuse of the comparative method—which abuse in turn is due to the lack of a proper method of interpretation. Comparison as currently employed is defective—even perverse—in at least three respects. In the first place, it is used indiscriminately and arbitrarily. Facts are torn loose from their context in social and natural environment and heaped miscellaneously together, because they have impressed the observer as alike in some respect. Upon a single page of Spencer[1] which I chanced to open looking for an illustration of this point appear Kamschadales, Kirghiz, Bedouins, East Africans, Bechuanas, Damaras, Hottentots, Malays, Papuans, Fijians, Andamanese—all cited in reference to establishing a certain common property of primitive minds. What would we think of a biologist who appealed successively to some external characteristic of, say, snake, butterfly, elephant, oyster, and robin in support of a statement? And yet the peoples mentioned present widely remote cultural resources, varied environments, and distinctive institutions. What is the scientific value of a proposition thus arrived at.

In the second place, this haphazard, uncontrollable selection yields only

Psychological Review, IX (May, 1902), 217–30. Reprinted by permission of the American Psychological Association.

static facts—facts which lack the dynamic quality necessary to a genetic consideration. The following is a summary of Mr. Spencer's characterizations of primitive man, emotional and intellectual:

He is explosive and chaotic in feeling, improvident, childishly mirthful, intolerant of restraint, with but small flow of altruistic feeling, attentive to meaningless detail, and incapable of selecting the facts from which conclusions may be drawn, with feeble grasp of thought, incapable of rational surprise, incurious, lacking in ingenuity and constructive imagination. Even the one quality which is stated positively, namely, keenness of perception, is interpreted in a purely negative way, as a character antagonistic to reflective development. "In proportion as the mental energies go out in restless perception, they cannot go out in deliberate thought." And this from a sensationalist in psychology!

Such descriptions as these also bear out my first point. Mr. Spencer himself admits frequent and marked discrepancies, and it would not be difficult to bring together a considerable mass of proof-texts to support the exact opposite of each of his assertions. But my point here is that present civilized mind is virtually taken as a standard, and savage mind is measured off on this fixed scale.

It is no wonder that the outcome is negative; that primitive mind is described in terms of "lack," "absence": its traits are incapacities. Qualities defined in such fashion are surely useless in suggesting, to say nothing of determining, progress and are correspondingly infertile for genetic psychology, which is interested in becoming, growth, development.

The third remark is that the results thus reached, even passing them as correct, yield only loose aggregates of unrelated traits—not a coherent scheme of mind. We do not escape from an inorganic conglomerate conception of mind by just abusing the "faculty" psychology. Our standpoint must be more positive. We must recognize that mind has a pattern, a scheme of arrangement in its constituent elements, and that it is the business of a serious comparative psychology to exhibit these patterns, forms, or types in detail. By such terms, I do not mean anything metaphysical: I mean to indicate the necessity of a conception such as is a commonplace with the zoologist. Terms like "articulate" or "vertebrate," "carnivore" or "herbivore," are "pattern" terms of the sort intended. They imply that an animal is something more than a random composite of isolated parts, made by taking an eye here, an ear there, a set of teeth somewhere else. They signify that the constituent elements are arranged in a certain way; that in being co-adapted to the dominant functions of the organism they are of necessity co-related with one another. Genetic psychology of mind will advance only as it discovers and specifies generic forms or patterns of this sort in psychic morphology.

It is a method for the determination of such types that I wish to suggest here. The biological point of view commits us to the conviction that mind, whatever else it may be, is at least an organ of service for the control of environment in relation to the ends of the life process.

If we search in any social group for the special functions to which mind is thus relative, occupations at once suggest themselves.[2] Occupations determine the fundamental modes of activity, and hence control the formation and use of habits. These habits, in turn, are something more than practical and overt. "Apperceptive masses" and associational tracts of necessity conform to the dominant activities. The occupations determine the chief modes of satisfaction, the standards of success and failure. Hence they furnish the working classifications and definitions of value; they control the desire processes. Moreover, they decide the sets of objects and relations that are important, and thereby provide the content or material of attention and the qualities that are interestingly significant. The directions given to mental life thereby extend to emotional and intellectual characteristics. So fundamental and pervasive is the group of occupational activities that it affords the scheme or pattern of the structural organization of mental traits. Occupations integrate special elements into a functioning whole.

Because the hunting life differs from, say, the agricultural, in the sort of satisfactions and ends it furnishes, in the objects to which it requires attention, in the problems it sets for reflection and deliberation, as well as in the psychophysic coordinations it stimulates and selects, we may well speak, and without metaphor, of the hunting psychosis or mental type. And so of the pastoral, the military, the trading, the manually productive (or manufacturing) occupations, and so on. As a specific illustration of the standpoint and method, I shall take the hunting vocation, and that as carried on by the Australian aborigines. I shall try first to describe its chief distinguishing marks; and then to show how the mental pattern developed is carried over into various activities, customs, and products, which on their face have nothing to do with the hunting life. If a controlling influence of this sort can be made out—if it can be shown that art, war, marriage, etc., tend to be psychologically assimilated to the pattern developed in the hunting vocation —we shall thereby get an important method for the interpretation of social institutions and cultural resources—a psychological method for sociology.

The Australian lives in an environment on the whole benign, without intense or violent unfavorable exhibition of natural forces (save in alternations of drought and flood in some portions), not made dangerous by beasts of prey, and with a sufficient supply of food to maintain small groups in a good state of nutrition though not abundant enough to do this without continual change of abode. The tribes had no cultivated plants, no domesticated animals (save the dingo dog), hence no beasts of burden, and no knowledge or use of metals.[3]

Now as to the psychic pattern formed under such circumstances. How are the sensory-motor coordinations common to all men organized, how stimulated and inhibited into relatively permanent psychic habits, through the activities appropriate to such a situation?

By the nature of the case, food and sex stimuli are the most exigent of all excitants to psychophysic activity, and the interests connected with them are the most intense and persistent. But with civilized man, all sorts of intermediate terms come in between the stimulus and the overt act, and between the overt act and the final satisfaction. Man no longer defines his end to be the satisfaction of hunger as such. It is so complicated and loaded with all kinds of technical activities, associations, deliberations, and social divisions of labor that conscious attention and interest are in the process and its content. Even in the crudest agriculture, means are developed to the point where they demand attention on their own account and control the formation and use of habits to such an extent that they are the central interests, while the food process and enjoyment as such are incidental and occasional.

The gathering and saving of seed, preparing the ground, sowing, tending, weeding, care of cattle, making of improvements, continued observation of times and seasons, engage thought and direct action. In a word, in all post-hunting situations the end is mentally apprehended and appreciated, not as food satisfaction, but as a continuously ordered series of activities and of objective contents pertaining to them. And hence the direct and personal display of energy, personal putting forth of effort, personal acquisition and use of skill are not conceived or felt as immediate parts of the food process. But the exact contrary is the case in hunting. There are no intermediate appliances, no adjustment of means to remote ends, no postponements of satisfaction, no transfer of interest and attention over to a complex system of acts and objects. Want, effort, skill, and satisfaction stand in the closest relations to one another. The ultimate aim and the urgent concern of the moment are identical; memory of the past and hope for the future meet and are lost in the stress of the present problem; tools, implements, weapons, are not mechanical and objective means but are part of the present activity, organic parts of personal skill and effort. The land is not a means to a result but an intimate and fused portion of life—a matter, not of objective inspection and analysis, but of affectionate and sympathetic regard. The making of weapons is felt as a part of the exciting use of them. Plants and animals are not "things," but are factors in the display of energy and form the contents of most intense satisfactions. The "animism" of primitive mind is a necessary expression of the immediacy of relation existing between want, overt activity, that which affords satisfaction, and the attained satisfaction itself. Only when things are treated simply as *means*, are marked off and held off against remote ends, do they become "objects."

Such immediacy of interest, attention, and deed is the essential trait of the nomad hunter. He has no cultivated plants, no system of appliances and tending and regulating plants and animals; he does not even anticipate the future by drying meat. When food is abundant, he gorges himself, but does not save. His habitation is a temporary improvised hut. In the interior, he does not even save skins for clothes in the cold of winter but cooks them with the rest of the carcass. Generally even by the water he has no permanent boats, but makes one of bark when and as he needs it. He has no tools or equipment except those actually in use at the moment of getting or using food—weapons of the chase and war. Even set traps and nets which work for the savage are practically unknown. He catches beast, bird, and fish with his own hands when he does not use club or spear; and if he uses nets he is himself personally concerned in their use.

Now such facts as these are usually given a purely negative interpretation. They are used as proofs of the incapacities of the savage. But in fact they are parts of a very positive psychosis which, taken in itself and not merely measured against something else, requires and exhibits highly specialized skill and affords intense satisfactions—psychical and social satisfactions, not merely sensuous indulgencies. The savage's repugnance to what we term a higher plane of life is not due to stupidity or dullness or apathy or to any other merely negative qualities—such traits are a later development and fit the individual only too readily for exploitation as a tool by "superior races." His aversion is due to the fact that in the new occupations he does not have so clear or so intense a sphere for the display of intellectual and practical skill, or such opportunity for a dramatic plan of emotion. Consciousness, even if superficial, is maintained at a higher intensity.[4]

The hunting life is of necessity one of great emotional interest, and of adequate demand for acquiring and using highly specialized skills of sense, movement, ingenuity, strategy, and combat. It is hardly necessary to argue the first point. Game and sport are still words that mean the most intense immediate play of the emotions, running their entire gamut. And these terms still are applied most liberally and most appropriately to hunting. The transferred application of the hunting language to pursuit of truth, plot interest, business adventure and speculation, to all intense and active forms of amusement, to gambling and the "sporting life," evidences how deeply imbedded in later consciousness is the hunting pattern or schema.[5]

The interest of the game, the alternate suspense and movement, the strained and alert attention to stimuli always changing, always demanding graceful, prompt, strategic, and forceful response; the play of emotions along the scale of want, effort, success or failure—this is the very type, psychically speaking, of the drama. The breathless interest with which we hang upon the movement of play or novel are reflexes of the mental attitudes evolved in the hunting vocation.

The savage loses nothing in enjoyment of the drama because it means life or death to him.[6] The emotional interest in the game itself is moreover immensely reinforced and deepened by its social accompaniments. Skill and success means applause and admiration; they mean the possibility of lavish generosity—the quality that wins all. Rivalry and emulation and vanity all quicken and feed it. It means sexual admiration and conquests—more wives or more elopements. It means, if persistent, the ultimate selection of the individual for all tribal positions of dignity and authority,

But perhaps the most conclusive evidence of the emotional satisfactions involved is the fact that the men reserve the hunting occupation to themselves and give to the women everything that has to do with the vegetable side of existence (where the passive subject matter does not arouse the dramatic play), and all activity of every sort that involves the more remote adaptation of means to ends—and hence drudgery.[7]

The same sort of evidence is found in the fact that, with change to agricultural life, other than hunting types of action are (if women do not suffice) handed over to slaves, and the energy and skill acquired to go into the game of war. This also explains the apparent contradiction in the psychic retrogression of the mass with some advances in civilization. The gain is found in the freed activities of the few, and in the cumulation of the objective instrumentalities of social life, and in the final development, under the discipline of subjection, of new modes of interest having to do with remoter ends—considerations, however, which are psychologically realized by the mass only at much later periods.

As to the high degree of skill, practical and intellectual, stimulated and created by the hunting occupation, the case is equally clear—provided, that is, we bear in mind the types of skill appropriate to the immediate adjustments required, and do not look for qualities irrelevant because useless in such a situation.

No one has ever called a purely hunting race dull, apathetic, or stupid. Much has been written regarding the aversion of savages to higher resources of civilization—their refusal to adopt iron tools or weapons, for example, and their sodden absorption in routine habits. None of this applies to the Australian or any other *pure* hunting type. Their attention is mobile and fluid as is their life; they are eager to the point of greed for anything which will fit into their dramatic situations as so to intensify skill and increase emotion. Here again the apparent discrepancies strengthen the case. It is when the native is forced into an alien use of the new resources, instead of adapting them to his own ends, that his workmanship, skill, and artistic taste uniformly degenerate.

Competent testimony is unanimous as to the quickness and accuracy of apprehension evinced by the natives in coming in contact even for the first time with complicated constructive devices of civilized man, provided only these appliances have a direct or immediate action-index. One of the commonest remarks of travelers, hardly prepossessed in favor of the savage, is their superiority in keenness, alertness, and a sort of intelligent good humor to the average English rustic. The accuracy, quickness, and minuteness of perception of eye, ear, and smell are no barren accumulation of meaningless sense detail, as Spencer would have it; they are the cultivation to the highest point of skill and emotional availability of the instrumentalities and modes of a dramatic life. The same applies to the native's interest in hard and sustained labor, to his patience and perseverance as well as to his gracefulness and dexterity of movement—the latter extending to fingers and toes to an extent which makes even skilled Europeans awkward and clumsy. The usual denial of power of continued hard work, of patience, and of endurance to the savage is based once more upon trying him by a foreign standard—interest in ends which involve a long series of means detached from all problems of purely personal adjustment. Patience and persistence and long-maintained effort the savage does show when they come within the scope of that immediate contest situation with reference to which his mental pattern is formed.

I hardly need say, I suppose, that in saying these things I have no desire to idealize savage intelligence and volition. The savage paid for highly specialized skill in all matters of personal adjustment by incapacity in all that is impersonal, that is to say, remote, generalized, objectified, abstracted. But my point is that we understand their incapacities only by seeing them as the obverse side of positively organized developments; and, still more, that it is only by viewing them primarily in their positive aspect that we grasp the genetic significance of savage mind for the long and tortuous process of mental development, and secure from its consideration assistance in comprehending the structure of present mind.

I come now to a brief consideration of the second main point—the extent to which this psychic pattern is carried over into all the relations of life, and becomes emotionally an assimilating medium. First, take art. The art of the Australian is not constructive, not architectonic, not graphic, but dramatic and mimetic.[8] Every writer who has direct knowledge of the Australian corroborees, whether occasional and secular or state and ceremonial, testifies to the remarkable interest shown in dramatic representation. The reproduction by dances of the movements and behavior of the animals of the chase is startling. Great humor is also shown in adapting and reproducing recent events and personal traits. These performances are attended with high emotional attacks; and all the accompaniments of decoration, song, music, spectators' shouts, etc., are designed to revive the feelings appropriate to the immediate conflict-situations which mean so much to the savage. Novelty is at a distinct premium; old songs are discarded; one of the chief interests at an intertribal friendly meeting is learning new dance songs; and acquisition of a new one is often sufficient motive for invitation to a general meeting.

The ceremonial corroborees are of course more than forms of art.[9] We have in them the sole exception to the principle that the activities of the hunter are immediate. Here they are weighted with a highly complicated structure of elaborated traditional rites—elaborated and complicated almost beyond belief.[10] But it is an exception which proves the rule. This apparatus of traditionary agencies has no reference to either practical or intellectual control, it gets nowhere objectively. Its effect is just to reinstate the emotional excitations of the food conflict situations; and particularly to frame in the young the psychic disposition which will make them thoroughly interested in the necessary performances.[11]

It is a natural transition to religion. Totemism and the abundance of plant and animal myths (especially the latter) and the paucity of cosmic and cosmogonic myths testify to the centering of attention upon the content of the combat, or hunting, situation. It would be absurd to attempt in a parenthesis an explanation of totemism, but certainly any explanation is radically defective which does not make much of the implication of tribe and animal in the same emotional situation. Hunter and hunted are the factors of a single tension; the mental situation cannot be defined except in terms of both. If animals get away, it is surely because they try; and, if they are caught, it is surely because after all they are not totally averse—they are friendly. And they seal their friendliness by sharing in one of the most intense satisfactions of life—savory food to the hungry. They are, as a matter of fact, co-partners in the life of the group. Why, then, should they not be represented as of close kin? In any case, attention and interest center in animals more persistently than in anything else; and they afford the content of whatever concentrated intellectual activity goes on. The food taboos, with their supernatural sanctions, certainly create tensions or reinstate conflict-situations in the mind and thus serve to keep alive in consciousness values which otherwise would be more nearly relegated to the mechanically habitual, or become sensuous, not idealized or emotionalized.

I turn now to matters of death and sickness, their cause and cure, or, if cure is hopeless, their remedy by expiation. Here the assimilation to the psychosis of the hunting activity is obvious. Sickness and death from sickness are uniformly treated as the results of attacks of other persons, who with secret and strange weapons are hunting their victim to his death. And the remedy is to hunt the hunter, to get the aid of that wonderful pursuer and tracker, the medicine man, who by superior ability runs down the guilty party, or with great skill hunts out the deadly missile or poison lodged in the frame of his victim.

If death ensues, then we have the devices for tracking and locating the guilty party. And then comes actual conflict, actual man-hunting. Death can be avenged only by the ordeal of battle—and here we have the explanation of the wars and warlike performances of which so much has been made. It is, however, now generally admitted that the chief object of these warlike meetings is to reinstate the emotion of conflict rather than to kill. They are, so to speak, psychological duels on a large scale—as one observer says, they are "fights with a maximum of noise, boast, outward show of courage, and a minimum of casualties."[12] But the maneuvering, throwing, and dodging that take place are a positive dramatic exercise in the utilities of their occupational pursuits.

Finally, as to marriage and the relations between the sexes. What was said concerning the impossibility of an adequate account of totemism applies with greater force to the problem of the system of group relationships which determine marital possibilities. It is clear, however, that the system of injunctions and restrictions serves to develop a scheme of inhibitions and intensified stimuli which makes sex satisfaction a matter of pursuit, conflict, victory, and trophy over again. There is neither complete absence of inhibition, which, involving little personal adjustment, does not bring the sexual sensations into the sphere of emotion as such; nor is there a system of voluntary agreement and affection, which is possible only with a highly developed method of intellectual control, and large outlooks upon a long future. There is just the ratio between freedom and restraint that develops the dramatic instinct and gives courtship and the possession of women all the emotional joys of the hunt—personal display, rivalry, enough exercise of force to stimulate the organism; and the emotion of prowess joined to the physical sensations of indulgence. Here, as elsewhere in the hunting psychosis, novelty is at a premium, for the mind is dependent upon a present or immediate stimulus to get activity going. It requires no deep scientific analysis to inform us that sex relations are still largely in the dramatized stage; and the play of emotion which accompanies the enacting of the successive stages of the drama gives way to genuine affection and intelligent foresight only slowly, through great modifications of the whole educative and economic environment. Recent writers, I think, in their interest in the institutional side of marriage (for we are going through a period of reading back Aryan legal relationships just as we formerly read back Aryan theogonies and mythologies), have overlooked the tremendous importance of the immediate play of psychic factors congruous to hunting as such.[13]

In conclusion, let me point out that the adjustment of habits to ends, through the medium of a problematic, doubtful, precarious situation, is the structural form upon which present intelligence and emotion are built. It remains the ground pattern. The further problem of genetic psychology is then to show how the purely immediate personal adjustment of habit to direct satisfaction in the savage became transformed through the introduction of impersonal, generalized, objective instrumentalities and ends; how it ceased to be immediate and became loaded and surcharged with a content which forced personal want, initiative, effort, and satisfaction further and further apart, putting all kinds of social divisions of labor, intermediate agencies, and objective contents between them. This is the problem of the formation of mental patterns appropriate to agricultural, military, professional, technological, and trade pursuits, and the reconstruction and overlaying of the original hunting schema.

But by these various agencies we have not so much destroyed or left behind the hunting structural arrangement of mind as we have set free its constitutive psychophysic factors so as to make them available and interesting in all kinds of objective and idealized pursuits—the hunt for truth, beauty, virtue, wealth, social well-being, and even for heaven and for God.

NOTES

1 In *Sociology*, I, 57.

2 We might almost say, in the converse direction, that biological genera are "occupational" classifications. They connote different ways of getting a living with the different instrumentalities (organs) appropriate to them, and the different associative relations set up by them.

3 All these points are important, for the general hunting psychosis exhibits marked differentiations when developed in relation to ferocious beasts; in relation to a very sparse or very abundant food supply; in relation to violently hostile natural forces; and when hunting is pusued in connection with various degrees of agriculture or domesticated herds or flocks. For economy of space, I have omitted reference to the few portions of Australia where the food supply (generally fish in such circumstances) is sufficiently abundant to permit quasi-permanent abodes, though the psychological variations thus induced are interesting.

4 For good statements by competent authorities of the Australian's aversion to agriculture, etc., see Hodginkson, *Australia, from Port Macquaria to Moreton Bay*, p. 243; and Grey, *Two Expeditions*, etc., II, 279.

5 See Thomas's "The Gaming Instinct," *American Journal of Sociology*, VI, 750. I am indebted to Dr. Thomas (through personal conversation as well as from his articles) for not only specific suggestions, but for the point of view here presented to such an extent that this article is virtually a joint contribution.

6 Though some writers even say that the savage's interest in the game of hunting is so great that he hunts for the excitement rather than for food. See Lumholtz, *Among Cannibals*, pp. 161 and 191.

7 This collateral development of a different mental pattern in women is a matter of the greatest significance, in itself, in its relation to subsequent developments, and in relation to present mental interests.

8 There are, of course, pictures, but, comparatively speaking, few and crude. Even the carvings, if originally pictorial, have mostly lost that quality and become conventional.

9 It is, of course, a historic fact that the actual origin of dramatic art (through the Greeks) is in mimetic dances of a festival and ceremonial sort.

10 The best account is, of course, Spencer and Gillen. Certain ceremonies take weeks.

11 Not, of course, that all these ceremonies are initiatory in character; on the contrary, many are "magical," intended to promote the productivity of their chief food supplies. But even these were conducted in dramatic fashion, and in such way as to reproduce the emotional disposition involved in the actual occupational life.

12 Horn, *Expedition*, IV, 36.

13 For a statement doing justice to the psychophysic factors involved, see Thomas, "Der Ursprung der Exogamie," *Zeitschrift für Socialwissenschaft*, V, 1.

II

GEORGE HERBERT MEAD

A Behavioristic Account of the Significant Symbol

THE STATEMENT I wish to present rests upon the following assumptions, which I can do no more than state: I assume, provisionally, the hypothesis of the physical sciences, that physical objects and the physical universe may be analyzed into a complex of physical corpuscles. I assume that the objects of immediate experience exist in relationship to the biologic and social individuals whose environments they make up. This relationship involves on the one hand the selection through the sensitivities and reactions of the living forms of those elements that go to make up the object. On the other hand these objects affect the plants and animals whose natures are responsible for them as objects; e.g., food exists as an immediate experience in its relation to the individuals that eat it. There is no such thing as food apart from such individuals. The selection of the characters which go to make up food is a function of living individuals. The effect of this food upon the living individuals is what we call adaptation of the form to the environment or its opposite. Whatever may be said of a mechanical universe of ultimate physical particles, the lines that are drawn about objects in experience are drawn by the attitudes and conduct of individual living forms. Apart from such an experience involving both the form and its environment, such objects do not exist.

On the other hand, these objects exist objectively, as they are in immediate experience. The relation of objects making up an environment to the plants and the animals in no sense renders these objects subjective. What are termed

Journal of Philosophy, XIX (1922), 157–63. Reprinted by permission of *The Journal of Philosophy*.

the natures of objects are in the objects, as are their so-called sensuous qualities, but these natures are not in the objects either as external or internal relations; they are of the very essence of the objects and become relations only in the thought process. The so-called sensuous qualities exist also in the objects, but only in their relations to the sensitive organisms whose environments they form.

The causal effect of the living organisms on their environment in creating objects is as genuine as the effect of the environment upon the living organism. A digestive tract creates food as truly as the advance of a glacial cap wipes out some animals or selects others which can grow warm coats of hair. An animal's sensitiveness to a particular character in an object gives the object in its relation to the animal a peculiar nature. Where there is sensitiveness to two or more different characters of the object, answering to reactions that conflict and thus inhibit each other, the object is in so far analyzed. Thus the width of a stream would be isolated from the other characters of the stream through the inhibition of the animal's tendency to jump over it. In the immediate experience in which the animal organism and its environment are involved, these characters of the objects and the inhibited reactions that answer to them are there or exist as characters, though as yet they have no significance nor are they located in minds or consciousnesses.

Among objects in the immediate experience of animals are the different parts of their own organisms, which have different characters from those of other objects—especially hedonic characters and those of stresses and excitements—but characters, not referred to selves until selves arise in experience. They are only accidentally private—i.e., necessarily confined to the experience of single individuals. If—after the fashion of the Siamese Twins—two organisms were so joined that the same organ were connected with the central nervous system of each, each would have the same painful or pleasurable object in experience. A toothache or a pleased palate are objects for a single individual for reasons that are not essentially different from those which make the flame of a match scratched in a room in which there is only one individual an object only for that individual. It is not the exclusion of an object from the experience in which others are involved which renders it subjective; it is rendered subjective by being referred by an individual to his self, when selves have arisen in the development of conduct. Exclusive experiences are peculiarly favorable for such reference, but characteristics of objects for everyone may be so referred in mental processes.

Among objects that exist only for separate individuals are so-called images. They are *there*, but are not necessarily *located* in space. They do enter into the structure of things, as notably on the printed page or in the hardness of a distant object; and in hallucinations they may be spatially located. They are dependent for their existence upon conditions in the organism—especially those of the central nervous system—as are other objects in experience, such as mountains and chairs. When referred to the self they become memory images, or those of a creative imagination, but they are not mental or spiritual stuff.

Conduct is the sum of the reactions of living beings to their environments, especially to the objects that their relation to the environment has "cut out of it," to use a Bergsonian phrase. Among these objects are certain that are of peculiar importance to which I wish to refer—viz., other living forms which belong to the same group. The attitudes and early indications of actions of these forms are peculiarly important stimuli and, to extend a Wundtian term, may be called "gestures." These other living forms in the group to which the organism belongs may be called social objects and exist as such before selves come into existence. These gestures call out definite and, in all highly organized forms, partially predetermined reactions, such as those of sex, of parenthood, of hostility, and possibly others, such as the so-called herd instincts. In so far as these specialized reactions are present in the nature of individuals, they tend to arise whenever the appropriate stimulus or gesture calls them out. If an individual uses such a gesture, and he is affected by it as another individual is affected by it, he responds or tends to respond to his own social stimulus, as another individual would respond. A notable instance of this is in the song or vocal gesture of birds. The vocal gesture is of peculiar importance because it reacts upon the individual who makes it in the same fashion that it reacts upon another, but this is also true in a less degree of those of one's own gestures that he can see or feel.

The self arises in conduct when the individual becomes a social object in experience to himself. This takes place when the individual assumes the attitude or uses the gesture which another individual would use and responds to it himself, or tends so to respond. It is a development that arises gradually in the life of the infant and presumably arose gradually in the life of the race. It arises in the life of the infant through what is unfortunately called imitation and finds its expression in the normal play life of young children. In the process the child gradually becomes a social being in his own experience, and he acts toward himself in a manner analogous to that in which he acts toward others. Especially he talks to himself as he talks to others, and in keeping up this conversation in the inner forum constitutes the field which is called that of mind. Then those objects and experiences which belong to his own body, those images which belong to his own past, become part of this self.

In the behavior of forms lower than man, we find one individual indicating objects to other forms, though without what we term signification. The hen that pecks at the angleworm is directly though without intention indicating it to the chicks. The animal in a herd that scents danger in moving away indicates to the other members of the herd the direction of safety and puts them in the attitude of scenting the same danger. The hunting dog points to the hidden bird. The lost lamb that bleats and the child that cries each points himself out to his mother. All of these gestures, to the intelligent observer, are significant symbols, but they are none of them significant to the forms that make them.

In what does this significance consist in terms of a behavioristic psychology? A summary answer would be that the gesture not only actually brings the stimulus-object into the range of the reactions of other forms, but that the nature of the object is also indicated; especially do we imply in the term "significance" that the individual who points out indicates the nature to *himself*. But it is not enough that he should indicate this meaning—whatever meaning is—as it exists for himself alone, but that he should indicate the meaning as it exists for the other to whom he is pointing it out. The widest use of the term implies that he indicates the meaning to any other individual to whom it might be pointed out in the same situation. In so far, then, as the individual takes the attitude of another toward himself, and in some sense arouses in himself the tendency to the action that his conduct calls out in the other individual, he will have indicated to himself the meaning of the gesture. This implies a definition of meaning—that it is an indicated reaction that the object may call out. When we find that we have adjusted ourselves to a comprehensive set of reactions toward an object, we feel that the meaning of the object is ours. But that the meaning may be ours, it is necessary that we should be able to regard ourselves as taking this attitude of adjustment to response. We must indicate to ourselves not only the object but also the readiness to respond in certain ways to the object, and this indication must be made in the attitude or role of the other individual to whom it is pointed out or to whom it may be pointed out. If this is not the case, it has not that common property that is involved in significance. It is through the ability to be the other at the same time that he is himself that the symbol becomes significant. The common statement of this is that we have in mind what we indicate to another that he shall do. In giving directions, we give the direction to ourselves at the same time that we give it to another. We assume also his attitude of response to our requests, as an individual to whom the direction has the same signification in his conduct that it has to ourselves.

But signification is not confined to the particular situation within which an indication is given. It acquires universal meaning. Even if the two are the only ones involved, the form in which it is given is universal—it would have the same meaning to any other who might find himself in the same position. How does this generalization arise? From the behavioristic standpoint it must take place through the individual's generalizing himself in his attitude of the other. We are familiar enough with the undertaking in social and moral instruction to children and to those who are not children. A child acquires the sense of property through taking what may be called the attitude of the generalized other. Those attitudes which all assume in given conditions and over against the same objects become for him attitudes which everyone assumes. In taking the role which is common to all, he finds himself speaking to himself and to others with the authority of the group. These attitudes become axiomatic. The generalization is simply the result of the identity of responses. Indeed, it is only as he has in some sense amalgamated the attitudes of the different roles in which he has addressed himself that he acquires the unity of personality. The "me" that he addresses is constantly varied. It answers to the changing play of impulse, but the group solidarity, especially in its uniform restrictions, gives him the unity of universality. This I take to be the sole source of the universal. It quickly passes the bounds of the specific group. It is the vox populi, vox dei, the "voice of men and of angels." Education and varied experience refine out of it what is provincial, and leave "what is true for all men at all times." From the first, its form is universal, for differences of the different attitudes of others wear their peculiarities away. In the play period, however, before the child has reached that of competitive games—in which he seeks to pit his own acquired self against others —in the play period this process is not fully carried out, and the child is as varied as his varying moods; but in the game he sees himself in terms of the group or the gang and speaks with a passion for rules and standards. Its social advantage and even necessity makes this approach to himself imperative. He must see himself as the whole group sees him. This again has passed under the head of passive imitation. But it is not in uniform attitudes that universality appears as a recognized factor in either inner or outer behavior. It is found rightly in thought, and thought is the conversation of this generalized other with the self.

The significant symbol is, then, the gesture, the sign, the word that is addressed to the self when it is addressed to another individual, and is addressed to another, in form to all other individuals, when it is addressed to the self.

Significance has, as we have seen, two references, one to the thing indicated and the other to the response, to the instance, and to the meaning or idea. I denotes and connotes. When the symbol is used for the one, it is a name.

When it is used for the other, it is a concept. But it neither denotes nor connotes except when, in form at least, denotation and connotation are addressed both to a self and to others, when it is in a universe of discourse that is oriented with reference to a self. If the gesture simply indicates the object to another, it has no meaning to the individual who makes it, nor does the response that the other individual carries out become a meaning to him unless he assumes the attitudes of having his attention directed by an individual to whom it has a meaning. Then he takes his own response to be the meaning of the indication. Through this sympathetic placing of themselves in each other's roles and finding thus in their own experiences the responses of the others, what would otherwise be an unintelligent gesture acquires just the value which is connoted by signification, both in its specific application and in its universality.

It should be added that in so far as thought—that inner conversation in which objects as stimuli are both separated from and related to their responses—is identified with consciousness—that is, in so far as consciousness is identified with awareness—it is the result of this development of the self in experience. The other prevalent signification of consciousness is found simply in the presence of objects in experience. With the eyes shut we can say we are no longer conscious of visual objects. If the condition of the nervous system or certain tracts in it cancels the relation of individual and his environment, he may be said to lose consciousness or some portion of it; i.e., some objects or all of them pass out of experience for this individual. Of peculiar interest is the disappearance of a painful object; e.g., an aching tooth under a local anesthetic. A general anesthetic shuts out all objects.

As above indicated, analysis takes place through the conflict of responses that isolates separate features of the object and both separates them from and relates them to their responses, i.e., their meanings. The response becomes a meaning when it is indicated by a generalized attitude both to the self and to others. Mind, which is a process within which this analysis and its indications take place, lies in a field of conduct between a specific individual and the environment, in which the individual is able, through the generalized attitude he assumes, to make use of symbolic gestures, i.e., terms, which are significant to all including himself.

While the conflict of reactions takes place within the individual, the analysis takes place in the object. Mind is, then, a field that is not confined to the individual much less located in a brain. Significance belongs to things in their relations to individuals. It does not lie in mental processes which are enclosed within individuals.

Part Two: Later Perspectives

I

HANS SPEIER

The Social Determination of Ideas[1]

RELATIVISTS WHO point out the futility of any philosophy that concerns itself with human nature in general, since this nature is time and spacebound, are sometimes unaware of the fact that their own relativism, whether it be social-historical, racial, psychological, or any other brand, presupposes a "philosophical anthropology": it happens to be no less general than the generalization it would discredit. All theories of the relation between ideas and the world we call social have philosophical implications. They imply general propositions concerning the nature of social reality, history, man and reason.

One can understand quite well that the philosophical character of these propositions will incline the sociologist to declare himself uninterested in their discussion. His concern in the field of intellectual history is the study of the concrete complex composed of ideas, institutions, and social relationships. But the nature of his investigation forces him twice into the philosophical arena. When he formulates a working hypothesis he in fact formulates a tentative philosophy which provides him with a frame of reference for his research. Again, when he comes to develop generalizations on the basis of his findings, he is taking a philosophical stand.

The issue is indeed not a question of whether these basic problems should be included in, or excluded from, sociological theory but simply whether or not the sociologist is aware of the fact that he has to take them into account. The value of theoretical considerations in the field of sociology of knowledge will only be impaired by their neglect.

Social Research, V (July, 1938), 182–205. Reprinted by permission of *Social Research* and the author. This paper is also Chapter 8 in Hans Speier, *Social Order and the Risks of War* (Cambridge, Mass.: The M.I.T. Press, 1965).

Three questions in particular seem to be in the way of a satisfactory account of the relations between thinking and social reality: a certain ambiguity in the term "human needs" and a subsequent confusion as regards the meaning of theoretical reasoning; a disregard for certain kinds of social action; finally, a petrification of the basis-superstructure scheme which figures perhaps more prominently in contemporary Marxism than in the writings of Marx and Engels.

The following considerations are sketchy. Despite the possible misunderstandings which they for that reason invite they are offered as critical remarks in order to make way for the discussion that follows. In that discussion will be outlined an approach to a sociology of knowledge that tries to avoid the pitfall of sociological determinism.

I

Let us start from the proposition that social reality exists in the form of social actions which satisfy needs. The general (natural) and the specific (cultural) aspects of these needs can be distinguished only by the analyst, not by the agent as agent. Man must always eat in order to live, but the way he satisfies his need for food depends on the existing state of social organization.

The theories which claim that ideas are socially determined regard thinking as instrumental to action.[2] The relation between ideas and social reality is therefore constituted in the medium of deeds. A direct relationship exists when thinking offers efficient means for satisfying a given need and when the satisfaction of specific needs is encouraged in preference to others that are possibly disparaged. These modes of thinking may be called *technical* and *promotive* (persuasive). There is another kind of reasoning. It does not overtly suggest means for reaching a given end, nor can it be adequately defined as persuasion for the adoption of a specific policy, although it may concern itself with both technical and promotive questions.[3] This reasoning may be called *theoretical*.

The difference between these two types of thinking is admitted even by naturalistic theories of reasoning that point out that the structure of thought processes resembles that of actions. Even if one considers reasoning as "doing in thought or imagination what was originally done by actual trial" (Rignano), it is at least implicitly conceded that the thinking involved in actual trial differs in character from thinking "in thought." Similarly, Pillsbury's distinction between inventive reasoning, which arises when man is confronted with a definite physical obstacle, and scientific reasoning, which appears "when some event is not understood, when it fails to fall into any of the classes previously known," is more important than his irritating suggestion that scientific reasoning represents "the more passive type" of the two kinds of thinking.[4]

Whether theoretical reasoning is concerned with nature, God, the social-cultural world or with itself, it has no immediate and not necessarily intended relationship to change which is to be brought about by human agents. Its objective is to understand something rather than to deal with something that presents obstacles to action and calls for their removal. The emphasis upon the cognitive implications of will, action, and feeling should not blur the fact that, however practical the origin of cognition may indeed be in certain spheres of knowledge, as in ethics for example, the specific truth contained in cognition cannot be identified with or reduced to anything in the practical sphere.[5]

Theoretical reasoning too may be dealt with in terms of human needs and satisfactions. If a mathematician, in working upon a problem, hopes to accomplish something apart from the successful completion of his work, be it power, economic gain, or increase in prestige, he has needs that are human but obviously irrelevant as far as his solving the problem is concerned. He may rightly expect to be honored and to become influential or rich when he succeeds in his task. But it is obvious that preoccupation with those needs will actually interfere with the completion of his work. The same holds true of any needs he may have for "applying" the possible result of his investigation to a practically important field of action. On the other hand, it would be absurd to deny that he has a need for finding the truth when he is engaged in endeavors to reach it. Thus it may be said that both needs and satisfactions may be either *irrelevant* or *pertinent* to the accomplishment of the thought process. Pertinent satisfactions are those which accrue from the accomplishment as such; they are impersonal and consist only in having found the truth. Irrelevant satisfactions are derived from the fact that the new knowledge may figure as a means in a chain of actions or in personal relationships with others. Irrelevant satisfactions are meaningful in a context composed of obstacles to actions and efficient means for overcoming them, or in a context composed of the agent and the others; the truth is instrumental in these contexts. Pertinent satisfactions are meaningful only in relation to the self-contained truth that has been reached.

If one holds that ideas are socially determined one might be inclined to discard such considerations as "psychological" and consequently irrelevant in a sociological setting of the problem. In the theories of the social determination of ideas the "psychological" aspect of the problem is either altogether disregarded or is disguised in terms which baffle empirical investigation, as in the case of Karl Mannheim's basic contention that the thinking individual participates in "unconscious motives" of social classes or groups.

The terms which are used to define the relation between ideas and social reality differ widely. They include condition, dependence, reflection, influence, determination, and many others; sometimes they are meant to pertain to the mere selection of the problem, sometimes to the truth discovered, or to the way in which a problem is put, or to the time at which it is raised, or to the methods of coping with it. They are put forward sometimes alone and sometimes in combination.

In any case it is difficult to conceive concretely of a social determination of ideas without assuming that the thinking individual identifies himself with certain needs of others who do not think and who want to act rather than to think. There are situations in which it does not appear farfetched to make this assumption. For example, the increase of nautical and geographical research in seventeenth-century England may be understood with reference to the needs of those men who profited from progress in these sciences, lent their financial support to the research, and associated socially with many scientists of the day.[6] But even in such lucid situations it remains a fact that every piece of research requires men actuated by the desire to know, men who are dependent on an intellectual tradition and equipped with the ability to detach themselves from needs irrelevant to their scientific thinking.

It is not unusual to regard the practical application of theoretical thinking as proof of the contention that the theory itself was called forth by the specific needs which it ultimately helped to satisfy. This attempt to solve the problem of the actual relation between thinking and social reality involves a methodological fallacy if the practical application was not foreseen, and precisely this lack of foresight has been a frequent incident in intellectual history. Nor can this interpretation account for the fact that often in history urgent economic needs remained unsatisfied while the technique of satisfying other needs happened to be improved by the practical application of scientific discoveries. "Boyle foresaw that chemistry, geology, botany, genetics ought to be able to transform agricultural methods; but for more than a century after this time they were still only groping towards the cardinal discoveries which enabled them to do so."[7]

G. N. Clark has given an instructive account of the various influences affecting the scientific movement in the age of Newton. He has shown that they by no means arose only from economic interests, but that they derived also from war, the arts, religion, medicine, and "the desire to know." His critical discussion of Hessen's thesis that the philosophy of Newton embodies the characteristic traits of the rising bourgeoisie closes with a charming anecdote. "A friend to whom he had lent a copy of Euclid's *Elements* asked

Newton of what 'use or benefit in life' the study of the book could be. That was the only occasion on which it is recorded that Newton laughed."[8]

The need that is pertinent to theoretical reasoning is the desire to know. This need is "natural," although its satisfaction may be stifled or facilitated by the specific conditions under which man lives. Some of the theories that insist on the social determination of ideas do not confine themselves to analyzing the conditions of this determination but are anxious to interpret the specific results of reasoning in terms of the specific needs present in the social situation. Instead of determining these needs concretely, which is, to be sure, not an easy task, they are likely to proceed on the assumption that certain needs are necessarily basic, so that inquiry into the structure of needs in a given situation appears superfluous. The economic need for gain, the political need for power, the social need for recognition figure prominently in the theories that attempt to uphold the social determination of ideas.

The satisfaction of these needs is comparable in that in each case it makes for differential security among the members or groups of society. One may add, therefore, that these "basic" needs are conceived as functions of differential insecurity. Social action, then, is considered to have as its natural objective an egoistic shift in the balance of security. When reason is regarded as instrumental to social action thus conceived, it is only logical to distrust reason's claim to universal validity, because in a competitive situation of unequal distribution of security this claim must be dismissed as unwarranted and "selfish"; it can merely reflect the need of one relatively secure group to maintain the status quo or the need of another relatively insecure group to improve its situation.

When the relations between ideas and social reality are analyzed on these grounds, a derogation of theoretical reasoning is indeed inevitable. It becomes intrinsically connected with the narrow conception of social action to which it refers. In a view which understands human nature only on the basis of its comparative insecurity, man's thinking as well as his acting is distorted. We do not think well when we are afraid.

It may be well to recall a few illustrations of this derogation of reason.

The most outstanding of these is Nietzsche's theory that truth is merely the result of a covenant concluded by the weaklings, who resort to reason and language because they have no stronger arms with which to secure safety in a state of dangerous nature.[9] This theory anticipates the psychological opinions which converge in the notion that speculation results from and indicates an imperfect satisfaction of desires which are more readily understood than the desire for speculation itself. Especially can religious and metaphysical thinking be represented as expressions of sublime egoism, since they offer spiritual security to men who cannot derive their feeling of security from solidarity and collective action with others.

The young Karl Marx, in whose critique of Hegel and the left-wing Hegelians the contention that ideas are socially determined appears in a powerful modern form, introduced the phenomenon of "consciousness" in his theory of man after pointing out that it is not fundamental and that "production" is prior. Man seeks to satisfy economic needs, produces means of satisfaction, creates new needs and reproduces himself—and in these four activities he cooperates with other men. Only after we have recognized these four aspects of the original historical relations, Marx declares, do we find that man also has consciousness.[10] "Contemplation" was subsequently presented as a socially necessary illusion of man living in capitalistic society; the so-called fetish character of that society serves to account for the contemplative attitude of philosophers who, failing to appreciate the dynamic and dialectical nature of the social structure, have no material interest in changing it.[11]

Contemplation has been dealt with by Karl Mannheim, not as a product of comparatively recent social developments, but as a residue of early human experience. He has suggested that "contemplation" is historically traceable to "the mystic vision of seers."[12] Today it is obsolete and rare. This argument bears a resemblance to the way in which Comte dealt with theology and metaphysics in his law of the three stages.[13] It is not reconcilable, however, with the tradition of the term. In classical Greek and Roman philosophy the terms *bios theoretikos* and *vita contemplativa* had not the meaning we often connect with contemplation: they did not indicate passivity.[14] The "quietistic" meaning of the word is oriental in origin and was introduced into Western philosophy by the skeptics. In any case, it is worth noting that popular interpretations of contemplation as something old and useless do not take cognizance of the idea that has to be refuted if contemplation is really to be devalued. This idea is that "practical" thinking is not that which is incident to the success of an action but that which is undertaken for the sake of and leads to truth.[15]

Another argument of Mannheim's against the value of contemplation is derived from the contention that cognition of the social-cultural world is only for those who want something from history. Only an active participation in the historical struggle of specific groups can yield understanding and hold any truth. Again, the apparent meaning of this contention is that to want the truth as such is not only a futile desire which cannot possibly be gratified but also a desire begotten by "illusion"—an illusion which itself is dependent on a particular social situation.

These illustrations, which could easily be multiplied, are sufficient to indicate the arguments used in the derogation of reason. Theoretical reasoning is said to be obsolete, illusory, and useless in so far as it is detached from kinds of action that are useful with reference to safety and power, economic gain, and social esteem. For the sake of brevity these may be called *distrustful actions*, because they are competitive in a situation of differential insecurity and thus can always be understood as efforts to prevent disadvantages that might accrue to the agents from the action of others.

According to those who attempt to devalue reason by identifying truth with success, only those ideas can ultimately be called true which are instrumental to the success of distrustful actions. In other words, reason assumes the nature of cunning, and philosophy is transformed into history,[16] sociology, and rhetoric. The result of this development has been characterized by Carl Becker, who has said: "Let Saint Thomas ask *us* to define anything—for example, the natural law—let him ask us to tell him what it *is*. We cannot do it. But given time enough we can relate for him its history."[17]

The predominance which distrustful actions assume over ideas necessarily leads to a fallacious conception of actions which are social but not distrustful. In particular, religious observances, educational guidance, and moral action will—like contemplation—be dealt with in such terms as power, esteem, and economic satisfactions.

Once the sphere of actions is reduced to the level of mutual distrust, not only ideas but also actions themselves either become intelligible only as a step toward a security goal within a given historical situation of power, esteem, and economic gains, or they remain "irrational" as a form of socially tolerated madness, as a sign of cultural "inertia" or the like. Put in a different way, one alternative is to treat religion, art, education, and morality as forms of social control and propaganda, glorification or legitimation of status, justification of material interests, indoctrination of historically relative values, and in other instrumental respects.[18] Exploration of the meaning of religion, art, education, moral norms is left then to the "dogmatic sciences"—theology, aesthetics, jurisprudence, logic, ethics—with the understanding that the findings of these endeavors will in turn be interpreted as "ideologies" determined by social forces originating in differential insecurity. The truth they contain is supposed to be a function of distrustful actions that have been successful. The other alternative is to conceive of religion and metaphysics as illusions—as far as nobody profits from them; to consider art as "escapism"—if it fails to take a stand in the social struggle; to treat moral precepts as "ideological"—if they have no demonstrable utility with reference to the interests of a group; and finally education, apart from being the transmission of skills and apart from increasing the efficiency of the social organization by indoctrinating the socially accepted valuations, would appear as waste and be considered to create only unhappiness.

Thus the search for the social determination of ideas involves not only a derogation of ideas themselves—that is, an identification of needs that call for action with those that result in theoretical reasoning—but also a derogation of those social actions that are not distrustful. If it is alleged that man's pertinent desire to know can be reduced to needs which are in fact incidental to the attainment of truth, one cannot expect a recognition of man's ability to act without regard to his comparative security.

What is the character of actions that are not distrustful? It may here suffice to say that such actions, instead of being related to differential gains of security, refer to non-egoistic accomplishment and to norms. In contrast to distrustful actions they necessarily imply an element of confidence. They are the *practical* manifestations of that property of human nature which enables man to search for truth.

In the theory that ideas are socially determined, much stress is put on the historical character of social-cultural life. But this understanding is significantly limited. History is recognized only in so far as the changing "social basis" entails changes in the "superstructure," and the specific dependence of the superstructure upon the basis is considered to be an "essential" relationship which does not change. Actions pertaining to power, social esteem, and economic gain are exempted from both moral and historical appreciation. They are considered to be natural, are judged by efficiency and can at best be subjected to standards of moral "conventions" which have a historically relative validity. It is here where the doctrine that ideas are socially determined reveals its unhistorical implications. One might say that the historical approach is based upon a natural law governing the structural relation of "ideal" and "real" factors. This dogmatism seriously interferes with an unbiased analysis of any complex of social actions because it presents as a law of dependence what might be merely a specific pattern among many possibilities.

Various attempts, however, have been made by sociologists to take cognizance of the historical character of the "pattern of dependence." Even Marx intimated that the economic factor has not always been the "basis" of society. Lukács has explicitly discussed the historical range of dialectical materialism.[19] Max Scheler has suggested a historical law concerning the varying predominance of the different material factors—that is, the vital, political, and economic factors—in the course of history.[20] Sorokin's "dynamic sociology" is based on what he calls "the principle of varying efficiency of the same factor in different cultures and societies."[21] And Karl

Mannheim in some of his earlier writings has pointed out that "shifts of the center of life" have occurred in history. What he called the "positivistic feeling of existence" was once presented by him as a specifically modern phenomenon brought about by a "shift of the center of life from spiritual, religious realities to the social and economic."[22] He asserted, furthermore, that "positivism" was "genuine," in other words, was the sincere expression of this shift of the center of life. Equally genuine was the positivistic "belief" in the empirical. He concluded that all this is still valid for us, "because it is genuine."[23] In his *Ideology and Utopia* Mannheim characterizes the modern methods of imputing ideas to the unconscious motivations of groups as "psychic annihilation,"[24] proposes that it was in the political discussions of modern democracies that the influence of unconscious collective motives was "for the first time" "discovered," and retreats from his previous historical position to one that is ahistorical. He holds that this recently discovered law of dependence has always existed. This is a simplification of the problem: it leads to an identification of a modern political method of "psychic annihilation" with a general sociological method to be applied not only to certain types of political thinking in modern times but to many other types of thinking—such as ethics, metaphysics, epistemology—at all times.

All the scholars have recognized that the problem of history is not merely that of changing "material" and "ideal" data, but also that of structural changes in the interdependence of various domains of life. Their statements would suggest the inference that there is in history a pluralism of patterns of dependence which should at least prevent the investigator from imposing the pattern of dependence of one society—usually that of his own—upon totally different historical situations.

The term "pluralism of patterns of dependence," however, must be rid of its vagueness and ambiguity. This pluralism postulates a conception of social reality which makes it impossible to conceive of the relation between ideal and social forces in the way we have so far followed. The problem is not to find the answer to the question as to what is "basis," what is "superstructure," but how the question itself must be put. I shall briefly indicate the meaning and a few implications of these statements.

II

Society is a reality in which there is a convergence of material, vital, and spiritual forces.[25] Therefore no sociological investigation of the relation between the social world and ideas in a given historical situation will ever find this relation corresponding to the dualisms matter-mind, profane-sacred, material-ideal; these dualisms are implicit in social life itself.

In the terms used in the preceding discussion, any social structure can be analyzed as composed of typical actions which satisfy needs and also of tensions which represent unsatisfied needs. These needs by no means refer necessarily to gain and loss, power and submission, esteem and deference; they are also spiritual, such as the needs for justice, worship, order, compliance with moral norms. In other words, the basic actions are not naturally distrustful actions. The importance of one class of actions, say, distrustful actions, in relation to other classes differs in different structures and even in different momentary situations of the same structure, according to material goods available, traditions, conflicts or friendly relations with other structures and many other factors. History as history cannot therefore be the basis of a general theory of what is natural in social life, or, rather, any typical action to be found in history is "natural," religious observance as well as economic exploitation, tabu as well as license.

Not only may social actions result from urgent spiritual needs; it may also happen that the same action satisfies needs of different character: the crusaders were "interested" both in fighting for the glory of God and in the acquisition of fiefs. A preconceived notion of the "natural" origin of social action is likely to lead to misapprehensions, no matter whether the notion be "idealistic" or "materialistic."

Again the needs or interests of individuals and groups are not natural in the sense that they can be inferred either from the nature of power, economic chance and prestige, or from the nature of justice, order, and mutual help. Definitions of interests and the formation of interest groups depend on the ethos of the agents, and this is shaped by a denial or acceptance of the prevailing ethos of society.[26] The ethos is the basic emotional structure of value preferences and value repugnances of a person, a group, or a culture—the spiritual, evaluative implication of a social structure; in it is founded the actual relationship between different needs, displayed by typical actions and tensions. Thus the ethos indicates the distance of actuality from the right life. It is the task of moral and political philosophy, not of historical research, to demonstrate in the light of reason the relative value of different needs in the right life.

The agents need not be fully aware of the ethos. Nor need their private value judgments be derived from it. In fact, man does not always act in order to obey moral precepts. But the ethos of a society is embodied in its institutions and in the principles of public blame and praise according to which esteem is distributed.[27] Thus the prevailing ethos of a society manifests itself primarily as institutional pressure—through which the given social reality assumes a quasi-objective character to the agents—and as social images

—which are symbols of the most highly honored type of activity and conduct.

The ethos of a society in which its material elements assume a social significance, differs with the contingencies of time and space. It is a cultural phenomenon. Therefore it may appear that a recourse to social-historical relativism is inevitable. As a matter of fact, the conception of social reality that underlies the foregoing theories of the social determination of ideas may seem less relativistic than the one here outlined. They revealed a dogmatic, unhistorical contention which resulted from a preoccupation with the differential insecurity of human nature. This notion is discarded in favor of a more comprehensive consideration of social action when it is held that social actions differ according to the social structure in which they occur. This, to be sure, is relativism, but it is a relativism without philosophical repercussions. It refers only to social life, which, because of its dualistic character, is indeed contingent; it does not encroach upon reason and upon reasonable action.

Moreover, it should be noted that differences in external actions, or in their valuations in the ethos of the agents, may be only apparent. A closer analysis often reveals that the apparent differences result only from differences of situational contingency, and that different actions or valuations have identical functional meanings in relation to the structure in which they occur. A quotation from Adam Ferguson, whose moral philosophy contains an instructive discussion of sociological relativism, may illustrate this point:

> We are at a loss . . . when we are told that what is punished as a crime in one country is rewarded or commended in another. . . . This defect, however, may be easily supplied if we consider, first of all, that men have different opinions respecting external objects; further, that many of the actions of men are considered more as *expressions* of what they mean or intend than as operations materially beneficial or hurtful. In the first instance, men proceed upon different notions of what is beneficial or hurtful; in the other they express or interpret their intentions differently.[28]

The common denominator through which much apparent "relativism" of actions disappears is the functional relationship between action and structure. It is here that the empirical research of the sociologist may make a real philosophical contribution, since philosophy is concerned with what is common in social actions in different societies, that is, with the meaning of social life rather than with its contingency.

At the time it must be noted also that the meaning of data which appear similar may differ in different stituations. Whether starvation of a part of the population entails revolution or strengthening fatalism in a society cannot be determined by analyzing starvation but only by understanding the meaning it has in the structure in which it occurs. Similarly, whether or not ideas are impotent to bring about a change of the prevailing ethos cannot be determined with reference to the nature of "mind" and its general relation to "matter." It depends on the structural value of ideas. A sermon may influence the conduct of one person and have no influence on another. There are societies in which religion has an important bearing on social action, others where it has not. Again, in so far as theories are popular that speak of the natural priority of distrustful actions, they may not only voice a socially prevailing ethos but even strengthen it. Thus even the question of the relativism of social actions can be properly answered only when the functional problems have been investigated on an empirical basis.

Once the so-called pluralism of dependence patterns is redefined in terms of a different conception of social reality, the relation between ideas and social life presents itself in a different form.

Technical and promotive reasoning can obviously be analyzed sociologically. Sociology cannot decide whether or not the means which technical reasoning offers for satisfying a given need are efficient. But it may interpret the existence of the needs in terms of the social situation, and possibly the choice of particular means as well. For example, the sociologist cannot judge about the efficiency of modern military discipline when it was recovered in sixteenth-century Netherlands from Roman literary sources. But he may interpret the need of the Dutch for such measures in their conflict with the Spaniards. He may also be able to show the bearing of various factors in the situation upon the adoption of the measures: such as the humanistic tradition of the scholar who translated the sources; the wealth of the country which enabled it to meet the prerequisite of military discipline, namely regularity of pay; the influence of the Protestant religion on the receptivity to discipline among the soldiers.

In promotive reasoning, which urges that one end be pursued in preference to another, sociology is faced with a phenomenon that in its most general terms may be called the quest for a public by a promoter. Research in this field has three main objectives. First, it may concern itself with the social composition and the specific ethos of the public, that is, the quasi-objective conditions which allow the promoter to operate, which permit him special esteem, and the like.

Second, it is possible to explain in terms of those conditions the specific type of promoter whose emergence is structurally possible. To illustrate, the sociologist will be concerned with such problems as: which social factors in the period of Greek enlightenment must be taken into account in order to understand the emergence of the sophists; whether the sophists' migratory existence can be understood with reference to their interest in evading taxation, and to what extent it can be accounted for by the composition of their public; which interests had a bearing upon the rise of the second sophistic movement in Hellenistic society.[29] Or in other contexts he will consider which factors throw light on the rhetorical influence of the humanists as envoys, lawyers, and statesmen; what has been the influence of the journalist upon terror in modern times;[30] what accounts for the power of the demagogue in modern enlightened society in general; what is the characteristic social set-up for the charlatan to become a conspicuous social type.[31]

The third concern of research is the means of diffusing ideas. The existing state of technology and social organization has an obvious bearing on the methods of persuasion. In analyzing these factors the sociologist must guard against assuming that the mere existence of certain facilities, such as the printing press or the radio, the lending library or the coffee-house, is a sufficient explanation of the purpose for which they are used. Their use and abuse are determined by the ethos of society in general and of the promoter in particular.

One might add that he who persuades takes heed of the needs and interests of his public. As Plato said, the rhetorician has studied the opinions of the multitude. The public success of an idea depends on its capacity to confirm pre-existing value attitudes, because it pleases man to hear that he was right. But it is also possible that success results from man's ability to understand that he was wrong or did not know, in which case, however, he is not persuaded but is guided to learn.

Different from the promoter is the one who thinks for the sake of finding truth, and correspondingly different are the tasks of sociology of knowledge, if knowledge is to designate something that is true. To begin with, it is characteristic of the philosopher and the scientist to doubt whether opinions are right, to ask whether existing values or interests are reasonable, to examine the ethos within which they are defined. The aim of theoretical reasoning is not success in public but simply truth.

From the fact that ideas are constantly being functionalized for the satisfaction of needs it cannot be inferred that they are indeed functions of those needs. It is impossible to impute them to a given social situation because the ethos of a society never coincides with the ethos of theoretical reasoning; that is, the social order is never wholly reasonable. So far as it is not, ideas must be "ideological," must transcend the contingencies of the social reality in which they occur, because the nature of the ideal reality does not contain the dualism which is to be found in the social.

It would be ridiculous to deny that the philosophers or the scientists are themselves entangled in these contingencies. Even as members of a leisure class they depend on the economic order which permits the existence of such a class. They are economically dependent on a patron or on collective patronage or on publishers, critics, and the literary market, or on the state or on a church. They would not be human if they did not depend somehow, somewhere, on somebody. In the sociology of knowledge there is no room for Alfred Weber's construction of a "socially detached" intelligentsia. The sociological question to be answered concretely in every concrete case is not whether a thinker is dependent, but in which specific interests—ecclesiastic, political, economic or otherwise—he is entangled.

This inevitable dependence on private or public needs and interests does not mean that his ideas are "perspectivistic," that they depend on those needs which are irrelevant to theoretical reasoning. The existence of needs may account for the selection of certain problems, and here is a fruitful field for sociological analysis. For example, the rise of modern science may be traced, and has often been traced, to specific interests and to a specific ethos which stressed the value of man's power over nature. But, to repeat, it is absurd to say that the truth of any scientific statement is socially determined. Nor can it be overlooked that a great number of philosophical problems are given by human existence as such, independent of any historical constellation of needs.

The fact that "perspectivism" of opinions results from the historical, social, and personal diversity of needs and interests has been known to the philosophers, jurists, and historians of all times. Modern sociology would merely reveal ignorance if it claimed to have discovered a commonplace. What it must do is to analyze this "perspectivism" systematically and empirically. It will have to make considerable efforts to equal the systematic stringency of analysis which distinguishes earlier writers in the field.

If this "perspectivism" were final and could not in some sense be overcome, one could not account for the fact that man, having recognized it, still tried to find the truth. The history of philosophy would be a chain of follies. Conversely, everyday experience teaches us that an opinion that we have and possibly share with others (group opinion) is not true simply because we happen to have it. Thus, through the ages, a prominent method of revealing the contingent character of mere opinion has been to consider it in the light of another. Even from the standpoint of sociological relativism it must be admitted that the thinking individual is able to take cognizance of opinions satisfactory to interests that are not his own. Nor can one deny that it is possible to take account of what has been thought in previous ages. The promoter, to be sure, is absorbed in the historical situation of needs in his time. Philosophers have access to the thinking of all times. Thus their "environment" extends beyond the contingencies of the interests which they happen to experience. Moreover, any critical consideration of different opinions presupposes that the critic has access not only to opinions but to the subject matter itself to which they refer.

The scientific task of a sociology of knowledge in the field of moral and political science is not to show how needs and interests influence thinking. This is a question of the deficiencies of reason as far as they are traceable to social needs, and it may, at times, be politically both urgent and beneficial. The philosophical task of a sociology of knowledge, however, is to show to what extent philosophers have left immediate partisan interests behind them,[32] and how by doing this they may have incidentally exerted a profounder influence upon the ethos of man than those who by being merely today's thinkers are already of the eternal yesterday.

Whereas an analysis of how the promoter's public is composed sheds light on the possibilities of the promoter's success or failure, the sociological analysis of the social-cultural situation of the philosopher reveals only how far his freedom to search for truth is facilitated or stifled, and the direction or the source of certain of his intellectual interests. "Superstition," said Lichtenberg, "is local philosophy." The aphorism implies that philosophy is never local. The public of the philosopher is composed of his contemporaries only to the extent that they, too, are in the timeless ranks of those who seek the truth.

NOTE ON THE PREDECESSORS OF THE SOCIOLOGY OF KNOWLEDGE

Especially important is Nicholas Malebranche's investigation of the relation between reasoning and "needs" in his *De la recherche de la vérité*, published in 1675. Malebranche recognized that

> the difference observable in Men, as to their Ways and Purposes in Life, are almost infinite. Their different conditions, different Imployments, different Posts and Offices and different Communities are innumerable. These Differences are the Reason of Man's acting upon quite different Designs; and Reasoning upon different Principles. Even in the same Community, wherein there should be but one Character of Mind, and all the same Designs; you shall rarely meet with several Persons, whose Aims and Views are not different. Their various Employments and their many adhesions necessarily diversify the Method and Manner they would take to accomplish those very things wherein they agree. [English translation by T. Taylor (Oxford, 1964), p. 75.]

That Bacon was aware of the problems of a sociology of knowledge can be seen from the following quotations. He complained that knowledge of the "divisions of man's nature" as they are contained in the traditions of astrology, the Italian *relationes* and in "every day's conference" "wandereth in words but is not fixed in inquiry." "No man bringeth them to the confectionary, that receipts might be made of them for the use of life." "Of much like kind are those impressions of nature, which are imposed upon the mind by the sex, by the age, by the region, by health and sickness, by beauty and deformity and the like, which are inherent and not extern; and again, those which are caused by extern fortune; as sovereignty, nobility, obscure birth, riches, want, magistracy, privateness, prosperity, adversity, constant fortune, variable fortune, rising per saltum, per gradus, and the like" (in *The Advancement of Learning* [Everyman's Library edition], pp. 169 ff.). The significance of Bacon for the development of the modern sociology of knowledge deserves a special study. In the meantime, cf. Edwin Greenlaw, *The Province of Literary History* (Baltimore, 1931).

Of later writers Johann Martin Chladenius (1710–59) is most prominent; cf. especially his *Einleitung zur richtigen Auslegung vernünftiger Reden und Schriften* (Leipzig, 1742), and his *Allgemeine Geschichtswissenschaft* (Leipzig, 1752). He pointed out that the recognition of a historical event requires a "spectator" or "originator" and that there are as many different kinds of spectators as there are social relations. The viewpoint (*Sehepunkt*) of the spectator is determined by evaluations, by psychological and cultural factors, by his social position and by his participation in the event. Differences in viewpoint lead to different judgments concerning the same event. Chladenius also developed a fruitful classification of the origins of these differences and of deviations from truth by enlargement, reduction, mutilation, distortion, illustration, termination, discontinuation, expansion, omission, abridgment, etc. A series of persons of whom one is the originator and the others merely "repetitors" (*Nachsager*) he called a "channel." He realized the importance of the channel for studying the diffusion of ideas and the change of the meaning of words. Ideas may "run," "stop," "propagate themselves," be "stimulated" or "renewed" in a channel. As an introduction to Chladenius, cf. Joachim Wach, *Das Verstehen*, II (Tübingen, 1933), 23–32 (Wach calls Chladenius' analyses exceedingly modern); Hans Stoltenberg, *Geschichte der deutschen Gruppwissenschaft* (Leipzig, 1937), pp. 163–68; and Hans Müller, *Johann Martin Chladenius* (Berlin, 1917).

Mention should be made also of Johann Christoph Gatterer, who in the *Allgemeine Historische Bibliothek*, V (1768), 3–29, published an essay on the "position and viewpoint of the historian," in which he pointed out the social-cultural dependence of historical knowledge. The essay contains an instructive illustration: a few pages from Livy are confronted with a few pages from Gatterer himself on the same subject matter, in order to demonstrate concretely how different positions and viewpoints entail different presentations.

For further material on the "forerunners" of the sociology of knowledge cf. the introduction by F. B. Kaye to Mandeville's *Fable of the Bees* (Oxford, 1924), and the historical part of Balduin Schwarz, *Der Irrtum in der Philosophie* (Münster, 1934).

NOTES

1 This article is based on a paper read at the annual meeting of the American Sociological Society, December, 1937. The author is indebted to Professor Max Wertheimer for valuable criticism.

2 This position is inevitable in such theories, though it is not always made explicit.

3 Aristotle's treatise on rhetoric is a notable case in point. Friedrich Blass has pointed out that Aristotle's *Rhetoric* has been of little use for practical purposes and has never made an orator; cf. his *Attische Beredsamkeit*, II, 393; Georgiana Paine Palmer, *The Τόποι of Aristotle's Rhetoric as Exemplified in the Orators* (Chicago, 1934), pp. 81 ff.; and Hans von Arnim, *Leben und Werke des Dio von Prusa* (Berlin, 1898).

4 W. B. Pillsbury, "Recent Naturalistic Theories of Reasoning," in *Scientia*, XXXVI (1924).

5 Cf. the disc in ussionHerman Schmalenbach, *Das Ethos und die Idee des (Erkennens)* (Tübingen, 1933).

6 Cf. E. G. P. Taylor, *Tudor and Early Stuart Geography 1583–1650* (London, 1934), and Louis B. Wright, *Middle-Class Culture in Elizabethan England* (Chapel Hill, N.C., 1935), chap. xiv.

7 G. N. Clark, *Science and Social Welfare in the Age of Newton* (Oxford, 1937), p. 90.

8 *Ibid.*, p. 91.

9 Friedrich Nietzsche, "Über Wahrheit und Lüge im aussermoralischen Simmt" (1878), in *Werke*, ed. by A. Baeumler, I, 605 ff.; cf. also Chaim Perelman, "Le statut social des jugements de vérité," in *Revue de l'institut de soziologie*, no. 1 (1933).

10 Karl Marx, *Der historische Materialismus, Die Frühschriften*, ed. by S. Landshut and J. P. Mayer (Leipzig, 1932), II, 20.

11 Cf. especially Georg Lukács, *Geschichte und Klassenbewusstsein* (Berlin, 1923), pp. 94–163.

12 Karl Mannheim, *Ideology and Utopia* (New York, 1936), p. 265; cf. also his *Mensch und Gesellschaft im Zeitalter des Umbaus* (Leyden, 1935), p. 170.

13 It should be noted that Comte's critical conception of theology and metaphysics as something old and for that reason useless rests on the same basis on which modern moral philosophy has attempted to devalue all virtues which do not fit in with the needs of modern society. The argument has become the rationalization of a value attitude which is one of the most characteristic traits of modern civilization.

14 The Greek term, however, seems to have had connotations that referred to the observers of the Panhellenic games; cf. Franz Boll, *"Vita Contemplativa,"* in *Sitzungeberichte der Heidelberger Akademie der Wissenschaften, Philosophisch-Historische Klasse* (1920), VIII.

15 Cf. Aristotle, *Politics*, VII, 3, 1325 b. Even the positivist Comte was aware of this when he traced the crisis of modern society to the unjustifiable metaphysical predominance of material considerations "which are so abusingly designated as practical"; cf. his *Sociologie*, chap. i.

16 For a lucid discussion of this transformation, cf. Leo Strauss, *The Political Philosophy of Hobbes* (Oxford, 1937), chap. vi; Strauss concludes that "The reason for the turning of philosophy to history [which occurred according to his opinion in the sixteenth century] is the conviction of the impotence of reason, added to the enhanced interest in man" (p. 93). Cf. especially the reference to Bodin, who spoke of the "incredible usefulness" of history, and to Bacon's critique of Aristotle. In both cases the turning to history was accompanied by a decision against the *vita contemplativa* in favor of the *vita activa*.

17 Carl Becker, *The Heavenly City of the Eighteenth-Century Philosophers* (New Haven, 1932), p. 19.

18 Cf. Kierkegaard's remark that "what the modern philosopher understands by faith is essentially what one calls an opinion" (in *Einubung im Christentum*, p. 181). A criticism of the anthropological approach to religion and a non-functional theory of cult, myth, and magic are contained in Walther F. Otto, *Dionysos* (Frankfurt, 1933). On the sociological interpretation of literature, cf. Horatio E. Smith, "Relativism in Bonald's Literary Doctrine," *Modern Philology*, XXII (November, 1924), 193–210, and the references given there; also Max Raphael, "Zur Kunsttheorie des dialektischen Materialismus," in *Philosophische Hefte* (1932), pp. 124–52.

For the obliteration of the distinction between education and propaganda, cf. Harold D. Lasswell's remark that: "Propaganda is the transmission of attitudes that are recognized as *controversial* within a given community. Education is a process of transmitting skill and *accepted* attitudes"—in H. D. Lasswell, R. D. Casey, and B. L. Smith, *Propaganda and Promotional Activities* (Minneapolis, 1935), p. 3; cf. also Leonard W. Doob, *Propaganda* (New York, 1935), pp. 79 ff.

The literature on sociological relativism in ethics is endless. For illustrations cf.: A. von Schelting, *Max Weber's Wissenschaftslehre* (Tübingen, 1934), pp. 143–45, which is a critical discussion of Mannheim's contention that the prohibition to take interest from loans derived from a social system in which consumption credit prevailed; Max Scheler, *Der Formalismus in der Ethik und die materiale Wertethik* (2d ed.; Haile, 1921), pp. 320–29, which is a critical discussion of Wundt's contention that in certain periods and among certain peoples murder has been considered an honorable action; also Herbert Spiegelberg, *Antirelativismus* (Zurich and Leipzig, 1935), and Georges Gurvitch, *Morale théorique et les sciences des moeurs* (Paris, 1937).

19 Lukács, *Geschichte und Klassenbewusstsein*, pp. 229–60; the references to Marx and Engels are on pp. 239 ff.

20 Max Scheler, *Die Wissensformen und die Gesellschaft* (Leipzig, 1926), pp. 34 ff.

21 Pitirim A. Sorokin, *Social and Cultural Dynamics* (New York, 1937), III, 374n.

22 Karl Mannheim, "Das Problem einer Soziologie des Wissens," in *Archiv für Sozialwissenschaft und Sozialpolitik*, LIII (1925), 587.

23 *Ibid.*, p. 599.

24 *Ibid.*, p. 35.

25 ". . . réalité à la fois matérielle, vitale, morale, spirituelle et même déjà réligieuse"— Maurice Blondel, *L'être et les êtres* (Paris, 1935), p. 116.

26 The term "ethos" was introduced into modern sociology by Max Scheler. He derived it from a conception of man as *ens amans* instead of *ens cogitans* or *ens volens*, though this is not relevant in our context. The ethos is neither identical with Sumner's concept of the mores nor is it a rational, logically formulated system of ethics. For an extended discussion, cf. Max Scheler, and his *Schriften aus dem Nachlass*, I (Berlin, 1933), 225–62. In American sociology the concept that comes closest to the ethos is Talcott Parsons' concept of "value attitude." The voluntaristic presuppositions of Parsons' interpretation of social action and of value make it difficult, however, for him to define value attitude; cf. his paper on "The Place of Ultimate Values in Sociological Theory," in the *International Journal of Ethics*, XLV (April, 1935), particularly 305 ff.

27 Cf. Parsons, "The Place of Ultimate Values in Sociological Theory," pp. 299–300, where institutions are treated as "normative rules" of social actions; cf. also my paper on "Honor and Social Structure," in *Social Research*, II (February, 1935), 74–97.

28 Adam Ferguson, *Principles of Moral and Political Science*, II (Edinburgh, 1792), 140–41.

29 For a concrete sociological analysis, cf. especially the introduction, "Sophistik, Rhetorik, Philosophie in ihrem Kampf und die Jugendbildung," to W. Arnim, *Leben und Werke des Dio von Prusa*; for minor corrections, cf. Hans Schulte, *Orator, Untersuchungen zum Ciceronianischen Bildungsideal* (Frankfurt, 1935).

30 For an illustration, cf. Kurt Baschwitz, "Schreckensherrschaften und ihre Presse," in *International Review for Social History*, I (Leyden, 1936), 273–310.

31 Cf. Grete de Francesco, *Die Macht des Charlatans* (Basel, 1937).

32 It is significant of the ethos of the modern sociology of knowledge that this question is systematically precluded from consideration.

2

TALCOTT PARSONS

An Approach to the Sociology of Knowledge[1]

IT SEEMS TO me that the tradition most explicitly associated with the concept of the sociology of knowledge, that in which the names of Marx and Mannheim are most prominent, has operated with too undifferentiated a conceptual scheme. The main framework of the problem has grown out of the tradition of German idealist-historicist thought and has concerned the relations between what are often called *Idealfaktoren* and *Realfaktoren*. The tendency has been to argue over which was the "most important," as for example in the case of Hegel's "idealism" versus Marx's "materialism," and, further, to neglect adequate differentiation of the components on either side of this "equation." Connected with this tendency to dichotomous, either-or thinking has been a strong tendency not to pay adequate attention to the methodological distinction between existential and evaluative judgments, a tendency to relativize all "objectivity" to a base in values or "interests." I should rather follow Max Weber in his insistence on distinguishing between the motives for interest in problems, which is inherently value-relative, and the grounds of the validity of judgments, which in the nature of the case cannot be relative in the same sense. In attempting to emphasize this and several other distinctions I consider basic to the sociology of knowledge, my approach is grounded in Weber's views as expressed both in his essays in the methodology of social science and in his studies in the sociology of religion, but also draws on other sources, notably Durkheim's analysis of social structure in relation to the problems of social solidarity. My general position is relatively close to that taken by Werner Stark in his recent book *The Sociology of Knowledge* (Glencoe, Ill.: The Free Press, 1958).

Transactions of the Fourth World Congress of Sociology, IV (Louvain: International Sociological Association, 1959), 25–49. Reprinted by permission of the International Sociological Association and the author.

SOME PRELIMINARIES

In order to place in context what I consider the relevant problems of a sociology of knowledge, I should like first to sketch a framework for the analysis of all human action conceived as a system. Action, so conceived, is an ordered system of components that root in the physical world and the living organism and that are controlled by cultural patterns and symbols. For the most general analytical purposes it is necessary to break action down into four primary subsystems which I should call the cultural system, the social system, the personality of the individual, and the behavioral organism. These four constitute a hierarchical order of control in the order named—i.e., from the cultural system "down." I see the problem area ordinarily known as the sociology of knowledge as involving the interdependence and the inter-penetration of what I have called the social system and the cultural system. But it should not be forgotten that the other two subsystems—personalities and biological organisms in a physical environment—are also concretely involved at every single point, for this classification is clearly analytical and not a classification of concrete entities. *All* human behavior is concretely at the same time cultural, social, psychological, and organic. Any concrete system of interacting persons is hence above all both a social system and a cultural system at the same time; these subsystems are only analytically distinguishable, not concretely separable except so far as cultural content can, for example, be "embodied" in physical artifacts like books or works of art.

To show how the cultural system and the social system are analytically distinct even though concretely interpenetrating, let us analyze each in turn into *its* four primary subsystems.

The Social System[2]

A social system is that aspect of action that is organized about the *interaction* of a plurality of human individuals. Its structure consists in the patterning of the relations of the individuals, and may be analyzed on four levels of generality so far as its units are concerned: (1) Individuals in roles are organized to form what we call (2) collectivities. Both roles and collectivities, however, are subject to ordering and control by (3) norms which are differentiated according to the functions of these units and to their situations, and by (4) values which define the desirable type of system of relationships. Like the subsystems of action, these four primary structural subsystems of the social system are both analytically distinguishable and concretely interpenetrating. Thus every social system in one sense "consists in" roles organized to form one collectivity, and if it is a complex system, many subcollectivities. But every role and collectivity is "governed" by norms and values, each of which category constitutes a differentiated system.

The Cultural System

A cultural system, on the other hand, is organized about patterns of the *meaning* of objects and the "expression" of these meanings through symbols and signs. Thus the "structure of culture" consists in patterns of meaning as such, i.e., what have often been called "ideas," "forms," etc. I would like to suggest four basic structural components (i.e., units) of cultural systems: (1) patterns of empirical existential ideas, defining the conceptual schemes in which empirical objects are "cognized"; (2) patterns of expressive symbolization defining the "forms" and "styles" in which objects are cathected and symbolically represented, or through which they acquire and express emotional meaning; (3) patterns of evaluation, or the patterns through which objects are evaluated as better or worse than each other; and (4) patterns of the grounding of meaning, or the modes of orientation in and to the world in which the "major premises" of all other components of culture are grounded. Like the above classifications of action subsystems and social subsystems, this classification also constitutes a hierarchy of control.[3] Similarly, these components must be conceived as interpenetrating with each other, as always all involved, though in different modes of relation.

But culture not only has a structure; it "functions" in action. As a component of action—as when defining roles and collectivities, or the goals and interests of persons—cultural patterns do not function "automatically" by some kind of "self-actualization" or "emanation," but only through integration with the other components of action, most importantly through what has come to be called institutionalization in the social system and internalization in the personality.

The Institutionalization of Values in the Social System

The primary focus of articulation between the social system and the cultural system is the institutionalization of patterns of evaluation from the cultural system into the social system to constitute its topmost controlling component. Thus every social system, even a total society, has a paramount value pattern. This in turn is differentiated, by a process I shall call "specification," to constitute values for the various differentiated and segmented subsystems of the larger system.

The concept of institutionalization is not confined to values in its relevance. The other three cultural components—empirical existential ideas, expressive symbols, and groundings of meaning—are also institutionalized, but they do not all have the same kind of relation to the social systems which are their "bearers." Though they ordinarily play secondary parts in most subsystems of a society, they can play a primary part in special types of subsystems which cannot subsist independently of the society. Thus, for example, what I call the grounding of meaning is the primary cultural component of religious collectivities, while the patterning of empirical knowledge is the primary cultural component of universities.

Values I conceive to be, in Clyde Kluckhohn's phrase, "conceptions of the desirable,"4 which I interpret to mean definitions of the directions of action commitment which are prescribed in the culture. The institutionalization of values is, sociologically considered, a complex matter; it constitutes an area of interpenetration of cultural and social systems. As components of the cultural system, values must be related to the rest of that cultural system, and hence to the modes of institutionalization of these other three cultural components. Secondly, however, as components of the social system itself, they must be related to the non-cultural components of social system functioning in such ways as to regulate the mechanisms by which social process occurs. Hence we need a double paradigm; on the one hand, one which places institutionalized values in the context of the rest of the institutionalized cultural system, and on the other hand, a paradigm which places the value components in their relations to the non-cultural components of the social system.

First Paradigm: *Relating Values to the Other Cultural Components*

As mentioned above, institutionalization of values in a society requires their specification to different subsystems of the society. On the highest level of cultural generality, values are couched in terms which are relevant to the comparative evaluation of different categories of object, both social and non-social. On the social level of specification, however, these more general bases of comparison are taken for granted and what is compared is different categories of social object. A societal value system, then, is the evaluative preference for a given type of society as compared to others. Further specification will lead to the conception of desirable types of subsystems within what is evaluated as a good society, in each case taking account of the place of the subsystem within the society.

Empirical Ideas. For these evaluations to take place, however, there must be some basis for discriminating empirically between the properties which are more and less highly evaluated. This means that the same cultural system must include, along with a value system, a set of empirical conceptions of the nature of the social systems and subsystems which are being evaluated, *and*, explicitly or implicitly, a set of empirical conceptions of the differences from and similarities to other social systems, historical or contemporary or even potentially occurring, which are differently evaluated.

It is in the *relation* between institutionalized values and empirical conceptions of the evaluated social systems that the problem of ideology arises. Clearly the actual evaluation of current social facts may vary on a positive-negative axis. Hence a whole society's value system may condemn certain aspects of a social status quo, such as crime and illness; these are by definition things the prevalence of which ought to be reduced. On the other hand, different groups within a society may evaluate the same social facts differently, resulting, for instance, in a bifurcation into "conservative" and "radical" values and ideologies.

Grounding of Meaning. Since values are always problematical with respect to their legitimation, societies also institutionalize patterns of meaning in terms of which their values "make sense." Here too there is a problem of specification in that there are different levels at which the problems of meaning can be raised. The one which is most directly relevant here is the meaning of the obligations and commitments of collectivities like the nation or profit-making business firms. It is a question of how the evaluation, positive or negative, can be backed by some sort of answer to the question why this evaluation should be accepted. In the most general terms, this meaning-complex is institutionalized in the religious system of the culture, but on occasion it may be a very prominent component in ideological systems which act as "political religions."

Expressive Symbolization. Finally, all social action requires motivational commitment on the part of individuals. No system of values can be adequately institutionalized unless it is integrated with a patterning of appropriate rewards and punishments that are contingent on various courses of behavior and hence the *meanings* of the objects, *individual* and *collective*, which reward and punish. Culturally these rewards involve the whole realm of expressive symbolization, and institutionalized patterns of style and taste are of course central to it. By definition, the moral component of institutionalized values must be distinguished from the reward component, but this does not negate the great importance of the relationship between them.

In my view, all four of these components of a cultural system are closely interdependent, so that no one of them can be institutionalized without important institutional questions being raised about the other three. But sociologists have historically tended to see the relation between values and empirical facts in terms of the problem of ideology, while the relation between grounds of meaning and personal motivation, as it was treated by Weber, has been seen as a problem of religious interests. Both pairs of relationships are rightly the concern of a sociology of knowledge, in my opinion, but in this paper I shall, for reasons of space, confine my attention to the former.

Second Paradigm: Relating Values to Non-cultural Components
The second paradigm referred to above concerns the problem of institutionalization at the level of functioning of the social system itself. Institutionalized values may of course be undermined at the cultural level, by changes focusing at any one or any combination of the four components just discussed, for instance by questioning the grounding of meaning, or by questioning the empirical tenability of conditions alleged to be necessary for implementing the values. Given legitimation through articulation with the cultural system, however, the institutionalization of values depends further on relative effectiveness in meeting the non-cultural conditions of their implementation.

Norms. First there is the need for spelling out the general values in terms of sufficiently specific operative norms which can adequately define the situation for the different categories of actors in the society. One might say that the value system must become incorporated in a "constitution," formal or informal, for individual commitment to values is not alone adequate to their implementation.

Collectivities. The second basic condition concerns the functions of the many types of collectivities within a society. Just as values need to be legitimated, so in turn they must, through legal or informal norms, legitimate the goals of different categories of collectivities, provided that the collectivities function so as to contribute to the maintenance and/or development of the society.

Roles. The final major condition for the implementation of values in the social system concerns individuals in roles. Through the socialization process the necessary congruence must be established between personal interests and responsibilities to the larger system.

In sum, values are only fully institutionalized when they have become adequately articulated with a differentiated system of normative order; with legitimation of the goals and functions of collectivities; and with the motivational commitments of individuals in roles, as internalized through the process of socialization.

WHERE THE SOCIOLOGY OF KNOWLEDGE FITS

As noted above, it seems to me that the main concern of the sociology of knowledge, especially in the tradition of Marx and of Mannheim, has been with the relation between two components outlined in the first of the two paradigms—between institutionalized value systems and empirical conceptions of societies and their subsystems. But in my opinion the sociology of knowledge should also (though not here) consider the relation between the cultural motivation of individuals and religious grounds of meaning, as this problem was analyzed in Max Weber's work in the sociology of religion.

The fact that Mannheim's attention was focused primarily on the former problem may have something to do with some of the ambiguities which have plagued discussion in this field, certain of which ambiguities start with the very term *Wissen*, which is the German word usually translated as "knowledge" in the phrase "sociology of knowledge." The focus has usually been on the concept of ideology as a structure of ideas, to be appropriately judged by the standards of empirical science. This clearly is at the center of Mannheim's thinking—the problem of the ways in which evaluative considerations enter into the allegedly empirical ideas current about societies, notably the societies in which the ideas themselves are produced, and how these may lead to distortion and selection and may or may not vitiate objectivity. The term *Wissen* is, however, also applicable in contexts which refer, not to empirical objects, but to the grounds of meaning, in what Weber would call "religious ideas." I should like to argue that the relation of this kind of *Wissen* to the social system is altogether different from Mannheim's problem of ideology.

But while both empirical science and the grounding of meaning are alike in referring to matters of what "is," of what "exists," in analytical independence of imperatives for action, the other two cultural categories— patterns of evaluation and of expressive symbolization—are so different from both of these that it is of dubious utility to include values and expressive symbols at all as forms of "knowledge." The essential issue is whether the sociology of knowledge should be treated as the "sociology of culture" in the most general possible sense, or whether it could reasonably be restricted to the aspects of culture here singled out. I shall proceed on the assumption that this restriction is reasonable.

THE RELATION OF VALUES TO EMPIRICAL SCIENCE

Having pointed out two areas of study for a sociology of knowledge, I shall narrow the scope of this discussion to one of them—the relation of values to empirical knowledge. My starting point is the conception that empirical-rational knowledge is an authentically independent component of all cultural systems, even in the most definitely non-literate societies.[5] The levels of its development of course vary enormously; modern science represents a phenomenon altogether without precedent in any other civilization. Science is characterized as a body of knowledge not only by its extension of the knowledge of facts, but, just as importantly, by its *organization* of facts in terms of generalized conceptual schemes.

Empirical knowledge is, furthermore, differentiated in terms of its objects of study, notably into physical, biological, psychological, social, and cultural sciences. While it is obvious that these "levels" of the empirical world interpenetrate intimately with one another, the older forms of positivistic reductionism, which would deny any genuine theoretical significance to such distinctions of level, must be regarded as definitely out of date and superseded.

Values, as was mentioned above, I understand to be *conceptions of the desirable*, applied to various objects and standing at varying levels of generality. Societal values are specified to the society itself as object; they are conceptions of the good type of society. When institutionalized, they are such conceptions as are held by the members of the society themselves, and to which they hold motivational commitments.

Within the cultural system—i.e., in terms of the first paradigm—values must meet certain imperatives. First, they must be *legitimized* through their relations to the ultimate grounds of meaning of the human situation. Secondly, they must be made motivationally meaningful through articulation of the desir*able* with the desir*ed*—i.e., through definition of appropriate rewards. The third imperative is, however, the one of most direct concern here. This concerns the relation between values and empirical knowledge. In this connection we should keep in mind that within a culture, the mutual relation to each other of empirical science and values is only one of several contexts in which each of these cultural categories is involved. Science is in particular also related to practical problems through its capacity for prediction and control, and to the cultural bases underlying the structure of theory. And social *values* are also related to the motivational commitments of individuals and to the grounds of the meaning of the values.

It should also be made clear at the start that both value systems and systems of empirical knowledge are graded into levels of generality. While for empirical knowledge the relevant scale is the hierarchy of the sciences from physical through biological to psychological, social, and cultural science, for values, it is the valuation of objects in these spheres, and of course in their subspheres. Therefore somewhat different problems arise according to what level of objects is being scientifically analyzed, on the one hand, and according to what level of specification in the system of values is involved, on the other. Our primary interest, in this paper, is clearly at the level of the relation between the values of the social system, on the one hand, and the scientific analysis of the social system, on the other. It is clear, further, that the social system referred to here is the total society. When we consider social classes or other subcategories of social structure, such as occupational status or ethnic groups within a society, another order of problems arises.

Bearing in mind these qualifications, we may say that there are here involved two fundamental problems—the "Kantian" problem and the "Weberian" problem. The Kantian problem relates in the first place to the basic scientific standards of empirical validity, which Weber called the "schema of empirical proof."[6] These basic standards are spelled out in three directions. The first, concerning the structure of the theoretical system, says that any inconsistency at theoretical levels is ground for questioning the validity of a given proposition—i.e., if this proposition is inconsistent which others believed to be validated. The other two sets of standards both concern particularized assertions about empirical objects. One concerns the empirical validity of the proposition, in terms of the well-known criteria of prediction and control; the other concerns the theoretical significance of the particular statement of fact. Put in the simplest terms, these two essential questions about a statement of fact are, "Is it empirically true?" and "Is it scientifically important?"

Empirical proof, however, is irrelevant without some conception of *problems* relative to which empirical propositions may be formulated. I would suggest that Kant's famous categories of the understanding constitute the formulation of the most general framework of the questions which are addressed to the empirical world. These categories are at the cultural level evaluative because they concern the categorization of what, for human beings, it is important to know about the empirical world. Clearly, the Kantian categories are rooted in the highest-level grounds of the validity of empirical knowledge, in what Kant called transcendental considerations. Thus the Kantian categories represent the level which comprises the significance of knowledge in all the empirical sciences—although clearly Kant was thinking primarily of physical science; in his time, problems of social science were hardly yet receiving serious philosophical consideration. This level would thus comprise interests of *all* categories of objects—physical, biological, social, etc.

In what sense could it be said that the Kantian categories are relative? I think the most likely sense is an evolutionary one. It is only when empirical knowledge becomes sufficiently developed and technical that such an elaborately differentiated scheme of categories becomes relevant. Such a relativity, however, does not affect the problem of validity as such, but rather the problem of human interests, i.e., the value of knowing different kinds of answers. Interests in this sense are subject to a process of differentiation through the development of culture.[7]

What I am calling the "Weberian" problem, as distinguished from the Kantian, arises at a lower level of generality which is more immediately relevant for the sociology of knowledge. This concerns the sense in which relatively specific social value systems (those of a particular society or sub-group in it) affect relatively specific bodies of knowledge. Here Weber's crucial concept is "value-relevance" (*Wertbeziehung*). Essentially what Weber said was that no matter how fully any given empirical propositions are validated, their inclusion in a body of knowledge about society is never completely independent of the value perspective from which those particular questions were asked to which these propositions constitute answers.

Weber's formulation could be said to be simply a statement of considerations at least implicit in the Kantian position. Weber, however, had the methodological problems of social science directly in mind, so it seems that there is a significant difference of level involved. In the study of a society by its own members, there is a different order of integration between values and empirical knowledge from that which exists between values and knowledge of the physical world. This is because the institutionalized values of a society constitute not merely a basis of selective *interest in* its phenomena, but are directly constitutive of the society's structure itself. This means that a different subject-object frame of reference is involved from that in the study of the physical world. The object is both "out there"—in Durkheim's sense an external object—and part of the observer himself, i.e., is internalized. There is doubtless a sense in which this is also true of physical objects, but it is somehow a remoter sense.

I should, however, not hesitate to apply the general methodological canons of scientific method to social theory as well as to physical theory. The position of the observer is in principle inherently involved in conceptualization of all objects—both social and physical—even though in social science it becomes in practice so much more salient that it must be explicitly analyzed to avoid serious implicit biases.[8]

These considerations do not seem to imply the *epistemological* relativism with the possibility of which Mannheim played. That this should be so depends on the conception of a fundamental unity of human culture and of the conditions of human orientation to the world. This is to say that there are universal criteria of empirical validity, a position taken clearly, following Weber, by both von Schelting and Stark. Within this framework, there is certainly variability, but it is not random variability, because neither human values nor the human situation vary at random. They vary on definable dimensions over limited ranges, ranges which are defined by the *relations* of empirical knowledge to the other three dimensions of cultural systems we have distinguished.[9]

The relativity of the empirical knowledge of social phenomena is thus not in essence, i.e., epistemologically, different from the relativity of physical knowledge.[10] We can, therefore, legitimately think in terms of an ideal type of objective scientific knowledge about a society, which is subject to all the fundamental canons of science, but which in selectivity (as distinguished from distortion) of content, and in the basis of its meaning within the society, is relative to the values of that society at a given time. This set of considerations merges with those previously discussed concerning the methodology of science itself, modifying them only by introducing explicitly the sense in which the content of any science, but most particularly of social science, contains an element of relation (and hence, in one sense, "relativity") to values.

THE VALUE-SCIENCE INTEGRATE AND IDEOLOGY

What Mannheim meant by the "general" conception of ideology[11] is very close to this ideal type of social science, relativized to the nature of the society in which it has arisen and gains some kind of acceptance. Interpreted in the present terms, it seems to me that Mannheim's "general ideology" should be regarded not just as a scientific explanation of the current state of the society, but as a "value-scientific integrate" at the cultural level. This is to say, it is a body of "ideas" which combine a conceptual framework for interpreting the empirical state of a society with a set of premises from which this state is evaluated positively or negatively. A "general ideology" is the most directly relevant general cultural framework within which a social system can be "seen" as an empirical object. It explicitly shows the relevance, besides the empirical scientific component itself, of the evaluative component, but it should not be forgotten that relations to the grounding of meanings and to expressive symbolization are also always implicitly relevant, even if they are not made explicit.

The value-science integrate, unlike Mannheim's "particular" conception, which I will refer to as "ideology,"[12] should be interpreted as theoretically independent of the degrees of integration of the actual social system with the values which constitute the premises of the value-science integrate. It is compatible with variations from the most "conservative" defense of the status quo to the most revolutionary repudiation of it in the name of an alternative state. Its essential criterion is consistency at the *cultural* level between empirical conceptions of the "social reality" and those evaluative patterns which define the *desirable* social system.

As we have noted, this conception does not impugn the objectivity of empirical social knowledge. It suggests that the *selection* of problems to which answers are given is a function of the values of the society in which such knowledge arises and becomes significant. In this sense, every social theory is relative to the society in which it belongs. But selection in this sense must be carefully distinguished both from a secondary type of selection and from *distortion*, which is realistically always present, but which analytically must be attributed to quite a different order of factors. Weber's concept of *Wert-beziehung*, in my opinion, adequately takes care of the concept of what may be called the "primary selectivity" involved in the value-science integrate. This is to say that even apart from limitations on the empirical resources available for validation, no social science integrated with the value system of a society can give answers to *all* the possible significant problems of societies, but only to those which have meaning within this integrate.

The more usual conception of ideology, which is close to what Mannheim meant by the "particular" conception, must be approached in terms of our *second* paradigm of institutionalization, which concerns not the sense in which different components of the institutionalized cultural system are integrated with *one another*, but the sense in which the normative culture thus institutionalized in fact determines concrete social action. What I have called the value-science integrate provides the essential set of standards of identifying a particular ideology, and the points of reference for analyzing its interdependence with those components of the social system which are by definition non-cultural.

Particular ideologies deviate from the value-science integrate in two significant respects. On the one hand they involve a further *selectivity*, in that among the problems and phenomena known to be significant for the social science of the time, they select some for emphasis, and neglect or play down others. Thus the business ideology, for instance, substantially exaggerates the contribution of businessmen to the national welfare and underplays the contribution of scientists and professional men. And in the current ideology of the "intellectuals," the importance of social "pressures to conformity" is exaggerated, and institutional factors in the freedom of the individual are ignored or played down.[13]

This type of selectivity, which may be called "secondary" to distinguish it from the "primary" type referred to above, shades off into *distortion*; indeed, the distinction between them depends on the level of generality at which the problem is considered. Thus, from the point of view of a full sociological analysis of American society as a whole, the "intellectuals'" neglect of the institutionalization of freedom could be called distortion, whereas at lower levels of generality, in discussions of particular organizational or peer-group phenomena, it may be considered to be selectivity. The criterion of distortion is that statements are made about the society which by social-scientific methods can be shown to be positively in error, whereas selectivity is involved where the statements are, at the proper level, "true" but do not constitute a balanced account of the available truth. It is clear that both secondary selectivity and distortion in an ideology violate the standards of empirical social science, in a sense in which the value-science integrate does not.

If these deviations from scientific objectivity are essential criteria of an ideology in this present sense, it does not follow that values have ceased to be relevant factors. The *relation* between values and empirical beliefs about the society continues to constitute the main axis of the problem. But in considering an ideology, values must be specified to the level of different subsystems of the society, like businessmen or intellectuals, and the degree of their compatibility with each of the non-cultural components distinguished in our second paradigm becomes problematical, whereas in the first paradigm it was not.

It should be made clear that my insistence on the indispensability of a standard of empirical validity for the analysis of ideology docs not imply that such analysis is possible only when the social sciences have reached perfection. What is required is not a standard of absolute correctness, but of relative validity, since the problem of ideology arises where there is a *discrepancy* between what is believed and what can be scientifically correct. Naturally the range over which such discrepancies can be demonstrated is a function of the advancement of social science. Science and ideology can be only analytically distinguished from each other; in its development, social science differentiates out from ideology since it emerges from the same roots in common sense.

Common sense is not necessarily ideological in the present meaning of the term, for it may formulate highly condensed and simplified versions of knowledge which can be scientifically demonstrated to be correct. The standard which is relevant here is not scientific proof or form of statement, but scientific correctness (including adequacy to the relevant problems). Persons who act on common sense may be themselves quite unable to explain why it is true, but so long as it *is* correct and neither selected nor distorted relative to the relevant action problems, it is not ideological.

The above discussion leads up to the proposition that the *problems* of the sociology of ideology cannot be clearly stated except in the context of an explicitly *cultural* reference. Secondary selection and distortion can only be demonstrated by reference to their deviation from the cultural standards of the value-science integrate, and if there is no such selection or distortion, the empirical beliefs in question must be classed as common sense, technological knowledge, or science. But once an ideology has been clearly identified by reference to deviation from these cultural standards, then the non-cultural considerations included in the second paradigm can be brought into play. Two aspects of the non-cultural problem may immediately be discriminated. One is the problem of explaining the *sources* of ideological selection and distortion; its reciprocal is the problem of the *consequences* to the social system of the promulgation and acceptance of ideological beliefs.

THE SOURCES OF IDEOLOGICAL SELECTION AND DISTORTION: THE CONCEPT OF STRAIN

The starting point for treatment of both of the above problems clearly lies in the relation of values to social structure through institutionalization. In terms of the second paradigm, it will be remembered, in order to be institutionalized, values have to be (1) specified not only to the society but to the relevant subsystems within the society; (2) legitimized as directly motivationally relevant to the particular groups involved and spelled out in terms of norms; (3) integrated, through the relevantly specified norms, with the goals of the collectivities concerned; and (4) integrated with the motivational commitments of individuals in roles.[14]

Since our concern in discussing ideologies is with deviance from an ideal type defined by a value-science integrate, the problem of locating the elements of deviance and their underlying sources can be broken down in terms of the above four subproblems. First, there is the possibility of malintegration of the value structure itself. This would take the form of a discrepancy in pattern between the society's higher-order values and the values of one or more relevant subsystems. This, for example, would be the case for an incomplete acculturated immigrant group that comes from a society having different values from those in the host society.

Second, even where values are adequately specified, there is the problem of defining norms the terms of which can be implemented in relatively concrete situations. Since social systems are systems of interactive *relationships* between units, a set of norms governing the action of two or more such units can never be tailored totally to the values, goals, or situation of *any one*. Norms thus have, above all, the function of integrating the "needs" of operative units with each other and of reconciling them with the needs of the system as a whole. In more detail, then, norms spell out expectations for collectivities and for persons acting in roles, and, in doing so, may bring to light discrepancies among these expectations.

Third, there may be discrepancy in the definition of the functions and goals of collectivities. A particularly prominent case has been the "profit motive" in modern Western society, which in my opinion is properly conceived as a goal of the business firm as a collectivity, not a "motive" of individuals. It is one of two primary institutionalized goals of firms, the other being "production" of goods and/or services. It has, of course, been an important focus of ideological preoccupation in modern society, particularly since industrial revolution.

Finally, a discrepancy may be located at the role level in terms of the motivation of the individual. A prominent example is the problem of institutionalizing commitment to marital patterns both as "love objects" and as co-leaders of the family. Thus the problem areas of sexual freedom and of divorce are foci of ideological thinking; comparable problems, though very different in specific content, concern commitment to occupational responsibilities, for instance, in discussions over the relative importance of work and leisure, such as Veblen's ironic treatment of the "leisure class."

In most concrete cases, discrepancies will exist at all four of these points, but they will have differential impacts on different groups in a society. All of them are, however, foci both of institutionalization and of internalization. Since social systems, cultural systems, and personality systems are independently variable, there will never be complete correspondence between them; some degree of discrepancy is inevitable.

Where these discrepancies can be shown to be specifically "built into" the social system, we may use the concept of *structured strain*.[15] So far as structured strain underlies ideologies, it can be said to focus on the relation between empirical conceptions of the society and its subsystems, and societal values and their subspecifications. It should be remembered, however, that the concept of strain is not in itself an explanation of ideological patterns, but a generalized label for the kind of factors to look for in working out an explanation. The above frame is meant to contribute to the interpretation of what underlies this label and its use in certain contexts.

In the above sketch, the point of reference is the factors involved in the orientations of certain categories of individuals. Persons looked at in this way are oriented in, and to, a situation external to themselves. It is, however, the crux of social systems analysis to keep continually in the forefront of attention the fact that what is a given category of actors is a set of patterned orientations from the point of view of the persons who compose that situation, and vice versa. The distinction between orienting actors and situation is hence inherently a relative distinction, relevant only at one level of analysis. This distinction is cut across by the distinction among institutionalized values, their grounding of meaning, motivational commitments, and empirical knowledge. All of these concepts apply, with different empirical content, of course, on *both* sides of the actor-situation dichotomy in any given case.

The imperatives described above for maintaining the ideal type of integration of objective social science with values entail certain balances in rates of input and output between particular roles and collectivities and other elements of the social system. The primary functional concern may be the maintenance and development of empirical knowledge, for instance, or the maintenance of values. Let us take empirical science, with special reference to social science, as an example.

Strains Affecting Social Science

The scientific community may be thought of as a social system which is organized about a type of *cultural* interest and commitment, in this case, the maintenance and extension of empirical knowledge. In analyzing such a system it is essential to distinguish clearly between institutionalized cultural standards themselves, on the one hand, and the institutionalized modes of their implementation in the corresponding social system, on the other. The first problem belongs in the first paradigm, the second in the second paradigm.[16]

Thus the cultural standards outlined above as "the schema of empirical proof" must be implemented in concrete processes of action. First, a system of scientific investigation must be organized to maximize the probability of attaining its goal of "discovery"—i.e., of making possible the statement of new empirical propositions. Secondly, however, discovery can only contribute to the cultural corpus of science through a process of empirical validation, in which the criteria of objectivity are paramount. Thirdly, the contribution of the isolated proposition, however valid, is limited unless it can be fitted into generalized conceptual schemes; hence building theory is just as important in investigation as a social process as is making empirical discoveries, or validating them.

The problem now is how far and by what processes the non-cultural conditions impinging on this process are successfully controlled in the interest of the cultural standards. Crucial though the creativeness of the individual scientist is, if he is to be a specialist in science, he and his family must find some basis of support in the division of labor. His incomprehensible, often uncanny and sometimes disturbing or dangerous activities and ideas must somehow be tolerated in the community. He must be provided with adequate facilities to do his work, including books and periodicals, laboratory equipment, and many other things. Scientists themselves must form a subcommunity with media of communication, modes of organization, and so on.

Clearly the basic mode of institutionalization of science in the modern Western world has come to be in the university, which provides scientists with a system of fully institutionalized occupational roles having a respected status in the community, financial support, facilities, and access to students and to a community of competent colleagues. Of course, a further highly significant development is the spilling over of science into other sectors of society, notably through its relation to the various kinds of technology employed in industry and in government.

The sociology of science, then, studies the conditions under which the cultural criteria of science can become institutionalized according to the first paradigm, and once they are institutionalized, the conditions necessary for their implementation in the concrete investigative process according to the second paradigm. Further, it deals with problems having to do with how far these scientific canons and implementing activities are accepted in the society outside the scientific community. It is in the nature of social systems that this acceptance cannot be limited to the scientific community itself; there must be articulation with more generalized values and the institutional structures in which nonscientists participate.

Broadly speaking, tolerance of the scientific attitude becomes more difficult the closer its subject matter comes to the direct constitution of the society and the personalities of its members. It seems highly probable that it is not only for technical, but also for societal, reasons that physical science, with its more remote subject matter, has been the first branch of science to achieve a high level of development, and that the development in our own time of the sciences dealing with human action documents a crucially important development in the society itself, as well as in science. It is not too much to say that in no previous society would this development have been possible. It is a fact, however, that social science has been a recently and rapidly developing thing; thus, the full institutionalization of the more general values of science, as defining the empirical role of the social scientist, cannot be taken for granted. There are "insecurities." Social scientists may lack support for scientific standards from their university as a collectivity which, to varying degrees, may have stable commitments to the goals of science. Or their own motivational commitments may be in varying respects and degrees incomplete and ambivalent; e.g., they may be more concerned with practical usefulness than they are with scientific achievement as such, or they may be overly "success"-oriented. Finally, the technical state of their own field may be so imperfect that it is difficult to use genuinely technical standards to resist these pressures when the primary rewards for genuine scientific achievement—self-respect or recognition from colleagues or both —may be too sparse for full efficacy over a long period.

There are thus built-in vulnerabilities to ideological "bias" at the very core of the social-scientific endeavor itself (and indeed, in somewhat lesser degree, in all science). But beyond this, what I have called the scientific community is at best only partially insulated, both culturally and socially, from those other elements in society which in the nature of *their* structural positions cannot give primacy to scientific subvalues and standards of empirical investigation. In these outside circles, commitments to other subvalues in the society are likely to be reflected in ambivalent or negative attitudes toward the scientist's role commitments (or, what in some respects is as disturbing, in the overidealization of the scientist as a "magician"). And the layman is likely to hold positive empirical beliefs which more or less disagree with those of scientific specialists in various fields.

This is essentially to say that the input–output balance between the scientific community and other societal subsystems is likely to be precarious, with an almost inherent tendency for strong pressures to exact "concessions" from the scientific community to these outside orientations. Underlying this situation is the fact that scientists are not as such politically powerful or in command of large economic resources; they are inherently dependent on other structural elements of the society for these resources as well as for their ultimate legitimation.

It is thus clear that members of the scientific community are in the nature of the case subject to such a complex of strains that it is not surprising if they are unable to control completely either their own belief systems or the currency of beliefs in the society at large about their fields of competence. The other side of the picture is, of course, the operation, over the long run, of selfcorrective mechanisms. Empirical propositions do get validated; the valuation of truth in this area does get progressively farther institutionalized. At certain points, practical "pay-offs" result in benefits which would not be available without such knowledge. Were these positive mechanisms not operative, it would be difficult to explain why the symbol "science" is clearly a modern prestige symbol which is widely, if sometimes dubiously, appropriated, as in the phrases "Christian *Science*" or "*scientific* socalism." Without the prestige of science, this would not make sense, and it would be difficult to understand that prestige if authentic science in fact had no independent importance.

It is also to be expected in terms of our analysis that as one goes from the inner core of what is here called the scientific community toward other groups in the social structure, there should be increasing prominence of selection and distortion relative to scientifically objective standards. Further, certain of these outside groups have special relations to selected portions of the scientific community because of their common "interests" in a particular subject matter. In the American type of society, there is first an obvious and natural relation between natural science and technology. Among the social sciences, then, a special relation obtains between the business community and economics, so that economics is peculiarly vulnerable to the operation of strains as between the scientific and the business communities. Similar considerations apply to the relations between political science and the political elements of the society, and between the legal system and academic law as a discipline. Finally, sociology, with values as a central part of its subject matter, stands in a relation of strain to those elements in the society that are particularly concerned with the guardianship of its values.

Since the strain to which the scientific community is inevitably subjected is likely to be fairly definitely structured rather than random, the chances are minimized of a completely "stark" confrontation of the scientific community with antithetical outside groups. This point calls attention to the very important role of the applied professions as "buffer institutions" in modern society. Historically, this has certainly involved the development of a professional clergy and a legal profession for the application of cultural values and norms in the social system, but more recently, the striking development is that of professions involving the application of various sciences. Medicine and engineering have taken the lead as applications of physical science, but there has been a steady spread of this development, above all to the psychological and social sciences.[17] It is commonplace to regard these applied professions as channels through which technical knowledge, generated in the scientific or otherwise predominantly cultural community, is diffused to and applied in sectors of the society which are not primarily devoted to cultural functions. This, of course, is correct, but it is only one side of the coin. The other is the sense in which the "applied" professions act as a buffer mitigating the pressures which impinge on the cultural community and which would otherwise constitute more seriously disturbing sources of strain.

These considerations are important for the study of ideology. The applied professions should constitute particularly strategic points for the study of the balance of forces operating on the scientific underpinnings of the intellectual culture of modern society, for these are the groups whose professional training has anchored them in the academic disciplines but who at the same time are in direct contact with the related nonacademic sectors of the society.

This point may be illustrated by mentioning a few empirical problems concerning American society, without attempting to enter into their analysis. One would be the problem of why "organized medicine" has come to be ideologically so closely assimilated to the predominant business ideology, thereby tending somewhat to cut itself off from university medicine. Another would be the problem of why, as documented in a recent study, the academic profession in the social sciences has leaned politically considerably to the left of other population groups of comparable income and social-prestige status.[18] Still another would be why the "intellectuals," particularly those outside the academic core, and with humanistic, literary interests, were so attracted by an ideology emphasizing the less attractive features of "mass culture," the dangers of "conformity," and the presumptive loss of "values" in contemporary society.[19]

Consideration of the ideologies of various professions connects with the problem of the ways in which groups not specifically trained in academic disciplines are predisposed to different orders of belief systems in the relevant areas. Examples would be the beliefs of the businessman or the trade unionist about the functioning of the economy, or the beliefs of the lay public concerning methods of child rearing and elementary education. With the increasing prominence of the intellectual disciplines in such areas, however, we cannot speak of ideological belief systems without reference to the ways "popular" beliefs attempt to articulate with those beliefs current in the relevant professional circles, which may themselves, of course, be ideologically selected and distorted.

SOME SOCIAL CONSEQUENCES OF IDEOLOGY

We may now turn briefly from the analysis of the *determinants* of ideological patterns to the obvious problem, that of the possible *effects* on a society of the currency of different ideological patterns. Systematic theoretical analysis of the articulation between cultural social systems is as necessary for this side of the problem as it is for dealing with the determination of ideas. In such analysis the two essential points of reference are again, on the one hand, the methodological criteria for objective empirical knowledge and, on the other hand, the conception of an integrated, institutionalized system of values.

The process by which a *new* value system may become institutionalized in a society or in one or more of its subsystems is clearly one version of the "influence of ideas," though not, as I see it, directly of "knowledge."[20] Here I would suggest, first, that in dealing with problems of ideology it is useful to treat the higher-level values of the society as given. Since the stability of such values is in general very important indeed for a social system, we may presume that perhaps the primary function of ideology is either to protect the stability of the institutionalized values, or conversely, in the case of a revolutionary ideology, to undermine the values, at least of such sub-systems as the "upper" classes and the business community, if not of the society as a whole; the latter case would present a different order of theoretical problem.

Broadly it can be said that within Western society there is at a high level a *common* value base underlying both conservative and radical ideologies. Instead of attempting to undermine these high-level values, the radical ideology tends to assert the unacceptability of the existing society from the point of view of values which everybody takes for granted, whereas the conservative ideology tends to assert that broadly the state of the society is acceptable, and that deliberate attempts to usher in change will be dangerous. Thus, questions of empirical fact about the state of the society have become especially salient with the emergence of the "ideological age" in the last century. An illustration that a radical ideology does not seek to overthrow the *whole* value complex of Western society is to be seen in the high value which "socialism," in *common* with "capitalism," places on economic production. This circumstance is one essential consideration for explaining the fact that the more radical version of socialism tends so drastically to lose its appeal in those societies which have achieved a relatively high level of industrial development and of economic welfare for the masses.[21]

A second social function of ideology is to facilitate acceptance, in the broader society, of scientific professionals and of the bodies of empirical knowledge they "produce." In spite of an ideology's selection and distortion, which are necessarily disturbing to those professionals, it may be conceived as a mechanism which mediates between their scientific standards and the values of those non-professional subgroups who also have an "interest" in various scientific fields. That is, *up to a certain limit*, which should be approximately definable in empirical terms, selection and distortion can still serve the function of integrating the main bearers of scientific culture with the other groups who have an "interest" in the subject matter. But somewhere there is a threshold beyond which the effect will tend to be the opposite. In contemporary society, the location of this threshold will affect the character of various versions of "anti-intellectualism." Thus the [Joseph] McCarthyite version of populism, for example, seems to have been clearly beyond this threshold with respect to demands for political loyalty in a democracy under severe political pressures.

A third function of ideology, vis-à-vis the maintenance of role-commitments by individuals, emerges when, in the process of structural differentiation within the framework of a relatively stable institutionalized value system, subsystem values no longer jibe sufficiently with the actual nature of those subsystems, thus raising questions about what is expected of classes of persons in different role positions in the society. When expectations are not adequately defined, it is impossible for performance and sanction to be accurately matched, and hence motivation to role performance is likely to be disturbed. Then, as psychological rationalization, adherence to an ideology can, within the personality, serve as a mechanism for bridging the gap. But here it is important to distinguish conceptually the consequences *for the social system* of this function of ideology, from its consequences in psychological terms *for the individual personality*, as well as more generally to discriminate between value problems at the cultural system level and role commitment problems at the social system level. We might indicate the distinction by saying that ideology is a category of culture more or less institutionalized in social systems, whereas the corresponding category for the personality is rationalization in the psychoanalytic sense. The degree to which rationalizations are socially shared is in principle problematical; for ideologies it is a defining criterion. Many discussions of ideology do not make these distinctions, which in terms of the present approach are crucial.

If it is indeed the case that ideology has a special relation to the process of structural differentiation in the society, it follows that it is in turn related to the problem of organic solidarity in Durkheim's sense. Perhaps it is not too much to say, in summary, that ideology is a special manifestation of the strains associated with the increasing division of labor, and that in turn it is an integrative mechanism which operates to mitigate those strains. More specifically, the strains particularly associated with structural differentiation are those of *anomie*, again in Durkheim's sense.[22] They concern inadequate clarity in the "definition of the situation," particularly at the normative level, since this level stands between values and the more specific goals of collectivities and role obligations of their members. On the whole, I would strongly suggest that a great prevalence of ideology is a symptom that the main disturbances in a society are *not* at the highest level of institutionalized values, but rather concern the integrative problems associated with the process of differentiation.

Unfortunately it is impossible, within the limits of this paper, to take space to follow out the implications of this interpretation further with the analysis of a few concrete examples, but such an attempt would be essential to a real demonstration of the usefulness of the approach.

CONCLUSION

This discussion has necessarily been a mere sketch of an exceedingly complicated area of problems. Its primary objective has been to try to put some problems which have grown up within the sociology of knowledge into a somewhat wider perspective made possible by the theory of action, which calls for the careful analysis of both cultural and social systems and their relations to each other. The term "knowledge" has seemed to me to refer to cognitively ordered orientations to objects, with reference both to empirical facts and to problems of meaning. The problem of ideology has been interpreted to concern the first context, expecially when the social system itself is the empirical object; Weber's problem of the sociology of religious ideas concerns primarily the second context. It seems important to keep these two problem areas clearly distinct, but also to relate them as the two primary branches of the sociology of knowledge.

Both involve fundamental relations to the values institutionalized in the social system. Indeed, this relation to values is the focus of the sociological problems which arise with respect to these two fundamental components of cultural systems. However, neither values nor motivational commitments and their symbolization in expressive terms are, by my definitions, legitimately referred to as forms of "knowledge." The sociology of knowledge should not be identified with the sociology of culture, which is a wider category. Only through an analysis of both social and cultural systems and of their interpenetration and interdependence, however, can an adequate sociology of knowledge be worked out.

NOTES

1 This paper constitutes a considerable condensation of the version submitted for the International Sociological Congress in Stresa, September, 1959. The difficult work of condensation has been very ably carried out, with complete fidelity to the author's meaning, by Mrs. Carolyn Cooper.

2 Cf. "An Outline of the Social System," Part II of General Introduction in Talcott Parsons, Edward A. Shils, Kaspas D. Naegele, and Jesse R. Pitts (eds). *Theories of Society*, (Glencoe, Ill.: The Free Press, 1961).

3 In one sense this classification is organized about the subject-object relationship. Seen from this point of view, empirical existential ideas and expressive symbol systems are patternings of the meaning *of objects*. Evaluative patterns and the grounding of meaning, on the other hand, put primacy in the orienting activity of the actor *as* subject; they are patternings of orientation which may be classified in such a way as to cut across any classification of the objects to which they are oriented. On the general basis of this classification, cf. "Culture and the Social System," Introduction to Part IV of *ibid.*

4 Clyde Kluckhohn, "Values and Value-Orientations in the Theory of Action: An Exploration in Definition and Classification," in Talcott Parsons and Edward A. Shils (eds.), *Toward a General Theory of Action* (Cambridge, Mass.: Harvard University Press, 1951), esp. p. 395.

5 Bronislaw Malinowski's well-known analysis in *Magic, Science and Religion* (1925) (Glencoe, Ill.: The Free Press, 1948), is perhaps the best reference point for this assertion.

6 Cf. Max Weber, "'Objectivity' in Social Science and Social Policy," in *Max Weber on the Methodology of the Social Sciences*, trans. and ed. by Edward A. Shils and Henry A. Finch (Glencoe, Ill.: The Free Press, 1949); Alexander von Schelting, *Max Weber's Wissenschaftslehre* (Tübingen: J. C. B. Mohr, 1934); also my own *The Structure of Social Action* (Glencoe, Ill.: The Free Press, 1940), chap. xv.

7 In our formal terms, this may be interpreted to mean that the canons of scientific *validity* root in the cultural complex which focuses on empirical knowledge, whereas the problem of the *importance* of empirical propositions roots in the evaluative complex.

8 It is partly for reasons of this sort that social science develops later in the evolution of culture than does physical science, and that successful handling of it requires higher levels of maturity in individual scientists, at least in the absence of full institutionalization. It might further be inferred that the establishment of an institutional framework for its handling was more difficult and more important than in the case of physical science.

9 It has been suggested above that there are three different bases of such variability, namely, institutionalized values, relations to the grounds of meaning, and to the interests of individuals in rewards for "acceptable" conduct. There are formal reasons to place these sets of selective factors in a hierarchy of control in the order named. For the benefit of those familiar with my analytical scheme it may be pointed out that the system of empirical knowledge is considered to be the adaptive subsystem of a system of culture. Its basic standards will be considered to be institutionalized in turn in *its* "pattern-maintenance" subsystem and thus relatively immune from influences emanating from other cultural subsystems. Of the three types of interchange with other cultural systems, however, the interchange with the value system should have the primarily *integrative* function. The relation to the grounding of meaning, then, should be particularly concerned with goal attainment of an empirical system, and that to the cultural patterning of the reward system should have primarily adaptive significance to it. If this formal set of relationships holds, it should follow that values should, in a cybernetic sense, control the other two sources of the variability relative to the basic cultural standards, the canons of validity. This might be regarded as a formal justification of Weber's emphasis on *value*-relevance as the primary focus of the problem of relativity of social-scientific knowledge. The formal scheme referred to here has been developed most fully so far

in published form in Talcott Parsons and Neil J. Smelser, *Economy and Society* (Glencoe, Ill.: The Free Press, 1956), chap. ii.

10 A point on which Weber unfortunately was not fully clear, since he was deeply imbued with the methodological importance of the distinction between the natural and the socio-cultural sciences, which was so prominent in the German intellectual milieu of his time.

11 Karl Mannheim, *Ideology and Utopia* (1929) (New York: Harcourt, Brace & Co., 1936), esp. p. 68, n. 2.

12 To avoid confusion with the more common conception of ideology (Mannheim's "particular" conception, which will be outlined below), I propose to avoid the use of the term "ideology" when referring to Mannheim's general conception, by substituting the phrase "value-science integrate."

13 Cf. F. X. Sutton, S. E. Harris, C. Kaysen, and J. Tobin, *The American Business Creed* (Cambridge Mass.: Harvard University Press, 1956); and Clyde Kluckhohn, "Have There Been Discernible Shifts in American Values During the Past Generation?" in Elting Morison (ed.), *The American Style* (New York: Harper & Bros., 1958).

14 It follows from this general description of the relations of values and norms to social structure that for the operative units of that structure—collectivities and persons in roles—their position in the structure is for most purposes the same thing as their relation to the societal value system and to its various subsystems specified to the relevant levels.

15 Cf. Sutton, Harris, Kaysen, and Tobin, *The American Business Creed*, for an important recent work which makes extensive use of this concept.

16 The scientific role must be institutionalized, but roles must fit into collectivities—in this case the most important is the university. Further, universities must enjoy freedom and encouragement under the normative order of the society. All these are steps of institutionalization *under* the cultural pattern of *valuation* of science.

17 A further most important development has been the increasing structural integration of these applied professions with the iniversity, especially through their training and through research. Cf. my paper "Some Problems Confronting Sociology as a Profession," *American Sociological Review*, XXIV (August, 1959), 547–59.

18 Paul F. Lazarsfeld and Wagner Thielens, Jr., *The Academic Mind* (Glencoe, Ill.: The Free Press, 1958).

19 Cf. Winston R. White, "The Ideology of American Intellectuals" (unpublished Ph.D. dissertation, Harvard University, 1960).

20 This process in the social system is directly analogous to that of the internalization of values in the personality through socialization. I have attempted to deal with an important societal case in "Christianity and Modern Industrial Society," in E. A. Tiryakian (ed.), *Essays in Honor of Pitirim A. Sorokin* (Glencoe, Ill.: The Free Press, 1961). A full discussion of the relation of subsystem values to the process of structural differentiation within a society is given in N. J. Smelser, *Social Change in the Industrial Revolution* (Chicago: University of Chicago Press, 1959). A paradigm for the case of personality was worked out by Talcott Parsons and James Olds, in Talcott Parsons and Robert F. Bales, *Family Socialization, and Interaction Process* (Glencoe, Ill.: The Free Press, 1955), chap. iv.

21 Cf. Seymour Martin Lipset, "Socialism—Left and Right—East and West," *Confluence*, VII (Summer, 1958), 173–92, and *Political Man* (Garden City, N.Y.: Doubleday and Co., 1960).

22 Cf. my paper, "Durkheim's Contribution to the Theory of Integration of Social Systems," in Kurt H. Wolff (ed.), *Emile Durkheim, 1858–1917: A Collection of Essays, with Translations and a Bibliography* (Columbus, Ohio: Ohio State University Press, 1961).

3

FLORIAN ZNANIECKI

Sociology and Theory of Knowledge

SOCIOLOGY IS STILL young and inclined to be imperialistic. Her fore-fathers claimed for her the entire domain of culture, and many of her faithful courtiers are trying to make those claims good by extending her sway over the fields of law, economics, technology, language, literature, art, religion, knowledge. These attempts conflict not only with the vested rights of the sciences that have of old dominated these fields but also with the counter-claims of sociology's equally aggressive rival—psychology, which is in turn encroaching upon sociological grounds. The resultant struggles have not been unproductive. New problems have been defined, new methods devised for their solution. On the other hand, however, many strictly socio-logical problems are still neglected or treated inadequately. It is all very well to cultivate the borderlands between the special sciences, but each science should first cultivate properly its own field by its own methods.

We are concerned here with that particular set of borderland problems that has recently been termed the "sociology of knowledge"—a term parallel to "sociology of religion," "sociology of art," "sociology of language."

Interest in these problems goes back to the very beginnings of modern sociological thought. The central idea of Comte's famous "law of three states" was that between certain types of philosophy or—more generally—of knowledge (theological, metaphysical, positive) and certain forms of social structure there exists a relationship of mutual dependence. Half a century later, the French sociological group centered around Durkheim tried in a series of highly significant studies to show the social origin of the funda-mental forms of human experience and thinking.[1] More recently, German

The Social Role of the Man of Knowledge (New York: Columbia University Press, 1940), pp. 1–22. Reprinted by permission of the Columbia University Press.

sociologists, especially Max Scheler and Karl Mannheim, have made systematic efforts to trace the dependence of knowledge on social conditions.[2]

The term "sociology of knowledge" seems to us rather unfortunate, for it suggests that knowledge as such is an object matter of sociological investigation. Now, every science deals with a specific class of systems and of processes. Sociology is primarily concerned with that class of systems which is called "social" (for example, a "social group," a "social relation") and with processes which occur within or between such systems. The distinctive characteristic of social systems is that their chief components are interacting men, whereas systems of knowledge, or theories (using this term in the most general sense), are obviously not social systems. Nor are linguistic, aesthetic, religious, or technical systems "social": there is little similarity between a compound sentence, a poem, a painting, a sacrifice, an automobile, on the one hand, and a political party, a club, a conjugal or parental relation, on the other hand, beyond the fact that each of them has an inner order holding its constituent parts together.

Of course, between social systems on the one hand and other kinds of cultural systems on the other hand there are many dynamic relationships of one-sided or mutual dependence, some of which we are going to investigate presently. But there are likewise relationships of dependence between other kinds of systems. If the existence of such relationships entitles us to use the terms "sociology of knowledge" and "sociology of art," by the same token we should be justified in speaking of "linguistics of religion," "religionistics of art," "economics of knowledge," and so on.

However, there is no need of wrangling about words. Since the expression "sociology of knowledge" has by now gained a wide recognition in sociological literature, we may as well adopt it with the emphatic reservation that it does not mean a "sociological theory of knowledge."[3] Otherwise, sociology would find itself in a curious position. As a theory of knowledge, a "science of the sciences," it would have to determine its own character as sociology; whereas as sociology it would determine its own character as a "science of the sciences."[4]

Many misunderstandings might be avoided if we had a fully constituted "science of knowledge," a comparative, inductive study of the various systems of knowledge which empirical research would disclose in the past and the present. Ever since antiquity, there has been indeed philosophy of knowledge—epistemology, logic, and methodology—trying to establish the general principles and norms upon which the validity of all knowledge depends, just as there has been a political and an ethical philosophy of social life. However, a science of knowledge parallel to modern sociology or linguistics would not attempt to standardize normatively the systems it studies but would view them simply as empirical realities, trying to reach by their comparative analysis theoretic generalizations about them. Such a science has only begun to emerge out of historical and ethnological studies. Its development is apparently a slow and difficult task, and the sociologist is hardly competent to participate in it.[5]

For an objective investigation of systems of knowledge in their composition, structure, and relationships must take fully into consideration that which is an essential characteristic of every system of knowledge: its claim to be *true*, that is, objectively valid. The sociologist, however, is not entitled to make any judgments concerning the validity of any systems of knowledge except sociological systems. He meets systems of knowledge in the course of his investigation only when he finds that certain persons or groups that he studies are actively interested in them, that they construct, improve, supplement, reproduce, defend, or popularize systems which they regard as true or else reject, oppose, criticize, or interfere with the propagation of systems which they consider untrue. In every such case the sociologist is bound to abide by whatever standards of validity those individuals or groups apply to the knowledge in which they take an active share. For, as an observer of cultural life, he can understand the data he observes only if he takes them with the "humanistic coefficient," only if he does not limit his observation to his own direct experience of the data but reconstructs the experience of the men who are dealing with them actively.[6] Just as a conjugal relation which he observes is to him really and objectively what it is to the conjugal partners themselves, or an association what it means to its members, a given system of knowledge must be to him also what it is to the people who participate in its construction, reproduction, application, and development. When he is studying their social lives, he must agree that, as to the knowledge which they recognize as valid, they are the only authority he need consider. He has no right as a sociologist to oppose his authority to theirs: he is bound by the methodical rule of unconditional modesty. He must resign his own criteria of theoretic validity when dealing with systems of knowledge which they accept and apply. It does not matter whether the type of knowledge which he finds these people cultivating be technical, normative or theoretic, theological, metaphysical or empirical, deductive or inductive, physical or humanistic, nor whether the particular system which they regard true be the physics of Thales, of Democritus, of St. Thomas, of Newton, or of Einstein, the biology of Aristotle or of Darwin, the psychology of Plato or of the behaviorists: it is their judgement, not the sociologist's, which conditions whatever influence their knowledge has on their social life, and vice versa.

But how ought the sociologist to behave when he finds that some people deny the validity of a system which other people regard as true? Does not this conflict of authorities compel him to make a decision? We do not think so. If we apply consistently the humanistic coefficient, we shall conclude that when a man takes a negative attitude toward a system of knowledge which others recognize, this is only a more or less interesting fact of his personal life, not affecting at all the objective composition, structure, or validity of the system which he rejects. In the same way, the fact that a person does not like the English language, impressionism in painting, or Calvinism in religion is entirely irrelevant to the intrinsic pattern and significance of those cultural systems as experienced by their adherents. Such a negative valuation may, however, be instructive in other respects. If a man rejects, for example, voluntaristic psychology because he applies to it the standards of behavioristic psychology which he recognizes as true, this fact (though it has no bearing upon voluntarism) throws light on the composition, structure, and claims to validity of behaviorism. In the same way, we learn something significant about the French language from the fact that some people do not like English because they judge it by French standards, or about the aesthetic pattern of cubism from a cubist who criticizes impressionism.

Let us accept as a "truth" any element of any system of knowledge taken with its humanistic coefficient, that is, taken from the standpoint of the men who believe that they understand this system, who are actively interested in it and regard it as containing objectively valid knowledge about the object matter to which it refers. How should such elements be defined? The sociologist is unable to answer this question; for the people who are actively interested in systems of knowledge variously conceive the nature of a "truth." "Truths" have been identified with names, sentences, propositions, artificial symbols and their relationships, ideas, representations, observations, concepts, judgments, intuitions, habits, responses to stimuli, and so on, and every such class may be variously defined; thus an "idea" of Plato's differs widely from an "idea" of Locke's. In observing, however, the actual functioning of these multiform "truths" in the sphere of active experience of the people who regard them as valid—in observing the influence which the recognition of certain truths has upon the conscious lives of people as experiencing and active subjects—we can say generally that whatever is regarded as a truth functions as a *norm of thinking*, imposes upon the conscious agent who recognizes it a distinctive selection and organization of some data of his experience. The data acquire thereby the character of object matter of knowledge. The "truth" itself—and even more so the whole system of which it is an element —possesses in the active experience of all those who recognize it an "objective" significance which makes its validity seem to them independent of their "subjective" emotions, wishes, representations. They *participate* in a system of knowledge, just as a leader or a member participates in a social group, a manager or a workman in that technical system which is called a "factory" or a "workshop."

Now, sociological investigation discovers that there are two kinds of connection between knowledge and social life. On the one hand, upon men's participation in a certain system of knowledge often depends their participation in some social system and their conduct within the limits of the latter. A person who is "instructed" or "learned" in certain theories is admitted to the perfomance of certain roles and to the membership of certain groups in which the "ignorant" are not allowed to share. A man who accepts the traditionalism of sacred, religious lore behaves differently as a member or functionary of particular groups from a man who recognizes the teleological rationalism of applied secular knowledge. The development and popularization of modern physical and biological sciences have markedly affected the composition and structure of many social groups, either directly by changing traditional beliefs or indirectly by the technological applications of those sciences.

On the other hand, the participation of men in certain social systems often determines (though perhaps not entirely or exclusively) in what systems of knowledge they will participate, and how. Many social groups require that all their members know certain sacred doctrines or the rudiments of some lay sciences, while some groups forbid their members to meddle with certain theories. Men who are destined for professional occupations must acquire the knowledge regarded as necessary for those occupations according to social rules and regulations. And there are various socially prescribed ways of participating in systems of knowledge. Sometimes men are expected and taught merely to memorize formulas in which knowledge is expressed, whereas at other times understanding of all the implications of a system is required. Exlusive emphasis may be put upon the practical application of the "truths" included in a system or, on the contrary, upon their purely theoretic significance. In many cases no modification of the system is allowed; in other cases it is regarded as not only permissible but meritorious to improve, develop, modify, supplement a system and in rare cases even to construct a new system.

Individual conformity with the various social demands relative to knowledge is obtained by specific methods of education, encouragement, and control. The success or failure of these methods in particular cases is conditioned, of course, by the psychological capacities and dispositions of the individuals to whom they are applied. But why individuals manifest such psychological capacities and dispositions as they possess by participating the way they do in certain systems of knowledge and not in others is a question which can be answered only by a study of the society in which those individuals live.

Thus, while admittedly systems of knowledge—viewed in their objective composition, structure, and validity—cannot be reduced to social facts, yet their historical existence within the empirical world of culture, in so far as it depends upon the men who construct them, maintain them by transmission and application, develop them, or neglect them, must in a large measure be explained sociologically. And this is what "sociology of knowledge" has actually been doing, whenever it was not vainly trying to become epistemology. Even thus limited, the task is sufficiently vast and difficult to occupy many sociologists for generations to come, especially as the conceptual framework hitherto used in dealing with these problems seems rather inadequate.

In our present outline we attempt to survey a certain portion of the field which "sociology of knowledge" tends to cover. We assume from experience and observation, direct and indirect, that knowledge as it has historically grown is the agglomerated product of specific cultural activities of numberless human individuals. Further, we are familiar with the fact that some individuals for longer or shorter periods of their lives specialize in cultivating knowledge, in distinction from other individuals who specialize in performing various other kinds of cultural activities—technical, economic, artistic, and so on. We call them "scientists," using the word in its etymological sense as derived from *scire*, "to know," and equivalent to "men of knowledge" (like the French term "savants"). This is obviously a different and much more extensive meaning than that in which this word is used by epistemologists and logicians, who define a "scientist" in terms of objective achievements in the field of knowledge. According to a conception prevalent in modern literature on the subject, an individual in order to be a scientist must produce some work which will qualify positively when judged by definite standards of validity. There are many writers who identify such standards with those of modern physical knowledge, to whom "science" means mathematics, astronomy, physics, and chemistry, with some portions of biology and perhaps geology grudgingly added; to them a "scientist" is only someone who efficiently works in one of those fields. Of course, as has been stated above, to us as sociologists, applying the humanistic coefficient to our data, all knowledge is valid which is regarded as such by the people who participate in it, and a "scientist" is any individual who is regarded by his social milieu and who regards himself as specializing in the cultivation of knowledge, irrespective of the positive or negative judgment which epistemologists or logicians may pronounce upon his work.

Now, individual specialization in any kind of cultural activity is generally recognized as a phenomenon which is socially conditioned. Sociologists have given considerable attention to it. Spencer was the first to treat it systematically in his *Principles of Sociology*, though we find some of his views anticipated in earlier works in social philosophy. For the most part, however, the attention of sociologists has centered upon the collective aspect of this phenomenon; viewing society as a whole, they regard individual specialization as a question of social structure, a differentiation of the total set of activities by which society is maintained. This is, for instance, what Durkheim emphasizes in his famous work *De la division du travail social*, in which progressive differentiation of functions is treated as the most significant collective process in the history of human societies.

But specialization has also an individual aspect: the persons who specialize in any kind of activity can be comparatively studied, irrespective of the part this activity plays in the total structure of a group or of society at large. Such studies may be psychological or sociological. In the former, attention centers upon the individual himself as a psychobiological being viewed apart from his social environment, and the problem is whether any typical psychological characteristics are associated with specialization in the given kind of activity and, if so, how this association is to be explained. There have been many monographic studies of this type in the course of the last half century, and they have been greatly stimulated by the development of psychotechnics and of vocational guidance, the purpose of which is to select for definite occupations individuals who possess or can easily develop the psychological characteristics which these occupations are supposed to require. In sociological studies of specialized persons, it is the connection between the individual and his social milieu which is the main object of interest; and his specialized activities are viewed with reference to the cultural setting in which they are performed. A classical example is Frazer's study of priests and kings in *The Golden Bough* (1935, Vols. I and II). Of course, a particular investigation may combine psychological and sociological problems, as exemplified in Sombart's monograph *Der Bourgeois*.

In sociology a conceptual framework for dealing with these problems has been gradually developing in the course of monographic investigations. In recent years the term "social role" has been used by many sociologists to denote the phenomena in question.[7] We say that a priest, a lawyer, a politician, a banker, a merchant, a physician, a farmer, a workman, a soldier, a house-wife, a teacher performs a specific social role. Furthermore, the concept (with certain variations) has proved applicable not only to individuals who specialize in certain activities but also to individuals as members of certain groups: thus an American, a Frenchman, a Methodist, a Catholic, a Communist, a Fascist, a club member, a member of the family (child, father, mother, grandparent) plays a certain social role.[8] An individual in the course of his life performs a number of different roles, successively or simultaneously; the synthesis of all the social roles he has ever performed from birth to death constitutes his social personality.

Every social role presupposes that between the individual performing the role, who may thus be called a "social person," and a smaller or larger set of people who participate in his performance and may be termed his "social circle" there is a common bond constituted by a complex of values which all of them appreciate positively. These are economic values in the case of a merchant or a banker and the circle formed by his clients; hygienic values for the physician and his patients; political values for a king and his subjects; religious values for the priest and his circle of lay believers; aesthetic values for the artist and the circle of his admirers and critics; a combination of various values which fill the content of family life between the child and his family circle. The person is an object of positive valuation on the part of his circle because they believe that they all need his cooperation for the realization of certain tendencies connected with these values. The banker's cooperation is presumably needed by those who tend to invest or borrow money; the physician's cooperation by those who wish to regain or to preserve their own health and the health of the people in whom they are interested; the child's cooperation by other family members for the maintenance of family life. On the other hand, the person obviously cannot perform his role without the cooperation of his circle—though not necessarily the cooperation of any particular individual within the circle. There can be no active banker without clients, no practicing physician without patients, no reigning king without subjects, no child-in-the-family without other family members.

The person is conceived by his circle as an organic and psychological entity who is a "self," conscious of his own existence as a body and a soul and aware of how others regard him. If he is to be the kind of person his social circle needs, his "self" must possess in the opinion of the circle certain qualities, physical and mental, and not possess certain other qualities. For instance, organic "health" or "sickness" affects his supposed capacity to perform most roles, but particularly occupational roles, such as the farmer's, the workman's, the soldier's, and the housewife's, which require certain bodily skills, while lack of training in the "proper" ways of moving and eating may exclude an individual from roles which require "society" manners. Some roles are limited to men, others to women; there are upper or lower age limits for every role; the majority of roles imply certain somatic racial characteristics and definite, though variable, standards of external appearance.

The psychological qualities ascribed to persons performing social roles are enormously diversified: in every Western language there are hundreds of words denoting supposed traits of "intelligence" and "character"; and almost every such trait has, or had in the past, an axiological significance, that is, is positively or negatively valued, either in all persons or in persons performing certain kinds of role. In naïve popular reflection, such psychological traits are real qualities of a substantial "mind" or "soul," whose existence is manifested by specific acts (including verbal statements) of the individual.

A person who is needed by a social circle and whose self possesses the qualities required for the role for which he is needed has a definite social *status*, that is, his circle grants him certain rights and enforces those rights, when necessary, against individual participants of the circle or outsiders. Some of those rights concern his bodily existence. For instance, he has an ecological position, the right to occupy a definite space (as home, room, office, scat) where he is safe from bodily injury, and the right to move safely over given territories. His economic position includes rights to use certain material values regarded as necessary for his subsistence on a level commensurate with his role. Other rights involve his "spiritual welfare": he has a fixed moral standing, can claim some recognition, social response, and participation in the nonmaterial values of his circle.

He, in turn, has a social *function* to fulfill; he is regarded as obliged to achieve certain tasks by which the supposed needs of his circle will be satisfied and to behave toward other individuals in his circle in a way that shows his positive valuation of them.

Such are the essential components which we believe, on the basis of previous studies, to be found in all social roles, although of course the specific composition of different kinds of social role varies considerably. But our knowledge of a social role is not complete if we know only its composition, for a role is a dynamic system and its components may be variously interconnected in the course of its performance. There are many different ways of performing a role, according to the dominant active tendencies of the performer. He may, for instance, be mainly interested in one of the components of his role—the social circle, his own self, the status or the function—and tend to subordinate other components to it. And, whatever his main interest, he may tend to conform with the demands of his circle or else try to innovate, to become independent of those demands. And, again, in either case he may be optimistically confident in the opportunities offered by his role and tend to expand it or else he may mistrust its possibilities and tend to restrict it to a perfectly secure minimum.

The possibility of reaching such general conclusions about all social roles and more specific, though still widely applicable, generalizations about social roles of a certain kind—such as the role of peasant, priest, merchant, factory worker, or artist—points obviously to the existence of essential uniformities and also of important variations among these social phenomena. Social roles constitute one general class of social system, and this class may be subdivided into less general classes, these into subclasses, and so on; for instance, within the specific class of factory worker there are hundreds of subclasses of workers employed in particular trades, and there is another line of differentiation according to the economic organization of the factories in which they are employed. Systematic sociology stands before a task similar to that of systematic biology with its still greater complication of classes and subclasses of living organisms; and here as there, only uniformities of specific systems make possible a further search for static and dynamic laws. But, manifestly, the source of uniformities in the social field is different from that in the field of biology.

Although in both fields differentiation is due to variations of individual systems, biological uniformities are due in the main to heredity; whereas uniformities of social systems, like those of all cultural systems, are chiefly the result of a reflective or unreflective use of the same *cultural patterns* in many particular cases. There is obviously a fundamental and universal, though unreflective, cultural pattern in accordance with which all kinds of lasting relationships between individuals and their social milieus are normatively organized and which we denote by the term "social role." The genesis of this pattern is lost in an inaccessible past, and so are the origins of what are probably its earliest variations, that is, those which everywhere differentiate individual roles according to sex and age.

But most of the patterns which have evolved during the history of mankind can be studied in the course of their becoming and duration. They originated usually by differentiation from older undifferentiated patterns, more seldom by entirely original, though gradual, invention. Many of these new patterns were short-lived or applied only within small collectivities, but some have lasted for thousands of years and spread over whole continents. In modern American society we find a number of patterns of social roles which can be traced back to prehistoric times, some still very vital, like the pattern of the rural housewife, others probably mere survivals destined soon to disappear, such as the patterns of the magician and the fortune teller.

Sometimes a pattern is explicitly formulated as a system of legal or ethical norms prescribing what all the roles of a given class within a particular political or religious society ought to be: such a pattern is then imposed by a dominant group upon all the candidates to those roles. For example, this is how the patterns of the several military, administrative, legislative, and judiciary roles are maintained and transmitted by state legislation; the patterns of priestly and medical roles are determined and stabilized in professional groups; the patterns of merchants, and artisans' roles in the Western world were perpetuated through centuries by the agency of guilds and corporations. In other cases, patterns of social roles are not explicitly rationalized but are included in the mores of a community and transmitted from old to young through a process of educational guidance and imitation; such has been the process of perpetuation of the role patterns of aristocrats, farmers, house-wives, servants. Sometimes, again, mores have been supplemented and modified by normative group regulation.

As to the diffusion of the patterns of social roles, or their spread from community to community and from society to society, there are various well-known ways by which this process goes on: borrowing from neigh-boring cultures, travel, trade, migration, colonization, conquest, dissemination of book lore. But not all the similarities of roles found in different communities or societies can be thus accounted for; in many cases we must admit independent evolution along similar lines. The world-wide similarity of the roles of warrior, priest, and small agriculturalist must be explained in all probability by a combination of diffusion and parallel evolution.

The conception of social roles here outlined furnishes the background for our present problems in the "sociology of knowledge." First of all, we presume hypothetically that individuals who specialize in cultivating knowledge and are therefore called "scientists" perform social roles of a definite class. This means that there must be social circles to whom knowledge in general or systematic knowledge in particular appears to be positively valuable. Participants in these circles must be convinced that they need the cooperation of "scientists" to realize certain tendencies connected with this valuable knowledge. In order to be qualified as a scientist whom his circle needs, a person must be regarded as a "self" endowed with certain desirable characteristics and lacking certain undesirable characteristics. Social status must be granted to a person who is thus needed and qualified as a scientist. And this person must perform social functions which will satisfy the needs of his circle in the matter of knowledge; in other words, he must cultivate knowledge for the benefit of those who grant him social status.

Are there indeed such social roles? If so what is their essential composition and structure? Are there any specific varieties among them? How are they as a class related logically to other classes of social role? And since in the social just as in the biological field genetic relationships between classes throw some light upon their logical relationships, we may ask: What is the origin of scientists' roles in general, and how did specific variations of those roles evolve?[9]

This gives us our first set of problems. They are of the same kind as all problems of systematic description and classification of social phenomena. But because this is a study in the "sociology of knowledge," there are other borderland problems which we have to face. Are there any relationships of functional dependence between the social roles which scientists perform and the kind of knowledge which they cultivate? More specifically: Are the systems of knowledge which scientists build and their methods of building them influenced by the social patterns with which scientists are expected to conform as participants in a certain social order and by the ways in which they actually realize those patterns?

NOTES

1 See Émile Durkheim, *Les Formes élémentaires de la vie religieuse* (Paris: Alcan, 1912), for a general outline of the sociological approach to knowledge. É. Durkheim and Marcel Mauss, in "Des quelques formes primitives de la classification," *L'Année sociologique, VI* (1901–2), show cases in which logical classes are determined by the subdivision of social groups. Lucien Lévy-Bruhl in his famous series of works on primitive thinking, *Les Fonctions mentales dans les sociétés inférieures* (Paris: Alcan, 1910), *La Mentalité primitive* (1922), *L'Ame primitive* (1927), *Le Surnaturel et la nature dans la mentalité primitive* (1931), *L'Expérience mystique et les symboles chez les primitifs* (1930), tends to prove that "primitive —or, rather, "preliterate" (Faris)—peoples use logical principles and categories different from ours: the obvious suggestion is that both theirs and ours are socially conditioned. Maurice Halbwachs, in *Les Cadres sociaux de la mémoire* (Paris: Alcan, 1924), shows that our memory, and consequently also our experience of time, is organized by a socially established and regulated framework of succession and simultaneity within which the facts of collective life are fitted. S. Czarnowski applied the sociological approach to space, particularly in his monograph "Le Morcellement de l'étendue," *Revue de l'histoire des religions* (1927).

2 Cf. Max Scheler (ed.), *Versuche zu einer Soziologie des Wissens* (Munich, 1924) and *Die Wissensformen und die Gesellschaft* (Leipzig, 1926); Karl Mannheim, *Ideology and Utopia*, trans. by L. Wirth and E. Shils (New York, 1936); Mannheim's article, "Wissenssoziologie," in A. Vierkandt, *Handwörterbuch der Soziologie* (Stuttgart, 1931).

3 I am borrowing this distinction from an unpublished paper by Mr. Edwin Anderson on Durkheim's sociological approach to knowledge.

4 Cf. Alexander von Schelting's criticism of Mannheim, in *American Sociological Review* (August, 1936).

5 One of the most interesting cooperative efforts to build such a science from monographic contributions is represented by twenty volumes of the periodical *Nauka Polska* (Polish Science), ed. by S. Michalski (Warsaw, 1920–39).

6 Florian Znaniecki, *The Method of Sociology* (New York, 1934).

7 Some sociologists prefer the term "personal role." The concept may be traced back to C. H. Cooley's *Human Nature and the Social Order* (1902). R. E. Park, E. W. Burgess, G. H. Mead, E. T. Hiller, and others have developed it since then. In the form here presented, it has been utilized in a series of monographic investigations based on first-hand materials and carried on for a number of years by myself and my assistants. These investigations covered the following classes of social role: peasant, peasant housewife, farm laborer, industrial worker, unemployed worker, child in family, pupil in school, youthful member of playgroup, soldier, teacher, artist. Materials have been drawn in each case from several national societies. Some of these studies have been published, mostly in Polish. The first outline of the present study was published in the *Polish Sociological Review* (1937).

8 Cf. Znaniecki, "Social Groups as Products of Cooperating Individuals," *American Journal of Sociology* (May, 1939).

9 Cf. Znaniecki, *The Method of Sociology*, chap. vi, "Analytic Induction."

4
KURT H. WOLFF

A Methodological Note on the Empirical
Establishment of Culture Patterns[1]

I. THE CULTURAL APPROACH

FUNDAMENTALLY, THE scientific study of a culture exemplifies one of two approaches. One is followed in most of the monographic anthropological literature. The other is implied in some of the more theoretically oriented anthropological writings[2] and especially in certain concepts of the sociology of knowledge;[3] yet it has not, to my knowledge, been made the explicit theoretical basis of the empirical study of a culture or community. The two approaches may be distinguished, first, on the philosophical-methodological level and, second, on what may be called the contentual level.

Philosophically and therefore methodologically, the first approach proceeds on the assumption that a person can and should study a culture as the natural scientist studies nature.[4] The culture is *there*—the task is to learn about it; and we learn about it with the help of rules which will be perfected in the course of scientific progress. It is true that many students of this school are aware of the "personal equation," which refers to the investigator's biases, emotions, prejudgments, or even to his own cultural "mold."[5] Yet this personal equation is considered merely a flaw which each individual student must try his best to eliminate so that objectivity may be preserved as much as possible.[6] For this process of elimination he relies on rules of science which are widely held and often taken for granted, such as the careful formulation of a hypothesis, the systematic search for the negative case,

---

Expanded version of an article originally published in *American Sociological Review*, X (April, 1945), 176–84. Reprinted by permission of the American Sociological Association and the author.

various pragmatic aspects and others.[7] By contrast, for the second approach to the scientific study of cultures, the "personal equation" is not a necessary evil, but the explicitly acknowledged basis. The personal, or better, cultural equation determines what *can be* perceived and interpreted of the culture under study, and *as what* it can be perceived and interpreted. For reasons of simplified reference, I call the first, the "objective "approach, and the second, the "cultural" approach. On the philosophical-methodological level, then, the contrast between the two can be pointedly summarized as follows: For the former, the objective approach, the relation between the student and the culture which he examines is taken for granted, and the central concept is that of scientific procedure, under which aspects of the relation between student and culture under study which have become problematical are subsumed as technicalities. For the latter, the cultural approach, the scientific procedure is taken for granted, and the central concept is that of cultural equation, under which aspects of scientific procedure which have become problematical are subsumed as technicalities.

Yet, furthermore, the follower of the objective school not only finds his work largely predetermined by scientific rules but also by what may be labelled "contentual" rules. His teachers have not only told him *how* to study a culture but also *what* to study. If he is a sociologist he may, for instance, take *Middletown* as a model and study his community by beginning with "Getting a Living" and following the chapters down the line until he comes to an outlook on the future. If he is an anthropologist he probably has in mind a number of important aspects of a culture, such as economics, social relations, child-rearing and education, and the like. He takes it for granted that some such "division" obtains in the culture he wants to study, no matter which, because such a division makes sense in his own culture.[8] Yet suppose that a Tasmanian, or even a Spanish-American, studies the culture of New York or Seattle:[9] would he take for granted the same aspects which an American student of a Tasmanian tribe or of a Mexican or New Mexican community takes for granted? I imagine he would not. I cannot prove it because to my knowledge no Tasmanian, or even Spanish-American, has studied a U.S. community, or else he was trained in the objective school. In fact, unless he was thus trained, we might be inclined not to consider his study scientific but merely a curious and naïve document. This reflection, though in a roundabout way, proves the highly specific, i.e., cultural, character of our social science and should therefore, at least, make it clear that its approach is only one among others.[10]

Perhaps the contrast with the second approach can be pointed out most sharply on this contentual level. Instead of treating a culture by contentual divisions,[11] the cultural approach proposes to treat it in terms of its patterns. The concept of pattern overrides contentual distinctions. Rather, it considers any contents as materials which may be patterned. From the standpoint of the members of the culture under study, the contentual is that to which patterns may apply; from the standpoint of the student of the culture, the contentual is the heuristic sphere of observation where patterns may be discerned. Clyde Kluckhohn[12] has clearly presented a list of types of patterns. Yet two decisive questions have not been raised, much less answered. One is the question of selection; namely, which observations of materials or inferences or constructs does the student call "patterns" and which does he not call so? The other is the question of method, namely: how does the student establish patterns empirically,[13] i.e., so that another student can check on them; and how does he prove his patterns to be adequate as an interpretation of the culture under study? In the following, preliminary answers to these two questions are given. They are based on five months of field work in a small Spanish-Anglo community in New Mexico.[14]

II. SELECTION OF PATTERNS

Tentative answers to both questions may be found if it is remembered, first, that the pattern concept is typical of the cultural approach and that the central concept of this approach is the "cultural equation," and, second, that the cultural equation determines what *can be* perceived and interpreted of the culture under study, and *as what* it can be perceived and interpreted. It may be assumed that in any culture under study a certain type of phenomena is perceived in such a way as to call for interpretation. It is these phenomena which strike the student as different from the ones that form part of his, and his group's, universe of discourse;[15] phenomena which therefore are not readily incorporable into this universe of discourse and which, consequently, call for some procedure by means of which they can be incorporated. This picture seems to be the more clear-cut the more different the two respective universes of discourse, or cultures, are—that under study and that of the student. A ritual among the Iatmül at once and undoubtedly appears to be part of a culture which the student does not share, and hence calls for subsumption under a larger "whole" which in turn is incorporated into the student's own culture. Or, to express the same thought in more customary terms: the student tries to understand the ritual within that larger complex and in turn tries to understand that complex itself. The picture seems least clear-cut where the two cultures are most similar. In contrast to the study of an exotic culture we have the sociological community study, where the student is struck by relatively minor nuances of his own culture.[16] The middle is held by "folk cultures."[17] They partake of the urban civilization of which the student is a member, but also of another culture which he wants to detect and describe in its fusion with his own. In many cases, therefore, it is difficult to ascertain whether an observation "belongs" to a whole that has the same significance as it has in his own culture, or whether it betrays hitherto unsuspected or suspected features. This is but to say that in folk cultures, diversities are not as striking as in exotic cultures, and likenesses not as striking as in urban communities.

The first step, then, toward an answer to the question of which observations are dignified by the term "pattern," is a preliminary classification of the culture under study in such terms as "exotic," "folk," or "urban." This classification is usually performed spontaneously and without much or any regard to the methodological consequences here discussed. If made with the awareness of its methodological implications, however, a sharper focus on the selection of patterns is produced. Suppose the culture under consideration is classified as belonging in the broad category of folk culture. The student thus expects to find patterns that this culture shares with his own—perhaps, e.g., in the field of attitudes toward money and the manipulation of it—and others which are not shared by the urban culture—perhaps, e.g., in the field of certain beliefs about planting or stars. Now, it must never be forgotten that this division of potential patterns is the student's own division —very likely not that of the members of the culture under study. It is a theoretical distinction on the level of classification and heuristic hypothesis or, to use a term of Karl Mannheim's,[18] of "sociological interpretation." It has not proceeded to the level of understanding, or of "immanent interpretation." It does not, as yet, interpret the culture under study in terms of its members.[19] The real difficulty, or the proper task, of the student of a folk culture is to study the mutual interdependence and the mutual shaping of patterns which he has preliminarily ascribed to urban or to "native" influences. Thus, patterns expressing attitudes toward money, e.g., must be examined with reference to their possible relation to, or influence on, patterns expressing beliefs in stars. The empirical ascertainment of interactions of this kind allows the student to describe the uniqueness of the folk culture which he is examining.[20]

The student, aware of a preliminary classification of the culture he wants to study, and of the difference between a classificatory and an immanent interpretation of what he will observe, now proceeds to the actual field work. To put it bluntly, he is about to fill his theoretical, or rational, framework empirically. He is now interested in answering the question of how this particular folk culture is made up in terms of his theoretical approach.

According to his individual disposition he may quickly formulate hypotheses and search for checks on them; or he may record anything that comes under his observation and try to piece together patterns in a slower manner. In either case, his cultural and personal sensitivity, enriched and sharpened by theoretical thinking, puts the limit on what he can perceive and interpret.[21]

In the field, then, the question of selection is answered in the following order: avid collection of empirical materials, immanent interpretation of these materials, their classification, classification of the culture. This is the reverse order of that which characterized the theorizing stage preceding the field work, where it was: preliminary classification of the culture, classificatory expectations regarding the materials to be collected. The three last steps in the field—immanent interpretation of materials, their classification, classification of the culture—in fact answer the question of selection. They determine (a) what patterns appear when the materials are interpreted as constituents of a meaningful presentation of the culture; (b) how the materials are to be classified—because constituents of this presentation—as imputable to other presentations (types) of cultures; (c) how the culture itself is to be classified. *When* each of these steps is taken probably depends on the investigator's disposition.[22]

III. EMPIRICAL ESTABLISHMENT OF PATTERNS

The answer to the first question—of selection—remains not quite clear as long as there is none to the second, namely, how the student establishes patterns empirically and how he proves them to be adequate as an interpretation of the culture. In other words, after it has been shown how patterns are looked for and found, it must now be demonstrated how they can be ascertained. While the preceding discussion did justice to any meaning the reader may reasonably have been expected to attribute to "pattern," it now becomes necessary to introduce a formal, though still provisional definition of it. A pattern is a uniformity of emotion, attitude, thoughtway, or knowledge.[23] In this definition it is implied that a pattern may be characteristic of an individual, of a group, or of all members of the culture under study. Therefore, to find out to which of these three categories the pattern applies is a statistical proposition. Theoretically, this is all that has to be said in answer to the question of how patterns are established empirically—by statistics.[24] In practice, however, there is more to the answer to this question. In most cases a sample technique must be devised. This, not only because it would be impossible, even in a culture shared by very few individuals, to test all patterns by a complete coverage, but also because it is not necessary to do so. In fact, in many cases it is scientifically legitimate to do without a statistically valid sample, as I shall try to show. *When* this is possible depends on the nature of the pattern under examination and on the purpose of the study.

If we want to know how many members of a culture own a house, are married, belong to a certain organization, have given occupations, or similar uniformities, there is no substitute for at least a statistically valid sample count. According to the conception of society and culture current in our universe of discourse, counts of this sort are held to be necessary for the presentation of a general picture of the culture under study. They are customarily dealt with under such contentual models as, respectively, "property," "marriage and family," "organizations and institutions," and "occupational distribution." It is not important here to answer the question whether uniformities of this nature should be called patterns or not; they could be only by stretching our definition considerably.[25] If the task of the student is to give a "total picture" of the culture, they are, at least, not of primary importance.[26] Yet they bridge the two cultures or universes of discourse (the student's and his readers', and the one to be studied) in such a way as to function as "background materials" for the culture to be incorporated: they can be grasped as readily understood things by the same means as they would be in the study of a culture very similar to that of the student's and readers'—an American urban or even rural community, for instance.

At this point the implication of "immanent interpretation" must be more closely examined. "Immanent interpretation" has two referents, of which Mannheim has discussed only one.[27] "Immanent interpretation of patterns" is, first, the description of the meaning which an individual or group gives to the uniformity of emotion, attitude, thoughtway, or knowledge. In this sense, it is the description of what meaning a person or group gives, e.g., to being in a reverent mood when at church (emotion), to liking beer, children, nature, or to hating Negroes, Jews, Mexicans (attitude), to conceptions of the war, of time, of money (thoughtways), or to orientation in time and space, to acquaintance with and use of herbs, sewing machines, wells, radios (knowledge). In other words, it is the recording of interpretations given by the members of the culture under study (and in some cases interpretations may be "rationalizations"). This is the referent Mannheim discusses. But "immanent interpretation" has another referent, and it is the more important one denoted in the expression, the "immanent interpretation of the materials." This expression was used to designate the first step which the student takes toward a presentation of the culture he studies. When this step was discussed it was defined as the interpretation of the materials "as constituents of a meaningful presentation of the culture." The significance of this statement must be made more explicit.

"Meaningful presentation of the culture" is its reinterpretation in such a way as to make its uniqueness incorporable into the universe of discourse of the student's and of his readers'. The ideal-theoretical extreme of meaningfulness is identification with this culture.[28] However, this is not only practically impossible to attain, but such identification would also be unformulable objectively, and hence unscientific (but rather artistic-intuitive). Yet even if we do not go beyond the establishment of patterns, their scientifically desirable statistical bases are not always either obtainable or called for. I have shown for which types of uniformities (usually not called patterns) they are obtainable as well as called for—for those which, in the cultural approach, make up background materials.[29] For patterns, i.e., uniformities of emotion, attitude, thoughtway, knowledge, something else is both obtainable and called for, namely, the presentation of the interrelatedness of patterns in such a way as to enable us to understand and predict the culture under study.

Suppose[30] the student has observed that a girl of eight years is afraid to cross a small creek. He has also observed fear in other individuals of the same culture on other occasions. He tentatively formulates fear as a pattern of reacting to certain things. It is impossible for him to ascertain statistically all things to which all members of the culture react with fear. Rather, he keeps his preliminary fear pattern—a uniformity of emotion and/or attitude —in mind while continuing his observations and preliminary formulations of other patterns. One of these, he observes, is the economical handling of language in speech, and its unaccomplished semi-illiterate handling in writing —a uniformity of thoughtways. He also remembers, from his background materials, statistical figures on literacy, formal education, and the like. Again it is impossible for him to ascertain statistically all situations in which all members of the culture express themselves linguistically. Nor is this called for, for what the student is interested in is the question of the interrelatedness of the fear pattern and the language pattern. Is there a connection between fear as a norm of reacting to certain things accepted by the members of this culture, and the likewise accepted economic handling of language as a norm of manipulating (expressing, withholding, implying) one's thoughts? Is perhaps economic insecurity a link between the two patterns? Here again the student adduces his background figures on property, income, indebtedness, budgets, etc.

In this example a number of methodological questions have been ignored, but it is hoped that the answer to the first part of our second question now becomes clearer: the student establishes patterns empirically by the presentation of the interrelatedness of patterns in such a way as to enable us to understand and predict the culture we study. It should be added that in establishing the interrelatedness of patterns the student makes use, as much as his sensitivity and integrity as a scientist force him to, of scientific rule. He will try to obtain some statistical basis, which alone enables him to ascertain whether the pattern he has hypothetically formulated applies to an individual, to a group, or to all members of the culture. Both for this purpose and for the purpose of throwing light on the interrelatedness of patterns, it is necessary to search for negative cases. These two examples once more illustrate what is meant, with reference to the empirical establishment of patterns, by the fact that scientific rule is taken for granted in the cultural approach.

It will have been seen that the answer to the question of how patterns are established empirically is intimately connected with the answer to the question of their selection. Even more closely related to the problem of empirical ascertainment of patterns is the last question, namely, how the student proves that the patterns he has established are indeed adequate as an interpretation of the culture. In fact, the answer to this question is implied in the statement that he establishes patterns empirically by the presentation of their interrelatedness. The answer only needs to be made explicit. His patterns are proved to be adequate when they make it possible to understand and predict the culture presented in their terms. What is meant by predictability, i.e., the anticipation of the reaction of the culture to certain changes and its change with these changes, is connoted by the colloquial meaning of this term itself. The prediction value of the presentation can be judged only by the future. As regards understanding, the meaning of this term has been made clear by the discussion of the pattern approach: it is precisely this approach which is held to be most appropriate to our understanding of a culture. It should be noted, however, that the understanding of certain aspects of a culture, made possible through the presentation of certain patterns, does not guarantee the understanding of other aspects. In other words, the fact that a presentation "makes sense" or is plausible does not prove that important things have not been overlooked—the future may, or may not, find the student out. Other than this, his only probability of having understood the culture is the maximum collection of materials, the most rigorous search for negative cases, and the most imaginative testing of varieties of alternatives in explanations and pattern combinations. Here again his sensitivity, trained by theoretical thinking, is of the essential importance.

In comparison with the immanent interpretation of a culture, its classification is easier, less urgent, and less exclusively the responsibility of the student. For once he has presented the culture, others may classify it according to their theories. The original presentation may enrich a relatively wide public's universe of discourse by a new conception of human society and culture. The classification will enrich the universe of discourse of a more specialized public—those interested in sociological and anthropological theory and, especially, in types or continua of cultures. This is not to say, however, that the classificatory phase is less important. For science itself it is the most important aspect of the study, since science progresses by a refinement of theory. Therefore, the decisive contribution to the advancement of science, made by the cultural approach through the presentation of a culture, is its contribution to scientific theory.

IV. SUMMARY OF THE THEORY PRESENTED IN THIS PAPER

A summary of the contrast between the two approaches to the study of a culture and of the methodological bases of the cultural approach may be given as follows:

(*A*) Two approaches to the scientific study of a culture.

(*1*) "Objective": central concept, the scientific (natural-science) procedure; personal equation taken for granted and sought to be eliminated as far as possible.

(*2*) "Cultural": central concept, the cultural equation; scientific procedure taken for granted and followed as far as possible.

(*B*) Characteristics of the cultural approach.

(*1*) Overriding of model contentual aspects of cultures by the pattern concept.

(*2*) Steps in the study of a culture:

(*a*) Preliminary comparison of the culture with that of the student's; hence its preliminary classification; hence expectations regarding types of patterns.

(*b*) Establishment of patterns. Hypothetical patterns arrived at through observation and tentative interpretation; their immanent interpretation, i.e., recording of interpretations given by the members of the culture, plus the establishment of the interrelatedness of the patterns in such a way as to make possible the understanding and predicting of the culture.

(*3*) Methodological elements characterizing the cultural-approach study:

(*a*) Presentation of statistically reliable background materials and of the connection between these and the patterns.

(*b*) Presentation of patterns and of their immanent interpretation.

(*c*) Demonstration of the application of the patterns to individuals, groups, or all members of the culture.

(*d*) Demonstration of the connection between the patterns and culture types (cf. *B2a*); the problems of history and culture change (especially important in the study of folk cultures).

(*e*) Demonstration of the adequacy of the patterns for understanding and predicting the culture, by discussion of negative cases and of alternative interpretations of materials and patterns.

(*f*) Classification of the culture in terms of types of cultures or of other theories.

V. AN ILLUSTRATION: PRELIMINARY HYPOTHESES REGARDING THE CULTURE OF THE SPANISH-SPEAKING PEOPLE OF XY[31]

It may be useful to illustrate some of the ideas expressed in this paper by a few remarks about the culture of *XY*. These remarks are made at the stage of investigation described under *B2b* in the preceding summary (IV, above). They contain (*1*) a list of some features of the culture of *XY* which are thought to be patterns (although it cannot yet be demonstrated that they are, much material collected in the field points in this direction); (*2*) an attempt to show the interrelatedness of these features or possibly patterns "in such a way as to make possible the understanding and predicting of the culture"; and also some remarks on change (cf. *B3d*). It should be emphasized once more and it should be kept in mind while reading what follows that it is preliminary, fragmentary, and presented only by way of illustration.

(1) List of Some Hypothetical Patterns of the Culture of XY[32]

Acceptance. Preliminary definition:[33] the unreflective acceptance of what comes or is. Illustrations:[34]

> *J* [Anglo] very kindly brought us a pound-box of candies . . . which we produced again yesterday after *lonche* [lunch] and of course offered *R* [our maid]. The candies are individually packed in the customary brown folded paper cups. *R* ate hers with a spoon in the paper cup using it as a kind of plate and said from time to time "*muy dulce*" [how sweet], "*dulcito*," and similar. This struck me as the acceptance of life—sweet or bitter, good or bad, not much fuss about anything. Other example: when I stopped in at *P*'s waiting for *Fr* [Anglo] to bring me to . . . [the county seat] to pick up the family, *P* said a nephew of hers . . . was *enfermo* [sick], *en la cabeza, tumor* [in the head, a tumor]—*muy triste* [very sad]; he had been in Italy (which I had learned the day before), but now in *Norte America*, and what that was, and I said that must be this country. Later *Fr* told me they [the *M*'s] had just received a telegram from the War Department that he was seriously ill, cerebral tumor, was in the North American area . . . They had not indicated to me that they had just

received the wire that morning. *R* mentioned nothing about this yesterday after she had undoubtedly learned of it.[35]

C [my wife] had picked up an ant which had gotten into her bed. Called *R*'s attention to it. *R* suggested it might be *chinches* [bedbugs]. *C* showed terror, quite in contrast to *R* who wiped a wooden board in her bed (otherwise iron bed) with vinegar. Hence *C* mentioned that *E* and *P* [visiting friends of ours who had spent a night in the *M* house] had found bedbugs in *A*'s [*R*'s brother] bed [in which *E* and *P*, in *A*'s absence, had slept]. "*Siento mucho*" [I am very sorry], but *A* sleeps outside for this reason—every night he takes his blankets and sleeps under a tree. Not the slightest moral indignation was mixed in *R*'s reaction—as it would have been in that of a *Hausfrau* or even an American housewife . . . Are bedbugs necessary evils which are accepted similar to the death of five out of fourteen children, say, lacking knowledge of birth control and disease prevention?[36]

Economics. P.d.: a social institution, i.e., a phenomenon virtually composed of heterogeneous elements but constituting a unit in the universe of discourse of the members of the culture under study. Ills:

R came later today with the news that *A* had suddenly arrived. The FSA to which he has owed $170 for 2–3 years . . . wired his company in . . . ordering him back because he had to attend to his farm. . . . *R* rightly said that the farm is well taken care of and that *A* can pay his debt much better working for wages than staying here. In fact, he already sent $130 home . . . [This sum] was, as *A* wrote, for their (family's) use, but when he now came they told him that they hadn't used a cent of it, keeping it for the payment of the debts, since "*tenemos suficiente*" [we have enough anyway]. Aside from the FSA loan, *A* also owes . . . the county and the state—taxes since 1931; although in some years he managed to pay back a little. *R* said he had nothing to do at home; of course, they were glad he is with them . . . Now that he makes no more money, *R* said, "*Yo no sé como lo haremos, pero ahora que está* A, *lo arreglara todo—y si no, todavia estamos muy contentos que esté*" [I don't know how we shall do it, but now that *A* is here he'll adjust everything—and if not, still we're very glad that he is here]. This remark most clearly shows how the family relation at least counterbalances economic stress.[37]

Family. P.d.: as under economics. Ills.: last part of preceding quotation, and:

It is very bad when families separate, *P* likes it when all stay together, but nowadays many go away, yet almost all come back. I said how happy she must be with her large family, and she broke out into almost a hymn to *el Señor* [the Lord] who blessed her with so good and large a family——and it was the *menor* [youngest (daughter)] who produced so many children . . . she counted on her fingers all . . . children by name, first the seven sons, then the three daughters. She repeated, hymn-like, "*por eso que estoy tan contenta, contenta, contenta*" [it is for this that I am so happy, happy, happy]—what more can I ask for but that I am here with my family all together? "*Bueno es estar juntos, pero cuando van afuera se debe andar al correo*" [It is good to stay together, but when they leave one has to go to the post office]—as now regarding *A*.[38]

Happiness. P.d.: happy state of mind, in the colloquial sense of the expression, induced by certain culture elements, e.g., physical presence of kin in the family's house, etc. Ills.: preceding quotation, and:

The *M*'s were having supper when I came back, and of course invited me, finally pressed a cup of coffee upon me. The family . . . was obviously very happy. *A* said to me that he had wanted to eat *quelite* [kind of spinach] . . . , which he got . . . *R* [had] beamed all day long as if the arrival of the brother [*A*], in spite of the [negative] economic implications, were the fulfillment of her wishes, which it most likely is . . .[39]

When the baby [ours] laughs, *R* laughs quite cordially too. This is probably an occasion engendering happiness because fitting in their own culture set-up (laughter of children, fine weather, flowers, and the like) . . . *R*, beaming, brought a telegram from *F* [her nephew] saying he is in this country, fine, and expecting to come to a hospital nearer home where he expects his parents to visit him. "*Que buenas nuevas—ayer* A, *y en la tarde la nueva de* F" [What good news—yesterday *A*, and this afternoon the news from *F*].[40]

Hospitality. Ills.: beginning of first quotation under Happiness, and:

C asked *R* yesterday whether she could take a few apricots from the tree, to cook for the child. *R*, after a moment of surprise at the question, so it seemed to *C*, opened her arms and said, but that *todo, todo* [everything] was ours—what a question. She then expanded that at this time of the year one didn't have to buy fruit; that after the apricots came the plums . . . This is another instance of . . . the instant transformation of persons when acting as hosts.[41]

Houses. P.d.: as under Economics; the fact that acting in one's own house with fellow residents (usually family) or toward a stranger gives a feeling of

security, pride, contentment, etc., not enjoyed outside the house. Ills.:
preceding quotation, and:

> *R* thanked me after we were through with the door work [done at my
> suggestion and for my convenience] as if I had helped her improve the
> house. That she found it an improvement was obvious, for she commented
> most favorably to *C* and me about it. Also, after I came home I suggested
> to put a . . . [curtain] in front of my clothes, and while we were looking for
> rods, etc., she called to *C*, "*ya tenemos una nueva idea*" [already we have a
> new (good) idea] . . . *C* asked her in connection with this and with the
> door how *A* [her brother, the owner of the house] would like it (that we
> made so many changes in the house), and she said of course he would,
> for he liked air and sun, which now could enter more easily than before.[42]

> The house in which one lives seems to be part of the happiness complex.
> At coffee we talked about things *R* and I had planned to do, such as the
> cleaning of the well. *A* inquired whether the roof had leaked. This set off
> a number of things he wanted to do in case he stays *algunos dias* [for several
> days]—put new dirt on the roof, dig a well near the kitchen (*no más 12 o
> 15 pies, no más dos, tres días de trabejo* [no more than 12 or 15 feet (to dig),
> no more than two, three days of labor]) . . . He was greatly interested.[43]

Mañana. P.d.: enjoyment of the now; acting on impulse relatively freer
from other considerations than is true in our culture; absence of time-is-
money complex. Cf. also under Organization, Time, To the Point. Ills.:

> When I'd just started typing the above, *A* came in with a bunch of herbs,
> sat down murmuring something about my being busy, but then started
> explaining [the herbs].[44]

> *A* came twice today to bring me more herbs, no matter whether I was
> busy or not, but immediately understanding that the first time I had to go
> to the post office, the second up to *Fr*.[45]

> *C*'s [our child's] birthday . . . There is some truth to Campa's "Mañana is
> today,"[46] but it is journalistic in that it does not attempt, even, to determine
> how far the today extends: there is some provision for the future, some
> planning among the people here . . . [Although] *Cr* made the quilt for the
> baby only last night (*Fr* saw it unfinished yesterday), and badly enough . . . ,
> it was ready, as were her cake (paid for) and one (gift) made by *Pa* and
> *Cl*, . . . while *R* had even as long as a week ago bought three flower-
> painted drinking glasses (for baby and his parents).[47]

Organization. P.d.: greater lack of capacity for coordination of thoughts, activities, persons, functions, than is found in our culture. Cf. also under Mañana, Time, To the Point. Ills.:

J and *Fr* [Anglos] reported that . . . [their dog] had died; they found him dead this morning and think, as does *JA*, that he was poisoned by eating some bran which some people put on their alfalfa against grasshoppers: it is mixed with arsenic lead. They remarked upon the fact that there was no notice posted of the spread poison, with shrugging shoulders. *A* explained how it was *tirado con la mano* [scattered with the hand] and that it was only within *cercos* [fences], but that *un animal mediano* [a (small) medium-sized animal] could pass through [the fence] and be poisoned.[48]

R said she had told yesterday . . . [the store-keeper] to direct the doctor to her (*P*'s) house. This remarkable foresight is probably due to the importance of the case—her mother's health, . . . the lack of organization is overcome through the significance of the event. In other words, here Mañana includes the tomorrow.[49]

She [*P*] said she went to see the doctor [in the county seat], but he was away for two weeks. (Re "Organization": she made a trip, difficult for her, only to find that it was in vain, since she hadn't made sure before going whether the doctor was available. However, . . . the lack of organization is observed by me in terms of what we—members of "my" culture—think about organization. In other words, it is a lack of organization or of planning in terms of our, not of their, culture. What is it in terms of their culture? The answer to this question could be approached only by "immanent interpretation," i.e., by what *P* herself says about this unsuccessful trip. The trouble is that she cannot interpret it. All she could . . . interpret she has already said: she went, and the doctor wasn't there, and that is too bad.)[50]

Time. P.d.: conceptions of time exemplified in unpunctuality, vague knowledge and designation of periods of time, etc.; psychological distribution of events in time.[51] Cf. also under Mañana, Organization, To the Point. Ills.:

I asked *R*, "*no está muy lejos para andar a Fr*" [it isn't very far to go to *Fr*] . . ., and she answered, "*no, no está muy lejos*" [no, it isn't very far] . . . but since I was anxious to get there and was tired and hungry, I asked further, "*Como diez minutos?*" [about ten minutes], and she answered, "*O sí, como diez minutos, veinte*" [O yes, something like 10 minutes, 20]. . . .

The fact is it is at least 20 minutes to go up there, crossing four fence gates
. . . I remember . . . when I asked old Mrs. *P* how old *Cr* and *R* [her daugh-
ters] were, and she didn't know it and had to figure it out asking them,
asking *A* [her son], reckoning by other dates, etc.; or, when I asked *MM*
yesterday how old her son was, of whom she was so proud, and she
hesitated and asked her husband—19 months.[52]

I was waiting for *Fr* and observed to the *M*'s that their clock (alarm) was
about half an hour late . . . To my surprise, *P*, who very probably can't
read the clock, asked me how I *arreglo mi reloj* [regulate my watch]—thus
"imprecision" re time does not preclude awareness of it, and chronological
at that, even in the . . . illiterate *P*. I explained that some days before I had
adjusted it [my watch] after the *V*'s radio time. Yet they didn't do a thing
about adjusting their clock. *Cr* remarked that when the school bell rang
at nine (it rings at nine and at one) theirs showed . . . [about half past
eight]—but nothing was done about it.[53]

Mrs. *H* has to go to . . . [the county seat] for her OAA insurance to be
transferred to her name [her husband having died a few days before]. She
was there Saturday, but thought she was only 60 or 61 years old. She
looked up her *fé de bautismo* [certificate of baptism] and found she was 71
and hence entitled to OAA; therefore she has to go and produce the
certificate of baptism as the "welle-fare."[54]

To the Point. P.d.: the relation of what is immediately given and what the
given implies is different in the *XY* culture than in ours so that it appears that
in the *XY* culture there is only a reaction to and grasp of the given, rather
than of its implications also. Cf. also under Mañana, Organization, Time.
Ills.

This morning, *R*, upon my question re the San Ysidro service today, said
that there wasn't going to be any; Mrs. *S* (in possession of the church keys)
told her that Mrs. *AS* was in . . . [the county seat] and hadn't come back
yet. So I asked about the significance of Mrs. *AS*, and *R* said she was
mayordoma de la iglesia [church stewardess], which she hadn't told me
yesterday. Gradually then I found out that there are always not two
persons, as I thought yesterday, but two couples who make the *mayor-
domos* . . . Tentatively stated, the "pattern" would be to give information
only to the point, but not thinking in terms of "complexes" or, better,
"topics."[55]

Waste. P.d.: the almost "automatic" conservation of waste matters which
in our culture would more generally be thrown away; at the same time, the

frequent forgetting that something has been preserved, and its consequent spoiling. Ills.:

> R today cleaned a head of lettuce which was about to spoil, conserving small still-fresh particles and putting the whole saved into a jar.[56]

> R saves the tin lids removed, with the can opener, from sardine cans and the like, to use them as curl rollers for her hair, since curl rollers are no longer available.[57]

> C's information . . . Example: I left a potato on a shelf, raw and cut in half—I forgot it, having taken the other half for the baby. Although R sees the shelf many times a day, she didn't throw this potato away but left it there because she thought I could use it. Finally I threw it away into a bucket which she brings to the hogs. Example: she had *cuajada* [clabber] stand around for days till it got moldy and then told me she thought we couldn't use it any more; she asked me whether I didn't think she should throw it away. Example: she thinks I am utterly wasteful ("oh, you can use those things") if I throw away the green points of onions—she fries them with potatoes or meat, etc. Example: everywhere I see folded-up paper conserved.[58]

(2) Attempt at Interrelating the Features or Possibly Patterns Listed, and Some Others[59]

Acceptance, i.e., the unreflective acceptance of what comes or is; hence the conception of Time as something of relatively minor importance—time orientation is relatively vague; therefore Campa[60] is right but overlooks the limitation of the Mañana pattern as imposed by events which tradition has made outstanding and the meeting of which therefore calls for planning. Tradition is, of course, also a check on Acceptance, and on the other hand tradition enhances what little Organization there is patterned. Readiness to conceive of non-traditional complexes is slight: the To-the-Point pattern. Perhaps one could say that Acceptance, Mañana, and lack of Organization are expressions of what might be called the *Hic-et-Nunc* configuration.[61] It is based on a profound optimism which is shown, also, in spontaneous friendliness, Hospitality, confidence, and it finds its most literal expression in the picture of Happiness, which might be labeled by "here," "together"; in the significance of the Family and the Houses. It is possible also that the careful preservation of Waste matter, checked by lack of Organization (so that much of what has been preserved spoils or is forgotten), is an expression of *Hic-et-Nunc*, in part "channeled" through the precarious Economics situation.

If this picture of the emotional set-up of the *XY* culture (optimism, etc.) easily follows from that of the intellectual-conceptual setup (Acceptance, Time, etc.)[62] it must not be forgotten that there are important changes which have taken place and are taking place in all these patterns and therefore in the whole interrelatedness of the patterns (or "configuration" or "configurations").

On the whole the patterns have been changing in the direction of those prevailing in the Anglo culture which surrounds that of *XY*. The culture of *XY* would therefore appear to have undergone a process of losing its characteristics as (perhaps only "ideal-typically") outlined above. Probably some of the original patterns can be more clearly observed in this processs of change than they could if this process were not existent—as, e.g., the traditionally fixed temporal events such as the *fiesta*,[63] when contrasted with the present-day gliding of this fixity. At the same time, the vague Time conception and the Acceptance pattern appear to be predisposing to this change. The integrating role of the Family, even of the Houses, has decreased; the conceptions of Happiness, Hospitality, Mañana, have changed in the direction of the money-accentuated urban-American culture. Least changed have been those patterns which were characterized in negative terms above: they are tending to become liabilities in competing with the Anglos—lack of organization and planning (Organization), inability to see new wholes and complexes (To the Point);[64] even the conservation of Waste may change into the ever heavier stress of the second aspect of this pattern, namely, wasting the conserved matter through spoiling, or even forgetting that it has been conserved.

The great amount of petty thievery (cigarettes, small change, food, etc.) practiced by Spanish-speaking persons against Anglos, even against those with whom they are connected by the most cordial relations and friendships, as well as against other Spanish-speaking persons, may be a reaction to the competitive aspects of the change, a kind of stereotyped (patterned) revenge based on frustration, which in turn would be due mainly to felt economic inferiority.[65] At any rate, the role of petty thievery must be examined with reference to each pattern sketched.

In conclusion it should be reiterated once more that the whole of the foregoing "illustration" (V, above, has been given only to make the theoretical part of this paper more concrete—not to produce even a sketch of the culture of *XY*. Otherwise two points in it would appear as entirely invalidating weaknesses: the failure to utilize *all* materials for the discussion of patterns (e.g., religion, kinship, language, education, knowledge of herbs, magic, witchcraft, sex, and others for which voluminous field notes have been gathered), and the remaining conceptual insufficiency, especially as regards a distinction between patterns, traits, complexes, and configurations.

NOTES

1 Revision of a paper presented at the Summer Institute of the Society for Social Research at the University of Chicago, August 4, 1944. The research on which this paper is based was made possible by a postdoctoral fellowship of the Social Science Research Council. I am indebted to Dr. Sol Tax, University of Chicago, and to Dr. Melvin J. Tumin, Wayne University, for valuable criticisms and suggestions.

2 E.g., Gregory Bateson, *Naven* (Cambridge, Eng., 1936); or E. E. Evans-Pritchard, *Witchcraft, Oracles, and Magic Among the Azande* (Oxford, Eng., 1937); and the "culture pattern" school, of which below. Cf. also Gregory Bateson, "Experiments in Thinking about Observed Ethnological Material," *Philosophy of Science*, VIII (January, 1941), 53–68; and Clyde Kluckhohn, "The Place of Theory in Anthropological Studies," *Philosophy of Science*, VI (July, 1939), 328–44.

3 Cf. the works of George A. Lundberg, Read Bain, and others.

4 Especially Karl Mannheim's concept of "existential determination of knowledge,' in *Ideology and Utopia* (New York, 1936), pp. 237–40, esp. p. 239 and note, and its discussion by Robert K. Merton, "Karl Mannheim and the Sociology of Knowledge," unpaged reprint from *The Journal of Liberal Religion*, II, No. 3 (Winter, 1941); further discussion of Mannheim in Virgil G. Hinshaw, Jr., "The Epistemological Relevance of Mannheim's Sociology of Knowledge," *The Journal of Philosophy*, II (February 4, 1943), 57–72; and in H. Otto Dahlke, "The Sociology of Knowledge," in Barnes, Becker, and Becker, *Contemporary Social Theory* (New York and London, 1940), esp. pp. 82–85. For a concise general treatment of the problems of the sociology of knowledge (although with very little attention to Mannheim), see Gerard De Gré, *Society and Ideology* (New York, 1943).

5 Cf. Pauline V. Young, *Scientific Social Surveys and Research* (New York, 1939), pp. 134–35.

6 Cf., e.g., the general attitude as expressed by L. L. Bernard, "The Sources and Methods of Cultural and Folk Sociology," in L. L. Bernard (ed.), *The Fields and Methods of Sociology* (New York, 1934), esp. pp. 354–55; also the whole literature on "evaluation" vs. "fact" in the social sciences, from Rickert and Max Weber to Gunnar Myrdal, *An American Dilemma* (New York and London, 1944), pp. 1035–64.

7 Cf., e.g., M. R. Cohen and E. Nagel, *An Introduction to Logic and Scientific Method* (New York, 1934); John Dewey, *Logic: The Theory of Inquiry* (New York, 1938); A. D. Ritchie, *Scientific Method* (London, 1933); A. N. Whitehead, *Science and the Modern World* (New York, 1925); A. C. Benjamin, *The Logical Structure of Science* (London, 1936); G. H. Mead, "The Nature of Scientific Knowledge," in *The Philosophy of the Act* (Chicago, 1938), pp. 45–62; etc.

8 In this connection, Gunnar Myrdal's suggestion is highly stimulating (in *An American Dilemma*, p. 3): "America, compared to every other country in Western civilization, large or small, has the *most explicitly expressed* system of general ideals in reference to human interrelations. This body of ideals is more widely understood and appreciated than similar ideals are anywhere else."

9 Cf. R. H. Tawney's suggestion that a Maori anthropologist undertake a study of the British, in reciprocation of Firth's study of the Maori (in the preface to Raymond Firth, *Primitive Economics of the New Zealand Maori* [New York, 1929]), p. xvii.

10 Following the presentation of the first draft of this paper, Robert J. Havighurst suggested that this line of thought necessarily leads to the question of whether, in our own society,

a "middle-class" sociologist could adequately study a "lower-class" group. A thorough answer to this question needs, first, a distinct and comprehensive theory of "class" and, second, a distinct and comprehensive theory of the relations between our "subcultures" and our "culture." I do not think that at present we have either. (As to the first, certainly W. Lloyd Warner's and his followers' "class" theory is inadequate; cf. C. Wright Mills's review of Warner and Lunt, *The Social Life of a Modern Community* [New Haven, 1941], in *American Sociological Review*, VII [April, 1942], 263–71. On subcultures, cf. the stimulating discussion in Ralph Linton, *The Study of Man* [New York and London, 1936], pp. 275–76.) My offhand answer to the question raised by Professor Havighurst is that recent presentations of U.S. culture—esp. Robert S. Lynd, *Knowledge for What?* (Princeton, 1939); Clyde Kluckhohn, "The Way of Life," *The Kenyon Review*, III (Spring, 1941), 160–79; Margaret Mead, *And Keep Your Powder Dry* (New York, 1942)—would indicate that what our culture has in common is more pervasive than what it differentiates; so that the case of the "middle-class" sociologist studying a "lower-class" group would not seem to be an example in point of my thought, and that such documents as Shaw's studies of delinquents, Anderson's studies of the hobo, Thrasher's *The Gang*, Whyte's *Street Corner Society*, etc., are not fundamentally vitiated by the shortcoming which Professor Havighurst envisaged. (Cf. in this connection the critiques of Adler, Rank, Freud, Thomas and Znaniecki, Shaw, and others by John Dollard in his *Criteria for the Life History* [New Haven, 1935].)

11 The closeness to Malinowski's functionalism is obvious; functional anthropology "holds that the . . . laws [of the cultural process] are to be found in the function of the real elements of culture. The atomizing or isolating treatment of cultural traits is regarded as sterile, because the significance of culture consists in the relation between its elements..." (cf. Bronislaw Malinowski, "Culture," in *Encyclopedia of the Social Sciences* [1931], IV, 625). However, while Malinowski is predominantly interested in an explanation of culture as a human characteristic and, proceding on this basis, comes upon the concepts of need and institution (cf. his "Man's Culture and Man's Behavior," *Sigma Chi Quarterly*, XXIX [October, 1941], 182–96, and XX [January, 1942], 66–78); and *A Scientific Theory of Culture and Other Essays* [Chapel Hill N.C., 1944]), the cultural approach is predominantly interested in studying cultures and comes upon the concept of pattern (see below).

12 Clyde Kluckhohn, "Patterning as Exemplified in Navaho Culture," in Leslie Spier, A. Irving Hallowell, Stanley S. Newman (eds.), *Language, Culture, and Personality, Essays in Memory of Edward Sapir* (Menasha, Wis., 1941), pp. 109–30, esp. 114–29. This exposition by far surpasses the methodology of preceding studies, esp. Ruth Benedict's pioneering *Patterns of Culture* (Boston, 1934); or Carle C. Zimmerman's *The Changing Community* (New York and London, 1938), esp. 155–57; as well as philosophically related works, from Nietzsche's *Birth of Tragedy* to Sorokin's *Social and Cultural Dynamics* and Morris's *Paths of Life*.

13 Kluckhohn, "Patterning as Exemplified in Navaho Culture," pp. 120, 124, seems to answer this question in terms of statistics, but see below.

14 Space limitations have made impossible the inclusion of rather extensive field notes gathered during the course of this field study which would have served to illustrate the analysis presented in this paper. [See note 31, below, and pp. 329–36.]

15 "Universe of discourse" (of an individual or a group) is the totality of concepts used (by that individual or group), plus their implications. Cf. Kurt H. Wolff, "The Sociology of

Knowledge: Emphasis on an Empirical Attitude," *Philosophy of Science*, X (April, 1943), 109, n. 19. Cf. also George H. Mead, *Mind, Self, and Society* (Chicago, 1934), p. 269.

16 Cf. remarks made in note 10, above.

17 The most recent systematic presentation of folk culture known to me is Robert Redfield, *The Folk Society* (Chicago, August 12, 1942), hectographed.

18 Karl Mannheim, "Ideologische und soziologische Interpretation der geistigen Gebilde," in *Jahrbuch für Soziologie*, II (Karlsruhe, 1926).

19 It is, however, from the latter standpoint that Kluckhohn, "Patterning as Exemplified in Navaho Culture," has classified patterns.

20 It should be noted that the two "elements" of a folk culture, here designated in so oversimplified a form as "urban" and "non-urban," may, of course each need to be seen as consisting of various cultural strains. Thus the culture of the New Mexican community previously referred to, in its urban aspects, combines strains from a culture colored by international industrialization, from the "average American city culture," from regional cultural peculiarities, and from cultures of still more nearby "semi-urban" centers; in its non-urban aspects, it combines strains from Spanish, Mexican, rural, and Indian cultures—and all strains are differentiated in terms of the two main (and other) types of the members of this culture: Spanish-speaking and English-speaking persons.

21 My own experience is that for an initial period of field work I prefer the slower, more chaotic manner of recording anything that comes under my observation to the method of rapidly formulating hypotheses, because I am aware that a premature hypothesis, although checkable and corrigible, shapes one's chances of perception and interpretation. I am also aware, of course, that one cannot proceed without hypotheses. But those which I have advanced as a general theoretical approach to the study of cultures appear to me the minimal limitations-enrichments of my sensitivity.

22 From my own experience I should say that the initial period of avidly collecting materials comes to an end when their "sheer quantity" forces the student to begin his interpretation. It may be noted that this interpretation is likely to be based on a topical breakdown of the materials—a breakdown which has probably accompanied their collection itself.

23 Kluckhohn, "Patterning as Exemplified in Navaho Culture," unfortunately gives no explicit definition of "pattern." In contrast to "custom" and "trait," which are contentual, it is structural (pp. 114, 116); in contrast to "configuration," which applies to covert culture, it applies to overt culture (pp. 114, 124, 129); "overt" and "covert" are not defined, however.

24 It is understood (as is all scientific rule) that the method by which statistical data are arrived at depends on the nature of the pattern (it may be interview, casual conversation, questionnaire, etc., or any combination of them).

25 Namely, if Kluckhohn's distinction between structural (patterns) and contentual (traits) regularities were obliterated and, e.g., house-ownership (i.e., something in which the student is interested as in a contentual item) were considered in its interrelation with (structural) patterns. The study in which this is done to my knowledge has yet to be written. See above and below on interrelatedness of patterns.

26 They are paid no, or very little, attention in Benedict, *Patterns of Culture*.

27 And with reference to intellectual productions exclusively.

28 Cf. Wolff, "The Sociology of Knowledge," p. 113.

29 See above, esp. note 21.

30 The following discussion is simplified by overlooking a classification of the patterns mentioned according to Kluckhohn's scheme (in "Patterning as Exemplified in Navaho Culture," pp. 114–29).

31 The New Mexico community mentioned before. This section, reference to which is made in note 14, was not published in the original version of this article because of space limitations and is here published for the first time.

32 The following analytical features are omitted in this list or introduced only unsystematically: number and characteristics of population sharing these patterns, including the question of whether they are shared by individuals or populations outside *XY*—whether, e.g., they are typical of Spanish-speaking New Mexico, of rural people elsewhere, etc.; and classification of patterns according to Kluckhohn.

33 Henceforth "P.d." Given only if the concept here used deviates specifically from its colloquial usage.

34 Henceforth "Ills." These illustrations almost exclusively deal with members of one family, the *M*'s. For the sake of concreteness, as well as of sincerity, quotations are copied literally from my field notes (with the exception of the entry referred to in note 59). Omissions are indicated by ellipses; additions (mainly English renditions of Spanish expressions), brackets. Parentheses, except those within brackets, are in the original notes. "Anglo" is a traditionally and customarily English-speaking person. Spanish spelling is in accordance with Appleton's *New English-Spanish and Spanish-English Dictionary* (New York and London, 1943).

35 Kurt H. Wolff, "Field Notes" (ms.), p. 6, May 5, 1944.

36 *Ibid.*, pp. 173–74, June 26, 1944.

37 *Ibid.*, p. 127, June 12, 1944.

38 *Ibid.*, p. 26, May 9, 1944.

39 *Ibid.*, p. 130, June 12, 1944.

40 *Ibid.*, p. 133, June 13, 1944.

41 *Ibid.*, p. 398, August 25, 1944.

42 *Ibid.*, p. 65, May 22, 1944.

43 *Ibid.*, p. 131, June 12, 1944.

44 *Ibid.*, p. 290, July 23, 1944.

45 *Ibid.*, p. 297, July 24, 1944.

46 Arthur L. Campa, "Mañana Is Today," *The New Mexico Quarterly*, IX (February, 1939), 3–11.

47 Wolff, "Field Notes," p. 288, July 22, 1944.

48 *Ibid.*, p. 327, July 39, 1944.

49 *Ibid.*, p. 362, August 17, 1944.

50 *Ibid.*, pp. 337–38, August 13, 1944.

51 Cf. Pitirim A. Sorokin, *Sociocultural Causality, Space, Time* (Durham, N.C., 1943), pp. 158–225.

52 Wolff, "Field Notes," pp. 4–5, May 5, 1944.

53 *Ibid.*, p. 49, May 15, 1944.

54 *Ibid.*, p. 345, August 14, 1944.

55 *Ibid.*, p. 47, May 15, 1944.

56 *Ibid.*, p. 126, June 11, 1944.

57 *Ibid.*, p. 200, July 3, 1944.

58 *Ibid.*, p. 335, August 12, 1944.

59 The following is a slightly revised field-note entry (cf. *ibid.*, pp. 334–35, August 12, 1944).

60 Campa, "Mañana Is Today."

61 It will be noted that this term—"configuration"—is here used for the first time as a possible structural concept, because the relation between patterns and configurations has not yet become clear to me, nor does the justification of "configuration" as a concept denoting a step at which one can arrive empirically as yet appear to me demonstrated. Cf. note 23, above. On configurations, cf. Kluckhohn, "Patterning as Exemplified in Navaho Culture," pp. 124–29, and Florence R. Kluckhohn, "*Los Atarqueños*: A Study of Patterns and Configurations in a New Mexico Village" (unpublished Ph.D. dissertation, Radcliffe College, 1941), pp. 9, 12–31.

62 It would be inviting to develop a presentation of the *XY* culture in terms of a more systematic development of its emotional ("ethos") and intellectual ("eidos") aspects, as Bateson (in *Naven*, *l. c.* has attempted it for the Iatmül culture, but at this stage of the investigation I am not yet sure whether such a framework is ideal for the study of *XY*. For a comparison of the early-stage pattern approach (Benedict) with Bateson (and Margaret Mead), cf. S. F. Nadel, "The Typological Approach to Culture," *Character and Personality*, V (June, 1937), 267–84.

63 Or cf. the information about the San Ysidro celebration in 1944 in the illustration of To the Point, above.

64 Florence R. Kluckhohn (in "*Los Atarqueños*," pp. 27–28) discusses fear as one of the configurations of the Atarque culture. Although I have materials on fear in *XY*, I do not yet know either what role it plays there or whether it has not come to be accentuated only along with economic insecurity (and the inadequacy of "Spanish knowledge," i.e., knowledge regarding herbs, craft, witchcraft, cures, etc., to meet this insecurity).

65 For the theory underlying this sequence, see, e.g., John Dollard *et al.*, *Frustration and Aggression* (New Haven, 1939).

5

ROBERT K. MERTON

Paradigm for the Sociology of Knowledge

TO OUTLINE EVEN the main currents of the sociology of knowledge in brief compass is to present none adequately and to do violence to all. The diversity of formulations—of a Marx or Scheler or Durkheim; the varying problems—from the social determination of categorical systems to that of class-bound political ideologies; the enormous differences in scope—from the all-encompassing categorizing of intellectual history to the social location of the thought of Negro scholars in the last decades; the various limits assigned to the discipline—from a comprehensive sociological epistemology to the empirical relations of particular social structures and ideas; the pro-liferation of concepts—ideas, belief systems, positive knowledge, thought, systems of truth, superstructure, etc.; the diverse methods of validation—from plausible but undocumented imputations to meticulous historical and statistical analyses—in the light of all this, an effort to deal with both analytical apparatus and empirical studies in a few pages must sacrifice detail to scope.

To introduce a basis of comparability among the welter of studies which have appeared in this field, we must adopt some scheme of analysis. The following paradigm is intended as a step in this direction. It is, undoubtedly, a partial and, it is to be hoped, a temporary classification which will disappear as it gives way to an improved and more exacting analytical model. But it does provide a basis for taking an inventory of extant findings in the field; for indicating contradictory, contrary, and consistent results; setting forth the conceptual apparatus now in use; determining the nature of problems which have occupied workers in this field; assessing the character of the evidence which they have brought to bear upon these problems; ferreting out the

Reprinted with permission of The Macmillan Company from *Social Theory and Social Structure* by Robert K. Merton, pp. 460–88. The Free Press, a Corporation, 1957.

characteristic lacunae and weaknesses in current types of interpretation. Full-fledged theory in the sociology of knowledge lends itself to classification in terms of the following paradigm.

(*1*) Where *is the existential basis of mental productions located?*
a. social bases: social position, class, generation, occupational role, mode of production, group structures (university, bureaucracy, academies, sects, political parties), "historical situation," interests, society, ethnic affiliation, social mobility, power structure, social processes (competition, conflict, etc.)

b. cultural bases: values, ethos, climate of opinion, *Volksgeist*, *Zeitgeist*, type of culture, culture mentality, *Weltanschauungen*, etc.

(*2*) What *mental productions are being sociologically analyzed?*
a. spheres of: moral beliefs, ideologies, ideas, the categories of thought, philosophy, religious beliefs, social norms, positive science, technology, etc.

b. which aspects are analyzed: their selection (lack of attention), level of abstraction, presuppositions (what is taken as data and what as problematical), conceptual content, models of verification, objectives of intellectual activity, etc.

(*3*) How *are mental productions related to the existential basis?*
a. causal or functional relations: determination, cause, correspondence, necessary condition, conditioning, functional interdependence, interaction, dependence, etc.

b. symbolic or organismic or meaningful relations: consistency, harmony, coherence, unity, congruence, compatibility (and antonyms); expression, realization, symbolic expression, *Strukturzusammenhang*, structural identities, inner connection, stylistic analogies, logicomeaningful integration, identity of meaning, etc.

c. ambiguous terms to designate relations: correspondence, reflection, bound up with, in close connection with, etc.

(*4*) Why? *Manifest and latent functions imputed to these existentially conditioned mental productions.*
a. to maintain power, promote stability, orientation, exploitation, obscure actual social relationships, provide motivation, canalize behavior, divert criticism, deflect hostility, provide reassurance, control nature, coordinate social relationships. etc.

(5) When *do the imputed relations of the existential base and knowledge obtain?*

a. historicist theories (confined to particular societies or cultures).

b. general analytical theories.

There are, of course, additional categories for classifying and analyzing studies in the sociology of knowledge, which are not fully explored here. Thus, the perennial problem of the implications of existential influences upon knowledge for the epistemological status of that knowledge has been hotly debated from the very outset. Solutions to this problem, which assume that a sociology of knowledge is necessarily a sociological theory of knowledge, range from the claim that the "genesis of thought has no necessary relation to its validity" to the extreme relativist position that truth is "merely" a function of a social or cultural basis, that it rests solely upon social consensus and, consequently, that any culturally accepted theory of truth has a claim to validity equal to that of any other.

But the foregoing paradigm serves to organize the distinctive approaches and conclusions in this field sufficiently for our purposes.

The chief approaches to be considered here are those of Marx, Scheler, Mannheim, Durkheim, and Sorokin. Current work in this area is largely oriented toward one or another of these theories, either through a modified application of their conceptions or through counterdevelopments. Other sources of studies in this field indigenous to American thought, such as pragmatism, will be advisedly omitted, since they have not yet been formulated with specific reference to the sociology of knowledge nor have they been embodied in research to any notable extent.

THE EXISTENTIAL BASIS

A central point of agreement in all approaches to the sociology of knowledge is the thesis that thought has an existential basis in so far as aspects can be derived from extra-cognitive factors. But this is merely a formal consensus, which gives way to a wide variety of theories concerning the nature of the existential basis.

In this respect, as in others, Marxism is the storm center of *Wissenssoziologie*. Without entering into the exegetic problem of closely identifying Marxism—we have only to recall Marx's "*je ne suis pas Marxiste*"—we can trace out its formulations primarily in the writings of Marx and Engels. Whatever other changes may have occurred in the development of their theory during the half century of their work, they consistently held fast to the thesis are that "relations of production" constitute the "real foundation" for the superstructure of ideas. "The mode of production in material life determines the general character of the social, political, and intellectual processes of life. It is not the consciousness of men that determines their existence, but on the contrary, their social existence determines their consciousness."[1] In seeking to functionalize ideas, i.e., to relate the ideas of individuals to their sociological bases, Marx locates them within the class structure. He assumes, not so much that other influences are not at all operative, but that class is a primary determinant and, as such, the single most fruitful point of departure for analysis. This he makes explicit in his first preface to *Capital*: ". . . here individuals are dealt with *only in so far* as they are the personifications of economic categories, embodiments of particular class-relations and class-interests."[2] In abstracting from other variables and in regarding men in their economic and class roles, Marx hypothesizes that these roles are primary determinants and this leaves as an open question *the extent to which they adequately account for thought and behavior in any given case.* In point of fact, one line of development of Marxism, from the early *German Ideology* to the later writings of Engels, consists in a progressive definition (and delimitation) of the extent to which the relations of production do in fact condition knowledge and forms of thought.

However, both Marx and Engels, repeatedly and with increasing insistence emphasized that the ideologies of a social stratum need not stem only from persons who are *objectively* located in that stratum. As early as the *Communist Manifesto*, Marx and Engels had indicated that as the ruling class approaches dissolution, "a small section . . . joins the revolutionary class. . . . Just as, therefore, at an earlier period, a section of the nobility went over to the bourgeoisie, so now a portion of the bourgeoisie goes over to the proletariat, and in particular, a portion of *the bourgeois ideologists*, who have *raised themselves* to the level of comprehending theoretically the historical movement as a whole."[3]

Ideologies are socially located by analyzing their perspectives and presuppositions and determining how problems are construed: from the standpoint of one or another class. Thought is not mechanistically located by merely establishing the class position of the thinker. It is attributed to that class for which it is "appropriate," to the class whose social situation with its class conflicts, aspirations, fears, restraints and objective possibilities within the given sociohistorical context is being expressed. Marx's most explicit formulation holds:

One must not form the narrow-minded idea that the petty bourgeoisie wants on principle to enforce an egoistic class interest. It believes, rather, that the *special* conditions of its emancipation are the *general* conditions through which alone modern society can be saved and the class struggle avoided. Just as little must one imagine that the democratic representatives are all shopkeepers or are full of enthusiasm for them. *So far as their education and their individual position are concerned*, they may be as widely separated from them as heaven from earth. *What makes them representative of the petty bourgeoisie is the fact that in their minds* [im Kopfe] *they do not exceed the limits which the latter do not exceed in their life activities*, that they are consequently driven to the same problems and solutions in theory to which material interest and social position drive the latter in practice. *This is* ueberhaupt, *the relationship of the political and literary representatives of a class to the class which they represent.*[4] [Italics added].

But if we cannot derive ideas from the objective class position of their exponents, this leaves a wide margin of indeterminacy. It then becomes a further problem to discover why some identify themselves with the characteristic outlook of the class stratum in which they objectively find themselves whereas others adopt the presuppositions of a class stratum other than "their own." An empirical description of the fact is no adequate substitute for its theoretical explanation.

In dealing with existential bases, Max Scheler characteristically places his own hypothesis in opposition to other prevalent theories.[5] He draws a distinction between cultural sociology and what he calls the sociology of real factors (*Realsoziologie*). Cultural data are "ideal," in the realm of ideas and values: "real factors" are oriented toward effecting changes in the reality of nature or society. The former are defined by ideal goals or intentions; the latter derive from an "impulse structure" (*Triebstruktur*, e.g., sex, hunger, power). It is a basic error, he holds, of all naturalistic theories to maintain that real factors—whether race, geopolitics, political power structure, or the relations of economic production—unequivocally determine the realm of meaningful ideas. He also rejects all ideological, spiritualistic, and personalistic conceptions which err in viewing the history of existential conditions as a unilinear unfolding of the history of mind. He ascribes complete autonomy and a determinate sequence to these real factors, though he inconsistently holds that value-laden ideas serve to guide and direct their development. Ideas as such initially have no social effectiveness. The "purer" the idea, the greater its impotence, so far as dynamic effect on society is concerned. Ideas do not become actualized, embodied in cultural developments, unless they are bound up in some fashion with interests, impulses, emotions, or collective tendencies and their incorporation in institutional structures.[6] Only then—and in this limited respect, naturalistic theories (e.g., Marxism) are justified—do they exercise some definite influence. Should ideas not be grounded in the imminent development of real factors, they are doomed to become sterile Utopias.

Naturalistic theories are further in error, Scheler holds, in tacitly assuming the *independent variable* to be one and the same throughout history. There is no constant independent variable but there is, in the course of history, a definite sequence in which the primary factors prevail, a sequence which can be summed up in a "law of three phases." In the initial phase, blood ties and associated kinship institutions constitute the independent variable; later, political power, and, finally, economic factors. There is, then, no constancy in the effective primacy of existential factors but rather an ordered variability. Thus, Scheler sought to realize the very notion of historical determinants.[7] He claims not only to have confirmed his law of the three phases inductively but to have derived it from a theory of human impulses.

Scheler's conception of *Realfaktoren*—race and kinship, the structure of power, factors of production, qualitative and quantitative aspects of population, geographical and geopolitical factors—hardly constitutes a usefully defined category. It is of small value to subsume such diverse elements under one rubric, and, indeed, his own empirical studies and those of his disciples do not profit from this array of factors. But in suggesting a variation of significant existential factors, though not in the ordered sequence which he failed to establish, he moves in the direction which subsequent research has followed.

Thus Mannheim derives from Marx primarily by extending his conception of existential bases. Given the *fact* of multiple group affiliation, the problem becomes one of determining *which* of these affiliations are decisive in fixing perspectives, models of thought, definitions of the given, etc. Unlike "a dogmatic Marxism," he does not assume that class position is alone ultimately determinant. He finds, for example, that an organically integrated group conceives of history as a continuous movement toward the realization of its goals, whereas socially uprooted and loosely integrated groups espouse a historical intuition which stresses the fortuitous and imponderable. It is only through exploring the variety of group formations—generations, status groups, sects, occupational groups—and their characteristic modes of thought that there can be found an existential basis corresponding to the great variety of perspectives and knowledge which actually obtain.[8]

Though representing a different tradition, this is substantially the position taken by Durkheim. In an early study with Mauss of primitive forms of classification, he maintained that the genesis of the categories of thought is to be found in the group structure and relations and that the categories vary with changes in the social organization.[9] In seeking to account for the social origins of the categories, Durkheim postulates that individuals are more directly and inclusively oriented toward the groups in which they live than they are toward nature. The primarily significant experiences are mediated through social relationships, which leave their impress on the character of thought and knowledge.[10] Thus, in his study of primitive forms of thought, he deals with the periodic recurrence of social activities (ceremonies, feasts, rites), the clan structure and the spatial configurations of group meetings as among the existential bases of thought. And, applying Durkheim's formulations to ancient Chinese thought, Granet attributes their typical conceptions of time and space to such bases as the feudal organization and the rhythmic alternation of concentrated and dispersed group life.[11]

In sharp distinction from the foregoing conceptions of existential bases is Sorokin's idealistic and emanationist theory, which seeks to derive every aspect of knowledge, not from an existential social basis, but from varying "culture mentalities." These mentalities are constructed of "major premises": thus, the ideational mentality conceives of reality as "non-material, everlasting Being"; its needs as primarily spiritual and their full satisfaction through "self-imposed minimization or elimination of most physical needs."[12] Contrariwise, the sensate mentality limits reality to what can be perceived through the senses; it is primarily concerned with physical needs which it seeks to satisfy to a maximum, not through self-modification, but through change of the external world. The chief intermediate type of mentality is the idealistic, which represents a virtual balance of the foregoing types. It is these mentalities, i.e., the major premises of each culture, from which systems of truth and knowledge are derived. And here we come to the self-contained emanationism of an idealistic position: it appears plainly tautological to say, as Sorokin does, that "in a sensate society and culture the sensate system of truth based upon the testimony of the organs of senses has to be dominant."[13] For sensate mentality has already been *defined* as one conceiving of "reality as only that which is presented to the sense organs."[14]

Moreover, an emanationist phrasing such as this bypasses some of the basic questions raised by other approaches to the analysis of existential conditions. Thus, Sorokin considers the failure of the sensate "system of truth" (empiricism) to monopolize a sensate culture as evidence that the culture is not "fully integrated." But this surrenders inquiry into the bases of those very differences of thought with which our contemporary world is concerned. This is true of other categories and principles of knowledge for which he seeks to apply a sociological accounting. For example, in our present sensate culture, he finds that "materialism" is less prevalent than "idealism," "temporalism" and "eternalism" are almost equally current; so, too, with "realism" and "nominalism," "singularism" and "universalism," etc. Since there are these diversities within a culture, the over-all characterization of the culture as sensate provides no basis for indicating which groups subscribe to one mode of thought, and which to another. Sorokin does not systematically explore varying existential bases *within* a society or culture; he looks to the "dominant" tendencies and imputes these to the culture as a whole.[15] Our contemporary society, quite apart from the *differences* of intellectual outlook of divers classes and groups, is viewed as an integral exemplification of sensate culture. On its own premises, Sorokin's approach is primarily suited for an over-all characterization of cultures, not for analyzing connections between varied existential conditions and thought within a society.

TYPES OF KNOWLEDGE

Even a cursory survey is enough to show that the term "knowledge" has been so broadly conceived as to refer to every type of idea and every mode of thought ranging from folk belief to positive science. Knowledge has often come to be assimilated to the term "culture," so that not only the exact sciences but ethical convictions, epistemological postulates, material predications, synthetic judgments, political beliefs, the categories of thought, eschatological doxies, moral norms, ontological assumptions, and observations of empirical fact are more or less indiscriminately held to be "existentially conditioned."[16] The question is, of course, whether these diverse kinds of "knowledge" stand in the same relationship to their sociological basis, or whether it is necessary to discriminate between spheres of knowledge precisely because this relationship differs for the various types. For the most part, there has been a systematic ambiguity concerning this problem.

Only in his later writings did Engels come to recognize that the concept of ideological superstructure included a variety of "ideological forms" which differ *significantly*, i.e., are not equally and similarly conditioned by the material basis. Marx's failure to take up this problem systematically[17] accounts for much of the initial vagueness about *what* is comprised by the superstructure and how these several "ideological" spheres are related to the modes of production. It was largely the task of Engels to attempt this clarification. In differentiating the blanket term "ideology," Engels granted a degree of autonomy to law.

As soon as the new division of labor which creates professional lawyers becomes necessary, another new and independent sphere is opened up which, for all its general dependence on production and trade, still has its own capacity for reacting upon these spheres as well. In a modern state, law must not only correspond to the general economic position and be its expression, but, must also be an expression which is *consistent in itself*, and which does not, owing to inner contradictions, look glaringly inconsistent. And in order to achieve this, the faithful reflection of economic conditions is more and more infringed upon. All the more so the more rarely it happens that a code of law is the blunt, unmitigated, unadulterated expression of the domination of a class—this in itself would already offend the "conception of justice."[18]

If this is true of law, with its close connection with economic pressures, it it is all the more true of other spheres of the "ideological superstructure." Philosophy, religion, science are particularly constrained by the pre-existing stock of knowledge and belief, and are only indirectly and ultimately influenced by economic factors.[19] In these fields, it is not possible to "derive" the content and development of belief and knowledge merely from an analysis of the historical situation:

Political, juridical, philosophical, religious, literary, artistic, etc., development is based on economic development. But all these react upon one another and also upon the economic base. It is not that the economic position is the *cause and alone active*, while everything else only has a passive effect. There is, rather, interaction on the basis of the economic necessity, which ultimately always asserts itself.[20]

But to say that the economic basis "ultimately" asserts itself is to say that the ideological spheres exhibit some degree of independent development, as indeed Engels goes on to observe: "The further the particular sphere which we are investigating is removed from the economic sphere and approaches that of pure abstract ideology, the more shall we find it exhibiting accidents [i.e., deviations from the "expected"] in its development, the more will its curve run in zigzag."[21]

Finally, there is an even more restricted conception of the sociological status of natural science. In one well-known passage, Marx expressly distinguishes natural science from ideological spheres.

With the change of the economic foundation the entire immense superstructure is more or less rapidly transformed. In considering such transformations the distinction should always be made between the material transformation of the economic conditions of production *which can be determined with the precision of natural science*, and the legal, political, religious, aesthetic or philosophic—in short, ideological forms in which men become conscious of this conflict and fight it out.[22]

Thus, natural science and political economy, which can match its precision, are granted a status quite distinct from that of ideology. The conceptual content of natural science is not imputed to an economic base: merely its "aims" and "material." "Where would natural science be without industry and commerce? Even this 'pure' natural science is provided with an aim, as with its material, *only* through trade and industry, through the sensuous activity of men."[23] [Italics added]. Along the same lines, Engels asserts that the appearance of Marx's materialistic conception of history was itself determined by "necessity," as is indicated by similar views appearing among English and French historians at the time and by Morgan's independent discovery of the same conception.[24]

He goes even further to maintain that socialist theory is itself a proletarian "reflection" of modern class conflict, so that here, at least, the very content of "scientific thought" is held to be socially determined,[25] without vitiating its validity.

There was an incipient tendency in Marxism, then, to consider natural science as standing in a relation to the economic base different from that of other spheres of knowledge and belief. In science, the focus of attention may be socially determined but not, presumably, its conceptual apparatus. In this respect, the social sciences were sometimes held to differ significantly from the natural sciences. Social science tended to be assimilated to the sphere of ideology, a tendency developed by later Marxists into the questionable thesiss of a class-bound social science which is inevitably tendentious[26] and into the claim that only "proletarian science" has valid insight into certain aspects of social reality.[27]

Mannheim follows in the Marxist tradition to the extent of exempting the "exact sciences" and "formal knowledge" from existential determination but not "historical, political, and social science thinking as well as the thought of everyday life."[28] Social position determines the "perspective," i.e., "the manner in which one views an object, what one perceives in it, and how one construes it in his thinking." The situational determination of thought does not render it invalid; it does, however, particularize the scope of the inquiry and the limits of its validity.[29]

If Marx did not sharply differentiate the superstructure, Scheler goes to the other extreme. He distinguishes a variety of forms of knowledge. To begin with, there are the "relatively natural *Weltanschauungen*": that which is accepted as given, as neither requiring nor being capable of justification.

These are, so to speak, the cultural axioms of groups; what Joseph Glanvill, some 300 years ago, called a "climate of opinion." A primary task of the sociology of knowledge is to discover the laws of transformation of these *Weltanschauungen*. And since these outlooks are by no means necessarily valid, it follows that the sociology of knowledge is not concerned merely with tracing the existential bases of truth but also of "social illusion, superstitution and socially conditioned errors and forms of deception."[30]

The *Weltanschauungen* constitute organic growths and develop only in long time spans. They are scarcely affected by theories. Without adequate evidence, Scheler claims that they can be changed in any fundamental sense only through race mixture or conceivably through the "mixture" of language and culture. Building upon these very slowly changing *Weltanschauungen* are the more "artificial" forms of knowledge which may be ordered in seven classes, according to degree of artificiality: (1) myth and legend; (2) knowledge implicit in the natural folk language; (3) religious knowledge (ranging from the vague emotional intuition to the fixed dogma of a church); (4) the basic types of mystical knowledge; (5) philosophical-metaphysical knowledge; (6) positive knowledge of mathematics, the natural and cultural sciences; (7) technological knowledge.[31] The more artificial these types of knowledge, the more rapidly they change. It is evident, says Scheler, that religions change far more slowly than the various metaphysics, and the latter persist for much longer periods than the results of positive science, which change from hour to hour.

This hypothesis of rates of change bears some points of similarity to Alfred Weber's thesis that civilizational change outruns cultural change and to the Ogburn hypothesis that "material" factors change more rapidly than the "non-material." Scheler's hypothesis shares the limitations of these others as well as several additional shortcomings. He nowhere indicates with any clarity what his principle of classification of types of knowledge—so-called "artificiality"—actually denotes. Why, for example, is "mystical knowledge" conceived as more "artificial" than religious dogmas? He does not at all consider what is entailed by saying that one type of knowledge changes more rapidly than another. Consider his curious equating of new scientific "results" with metaphysical systems; how does one compare the degree of change implied in neo-Kantian philosophy with, say, change in biological theory during the corresponding period? Scheler boldly asserts a sevenfold variation in rates of change and, of course, does not emprically confirm this elaborate claim. In view of the difficulties encountered in testing much simpler hypotheses, it is not at all clear what is gained by setting forth an elaborate hypothesis of this type.

Yet only certain aspects of this knowledge are held to be sociologically determined. On the basis of certain postulates, which need not be considered here, Scheler goes on to assert:

> The sociological character of all knowledge, of all forms of thought, intuition and cognition is unquestionable. Although the *content* and even less the objective validity of all knowledge is not determined by the *controlling perspectives of social interests*, nevertheless this is the case with the selection of the objects of knowledge. Moreover, the "forms" of the mental processes by means of which knowledge is acquired are always and necessarily co-determined sociologically, i.e., by the social structure.[32]

Since explanation consists in tracing the relatively new to the familiar and known and since society is "better known" than anything else,[33] it is to be expected that the modes of thought and intuition and the classification of knowable things generally, are co-determined (*mitbedingt*) by the division and classification of groups which comprise the society.

Scheler flatly repudiates all forms of sociologism. He seeks to escape a radical relativism by resorting to a metaphysical dualism. He posits a realm of "timeless essences" which in varying degrees enter into the *content of judgments*; a realm utterly distinct from that of historical and social reality which determines the *act* of judgments. As Mandelbaum has aptly summarized this view:

> The realm of essences is to Scheler a realm of possibilities out of which we, bound to time and our interest, first select one set and then another for consideration. Where we as historians turn the spotlight of our attention depends upon our own sociologically determined valuations; what we see there is determined by the set of absolute and timeless values which are implicit in the past with which we are dealing.[34]

This is indeed counterrelativism by fiat. Merely asserting the distinction between essence and existences avoids the incubus of relativism by exorcizing it. The concept of eternal essences may be congenial to the metaphysician; it is wholly foreign to empirical inquiry. It is noteworthy that these conceptions play no significant part in Scheler's empirical efforts to establish relations between knowledge and society.

Scheler indicates that different types of knowledge are bound up with particular forms of groups. The content of Plato's theory of ideas required the form and organization of the platonic academy; so, too, the organization of Protestant churches and sects was determined by the content of their beliefs, which could exist only in this and in no other type of social organization, as Troeltsch has shown. And, similarly, *Gemeinschaft* types of society have a traditionally defined fund of knowledge which is handed down as conclusive; they are not concerned with discovering or extending knowledge. The very effort to test the traditional knowledge, in so far as it implies doubt, is ruled out as virtually blasphemous. In such a group, the prevailing logic and mode of thought is that of an *"ars demonstrandi"* not of an *"ars inveniendi."* Its methods are prevailingly ontological and dogmatic, not epistemologic and critical; its mode of thought is that of conceptual realism, not nominalistic as in the *Gesellschaft* type of organization; its system of categories, organismic and not mechanistic.[35]

Durkheim extends sociological inquiry into the social genesis of the categories of thought, basing his hypothesis on three types of presumptive evidence. (1) The fact of cultural variation in the categories and the rules of logic "prove that they depend upon factors that are historical and consequently social."[36] (2) Since concepts are imbedded in the very language the individual acquires (and this holds as well for the special terminology of the scientist) and since some of these conceptual terms refer to things which we, as individuals, have never experienced, it is clear that they are a product of the society.[37] And (3), the acceptance or rejection of concepts is not determined *merely* by their objective validity but also by their consistency with other prevailing beliefs.[38]

Yet Durkheim does not subscribe to a type of relativism in which there are merely competing criteria of validity. The social origin of the categories does not render them wholly arbitrary so far as their applicability to nature is concerned. They are, in varying degrees, adequate to their object. But since social structures vary (and with them, the categorical apparatus) there are inescapable "subjective" elements in the particular logical constructions current in a society. These subjective elements "must be progressively rooted out, if we are to approach reality more closely." And this occurs under determinate social conditions. With the extension of intercultural contacts, with the spread of intercommunication between persons drawn from different societies, with the enlargement of the society, the local frame of reference becomes disrupted. "Things can no longer be contained in the social molds according to which they were primitively classified; they must be organized according to principles which are their own. So logical organization differentiates itself from the social organization and becomes autonomous. Genuinely human thought is not a primitive fact; it is the product of history."[39] Particularly those conceptions which are subjected to scientifically methodical criticism come to have a greater objective adequacy. Objectivity is itself viewed as a social emergent.

Throughout, Durkheim's dubious epistemology is intertwined with his substantive account of the social roots of concrete designations of temporal, spatial, and other units. We need not indulge in the traditional exaltation of the categories as a thing set apart and foreknown, to note that Durkheim was dealing not with them but with conventional divisions of time and space. He observed, in passing, that differences in these respects should not lead us to "neglect the similarities, which are no less essential." If he pioneered in relating variations in systems of concepts to variations in social organization, he did not succeed in establishing the social origin of the categories.

Like Durkheim, Granet attaches great significance to language as constraining and fixing prevalent concepts and modes of thought. He has shown how the Chinese language is not equipped to note concepts, analyze ideas, or to present doctrines discursively. It has remained intractable to formal precision. The Chinese word does not fix a notion with a definite degree of abstration and generality, but evokes an indefinite complex of particular images. Thus, there is no word which simply signifies "old man." Rather, a considerable number of words "paint different aspects of old age": *k'i*, those who need a richer diet; *k'ao*, those who have difficulty in breathing, and so on. These concrete evocations entail a multitude of other similarly concrete images of every detail of the mode of life of the aged; those who should be exempt from military service; those for whom funerary material should be held in readiness; those who have a right to carry a staff through the town, etc. These are but a few of the images evoked by *k'i*, which, in general, corresponds to the quasi-singular notion of old persons, some sixty to seventy years of age. Words and sentences thus have an entirely concrete, emblematic character.[40]

Just as the language is concrete and evocative, so the most general ideas of ancient Chinese thought were unalterably concrete, none of them comparable to our abstract ideas. Neither time nor space were abstractly conceived. Time proceeds by cycles and is round; space is square. The earth, which is square, is divided into squares; the walls of towns, fields, and camps should form a square. Camps, buildings and towns must be oriented and the selection of the proper orientation is in the hands of a ritual leader. Techniques of the division and management of space—surveying, town development, architecture, political geography—and the geometrical speculations which they presuppose are all linked with a set of social regulations. Particularly as these pertain to periodic assemblies, they reaffirm and reinforce in every detail the symbols which represent space. They account for its square form, its heterogeneous and hierarchic character, a conception of space which could only have arisen in a feudal society.[41]

Though Granet may have established the social grounds of concrete designations of time and space, it is not at all clear that he deals with data comparable to Western conceptions. He considers traditionalized or ritualized or magical conceptions and implicitly compares these with our matter-of-fact, technical, or scientific notions. But in a wide range of actual *practices*, the Chinese did not *act* on the assumption that "time is round" and "space, square." When comparable spheres of activity and thought are considered it is questionable that this radical cleavage of "categorical systems" occurs, in the sense that there are no common denominators of thought and conception. Granet has demonstrated qualitative differences of concepts in *certain contexts*, but not within such comparable contexts as, say, that of technical practice. His work testifies to different foci of intellectual interests in the two spheres and within the ritualistic sphere, basic differences of outlook, but not unbridgeable gaps in other spheres. The fallacy which is most prominent in Lévy-Bruhl's concept of the "prelogicality" of the primitive mind thus appears in the work of Granet as well. As Malinowski and Rivers have shown, when comparable spheres of thought and activity are considered, no such irreconcilable differences are found.[42]

Sorokin shares in this same tendency to ascribe entirely disparate criteria of truth to his different culture types. He has cast into a distinctive idiom the fact of shifts of attention on the part of intellectual elites in different historical societies. In certain societies, religious conceptions and particular types of metaphysics are at the focus of attention, whereas in other societies, empirical science becomes the center of interest. But the several "systems of truth" coexist in each of these societies within certain spheres; the Catholic church has not abandoned its "ideational" criteria even in this sensate age.

In so far as Sorokin adopts the position of radically different and disparate criteria of truth, he must locate his own work within this context. It may be said, though an extensive discussion would be needed to document it, that he never resolves this problem. His various efforts to cope with a radically relativistic impasse differ considerably. Thus, at the very outset, he states that his constructions must be tested in the same way "as any scientific law. First of all the principle must by nature be logical; second, it must successfully meet the test of the 'relevant facts,' that is, it must fit and represent the facts."[43] In Sorokin's own terminology, he has thereby adopted a scientific position characteristic of a "sensate system of truth." When he confronts his own epistemologic position directly, however, he adopts an "integralist" conception of truth which seeks to assimilate empirical and logical criteria as well as a "supersensory, superrational, metalogical act of 'intuition' or 'mystical experience.' "[44] He thus posits an integration of these diverse systems. In order to justify the "truth of faith"—the only item which would remove him from the ordinary criteria used in current scientific work— he indicates that "intuition" plays an important role as a *source* of scientific discovery. But does this meet the issue? The question is not one of the psychological *sources* of valid conclusions, but of the *criteria* and *methods of validation*. Which criteria would Sorokin adopt when "supersensory" intuitions are not consistent with empirical observation? In such cases, presumably, so far as we can judge from his work rather than from his comments about his work, he accepts the facts and rejects the intuition. All this suggests that Sorokin is discussing under the generic label of "truth" quite distinct and not comparable types of judgments: just as the chemist's analysis of an oil painting is neither consistent nor inconsistent with its aesthetic evaluation, so Sorokin's systems of truth refer to quite different kinds of judgments. And indeed, he is finally led to say as much, when he remarks that "each of the systems of truth, within its legitimate field of competency, gives us genuine cognition of the respective aspects of reality."[45] But whatever his private opinion of intuition he cannot draw it into his sociology as a *criterion* (rather than a source) of valid conclusions.

RELATIONS OF KNOWLEDGE TO THE EXISTENTIAL BASIS

Though this problem is obviously the nucleus of every theory in the sociology of knowledge, it has often been treated by implication rather than directly. Yet each type of imputed relation between knowledge and society presupposes an entire theory of sociological method and social causation. The prevailing theories in this field have dealt with one or both of two major types of relation: causal or functional, and the symbolic or organismic or meaningful.[46]

Marx and Engels, of course, dealt solely with some kind of causal relation between the economic basis and ideas, variously terming this relation as "determination, correspondence, reflection, outgrowth, dependence," etc. In addition, there is an "interest" or "need" relation; when strata have (imputed) needs at a particular stage of historical development, there is held to be a definite pressure for appropriate ideas and knowledge to develop. The inadequacies of these divers formulations have risen up to plague those who derive from the Marxist tradition in the present day.[47]

Since Marx held that thought is not a mere "reflection" of objective class position, as we have seen, this raises anew the problem of its imputation to a determinate basis. The prevailing Marxist hypotheses for coping with this problem involve a theory of history which is the ground for determining whether the ideology is "situationally adequate" for a given stratum in the society: this requires a hypothetical construction of what men *would think and perceive* if they were able to comprehend the historical situation adequately.[48] But such insight into the situation need not *actually* be widely current within particular social strata. This, then, leads to the further problem of "false consciousness," of how ideologies which are neither in conformity with the interests of a class nor situationally adequate come to prevail.

A partial empirical account of false consciousness, implied in the *Manifesto*, rests on the view that the bourgeoisie control the content of culture and thus diffuse doctrines and standards alien to the interests of the proletariat.[49] Or, in more general terms, "the ruling ideas of each age have ever been the ideas of its ruling class." But this is only a partial account; at most it deals with the false consciousness of the subordinated class. It might, for example, partly explain the fact noted by Marx that even where the peasant proprietor "does belong to the proletariat by his position he does not believe that he does." It would not, however, be pertinent in seeking to account for the false consciousness of the ruling class itself.

Another, though not clearly formulated, theme which bears upon the problem of false consciousness runs throughout Marxist theory. This is the conception of ideology as being an *unwitting, unconscious* expression of "real motives," these being in turn construed in terms of the objective interests of social classes. Thus, there is repeated stress on the unwitting nature of ideologies: "Ideology is a process accomplished by the so-called thinker consciously indeed but with a false consciousness. The real motives impelling him remain unknown to him, otherwise it would not be an ideological process at all. Hence he imagines false or apparent motives."[50]

The ambiguity of the term "correspondence" to refer to the connection between the material basis and the idea can only be overlooked by the polemical enthusiast. Ideologies are construed as "distortions of the social situation";[51] as merely "expressive" of the material conditions;[52] and, whether "distorted" or not, as motivational support for carrying through real changes in the society.[53] It is at this last point, when "illusory" beliefs are conceded to provide motivation for action, that Marxism ascribes a measure of independence to ideologies in the historical process. They are no longer merely epiphenomenal. They enjoy a measure of autonomy. From this develops the notion of interacting factors in which the superstructure, though interdependent with the material basis, is also assumed to have some degree of independence. Engels explicitly recognized that earlier formulations were inadequate in at least two respects: first, that both he and Marx had previously overemphasized the economic factor and understated the role of reciprocal interaction;[54] and second, that they had "neglected" the formal side—the way in which these ideas develop.[55]

The Marx-Engels views on the connectives of ideas and economic substructure hold, then, that the economic structure constitutes the framework that limits the range of ideas that will prove socially effective; ideas that do not have pertinence for one or another of the conflicting classes may arise, but will be of little consequence. Economic conditions are necessary, but not sufficient, for the emergence and spread of ideas that express either the interests or outlook, or both, of distinct social strata. There is no strict determinism of ideas by economic conditions, but a definite predisposition. Knowing the economic conditions, we can predict the kinds of ideas that can exercise a controlling influence in a direction that can be effective. "Men make their own history, but they do not make it just as they please; they do not make it under circumstances chosen by themselves, but under circumstances directly found, given and transmitted from the past." And in the making of history, ideas and ideologies play a definite role: consider only the view of religion as "the opiate of the masses"; consider further the importance attached by Marx and Engels to making those in the proletariat "aware" of their "own interests." Since there is no fatality in the development of the total social structure, but only a development of economic conditions that make certain lines of change *possible* and probable, idea systems may play a decisive role in the selection of one alternative that "corresponds" to the real balance of power rather than another alternative that runs counter to the existing power situation and is therefore destined to be unstable, precarious, and temporary. There is an ultimate compulsive that derives from economic development, but this compulsive does not operate with such detailed finality that no variation of ideas can occur at all.

The Marxist theory of history assumes that, *sooner or later*, idea systems that are inconsistent with the actually prevailing and incipient power structure will be rejected in favor of those that more nearly express the actual alignment of power. It is this view that Engels expresses in his metaphor of the "zigzag course" of abstract ideology: ideologies may temporarily deviate from what is compatible with the current social relations of production, but they are ultimately brought back in line. For this reason, the Marxist analysis of ideology is always bound to be concerned with the "total" historical situation, in order to account both for the temporary deviations and the later accommodation of ideas to the economic compulsives. But for this same reason, Marxist analyses are apt to have an excessive degree of "flexibility," almost to the point where *any* development can be explained away as a temporary aberration or deviation; where "anachronisms" and "lags" become labels for the explaining away of existing beliefs which do not correspond to theoretical expectations; where the concept of "accident" provides a ready means of saving the theory from facts that seem to challenge its validity.[56] Once a theory includes concepts such as "lags," "thrusts," "anachronisms," "accidents," "partial independence," and "ultimate independence," it becomes so labile and so indistinct, that it can be reconciled with virtually any configuration of data. Here, as in several other theories in the sociology of knowledge, a decisive question must be raised in order to determine whether we have a genuine theory: how can the theory be invalidated? In any given historical situation, which data will contradict and invalidate the theory? Unless this can be answered directly, unless the theory involves statements that can be controverted by definite types of evidence, it remains merely a pseudo-theory which will be compatible with any array of data.

Though Mannheim has gone far toward developing actual research procedures in the substantive sociology of knowledge, he has not appreciably clarified the connectives of thought and society.[57] As he indicates, once a thought structure has been analyzed, there arises the problem of imputing it to definite groups. This requires not only an empirical investigation of the groups or strata which prevalently think in these terms, but also an interpretation of why these groups, and not others, manifest this type of thought. This latter question implies a social psychology which Mannheim has not systematically developed.

The most serious shortcoming of Durkheim's analysis lies precisely in his uncritical acceptance of a naïve theory of correspondence in which the categories of thought are held to "reflect" certain features of the group organization. Thus "there are societies in Australia and North America where space is conceived in the form of an immense circle, *because* the camp has a circular form . . . the social organization has been the model for the spatial organization and a reproduction of it."[58] In similar fashion, the general notion of time is derived from the specific units of time differentiated in social activities (ceremonies, feats, rites).[59] The category of class and the modes of classification, which involve the notion of a hierarchy, are derived from social grouping and stratification. Those social categories are then "projected into our conception of the new world."[60] In summary, then, categories "express" the different aspects of the social order.[61] Durkheim's sociology of knowledge suffers from his avoidance of a social psychology.

The central relation between ideas and existential factors for Scheler is interaction. Ideas interact with existential factors which serve as selective agencies, releasing or checking the extent to which potential ideas find actual expression. Existential factors do not "create" or "determine" the content of ideas; they merely account for the *difference* between potentiality and actuality; they hinder, retard or quicken the actualization of potential ideas. In a figure reminiscent of Clerk Maxwell's hypothetical demon, Scheler states: "in a definite fashion and order, existential factors open and close the sluice gates to the flood of ideas." This formulation, which ascribes to existential factors the function of selection from a self-contained realm of ideas is, according to Scheler, a basic point of agreement between such otherwise divergent theorists as Dilthey, Troeltsch, Max Weber, and himself.[62]

Scheler operates as well with the concept of "structural identities," which refers to common presuppositions of knowledge or belief, on the one hand, and of social, economic, or political structure on the other.[63] Thus, the rise of mechanistic thought in the sixteenth century, which came to dominate prior organismic thought is inseparable from the new individualism, the incipient dominance of the power-driven machine over the hand tool, the incipient dissolution of *Gemeinschaft* into *Gesellschaft*, production for a commodity market, rise of the principle of competition in the ethos of western society, etc. The notion of scientific research as an endless process through which a store of knowledge can be accumulated for practical application as the occasion demands and the total divorce of this science from theology and philosophy was not possible without the rise of a new principle of infinite acquisition characteristic of modern capitalism.[64]

In discussing such structural identities, Scheler does not ascribe primacy either to the socio-economic sphere or to the sphere of knowledge. Rather, and this Scheler regards as one of the most significant propositions in the field, both are determined by the impulse structure of the elite, which is closely bound up with the prevailing ethos. Thus, modern technology is not merely the application of a pure science based on observation, logic, and mathematics. It is far more the product of an orientation toward the control of nature, which defined the purposes as well as the conceptual structure of scientific thought. This orientation is largely implicit and is not to be confused with the personal motives of scientists.

With the concept of structural identity, Scheler verges on the concept of cultural integration or *Sinnzusammenhang*. It corresponds to Sorokin's conception of a "meaningful cultural system" involving interdependence of parts.[65] Having constructed his types of culture, Sorokin's survey of criteria of truth, ontology, metaphysics, scientific and technologic output, etc., finds a marked tendency toward the meaningful integration of these with the prevailing culture.

Sorokin had boldly confronted the problem of how to determine the *extent* to which such integration occurs, recognizing, despite his vitriolic comments on the statisticians of our sensate age, that to deal with the extent or degree of integration necessarily implies some statistical measure. Accordingly, he developed numerical indexes of the various writings and authors in each period, classified these in their appropriate category, and thus assessed the comparative frequency (and influence) of the various systems of thought. Whatever the technical evaluation of the validity and reliability of these cultural statistics, he has directly acknowledged the problem overlooked by many investigators of integrated culture or *Sinnzusammenhängen*, namely, the approximate degree or extent of such integration. Moreover, he plainly bases his empirical conclusions very largely upon these statistics.[66] And these conclusions again testify that his approach leads to a statement of the problem of connections between existential bases and knowledge, rather than to its solution. Thus, to take a case in point: "Empiricism" is defined as the typical sensate system of truth. The last five centuries, and more particularly the last century represent "sensate culture par excellence!"[67] Yet, even in this flood tide of sensate culture, Sorokin's statistical indices show only some 53 per cent of influential writings in the field of "empiricism." And in the earlier centuries of this sensate culture—from the late sixteenth to the mid-eighteenth—the indices of empiricism are consistently lower than those for rationalism (which is associated, presumably, with an idealistic rather than a sensate culture).[68] The object of these observations is not to raise the question whether Sorokin's conclusions coincide with his statistical data: it is not to ask why the sixteenth and seventeenth centuries are said to have a dominant "sensate system of truth" in view of these data. Rather, it is to indicate that, even on Sorokin's own premises, over-all characterizations of historical cultures constitute merely a first step, which must be followed by analyses of deviations from the central tendencies of the culture. Once the notion of *extent* of integration is introduced, the existence of types of knowledge which are not integrated with the dominant tendencies cannot be viewed merely as "congeries" or as "contingent." Their *social* bases must be ascertained in a fashion for which an emanationist theory does not provide.

A basic concept which serves to differentiate generalizations about the thought and knowledge of an entire society or culture is that of the "audience" or "public" or what Znaniecki calls "the social circle." Men of knowledge do not orient themselves exclusively toward their data nor toward the total society, but to special segments of that society with their special demands, criteria of validity, of significant knowledge, or pertinent problems, etc. It is through anticipation of these demands and expectations of particular audiences, which can be effectively located in the social structure, that men of knowledge organize their own work, define their data, seize upon problems. Hence, the more differentiated the society, the greater the range of such effective audiences, the greater the variation in the foci of scientific attention, of conceptual formulations and of procedures for certifying claims to knowledge. By linking each of these typologically defined audiences to their distinctive social position, it becomes possible to provide a *wissenssoziologische* account of variations and conflicts of thought within the society, a problem which is necessarily bypassed in an emanationist theory. Thus, the scientists in seventeenth-century England and France who were organized in newly established scientific societies addressed themselves to audiences very different from those of the savants who remained exclusively in the traditional universities. The direction of their efforts toward a "plain, sober, empirical" exploration of specific technical and scientific problems differed considerably from the speculative, unexperimental work of those in the universities. Searching out such variations in effective audiences, exploring their distinctive criteria of significant and valid knowledge,[69] relating these to their position within the society and examining the sociopsychological processes through which these operate to constrain certain modes of thought constitutes a procedure which promises to take research in the sociology of knowledge from the plane of general imputation to that of testable empirical inquiry.[70]

The foregoing account deals with the main substance of prevailing theories in this field. Limitations of space permit only the briefest consideration of one other aspect of these theories singled out in our paradigm: functions imputed to various types of mental productions.[71]

FUNCTIONS OF EXISTENTIALLY CONDITIONED KNOWLEDGE

In addition to providing causal explanations of knowledge, theories ascribe social functions to knowledge, functions which presumably serve to account for its persistence or change. These functional analyses cannot be examined in any detail here, though a detailed study of them would undoubtedly prove rewarding.

The most distinctive feature of the Marxist imputation of function is its ascription, not to the society as a whole, but to distinct strata within the society. This holds not only for ideological thinking but also for natural science. In capitalist society, science and derivative technology are held to become a further instrument of control by the dominant class.[72] Along these same lines, in ferreting out the economic determinants of scientific development, Marxists have often thought it sufficient to show that the scientific results enabled the solution of some economic or technological need. But the application of science to a need does not necessarily testify that the need has been significantly involved in leading to the result. Hyperbolic functions were discovered two centuries before they had any practical significance and the study of conic sections had a broken history of two millennia before being applied in science and technology. Can we infer, then, that the "needs" which were ultimately satisfied through such applications served to direct the attention of mathematicians to those fields, that there was, so to speak, a retroactive influence of some two to twenty centuries? Detailed inquiry into the relations between the emergence of needs, recognition of these needs by scientists or by those who direct their selection of problems and the consequences of such recognition is required before the role of needs in determining the thematics of scientific research can be established.[73]

In addition to his claim that the categories are social emergents, Durkheim also indicates their social functions. The functional analysis, however, is intended to account not for the particular categorical system in a society but for the existence of a system common to the society. For purposes of inter-communication and for coordinating men's activities, a common set of categories is indispensable. What the a priorist mistakes for the constraint of an inevitable, native form of understanding is actually "the very authority of society, transferring itself to a certain manner of thought which is the indispensable condition of all common action."[74] There must be a certain minimum of "logical conformity" if joint social activities are to be maintained at all; a common set of categories is a functional necessity. This view is further developed by Sorokin, who indicates the several functions served by different systems of social space and time.[75]

FURTHER PROBLEMS AND RECENT STUDIES

From the foregoing discussion, it becomes evident that a wide diversity of problems in this field require further investigation.[76]

Scheler had indicated that the social organization of intellectual activity is significantly related to the character of the knowledge which develops under its auspices. One of the earliest studies of the problem in this country was Veblen's caustic, impressionistic, and often perceptive account of the pressures shaping American university life.[77] In more systematic fashion, Wilson has dealt with the methods and criteria of recruitment, the assignment of status and the mechanisms of control of the academic man, thus providing a substantial basis for comparative studies.[78] Setting forth a typology of the roles of men of knowledge, Znaniecki developed a series of hypotheses concerning the relations between these roles and the types of knowledge cultivated; between types of knowledge and the bases of appraisal of the scientist by members of the society; between role definitions and attitudes toward practical and theoretical knowledge; etc.[79] Much remains to be investigated concerning the bases of class identifications by intellectuals, their alienation from dominant or subordinate strata in the population, their avoidance of or indulgence in researches which have immediate value implications challenging current institutional arrangements inimical to the attainment of culturally approved goals,[80] the pressures toward technicism and away from dangerous thoughts, the bureaucratization of intellectuals as a process whereby problems of policy are converted into problems of administration, the areas of social life in which expert and positive knowledge are deemed appropriate and those in which the wisdom of the plain man is alone considered necessary—in short, the shifting role of the intellectual and the relation of these changes to the structure, content, and influence of his work require growing attention, as changes in the social organization increasingly subject the intellectual to conflicting demands.[81]

Increasingly, it has been assumed that the social structure does not influence science merely by focusing the attention of scientists upon certain problems for research. In addition to the studies to which we have already referred, others have dealt with the ways in which the cultural and social context enters into the conceptual phrasing of scientific problems. Darwin's theory of selection was modeled after the prevailing notion of a competitive economic order, a notion which in turn has been assigned an ideological function through its assumption of a natural identity of interests.[82] Russell's half-serious observation on the national characteristics of research in animal learning points to a further type of inquiry into the relations between national culture and conceptual formulations.[83] So, too, Fromm has attempted to show that Freud's "conscious liberalism" tacitly involved a rejection of impulses tabooed by bourgeois society and that Freud himself was in his patricentric character, a typical representative of a society which demands obedience and subjection.[84]

In much the same fashion, it has been indicated that the conception of multiple causation is especially congenial to the academician, who has relative security, is loyal to the status quo from which he derives dignity and sustenance, who leans toward conciliation and sees something valuable in all viewpoints, thus tending toward a taxonomy which enables him to avoid taking sides by stressing the multiplicity of factors and the complexity of problems.[85] Emphases on nature or nurture as prime determinants of human nature have been linked with opposing political orientations. Those who emphasize heredity are political conservatives, whereas the environmentalists are prevalently democrats or radicals seeking social change.[86] But even environmentalists among contemporary American writers on social pathology adopt conceptions of "social adjustment" which implicitly assume the standdards of small communities as norms and characteristically fail to assess the possibility of certain groups achieving their objectives under the prevailing institutional conditions.[87] The imputations of perspectives such as these require more systematic study before they can be accepted, but they indicate recent tendencies to seek out the perspectives of scholars and to relate these to the framework of experience and interests constituted by their respective social positions. The questionable character of imputations which are not based on adequate *comparative* material is illustrated by a recent account of the writings of Negro scholars. The selection of analytical rather than morphological categories, of environmental rather than biological determinants of behavior, of exceptional rather than typical data is ascribed to the caste-induced resentment of Negro writers, without any effort being made to compare the frequency of similar tendencies among white writers.[88]

Vestiges of any tendency to regard the development of science and technology as *wholly* self-contained and advancing irrespective of the social structure are being dissipated by the actual course of historical events. An increasingly visible control and, often, restraint of scientific research and invention has been repeatedly documented, notably in a series of studies by Stern,[89] who has also traced the bases of resistance to change in medicine.[90] The basic change in the social organization of Germany has provided a virtual experimental test of the close dependence of the direction and extent of scientific work upon the prevailing power structure and the associated cultural outlook.[91] And the limitations of any unqualified assumption that science or technology represent the basis to which the social structure must adjust become evident in the light of studies showing how science and technology have been put in the service of social or economic demands.[92]

To develop any further the formidable list of problems that require and are receiving empirical investigation would outrun the limits of this chapter. There is only this to be said: the sociology of knowledge is fast outgrowing a prior tendency to confuse provisional hypothesis with unimpeachable dogma; the plenitude of speculative insights which marked its early stages are now being subjected to increasingly rigorous test. Though Toynbee and Sorokin may be correct in speaking of an alternation of periods of fact-finding and generalization in the history of science, it seems that the sociology of knowledge has wedded these two tendencies in what promises to be a fruitful union. Above all, it focuses on problems which are at the very center of contemporary intellectual interest.[93]

NOTES

1 Karl Marx, *A Contribution to the Critique of Political Economy* (Chicago: C. H. Kerr, 1904), pp. 11–12.

2 Karl Marx, *Capital*, I, 15; cf. Karl Marx and Friedrich Engels, *The German Ideology* (New York: International Publishers, 1939), p. 76; cf. Max Weber, *Gesammelte Aufsätze zur Wissenschaftslehre* (Tübingen, 1922), p. 205.

3 Marx and Engels, *The Communist Manifesto*, in *Karl Marx, Selected Works*, I, 216.

4 Karl Marx, *Der Achtzehnte Brumaire des Louis Bonaparte* (Hamburg, 1885), p. 36.

5 This account is based upon Max Scheler's most elaborate discussion, "Probleme einer Soziologie des Wissens," in his *Die Wissensformen und die Gesellschaft* (Leipzig: Der Neue-Geist Verlag, 1926), pp. 1–229. This essay is an extended and improved version of an essay in his *Versuche zu einer Soziologie des Wissens* (Munich: Duncker and Humblot, 1924), pp. 5–146. For further discussions of Scheler, see P. A. Schillp, "The Formal Problems of Scheler's Sociology of Knowledge," *The Philosophical Review*, XXXVI (March, 1927), 101–20; Howard Becker and H. O. Dahlke, "Max Scheler's Sociology of Knowledge," *Philosophy and Phenomenological Research*, II (March, 1942), 310–22.

6 Scheler, *Die Wissensformen und die Gesellschaft*, pp. 7, 32.

7 *Ibid.*, pp. 25–45. It should be noted that Marx had long since rejected out of hand a similar conception of shifts in independent variables which was made the basis for an attack on his *Critique of Political Economy*; see *Capital*, I, 94, *n*.

8 Karl Mannheim, *Ideology and Utopia*, (New York: Harcourt, Brace & Co., 1936), pp. 247–48. In view of the recent extensive discussions of Mannheim's work, it will not be treated at length in this essay. For the writer's appraisal, see Robert K. Merton, *Social Theory and Social Structure* (Glencoe, Ill.: The Free Press, 1957), chap. xiii.

9 Émile Durkheim and Marcel Mauss, "Des quelques formes primitives de la classification," *L'Année sociologique*, VI (1901–2), 1–72, ". . . even ideas as abstract as those of time and space are, at each moment of their history, in close relation with the corresponding social organization." As Marcel Granet has indicated, this paper contains some pages on Chinese thought which have been held by specialists to mark a new era in the field of sinological studies.

10 Émile Durkheim, *Elementary Forms of Religious Life* (New York: The Macmillan Co., 1915), pp. 443–44; see also Hans Kelsen, *Society and Nature* (Chicago: University of Chicago Press, 1943), p. 30.

11 Marcel Granet, *La Pensée chinoise* (Paris: La Renaissance du Livre, 1934), e.g., pp. 84–104.

12 Pitirim A. Sorokin, *Social and Cultural Dynamics* (New York, I, 1937, 72–73.

13 *Ibid.*, II, 5.

14 *Ibid.*, I, 73.

15 One "exception" to this practice is found in his contrast between the prevalent tendency of the "clergy and religious landed aristocracy to become the leading and organizing classes in the Ideational, and the capitalistic bourgeoisie, intelligentsia, professionals, and secular officials in the Sensate culture (*ibid.*, III, 250). And see his account of the diffusion of culture among social classes, in *ibid.*, IV, 221 ff.

16 Cf. Merton, *Social Theory and Social Structure*, pp. 133–35; Kurt H. Wolff, "The Sociology of Knowledge: Emphasis on an Empirical Attitude," *Philosophy of Science*, X, (1943), 104–23; Talcott Parsons, "The Role of Ideas in Social Action," in *Essays in Sociological Theory*, chap. vi.

17 This is presumably the ground for Scheler's remark—"A specific thesis of the economic conception of history is the subsumption of the laws of development of *all* knowledge under the laws of development of ideologies"—in *Die Wissensformen und die Gesellschaft*, p. 21.

18 Engels, letter to Conrad Schmidt, October, 27, 1890, in *Karl Marx, Selected Works*, I, 385.

19 *Ibid.*, I, 386.

20 Engels, letter to Heinz Starkenburg, January 25, 1894, in *ibid.*, I, 392.

21 *Ibid.*, I, 393; cf. Engels, *Feuerbach* (Chicago: C. H. Kerr, 1903), pp. 117 ff. "It is well known that certain periods of highest development of art stand in *no direct connection* with the general development of society, nor with the material basis and the skeleton structure of its organization"—Marx, introduction to *A Contribution to the Critique of Political Economy*, pp. 309–10.

22 Marx, *A Contribution to the Critique of Political Economy*, p. 12.

23 Marx and Engels, p. 103, above. See also Engels, *Socialism: Utopian and Scientific* (Chicago: C. H. Kerr, 1910), pp. 24–25, where the needs of a rising middle class are held to account for the revival of science. The assertion that "only" trade and industry provide the aims is typical of the extreme, and untested, statements of relationships which prevail especially in the early Marxist writings. Such terms as "determination" cannot be taken at their face value; they are characteristically used very loosely. The actual *extent* of such relationships between intellectual activity and the material foundations were not investigated by either Marx or Engels.

24 Engels, in *Karl Marx, Selected Works*, I, 393. The occurrence of parallel independent discoveries and inventions as "proof" of the social determination of knowledge was a repeated theme throughout the nineteenth century. As early as 1828, Macaulay in his essay on Dryden had noted concerning Newton's and Leibniz's invention of the calculus: "Mathematical science, indeed, had reached such a point, that if neither of them had existed, the principle must inevitably have occurred to some person within a few years." He cites other cases in point. Victorian manufacturers shared the same view with Marx and Engels. In our own day, his thesis, based on independent duplicate inventions, has been especially emphasized by Dorothy Thomas, Ogburn, and Vierkandt.

25 Engels, *Socialism: Utopian and Scientific*, p. 97.

26 V. I. Lenin, "The Three Sources and Three Component Parts of Marxism," in *Karl Marx, Selected Works*, I, 54.

27 Nikolai Bukharin, *Historical Materialism* (New York: International Publishers, 1925), pp. xi–xii; B. Hessen, in *Society at the Cross-Roads* (London: Kniga, 1932), p. 154; A. I. Timeniev, in *Marxism and Modern Thought* (New York: Harcourt, Brace, 1935), p. 310; "Only Marxism, only the ideology of the advanced revolutionary class is scientific."

28 Mannheim, *Ideology and Utopia*, pp. 150, 243; Mannheim, "Die Bedeutung der Konkurrenz im Gebiete des Geistigen," in *Verhandlungen des 6. deutschen Soziologentages* (Tübingen, 1929), p. 41.

29 Mannheim, *Ideology and Utopia*, pp. 256, 264.

30 Scheler, *Die Wissensformen und die Gesellschaft*, pp. 59–61.

31 *Ibid.*, p. 62.

32 *Ibid.*, p. 55.

33 See the same assumption of Durkheim, cited in note 10, above.

34 Maurice Mandelbaum, *The Problem of Historical Knowledge* (New York: Liveright, 1938), p. 150; Sorokin posits a similar sphere of "timeless ideas," e.g., in his *Sociocultural*

Causality, Space, Time (Durham, N.C.: Duke University Press, 1943), p. 215, *passim*.

35 Scheler, *Die Wissensformen und die Gesellschaft*, pp. 22–23; cf. a similar characterization of "sacred schools" of thought by Florian Znaniecki, *The Social Role of the Man of Knowledge* (New York: Columbia University Press, 1940), chap. iii.

36 Durkheim, *Elementary Forms of Religious Life*, pp. 12, 18, 439.

37 *Ibid.*, pp. 433–35,

38 *Ibid.*, p. 438.

39 *Ibid.*, pp. 444–45, 437.

40 Granet, *La Pensée chinoise*, pp. 37–38, and the whole of chap. i.

41 *Ibid.*, pp. 87–95.

42 Cf. Bronislaw Malinowski, *Magic, Science & Religion* (Glencoe, Ill.: The Free Press, 1948), p. 9—"Every primitive community is in possession of a considerable store of knowledge, based on experience and fashioned by reason." See also Emile Benoit-Smullyan, "Granet's *La Pensée Chinoise*," *American Sociological Review*, I (1936), 487–92.

43 Sorokin, *Social and Cultural Dynamics*, I, 36; cf. II, 11–12, *n.*

44 *Ibid.*, IV, chap xvi; Sorokin, *Sociocultural Causality, Space, Time*, chap. v.

45 Sorokin, *Sociocultural Causality, Space, Time*, pp. 230–31, *n.*

46 The distinctions between these have long been considered in European sociological thought. The most elaborate discussion in this country is that of Sorokin, *Social and Cultural Dynamics*, e.g., I, chaps. i–ii.

47 Cf. the comments of Hans Speier, pp. 263–81, above; C. Wright Mills, "Language, Logic and Culture," *American Sociological Review*, IV (1939), 670–80.

48 Cf. the formulation by Mannheim, *Ideology and Utopia*, pp. 175 ff.; Georg Lukács, *Geschichte und Klassenbewusstsein* (Berlin, 1923), pp. 61 ff.; Arthur Child, "The Problem of Imputation in the Sociology of Knowledge," *Ethics*, LI (1941), 200–14.

49 Marx and Engels, p. 105, above—"In so far . . . as they rule as a class and determine the extent and compass of an epoch, it is self-evident that they do this in their whole range, hence, among other things, rule also as thinkers, as producers of ideas, and regulate the production and distribution of the ideas of their age . . ."

50 Engels, letter to Mehring, July 14, 1893, in *Karl Marx, Selected Works*, I, 388–89; cf. Marx, *Der Achtzehnte Brumaire des Louis Bonaparte*, p. 33; Marx, *A Contribution to the Critique of Political Economy*, p. 12.

51 Marx, *Der Achtzenhte Brumaire des Louis Bonaparte*, p. 39, where the democratic Montagnards indulge in self-deception.

52 Engels, *Socialism: Utopian and Scientific*, pp. 26–27. Cf. Engels, *Feuerbach*, pp. 122–23—"The failure to exterminate the Protestant heresy *corresponded* to the invincibility of the rising bourgeoisie. . . . Here Calvinism proved itself to be the true religious disguise of the interests of the bourgeoisie of that time."

53 Marx grants motivational significance to the "illusions" of the burgeoning bourgeoisie, (in *Der Achtzehnte Brumaire des Louis Bonaparte*, p. 8).

54 Engels, letter to Joseph Bloch, September 21, 1890, in *Karl Marx, Selected Works*, I, 383.

55 Engels, letter to Mehring, July 14, 1893, in *ibid.*, I, 390.

56 Cf. Max Weber, *Gesammelte Aufsätze zur Wissenschaftslehre*, 166–70.

57 This aspect of Mannheim's work is treated in detail in Merton, *Social Theory and Social Structure.*

58 Durkheim, *Elementary Forms of Religious Life*, pp. 11–12.

59 *Ibid.*, pp. 10–11.

60 *Ibid.*, p. 148.

61 *Ibid.*, p. 440.

62 Scheler, *Die Wissensformen und die Gesellschaft*, p. 32.

63 *Ibid.*, p. 56.

64 *Ibid.*, p. 25; cf. pp. 482–84.

65 Sorokin, *Social and Cultural Dynamics*, I, chap. i, IV, chap. i.

66 Despite the basic place of these statistics in his empirical findings, Sorokin adopts a curiously ambivalent attitude toward them, an attitude similar to the attitude toward experiment imputed to Newton: a device to make his prior conclusions "intelligible and to convince the vulgar." Note Sorokin's approval of Park's remark that his statistics are merely a concession to the prevailing sensate mentality and that "if they want 'em, let 'em have 'em"—Sorokin, *Sociocultural Causality, Space, Time*, p. 95, *n*. Sorokin's ambivalence arises from his effort to integrate quite disparate "systems of truth."

67 Sorokin, *Social and Cultural Dynamics*, II, 51.

68 *Ibid.*, II, 30.

69 The Richert-Weber concept of *Wertbeziehung* (relevance to value) is but a first step in this direction; there remains the further task of differentiating the various sets of values and relating these to distinctive groups or strata within the society.

70 This is perhaps the most distinctive variation in the sociology of knowledge now developing in American sociological circles, and may almost be viewed as an American acculturation of European approaches. This development characteristically derives from the social psychology of G. H. Mead. Its pertinence in this connection is being indicated by C. W. Mills, Gerard de Gré, and others. See Znaniecki's conception of the "social circle," in *The Social Role of the Man of Knowledge*. See, also, the beginnings of empirical findings along these lines in the more general field of public communications: Paul F. Lazarsfeld and R. K. Merton, "Studies in Radio and Film Propaganda."

71 An appraisal of historicist and ahistorical approaches is necessarily omitted. It may be remarked that this controversy definitely admits of a middle ground.

72 For example, Marx quotes from the nineteenth-century apologist of capitalism, Ure, who, speaking of the invention of the self-acting mule, says: "A creation destined to restore order among the industrious classes. . . . This invention confirms the great doctrine already propounded, that when capital enlists science into her service, the refractory hand of labor will always be taught docility"—in *Capital*, I, 477.

73 Cf. Hessen, *Society of the Cross-Roads*; R. K. Merton, *Science, Technology and Society in 17th Century England* (Bruges: Osiris History of Science Monographs, 1938), chap. vii–x; J. D. Bernal, *The Social Function of Science* (New York: The Macmillan Co. 1939); J. G. Crowther, *The Social Relations of Science* (New York: The Macmillan Co., 1941); Bernard Barber, *Science and the Social Order* (Glencoe, Ill.: The Free Press, 1952); Gerard De Gré, *Science as a Social Institution* (New York: Doubleday & Company, 1955).

74 Durkheim, *Elementary Forms of Religious Life*, p. 17; also pp. 10–11, 443.

75 Sorokin, *Sociocultural Causality, Space, Time, passim*.

76 For further summaries, see Louis Wirth's preface to Mannheim, *Ideology and Utopia*, pp. xxviii–xxxi; J. B. Gittler, "Possibilities of a Sociology of Science," *Social Forces*, XVIII (1940), 350–59.

77 Thorstein Veblen, *The Higher Learning in America* (New York: Huebsch, 1918).

78 Logan Wilson, *The Academic Man*; cf. E. Y. Hartshorne, *The German Universities and National Socialism* (Cambridge, Mass.: Harvard University Press, 1937).

79 Znaniecki, *The Social Role of the Man of Knowledge.*

80 Gunnar Myrdal in his treatise, *An American Dilemma*, repeatedly indicates the "concealed valuations" of American social scientists studying the American Negro and the effect of these valuations on the formulation of "scientific problems" in this area of research. See especially II, 1027–64.

81 Mannheim refers to an unpublished monograph on the intellectual; general bibliographies are to be found in his books and in Roberto Michels' article on "Intellectuals," in *Encyclopedia of the Social Sciences*. Recent papers include C. W. Mills, "The Social Role of the Intellectual," *Politics*, I (April, 1944); R. K. Merton, "Role of the Intellectual in Public Policy," presented at the annual meeting of the American Sociological Society, December 4, 1943 (chap. vii in *Merton, Social Theory and Social Structure*); Arthur Koestler "The Intelligentsia," *Horizon*, IX (1944), 162–75.

82 Keynes observed that "The Principle of the Survival of the Fittest could be regarded as one vast generalization of the Ricardian economics"—quoted by Talcott Parsons, *The Structure of Social Action* (Glencoe, Ill.: The Free Press, 1949), p. 113; cf. Alexander Sandow, "Social Factors in the Origin of Darwinism," *Quarterly Review of Biology*, XIII, 316–26.

83 Bertrand Russell, *Philosophy* (New York: W. W. Norton & Company, 1927), pp. 29–30. Russell remarks that the animals used in psychological research "have all displayed the national characteristics of the observer. Animals studied by Americans rush about frantically, with an incredible display of hustle and pep, and at last achieve the desired result by chance. Animals observed by Germans sit still and think, and at last evolve the solution out of their inner consciousness." Witticisms need not be mistaken for irrelevance; the possibility of national differences in the choice and formulation of scientific problems has been repeatedly noted, though not studied systematically. Cf. Richard Müller-Freienfels, *Psychologie der Wissenschaft* (Leipzig: J. A. Barth, 1936), chap. viii, which deals with national, as well as class, differences in the choice of problems, "styles of thought," etc., without fully acquiescing in the *echt-deutsch* requirements of a Krieck. This type of interpretation, however, can be carried to a polemical and ungrounded extreme, as in Max Scheler's debunking "analysis" of English cant. He concludes that, in science, as in all other spheres, the English are incorrigible "cantians." Hume's conception of the ego, substance, and continuity as biologically useful self-deceptions was merely purposive cant; so, too, was the characteristic English conception of working hypotheses (Maxwell, Kelvin) as aiding the progress of science but not as truth—a conception which is nothing but a shrewd maneuver to provide momentary control and ordering of the data. All pragmatism implies this opportunistic cant, says Scheler, in *Genius des Krieges* (Leipzig: Verlag der Weissenbuecher, 1915).

84 Erich Fromm, "Die gesellschaftliche Bedingtheit der psychoanalytischen Therapie," *Zeitschrift für Sozialforschung*, IV (1935), 365–97.

85 Lewis S. Feuer, "The Economic Factor in History," *Science and Society*, IV (1940), 174–75.

86 N. Pastore, "The Nature-Nurture Controversy: A Sociological Approach," *School and Society*, LVII (1943), 373–77.

87 C. Wright Mills, "The Professional Ideology of Social Pathologists," *American Journal of Sociology*, XLIX (1943), 165–90.

88 William T. Fontaine, "'Social Determination' in the Writings of Negro Scholars," *American Journal of Sociology*, XLIX (1944), 302–15.

89 Bernhard J. Stern, "Resistances to the Adoption of Technological Innovations," in National Resources Committee, *Technological Trends and National Policy* (Washington D.C.: U.S. Government Printing Office, 1937), pp. 39–66; "Restraints upon the Utilization of Inventions," *The Annals*, CC (1938), 1–19, and further references therein; Walton Hamilton. *Patents and Free Enterprise* ("TNEC Monograph No. 31;" 1941).

90 Bernhard J. Stern, *Social Factors in Medical Progress* (New York: Columbia University Press, 1927); *Society and Medical Progress* (Princeton: Princeton University Press, 1941); cf. Richard H. Shryock, *The Development of Modern Medicine* (Philadelphia: University of Pennsylvania Press, 1936); Henry E. Sigerist, *Man and Medicine* (New York: W. W. Norton and Company, 1932).

91 Hartshorne, *The German Universities and National Socialism.*

92 Only most conscpicuously in time of war; see Sorokin's observation that centers of military power tend to be centers of scientific and technologic development (in *Dynamics* IV, 249–51); cf. I. B. Cohen and Bernard Barber, *Science and War* (ms.); R. K. Merton, "Science and Military Technique," *Scientific Monthly*, XLI (1935), 542–45; Bernal, *The Social Function of Science*; Julian Huxley, *Science and Social Needs* (New York: Harper & Bros., 1935).

93 For extensive bibliographies, see Barber, *Science and the Social Order*; Mannheim, *Ideology and Utopia*; Harry E. Barnes, Howard Becker, and Frances B. Becker (eds), *Contemporary Social Theory* (New York: Appleton-Century, 1940).

6

PETER L. BERGER

Identity as a Problem in the Sociology of Knowledge

IT IS THROUGH the work of George Herbert Mead and the Meadian tradition of the "symbolic-interactionist" school that a theoretically viable social psychology has been founded. Indeed, it may be maintained that in this achievement lies the most important *theoretical* contribution made to the social sciences in America. The perspectives of the Meadian tradition have become established within American sociology far beyond the school that explicitly seeks to represent them. Just as it was sociologists who "discovered" Mead at the University of Chicago and diffused his ideas beyond the latter's confines, so the social psychology constituted on this foundation continues to be the one to which sociologists gravitate most naturally in their theoretical assumptions, a "sociologist's psychology," despite the later competition from psychoanalysis and learning theory.[1] By contrast, the sociology of knowledge has remained marginal to the discipline in this country, still regarded widely as an unassimilated European import of interest only to a few colleagues with a slightly eccentric penchant for the history of ideas.[2] This marginality of the sociology of knowledge is not difficult to explain in terms of the historical development of sociological theory in this country. All the same, it is rather remarkable that the theoretical affinity between the sociology of knowledge and social psychology in the Meadian tradition has not been widely recognized. One might argue that there has been an implicit recognition in the linkage of social psychology, by way of role theory and reference group theory, with the psychology of

---

Journal of Sociology, VII (1966), 105–15. Reprinted by permission of the *European Journal of Sociology* and the author.

cognitive processes, particularly in the work of Robert Merton, Muzafer Sherif and Tamotsu Shibutani.[3] In the case of Merton, however, the discussion of the cognitive implications of social-psychological processes occurs in a curious segregation from the treatment of the sociology of knowledge, while in the cases of Sherif and Shibutani there appears to be no conscious connection with the sociology of knowledge at all.

Understandable historically, this segregation is theoretically deplorable. Social psychology has been able to show how the subjective reality of individual consciousness is socially constructed. The sociology of knowledge, as Alfred Schütz has indicated, may be understood as the sociological critique of consciousness, concerning itself with the social construction of reality in general.[4] Such a critique entails the analysis of both "objective reality" (that is, "knowledge" about the world, as objectivated and taken for granted in society) and its subjective correlates (that is, the modes in which this objectivated world is subjectively plausible or "real" to the individual). If these shorthand descriptions of the two subdisciplines are allowed, then integration between them is not an exotic miscegenation but a bringing together of two partners by the inner logic of their natures. Obviously this paper cannot develop the details of such a project of theoretical integration, but it may indicate some general directions and implications.

Social psychology has brought about the recognition that the sphere of psychological phenomena is continuously permeated by social forces, and more than that, is decisively shaped by the latter. "Socialization" means not only that the self-consciousness of the individual is constituted in a specific form by society (which Mead called the "social genesis of the self"), but that psychological reality is in an ongoing dialectical relationship with social structure. Psychological reality refers here, *not* to scientific or philosophical propositions *about* psychological phenomena, but to the manner in which the individual apprehends himself, his processes of consciousness and his relations with others. Whatever its anthropological-biological roots, psychological reality arises in the individual's biography in the course of social process and is only maintained (that is, maintained in consciousness *as* "reality") by virtue of social processes. Socialization not only ensures that the individual is "real" to himself in a certain way, but that he will ongoingly respond to his experience of the world with the cognitive and emotive patterns appropriate to this "reality." For example, successful socialization shapes a self that apprehends itself exclusively and in a taken-for-granted way in terms of one or the other of two socially defined sexes, that "knows" this self-apprehension to be the only "real" one, and rejects as "unreal" any contrary modes of apprehension or emotionality. Self and society are inextricably interwoven entities. Their relationship is dialectical because the self, once formed, may act back in its turn upon the society that shaped it (a dialectic that Mead expressed in his formulation of the "I" and the "me"). The self exists by virtue of society, but society is only possible as many selves continue to apprehend themselves and each other with reference to it.[5]

Every society contains a repertoire of identities that is part of the "objective knowledge" of its members. It is "known" as a matter "of course" that there are men and women, that they have such-and-such psychological traits and that they will have such-and-such psychological reactions in typical circumstances. As the individual is socialized, these identities are "internalized." They are then not only taken for granted as constituents of an objective reality "out there" but as inevitable structures of the individual's own consciousness. The objective reality, as defined by society, is subjectively appropriated. In other words, socialization brings about symmetry between objective and subjective reality, objective and subjective identity. The degree of this symmetry provides the criterion of the successfulness of socialization. The psychological reality of the successfully socialized individual thus *verifies* subjectively what his society has objectively defined as real. He is then no longer required to turn outside himself for "knowledge" concerning the nature proper of men and women. He can obtain that result by simple introspection. He "knows who he is." He feels accordingly. He can conduct himself "spontaneously," because the firmly internalized cognitive and emotive structures make it unnecessary or even impossible for him to reflect upon alternative possibilities of conduct.[6]

This dialectic between social structure and psychological reality may be called the fundamental proposition of any social psychology in the Meadian tradition. Society not only defines but creates psychological reality. The individual *realizes* himself in society—that is, he recognizes his identity in socially defined terms and these definitions *become reality* as he lives in society. This fundamentally Meadian dialectic makes intelligible the social-psychological scope of W. I. Thomas' concept of the "definition of the situation" as well as of Merton's of the "self-fulfilling prophecy."[7]

The sociology of knowledge is concerned with a related but broader dialectic—that between social structure and the "worlds" in which individuals live, that is, the comprehensive organizations of reality within which individual experience can be meaningfully interpreted.[8] Every society is a world-building enterprise. Out of the near-infinite variety of individual symbolizations of experience society constructs a universe of discourse that comprehends and objectivates them. Individual experience can then be understood as taking place in an intelligible world that is inhabited also by others and about which it is possible to communicate with others. Individual meanings are objectivated so that they are accessible to everyone who co-inhabits the world in question. Indeed, this world is apprehended as "objective reality," that is, as reality that is shared with others and that exists irrespective of the individual's own preferences in the matter. The socially available definitions of such a world are thus taken to be "knowledge" about it and are continuously verified for the individual by social situations in which this "knowledge" is taken for granted. The socially constructed world becomes the world *tout court*—the only real world, typically the only world that one can seriously conceive of. The individual is thus freed of the necessity of reflecting anew about the meaning of each step in his unfolding experience. He can simply refer to "common sense" for such interpretation, at least for the great bulk of his biographical experience.[9]

Language is both the foundation and the instrumentality of the social construction of reality.[10] Language focalizes, patterns, and objectivates individual experience. Language is the principal means by which an individual is socialized to become an inhabitant of a world shared with others and also provides the means by which, in conversation with these others, the common world continues to be plausible to him.[11] On this linguistic base is erected the edifice of interpretive schemes, cognitive and moral norms, value systems and, finally, theoretically articulated "world views" which, in their totality, form the world of "collective representations" (as the Durkheimian school put it) of any given society.[12] Society *orders* experience. Only in a world of social order can there develop a "collective consciousness" that permits the individual to have a subjectively meaningful life and protects him from the devastating effects of *anomie*, that is, from a condition in which the individual is deprived of the social ordering processes and thus deprived of meaning itself. It is useful to remind oneself of the linguistic base of all social order whenever one theorizes about the latter, because language makes particularly clear just what is meant by the social construction of an objectively real world. Language is undeniably a social invention and a linguistic system cannot be credited with an ontological status apart from the society that invented it. Nevertheless, the individual learns his language (especially, of course, his native language) as an objective reality.[13] He cannot change it at will. He must conform to its coercive power. Typically, he is unable to conceive of either the world or of himself except through the conceptual modalities which it provides. But this facticity, externality, and coerciveness of language (the very traits that constitute the

Durkheimian *choseïté*, or thinglike character, of social phenomena) extends to all the objectivations of society. The subjective consequence is that the individual "finds himself" (that is, apprehends himself as placed, willy-nilly) in the social world as much as in nature.

It is important to stress that the social construction of reality takes place on both the pre-theoretical and the theoretical levels of consciousness, and that, therefore, the sociology of knowledge must concern itself with both. Probably because of the German intellectual situation in which the sociology of knowledge was first developed, it has hitherto interested itself predominantly in the theoretical side of the phenomenon—the problem of the relationship of society and "ideas."[14] This is certainly an important problem. But only very few people are worried over "ideas," while everyone lives in some sort of a world. There is thus a sociological dimension to the human activity of world-building in its totality, not only in that segment of it in which intellectuals manufacture theories, systems of thought, and *Weltanschauungen*. Thus, in the matter under discussion here, the sociology of knowledge has an interest not only in various theories *about* psychological phenomena (what one may call a sociology of psychology) but in these phenomena themselves (what one may then, perhaps impertinently, call a sociological psychology).

The relationship between a society and its world is a dialectic one because, once more, it cannot be adequately understood in terms of a one-sided causation.[15] The world, though socially constructed, is not a mere passive reflection of the social structures within which it arose. In becoming "objective reality" for its inhabitants it attains not only a certain autonomy with respect to the "underlying" society but even the power to act back upon the latter. Men invent a language and then find that its logic imposes itself upon them. And men concoct theories, even theories that may start out as nothing but blatant explications of social interests, and then discover that these theories themselves become agencies of social change. It may be seen, then, that there is a theoretically significant similarity between the dialectics of social psychology and of the sociology of knowledge, the dialectic through which society generates psychological reality and the dialectic through which it engages in world-building. Both dialectics concern the relationship between objective and subjective realities, or more precisely, between socially objectivated reality and its subjective appropriation. In both instances, the individual internalizes facticities that appear to him as given outside himself and, having internalized them to become given contents of his own consciousness, externalizes them again as he continues to live and act in society.[16]

These considerations, especially in the compressed form in which they have had to be presented here, may at first seem to be excessively abstract. Yet, if one asks about the combined significance of these root perspectives of social psychology and the sociology of knowledge for the sociological understanding of identity, one may answer in a rather simple statement: *Identity, with its appropriate attachments of psychological reality, is always identity within a specific, socially constructed world.* Or, as seen from the viewpoint of the individual: *One identifies oneself, as one is identified by others, by being located in a common world.*

Socialization is only possible if, as Mead put it, the individual "takes the attitude" of others, that is, relates to himself as others have first related to him. This process, of course, extends to the establishment of identity itself, so that one may formulate that social identification both precedes and produces self-identification. Now, it is possible that the Meadian process of attitude- and role-taking occurs between individuals who do not share a common world—for instance, between Columbus and the very first American Indians he met in 1492. Even they, however, soon identified each other within a world which they inhabited together, or more accurately, they together established such a world as they dealt with each other. Socializing each other in terms of this world, they could then take on the attitudes and roles appropriate within it. Columbus and his Spaniards, being (like parents in this respect) the stronger party, had the edge in this game of "naming"—the others had to identify themselves in the Spaniards' terms, namely, as *Indios*, while the Spaniards were probably little tempted to identify themselves with the mythological creatures as which they in turn were first identified by the others. In other words, the American Indian identified himself by locating himself in the Spaniard's world, though, to be sure, that world was itself modified as he became its co-inhabitant. In the more normal cases of socialization, occurring between individuals who already co-inhabit the same world, it is even easier to see how identification entails location in that world from the beginning. The parents give their child a name and then deal with him in terms appropriate to this identification. The literal act of "naming," of course, is already location in this sense (its exactitude depending upon the culture—"John Smith" being less satisfactory as an "address" than "Ivan Ivanovitch, Village Idiot," and so forth). However, as the full implications of the name and its location unfold in the course of socialization, the child appropriates the world in which he is thus located in the same process in which he appropriates his identity—a moral universe as he identifies himself as a "good baby," a sexual universe as a "little boy," a class universe as a "little gentleman"—and so on. One may expand the Meadian phrase, then, by saying that the individual takes the world of others as he takes their attitudes and roles. Each role implies a world. The self is always located in a world. The *same* process of socialization generates the self and internalizes the world to which this self belongs.

The same reasoning applies to psychological reality in general. Just as any particular psychological reality is attached to a socially defined identity, so it is located in a socially constructed world. As the individual identifies and locates himself in the world of his society, he finds himself the possessor of a pre-defined assemblage of psychological processes, both "conscious" and "unconscious" ones, and even some with somatic effects. The "good baby" feels guilty after a temper tantrum, the "little boy" channels his erotic fantasies toward little girls, the "little gentleman" experiences revulsion when someone engages in public nose-picking—and this revulsion may, under the proper conditions, affect his stomach to the point of vomitation. Every socially constructed world thus contains a repertoire of identities and a corresponding psychological system. The social definition of identity takes place as part of an overarching definition of reality. The internalization of the world, as it occurs in socialization, imposes upon consciousness a psychological as well as a cognitive structure, and (to a degree which has as yet not been adequately clarified scientifically) even extends into the area of physiological processes.[17] Pascal indicated the root problem of the sociology of knowledge when he observed that what is truth on one side of the Pyrenees is error on the other. The same observation applies to the good conscience and the bad (including the "unconscious" manifestations of the latter), to the libidinously interesting and the libidinously indifferent, as well as to what upsets and what relaxes the gastric juices. And, of course, a French identity differs appreciably from a Spanish one.[18]

A third dialectic may be analyzed if one now turns to the theoretical level of consciousness—that between psychological reality and psychological models. Men not only experience themselves. They also explain themselves. While these explanations differ in their degrees of sophistication, it would be difficult to conceive of a society without some theoretical explication of the psychological nature of man. Whether such explication takes the form of proverbial wisdom, mythology, metaphysics, or scientific generalization is, of course, a different question. What all these forms have in common is that they systematize the experience of psychological reality on a certain level of abstraction. They constitute psychological models, by means of which individual psychological process can be compared, typified, and thus "prepared for treatment." For example, individuals in a society may have all kinds of visionary experiences. Both the individuals themselves and those with whom they live are faced with the question of what these experiences signify. A psychological model that "explains" such occurrences allows them to compare any particular experience with the several species codified in the model. The experience may then be classified in terms of this typology—as a case of demon possession, say, or as a mark of sacred status, or as merely crazy in a profane mode. This application of the psychological model (the "diagnosis") then permits a decision on what to do about the occurrence (the "therapy"—to exorcize the individual, to beatify him, or possibly to award him the role of buffoon and of menace to disobedient children. In other words, the psychological model locates individual experience and conduct within a comprehensive theoretical system.[19]

It goes without saying that each psychological model is embedded in a more general theoretical formulation of reality. The model is part of the society's general "knowledge about the world," raised to the level of theoretical thought. Thus a psychological model that contains a typology of possession belongs to a religious conception of the world as such and a psychological theory of "mental illness," as understood by contemporary psychiatry, is located in a much wider "scientific" conception of the world and of man's place in it. *Psychological "knowledge" is always part of a general "knowledge about the world"*—in this proposition lies the foundation of what, a little earlier, was called the sociology of psychology. The import of this proposition can be conveyed by referring to the psychiatric concept of "reality orientation." A psychiatrist may decide that a certain individual is not adequately "oriented to reality" and, therefore, "mentally ill." The sociologist may then accept this description, but must immediately ask— *"which reality?"* Just as cultural anthropology has been able to demonstrate that the manifestations of the Freudian "pleasure principle" vary from one society to another, so the sociology of knowledge must insist on a similar sociocultural relativization of the Freudian "reality principle."[20]

This sociological perspective has far-reaching implications for the analysis of psychological theories. As has been indicated, every socially constructed world contains a psychological model. If this model is to retain its plausibility, it must have some empirical relationship to the psychological reality objectivated in the society. A demonological model is "unreal" in contemporary society. The psychoanalytic one is not. It is important to stress once again the matter of empirical verification. Just as the individual can verify his socially assigned identity by introspection, so the psychological theoretician can verify his model by "empirical research." If the model corresponds to the psychological reality as socially defined and produced, it will quite naturally be verified by empirical investigation of this reality.

This is not quite the same as saying that psychology is self-verifying. It rather says that the data discovered by a particular psychology belong to the same socially constructed world that has also produced that psychology.

Once more, the relationship between psychological reality and psychological model is a dialectic one. The psychological reality produces the psychological model, insofar as the model is an empirically verifiable representation of the reality. Once formed, however, the psychological model can act back upon the psychological reality. The model has *realizing* potency, that is, it can create psychological reality as a "self-fulfilling prophecy." In a society in which demonology is socially established, cases of demon possession will empirically multiply. A society in which psychoanalysis is institutionalized as "science" will become populated by people who, in fact, evince the processes that have been theoretically attributed to them. It should be clear that this self-fulfilling character of psychological models is grounded in the same dialectic of socialization that Mead first formulated with incisive clarity and which can be summarized by saying that men become that as which they are addressed.

The purpose of these brief considerations has been to indicate what theoretical gains might be expected from an integration of the approaches of social psychology in the Meadian tradition and the sociology of knowledge. This is obviously not the place to discuss the methodological issues or the numerous possibilities of empirical exploration arising from such integration.[21] Suffice it to say, in conclusion, that the theoretical viewpoint expressed here implies a serious reconsideration of the relationship between the two disciplines of sociology and psychology. This relationship has been characterized, at least in this country, by a theoretically unjustified timidity on the side of the sociologists and by a spirit of ecumenical tolerance that may have beneficial consequences for interdepartmental amity, but which has not always been conducive to clear sociological thinking.

NOTES

1 On the "diffusion" of Meadian social psychology among American sociologists, cf. Anselm Strauss (ed.), *George Herbert Mead on Social Psychology* (Chicago: University of Chicago Press, 1964), pp. vii ff. For a critique of this Meadian "establishment," from a psychoanalytically oriented viewpoint, cf. Dennis Wrong, "The Over-Socialized Conception of Man in Modern Sociology," *Psychoanalysis and the Psychoanalytic Review*, XXXIX (1962), 53 ff.

2 Among American sociologists, the sociology of knowledge has remained rather narrowly associated with its conception by Karl Mannheim, who served as its principal

"translator" from the context of German *Geisteswissenschaft* to that of English-speaking social science. The writings of Max Scheler on *Wissenssoziologie* (the term was coined by him) remain untranslated today. American sociologists have also, in the main, remained unaffected by the development of the sociology of knowledge in the work of Alfred Schütz, not to mention recent contributions in the positivistic tradition (mainly by sociologists writing in German) and by Marxists (mainly in France). For the Mannheim-oriented reception of the sociology of knowledge in America, cf. Robert Merton, *Social Theory and Social Structure* (Glencoe, Ill.: The Free Press, 1957), pp. 439 ff.; and Talcott Parsons, pp. 282–306, above. For a conception of the subdiscipline more in the line of Scheler than of Mannheim (and with which the present writer would not associate himself fully, either), cf. Werner Stark, *The Sociology of Knowledge* (Glencoe, Ill.: The Free Press, 1958).

3　Cf. Merton, *Social Theory and Social Structure*, pp. 225 ff.; Muzafer Sherif and Carolyn Sherif, *An Outline of Social Psychology* (New York: Harper & Row, 1956); Tamotsu Shibutani, "Reference Groups and Social Control," in Arnold Rose (ed.), *Human Behavior and Social Processes* (Boston: Houghton Mifflin Co., 1962), pp. 128 ff.

4　This understanding of the scope of the sociology of knowledge, a much broader one than that of the Mannheim-oriented approach, has been strongly influenced by the work of Alfred Schütz. Cf. Alfred Schütz, *Der sinnhafte Aufbau der sozialen Welt* (Vienna: Springer, 1960); *The Problem of Social Reality* (The Hague: Nijhoff, 1962); *Studies in Social Theory* (The Hague: Nijhoff, 1964).

5　This dialectic between self and society can also be formulated in Marxian terms. Cf., for example, Joseph Gabel, *La Fausse conscience* (Paris: Editions de Minuit, 1962); and Jean-Paul Sartre, *Search for a Method* (New York: Alfred A. Knopf, 1963). For an attempt at integrating certain Marxian categories within a non-Marxian sociology of knowledge, cf. Peter Berger and Stanley Pullberg, "Reification and the Sociological Critique of Consciousness," *History and Theory*, IV (1965).

6　On the social structuring of conduct, cf. Arnold Gehlen, *Urmensch und Spätkultur* (Bonn: Athenaeum, 1956), where Gehlen proposes a biologically grounded theory of social institutions. On this very suggestive theory, which to date has remained practically unknown to American sociologists, also cf. Arnold Gehlen, *Anthropologische Forschung* (Hamburg: Rowohlt, 1961), and *Studien zur Anthropologie und Soziologie* (Neuwied/Rhein: Luchterhand, 1963).

7　Thomas' well-known dictum on the "real consequences" of social definition was presumably intended, and has been generally understood as intending, to say that once a "reality" has been defined, people will act *as if* it were indeed so. To this important proposition must be added an understanding of the *realizing* (that is, reality-producing) potency of social definition. This social-psychological import of Thomas' "basic theorem" was developed by Merton, *Social Theory and Social Structure*, pp. 421 ff. The sociology of knowledge, as this paper tries to indicate, would extend this notion of the social construction of "reality" even further.

8　Cf. Schütz, *The Problem of Social Reality*, pp. 207 ff.

9　Cf. *ibid.*, pp. 3 ff.

10　Cf. *ibid.*, pp. 287 ff. Also, cf. Ernst Cassirer, *An Essay on Man* (New Haven: Yale University Press, 1962), pp. 109 ff. The problem of language and "reality," neglected by American sociologists, has been extensively discussed in American cultural anthropology, *vide* the influence of Edward Sapir and the controversy over the so-called

"Whorf hypothesis." It has been a central problem for sociologists and cultural anthropologists in France ever since the Durkheim school. Cf. Claude Lévi-Strauss, *La Pensée sauvage* (Paris: Plon, 1962).

11 On the maintenance of "reality" by means of the "conversational apparatus," cf. Peter Berger and Hansfried Kellner, "Le Mariage et la construction de la réalité," *Diogène*, XLVI (1964), 3 ff.

12 One may say that the Durkheimian theory of "collective consciousness" is the positive side of the theory of *anomie*. The *locus classicus* of this is, of course, Durkheim's *Elementary Forms of Religious Life*. For important developments of this (all of great relevance for the sociology of knowledge), cf. Marcel Granet, *La Pensée chinoise* (Paris: Albin Michel, 1950); Maurice Halbwachs, *Les Cadres sociaux de la mémoire* (Paris: P.U.F., 1952); Marcel Mauss, *Sociologie et anthropologie* (Paris: P.U.F., 1960).

13 The fullest evidence on the "objectivity" of the child's language learning is to be found in the work of Jean Piaget.

14 The fixation of the sociology of knowledge on the theoretical level of consciousness is well expressed in the subtitle of the previously cited work by Stark—"An Essay in Aid of a Deeper Understanding of the History of Ideas." The present writer would consider Schütz's work as essential for arriving at a broader conception of the subdiscipline. For a broader approach based on Marxian presuppositions, cf. Henri Lefebvre, *Critique de la vie quotidienne* (Paris: L'Arche, 1958–61). For a discussion of the possibility of using Pareto for a critique of pre-theoretical consciousness in society, cf. Brigitte Berger, "Vilfredo Pareto's Sociology as a Contribution to the Sociology of Knowledge" (unpublished Ph.D. dissertation, New School for Social Research, 1964).

15 This problem is, of course, dealt with by Marx in his well-known conception of sub- and super-structure. The present writer would argue that, at least in Marx's early writings (as in the *Economic and Philosophic Manuscripts of 1844*), the relationship between the two is clearly a dialectic one. In later Marxism, the dialectic is lost in a mechanistic understanding of sub- and super-structure in which the latter becomes a mere epiphenomenon (Lenin—a "reflection") of the former. On the "reification" of Marxism in Communist ideology (perhaps one of the great ironies in the history of ideas), cf., for example, Joseph Gabel, *Formen der Entfremdung* (Frankfurt: Fischer, 1964), pp. 53 ff. Probably the most important work, within the Marxian tradition, which has tried to recapture the original dialectic in dealing with this problem is Georg Lukács' *Geschichte und Klassenbewusstsein* (1923), now virtually unobtainable in German, but available in an excellent French translation—*Histoire et conscience de classe* (Paris: Editions de Minuit, 1960).

16 The overarching dialectic of sociation indicated here can be analyzed in terms of three "moments"—externalization, objectivation, and internalization. The dialectic is lost whenever one of these "moments" is excluded from social theory. Cf. Berger and Pullberg, "Reification and the Sociological Critique of Consciousness."

17 For indications of the intriguing possibilities of such a "socio-somatics," cf. Georg Simmel's discussion of the "sociology of the senses," in his *Soziologie* (Berlin: Duncker & Humblot, 1958), pp. 483 ff. Also cf. Mauss's essay on the "techniques of the body," in *Sociologie et anthropologie*, pp. 365 ff.

18 It is not intended here to propose a "sociologistic" view of reality as *nothing but* a social construction. Within the sociology of knowledge, however, it is possible to bracket the final epistemological questions.

19 On the sociology-of-knowledge implications of diagnostic typologies, cf. Eliot Freidson, *The Sociology of Medicine* (Oxford: Blackwell, 1963), pp. 124 ff.
20 For a critique of the contemporary concept of "mental illness," coming from within psychiatry itself, cf. Thomas Szasz, *The Myth of Mental Illness* (New York: Hosber-Harper, 1961).
21 Cf. Peter L. Berger and Thomas Luckmann, *The Social Construction of Reality* (Garden City, N.Y.: Doubleday & Co., 1966).

Part Three: The Sociocultural Environment and Ideas

I

MAX WEBER

Asceticism and the Spirit of Capitalism

ALTHOUGH WE CANNOT here enter upon a discussion of the influence of Puritanism in all directions, we should call attention to the fact that the toleration of pleasure in cultural goods, which contributed to purely aesthetic or athletic enjoyment, certainly always ran up against one characteristic limitation: they must not cost anything. Man is only a trustee of the goods which have come to him through God's grace. He must, like the servant in the parable, give an account of every penny entrusted to him,[1] and it is at least hazardous to spend any of it for a purpose which does not serve the glory of God but only one's own enjoyment.[2] What person, who keeps his eyes open, has not met representatives of this viewpoint even in the present?[3] The idea of a man's duty to his possessions, to which he subordinates himself as an obedient steward, or even as an acquisitive machine, bears with chilling weight on his life. The greater the possessions the heavier, if the ascetic attitude toward life stands the test, the feeling of responsibility for them, for holding them undiminished for the glory of God and increasing them by restless effort. The origin of this type of life also extends in certain roots, like so many aspects of the spirit of capitalism, back into the Middle Ages.[4] But it was in the ethic of ascetic Protestantism that it first found a consistent ethical foundation. Its significance for the development of capitalism is obvious.[5]

This worldly Protestant asceticism, as we may recapitulate up to this point, acted powerfully against the spontaneous enjoyment of possessions; it restricted consumption, especially of luxuries. On the other hand, it had the

The Protestant Ethic and the Spirit of Capitalism, translated by Talcott Parsons (New York: Charles Scribner's Sons, 1958), pp. 170–83. Reprinted by permission of Charles Scribner's Sons, Inc., and George Allen and Unwin, Ltd.

psychological effect of freeing the acquisition of goods from the inhibitions of traditionalistic ethics. It broke the bonds of the impulse of acquisition in that it not only legalized it, but (in the sense discussed) looked upon it as directly willed by God. The campaign against the temptations of the flesh, and the dependence on external things, was, as besides the Puritans the great Quaker apologist Barclay expressly says, not a struggle against the rational acquisition, but against the irrational use of wealth.

But this irrational use was exemplified in the outward forms of luxury which their code condemned as idolatry of the flesh,[6] however natural they had appeared to the feudal mind. On the other hand, they approved the rational and utilitarian uses of wealth which were willed by God for the needs of the individual and the community. They did not wish to impose mortification[7] on the man of wealth, but the use of his means for necessary and practical things. The idea of comfort characteristically limits the extent of ethically permissible expenditures. It is naturally no accident that the development of a manner of living consistent with that idea may be observed earliest and most clearly among the most consistent representatives of this whole attitude toward life. Over against the glitter and ostentation of feudal magnificence which, resting on an unsound economic basis, prefers a sordid elegance to a sober simplicity, they set the clean and solid comfort of the middle-class home as an ideal.[8]

On the side of the production of private wealth, asceticism condemned both dishonesty and impulsive avarice. What was condemned as covetousness, Mammonism, etc., was the pursuit of riches for their own sake. For wealth in itself was a temptation. But here asceticism was the power "which ever seeks the good but ever creates evil"[9] what was evil in its sense was possession and its temptations. For in conformity with the Old Testament and in analogy to the ethical valuation of good works, asceticism looked upon the pursuit of wealth as an end in itself as highly reprehensible; but the attainment of it as a fruit of labor in a calling was a sign of God's blessing. And even more important: the religious valuation of restless, continuous, systematic work in a worldly calling, as the highest means to asceticism, and at the same time the surest and most evident proof of rebirth and genuine faith, must have been the most powerful conceivable lever for the expansion of that attitude toward life which we have here called the spirit of capitalism.[10]

When the limitation of consumption is combined with this release of acquisitive activity, the inevitable practical result is obvious: accumulation of capital through ascetic compulsion to save.[11] The restraints which were imposed upon the consumption of wealth naturally served to increase it by making possible the productive investment of capital. How strong this influence was is not, unfortunately, susceptible of exact statistical demonstration. In New England the connection is so evident that it did not escape the eye of so discerning a historian as Doyle.[12] But also in Holland, which was really only dominated by strict Calvinism for seven years, the greater simplicity of life in the more seriously religious circles, in combination with great wealth, led to an excessive propensity to accumulation.[13]

That, furthermore, the tendency which has existed everywhere and at all times, being quite strong in Germany today, for middle-class fortunes to be absorbed into the nobility, was necessarily checked by the Puritan antipathy to the feudal way of life, is evident. English Mercantilist writers of the seventeenth century attributed the superiority of Dutch capital to English to the circumstance that newly acquired wealth there did not regularly seek investment in land. Also, since it is not simply a question of the purchase of land, it did not there seek to transfer itself to feudal habits of life, and thereby to remove itself from the possibility of capitalistic investment.[14] The high esteem for agriculture as a peculiarly important branch of activity, also especially consistent with piety, which the Puritans shared, applied (for instance in Baxter) not to the landlord, but to the yeoman and farmer, in the eighteenth century not to the squire, but the rational cultivator.[15] Through the whole of English society in the time since the seventeenth century goes the conflict between the squirearchy, the representatives of "merrie old England," and the Puritan circles of widely varying social influence.[16] Both elements, that of an unspoiled naïve joy of life, and of a strictly regulated, reserved self-control, and conventional ethical conduct are even today combined to form the English national character.[17] Similarly, the early history of the North American Colonies is dominated by the sharp contrast of the adventurers, who wanted to set up plantations with the labor of indentured servants and live as feudal lords, and the specifically middle-class outlook of the Puritans.[18]

As far as the influence of the Puritan outlook extended, under all circumstances—and this is, of course, much more important than the mere encouragement of capital accumulation—it favored the development of a rational bourgeois economic life; it was the most important, and above all the only consistent influence in the development of that life. It stood at the cradle of the modern economic man.

To be sure, these Puritanical ideals tended to give way under excessive pressure from the temptations of wealth, as the Puritans themselves knew very well. With great regularity we find the most genuine adherents of Puritanism among the classes which were rising from a lowly status,[19] the small bourgeois and farmers, while the *beati possidentes*, even among Quakers, are often found tending to repudiate the old ideals.[20] It was the same fate which again and again befell the predecessor of this worldly asceticism, the monastic asceticism of the Middle Ages. In the latter case, when rational economic activity had worked out its full effects by strict regulation of conduct and limitation of consumption, the wealth accumulated either succumbed directly to the nobility, as in the time before the Reformation, or monastic discipline threatened to break down, and one of the numerous reformations became necessary.

In fact, the whole history of monasticism is in a certain sense the history of a continual struggle with the problem of the secularising influence of wealth. The same is true on a grand scale of the worldly asceticism of Puritanism. The great revival of Methodism, which preceded the expansion of English industry toward the end of the eighteenth century, may well be compared with such a monastic reform. We may hence quote here a passage[21] from John Wesley himself which might well serve as a motto for everything which has been said above. For it shows that the leaders of these ascetic movements understood the seemingly paradoxical relationships which we have here analyzed perfectly well, and in the same sense that we have given them.[22] He wrote:

> I fear; wherever riches have increased, the essence of religion has decreased in the same proportion. Therefore I do not see how it is possible, in the nature of things, for any revival of true religion to continue long. For religion must necessarily produce both industry and frugality, and these cannot but produce riches. But as riches increase, so will pride, anger, and love of the world in all its branches. How then is it possible that Methodism, that is, a religion of the heart, though it flourishes now as a green bay tree, should continue in this state? For the Methodists in every place grow diligent and frugal; consequently they increase in goods. Hence they proportionately increase in pride, in anger, in the desire of the flesh, the desire of the eyes, and the pride of life. So, although the form of religion remains, the spirit is swiftly vanishing away. Is there no way to prevent this—this continual decay of pure religion? We ought not to prevent people from being diligent and frugal; *we must exhort all Christians to gain all they can, and to save all they can; that is, in effect, to grow rich.*[23]

There follows the advice that those who gain all they can and save all they can should also give all they can, so that they will grow in grace and lay up a treasure in heaven. It is clear that Wesley here expresses, even in detail, just what we have been trying to point out.[24]

As Wesley here says, the full economic effect of those great religious movements, whose significance for economic development lay above all in their ascetic educative influence, generally came only after the peak of the purely religious enthusiasm was past. Then the intensity of the search for the Kingdom of God commenced gradually to pass over into sober economic virtue; the religious roots died out slowly, giving way to utilitarian worldliness. Then, as Dowden puts it, as in *Robinson Crusoe*, the isolated economic man who carries on missionary activities on the side,[25] takes the place of the lonely spiritual search for the Kingdom of Heaven of Bunyan's pilgrim, hurrying through the market-place of Vanity.

When later the principle "to make the most of both worlds" became dominant in the end, as Dowden has remarked, a good conscience simply became one of the means of enjoying a comfortable bourgeois life, as is well expressed in the German proverb about the soft pillow. What the great religious epoch of the seventeenth century bequeathed to its utilitarian successor was, however, above all an amazingly good, we may even say a pharisaically good, conscience in the acquisition of money, so long as it took place legally. Every trace of the *deplacere vix potest* has disappeared.[26]

A specifically bourgeois economic ethic had grown up. With the consciousness of standing in the fullness of God's grace and being visibly blessed by Him, the bourgeois businessman, as long as he remained within the bounds of formal correctness, as long as his moral conduct was spotless and the use to which he put his wealth was not objectionable, could follow his pecuniary interests as he would and feel that he was fulfilling a duty in doing so. The power of religious asceticism provided him in addition with sober, conscientious and unusually industrious workmen, who clung to their work as to a life purpose willed by God.[27]

Finally, it gave him the comforting assurance that the unequal distribution of the goods of this world was a special dispensation of Divine Providence, which in these differences, as in particular grace, pursued secret ends unknown to men.[28] Calvin himself had made the much-quoted statement that only when the people, i.e., the mass of laborers and craftsmen, were poor did they remain obedient to God.[29] In the Netherlands (Pieter de la Court and others), that had been secularized to the effect that the mass of men only labor when necessity forces them to do so. This formulation of a leading idea of capitalistic economy later entered into the current theories of the productivity of low wages. Here also, with the dying out of the religious root, the utilitarian interpretation crept in unnoticed, in the line of development which we have again and again observed.

Medieval ethics not only tolerated begging but actually glorified it in the mendicant orders. Even secular beggars, since they gave the person of means opportunity for good works through giving alms, were sometimes considered an estate and treated as such. Even the Anglican social ethic of the Stuarts was very close to this attitude. It remained for Puritan Asceticism to take part in the severe English Poor Relief Legislation which fundamentally changed the situation. And it could do that, because the Protestant sects and the strict Puritan communities actually did not know any begging in their own midst.[30]

On the other hand, seen from the side of the workers, the Zinzendorf branch of Pietism, for instance, glorified the loyal worker who did not seek acquisition, but lived according to the apostolic model, and was thus endowed with the *charisma*[31] of the disciples.[32] Similar ideas had originally been prevalent among the Baptists in an even more radical form.

Now naturally the whole ascetic literature of almost all denominations is saturated with the idea that faithful labor, even at low wages, on the part of those whom life offers no other opportunities, is highly pleasing to God. In this respect Protestant Asceticism added in itself nothing new. But it not only deepened this idea most powerfully, it also created the force which was alone decisive for its effectiveness: the psychological sanction of it through the conception of this labor as a calling, as the best, often in the last analysis the only means of attaining certainty of grace.[33] And on the other hand it legalized the exploitation of this specific willingness to work, in that it also interpreted the employer's business activity as a calling.[34] It is obvious how powerfully the exclusive search for the Kingdom of God only through the fulfillment of duty in the calling, and the strict asceticism which Church discipline naturally imposed, especially on the propertyless classes, was bound to affect the productivity of labour in the capitalistic sense of the word. The treatment of labor as a calling became as characteristic of the modern worker as the corresponding attitude toward acquisition of the businessman. It was a perception of this situation, new at his time, which caused so able an observer as Sir William Petty to attribute the economic power of Holland in the seventeenth century to the fact that the very numerous dissenters in that country (Calvinists and Baptists) "are for the most part thinking, sober men, and such as believe that Labor and Industry is their duty toward God."[35]

Calvinism opposed organic social organization in the fiscal-monopolistic form that it assumed in Anglicanism under the Stuarts, especially in the conceptions of Laud, this alliance of Church and State with the monopolists on the basis of a Christian-social ethical foundation. Its leaders were universally among the most passionate opponents of this type of politically privileged commercial, putting-out, and colonial capitalism. Over against it they placed the individualistic motives of rational legal acquisition by virtue of one's own ability and initiative. And while the politically privileged monopoly industries in England all disappeared in short order, this attitude played a large and decisive part in the development of the industries which grew up in spite of and against the authority of the State.[36] The Puritans (Prynne, Parker) repudiated all connection with the large-scale capitalistic courtiers and projectors as an ethically suspicious class. On the other hand, they took pride in their own superior middle-class business morality which formed the true reason for the persecutions to which they were subjected on the part of those circles. Defoe proposed to win the battle against dissent by boycotting bank credit and withdrawing deposits. The difference of the two types of capitalistic attitude went to a very large extent hand in hand with religious differences. The opponents of the Nonconformists, even in the eighteenth century, again and again ridiculed them for personifying the spirit of shopkeepers, and for having ruined the ideals of old England. Here also lay the difference of the Puritan economic ethic from the Jewish; and contemporaries (Prynne) knew well that the former and not the latter was the bourgeois capitalistic ethic.[37]

One of the fundamental elements of the spirit of modern capitalism, and not only of that but of all modern culture: rational conduct on the basis of the idea of the calling, was born—that is what this discussion has sought to demonstrate—from the spirit of Christian asceticism. One has only to reread the passage from Franklin, quoted at the beginning of this essay, in order to see that the essential elements of the attitude which was there called the spirit of capitalism are the same as what we have just shown to be the content of the Puritan worldly asceticism,[38] only without the religious basis, which by Franklin's time had died away. The idea that modern labor has an ascetic character is of course not new. Limitation to specialized work, with a renunciation of the Faustian universality of man which it involves, is a condition of any valuable work in the modern world; hence deeds and renunciation inevitably condition each other today. This fundamentally ascetic trait of middle-class life, if it attempts to be a way of life at all, and not simply the absence of any, was what Goethe wanted to teach, at the height of his wisdom, in the *Wanderjahren*, and in the end which he gave to the life of his *Faust*.[39] For him the realization meant a renunciation, a departure from an age of full and beautiful humanity, which can no more be repeated in the course of our cultural development than can the flower of the Athenian culture of antiquity.

The Puritan wanted to work in a calling; we are forced to do so. For when asceticism was carried out of monastic cells into everyday life, and began to dominate worldly morality, it did its part in building the tremendous cosmos of the modern economic order. This order is now bound to the technical and economic conditions of machine production which today determine the lives of all the individuals who are born into this mechanism, not only those directly concerned with economic acquisition, with irresistible force. Perhaps it will so determine them until the last ton of fossilized coal is burnt. In Baxter's view the care for external goods should only lie on the shoulders of the "saint like a light cloak, which can be thrown aside at any moment."[40] But fate decreed that the cloak should become an iron cage.

Since asceticism undertook to remodel the world and to work out its ideals in the world, material goods have gained an increasing and finally an inexorable power over the lives of men as at no previous period in history. Today the spirit of religious asceticism—whether finally, who knows?—has escaped from the cage. But victorious capitalism, since it rests on mechanical foundations, needs its support no longer. The rosy blush of its laughing heir, the Enlightenment, seems also to be irretrievably fading, and the idea of duty in one's calling prowls about in our lives like the ghost of dead religious beliefs. Where the fulfillment of the calling cannot directly be related to the highest spiritual and cultural values, or when, on the other hand, it need not be felt simply as economic compulsion, the individual generally abandons the attempt to justify it at all. In the field of its highest development in the United States, the pursuit of wealth, stripped of its religious and ethical meaning, tends to become associated with purely mundane passions, which often actually give it the character of sport.[41]

No one knows who will live in this cage in the future, or whether at the end of this tremendous development entirely new prophets will arise, or there will be a great rebirth of old ideas and ideals, or, if neither, mechanized petrification, embellished with a sort of convulsive self-importance. For of the last stage of this cultural development, it might well be truly said: "Specialists without spirit, sensualists without heart; this nullity imagines that it has attained a level of civilization never before achieved."

But this brings us to the world of judgments of value and of faith, with which this purely historical discussion need not be burdened. The next task would be rather to show the significance of ascetic rationalism, which has only been touched on in the foregoing sketch, for the content of practical social ethics, thus for the types of organization and the functions of social groups from the conventicle to the State. Then its relations to humanistic rationalism,[42] its ideals of life and cultural influence; further to the development of philosophical and scientific empiricism, to technical development and to spiritual ideals would have to be analyzed. Then its historical development from the medieval beginnings of worldly asceticism to its dissolution into pure utilitarianism would have to be traced out through all the areas of ascetic religion. Only then could the quantitative cultural significance of ascetic Protestantism in its relation to the other plastic elements of modern culture be estimated.

Here we have only attempted to trace the fact and the direction of its influence to their motives in one, though a very important point. But it would also further be necessary to investigate how Protestant Asceticism was in turn influenced in its development and its character by the totality of social conditions, especially economic.[43] The modern man is in general, even with the best will, unable to give religious ideas a significance for culture and national character which they deserve. But it is, of course, not my aim to substitute for a one-sided materialistic an equally one-sided spiritualistic causal interpretation of culture and of history. Each is equally possible.[44] but each, if it does not serve as the preparation, but as the conclusion of an investigation, accomplishes equally little in the interest of historical truth.[45]

NOTES

1 Thus Baxter in the passage cited above, I, 108, and below.

2 Cf. the well-known description of Colonel Hutchinson (often quoted, for instance, in Sanford, *Studies and Reflections of the Great Revolution*, p. 57) in the biography written by his widow. After describing all his chivalrous virtues and his cheerful, joyous nature, it goes on: "He was wonderfully neat, cleanly, and genteel in his habit, and had a very good fancy in it; but he left off very early the wearing of anything that was costly." Quite similar is the ideal of the educated and highly civilized Puritan woman who, however, is penurious of two things: (1) time, and (2) expenditure for pomp and pleasure, as drawn in Baxter's funeral oration for Mary Hammer (*Works of the Puritan Divines* [London, 1845–48], p. 533).

3 I think, among many other examples, especially of a manufacturer unusually successful in his business ventures, and in his later years very wealthy, who, when for the treatment of a troublesome digestive disorder the doctor prescribed a few oysters a day, could only be brought to comply with difficulty. Very considerable gifts for philanthropic purposes which he made during his lifetime and a certain openhandedness showed, on the other hand, that it was simply a survival of that ascetic feeling which looks upon enjoyment of wealth for oneself as morally reprehensible, but has nothing whatever to do with avarice.

4 The separation of workshop, office, of business in general and the private dwelling, of firm and name, of business capital and private wealth, the tendency to make of the business a *corpus mysticum* (at least in the case of coporate property) all lay in this direction. On this, see my *Handelsgesellschaften im Mittelalter* (*Gesammelte Aufsätze zur Sozial- und Wirtschaftsgeschichte*, pp. 312 ff.).

5 W. Sombart in his *Kapitalismus* (first edition) has already well pointed out this characteristic phenomenon. It must, however, be noted that the accumulation of wealth springs from two quite distinct psychological sources. One reaches into the dimmest antiquity and is expressed in foundations, family fortunes, and trusts, as well as much more purely and clearly in the desire to die weighted down with a great burden of material goods; above all to insure the continuation of a business even at the cost of the personal interests of the majority of one's children. In such cases it is, besides the desire to give one's own creation an ideal life beyond one's death, and thus to maintain the *splendor familiæ* and extend the personality of the founder, a question of, so to speak, fundamentally egocentric motives. That is not the case with the bourgeois motive with which we are here dealing. There the motto of asceticism is *Entsagen sollst du, sollst entsagen* in the positive capitalistic sense of *Erwerben sollst du, sollst erwerben*. In its pure and simple non-rationality it is a sort of categorical imperative. Only the glory of God and one's own duty, not human vanity, is the motive for the Puritans; and today only the duty to one's calling. If it pleases anyone to illustrate an idea by its extreme consequences, we may recall the theory of certain American millionaires, that their millions should not be left to their children, so that they will not be deprived of the good moral effects of the necessity of working and earning for themselves. Today that idea is certainly no more than a theoretical soap-bubble.

6 This is, as must continually be emphasized, the final decisive religious motive (along with the purely ascetic desire to mortify the flesh). It is especially clear in the Quakers.

7 Baxter (*Saints' Everlasting Rest*, p. 12) repudiates this with precisely the same reasoning as the Jesuits: the body must have what it needs, otherwise one becomes a slave to it.

8 This ideal is clearly present, especially for Quakerism, in the first period of its development, as has already been shown in important points by Weingarten in his *Englische Revolutionskirchen*. Also Robert Barclay's thorough discussion (*The Inner Life of the Religious Societies of the Commonwealth* [1876], pp. 519 ff., 533) shows it very clearly. To be avoided are: (1) Worldly vanity; thus all ostentation, frivolity, and use of things having no practical purpose, or which are valuable only for their scarcity (i.e., for vanity's sake). (2) Any unconscientious use of wealth, such as excessive expenditure for not very urgent needs above necessary provision for the real needs of life and for the future. The Quaker was, so to speak, a living law of marginal utility. "Moderate use of the creature" is definitely permissible, but in particular one might pay attention to the quality and durability of materials so long as it did not lead to vanity. On all this cf. *Morgenblatt für gebildete Leser* (1846), pp. 216 ff. Especially on comfort and solidity among the Quakers, cf. Schneckenburger, *Vorlesungen*, pp. 96 ff.

9 Adapted by Weber from Faust, Act I. Goethe there depicts Mephistopheles as "*Die Kraft, die stets das Böse will, und stets das Gute schafft*"—trans.

10 It has already been remarked that we cannot here enter into the question of the class relations of these religious movements (see the essays on the *Wirtschaftsethik der Weltreligionen*). In order to see, however, that for example Baxter, of whom we make so much use in this study, did not see things solely as a bourgeois of his time, it will suffice to recall that even for him in the order of the religious value of callings, after the learned professions comes the husbandman, and only then mariners, clothiers, booksellers, tailors, etc. Also, under mariners (characteristically enough) he probably thinks at least as often of fishermen as of shipowners. In this regard several things in the *Talmud* are in a different class. Cf., for instance, in Wünsche, *Babyl. Talmud*, II, 20, 21, the sayings of Rabbi

Eleasar, which though not unchallenged, all contend in effect that business is better than agriculture. In between, see II, 2, 68, on the wise investment of capital: one-third in land, one-third in merchandise, and one-third in cash.

For those to whom no causal explanation is adequate without an economic (or material-istic, as it is unfortunately still called) interpretation, it may be remarked that I consider the influence of economic development on the fate of religious ideas to be very impor-tant and shall later attempt to show how in our case the process of mutual adaptation of the two took place. On the other hand, those religious ideas themselves simply cannot be deduced from economic circumstances. They are in themselves, that is beyond doubt, the most powerful plastic elements of national character, and contain a law of development and a compelling force entirely their own. Moreover, the most import-ant differences, so far as non-religious factors play a part, are, as with Lutheranism and Calvinism, the result of political circumstances, not economic.

11 That is what Eduard Bernstein means to express when he says, in his *Geschichte des Sozialismus* (Stuttgart, 1895), pp. 625, 681, "Asceticism is a bourgeois virtue." His discussion is the first which has suggested these important relationships. But the con-nection is a much wider one than he suspected. For not only the accumulation of capital, but the ascetic rationalization of the whole of economic life was involved.

For the American Colonies, the difference between the Puritan North, where, on account of the ascetic compulsion to save, capital in search of investment was always available, from the conditions in the South has already been clearly brought out by Doyle.

12 Doyle, *The English in America*, II, chap. i. The existence of ironworks (1643), weaving for the market (1659), and also the high development of the handicrafts in New England in the first generation after the foundation of the colonies are, from a purely economic viewpoint, astounding. They are in striking contrast to the conditions in the South, as well as the non-Calvinistic Rhode Island with its complete freedom of conscience. There, in spite of the excellent harbor, the report of the Governor and Council of 1786 said: "The great obstruction concerning trade is the want of merchants and men of considerable estates amongst us" (M. Arnold, *History of the State of Rhode Island*, p. 490). It can in fact hardly be doubted that the compulsion continually to reinvest savings, which the Puritan curtailment of consumption exercised, played a part. In addition there was the part of Church discipline which cannot be discussed here.

13 That, however, these circles rapidly diminished in the Netherlands is shown by Busken-Huet's discussion (*Het Land van Rembrandt*, II, chaps. iii and iv). Nevertheless, Groen van Prinsterer says (*Handb. der Gesch. van het Vaderland* [3rd ed.] par. 303, note p. 254), "*De Nederlanders verkoopen veel en verbruiken wenig*," even of the time after the Peace of Westphalia.

14 For England, for instance, a petition of an aristocratic Royalist (quoted in Ranke, *Engl. Geschichte*, IV, 197), presented after the entry of Charles II into London, advocated a legal prohibition of the acquisition of landed estates by bourgeois capital, which should thereby be forced to find employment in trade. The class of Dutch regents was distin-guished as an estate from the bourgeois patricians of the cities by the purchase of landed estates. See the complaints, cited by Fruin, *Tien jaren uit den tachtigjarigen oorlog*, of the year 1652, that the regents have become landlords and are no longer merchants. To be sure, these circles had never been at bottom strictly Calvinistic. And the notorious scramble for membership in the nobility and titles in large parts of the Dutch middle

class in the second half of the seventeenth century in itself shows that at least for this period the contrast between English and Dutch conditions must be accepted with caution. In this case the power of hereditary moneyed property broke through the ascetic spirit.

15 Upon the strong movement for bourgeois capital to buy English landed estates followed the great period of prosperity of English agriculture.

16 Even down into this century Anglican landlords have often refused to accept Nonconformists as tenants. At the present time the two parties of the Church are of approximately equal numbers, while in earlier times the Nonconformists were always in the minority.

17 H. Levy (article in *Archiv für Sozialwissenschaft und Sozialpolitik*, XLVI, 605) rightly notes that according to the native character of the English people, as seen from numerous of its traits, they were, if anything, less disposed to welcome an ascetic ethic and the middle-class virtues than other peoples. A hearty and unrestrained enjoyment of life was, and is, one of their fundamental traits. The power of Puritan asceticism at the time of its predominance is shown most strikingly in the astonishing degree to which this trait of character was brought under discipline among its adherents.

18 This contrast recurs continually in Doyle's presentation. In the attitude of the Puritan to everything the religious motive always played an important part (not always, of course, the sole important one). The colony (under Winthrop's leadership) was inclined to permit the settlement of gentlemen in Massachusetts, even an upper house with a hereditary nobility, if only the gentlemen would adhere to the Church. The colony remained closed for the sake of Church discipline. The colonization of New Hampshire and Maine was carried out by large Anglican merchants, who laid out large stock-raising plantations. Between them and the Puritans there was very little social connection. There were complaints over the strong greed for profits of the New Englanders as early as 1632 (see Weeden's *Economic and Social History of New England*, I, 125).

19 This is noted by Petty (*Pol. Arith.*), and all the contemporary sources without exception speak in particular of the Puritan sectarians, Baptists, Quakers, Mennonites, etc., as belonging partly to a propertyless class, partly to one of small capitalists, and contrast them both with the great merchant aristocracy and the financial adventurers. But it was from just this small capitalist class, and not from the great financial magnates, monopolists, government contractors, lenders to the King, colonial entrepreneurs, promoters, etc., that there originated what was characteristic of Occidental captalism: the middle-class organization of industrial labor on the basis of private property (see Unwin, *Industrial Organization in the Sixteenth and Seventeenth Centuries* [London, 1914], pp. 196 ff.). To see that this difference was fully known even to contemporaries, cf. Parker's *Discourse Concerning Puritans* of 1641, where the contrast to promoters and courtiers is also emphasized.

20 On the way in which this was expressed in the politics of Pennsylvania in the eighteenth century, especially during the War of Independence, see Sharpless, *A Quaker Experiment in Government* (Philadelphia, 1902).

21 Quoted in Southey, *Life of Wesley*, chap. xxix (second American edition, II, p. 308). For the reference, which I did not know, I am indebted to a letter from Professor Ashley (1913). Ernst Troeltsch, to whom I communicated it for the purpose, has already made use of it.

22 The reading of this passage may be recommended to all those who consider themselves

today better informed on these matters than the leaders and contemporaries of the movements themselves. As we see, they knew very well what they were doing and what dangers they faced. It is really inexcusable to contest so lightly, as some of my critics have done, facts which are quite beyond dispute, and have hitherto never been disputed by anyone. All I have done is to investigate their underlying motives somewhat more carefully. No one in the seventeenth century doubted the existence of these relationships (cf. Manley, *Usury of 6 per Cent. Examined* [1669], p. 137). Besides the modern writers already noted, poets like Heine and Keats, as well as historians like Macaulay, Cunningham, Rogers, or an essayist such as Matthew Arnold, have assumed them as obvious. From the most recent literature see Ashley, *Birmingham Industry and Commerce* (1913). He has also expressed his complete agreement with me in correspondence. On the whole problem now cf. the study by H. Levy referred to in note 17, above.

23 Weber's italics—trans.

24 That exactly the same things were obvious to the Puritans of the classical era cannot perhaps be more clearly shown than by the fact in Bunyan Mr. Money-Love argues that one may become religious in order to get rich, for instance to attract customers. For why one has become religious makes no difference (see p. 114, Tauchnitz edition).

25 Defoe was a zealous Nonconformist.

26 Spener also (*Theologische Bedenken*, 426, 429, 432 ff.), although he holds that the merchant's calling is full of temptations and pitfalls, nevertheless declares in answer to a question: "I am glad to see, so far as trade is concerned, that my dear friend knows no scruples, but takes it as an art of life, which it is, in which much good may be done for the human race, and God's will may be carried out through love." This is more fully justified in other passages by mercantilist arguments. Spener, at times in a purely Lutheran strain, designates the desire to become rich as the main pitfall, following I Tim. vi, viii, and ix, and referring to Jesus Sirach, and hence rigidly to be condemned. But, on the other hand, he takes some of it back by referring to the prosperous sectarians who yet live righteously. As the result of industrious work wealth is not objectionable to him either. But on account of the Lutheran influence his standpoint is less consistent than that of Baxter.

27 Baxter, II, 16, warns against the employment of "heavy, flegmatic, sluggish, fleshly, slothful persons" as servants, and recommends preference for godly servants, not only because ungodly servants would be mere eye-servants, but above all because "a truly godly servant will do all your service in obedience to God, as if God Himself had bid him do it." Others, on the other hand, are inclined "to make no great matter of conscience of it." However, the criterion of saintliness of the workman is not for him the external confession of faith, but the "conscience to do their duty." It appears here that the interests of God and of the employers are curiously harmonious. Spener also (*Theologische Bedenken*, III, 272), who otherwise strongly urges taking time to think of God, assumes it to be obvious that workers must be satisfied with the extreme minimum of leisure time (even on Sundays). English writers have rightly called the Protestant immigrants the pioneers of skilled labor. See also proofs in H. Levy, *Die Grundlagen des ökonomischen Liberalismus in der Geschichte der englischen Volkswirtschaft* (Jena, 1912), p. 53.

28 The analogy between the unjust (according to human standards) predestination of only a few and the equally unjust, but equally divinely ordained, distribution of wealth, was too obvious to be escaped. See for example Hoornbeck, *Theologia practica*, I, 153.

Furthermore, as for Baxter, I, 280, poverty is very often a sympton of sinful slothfulness.

29 Thomas Adams (*Works of the Puritan Divines*, p. 158) thinks that God probably allows so many people to remain poor because He knows that they would not be able to withstand the temptations that go with wealth. For wealth all too often draws men away from religion.

30 See the study of Levy (*Die Grundlagen des ökonomischen Liberalismus in der Geschichte der englischen Volkswirtschaft*. The same is noted in all the discussions (thus by Manley for the Huguenots.)

31 *Charisma* is a sociological term coined by Weber himself. It refers to the quality of leadership which appeals to non-rational motives. See *Wirtschaft und Gesellschaft* (Tübingen, 1925), pp. 140 ff.—trans.

32 Similar things were not lacking in England. There was, for example, that Pietism which, starting from Law's *Serious Call* (1728), preached poverty, chastity, and, originally, isolation from the world.

33 Baxter's activity in Kidderminster, a community absolutely debauched when he arrived, which was almost unique in the history of the ministry for its success, is at the same time a typical example of how asceticism educated the masses to labor, or, in Marxian terms, to the production of surplus value, and thereby for the first time made their employment in the capitalistic labor relation (putting out industry, weaving, etc.) possible at all. That is very generally the causal relationship. From Baxter's own viewpoint he accepted the employment of his charges in the capitalistic production for the sake of his religious and ethical interests. From the standpoint of the development of capitalism these latter were brought into the service of the development of the spirit of capitalism.

34 Furthermore, one may well doubt to what extent the joy of the medieval craftsman in his creation, which is so commonly appealed to, was effective as a psychological motive force. Nevertheless, there is undoubtedly something in that thesis. But in any case asceticism certainly deprived all labor of this worldly attractiveness, today forever destroyed by capitalism, and oriented it to the beyond. Labor in a calling as such is willed by God. The impersonality of present-day labor, what, from the standpoint of the individual, is its joyless lack of meaning, still has a religious justification here. Capitalism at the time of its development needed laborers who were available for economic exploitation for conscience's sake. Today it is in the saddle, and hence able to force people to labor without transcendental sanctions.

35 W. Petty, *Political Arithmetick*, *Works*, ed. by Hull, I, 262.

36 On these conflicts and developments see H. Levy in *Die Grundlagen des ökonomischen Liberalismus in der Geschichte der englischen Volkswirtschaft*. The very powerful hostility of public opinion to monopolies, which is characteristic of England, originated historically in a combination of the political struggle for power against the Crown—the Long Parliament excluded monopolists from its membership—with the ethical motives of Puritanism; and the economic interests of the small bourgeois and moderate-scale capitalists against the financial magnates in the seventeenth century. The Declaration of the Army of August 2, 1652, as well as the Petition of the Levellers of January 28, 1653, demand, besides the abolition of excises, tariffs, and indirect taxes, and the introduction of a single tax on estates, above all free trade, i.e., the abolition of the monopolistic barriers to trade at home and abroad, as a violation of the natural rights of man.

37 Cf. *ibid.*, pp. 51 ff.

38 That those other elements, which have here not yet been traced to their religious roots, especially the idea that honesty is the best policy (Franklin's discussion of credit), are also of Puritan origin, must be proved in a somewhat different connection. Here I shall limit myself to repeating the following remark of J. A. Rowntree (*Quakerism, Past and Present*, pp. 95–96), to which E. Bernstein has called my attention: "Is it merely a coincidence, or is it a consequence, that the lofty profession of spirituality made by the Friends has gone hand in hand with shrewdness and tact in the transaction of mundane affairs? Real piety favors the success of a trader by insuring his integrity and fostering habits of prudence and forethought, important items in obtaining that standing and credit in the commercial world, which are requisites for the steady accumulation of wealth." "Honest as a Huguenot" was as proverbial in the seventeenth century as the respect for law of the Dutch, which Sir W. Temple admired, and, a century later, that of the English as compared with those Continental peoples that had not been through this ethical schooling.

39 Well analyzed in Bielschowsky's *Goethe*, II, chap. xviii. For the development of the scientific cosmos Windelband, at the end of his *Blütezeit der deutschen Philosophie* (Vol. II of the *Gesch. d. Neueren Philosophie*), has expressed a similar idea.

40 Baxter, *Saints' Everlasting Rest*, chap. xii.

41 "Couldn't the old man be satisfied with his $75,000 a year and rest? No! The frontage of the store must be widened to 400 feet. Why? That beats everything, he says. In the evening when his wife and daughter read together, he wants to go to bed. Sundays he looks at the clock every five minutes to see when the day will be over—what a futile life!" In these terms the son-in-law (who had emigrated from Germany) of the leading dry-goods man of an Ohio city expressed his judgment of the latter, a judgment which would undoubtedly have seemed simply incomprehensible to the old man. A symptom of German lack of energy.

42 This remark alone (unchanged since his criticism) might have shown Brentano (*Die Anfänge des modernen Kapitalismus* [1916]) that I have never doubted its independent significance. That humanism was also not pure rationalism has lately again been strongly emphasized by Borinski in the *Abhandl. der Münchener Akad. der Wiss.* (1919).

43 The academic oration of v. Below, *Die Ursachen der Reformation* (Freiburg, 1916), is not concerned with this problem, but with that of the Reformation in general, especially Luther. For the question dealt with here, especially the controversies which have grown out of this study, I may refer finally to the work of Hermelink, *Reformation und Gegenreformation*, which, however, is also primarily concerned with other problems.

44 For the above sketch has deliberately taken up only the relations in which an influence of religious ideas on the material culture is really beyond doubt. It would have been easy to proceed beyond that to a regular construction which logically deduced everything characteristic of modern culture from Protestant rationalism. But that sort of thing may be left to the type of dilettante who believes in the unity of the group mind and its reducibility to a single formula. Let it be remarked only that the period of capitalistic development lying before that which we have studied was everywhere in part determined by religious influences, both hindering and helping. Of what sort these were belongs in another chapter. Furthermore, whether, of the broader problems sketched above, one or another can be dealt with in the limits of this Journal [the essay first appeared in the *Archiv für Sozialwissenschaft und Sozialpolitik*—Trans.] is not certain in view of the problems to which it is devoted. On the other hand, to write heavy tomes,

as thick as they would have to be in this case, and dependent on the work of others (theologians and historians), I have no great inclination (I have left these sentences unchanged).

For the tension between ideals and reality in early capitalistic times before the Reformation, see now Strieder, *Studien zur Geschichte der kapit. Organizationsformen* (1914), Book II. (Also as against the work of Keller [*Unternehmung und Mehrmert*, Publications of the Goerres-Gesellschaft, XII], which was utilized by Sombart.)

45 I should have thought that this sentence and the remarks and notes immediately preceding it would have sufficed to prevent any misunderstanding of what this study was meant to accomplish, and I find no occasion for adding anything. Instead of following up with an immediate continuation in terms of the above program, I have, partly for fortuitous reasons, especially the appearance of Troeltsch's *Die Soziallehren der christlichen Kirchen und Gruppen*, which disposed of many things I should have had to investigate in a way in which I, not being a theologian, could not have done it; but partly also in order to correct the isolation of this study and to place it in relation to the whole of cultural development, determined, first, to write down some comparative studies of the general historical relationship of religion and society.

2

IAN D. CURRIE

*The Sapir-Whorf Hypothesis**

INTRODUCTION

IN A SERIES of papers published posthumously in 1952,[1] an American linguist, Benjamin Lee Whorf, gave fresh and striking expression to the view that the characteristics of language have determining influences on thought. As the languages of mankind differ greatly with respect to their structural, lexical, and other characteristics, he suggested that monolingual individuals speaking very different languages should, as a result, differ in symbolically mediated behavior. He stimulated a renewed interest in this problem among linguists and anthropologists, and, in time, among semanticists, psychologists, and sociologists. Currently, interest in the Whorf hypothesis is intense— the more so as a divergence of opinion exists over its proper interpretation, its limits, its verifiability, and its validity.[2] This paper briefly reviews the history of the hypothesis, and presents a discussion of the Whorfian formulation and the critical and empirical work to which this formulation has been subjected.

WHORF'S PREDECESSORS

Some of the elements comprising the Whorfian hypothesis can be traced a considerable distance back in time—as far back as the latter part of the eighteenth century. The idea that language presents his world to man was a European scholarly tradition, particularly in the German-speaking world.

* I am indebted to Randall Collins, Margaret Currie, Barclay Johnson, and Leo Lowenthal, who read an earlier version of this paper, and responded with many helpful comments and suggestions.

Berkeley Journal of Sociology, XI (1966), 14–31. Reprinted by permission of the *Berkeley Journal of Sociology* and the author.

Wilhelm von Humboldt in the 1790's, Ernst Cassirer and other contemporary or near-contemporary German scholars, and, more recently, Franz Boas, the anthropologist, and Edward Sapir, Whorf's immediate intellectual predecessor, all dealt with this same basic idea.

Whorf derived his generalizations on the relation of thought and behavior to language primarily from his analyses of certain exotic linguistic systems, notably those of the Hopi, Shawneee, and Nootka Indian cultures, which he compared with European languages.[3] He regarded the differences that he found among the latter as so insignificant that he grouped them all together under the term Standard Average European (SAE).[4] Whorf denies the widely held notion that the thought processes of all human beings possess a common logical structure (called by Whorf "natural logic") which operates before and independently of language. Linguistic patterns themselves determine what the individual perceives and how he thinks about it. Because these patterns vary widely, the ways of thinking and perceiving in groups using different linguistic systems will produce basically different world views. In short, according to Whorf, language shapes our ideas rather than merely expressing them.

THE WHORFIAN TREATMENT OF THE LINGUISTIC RELATIVITY HYPOTHESIS

While Sapir was interested in the hypothesis of linguistic relativity and was convinced of its validity, his principal empirical and speculative writings were concerned with other problems. Whorf, on the other hand, devoted himself to the investigation of the hypothesis which now bears the names of the two men from almost the very beginning of his systematic work in linguistics until the time of his premature death.

The major result of Whorf's work was a theory of the influence of language on perception and thought, summarized as follows.

No individual is free to describe nature with absolute impartiality, but is "constrained to certain modes of interpretation even while he thinks himself most free. . . . We are thus introduced to a new principle of relativity, which holds that all observers are not led by the same physical evidence to the same picture of the universe, unless their linguistic backgrounds are similar, or can in some way be calibrated."[5] The linguistic relativity principle means that "users of markedly different grammars are pointed by their grammars toward different types of observations and different evaluations of externally similar acts of observation, and hence are not equivalent as observers but must arrive at some different views of the world."[6]

For instance, experience of nature is segmented in a particular manner by particular linguistic patterns. English and similar languages deal with nature as a series of distinct *things* and *events*, a view implicit in classical physics and astronomy. The concepts of time and matter basic to Western European science are dependent upon the nature of the language in which they have been developed.

SAE objectifies time as if it were a ribbon or scroll marked off in equal spaces, a conception incompatible with the Hopi linguistic pattern, which is essentially ahistorical; the past for the Hopi is always implicit in the present. Whorf notes that a cultural result of the Western European view of our time is our linguistically conditioned interest in record-keeping, diaries, histories, and the concern with the "past" generally, as well as our emphasis on devices such as clocks, calendars, and time graphs, for the exact quantification of time.[7]

Perhaps the most important example of the relativity principle is found in the "use of language on date" that has made possible the scientific world view so characteristic of Western European cultures. Whorf, however, is very careful to state that Western European science is not *caused* by language but is "simply colored by it." Historic, economic, and other forces fortuitously converged in an area of the world where certain linguistic patterns (SAE) were dominant, and resulted in the kind of thinking, and, as Whorf would say, talking, which we know as science. The kind of science which resulted in Western Europe could, in Whorf's opinion, only have come about in a culture with linguistic patterns of a particular character.[8]

This linguistic relativism of Whorf is a special type of cultural-relativistic theory, whose special character lies in the central role he assigns to linguistic patterns.[9]

WHORF'S EVIDENCE

Whorf collected a great deal of data on vocabulary differences between languages, positing that these were related to differences in perception and cognition. Language X has a single term for phenomenon x, whereas language Y either does not possess such a term at all (and therefore refers to the phenomenon concerned either not at all, or else only by way of a circumlocution), or it has three terms, all differing in meaning and within the same area of reference. The result is that it is much *easier* to refer to certain phenomena or to certain nuances of meaning in some languages than in others. Whorf thus reasoned that the world appears differently to speakers of different languages. As a result of vocabulary differences in these languages, the attention of their speakers is differentially called to different aspects of the environment. This data Whorf drew largely from American Indian languages, which he contrasted mainly with American English. For example, English has different words for "pilot," "fly" (noun), and "airplane," but Hopi has only one. Eskimo has many words for different kinds of "snow," whereas English has only one. On the other hand, Aztec has only one word for our separate words "cold," "ice," and "snow." Many other examples could be given from the vocabulary of color perception, kinship terminology, and so on. Whorf contended that these vocabulary differences help speakers of certain languages to be more easily aware of some aspects of their environment and to communicate more easily about them, while constraining them to leave other distinctions unnoticed which speakers of other languages habitually make.[10]

Whorf regarded inflections, or grammatical forms, as an even more pervasive influence on perception than vocabulary, as inflections are less subject to change. They affect thought by calling attention to certain aspects of experience rather than to others. The way in which inflections most often operate can be most conveniently illustrated with a hypothetical example. Verb stem A, at some earlier stage of the language, was used by itself. Subsequently, it came to seem desirable that tense indicators representing past, present, and future be added to the verb. These indicators might be suffixes, and the verb can hence be symbolically represented as Ax, Ay, and Az. Because every situation in which A was formerly used was one in which a suffix was applicable, a simplification would naturally suggest itself. The stem form was now no longer needed by itself, because one of the suffixed forms would always be appropriate, and yet it was easier to pronounce than any of them. It would naturally, therefore, be used in place of one of the suffixed forms, with the meaning of that form. Thus, Ax might be abbreviated to A. While this would be conversationally convenient, it would, in effect, deprive the language of any word having the original meaning of A. This might, of course, be no loss, but an increase in thought would be required in order to use the language. Now one could no longer simply notice that the conditions for the application of the stem word were present and proceed to use it. It would be necessary to notice in addition which of the suffixes applied. Hence, in order to speak of one aspect of experience, it would be necessary to notice—and speak of—another as well. This phenomenon might be termed a *forced observation* induced by inflection. Tense, which has been used here as an example, constitutes only one sort of forced observation. The use of an English verb, for example, requires observations regarding number and person as well.[11] The observations that are forced differ in different languages. For example, with respect to English and Navaho:

English stops with what from the Navaho point of view is a very vague statement—"I drop it." The Navaho must specify four particulars which the English leaves either unsettled or to inference from context:

(1) Whether "it" is definite or just "something."

(2) . . . whether the object is round, or long, or fluid, or animate, etc.

(3) Whether the act is in progress, or just about to start, or just about to stop, or habitually carried on, or repeatedly carried on. . . .

(4) The extent to which the agent controls the fall.[12]

Similarly, Wintu requires that the evidence on which a statement is based be indicated by suffixes, thus forcing this observation:

He (the Wintu) cannot say simply *the salmon is good*. That part of *is good* which implies the tense (now) and the person (it) further has to contain one of the following implications: (the salmon is good) I see, I taste, (or know through some sense other than sight), I infer, I judge, I am told.[13]

Because, in English, the time of an action must be indicated, it is more likely to receive the attention of a speaker of English than that of a speaker of Wintu. The Wintu speaker, on the other hand, would be more likely to perceive the evidence upon which the statement is based than would the speaker of English, a language in which it is easier to make a statement without making such a specification.

The sentence structure peculiar to a language was another factor to which Whorf devoted a great deal of attention. An example of his work in this area is provided by a study which he made of differences between SAE and Hopi.

With reference to English and the SAE languages generally, two dominant forms of sentence seem to exist: first, what may be called the subject-predicate type of statement, of which "The book is red" will serve as a paradigm; and second, what may be termed the actor-action type, of which "John runs" or "John loves Mary" are representative. In the first type, no action takes place; a quality is merely attributed to a subject. In the second type, the subject is conceived as taking an action. In both cases, however, the subject is typically an enduring object, something recognizable through time, and even when it is not, the tendency is to speak as if it were. For example, an automobile mechanic may talk of fixing "the timing" on a car in much the same way that he speaks of fixing the tire, even though "the timing" is not, like the tire, an object, but rather a relation of events. Speaking of the timing in this fashion is perhaps merely metaphorical, but even if this is so, the metaphor still proceeds via the conception of a stable physical object.[14]

Whorf noted the pervasiveness in our language of this tendency to speak of events as if they were stable objects, and hence to lose, in speech at least, much of the fluidity of passing experience. This tendency extends to time itself, which is spoken of and thought of as a substance of indefinite extent. A segment of time may be isolated "in the same sense that we may cut a link of sausage, and we may save five minutes in something like the sense that we save a scrap of meat."[15]

Such ways of looking at the world are, in Whorf's opinion, of importance not merely in the organization of the details of experience, but are also of importance in philosophy, in particular for logic and metaphysics. Classical logic held that the subject-predicate form of statement was basic. It insisted that all logical manipulations be confined to this form, and it classified and tested arguments in terms of the relations between subject and predicate. While this conception of logic is almost completely discredited at present, it was undoubtedly a major influence on thought up to the present century.[16]

In metaphysics, subject and predicate are conceived in a somewhat different form. One of the classic philosophic problems has been to explain the integration and organization of our sense perception, the classic answer being that the universe is composed of *substances* and that everything perceived is an attribute of some substance. Hence, according to most of the Western philosophic tradition, the most abstract description of the universe would be that it consists of substances and their attributes.

Much of the philosophy of the twentieth century has been a polemic against these conceptions. Thus, Russell has insisted: " 'Substance,' in a word, is a metaphysical mistake, due to the transference to the world-structure of the structure of sentences composed of a subject and a predicate."[17]

CRITICAL ASSESSMENT

When Whorf tells us that "there is a precarious dependence of all we know upon linguistic tools which themselves are largely unknown or unnoticed,"[18] he strikes at all of us in a sensitive area—the foundations of our certainty in our scientific findings and in our everyday decisions. When he attacks the view that grammars are "merely norms of conventional and social correctness" and claims that they are, instead, the very means by which we fashion experience, our reaction is that he must either be drawing attention to a popular fallacy of which we have been unaware, or tilting at non-existent windmills. In short, Whorf, like Freud, impugns our objectivity and rationality.[19] It is not surprising then that many logical as well as experimental efforts have been made to re-evaluate the grounds upon which his formulations are based. We will consider some of the critical objections and some of the empirical investigations to which these formulations have been subjected.

1. *Syntactic Variation Not Related to Changes in Philosophical Ideas*

Whorf has suggested that the syntax of a language tends to be projected by speakers into their conceptions of reality. Linguistic determinants, of which the individual is unconscious, are thus held to influence his metaphysical outlook. In a recent paper,[20] Feuer cites a number of instances in which this process does not appear to have occurred. For example, in Danish, Russian, and English, the subjunctive mood has been gradually disappearing. This mood has traditionally expressed statements denoting hesitation, doubt, or anxiety concerning the reality of a situation. However, the philosophic speculations which have appeared in these languages do not appear to be correlated with this decline. Kierkegaard, for example, had no difficulty expressing his uncertainty and anxiety in an idiom which was abandoning the subjunctive mood. Further, French metaphysicians and French positivists use the same idiom with the same structure. The grammar they employ has not predetermined them to a common mold, and philosophers as diverse in thought as Descartes, Comte, and Bergson were able to state their ideas clearly in the same syntax. Similarly, Feuer notes such phenomena as gender, double or cumulative negation, and different tense-systems in a number of languages but finds no corresponding determination of metaphysical thought.[21] (On the other hand, Jakobson and others cite many examples of the semantic vitality of such large and *apparently* semantically dead syntactic categories as the genders of languages such as German and Chinook. These categories may influence thought.)[22]

2. *The Diffusion of a Common Philosophy Through Different Syntaxes*

Feuer points out that the Aristotelian metaphysics, for example, has not been the exclusive property of the Indo-European languages, but was propounded and developed by Arabic and Hebrew thinkers before it was espoused by the medieval Christian philosophers. Although the syntax of the Semitic languages differs markedly from that of the European tongues, Semitic syntactical rules provided no obstacle to the formulation of Aristotelian ideas. For example, the ideas of "being" were explicated in classical Hebrew, although ordinary noun clauses are without a copula of any kind in that language, which, in addition, possesses no abstract verb "to exist."

While some misrepresentation of Aristotle's ideas did occur as they were refracted from one linguistic medium to another—Syriac, Arabic, Hebrew,

Latin—"the outstanding fact . . . is that problems of syntax and terminology were surmounted with relative ease to achieve an expression of Aristotelian metaphysics in these languages."[23]

3. *The Translation Fallacy*

Whorf often tries to prove that differences in "world view" derive from differences in vocabulary and syntax by translating utterances from one language quite literally into another, usually English. We find what we would call "a dripping spring" being translated from Apache as "as water, or springs, whiteness moves downward," and Whorf concluding from the differences *in the two English renderings* that the Apache "world view" is very different from ours. However, the two English phrases are *not comparable* because Whorf has not given the general meanings of the English morphemes. Indeed, if we were to translate the English phrase *a/drip(p)/ing spring/* into its most literal and abstract terms, we would obtain something like "An instance of the general class, characterized by liquid falling in small, natural segments, process ongoing, eruption of water,"[24] and most speakers of English would fail to recognize their own "world view"! Whorf's translation method as a technique for establishing linguistic relativity also distorts the significance of metaphors, the literal significance of which never in fact penetrates the consciousness of speakers. Two examples will suffice. Suppose a Hopi linguist were to translate literally the English word *breakfast* as "the termination of a period of religious abstinence from food." He might then conclude that contemporary speakers of English must conceive of each night's sleep as a religious experience, because each morning's meal serves to break a fast![25] Another example of this fallacy may be drawn from Cassirer's work. To illustrate the mentality of certain African tribes, Cassirer writes:

> The languages of the Sudan usually express the circumstance that a subject is in process of action by means of a locution which really means [NB] that the subject is *inside* that action. But since, moreover, this *inside* is usually expressed very concretely, phrases result such as *I am on the inside of walking, I am the belly of walking*, for "I am in the process of walking."[26]

Results comparable in grotesqueness to the above example could be produced by the literal translation of a host of English metaphors, for instance, *everybody, in the face of, beforehand* and *inside*. In the classroom where European languages are taught, it is customary to avoid the odd results of literal translation by assuming a similarity of psychological processes and by liberalizing translation procedures so as to produce equivalent meanings. With Shawnee, Nootka, Apache, and Hopi (though never with the European languages) Whorf did not follow this procedure, insisted on a literal translation, and concluded that world views differ.[27] The evidence of literal translation does not establish the validity of the linguistic relativity hypothesis. Whorf's "unsympathetic" translation procedures, however, were the result of his initial assumption of such validity.[28]

4. *Whorf's Treatment of the Structural Features of Language*

Members of structural categories in a language have no common phonetic feature, but are grouped together because they have the same structural relations with other forms in the language. In English, for example, nouns constitute a structural category; its members can appear with definite and indefinite articles, form plurals in certain ways, and so forth. In French, all nouns of the feminine gender belong to one structural category because they all require the feminine articles and suffixes. Whorf usually assumes that structural categories are also symbolic categories. When he finds structural differences in languages, he concludes that there are parallel cognitive differences. For example, there exist in Hopi two structural categories rather similar to our verb and noun categories, with the difference that one of the Hopi classes includes only the names for such short-term events as lightning, flame, and spasm, while the other includes only such long-term events as man, house, and lifetime. From this Whorf concludes that the Hopi organize their world on a dimension which we usually overlook, and, indeed, when the structural class possesses such obvious semantic properties, his conclusions have a kind of plausibility.[29] However, very few structural classes have such clear and consistent meanings, and, in Indo-European languages, many structural categories have *no* discernible meaning. For example,

> In French . . . it is not clear that the gender of a form signifies anything to a speaker. Certainly it is difficult to find any common attributes in the references for French nouns of feminine gender. Not even the majority of them manifest sexuality—even in the extended sense of Freud. . . . The linguistic Charles Fries[30] has shown how difficult it is to describe a semantic for the English "parts of speech." If the noun can be defined as "the name of a person, place or thing," this is only because "thing" is left unexplicated. It serves handily to designate whatever is nominalized and yet is neither person nor place.[31]

Further, even when the ethnolinguist is able to discover consistent structural meanings, *it does not follow that these meanings are present to the native speakers of a language.* Even if there *were* some semantic to French gender, for example, one could speak the language without detecting it. As Brown and Lenneberg have recently pointed out, no legitimate inferences about thought can be derived from the simple existence of the structural classes which Whorf has described. It is clear that psychological in addition to linguistic data would be essential to justify any conclusions about the influence of the structural features of language upon thought.

5. *The Inadequacy of Whorf's Material as a Test of his Hypothesis*

One of the greatest pitfalls in the way of research upon the influence of language on thought is *circulatory of inference.* Whorf asserts that people in different cultures have different "world views" *because* their languages differ. For instance, the Hopi are regarded as having different time conceptions because their language uses a different tense system. Or, to give another example, Whorf translates the Apache phrase to which we have had reference previously as "as water, or springs, whiteness moves downward," from which he concludes, "How utterly unlike our way of thinking!"[32] But nothing about Hopi or Apache *thinking* has actually been observed. To claim that Hopi speakers must perceive time and Apache speakers must perceive springs differently from us because their way of talking about them is different, and then to infer how they perceive solely from how they talk, is tautological. Unfortunately, much of the "evidence" both for and against Whorf's hypothesis has remained at this level.[33] In order to escape from this trap, the independent and dependent variables, language structure and "world view," must be independently measured.

There are further problems with regard to the reliability and validity of Whorf's evidence. For a given language, his procedure in attempting to discern its cognitive "style" is to note a particular principle or theme, and then trace and elaborate it wherever else he feels he detects it. As Hymes has quite correctly pointed out, this procedure may be invaluable as a source of insight, but it is quite inadequate as a demonstration of the *validity* of the insight:

> One difficulty is that control may relax, as one naturally enough seeks to enhance the significance of the insight by assimilating more and more to it. The insight, or its cover term, may easily become inflated (or watered down), and the connection between the features subsumed under it may become tenuous and metaphorical at best. It should be possible to state what cannot fit and why; other insights should be considered, and what may fit into them as carefully sought.[34]

In short, with respect to any given hypothesis, the linguistic evidence, both positive and negative, should be systematically, rather than merely impressionistically, examined. Whorf's material is, however, largely impressionistic, anecdotal, and illustrative. Therefore it is capable of suggesting his hypothesis, but not of testing it.

THE EXPERIMENTAL EVIDENCE

The critical objections to Whorf's formulations and research techniques which we have cited above do not "disprove" his hypothesis, just as his own efforts on its behalf have not "proven" it. Rather, their consideration in relation to Whorf's work make it clear that attempts at grossly "proving" or "disproving" the hypothesis must be abandoned in favor of meticulous and sophisticated experimental efforts which would "delimit more sharply the types of language structures and the types of non-linguistic behaviors that do or do not show the Whorfian effect as well as [to delimit] the degree and the modifiability of this involvement when it does obtain."[35] In this final section, we consider some of these experimental efforts to specify the hypothesis.

Most of this experimental work has been done in connection with what has been christened the Southwest Project in Comparative Psycholinguistics, conducted with groups speaking Navaho, Hopi, Zuni, Spanish-American, Hopi-Tewa, Tewa, and English. The scholars involved in this project felt that research on the Whorf hypothesis and similar formulations had suffered from methodological confusion and failure to state hypotheses in testable form. The Southwest Project has been designed to alleviate this situation. Its researchers wish to set up experimental situations in which relations between codification, cognition, and behavior can be systematically and meticulously examined. By *codification* they mean all of those aspects of speech behavior which are forced upon the individual speaker by his language, infringement of which would result in defective communication. This includes the phonemic, morphemic, and syntactic structure of the language, as well as its lexicon. For example, if the speaker wishes to communicate about colors, he must employ the color-terms available in his language (and languages will differ in how their color terminology divides the spectrum). He must also follow the grammatical rules by which lexicon items are compounded in his language. By *cognition* they refer to "those representational processes in language users whereby certain stimulus patterns (signs) come to stand for other stimulus patterns (significates),"[36] and regard cognitive processes as functioning in such total activities as perceptual organization, recognition, retention, thinking, concept formation, and problem solving. By *behavior* they mean nothing more than these total activities—perceptual organization (for example, sorting colored yarns into discrete piles), recognition (for example, indicating those color patches, previously shown amongst a larger number), and so forth. The major hypothesis under test is, of course, that these performances will vary as a function of codification of language.[37]

The first of these experiments that we will discuss concerns the color lexicon. The color spectrum is an ideal aspect of the environment to study psycholinguistically because the evidence indicates that human beings perceive it as a continuum, regardless of their language background,[38] whereas color terminologies are categorical and differ notably among different languages.[39] Recent work by Brown and Lenneberg[40] and Lenneberg and Roberts[41] has shown that for English speakers as well as for Zuni speakers, various sections of the spectrum (these sections are different for each language) vary in their *codability*; that is, the ease and unambiguity with which speakers of a given language can name a particular color varies. Some colors are quickly given an identical name by all subjects, which means that their codability is high, whereas other colors have low codability in that they are labeled slowly, variably among subjects, and with phrases and circumlocutions rather than by a single term. The psycholinguistic question asked was whether differences in codability could be related to some independently measurable thought process such as the recognition of colors previously shown to the subject as part of a larger group of colors. It was found that recognition varied directly with codability. Lenneberg and Roberts then compared English and Zuni speakers and found that they differed in their recognition of colors in ways that were predictable from the codability of the colors in the two languages. A rather dramatic example of this can be provided. In English, yellow and orange are the most sharply defined, that is, highly codable, color categories, and, accordingly, English speakers never confused them. The highest recognition scores were associated with these two colors. The Zuni color lexicon, by constrast, does not distinguish between these colors. It refers to them both by a single term. Accordingly, in their recognition task, not a single monolingual Zuni correctly identified either orange or yellow.[42] Furthermore, "bilingual Zunis who knew English fell between the monolingual Zuni and the native speakers of English in the frequency with which they made these errors."[43]

Further experiments connected with the Southwest Project are those of Carroll and Casagrande, who carried out two cross-cultural studies of the influence of certain lexical and grammatical categories upon thought and behavior. In the first experiment, fluent Hopi speakers were compared with a group of English speakers with respect to the classification and sorting of pictures. Using lexical data, the investigators offered the hypothesis that for each of several sets of three pictures, Hopi speakers would more frequently classify a certain subset of two as belonging together (because in Hopi the seemingly dissimilar activities depicted were nevertheless commonly referred to by a single verb), whereas English speakers would more frequently classify a different subject of two as belonging together (because in English a single verb was commonly used to refer to them). While the data that they obtained do not demonstrate a uniform association between "Hopi categorizing responses" and the classifications of Hopi speakers, or between "English categorizing responses" and the classifications of English speakers, they nevertheless do reveal a strong tendency in that direction.[44] The second experiment was concerned with the influence of grammatical categories. The grammatical features of interest to them were the particular verb forms required in Navaho for referring to objects in accordance with such physical attributes as their shape, flexibility, or flatness. The non-linguistic data were the object-classifying actions of their subjects when presented first with a pair of objects which differ from each other in *two* respects (such as color and shape) and then with a third object similar to each member of the original pair in one of the two relevant features. The subjects were asked to indicate which member of the original pair went best with the third object shown them. If their reactions were determined by the Navaho verb form, they would have to select a certain one of the original set of objects. The researchers' hypotheses are stated explicitly:

[a] . . . that this feature of the Navaho language would affect the relative potency or order of emergence of such concepts as color, size, shape or form, and number in the Navaho-speaking child [specifically, that perception of shape or form would, in the Navaho child, develop earliest and increase more regularly with age, since this is the aspect provided for in the verb forms themselves], and [b] that he [the Navaho child] would be more inclined to perceive formal similarities [similarities of shape or form] between objects than would English-speaking Navaho children of the same age.[45]

The investigators assure us as well that the grammatical rules governing the verb stems in question

. . . operate well below the level of conscious awareness. Although most Navaho-speaking children, even at age three or four, used these forms unerringly, they were unable to tell *why* they used a particular form with any particular object. Even when a child could not name an object—or may not have seen one like it before—in most cases he used the right verb form according to the nature of the object.[46]

Their subjects were two groups of Navaho children, one being described as "Navaho-dominant," consisting of subjects who were either monolingual speakers of Navaho or else bilinguals in whom Navaho was dominant over English, and the other as "English-dominant." A further control group was also used, consisting of white middle-class children from the Boston area. In many respects the authors' findings are highly favorable for the Whorf hypothesis: the Navaho-dominant subjects do in fact make the choices predicted on the basis of Navaho verb-stem requirements with a significantly greater frequency than do the English-dominant Navaho subjects. There is, also, a consistent increase in the "Navaho-required responses" as the age of the subjects increases. Thus, although there is far from a one-to-one relationship between language dominance and object-classification behavior, the evidence of these two groups of subjects is quite favorable to the Whorf hypothesis. However, when the data from the white middle-class Boston subjects are considered, some intriguing problems of interpretation appear, for they are even more "Navaho" in their object-classifying behavior than are the Navaho-dominant subjects! This anomalous finding is, however, of great value for "it forces a consideration not only of the absence or presence of linguistic relativity in cognitive processes, but of the degree ('strength') of this relativity as well as of its relative strength in comparison to other factors that may affect . . . cognitive processes in various human groups."[47] It led them to amend their hypothesis as follows:

> The tendency of a child to match objects on the basis of form or material rather than size or color increases with age and may be enhanced by either of two kinds of experiences: (a) learning to speak a language, like Navaho, which because of the central role played by form and material in its grammatical structure, requires the learner to make certain discriminations of form and material in the earlier stages of language learning in order to make himself understood at all; or (b) practice with toys and other objects involving the fitting of forms and shapes, and the resultant greater reinforcement received from form-matching.[48]

This experiment suggests the complexity of testing the linguistic relativity hypothesis by predicting specific behavioral responses. Its results, in conjunction with others produced by the Southwest Project, indicate that language does have some influence upon thought, but show how difficult this influence is to measure and specify.

Some further evidence bearing on the Whorf hypothesis has been gained by use of the semantic differential, a technique for measuring the meaning of words. Concepts such as *mother* or *President Johnson* are rated by subjects in a series of seven-point descriptive scales defined by a pair of opposite adjectives: good-bad, hot-cold, active-passive, sweet-sour, crooked-straight, and so on. For example, if we were interested in the meaning of the English word *man*, we might ask native speakers of English to locate the word in various dimensions of meaning, as defined by certain scales such as:

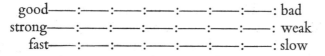

The semantic differential is a method of measurement, not a specific test. Thus the scales and concepts used when this method is employed will vary with the purpose of the investigation. However, research with the semantic differential suggests that there are three primary dimensions in the organization of semantic judgments. These are the *evaluative* (good-bad), the *potency* (strong-weak), and the *activity* (fast-slow) dimensions.[49]

Some of the experimental work on the Whorf hypothesis, as we have indicated, suggests that certain differences in language do produce corresponding differences in thought. But the work of Osgood and others, who have used the semantic differential for the comparative study of such languages as English, Japanese, Korean, Greek, Hopi, Zuni, Navaho, and Spanish, "strongly supports the position that, for certain aspects of cognitive behavior at least, 'world view' may remain relatively constant despite differences in both language and culture."[50] To provide two brief examples from one such study:

If one examines only those cases where there is significant intracultural agreement on a rating, it appears that there is a very high degree also of cross-cultural agreement. Thus in all four groups of informants—Navaho, Mexican-Americans, Japanese visiting students, and American students—over 80 per cent of each group said that BAD was closer to a thick than to a thin line, to a colorless than to a colored circle, to a black than to a white circle, to a crooked than to a straight line. The lowest level of over-all agreement for such items, 86 per cent, was between Navahos and the Anglos.

A second issue was whether the words presented were functionally antonyms in all the groups, that is, whether they were given opposite . . . ratings. For eleven out of twelve of the pairs of English opposites, functional opposition also appeared in all the other groups. The exception was

FAST-SLOW, which in Navaho are adverbial forms which would appear with a description of movement and may therefore both imply movement [and hence would not, presumably, be opposed, as they are in English]. In other cases, the opposition was present but weaker than in English. Thus, in Navaho MAN and WOMAN, and EXCITEMENT and CALM, were not in strong opposition; in Japanese, ENERGETIC and LAZY and, in Spanish, STRONG and WEAK were in least opposition.[51]

The apparent conflict between the findings of Osgood and others can perhaps be resolved if we make a distinction between two general classes of cognition, termed by Osgood *connotative* and *denotative*. Connotative phenomena are general to human groups regardless of language or culture differences, while denotative linguistic phenomena depend on grammatical and vocabulary differences and vary from one language group to another. The meagre evidence available seems to be consistent with this interpretation, which Osgood puts forward merely as a suggestion.[52]

He also offers a number of hypotheses in explanation of these intriguing similarities in connotative systems despite language differences. For instance, the similarity of biological reactions to some situations might result in common emotional reactions. Or, experience general to mankind, such as that of the color and temperature of fire or of water, might engender other common associations—for example, that between the red end of the color spectrum and the sensation of warmth, or between the blue end and the sensation of coldness.[53]

THE PRESENT STATUS OF THE SAPIR-WHORF HYPOTHESIS

Whorf's three main contentions: that language influences perception of direct natural experience, that it creates non-perceptual categories that influence world views, and that it directs social perceptions, have been subjected to varying amounts of testing and so far found to differ widely in validity.

The Southwest Project seems to have established that the first is true—monolingual subjects see or do not see natural objects or conditions, such as color, as their language provides or does not provide the relevant vocabulary. Further experimentation is attempting to show the mechanics of this process.

The second assertion, of powerful linguistic influence on world views, seems to be generally unfounded. A persuasive idea or an intense need for intellectual endeavor in a particular field is well able to overcome linguistic barriers. Not only the comparative evidence cited on the spread of philosophic attitudes across Europe and Asia Minor, but also the fact that modern science and philosophy has emancipated itself from the Aristotelian logic inherent in European languages, seem to disprove any contention that the grip of language on thought cannot be broken.

Whether social perceptions are formed by language has been the least examined contention and is still the most problematic part of the hypothesis.

More research, and especially, more research on specifically designated and separate sections of the hypothesis, is, in fact, needed urgently. From the failure of the Southwest Project and of Osgood's semantic differential research to uncover strong, positive evidence of the effects of language on thought, some students[54] have drawn the negative conclusion that such effects do not exist. In Hymes' opinion, however, the conclusion to be drawn is, rather, that the meticulous study of the problem is so complex and difficult that the time spent to date on the testing and development of instruments for the first experimentally designed field studies of it is obviously insufficient to produce any but exploratory data and the rather tentative conclusions appropriate to them.[55] Further refinements and more rigorous conclusions will result if investigators undertake researches in an attempt to separate specific processes in the language-thought symbiosis.

NOTES

1 Benjamin Lee Whorf, *Language, Thought and Reality*, ed. by John B. Carroll (New York: John Wiley & Sons, 1956).

2 Joshua A. Fishman, "A Systematization of the Whorfian Hypothesis," *Behavioral Science*, V (1960), 323.

3 Franklin Fearing, "An Examination of the Conceptions of Benjamin Whorf in the Light of Theories of Perception and Cognition," in Harry Hoijer *et. al.* (eds.), *Language in Culture*, p. 47.

4 Paul Henle, "Language, Thought and Culture," in Paul Henle *et al.* (eds.), *Language, Thought and Culture* (Ann Arbor: University of Michigan Press, 1958), p. 2.

5 Benjamin Lee Whorf, *Collected Papers in Metalinguistics* (1952), p. 5, cited by Fearing, in Hoijer *et al.*, *Language in Culture*, p. 48.

6 Whorf, *Collected Papers in Metalinguistics*, p. 11, cited by Fearing, in *ibid.*

7 *Ibid.*, p. 49.

8 *Ibid.*

9 *Ibid.*

10 Fishman, "A Systematization of the Whorfian Hypothesis," p. 327.

11 Henle, "Language, Thought and Culture," pp. 8–9.

12 Clyde Kluckhohn and Dorothea Leighton, *The Navaho* (Cambridge, Mass., 1948), p. 204, cited in *ibid.*, pp. 9–10.

13 Dorothy D. Lee, "Conceptual Implications of an Indian Language," *Philosophy of Science*, V (1936), 90, cited in *ibid.*, p. 10.

14 *Ibid.*, pp. 10–11.

15 *Ibid.*, p. 11.

16 *Ibid.*

17 Bertrand Russell, *History of Western Philosophy* (New York, 1945), p. 202, cited in *ibid.*, p. 12.

18 Fishman, "A Systematization of the Whorfian Hypothesis," p. 326.

19 *Ibid.*

20 Lewis S. Feuer, "Sociological Aspects of the Relation Between Language and Philosophy," *Philosophy of Science*, XX, No. 2 (1953), 85–100.

21 *Ibid.*, pp. 86–88.

22 Dell H. Hymes, "On Typology of Cognitive Styles in Language (with Examples from Chinookan)," *Anthropological Linguistics*, III, No. 1, 34.

23 Feuer, "Sociological Aspects of the Relation Between Language and Philosophy," pp. 90–91.

24 Donald E. Walker, James J. Jenkins, and Thomas A. Sebeck, "Language, Cognition and Culture," in Charles E. Osgood (ed.), *Psycholinguistics: A Survey of Theory and Research Problems*, "Memoir 10 of the International Journal of American Linguistics", p. 194.

25 Charles E. Osgood, "Psycholinguistic Relativity and Universality" (unpublished paper prepared for the International Congress of Psychology, Bonn, West Germany, August, 1960), p. 3.

26 Ernst Cassirer, *Philosophie der symbolischen Formen: Die Sprache*, I (Berlin, 1923), 168–69 (Cassirer's source is D. Westermann, *Sudansprachen*), cited in Eric H. Lenneberg, "Cognition in Ethnolinguistics," *Language*, XXIX (1953), 466.

27 Roger Brown, *Words and Things* (Glencoe, Ill.: The Free Press, 1958), p. 231.

28 *Ibid.*, p. 233.

29 Roger Brown and Erich H. Lenneberg, "A Study in Language and Cognition," *Journal of Abnormal and Social Psychology*, XLIX (1954), 456.

30 Charles C. Fries, *The Structure of English* (New York: Harcourt, Brace, 1952), cited in *ibid.*

31 *Ibid.*

32 Whorf, *Language, Thought and Reality*, p. 241, cited in Osgood, "Psycholinguistic Relativity and Universality," p. 4.

33 *Ibid.*

34 Hymes, "On Typology of Cognitive Styles in Languages," p. 37.

35 Fishman, "A Systematization of the Whorfian Hypothesis," p. 337.

36 Walker, Jenkins and Sebeck, "Language, Cognition and Culture," p. 193.

37 *Ibid.*, pp. 193–94.

38 Lenneberg, "Cognition in Ethnolinguistics," *Language*, p. 469.

39 Osgood, "Psycholinguistic Relativity and Universality," p. 4.

40 Brown and Lenneberg, "A Study in Language and Cognition."

41 Eric H. Lenneberg and John M. Roberts, *The Language of Experience* ("Memoir 13 of the International Journal of American Linguistics"; 1956).

42 *Ibid.*, p. 31.

43 Brown and Lenneberg, "A Study in Language and Cognition," p. 461.

44 John B. Carroll and Joseph B. Casagrande, "The Functions of Language Classifications

in Behavior," in Eleanor E. Maccoby, Theodore M. Newcomb, and Eugene L. Hartley, *Readings in Social Psychology* (3d ed.; New York: Holt, 1958), pp. 22–26, cited in Fishman, "A Systematization of the Whorfian Hypothesis," p. 330.

45 Carroll and Casagrande, "The Functions of Language Classifications in Behavior," p. 27, cited in *ibid.*, p. 334.

46 *Ibid.*

47 *Ibid.*, p. 335.

48 Carroll and Casagrande, "The Functions of Language Classifications in Behavior," p. 31.

49 Howard Maclay and Edward E. Ware, "Cross-Cultural Use of the Semantic Differential," *Behavioral Science*, VI, No. 3 (1961), 186.

50 Charles E. Osgood, "The Cross-Cultural Generality of Visual-Verbal Synesthetic Tendencies," *Behavioral Science*, V (1960), 168.

51 *Ibid.*, in an abstract of this paper by Susan Erwin, *International Journal of American Linguistics*, XXVII, No. 3 (1961), 261–62.

52 Osgood, "The Cross-Cultural Generality of Visual-Verbal Synesthetic Tendencies," p. 168.

53 *Ibid.*

54 Joseph H. Greenberg, "Current Trends in Linguistics," *Science*, CXXX, No. 3383 (1959), 1169.

55 Dell H. Hymes, "Linguistic Aspects of Cross-Cultural Personality Study," in Bert Kaplan *et al.* (eds.), *Studying Personality Cross-Culturally* (New York: Harper & Row, 1961), p. 329.

3

JULES J. WANDERER

An Empirical Study in the Sociology of Knowledge

INTRODUCTION

IN PURSUIT OF traditionally defined goals,[1] investigations in the sociology of knowledge typically focus upon *substantive* materials in their examination of the relationship between a social existential base and a mode of thought.[2] This work demonstrates the possibility of supplementing such substantive considerations with materials developed through an analysis of intellectual systems for underlying *structural* dimensions.

The central issue raised here concerns the character of the selected representation of the mode of thought, i.e., the property of the mode of thought that is selected to represent it. In so far as studies in the sociology of knowledge take some substantive property of a mode of thought and seek to understand its social origin, their point of departure is not the mode of thought per se but certain of its substantive properties. Weber, for example, in his discussion of the spirit of capitalism, characterized capitalism substantively: "Nevertheless, we provisionally use the expression spirit of (modern) capitalism to describe that attitude which seeks profit rationally and systematically in the manner which we have illustrated by the example of Benjamin Franklin."[3]

That representations of modes of thought have traditionally been substantive does not preclude the possibility of representing them otherwise. Rather than examine the correspondence of some particular substantive

Sociological Inquiry, XXXIX, No. 1 (Winter, 1969), 19–26. Reprinted by permission of *Sociological Inquiry* and the author.

property of a mode of thought to a social existential base, one might focus upon the structural properties of particular intellectual systems, or "mental productions."[4] It will be shown that new materials for the sociology of knowledge emerge from the examination of intellectual systems for structural commonalities, especially commonalities related to the ways in which demonstrations of proof on intellectual systems are structured.

The view taken here is that just as an intellectual system may be identified in terms of its subject matter, for example, a sociological theory, an economic theory, a philosophical system, or a geometry, certain intellectual systems may also be examined for the manner in which their *proofs are structured*. In so far as the structures of such systems of proof are underlying dimensions, they must be uncovered. Once uncovered, they may be taken as data for the sociology of knowledge. The structural properties of intellectual systems may then be compared one with another for differences and similarities. One may then also pursue the traditional sociological inquiry into the social existential props for such structures of proof and examine both the historical and functional implications of the relationship between society and what is taken as a valid demonstration of proof.

Euclidean geometry, for example, may be understood through an examination of the social existential conditions characterizing Euclid's world. Similarly one may investigate the social existential conditions characterizing Spinoza's time. But what if it could be shown empirically that a significant structural property underlying Spinoza's system of proof and Euclid's system of proof is common to both?

If a common underlying dimension can be empirically ascertained among intellectual systems with content as different as Spinoza's and Euclid's, and if these intellectual systems can be said to be representative of a tradition of thought, i.e., Western thought, then one might conclude that the constituent structural properties of the intellectual systems are also constituent properties of the tradition that issued them. A further generalization suggests itself: the extent to which an intellectual system is taken seriously within the context of a tradition of thought is as dependent upon its substantive properties as its measure of conformity to the prescriptions governing the structure of its demonstration of proof.[5]

This paper reports a unique application of Guttman scale analysis to uncover a common structural property underlying the intellectual work of two renowned thinkers separated by many centuries and distinguished by diverse subject matter: Benedict de Spinoza (1632–77) and Euclid (*ca.* third century B.C.). In so far as Guttman scales have known properties, an intellectual system that can be scaled can be said to possess those properties. The research reported here focuses primarily upon the identification and description of the characteristics of the common structural property.[6]

Briefly stated, Guttman scaling makes possible the generation of an ordinal relationship among qualitatively defined variables if, in fact, a single dimension exists to which the variables are related. The scale, or ordinal relationship, merely orders the variables along the common continuum. The continuum, in turn, has known properties: the variables located along it are cumulatively related, and the continuum is unidimensional.[7]

Unidimensionality is of significant importance in the social sciences. We are often interested in developing scalable instruments that measure some sociological or social psychological dimension, for example, integration. The instrument consists of items that the investigator believes are more or less related to integration. The items should vary from statements highly unfavorable to integration to those highly favorable to integration. A respondent is given that score which represents his total response pattern to all items; the score of twenty-five for example, means that he answered "yes" to all twenty-five items and is therefore distinguished from the respondent with a total score of zero. Any combination of "yes" and "no" responses is possible, and each total score places one respondent in relation to another.

If the items and respondents are related to each other so that they can be ranked from most to least in a systematic and cumulative way enabling a single response to locate the respondent along the dimension, then a Guttman type scale is achieved. The internal reliability of the items (or the extent to which the items hang together along the dimension) is reflected by the fact that they scale. A good scale is composed of items that do so with a minimum of error. Error limits have been traditionally set so that an acceptable scale contains less than ten per cent error.[8]

SCALING INTELLECTUAL MATERIALS

The Guttman scaling technique has obvious application for the examination of an intellectual system in which there are clearly stated propositions to be proved by one or more of a set of items of proof. If the intellectual system can be coded so that each proposition may be identified in terms of the materials that are used to prove it, then the system can be tested for unidimensionality and for the consistency of the cumulative property of its demonstration of proof, that is to say, how well it scales. If the materials scale, then the cumulative property of the demonstration of proof would be seen in the fact that the propositions fall along a continuum from hardest to easiest to prove. It follows that the propositions that are harder to prove would take as proof all of the items of proof taken by propositions that were easier to prove.

The consistent and cumulative utilization of the items of proof to demonstrate a series of propositions must be done rigorously by the thinker because the Guttman scale tests exactly that: the consistent application of the cumulative property of the system along a single dimension. If the intellectual system is predicated upon a demonstration of proof that is multidimensional, it would not satisfy the criteria of Guttman scaling.

In order to use Guttman scaling with intellectual materials, a number of assumptions must be made. To facilitate the mechanics of scaling, it is assumed that propositions in an intellectual system may be viewed as a population of "respondents." Each proposition, in turn, is treated as an individual proposition in the same way as an individual respondent's responses are treated in a conventional application of Guttman scale analysis. Just as each respondent to whom an instrument is administered may be represented by his configuration of dichotomized "yes" and "no" responses to a series of items, so may the individual proposition be represented by its configuration of "takes as proof" or "does not take as proof" responses for each item of proof. An analog is suggested: the respondent responds to a series of items as the individual proposition employs or does not employ "items" for its proof. The resulting matrices are comparable: respondents by items, propositions by "items" of proof.

THE CODING PROCEDURE

In so far as the application of Guttman scaling for the analysis of the structure of proof underlying intellectual systems departs somewhat from the conventional application of that technique, a brief description of the coding procedure employed in the analysis of Euclid and Spinoza is offered here. First, assume that there are only five propositions in an intellectual system; these propositions are numbered *one, two, three, four,* and *five*. These numbers, it should be noted, are merely labels naming the propositions. There are four items of proof employed in the demonstration of proof of the propositional system; these items of proof are lettered *a, b, c,* and *d*.

The substantive presentation of the materials is as follows: *Proposition one* is proved by *item b* and *item d*. *Proposition two* is proved by *items a, b, c,* and *d*. *Proposition three* is proved by *item a* and *proposition one*. It should be noted that *proposition one* is not itself coded as an item of proof, but instead it is represented by the items of proof that were employed in its demonstration, that is to say, the items of proof employed to prove it. Thus *proposition three* may be said to employ in its proof *item a, item b,* and *item d*. *Proposition four* is proved by *item b* and *item d*. *Proposition five* is proved by *item b*. These data may be presented in the following matrix. The symbol *x* denotes employment of the item.

| | Items of Proof | | | |
	a	b	c	d
Proposition one		x		x
Proposition two	x	x	x	x
Proposition three	x	x		x
Proposition four		x		x
Proposition five		x		

This raw data matrix may be treated as conventional materials in Guttman scaling, and both the propositions and the items of proof may be ordered from most to least. In this example, a perfect scale is obtained.

The application of this procedure for the intellectual systems presented by Euclid and Spinoza involves these steps: First, every item of proof is listed. To ascertain the total number of items of proof, every proposition is examined in order to see what the thinker employed in its proof. The items of proof are arbitrarily numbered from *1* to *N*. Secondly, each proposition is examined again to see what the thinker employed for its proof. For those items of proof mentioned by the thinker, the proposition is coded a "yes"; for all other items of proof the proposition is coded a "no."

Certain intellectual systems easily lend themselves to such a representation. Both Euclid and Spinoza, for example, provide the reader with systems of proof composed of unambiguously identified propositions to be proved, and unambiguously identified items of proof. It should be noted that these authors were deliberately selected because their intellectual works required a minimum of interpretative work on the part of the researcher. As will be shown below, the materials presented by each author clearly indicated whether or not a given item of proof was utilized in the demonstration of each proposition. It will be seen that an application of the analytical technique suggested in this paper to less well-structured intellectual systems or to systems presented in narrative form would involve the researcher in difficult coding problems.

SPINOZA

The Guttman scale on the structure of Spinoza's proof was constructed with the materials presented in *Ethics*.[9] These materials consisted of the total population of forty-nine propositions, and eight of the corollaries[10] as the materials to be proved, and thirty-four items of proof consisting of postulates, corollaries, axioms, lemmas, definitions, and propositions pre-viously demonstrated in "Part I." In addition to these items of proof, Spinoza also employed propositions which were themselves demonstrated early in "Part II" in the demonstration of later propositions in "Part II." Proposition I, for example, was used once in a later proof, while the corollary of Proposition XI was used twelve different times. The average appearance of those forty-three propositions that were actually used in the demonstration of later propositions was 2.9.

The demonstrations of proof took a variety of forms. Some propositions in "Part II" were demonstrated with materials from "Part I" only, for ex-ample, Propositions V, VI, and VII; others were demonstrated entirely with materials previously demonstrated in "Part II" themselves, for example, Propositions XXII and XXIII. Most propositions, however, were demon-strated with a mixture of materials, i.e., both previously demonstrated materials and new materials. For example, in his demonstration of Proposi-tion XLIV Spinoza stated:

> Proposition XLIV. *It is not of the nature of reason to consider things as con-tingent but as necessary.*
> Demonstration. It is in the nature of reason to perceive things truly (Prop. 41, pt. 2), that is to say (Ax. 6, pt. 1), as they are in themselves, that is to say (Prop. 29, pt. 1), not as contingent but as necessary.[11]

It is clearly seen that the items used by Spinoza as items of proof in the demonstration of Proposition XLIV included two previously demonstrated propositions and one axiom. Coding Proposition XLIV involved a "yes" for Axiom 6, a "yes" for all of the materials of proof used in the demon-stration of Propositions 29 and 41, and a "no" for all of the remaining items of proof.[12]

The scale thus generated included a total of fifty-seven propositions and corollaries to be proved by thirty-four items of proof. Only those items of proof that were actually used by Spinoza in "Part II" were included in the scale. It should be noted that the construction of the scale conformed to the conventional rule governing removals from Guttman scales, i.e., propo-sitions to be proved operating as respondents were never omitted. The coefficient of reproducibility of this scale was .96.

Since some of the items of proof were employed infrequently, i.e., em-ployed in the demonstration of few propositions, it might be assumed that the resulting small marginals were decreasing scalability and inflating the coefficient of reproducibility. Consequently, those items of proof that were employed less than four times were removed from the scale. The resulting

Guttman scale consisted of fifty-seven propositions to be proved by twenty-two items of proof. Figure 1 shows the scale thus reconstructed. The co-efficient of reproducibility was .955.[13]

It has been shown that the structure of Spinoza's system of proof satisfies the criteria of Guttman scaling. Consequently it may be said that the structural dimension underlying the system of proof is unidimensional and cumulative.

EUCLID

The Guttman scale on the structure of proof employed by Euclid was constructed with the materials presented in "Book II" of the *Elements*.[14] These materials consisted of all forty-eight propositions as items to be proved, and thirteen items of proof-five postulates, three definitions, and five common notions. Each proposition was coded "yes" or "no" for each of the items of proof. If a proposition employed in its demonstration of proof a previously demonstrated proposition, it was assigned all of the materials used to prove that proposition.

The following abstract is part of Euclid's demonstration of Proposition 13 and is included here to illustrate the flavor of the Euclidean materials.

Proposition 13

If a straight line set up on a straight line make angles, it will make either two right angles or angles equal to two right angles.

For let any straight line AB set up on the straight line CD make the angles CBA, ABD;

I say that the angles CBA, ABD are either two right angles or equal to two right angles.

Now, if the angle CBA is equal to the angle ABD, they are two right angles. (Def. 10)

But, if not, let BE be drawn from the point B at right angles to CD; (I. 11)

therefore the angles CBE, EBD are two right angles.

Then, since the angle CBE is equal to the two angles CBA, ABE,

let the angle EBD be added to each;

therefore the angles CBE, EBD are equal to the three angles CBA, ABE, EBD. (C.N. 2)[15]

Proposition 13 was assigned a "yes" for Definition 10, a "yes" for Proposition 11, a "yes" for Common Notion 2, a "yes" for Common Notion 1 (which appears later in the demonstration and is not included in the above abstract), and a "no" for all of the remaining items of proof.

FIGURE 1 SPINOZA

Items of Proof

```
 36 xxxxxxxxxxxxxxxxxxxxxxxx
 28 xxxxxxxxxxxxxxxxxxxxxx
c29 xxxxxxxxxxxxxxxxxxxxxx
 24 xxxxxxxxxxxxxxxxx xxx
c44 xxxxxxxxxxxxxxxxx      x
 23 xxxxxxxxxxxxxxxxxxx
c38 xxxxxxxxxxxxxxxxxxx
c26 xxxxxxxxxxxxxxxxxxx
 47 xxxxxxxxxxxxxxxxxxx
 26 xxxxxxxxxxxxxxxxxx
 29 xxxxxxxxxxxxxxxxxx
 38 xxxxxxxxxxxxxxxxxx
 39 xxxxxxxxxxxxxxxxxx
 46 xxxxxxxxxxxxxxxxxx
 19 xxxxxxxxxxxxxxxxxx
 15 xxxxxxxxxxxxxxxxxx x
 13 xxxxxxxxxxxxxxxxxx
 21 xxxxxxxxxxxxxxxxx
 22 xxxxxxxxxxxxxxxxx
 43 xxxxxxxxxxxxxx           x
 18 xxxxxxxxxxxxxx      x
c17 xxxxxxxxxxxxxx      x
 17 xxxxxxxxxxxxxx      x
 14 xxxxxxxxxxxxxx         x
 12 xxxxxxxxxxxxxx
 20 xxxxxxxxxxxxxx
 30 xxxxxxxxxxxxxx
c 9 x       xxxxxxx
 44 xxxxxxx                  x
 41 xxxxxxx                  x
 49 xxxxxx x
 48 xxxxxx x
c49 xxxxxx x
 34 xxxxxx                   x
 40 xxxxxx
 42 xxxxxx
 11 xxxxxx
c10  x      x x
 45 x      x  xx
 25 x       x x        x
 35 x      x              x
 33 x      x              x
  5 x         xx
  9 x        x x
 32 x                     x
 27 x                 x
 16 x                 x
  6 x         x
  7 x
  8 x
  3        x x xxx
 37          x xx
  2          x xx
  1          x xx
 10  x
 31        x
  4
```

Propositions and Corollaries

FIGURE 2 EUCLID

Items of Proof

```
48 xxxxxxxxxxxxx
47 xxxxxxxxxxxxx
46 xxxxxxxxxxxxx
45 xxxxxxxxxxxxx
44 xxxxxxxxxxxxx
42 xxxxxxxxxxxxx
41 xxxxxxxxxxxxx
40 xxxxxxxxxxxxx
39 xxxxxxxxxxxxx
38 xxxxxxxxxxxxx
37 xxxxxxxxxxxxx
36 xxxxxxxxxxxxx
33 xxxxxxxxxxxxx
32 xxxxxxxxxxxxx
43 xxxxxxxxxxx  x
35 xxxxxxxxxxx  x
34 xxxxxxxxxxx  x
31 xxxxxxxxxxxx
28 xxxxxxxxxxxx
27 xxxxxxxxxxxx
26 xxxxxxxxxxx
25 xxxxxxxxxxx
24 xxxxxxxxxxx
23 xxxxxxxxxxx
22 xxxxxxxxxxx
21 xxxxxxxxxxx
20 xxxxxxxxxxx
19 xxxxxxxxxxx
18 xxxxxxxxxxx
17 xxxxxxxxxxx
16 xxxxxxxxxxx
30 xxxxxxxxxxx
29 xxxxxxxxxxx
15 xxxxxxxxxx
14 xxxxxxxxxx
13 xxxxxxxxx
12 xxxxxxxx
11 xxxxxxxx
10 xxxxxxx
 9 xxxxxxx
 8 xxxxxxx
 7 xxxxxxx
 5 xxxxxxx
 3 xxxxxx
 2 xxxxxx
 1 xxxx
 4         x
 6
```

Propositions

Figure 2 shows the Guttman scale for Euclid's proof. With only six scale errors, the coefficient of reproducibility was .99. It might be noted that modern geometry considers Proposition 4 an axiom rather than a proposition as Euclid did. However, in conformity with Euclid's presentation, the item is treated as a proposition even though it contributes one of the scale errors. Thus the identification of a scale error corresponds to the logical reconstruction of Euclid's system by subsequent mathematicians.

The reader will note that Proposition 6 employed none of the items of proof in its demonstration. Euclid did not demonstrate Proposition 6 as he did the others. As Heath pointed out in an editorial comment, "We have here used, for the first time in the *Elements*, the method of *reductio ad absurdum*. . . ."[16] Proposition 6 is the converse of Proposition 5.

DISCUSSION

The intellectual systems of Euclid and Spinoza conform to the criteria for a Guttman scale. Both systems generate coefficients of reproducibility well above the minimum standard. Consequently, it may be said that both Spinoza and Euclid present unidimensional and cumulative arguments.[17]

The virtue of an intellectual system is in part related to the extent to which it approximates the normative rationality of its time. A thought system is tied to the social existential base in so far as it must utilize in its demonstration of proof the ongoing normatively rational structure of proof. One structural element of Western rationality has been shown to underlie the intellectual work of both Euclid and Spinoza. As representatives of Western thought they both employed lineal demonstrations of proof. Assertions of pre-Grecian arational thought systems[18] suggest the possibility of other normative standards. There is, in addition, some evidence to indicate the more recent use of nonlineal codification.[19]

This paper has delineated as a consequence of empirical inquiry one of the structural components underlying the intellectual work of two representatives of Western thought.[20] The implications for the sociology of knowledge are clear: it is possible to uncover structural regularities characterizing substantively different intellectual systems; it is possible to examine and describe these structural components; it is possible to examine these components in light of their social origins; finally, it is possible to compare structurally different standards of normative rationality using the same methods employed in traditional comparative studies.

NOTES

1 Mannheim noted that "the principal thesis of the sociology of knowledge is that there are modes of thought which cannot be adequately understood as long as their social origins are obscured"—Karl Mannheim, *Ideology and Utopia* (New York: Harcourt, Brace & Co., 1936), p. 2.

2 See, for example, Robert K. Merton, *Social Theory and Social Structure* (Glencoe, Ill.: The Free Press, 1957), pp. 456–88 [most of which appears above, pp. 342–72], especially the "Paradigm for the Sociology of Knowledge," sec. 2b, pp. 343–44, above.

3 Max Weber, *The Protestant Ethic and the Spirit of Capitalism*, trans. by Talcott Parsons (New York: Charles Scribner's Sons, 1930), p. 64.

4 Merton, pp. 343–44, above. The reader will note that I have adopted the terminology "intellectual system" to represent one particular type of mental production or mode of thought.

5 Van Nieuwenhuijze noted that "proof is a flashback from the system to the single fact. An explanation is true, is proven, when a system will 'hold' a fact at its allotted place"— C. A. O. Van Nieuwenhuijze, *Society As Process* (The Hague, The Netherlands: Mouton & Co., 1962), pp. 123–24, note 16.

6 The reader who seeks to pursue the implications of this research for the sociology of knowledge is referred to the works of scholars who have concerned themselves with the problems of lineal codification and process analysis. See Dorothy Lee, *Freedom and Culture* (Englewood Cliffs, N.J.: Spectrum Books, 1959), pp. 105–20, for a discussion of lineal codification; and Van Nieuwenhuijze, *Society As Process*, for a discussion of process analysis.

7 Details on Guttman scaling may be found in various writings, for example, Allen L. Edwards, *Technique of Attitudes Scale Construction* (New York: Appleton-Century-Crofts, 1957), pp. 172–99, to name just one.

8 *Ibid.*, p. 183.

9 Benedict de Spinoza, *Ethics*, "Part II," ed. by James Gutmann (New York: Hafner Publishing Company, 1949), pp. 79–126.

10 The corollaries that were included in the scale employed in their proof different materials than the propositions from which they were derived. If a corollary employed identical materials, it was not included.

11 *Ibid.*, p. 115.

12 Proposition 41 had previously been demonstrated by Proposition 35 and 34, "Part II," and Proposition 29 by Axiom 6 "Part I," Proposition 13 and 27 "Part II." At first glance it might appear that the cumulative property of the relationship among items is strongly determined by the coding procedure adopted. While in a few cases it is found that scale types use identical materials, more frequently scale types are generated by different combinations of materials of proof with similar outcomes (scale types) as a consequence.

13 As a consequence of omitting those items of proof that were employed less than four times, Proposition IV was transformed into a scale artifact, that is, appears in the scale without any apparent proof. The two items of proof employed in the demonstration of Proposition IV were removed according to the above noted criterion.

14 T. L. Heath, *The Thirteen Books of Euclid's Elements*, "Book I, Propositions" (Cambridge, Eng.: The University Press, 1908), pp. 241–369.

15 *Ibid.*, p. 275. In the continuation of this rather lengthy proof, Euclid introduces only one additional item of proof, Common Notion 1.

16 *Ibid.*, p. 256.
17 I interpret the properties of unidimensionality and cumulativeness as evidence of linearity or lineal codification.
18 Van Nieuwenhuijze, *Society As Process.*
19 Lee, *Freedom and Culture.*
20 No attempt has been made to compare the relative merits of different codification schemes although the problems of comparative validity and efficacy are worthy of study.

4

VERNON K. DIBBLE

Occupations and Ideologies

OCCUPATIONAL CULTURES have often been studied seriatim, with more attention to the distinctive features of a particular line of work than to explicit comparisons, and with little concern for the relationships between occupational ideologies and other systems of belief.[1] But since occupational ideologies are virtually ubiquitous, they must have consequences for the acceptance of political doctrines, social creeds, or generalized world views by groups that include the practitioners of different occupations. If highly developed and strongly held, they might limit the variations which are possible in transoccupational ideologies. Or, to take a cue from Durkheim's contention that the *conscience commune* "consists increasingly of ways of thinking and of feeling which are very general and very indeterminate" as organic solidarity becomes more predominant,[2] the existence of countless occupational ideologies in a society might require that class or other trans-occupational ideologies be expressed in a highly abstract form which allows for a variety of interpretations.

Such tendencies might be held in check, however, by the dissemination of occupational ideologies beyond the groups in which they first emerge. The practitioners of an occupation would then share a set of values and beliefs with others. There would presumably be less call for a more abstract system of beliefs under which the ideologies of diverse groups could be subsumed. In other words, one might return to Durkheim's problem—the conditions of cultural consensus in a highly differentiated society—from a rather oblique angle. Instead of asking how the belief systems of different substructures do or do not become linked to an over-all system, one might investigate the

American Journal of Sociology, LXVIII (September, 1962), 229–41. Reprinted by permission of The University of Chicago Press and the author.

conditions under which consensus will or will not ensue from acceptance by some groups of beliefs which had emerged out of the conditions peculiar to other groups. For purposes of this paper, this highly general formulation becomes the question: Under what conditions is an occupational ideology disseminated beyond the occupation in which it is first espoused?

PAROCHIAL AND ECUMENIC IDEAS

Three simple ideas provide points of departure for further propositions. First, people are more likely to become aware of ideas which seem relevant to their problems than of ideas which seem irrelevant, and they tend to adopt those which seem helpful in solving their problems. Second, since people in different occupations pursue different goals and confront different obstacles, they also have different problems. The everyday worries of bankers and of bootblacks are quite dissimilar. Third, people in different lines of work therefore have different views of the life about them that in greater or lesser degree add up to distinctively occupational ideologies.

If these contentions be true, then the ideology of an occupation will not be diffused into other groups unless it contains a high proportion of ideas which are not parochial. The ideas of cabdrivers about "public transportation types" or of professors about the relative merits of teaching and research are examples of parochial ideas. Such ideas are hardly meaningful or important unless one is at least close to the occupation in question.

Somewhat less parochial are ideas which explain and justify an occupation. Lawyers do not stir up trouble. They mitigate conflict by providing orderly procedures. Accountants do not mess up straightforward notions of profit and loss with their esoteric methods. They prevent the nation's business from falling into chaos. Politicians are not out for power. They are practical men who can get things done for the common good.

Such ideas are meant to justify an occupation and its claims. But laymen can always counter with ideas of their own which justify their own occupations. These semiparochial ideas may influence laymen or clients in their dealings with the occupation in question. But it is quite another thing for laymen to bring ideas to the performance of their own roles and to the pursuit of their own goals in a variety of social relationships. For this process to take place, an occupational ideology must include ideas which are ecumenic rather than parochial. That is, must include ideas which are relevant to the concerns of laymen entirely apart from their dealings with the occupation in question.

The legal profession provides an apt example. It has ideas on how to attain justice—and what goal could be more ecumenic than that? Some of these ecumenic ideas are answers to outsiders who question the profession's highly parochial behavior. Lawyers espouse causes in return for money, fight with each other in public, and then leave the courtroom together as friends and colleagues. Since laymen do not act that way, the attorneys' peculiar performance is suspect.

The legal profession explains this parochial behavior by showing its relationship to ecumenic goals. In the long run, it contends, justice is best served if each party to a dispute has the best advocacy he can command. This is possible only if attorneys who accept a case devote themselves unreservedly to their clients' cause. If both sides do so, then more facts, more points of law, and more questions of justice and public policy will be argued than would otherwise be possible. Hence, judge or jury have a more solid basis for making informed decisions.

This idea, clearly, is not parochial. It might be adapted by other institutions. Analogous arrangements are seen in the canonization procedures of the Catholic church. But further examples of institutionalized advocacy are rare. The idea might be taken up by ideologues concerned with justice and civil liberties. But civil libertarian concern with the right to legal counsel is restricted to a small fraction of all cases heard before the courts. When this concern does apply, as in politically controversial cases, it becomes absorbed into rights to a fair trial and to due process. It is not extended to the right to an attorney who will "hypocritically" devote himself without reservation to his client's cause.

This idea is, of course, part of a generalized outlook. Bureaucrats tend to see social reality in terms of a few fixed categories under which recurrent events and permanent situations are subsumed.[3] In contrast, lawyers regard virtually all events as at least provisionally arguable. For, in the legal outlook, there are inevitable discrepancies between general categories and particular events. Analogy, rather than simple subsumption, most accurately describes the way in which categories and events are related to each other in legal thought.[4] And analogies are notoriously arguable. But if neither the particular idea nor the general outlook is limited in relevance to the concerns of a single occupational group, they still do not become widely diffused beyond the profession in which they are held. Particular ideas and general outlooks that are not parochial seem to be a necessary but not sufficient condition under which this process will take place.

SOME CONSEQUENCES OF STRATIFICATION

It is necessary to bring other variables into the argument. One such variable, itself also relevant to the degree of parochialism in an occupational ideology, is the position of an occupation in a society's system of stratification. Osgood and Tannenbaum have shown that a person's acceptance of a "message," that is, of an idea or opinion, is a function of its content, of the recipient's prior attitude toward the object, and of the recipient's prior evaluation of the source.[5] To be concrete, if Eisenhower says that the King of Thailand is a great statesman, or if Louis Armstrong says that the king is a great jazz musician, then, in the absence of any prior images of the royal persona in question, one's acceptance of the message depends upon one's prior evaluations of Eisenhower and of Armstrong, respectively.

The authors cited are interested primarily in the psychology of opinion change. But evaluations of sources of messages vary with the sources' positions within social structures. It is therefore possible to examine the operation of the principles that these authors enunciate as these principles apply in a variety of structural contexts. Their applicability to the position of a "source" in a society's system of stratification is obvious. They suggest that most people will not allow themselves to be tainted with ideas and outlooks which bear the stamp of lowly origin: the downward mobility of ideas proceeds more easily and with greater frequency than their upward mobility.[6]

The relevance of an occupation's rank to our problem is somewhat complicated, however. For certain consequences of high rank erect barriers to the dissemination of occupational ideologies. It would at first seem that these consequences facilitate dissemination. First, higher-ranking occupations are more likely than lower-ranking occupations to have highly developed ideologies. This is relevant to our problem, for surely an ideology must exist before it can be disseminated. Second, the ideologies of higher-ranking occupations are likely to be less parochial than the ideologies of lower-ranking occupations. Each of those contentions can be derived from propositions that are of more general relevance than the problems discussed here and that are valid in diverse areas of social life.

On what grounds can it be maintained that higher-ranking occupations are likely to have more highly developed ideologies than lower-ranking occupations? People do not generally accord equal value to the various positions they hold in various groups and organizations. The value they place upon their affiliation with a given social system varies, among other things, with the rank of their position within that system. As everyone knows, the job of chairman of the board is accorded greater value than the job of janitor. This is true with reference to two different points of comparison. First, within the economy, people in higher-ranking occupations value their jobs more highly than people in lower-ranking occupations.[7] Among the latter, the job is often "a necessary evil to be endured because of the weekly pay check."[8] Second, moving between the economy and other areas of society, people in higher-ranking occupations value their jobs more highly than most other positions that they also occupy, while those in lower-ranking occupations value other affiliations, outside the economy, more highly than they value their jobs. Friendships and other primary-group relationships, for example, are often more important in the working class than in other groups. This difference is indicated in the contrast between the working-class "ethics of reciprocity" and the middle-class "ethics of individual responsibility."[9] A number of other observations bear on the same general issue. The difference between the craft orientation of artisans' unions and the greater class orientation of the unions of lower-ranking workers, and the fact that the most enthusiastic religious sects throughout history have almost invariably been lower-class movements, are both cases in point.

As these diverse examples suggest, those in lower-ranking occupations may not become involved in much of anything at all beyond their immediate circle of primary-group relations.[10] But, if and when they do become involved, in a mass or organized way, their involvement will not have a narrow occupational focus. It may be oriented to class, to religion, or whatever, but not to occupation.[11]

These observations all constitute another way of stating the proposition that the higher the rank of an occupation the more likely it is to have a highly developed occupational ideology. It is possible to derive this proposition in a systematic fashion, simply by bringing together the various considerations just presented. First, a person has more ideas about the problems which are of greater concern to him and fewer ideas about the problems which are of lesser concern to him. Second, the problems posed by more highly valued social positions are of greater concern to the individual than those posed by less salient ones. Third, jobs are more highly valued by those in high-ranking occupations and are less salient to those in lower-ranking occupations. It follows, therefore, that people in higher-ranking occupations develop more ideas about the problems posed by their occupational life than people in lower-ranking occupations. If sheer quantity of ideas measures the degree of development of an occupational ideology, then our initial hypothesis is thus derivable from these three familiar propositions.

The contention that higher rank results in less parochial occupational ideologies can be derived from two propositions. First, ideas addressed to a socially heterogeneous audience are likely to be less parochial than ideas addressed to a socially homogeneous audience. This proposition is implied in Marx's observation that revolutionary classes have to propagate "ideal formulae" because they need a wider base of support than that on which the existing ruling class rests.[12] Second, higher-ranking occupations feel more constrained than lower-ranking ones to address their occupational ideologies to socially heterogeneous audiences. If both of these propositions are true, then it follows that the ideologies of higher-ranking occupations exhibit less parochialism than those of lower-ranking occupations.

First, why should higher-ranking occupations feel more constrained than lower-ranking occupations to address their ideologies to a heterogeneous public? As is well known, rank, power over others, and rewards bestowed by, or extracted from, others go along together. To the extent that a society is held together by consensus and not by force alone, those who do not possess power and rewards call into account those who do. Or those who possess power anticipate the need to legitimize their position in the eyes of those who do not. For where consensus obtains, the unequal distribution of power and rewards is the unequal distribution of values, or of access to values, which are held both by those who are in the higher ranks and those who are not. Those who have rewards from others and who control others must explain to the rest of society why they possess values which others share but are not allowed to enjoy.[13]

Second, the proposition that ideas addressed to a heterogeneous public will be less parochial than those which are not so addressed can be related to the simple contention stated above concerning the relationship between the solving of problems and the acceptance of ideas. Since problems vary with one's station in life, the more heterogeneous an audience the smaller the number of ideas which all or most people in the audience are ready to accept in common. This fact of everyday experience soon becomes known to publicists, propagandists, and the like. Hence, those who want to convince everyone in a heterogeneous audience feel constrained to broadcast ecumenic ideas. This can be done in at least two ways. One can link the parochial goals and claims of a particular occupational group to values held in common throughout a society. This practice is typical of the learned professions. Medicine is a matter of life and death, but the medical profession argues that goals that all men desire are best served if society accords to the profession that privileged position of internal autonomy which it wants. Or, instead of linking parochial ideas to generally held values, one might so generalize the ideas which emerge out of one's occupational subculture as to make them appear applicable to the society at large. This practice is typical of American business. The particular kind of responsibility, and the concomitant ethic of self-reliance and accountability, to which businessmen are subjected has become a generalized ethic, rather than simply an occupational morality for use on the job. Not only the businessman, but others too should be self-reliant and judged rigorously by their objective achievements. Those who are not called to account in the same way are morally inferior to him; politicians, bureaucrats, intellectuals, academicians, reformers, union leaders. If he finds the discipline of the balance sheet an exacting one, he likes to believe that a similar discipline should and ultimately does govern affairs outside the business enterprise. Eventually everyone must be brought to account: those who think otherwise are impractical and immoral.[14]

For example, although government debt and deficit financing often further the economic interests of at least some kinds of business, they are anathemas to the business creed. For they are examples of politicians getting away with practices inconsistent with a particular occupational ideology, generalized so as to apply to political institutions as well as to business firms. The ultimate stage in this process is, of course, "What's good for General Motors is good for the country," or a character named "Industry" in a newspaper advertisement saying "I am the people . . . all my brains and brawn strain for the good of the many . . . I am the American Way."[15]

These, then, are the two ways: one may link the parochial ideas of a particular group to generally held values, or one may generalize parochial ideas so as to make them applicable throughout an entire society. There are interesting differences between these two practices. The first is much closer than the second to the kind of cultural integration which Durkheim envisages in *The Division of Labor*. It implies a more "organic," even *staendisch*, image of society, for it assumes that societies consist of differentiated parts and goes on to claim that the jobs that the whole wants done can best be performed by delegating them to the various parts in which those especially suited to perform them are found. Why the learned professions should adopt this model while business, at least in the United States, uses the second technique is itself an important question. This difference in ideological practice is apparently caused by certain rather striking differences in the individual and corporate positions of businessmen and professionals. The professional man's clients acknowledge their need of him, and their inability to solve their own problems, by seeking him out: the businessman, driven by the need to maximize profits or to maintain a competitive position, must seek out customers whether they need him or not. Practitioners of a well-established profession see their position legitimized by laymen who come to them daily. They feel less need, therefore, to defend their claims by generalizing their parochial outlook into an "American Way of Life." They need only link their parochial ways to generally held values in order to legitimize a limited area of freedom and autonomy. Businessmen, in contrast, cannot rest content with a limited area of freedom and autonomy. Exercising more power in the society, being subjected to greater attack, and having more at stake in the perpetuation of a particular kind of society, they leave almost no area untouched by the generalized business creed.

For present purposes, however, both techniques can be contrasted with the predominance of parochial ideas in the explicit ideologies or in the inarticulate attitudes toward the job among practitioners of lower-ranking occupations. The occupational ideology of crafts, group control over scarce opportunity, demands from others the recognition of certain claims which craftsmen set forth.[16] It does not claim that what is good for bricklayers is good for the country. On the contrary, certain functions which the ideology recognizes as legitimate and necessary, such as the investment of capital at a risk, are left for other people to perform and to think about as best they see fit.[17] Where the job is less meaningful, as among unskilled or semiskilled industrial workers, occupational ideas and attitudes are quite parochial. Chinoy's auto workers "limited their demands in the plant to adequate wages, some measure of security, and the avoidance of physical strain and discomfort."[18] Many of their standards for evaluating jobs were explicitly negativistic: they wanted jobs which were "not too heavy," "not too noisy," "not too dirty," or not too closely supervised, and they wanted to avoid jobs in which one could not smoke or go to the men's room. And, one suspects, those desiderata which are phrased in positive terms, money and job security, are really experienced with a heavy dose of negativism. Money probably means the avoidance of too much debt, just as job security means the avoidance of too much unemployment. These standards indicate how one can perhaps make the best of a bad deal. They are relevant only to the concerns of those who find themselves trapped in similar bad deals. There is a meager stock of ideas in this incipient occupational ideology, and those which do exist are all parochial. The alienation of workers from their jobs has directed their aspirations toward goals which can be realized elsewhere, and to which the weekly pay check is only a means.

The point is not only that the ideologies of higher-ranking occupations are more highly developed than those of lower-ranking occupations, but also that they are more ecumenic. When one adds to these conclusions the contention stated earlier that high rank per se facilitates the dissemination of one's ideas, then it would appear that the ideologies of higher-ranking occupations would often be widely diffused throughout the society.

It was said above, however, that high rank seems to make for the diffusion of occupational ideologies only at first glance. Other processes set in motion by this factor erect barriers to dissemination. The most obvious point is that everything said here about one high-ranking occupation applies to all others. The job is highly valued in all of them. They all have highly developed occupational ideologies. They all attempt to propagate ecumenic ideas in order to convince a diffuse and heterogeneous public. They are competing with one another in matters which are felt to be of great importance and for which highly developed batteries of ideas are ready at hand. The result is the "mild paranoia" in the images which the professions have of each other, or C. P. Snow's two cultures, or the muted suspicion with which the practitioners of the diverse social sciences view one another's work.[19]

Because of the rivalries and suspicions between higher-ranking occupations, the outlook of one will not be accepted by others. And if high-ranking groups are split off from one another ideologically, then there is less likelihood that lower-ranking groups will take over ideas from the ideology of any single high-ranking occupation. For they will receive contradictory, or at least different, messages from on high. Those in the higher ranks may agree on the basic outlines of the society, on morality, motherhood, and the American Way. But since they do not coalesce around any set of ideas from specifically occupational ideologies, lower-ranking groups are beyond their influence so far as these kinds of ideas are concerned. Hence, although higher rank has a direct affect on increasing the likelihood that ideas will be disseminated, and an indirect effect by widening the audience to which they are addressed and by diminishing parochialism, high rank and ecumenic thinking are not sufficient to bring about the wider dissemination of occupational as distinguished from class ideologies.

PRACTITIONERS AND LAYMEN

Clearly, then, something else is needed. A relevant factor is the range of strata and subcultures in the society with which an occupation has dealings. Collectively, lawyers, doctors, teachers, plumbers, and bureaucrats interact with virtually every stratum in society. Professors, interior decorators, astrologers, and governesses interact with people from very restricted subcultures. The greater the diversity of subcultures with which an occupation deals, the wider the range of opportunities it has to insinuate its ideas into other groups. What is more, the more heterogeneous the collective clientele, the less likely it is that the occupational ideology will be parochial. Those who must come to terms with a wide variety of people must adjust their ideas accordingly. But, of course, much more has to be said.

First, the ideologies of many occupations whose practitioners deal with a wide variety of groups are not taken up by others because of the low rank of these occupations. Second, the possibilities indicated above appear likely only in occupations in which the problems of managing people, and not simply the sale and purchase of good or services, is a large segment of the total occupational task. News vendors and their customers encounter no problems in one another, regardless of the attitudes or beliefs held on either side. Third, we must look further into the structural context of interaction between practitioners and laymen.

People in modern societies occupy a number of positions in various groups and organizations, and it is important to note which one of the layman's affiliations is at stake in his dealings with a practitioner. In some cases the layman is pursuing goals which appertain to his most highly valued positions. He might be an industrialist who needs the advice of a lawyer on a business problem or the consent of a banker to a projected expansion. In other cases the layman is pursuing interests and values which do not appertain to his most salient affiliations. He might be a businessman who occasionally goes to a concert. In the former type of relationship there is greater potentiality for the transmission of ideas from practitioners to laymen than in the latter.

Once again we draw upon the proposition that a person's receptivity to an idea varies, among other things, with his prior evaluation of its source. One reason to value another person highly is that the other person is instrumental in the realization of one's own goals. This does not happen, of course, if the instrumental person is of low rank, is subordinate, or is powerless vis-à-vis one's self. In these cases other people become instruments to be wielded, organized, commanded. Where wielding is not possible, however, a high evaluation of the instrumentally significant person is likely to develop. In return for this manifested evaluation, the instrumentally significant person carries out his end of the exchange by acting to further the other's goals. In all occupations both practitioner and client are instrumentally significant to each other in some degree. But sometimes the goals at stake are not important: no one really needs the services of a pedicurist. And sometimes alternative instruments are available: you can tell your troubles to a friend, to a bartender, or to a spiritualist. The elimination of alternative instruments is, of course, an important element in the process of professionalization. When alternative instruments have been eliminated, and when the practitioner is of great instrumental significance to the client's central goals, as held by virtue of his most salient affiliations, then his receptivity to the practitioner's ideas is stronger. Executives of large corporations in twentieth-century America have taken over bits and pieces from the occupational ideologies of engineers, lawyers, accountants, and other professionals on whom they must for certain purposes rely. In the case of "scientific management," for example, executives were influenced by an engineering out-look.[20] If, on the other hand, a variety of instruments is available, or if the practitioner is of lesser instrumental significance, or if the goals at stake are peripheral in the client's life, then the client's receptivity to the practitioner's idea is weaker.

Even through an occupation may provide the only instruments available, and even though its collective clientele may be socially heterogeneous, one must still examine its internal organization. Occupations that are similar to one another in the extent to which their practitioners collectively interact with a wide variety of groups differ in their internal structure. People from every class and subculture are among the clients of physicians. But when one looks at individual practitioners, the picture immediately changes. The physician on Fifth Avenue and the physician on the Lower East Side have very different clienteles. The practitioner with the lower-class clientele has less prestige within the profession. This uncomfortable position can be mitigated if he minimizes his ties with the elites. The elites, in turn, are happy to respond in kind.[21] This process weakens the ideological unity of a profession and makes it less likely to present a united ideological front to outsiders. Moreover, such processes may prevent the occupational ideology from becoming as fully developed as it would be otherwise. Practitioners with different clienteles must adjust to the different milieu in which they work. Those who might otherwise push for particular ideas will be held back, lest they weaken the unity of the professional group which serves to protect the profession as a whole in its assertion of claims, privileges, and rights.[22]

In law or medicine if you can get clients to support you, then you can at least survive. Success in such occupations is not completely determined by organizational superiors or by occupational elites. Where self-employment is more limited, as in science or social work, differences in clientele do not lead to the cutting of ties with the profession and to the consequences outlined above. This is even more true for academicians or bureaucrats who are employed only by formal organizations. Organizations are ranked, to be sure, and one's closest ties are likely to be with colleagues in organizations whose rank is similar to one's own. But the simultaneous existence of organizational and occupational affiliations restrains the tendencies of individuals to become absorbed into their immediate situations and into diverse clienteles.

It is only in occupations where the processes illustrated by the physician with a lower-class clientele cannot take place that the social heterogeneity of the profession's collective clientele is of great relevance to our problem. For only in such professions are practitioners with diverse clienteles prevented from becoming absorbed into the subcultures of their clients. Only with this kind of internal organization are practitioners with diverse clienteles forced to remain in sustained interaction with each other. And only in this way can diversity of clientele have strong influence upon those within the profession, who in turn take their common outlooks back to their relationships with very diverse clients.

Although our discussion has dealt primarily with the point of contact between the practitioners of a given occupation and the potential recipients of their ideology, it has been necessary also to consider the internal organization of occupational groups. For the consequences of the relationship between professional and outsider vary with the internal organization of the profession. The same must also be said of the potential recipients. The consequences of the relationship between practitioners and laymen vary with the kind of social system from which the laymen come. The social position of the recipient becomes especially crucial when one considers the dissemination of generalized outlooks, rather than particular ideas.

IDEAS AND OUTLOOKS

We have thus far done little more than allude to this distinction, but it is an important one. Industrial workers believe that "something would happen" if they complied with the manifest wishes of management by producing and earning as much as an incentive system allows. Spokesmen for management, and some social scientists, have regarded this fear as foolish and unfounded. Here are two particular ideas which contradict each other. Hence, if they used an incentive system to make more money than the foreman, let us say, "something" would indeed have to happen.[23] In the generalized outlook of managers, however, people are classed with machines, capital, land, and raw materials as instruments of production. It is their productive activities, not their structural positions, which are crucial. Since the social structure of the plant is largely taken for granted, the generalized outlook of managers emphasizes purely economic pursuits, torn from the social context in which they take place. Hence, if a worker uses the incentive system to make twice as much money, so what? That's all to the good. There are, in short, particular ideas and general outlooks.

One would expect barriers to the dissemination of ideas to operate even more strongly in the case of outlooks which characterize an ideology as a whole. Ideas are continually bruited about. One can pick them up without necessarily accepting, or without even being aware of, the generalized outlook of which they are a part. They can then be assimilated into one's own outlook. For a particular idea may be congruent with a wide variety of outlooks. The idea that institutionalized advocacy best serves justice in the long run is consistent with a generalized view of the inherent arguability of human events, with a generalized skepticism about human motives, or with a generalized view of the frailty of human reason.

But the extent to which the same outlook can embrace different ideas or the same idea can be assimilated into a variety of outlooks soon reaches its limits. Although the idea that justice is best served by institutionalized and even "hypocritical" advocacy is relevant to the concerns of civil libertarian ideologues, the outlook of which it is a part, or those which it might imply, are not consistent with the outlook of the ideologue. Neither a generalized view of the inherent arguability of human events, nor a generalized skepticism about human motives, nor a generalized view of the frailty of human reason is consistent with the division of human events into those which conform to the true principles of justice and freedom and those which do not. With such outlooks one cannot proceed to *écraser l'infâme*. Though all of the social conditions conducive to the dissemination of an idea be present, the potential recipients of the idea might still resist because it is inconsistent with their general outlooks. People avoid ideas—particular sights—which are inconsistent with outlooks—generalized ways of seeing.

If this is so, then how can outlooks ever be disseminated from one group to another? Life soon wipes out any cognitive *tabula rasa* which the newborn babe might have. One must look to variations in the strength of the social constraints which bind differently situated people to their outlooks; more specifically, to variations in the controls imposed by one's immediate working environment and in the degree of specificity with which adequate performance is defined.

SOCIAL CONTROL AND THE TRANSMISSION OF IDEOLOGIES

The idea can best be stated with reference to two examples. Bureaucrats must continually interact with superiors, with subordinates, and with outsiders in their agency's jurisdiction. The norms which govern these relationships are, in large measure, formally defined. They are defined at least in part by superiors who, in speaking these norms to subordinates and to each other, are acting in terms of their own most central affiliations. Compare this situation with that of free-lance artists, of the *freischwebende Intelligenz*, or, in somewhat lesser degree, of regularly employed academicians. In these positions one's social relationships can be limited for the most part to interactions with others of one's own kind. This fact is variously referred to as Bohemia or as the ivory tower. The role expectations for the occupants of these positions, especially the first two, are vaguely diffuse in our culture.

In the absence of a thought police or a Ministry for Propaganda and Enlightenment, they are not defined by occupants of particular organizational positions. Further, outsiders who define these role expectations—be they purchasers of paintings or trustees of a university—are usually acting in terms of positions which are peripheral within their own range of memberships and affiliations. They may enter into artistic or intellectual circles primarily in search of suitable adornments with which to embellish their more primary statuses. They therefore have less motivation to exert sustained and enduring control. Other controls, to be sure, are not intermittent and are not exerted by people who are acting in their more peripheral statuses. Critics, dealers, and publishers are permanently on the scene.

The point of the comparison holds up, nonetheless. Of the two groups in question, bureaucrats are subjected to more intense and more visible controls in the three respects mentioned: they must engage in more sustained interactions with a wider variety of role partners; the norms governing these interactions are formally defined; those who define the norms are permanently on the scene and are more highly motivated to exert sustained control because in the process of doing so they are performing their main job. The social relationships in which the bureaucrat participates are more tightly structured and more explicitly defined. Differences in cognitive orientations to these relationships are therefore more visible and, so far as these orientations are given normative sanction, are more quickly punished or rewarded.[25]

Since contemporary intellectuals or artists live in more loosely structured environments, the social constraints which bind them to particular outlooks are weaker. Their receptivity to other outlooks is therefore greater. They can act as catalysts, picking up outlooks present in other groups, formalizing or reshaping them, adding rationales of their own, and presenting them in turn to whoever will pay heed.[26]

One may be subjected to close and enduring controls on the job and still be open to extra-occupational influences. This is the case when jobs are "a necessary evil to be endured because of the weekly pay check." Behavioral conformity in such instances greatly exceeds actual internalization of standards imposed by superiors, and alienation from work makes for both a greater receptivity to outside influences and for less of an occupational ideology to stand in the way of these influences.

These points are relevant to the understanding of a wide variety of typically working-class phenomena. Millenarianism or other forms of religious enthusiasm and the "ethics of reciprocity" mentioned above must stem in part from the experience of work as a necessary evil, important largely as a means to the realization of non-economic goals. Similarly, the unending quest for consumer goods—often noted among American workers today—is not a search for symbols appropriate to one's station in life, as defined by one's job. This would be the case with the corporate executive, say, who needs a larger house because he has passed beyond a certain level in the corporate hierarchy. Rather, it appears to be a search for signs of a good life which can be led apart from the world of work. Both proletarian revolutions and the sale of gadgets are furthered by the rejection of occupational life per se and by the concomitant susceptibility to wider identifications.

Numerous studies have shown that members of working classes tend to live within the narrow confines of their own immediate experience. The present argument suggests, however, that their very lack of commitment to occupational life, their alienation from the job, can sometimes make for working-class cosmopolitanism, or at least for gropings toward wider horizons. Millenarianism, revolutionary doctrines, and the new TV set can all, under varying circumstances, take on this single meaning. To the extent that such processes take place, industrial workers share with free-lance intellectuals a greater receptivity to outlooks disseminated from other groups in society. Intellectuals are less subject to sustained control and to specifically defined role expectations: workers are subject to controls in a social system which cannot capture their most basic commitments.

CONCLUSION

When one considers the full range of conditions which brings about the wider dissemination of occupational ideologies, it becomes clear that few occupations in few historical periods meet all the prerequisites simultaneously. The attempt to answer the question posed at the beginning has, in effect, answered a very different question: Why does this wider diffusion take place so infrequently? This is not to say that laymen rarely accept anything at all from occupational ideologies. Most occupations are successful in propagating the images of themselves that they wish others to hold. But these phenomena are slightly beside the point. They are quite different from the acceptance of a generalized occupational outlook by other groups, which, in turn, carry this outlook with them to the performance of their own roles and to the pursuit of their own goals. It is this phenomenon which is extremely infrequent. It has nonetheless been known to happen. In various times and places one finds scientism outside of science, commercialism outside of commerce, and militarism outside the military. In some cases, when a particular occupation is very powerful in a society, its outlook has in remarkable degree been diffused throughout an entire culture—as with businessmen in the United States or professional bureaucrats in Imperial

Germany. Much more frequently, one group picks up a single aspect of another's occupational ideology. Why have social workers taken over the academicians' notion that it is important to do research while nurses, for example, have failed to do so? Why has corporate management, but not governmental or academic management, taken over aspects of an engineering outlook? Answers to these questions would shed light not only on particular occupations but also on the flow of ideas and outlooks throughout an entire society.

NOTES

1 This description does not apply to many studies of occupational cultures. It does apply to such works as the following: Howard S. Becker, "The Professional Dance Musician and His Audience," *American Journal of Sociology*, LVII (September, 1951), 136–44; Fred Davis, "The Cabdriver and His Fare: Facets of a Fleeting Relationship," *American Journal of Sociology*, LXV (September, 1959), 158–65; George Devereux and Florence R. Weiner, "The Occupational Status of Nurses," *American Sociological Review*, XV (October, 1950), 628–43; Ray Gold, "Janitors Versus Tenants: A Status-Income Dilemma," *American Journal of Sociology*, LVII (March, 1952), 486–93; S. Kirson Weinberg and Henry Arond, "The Occupational Culture of the Boxer," *American Journal of Sociology*, LVII (March, 1952), 460–69.

2 Émile Durkheim, *De la division du travail social* (5th ed.; Paris: Felix Alcan, 1926), pp. 146–47.

3 This has been noted by Mannheim, Merton, and others. Cf., *inter alia*, James G. March and Herbert Simon, *Organizations* (New York: John Wiley & Sons, 1958), p. 39.

4 Edward H. Levi, *An Introduction to Legal Reasoning* (Chicago: University of Chicago Press, 1949), pp. 2–4.

5 C. E. Osgood and P. Tannenbaum, "The Principle of Congruity and the Prediction of Attitude Change," *Psychological Review*, LXII (1955), 42–55.

6 Evidence for this contention and certain necessary qualifications are found in Elihu Katz and Paul F. Lazarsfeld, *Personal Influence: The Part Played by People in the Flow of Mass Communications* (Glencoe, Ill.: The Free Press, 1955).

7 Cf., e.g., Table 1 in Alex Inkeles, "Industrial Man: The Relation of Status to Perception, Experience, and Value," *American Journal of Sociology*, LXVI (July, 1960), 1–31.

8 Ely Chinoy, *Automobile Workers and the American Dream* (Garden City, N.Y.: Doubleday & Co., 1955), p. 130.

9 Albert K. Cohen, *Delinquent Boys: The Culture of the Gang* (Glencoe, Ill.: The Free Press, 1955), pp. 89, 96–97.

10 Genevieve Knupfer, "Portrait of an Underdog," *Public Opinion Quarterly*, XI (Spring, 1947), 103–14.

11 Although direct extrapolations from experimental groups to larger social systems are often misleading, it might be noted that this contention is consistent with experimental findings reported by Harold H. Kelley. He reports that "the more unpleasant is a

position in a hierarchy, the stronger are the forces on a person to communicate task-irrelevant content, this holding true whether the communication is directed to one's own level or to the other level" (in "Communication in Experimentally Created Hierarchies," in Dorwin Cartwright and Alvin Zander [eds.], *Group Dynamics: Research and Theory* [Evanston, Ill.: Row, Peterson & Co., 1953], p. 460).

12 Karl Marx and Friedrich Engels, *Werke* (Berlin: Dietz Verlag, 1958), III, 47–48.

13 On some of these points, cf. Sigmund Diamond, *The Reputation of the American Business-man* (Cambridge, Mass.: Harvard University Press, 1955), pp. 176–82.

14 Francis X. Sutton, Seymour E. Harris, Carl Kaysen, and James Tobin, *The American Business Creed* (Cambridge, Mass.: Harvard University Press, 1956), p. 352. The point which follows, concerning government debt and deficit financing, is also taken from this source.

15 From an advertisement of the General Cable Corporation, in *The New York Times*, April 18, 1952, quoted in *ibid.*, pp. 35–36.

16 This characterization is taken from Selig Perlman, *A Theory of the Labor Movement* (New York: Augustus M. Kelley, 1949). Perlman, writing in the 1920's, felt that he was describing the outlook of all "manualists," but he tended to extend the outlook of artisans to workers in general.

17 *Ibid.*, p. 239.

18 Chinoy, *Automobile Workers and the American Dream*, p. 83.

19 On the "mild paranoia," cf. Theodore Caplow, *The Sociology of Work* (Minneapolis: University of Minnesota Press, 1957), p. 131.

20 For a brief discussion of the relationships between executives and professionals and of the ways in which the thinking of executives has been influenced by these relationships, see Robert Aaron Gordon, *Business Leadership in the Large Corporation* (Berkeley: University of California Press, 1961), pp. 258–66. (This work was first published in 1945.)

21 Cf., e.g., Joe L. Spaeth, "Industrial Medicine: A Low-Status Branch of a Profession" (unpublished Master's thesis, University of Chicago, 1958). Industrial physicians are affiliated with few hospitals and only with the less prestigeful ones. They are socially peripheral to the profession in various other ways and, concomitantly, are ideologically defiant as well. Spaeth finds that their view of their practices is more commercial and less professional than in the profession as a whole.

22 Some of the processes mentioned here are analyzed for the legal profession by Karl Llewellyn in "The Bar Specializes—with What Results?" *Annals of the American Academy of Political and Social Science*, CLXVIII (1933), 177–92.

23 This point was suggested by William J. Goode in a private communication.

24 This statement refers, of course, to one variety of "cognitive dissonance" (see Leon Festinger, *A Theory of Cognitive Dissonance* [Evanston, Ill.: Row, Peterson & Co., 1957]).

25 The notion of "tightly" and "loosely" structured social systems was presented by the late John Embree in his analyses of Thai society and was developed by Bryce Ryan and Murray Strauss in "The Integration of Sinhalese Society," *Research Studies of the State College of Washington*, XXII (1954), 179–227. Although the notion is used here in a slightly different sense, the suggestion by Ryan and Strauss that loosely structured systems are more susceptible to cultural influence from the outside and that these influences are less disruptive in loosely structured than in tightly structured systems is similar to the argument stated here.

26 This discussion should be compared with Mannheim's treatment of "The Sociological Problem of the 'Intelligentsia,' " in *Ideology and Utopia*, translated by Louis Wirth and Edward Shils (New York: Harvest Books, 1936), pp. 153–64. This discussion is in part a restatement of Mannheim's distinction between those who "have their outlooks and activities directly and exclusively determined by their specific social situation" and those who are "enabled . . . to develop the social sensibility that was essential for becoming attuned to the dynamically conflicting forces."

5

MELVIN SEEMAN

Intellectual Perspective and Adjustment to Minority Status

IN THE STUDY of the consequences of social marginality, two opposed, though not mutually exclusive, viewpoints find clear expression: on the one hand, that marginal status is a misfortune involving inescapable psychological penalty; and, on the other hand, that substantial good may flow from the fact of marginality. This paper adopts the latter view, and presents empirical evidence bearing on the possibility of such positive consequences.

The significance of this evidence lies partially in the fact that the negative view is now so dominant in the literature. One could document at length Riesman's contention that "we tend all too often in social science to look at the punishing aspects of such phenomena as alienation, marginality and social mobility."[1] The theme which emerges from this negative view is nicely put by Jessie Bernard at the outset of her paper on "biculturality"; "There is no happier fate for any man than to live his life in a culture never challenged, a culture he is never called upon to justify; to eat and speak and dress and pray without ever realizing that there are other ways of doing these simple things."[2]

Though the negative stance toward marginality is more abundant and powerful in impact, the alternative view has, nevertheless, a respectable history: Park, Simmel, and Veblen are among those who have stressed the potential good that may issue from the fact of marginality. Simmel, for example, treats the "stranger" as a marginal person, and one consequence of this marginality is the "objectivity of the stranger":

Social Problems, III (1956), 142–53. Reprinted by permission of The Society for the Study of Social Problems and the author.

He is not radically committed to the unique ingredients and peculiar tendencies of the group and therefore approaches them with the specific attitude of "objectivity." But objectivity does not simply involve passivity and detachment; it is a particular structure composed of distance and nearness, indifference and involvement. . . . Objectivity may also be defined as freedom: the objective individual is bound by no commitments which could prejudice his perception, understanding, and evaluation of the given.[3]

In a sense, Simmel and Veblen are the points of origin for the thesis advanced here. Our thesis is that marginal status (in the present case, the position as Jew in a Gentile world) provides the opportunity for the development of perspective and creativity in the realm of ideas, and that the realization of this opportunity depends upon the individual's adjustment to marginality.[4] We incorporate, in what follows, both Simmel's view of the marginal person as one who is uniquely equipped to challenge the "givens" in society; and Veblen's view that the marginality of the Jew, in particular, has been an important factor in his emergence "as a creative leader in the world's intellectual enterprise":

It is by loss of allegiance, or at the best by force of a divided allegiance to the people of his origin, that he finds himself in the vanguard of modern inquiry. [Such intellectual enterprise] presupposes a degree of exemption from hard-and-fast preconceptions, a skeptical animus, *Unbefangenheit*, release from the dead hand of conventional finality. The intellectually gifted Jew is in a peculiarly fortunate position in respect of this requisite immunity from the inhibition of intellectual quietism. But he can come in for immunity only at the cost of losing his secure place in the scheme of conventions into which he has been born, and at the cost, also, of finding no similarly secure place in that scheme of Gentile conventions into which he is thrown.[5]

We are not here interested in the question of whether the Jew has, as Veblen argues, contributed "more than an even share to the intellectual life of modern Europe"; but in the question of whether marginality of any kind (using the Jews as a clear case in point) can be one of the conditions for the development of intellectual perspective. Our guess was that a successful experience with marginality increases the likelihood of high perspective. The guess is one which can be rationalized as a simple learning phenomenon: the individual whose attempt to accommodate to the conflict in values which marginality imposes is reinforced by success will, by the same token, learn the value of (and technique for) questioning "givens" and seeking new solutions.

INSTRUMENTS, SCORING PROCEDURE, AND SAMPLE

To test such a notion, we developed two major instruments for use with a Jewish sample. One of these was an Incomplete Sentences Blank (ISB) composed of twenty-eight stems to be made into sentences by the respondent. Fourteen of the stems were Jewish-relevant in content (e.g., "Jewish radicals . . ."; "Passover . . ."); and fourteen were neutral stems ("I regret . . ."; "I secretly . . ."). The neutral and Jewish stems were alternated, with the neutral stems providing an index of general personality adjustment as distinct from adjustment to minority status.[6]

The second instrument consisted of six brief descriptions of problem situations. The subjects were asked to "state and discuss your reaction to such a situation in *twenty-five or more words.* Each situation dealt with a controversial issue involving multiple-value viewpoints from which the social conflict might be approached. The first of these six items is reproduced here in full:

> Legislators, parents, and professional educators have been concerned about the menace of comic books to children. Many communities are searching for a way of handling this problem, with censorship being a key issue. What stand would you take in this issue? Why?

The remaining five situations dealt with enforcement of the Supreme Court's desegregation ruling, interreligious dating, homosexuality in athletics, a legitimate but unwanted child being put up for adoption, and Communist authorship of a physics text used in high schools.

The responses to these six situations were scored on a five-point "Scale for the Measurement of Intellectual Perspective." The scale is intended as an index of creativity in intellectual approach, where "creativity" is defined essentially as "the capacity to make the given problematic." Thus, scale point 1 is used for responses which treat "values as standardized givens"; and scale point 5 for responses which treat "values as experimental emergents." But since these two rather cryptic definitions of the end points of the scale were hardly enough for scorers to use in judging responses to the situational items, a set of descriptions of each of the five positions on the scale was worked out. Those descriptions are presented as Figure 1.[7]

The three descriptions were intended for clarification only: each situational item received one score—a score which, as we proceed from 1 through 5, represents an increasing degree of readiness to entertain an uncategorical, multiple-value perspective toward situations which are inherently complex. The respondent's total score on intellectual perspective was simply the sum

FIGURE 1

A Scale for the Measurement of Intellectual Perspective

	Scale Point 1	2	3	4	Scale Point 5
1. *Scorer judgment*	A given value, alternative, or position taken as obviously right, unconditional, categorical. Shows no awareness of the relevance of multiple values to the situation. *Treats values as standardized givens.*	Shows awareness of other positions and values; but clear commitment to one.	Recognizes the legitimacy of other positions in spite of own commitment; the "undecideds" also go here.	Shows clear evidence that alternatives are possible for him; that under different conditions, different choices may be made; that multiple values are involved in decision.	Seeks a creative alternative which synthesizes the viewpoints possible. *Treats values as experimental emergents.*
2. *Inferred thought process*	"X is the only possible right way."	"I think X is right; but I know some people think Y is right."	"I think X is right; but after all you have to take into account that some people hold to Y and they may have some justification for their view."	"I think you have to weigh the values that may be involved from a number of points of view, and realize that your decision is not an absolute choice but relative to the situation; under the circumstances I choose X; but I can conceive of myself choosing Y, and my choice is a choice of relative goods."	"I think there are a number of right ways of dealing with this, and a number of important values involved—the job is to find a solution that may go off the beaten path and may in the process set a new standard without sacrificing any one good for another."
3. *Presumed behavior tendencies*	*Behavior is a function of standardized right answers.*	*Behavior is a function choice between tenable and untenable alternatives (the latter being considered in some degree but rejected).*	*Behavior is a compromise between a "right" position and a legitimate minority view not personally subscribed to.*	*Behavior is a function of seen multiple ends which may be served in complex social situations.*	*Behavior is a function of the search for new solutions where multiple tenable values are involved.*

of his six item scores. To minimize contamination, each of the six items was scored independently.

"Minority maladjustment" and "conflict" scores were derived from the responses to the ISB. The fourteen neutral items of this test were scored for "conflict" on a seven-point continuum, according to the method described in the Rotter manual.[8] Scoring was performed by an advanced graduate student in clinical psychology.

The individual's maladjustment to minority status was obtained by scoring the fourteen Jewish-relevant stems of the ISB on a five-point scale.[9] Here, only the end-points of the scale were defined; the scale as used by the judges appears in Figure 2. The total score on minority maladjustment is an index of the extent to which the individual responds to his minority position with efforts at escape and denial (assimilationist responses) or at defense (chauvinist responses), as against a positive acceptance of the fact of marginality without overreaction to stereotypes. The view of adjustment embodied in this scoring borrows heavily from Lewin's analysis of self-hatred among Jews[10] and from Clement Greenberg's essay on Jewish chauvinism.[11] Lewin was concerned almost exclusively with the individual who manifests escape tendencies, but Greenberg argues that this overly anti-Jewish adjustment may be matched on the other side by the so-called "positive Jew" who "asserts, seeks out, and revels in his Jewishness." About this type, Greenberg says:

> But what do I see when I take a longer look? That the Jewishness of so many of these "positive" Jews is truculent and very sensitive to criticism; and that it is also aggressive and uncharitable; that it points to itself too challengingly and has too little patience with conceptions of Jewishness other than its own . . . It is this absence of ease that makes me suspect that a certain familiar psychological mechanism is at work here. By projecting it upon others and attacking it violently in others, these "positive" Jews may be exorcizing from their own consciousness an image of the Jew that is no less "negative" than that in the mind of the most cringing "assimilationist."[12]

The description of minority adjustment given in Figure 2 attempts to put these conceptions to work in empirical fashion. The view of adjustment which the scale represents clearly involves certain value premises—as, for that matter, does the "conflict" scale and, indeed, any measure of maladjustment. So long, however, as these premises are clear, and the scoring derived from them reliable, the reader may judge for himself how far he wishes to go in accepting the implications of the data presented in the following section.

A total of seventy usable protocols was obtained from a fairly diversified

FIGURE 2

A RATING SCALE FOR MINORITY MALADJUSTMENT

	Scale Point 1	2	3	4	Scale Point 5
1. *Identification with Jewishness*	Jewishness not categorically rejected; but accepted with neither belligerence nor defensiveness				Categorical identification, or categorical rejection (by way of idealizing of Jewish membership and associations; or rejection of "bad" Jews)
2. *Treatment of stereotypic qualities*	Stereotypes of either own group or outgroup are not accepted as adequate basis for response: there is qualification; causal review; speculation; search for the meaning of differences, rather than outright acceptance or rejection of stereotypes				Stereotypes are accepted with no qualification as the basis for response, either by way of approval or disapproval of the quality seen
3. *Conflict over Jewishness*	Openly discussed; or takes the form of admitted difficulties to be positively and rationally assessed				Denial of conflict; or exaggeration of personal doubt or persecution

sample of respondents. The original plan was to distribute the questionnaires to a random list of persons contributing to the United Jewish Appeal in the city of Columbus, Ohio. It quickly became clear, however, that an adequate return could not be achieved in this way, partly because of the length and difficulty of the instruments. Out of a total of 100 questionnaires distributed to the random list, only twenty complete forms were returned. The following groups were then personally contacted and their aid enlisted: two groups of members of Jewish women's organizations; a social club and an evening class at the local Jewish Center; and a student group meeting at the university center for Jewish students. The returns from these groups averaged 64 per cent, a total of eighty-seven questionnaires having been distributed among them.[13]

TABLE 1

INTER-SCORER AGREEMENT AND SPLIT-HALF RELIABILITIES OF THE MINORITY MALADJUSTMENT, INTELLECTUAL PERSPECTIVE, AND CONFLICT SCALES

	Inter-Scorer Correlations		Corrected Split Half Reliability**	
	N	r	N	r
Minority maladjustment	72	.73	72	.79
Intellectual perspective	18	.68	75	.86
Conflict	*	*	53	.73

* Since considerable material is already available on the reliability of "conflict" scoring, and since the judge in this case was thoroughly familiar with the use of the Rotter manual, no multiple judging for "conflict" was attempted.
** The correlation between odd and even halves of each test was corrected by the Spearman-Brown prophecy formula.

The reliability of judgments, as well as total score reliabilities in the conventional sense, are always a primary question in work of this kind, where open-ended material is scored. The agreement among independent judges and the corrected split-half reliabilities for the three major scores are presented in Table 1. All of the available evidence indicates that the judgments and the scores used here have a satisfactory reliability.

RESULTS

The correlations of primary interest—those among the three main variables of minority maladjustment, intellectual perspective, and conflict—are

TABLE 2

CORRELATIONS AMONG MINORITY MALADJUSTMENT,
INTELLECTUAL PERSPECTIVE, AND CONFLICT SCORES
(*N*= 70)

	Minority Maladjustment	Intellectual Perspective
Intellectual perspective	− .44[*]	—
Conflict	.03	.03

[*] Significant at the 1 per cent level of confidence.

presented in Table 2. They show first a significant inverse association, as we anticipated, between minority maladjustment and intellectual perspective. The "highs" in minority maladjustment, who have not solved the problems which their marginality imposes, are low in intellectual perspective; while the "lows," who have experienced marginality and resolved it, are high in intellectual perspective. Second, they show no association between conflict and minority maladjustment, indicating that the minority score is a fairly specific index of the individual's reaction to marginality rather than a measure of general personality adjustment.

Since our thesis is that successful experience with marginality, not personality conflict in general, is a crucial factor in the development of perspective, the independence here established between the two measures is important. It is an independence, too, which makes considerable sense on logical grounds, since the sources of personality conflict are so varied, and so often unconnected with marginality (as in the case of many intrafamily difficulties, for example). At any rate, we discover here that conflict and minority maladjustment are independent, and that the latter, not the former, is significantly tied to intellectual perspective.[14]

Beyond this bald statement of relationships, however, several important considerations remain. It might be asked, for example, whether the correlation of − .44 between minority maladjustment and perspective is consistent from item to item in the perspective scale. The correlations of minority maladjustment with responses to each item of the perspective scale are given in Table 3, where considerable consistency in association with all items is indicated. This consistency is all the more notable when we recall that the six items of the scale were scored "blind"—i.e., the consistency is presumably not a function of scorer "halo."

TABLE 3

CORRELATIONS BETWEEN MINORITY MALADJUSTMENT
SCORES AND ITEM RESPONSES ON INTELLECTUAL PERSPECTIVE
(N= 70)

Item Number	Item Content	r
1.	Comics and the problem of censorship	− .49*
2.	Enforcement of desegregation	− .27**
3.	Adoption of unwanted children	− .32*
4.	Inter-religion dating and marriage	− .32*
5.	Homosexuality in athletics	− .36*
6.	Communist authorship of physics text	− .25**

*Significant at the 1 per cent level of confidence.
**Significant at the 5 per cent level of confidence.

A more crucial question, however, is whether the relationship between minority maladjustment and intellectual perspective holds regardless of the schooling, occupational level, or age of the respondent. The relevant *r*'s needed for partial correlation are given in Table 4, and the partial correlations themselves in Table 5. The relationship between minority maladjust-

TABLE 4

YEARS OF SCHOOLING, OCCUPATIONAL PRESTIGE, AND
AGE OF RESPONDENTS CORRELATED WITH MINORITY
MALADJUSTMENT AND INTELLECTUAL PERSPECTIVE
(N= 70)

	Minority Maladjustment	Intellectual Perspective
Years of schooling	− .35*	.43*
Occupational prestige**	− .22	.35*
Age	.14	− .21

*Significant at the 1 per cent level of confidence.
**Prestige scores were obtained by rating the respondent's occupation (or husband's occupation) by reference to an extended North-Hatt scale. (National Opinion Research Center, "Jobs and Occupations," in *Class, Status, and Power,* ed. by R. Bendix and S. M. Lipset [Glencoe, Ill.: The Free Press, 1953], pp. 411–26.)

TABLE 5

PARTIAL CORRELATIONS BETWEEN MINORITY MALADJUSTMENT
AND INTELLECTUAL PERSPECTIVE WITH SCHOOLING,
OCCUPATIONAL PRESTIGE, AND AGE HELD CONSTANT
($N = 70$)

Variable Held Constant	Partial Correlation	"t" Value
Years of schooling	− .34	2.983★
Prestige	− .40	3.545★
Age of respondent	− .43	3.877★

★Significant at or beyond the 1 per cent level of confidence. The significance of partial *r* was computed according to the procedure described in McNemar. (Q. McNemar, *Psychological Statistics* [New York: John Wiley & Sons, 1949], p. 227.)

ment and intellectual perspective remains quite stable when the influence of these three possible "hidden factors" is eliminated. In all three instances, the key correlation retains its statistically significant character. This does not demonstrate, of course, that minority adjustment *causes* high perspective, but it seems clear that there is *some reliable relationship* between the two.

In order to explore more fully the nature of that relationship, the total sample was divided into four adjustment types: assimilationists, chauvinists, ambivalents, and adjustors. In scoring the Jewish-relevant items, all responses which deviated from the adjustment end of the scale, and which could be clearly typed as assimilationist or chauvinist in tendency, were so designated. Responses were scored "assimilationist" when they reflected the premise that Jewish differences are the root of the minority's troubles and these differences should, therefore, be done away with. For example, in completing the stem "Jewish doctors . . . ," one respondent wrote: "Seem to judge each other by the amount of money they make." Chauvinist responses, by contrast, reflect the premise that Jewish differences are either inherently superior or require extravagant defense. In response to the same stem, "Jewish doctors . . . ," a characteristic chauvinist response was: "Are very brilliant." Thus, a given response might be scored "3—chauvinist," while another, equally indicative of maladjustment, might be scored "3—assimilationist."

The "chauvinist" type category was made up of the seventeen respondents scoring highest on minority maladjustment in the chauvinist direction; similarly, the seventeen highest scorers in the assimilationist direction constituted the "assimilationist" category. Two of the more ambiguous cases were omitted to provide equal *n*'s in an analysis of variance design. Then the seventeen lowest scores on minority maladjustment were labeled "adjustors," and the remaining seventeen cases, neither low in maladjustment nor conspicuously high in either a chauvinist or an assimilationist direction, were termed "ambivalents."

The mean scores and standard deviations for each of these types on the three major variables of perspective, conflict, and minority maladjustment are presented in Table 6. The data on minority maladjustment are given for

TABLE 6

MEANS AND STANDARD DEVIATIONS OF SCORES ON
INTELLECTUAL PERSPECTIVE, CONFLICT, AND MINORITY
MALADJUSTMENT, BY ADJUSTMENT TYPE

Adjustment Type	N	INTELLECTUAL PERSPECTIVE		CONFLICT		MINORITY MALADJUSTMENT	
		Mean	S.D.	Mean	S.D.	Mean	S.D.
Adjustors	17	4.76	1.80	4.35	1.97	1.24	1.00
Chauvinists	17	2.71	1.32	4.76	2.01	6.18	3.88
Assimilationists	17	4.23	2.65	5.76	2.01	5.82	2.09
Ambivalents	17	3.76	2.42	4.24	1.99	4.35	1.28

purposes of inspection only (the breakdown into types being itself dependent upon this score), and these data may be dismissed with one comment. The mean scores on minority maladjustment vary as the selection procedure dictates—i.e., the adjustors are low, while the chauvinists and assimilationists are high—but it is notable that the chauvinists and assimilationists are equally high in maladjustment.

It is, however, the perspective and conflict scores in Table 6 which are of greatest interest. Both the means and the standard deviations for "intellectual perspective" vary widely among adjustment types. The standard deviations, in fact, turned out to be significantly different at the 5 per cent level of confidence, and it was necessary to apply a square root transformation to the original perspective scores to meet the conditions for an analysis of variance among adjustment types. With the data thus transformed, an analysis of variance was conducted to determine whether the adjustment types differ significantly in intellectual perspective. The resulting "F" ratio of 1.935 does not reach a statistically significant level.

As far as perspective is concerned, therefore, there are two outcomes of this analysis by type. Although, apparently, the four types do not differ significantly in their average level of intellectual perspective, there are differences among types in the amount of variation in perspective (i.e., in the clustering or spread of scores). In this light, the data of Table 6 are suggestive. The assimilationists score substantially the same as the adjustors in intellectual perspective, but their scores are the most variable of the four types. The chauvinists, on the other hand, do have the lowest score on intellectual perspective,[15] and, at the same time, their scores vary the least. Our sample here is quite small, given the four-way typology; but there is a sense, it seems, in which Greenberg may be perfectly correct in his doubts about the "positive" Jewish adjustment. Judged, at least, in terms of consequences (and here intellectual perspective is viewed as one such consequence), the chauvinists are not only the poorest in perspective, but they are homogeneously so.[16]

If we look, now, at the data on "conflict" in Table 6, the pattern found in the over-all correlations is repeated in the analysis by types—i.e., the pattern of no association. The standard deviations do not differ significantly, nor are there significant differences of means among the four adjustment types. Apparently, general personality conflict is consistently unrelated to the main issues in our analysis.

THE PROBLEM OF "INAUTHENTICITY"

One further type of scoring was attempted. For each respondent, a "conversion" score was computed, indicating the number of times a neutral stem on the ISB was completed with Jewish-relevant material. With fourteen neutral items, the theoretical range of this conversion score was from zero to fourteen; the obtained range was from zero to twelve. The engaging aspect of this score, as with all indirect measures, is that the respondent has little opportunity to "manipulate" his replies, since the the very existence and meaning of the score is relatively hidden.

It is difficult to give a definitive label to the conversion score, but one way to describe it is through the concept of "inauthenticity," a notion first introduced by Sartre. For Sartre, "what characterizes the inauthentic Jews is that they deal with their situation by running away from it; they have chosen to deny it..."[17] This is only one form of "inauthenticity," however. The more general referent of the term is *overreaction to the occupancy of a given status*.

An adequate general definition of "overreaction" is, of course, difficult to provide, but instances of it point fairly clearly to the phenomena that "inauthenticity" is intended to cover: the female scientist who guides her behavior as scientist (e.g., in a discussion of physical principles) by letting her position as a woman intrude into the decision as to what she should or should not say; or, more pertinently, the Jew who guides his behavior by the stereotype of the "bad Jew," and reveals extreme sensitivity to the behavior of other Jews.[18]

The conversion score represents an effort to explore empirically this idea of inauthenticity conceived as overreaction to status position. Viewed in this way, the extremes in conversion are of major interest, since it is possible to "overreact" in two ways: to evade the issue of one's Jewish status by permitting no overlap between the neutral stems and the relevant stems; or to overassert, by allowing the fact of Jewishness to determine response to all of the items regardless of their neutrality.

The question, then, is whether the conversion score—taken as a measure of inauthenticity—is significantly associated with degree or type of minority maladjustment. We would not anticipate, however, simple straightline relationships, since the extreme cases of conversion (whether low or high) are seen as being more alike, insofar as inauthenticity is concerned, than the middle group who convert to some extent. As one would guess, following this logic, the linear r's between conversion and the three major variables in this study are quite low and statistically insignificant: the correlation of conversion with intellectual perspective is .09; with minority maladjustment, .03; and with conflict, .21. Nor, on the other hand, was there a significant departure from linearity of relationship, a departure that the logic of the argument *would* lead us to anticipate in the case of minority maladjustment and intellectual perspective. The correlation ratio between conversion and intellectual perspective was .33; between conversion and minority maladjustment, .36. Neither of these ratios reaches the .05 level of significance,

TABLE 7

MEANS AND STANDARD DEVIATIONS FOR CONVERSION SCORES,
BY ADJUSTMENT TYPE

Adjustment Type	N	Mean	S.D.
Adjustors	17	1.59	1.75
Chauvinists	17	2.29	2.98
Assimilationists	17	1.88	2.08
Ambivalents	17	1.06	1.35

though the trend of the relationship in both cases is in the expected direction (high and low conversion associated with high maladjustment and low perspective).

The analysis of conversion scores by adjustment types was based upon the information in Table 7. As with the perspective scores, the conversion data show no difference in mean scores for the several types (again, using transformed data), but the standard deviations are significantly different at the 5 per cent level of confidence (chi square = 8.895). These results conform to expectation, in that there is no sure ground (where conversion extremes are equally inauthentic) to anticipate *mean* differences, but there is ground for expecting the spread of scores on conversion to vary. It is notable that the two groups which show the widest spread are the chauvinists and the assimilationists, the two groups which, on a priori grounds, are most likely to be "inauthentics."

These results on "conversion" tell us very little of a substantial nature about the relation of inauthenticity to minority maladjustment or intellectual perspective. As exploratory results they may nevertheless be important, for two reasons. First, they do suggest that the concept of inauthenticity can be usefully explored as an aspect of minority life. With a larger sample (where the correlation ratios, for example, would be less suspect due to a small number of cases in some of the arrays) and with supplementary information by way of interviews, there is ground for hope that this concept, heretofore a vehicle for the essayist, may be made empirically productive. Second, the consistency of some of the findings on conversion (where the respondent was totally unaware of the meaning or existence of the measure) with the results given earlier in this paper suggests that we are not dealing here with a fictitious association between minority maladjustment and perspective produced by the simple fact that some of our respondents are "sharper" than others in guessing what a "good" response is on the two instruments developed in this study.

CONCLUSION

No one would assert that this work has verified the assertions by Park, Simmel, Veblen, and others about the positive consequences of marginality. We have, at best, made these assertions more plausible. At the same time, we have laid out some tools and directions for further inquiry.

Such inquiry is surely one of the crucial tasks in the sociology of knowledge since it bears directly on the relationship of social position to creativity in intellectual work. There are many kinds of marginality—including national, sexual, religious, economic, and a host of other brands. We need, especially in these days when conformity rather than creativity is the rule, to examine with care, as well as with hope, any doctrine which directs our attention to such marginalities as potential sources of insight and perspective.

NOTES

1 D. Riesman, *Individualism Reconsidered* (Glencoe, Ill.: The Free Press, 1954), p. 159.

2 J. Bernard, "Biculturality: A Study in Social Schizophrenia," in *Jews in a Gentile World*, ed. by I. Graeber and S. H. Britt (New York: The Macmillan Co., 1942), p. 264.

3 Georg Simmel, *The Sociology of Georg Simmel*, ed. by K. H. Wolff (Glencoe, Ill.: The Free Press, 1950), pp. 404, 405.

4 This same view has been nicely put by Riesman: "our problem becomes one of seeing what positions in society are conducive, more or less, to insight and choice. Whether marginality fosters insight and choice depends, of course, on the given case. Marginality can freeze people with anxiety or nostalgia, while the absence of marginality can give people so much power that they need not choose, but can make all the other people choose" (in *Individualism Reconsidered*, p. 163).

5 T. Veblen, *Essays in Our Changing Order* (New York: Viking Press, 1934), pp. 225–27.

6 The original form of the ISB, with thirty-eight stems, was developed by Milton Feiner and used by him in a master's thesis. (M. Feiner, "Adjustment to Minority Group Status and Perspectival Freedom" [unpublished master's thesis, The Ohio State University, 1953].) The neutral stems were modeled after the items in the Rotter Incomplete Sentences Blank, a test designed to measure personality conflict. (J. B. Rotter and J. Rafferty, *Manual for the Rotter Incomplete Sentences Blank* [New York: Psychological Corporation, 1950].)

    I wish to express my special thanks to Mr. Feiner, who served as one of the judges for the Jewish-relevant responses—a laborious and difficult task, indeed, since it involved over 1,000 individual judgments on seventy-two protocols. I am indebted also to Mr. Walter Mischel for the judgments on the "neutral" stems, and to Mrs. Frances Mischel for the major share of scoring and computation on this project.

7 The spiritual items and the perspective scale were worked out in collaboration with Mary L. Bach, who used this scale in a master's thesis. (M. Bach, "The Relationship Between Measurements of Self-Insight and Value Perspective" [unpublished master's thesis, The Ohio State University, 1955].)

8 Rotter and Rafferty, *Manual for the Rotter Incomplete Sentences Blank*.

9 In this case, and in the scoring of conflict, responses were scored over the entire protocol on the theory that the meaning of the relatively short item responses could be better assessed with the total group of responses in view. This procedure represents, in a sense, a calculated risk of contamination in the interests of surer meaning for brief responses.

10 K. Lewin, *Resolving Social Conflicts* (New York: Harper & Bros., 1948), pp. 186–200.

11 C. Greenberg, "Self-Hatred and Jewish Chauvinism," *Commentary*, X (November, 1950), 426–33.

12 *Ibid.*, p. 427.

13 We have, obviously, no measure of marginality, but we assume that by the very nature of the sample, we are dealing with individuals who have had to come to terms in some

fashion with their marginal status as minority members. There are a number of problems which cannot be adequately discussed in this limited space, and one of these is the unclarity of the concept of marginality itself. We use it here as essentially synonymous with minority position, where minority is defined as a group against which categorical discrimination is practiced, and where, by implication, the minority individual is oriented toward the differing norms of both the minority and the majority group, while the full rewards of both are not accessible.

A second problem which cannot be explicated lies in the perspective scale. This scale, being oriented toward the individual's treatment of values, concerns only one kind of intellectual perspective. Further, we do not mean to imply that the behavior that we have labeled as scale point 5 is always the most desirable. This is a situationally relative matter; there are presumably times and circumstances in which "creativity" is not a functional response.

14 Feiner's results (in "Adjustment to Minority Group Status and Perspectival Freedom"), based on a sample of sixty-six Jewish respondents, are rather consistent with the data given in Table 2, but there are some important differences. He used the well-known "F" scale as his measure of intellectual perspective. Feiner reports an r of .72 between "F" and minority adjustment. This correlation is considerably higher than the r given here, though consistent in direction. Between conflict and minority maladjustment his correlation was .37 (significant at the 1 per cent level), while the obtained r between conflict and "F" was .27 (significant at the 5 per cent level). It was largely because of our dissatisfaction with the use of the "F" scale to measure intellectual perspective that the scale described above was developed.

15 Bernard, "Biculturality," p. 271.

16 The leads provided by this analysis are not dissipated when the three relevant control variables of age, occupational prestige, and education are brought into the picture. A comparison of the four adjustment types on these variables indicates the following: (a) for all three variables the standard deviations among types are homogeneous; (b) for age and occupational prestige, there are no significant differences of means among types; and (c) for education, the mean differences among types are significant at the 5 per cent level ($F = 3.918$), but the comparison of greatest interest here, that between assimilationists and chauvinists, yields a critical ratio which is not significant ($t = 1.854$).

17 Jean-Paul Sartre, *Anti-Semite and Jew* (New York: Schocken Books, 1948), p. 83.

18 Rinder and Campbell have analyzed some of the very real difficulties, both moral and conceptual, which the term "inauthenticity" presents. Their view is closely allied to the one presented here. At one point, for example, commenting on the Greenberg article ("Self-Hatred and Jewish Chauvinism"), they say: "In this insightful and perceptive essay, Greenberg has tried to show how both the Jewish chauvinist and the Jew manifesting self-hatred share the same motivational anomaly; namely, the behavior of both suffers from over-reference to the fact of their Jewishness." (I. D. Rinder and D. T. Campbell, "Varieties of Inauthenticity," *Phylon*, XIII [December, 1952], 271.)

6

DENNISON NASH

The Ethnologist as Stranger: An Essay in the Sociology of Knowledge

IF WE WERE to look at the culture of cultural anthropologists from their own point of view the custom of the field trip would appear very close to the culture focus (see Chapple, 1952: 341–42; Hart, 1947; Mead, 1952; Nadel, 1951: 20–24).* We would note that the manifest function of this ordeal is to provide data for scholarly analysis, the latent, to facilitate passing from one status to another. Concerning the objectives of "good" field work, our anthropologist informants might refer us to the sayings of the culture hero, Boas, who insisted that anthropologists should obtain from intimate association with a people a thoroughgoing, objective account of their culture (Boas, 1938: 666–86). Should we inquire further we would find that anthropologists, like other human beings, rarely attain their ideals in practice and that they are increasingly aware of the impossibility of doing so. Field trips, some of them know, must be conducted by humans; humans are, inevitably, biased; therefore, total objectivity is impossible in field work (see Nadel, 1951: 48–55). A clear, if somewhat embarrassing, demonstration of this dictum has been given by the anthropologist Bennett (1946), who has noted and analyzed the divergent views of the same (Pueblo) cultural reality by different field workers.

The proper way for scientists to deal with bias, as Nadel and others have

* Full documentation of sources cited in the text and notes of this chapter may be sound by referring to the appropriate entry in the Bibliography, pp. 484–87, below.—Eds.

Southwestern Journal of Anthropology, XIX (Summer, 1963), 149–67. Reprinted by permission of the *Southwestern Journal of Anthropology* and the author.

pointed out, is not to ignore it nor shove it under the rug, but to declare it and try, by understanding its sources, to diminish it (Nadel, 1951: 48–55). One important possible source of bias in anthropologists is the anthropological community itself. The novice anthropologist is recruited into and trained by a group with a particular formal and informal ideology which, to a greater or lesser extent, he absorbs and carries with him into the field. Another possible source of bias is the field situation, more specifically, the role which the ethnologist must play in it.[1] This essay is devoted to an analysis of the influence of this role on the ethnologist's point of view.

One way of approaching the problem of the influence of the field role on the ethnologist's viewpoint is to consider him to be faced with a problem of adaptation. How well or ill he adapts to the condition of his field role may determine what he sees, how he thinks, and therefore the nature of his report on the people he has studied. How may the most general role which the anthropologist plays in the field be described? The hypothesis of this essay is that the ethnologist in the field is a stranger, that he faces the problem of adapting to this role, and that the objectivity of his field report will, through the mechanisms of perception and cognition, reflect the nature of his adaptation. The discussion will be organized around a series of questions: What are the conditions of the stranger's role in the ideal-typical case and how do they tend to influence one's perception? How close does the role of ethnologist in the field approximate this ideal-typical case? If the ethnologist may be called a stranger, what is the nature of his adaptation to the role and what are the implications of this for his point of view?

THE STRANGER'S ROLE

Though each man is a stranger to every other, the degree of strangeness quite obviously varies from one relationship to another. Only a few social relationships would approach the acme of "nearness" and "farness" that Simmel, in his classic discussion of the stranger, accepts as strange. Speaking in the ideal-typical sense, Simmel (1950:402) says that "strangeness means that he who . . . is far is actually near." The optimum combination of spatial proximity with social distance, though produced at other times, is particularly evident when an alien has just entered the life space of an established group. Because he has come within the group's boundaries he must be recognized in some way by group members; but because he does not share those qualities which constitute the group's unique identity, because he brings foreign qualities into the group's space, he becomes a stranger. His strangeness will prevail until he acquires the necessary group qualities, i.e., some kind of acceptable frame of reference and behavioral repertoire that will enable him to be a regular member in good standing, or until he leaves. He is destined to be considered strange, to feel strange, and to experience the pressures of this position as long as he remains in sociological limbo between groups.

When Simmel (1950: 402) suggests that the stranger "has not quite over-come the freedom of coming and going" he gives a clue to what may be the most fruitful perspective for examining the stranger. The role of stranger is played at a particular point in time by a person who usually is on his way from one social location to another. It would be highly artificial to fix him in time and space, since he is not fixed in reality, The stranger as a person who is coming and going has a history, and it would appear difficult to obtain a satisfactory picture of his unique condition without resorting to this history. Seen from the diachronic point of view, what does the progress of the stranger look like?

Strangers begin as travelers, i.e., subject to displacement in space, time, and social position. Though there usually is some selection of travelers, let us for the moment consider one who is about to embark to be an average citizen of some home population, i.e., one who has effected some kind of average adjustment to it. What is likely to happen to this average citizen when he goes abroad?

All humans require group living in order to survive. Besides the necessary assistance derived from a division of labor, most of us need continual reinforcement by a group in which we are a member to hold on to that coherent frame of reference which seems to be necessary for mental well-being.[2] But travel inevitably cuts the traveler loose from his traditional bearings. He is cast adrift from traditional social controls and much of his activity may be understood in terms of the emotional state which frequently accompanies the loss of such controls. The extreme experience derived from the conditions of travel is the impression of vastly increased possibilities which leads to feelings of both pleasure and anxiety—the specific emotional state depending on the personality of the traveler.[3] All humans must adapt to the external world if they are to survive. Their adaptation is mediated by a frame of reference. Now, since the external world is changing for him, the traveler must re-orient himself. While he is a traveler and when he puts into some port and becomes a *bona fide* stranger, one of his problems is to create or maintain some frame of reference which will be both externally and internally adaptive.

To his hosts the newcomer is largely an unknown quantity. They see him and may have to deal with him, but usually they know little about him as a person. On the basis of what little evidence they have about him the hosts usually put him in some familiar category of persons such as enemy, missionary, tourist, trader, prophet. The stranger may or may not think of himself in these terms, but they constitute part of the initial social reality which he faces. How "powerful" a reality it is depends on the relative power of the hosts in their relations with the stranger.

The stranger is still very much "at sea" upon his arrival. The kaleidoscope of impressions he receives tend to load his experience with incongruity or ambiguity. The fairly stable perceptual scheme which heretofore has mediated between his needs and the external world is threatened by such conditions, and the stranger becomes increasingly concerned with extracting meaning from his experiences. The adaptable stranger will learn to organize his experiences more and more in terms of the realities of the new situation. He not only will become familiar with his surroundings, but he will, through the necessity of "taking the role of the other" in his transactions with hosts, tend to incorporate elements of their point of view. This occurs in cases of extreme conflict or discrimination. Minority immigrant groups, for example, who are kept down and out by the hosts, still have acquired host values.[4]

As the stranger's point of view moves inexorably in the direction of host norms, it might be supposed (especially if he is favorably received) that he feels an increasing affinity with them. The paradox is that he does not. As he becomes more like the hosts he feels (up to a certain point) more of an outsider. His greater familiarity with the hosts and their ways tend to make him more aware of the gulf which separates him from them. Where at first he may have thought that he could negotiate the distance between him and the hosts in terms of his home culture, the task may look more and more hopeless. At home some solution could be worked out simply by comparatively minor changes in one or the other party within culturally outlined limits. Now it becomes a matter of changing whole cultures within unknown limits. As the stranger discerns that the hosts with whom he deals are acting with the weight of a cultural heritage behind them, he begins to pass consciously into the limbo of marginality which will prevail until he either becomes a full-fledged member of the host group or departs.

What is the general character of the social condition in which the stranger exists throughout his progress, i.e., what are the general conditions of his role? Pre-eminent among them are normlessness and alienation. The stranger is an outsider in a world (for him) of ambiguity, inconsistency, and flux. The concept of anomie, originally used by Durkheim and later elaborated by other sociologists, seems to be an appropriate general term to apply to this situation. Though this novel experience may be in itself pleasurable, the ideal-typical situation of the stranger seems more likely to lead in the direction of anxiety, which in turn may elicit a number of psychological reactions.[5]

The term "culture shock" has been coined to refer to the negative effects on the individual of his experience as a stranger. Though it has achieved considerable popularity, its empirical referents still are not clear, and though its scope of explanation in the case of the stranger is no broader than of anomie it has no connections with a more general theory (see Cleveland, Mangone, and Adams, 1960; 26–45). For these reasons the concept of anomie is preferable for describing the conditions of the stranger's role, but the literature on culture shock is valuable for illustrations of this aspect of the stranger's progress.

What are the likely perceptual reactions to the condition of anomie inherent in the stranger's role? The average citizen at home has developed a more or less stable adaptive frame of reference which mediates between his needs and the external conditions of his society. When he becomes a stranger he is faced at the outset with a rapid and often incomprehensible change in external demands while his internal requirements remain nearly constant. Successful adaptation means that he must eventually change his frame of reference—and possibly his internal requirements as well—in the direction of the hosts' viewpoint. How much he must change and how readily he negotiates the transition will depend on the nature of the specific stranger-situation and the personal and other resources he brings to it.

The typical initial response of strangers is to assert the more valuable elements in the habitual frame of reference derived in part from their home reference group and to deny incongruous or threatening stimuli. They respond by denying what does not fit their preferred hypotheses and emphasizing what does. This reaction has been found in a number of experiments of the type carried out by Bruner and Postman (1949), in a small group experiment by Nash and Wolfe (1957), and in observations of travelers abroad. Such a response may be "socialized" by two or more like-minded strangers who form an enclave which becomes a kind of home away from home. This group, by developing what is in fact an adaptive division of labor, by providing a practice area, and by serving as a therapeutic haven, may tend to make the problem of individual adaptation less difficult.[6] With time, the norms of such an enclave (if it is adaptive) will, as in the case of the adaptive individual, tend to move in the direction of host group norms.

Various hostile reactions may accompany the stranger's initial response or appear shortly thereafter. The individual's inevitable frustrations in all areas, including the perceptual, may cause him to blame the external world, particularly the hosts. Thus, subjects who are confronted by incongruous stimuli in psychological experiments begin to find fault with them (see

Bruner and Postman, 1949). Travelers will complain about the conditions of their existence and the character of their hosts.[7] When these hosts appear strong such hostility may be turned inward and lead to the kind of Rorschach responses that DeVos (1961) has noted among people undergoing acculturation.

Through the remainder of his career, even if he is in a "fortified" enclave such as the one that Forster (1924) depicts so masterfully in *Passage to India*, the stranger probably will extend and deepen his contacts with the hosts and their culture. For the average citizen this process probably is more frustrating than rewarding. From the point of view of the stranger, as Schütz (1944: 506) notes, the host culture is "not a shelter, but a field of adventure, not a matter of course, but a questionable topic of investigation, not an instrument for disentangling problematic situations, but a problematic situation itself and one difficult to master." The structure of life which is in large part taken for granted by the hosts must be built up piece by piece by the stranger. It is unlikely, therefore, that he ever can establish the kind of organic connections with the host group which would develop by being socialized in it. The fact that he is ever an outsider may account for the objectivity of the stranger which Schütz (1944: 506) and Simmel (1950: 405) have noted. These authors undoubtedly are correct if they mean that the stranger looks at the hosts and the world from outside. If, however, by objectivity they mean an unbiased attitude, they would (if the stranger is an average citizen) seem to be wrong. The condition of anomie inherent in the stranger's role is unlikely to permit this. Rather, in such an anxiety-provoking situation one would expect an average citizen to develop and maintain strong, inflexible, "black and white" views and to display "perceptual sensitivity" and "perceptual defense" in keeping with them. If his anxiety were extreme, marked perceptual disorganization should result.[8] The stranger should become intolerant of the ambiguous experience which derives from the conditions of his role. As used by Frenkel-Brunswik (1949), "intolerance of ambiguity" means that he would tend to resolve his perceptual difficulties by constriction and rigidity. Some evidence exists in favor of this hypothesis, though it is far from conclusive. At least two studies (Roberts and Rokeach, 1956; Srole, 1956) have shown that people who score higher on Srole's scale of anomie (which is supposed to measure feelings of isolation from others) tend to be more authoritarian (and therefore, presumably, more "intolerant of ambiguity"). Now if subjective feelings of anomie are positively correlated with external conditions such as those found in the stranger's role, then the "authoritarian" perceptual reaction, intolerance of ambiguity, should be characteristic of strangers who have been average citizens.[9]

Let us suppose that the above hypothesis is correct. What specific form will the constrictive perceptual reaction take in strangers? Authoritarians tend to be conforming individuals, which suggests that they will tend to cling to the norms of the groups in their life space. In the usual case of the stranger these are the home and the host groups. It is to be expected, then, that the stranger's constrictive response will tend to polarize in the direction of home or host reference group norms, or both, and that he will cling to them with the desperation born of anxiety.[10] In Bennett's terms (1946), they will show approach or avoidance reactions in regard to their hosts.

FACTORS IN INDIVIDUAL ADAPTATION

The important parameters in the stranger's adaptation are the compatibility of home and host cultures, his treatment by the hosts, his relative power, the presence (or absence) of an enclave, and his own potential for adaptation.[11] So far it has been assumed that the cultures involved are quite incompatible, that host treatment of the stranger varies, that the stranger may be more or less powerful than they, and that he must effect an adaptation without the assistance of an enclave. Considering such situational factors as given, what may be said about qualities in the stranger's personality which may facilitate or retard adaptation?

Though the hypothetical stranger in this discussion is assumed to have been an average citizen in his home society, this is rarely the case in real life. In compulsory military service abroad or mass migrations, average citizens may be frequent, but most strangers do not appear to meet this assumption (see, e.g., Cleveland, Mangone, and Adams, 1960: 8–25). Clearly, there are "selective" factors, both voluntary and involuntary, operating to recruit people who travel abroad. The question of whether or not such selection produces individuals who are capable of adapting to their roles as strangers has barely been tapped by empirical research. Probably the selective process is not quite so dysfunctional (for Americans) as the parade of barely disguised horrors in *The Ugly American* (Lederer and Burdick, 1958) would indicate. One important project in evaluating the congruence of selection and adaptation of strangers is the identification of those personal qualities which facilitate adaptation to the stranger's role. Are there types of people who are particularly adaptive?

Social isolation or alienation and normlessness dominate the stranger's experience. An adaptive individual would take such experience as a matter of course. He would be able to cope with the conditions of the stranger's role without undue personality strain. Nash and Schaw (1962–63) in their study of Japanese immigrants in Cuba have identified two kinds of adaptive personality. One, the Transitional Man, brings with him personality traits which are compatible with the norms of a specific host group. These enable him (if situational factors are favorable) to fit quickly into the host group. He does not long remain a stranger. The other, the Autonomous Man, has the flexibility of personality which permits him to adapt rapidly to host norms or to remain in the limbo of marginality. His characteristic approach to the world may be described as detached involvement; his frame of reference is tolerant of ambiguity—he does not resort to "authoritarian" closure. The Autonomous Man is the ideal-typical stranger because he can negotiate short- or long-term strangership under the broad conditions that we took to be given. It may be such a man as he whom Schütz and Simmel had in mind when they spoke of the stranger's objectivity. The Autonomous Man is subject to very little bias by the conditions of any stranger's role. Ethnologists are supposed to be objective when they are in the field. If they can be counted as strangers, then, the problem will be to see to what degree they share the personal qualities of the Autonomous Man. If they share such qualities, the field situation as a source of ethnological bias may be minimized.

THE ETHNOLOGIST AS STRANGER

In the Golden Age of ethnology (the time of Franz Boas) it was customary for the ethnologist to pass through his ordeal by field work alone in some primitive society. More recently, underdeveloped and civilized societies have become approved objects of study, but the ideals of the anthropological community still refer to the primitive or archaic, and wholehearted acceptance has been reserved to those scholars who have "done" one such society (Dozier, 1955; Mead, 1952: 344; Nadel, 1951: 1–19). A career and a reputation may hinge on the ethnologist's brief (usually no more than a year-and-a-half) participation in the life of one of these societies. In making the jump from a civilized to a primitive situation, in establishing rapport, and in attempting to acquire fairly complete data on the culture in a few months, the ethnologist encounters an extreme condition of strangership which lends a "do or die" atmosphere to his expedition. For few other strangers is the adaptive problem so extreme, and for a few does so much hinge on successful adaptation.

Paul (1953: 442) points out that the aim of the field worker is "to gather and relate two sets of data, a description of the situation as he sees it, looking from the outside in, and a description of the situation as the native sees it, looking from the inside out." In this description he should strive to be as objective as possible. The ideal is to cover the whole culture in depth. In doing this he should let all the facts have their say, check them where possible, and not systematize them too quickly. This is a normal enterprise in social science, but the ethnologist must carry it out under extraordinary conditions which, for the average citizen, would lead in the direction of the "authoritarian" perceptual solution or possibly total disintegration. Other social scientists study humans, have their problems with cultural differences, personal bias, time limitations, mutual "impression management," and maintaining a precarious balance between participation and detachment, but for few others are adaptive difficulties raised to the point where their influence on perception becomes a significant problem.[12]

A great many specific adaptations, great and small, are required of the stranger-ethnologist. Climate, terrain, or the conformation and movements of heavenly bodies may be very different. He must survive bouts with exotic germs and learn to deal with new flora and fauna. The possibility of accident or sickness will increase, but if he is stricken he probably will not have access to western therapeutic procedures. His contacts with the hosts must expand if he is to do his job, and each new contact raises the problem of not only individual, but cultural, differences. Ethnologists have different opinions about how "forward" one may be in such proceedings, but, whether they go fast or slow, their mission imposes certain limitations on the ultimate *rapprochement* between the ethnologist and the people he is studying. As Paul (1953: 431) says, "The game of mutual understanding takes place within a field of restricted possibilities. The ethnologist's choices are limited by the range of role adaptations he is willing and able to play, as well as by the range of roles the natives find acceptable." The ethnologist ought to participate widely and deeply in the life of the hosts yet maintain the independence of decision necessary to chart the most effective avenue of penetration and the detachment necessary for objectivity. He seeks to belong in order to understand, but he must be an outsider if he is to remain an ethnologist (Paul, 1953: 435, 437). In short, the picture of the ideal field worker is very similar to Simmel's stranger (1950: 405), in whom the qualities of nearness and remoteness give the character of "objectivity." It is doubtful, however, that such objectivity (in the sense of unbiased perception) may be attained without extraordinary personal qualities.

Our knowledge about ethnologists' experiences in the field and their relations to them is severely limited by what appears to be a non-autobiographical tendency in the only possible source of such information, i.e., the ethnologists themselves. A fairly broad range of experience, both frustrating and rewarding, and positive and negative mental states are reported, but no systematic appraisal of the field experience as seen by the ethnologists themselves is possible with the evidence at hand.[13] There are two possible reasons why ethnologists do not publish very many auto-biographical accounts of their experience in the field: (*1*) They are hiding experiences which are significant to the validity of their report (and thus are a bunch of conscious or unconscious conspirators). (*2*) They experience nothing which they conceive to be significant to the validity of their report (and thus are superadaptors, not given to introspection, or both). Enough evidence exists to suggest the second alternative as an hypothesis. More specifically, it will be argued that the validity of the ethnologist's report is not greatly influenced by the field experience, because he is adaptive to the role of stranger, and therefore his perception is not seriously distorted by field conditions.

THE ETHNOLOGIST AS ADAPTOR

Ethnologists *are* biased. Bidney (1953), for example, has pointed out that they manifest a "romantic cultural pluralism." This tends to put them on the side of the people they study rather than their home society (see Lévi-Strauss, 1961: 381–92). In Bennett's terms this means that they would tend to be "approachers" rather than "avoiders" in regard to their hosts. In this essay the question is how much of this bias is due to the influence of the role of ethnologist-stranger. In the case of the average man we should expect a constrictive reaction which would polarize in terms of approach to, or avoidance of, host group norms. But anthropologists, as anyone who has associated with them knows, are not average citizens. Do their special attributes include qualities which will enable them to adapt to their role in the field?

Because authoritarian tendencies are strengthened in the stranger's role, and because these are inimical to the kind of perceptual adaptation which the ethnologist-stranger should achieve, the adaptive ethnologist ought to be non-authoritarian. Let us look first to see how he meets this criterion, then the broader criteria of the Autonomous Man who is also a social scientist. The values of the modern anthropological community, as Bidney (1953) has noted, are liberal-democratic, and Tax (1955: 321–23) and Hallowell (1960), among others, have traced a liberal, i.e., relativistic, strain back to the beginnings of anthropology. On the other hand, an early strain of cultural absolutism also existed, and this point of view was not reserved to armchair anthropologists.[14] This means that field work can be done by those who espouse a non-democratic-liberal point of view (whether it is field work of the kind Boas advocated is debatable). Furthermore, personal acquaintance with anthropologists shows us that some authoritarian types do exist in the community. These observations force us to eschew the short-cut of inferring the personality types of a group from its ideology.[15]

Unfortunately, no direct assessment of anthropologists' authoritarian tendencies—especially tolerance of ambiguity—has been made, and it seems reasonable to believe that, if it were, no such "naïve" instruments as the California scales could be used to obtain valid responses from the sophisticated anthropologists. However, a fairly extensive and intensive psychological study has been done by Ann Roe (1952a, 1952b) who, in publishing her results, has taken such care to protect the anonymity of her subjects as to render her data less useful than it might otherwise be. Still, she presents many useful generalizations, and it is possible to refer to them in assessing the capacity of anthropologists to function in the role of ethnologist-stranger.

In her project involving a number of kinds of research scientists, Roe interviewed and tested eight eminent anthropologists and gave group Rorschachs to twenty-five anthropologists on five faculties. Her claim (1952b: 223) that "the research scientists studied individually . . . show precisely the differences (on the Rorschach) between fields that the subjects studied in groups do" appears valid. In their Rorschach responses, anthropologists are most like psychologists and least like biologists and physical scientists (Roe, 1952b: 222–23). However, it was not possible to specify differences between different fields of anthropology, e.g., between archaeology, physical anthropology, and social or cultural anthropology. Roe's generalizations, therefore, cover a broader universe than is being considered in this essay, i.e. cultural anthropology and its field practitioners. Nevertheless, if the general characteristics of Roe's sample suggest some adaptive potential for the role of ethnologist-stranger, we may be encouraged to undertake further studies with more refined samples to reach more firm conclusions.

The anthropologists studied are Americans. The mean age of the group of twenty-five was about forty-two, of the eight eminent men, about forty-nine. The information available suggests that they did their first field work in the Golden Age of ethnology. These scientists emerge as intelligent, independent-minded achievers who have a strong interest in people. Roe proposes that this interest stems from early problems in relations within their upper-status families and is now channeled—for the most part, successfully—into a vocation where the anthropologists' sense of social superiority "permits a somewhat Jovian survey of their own society as well as others and maintains [them] in a state of superiority just because [they] are able to make the survey" (Roe 1952a: 50). In addition, the anthropologists show a capacity for rapport with people and a tendency to be unconventional, though not asocial. These qualities suggest the requisite interest and abilities to establish, maintain, and endure that kind of involved detachment with a people that the role of ethnologist requires.

The manner in which these scientists approach the Rorschach indicates how they may deal with exotic and ambiguous experiences which one encounters in the role of ethnologist-stranger. They are very sensitive and receptive to a broad range of experience, especially the exotic, but they tend not to be concerned with the formal qualities of the blots and a methodical succession of percepts. This leads Roe (1952a: 43) to conclude that they display "a sort of haphazard use of rational controls"—that is, that they can be rational when they wish to be, but generally feel no compulsion to make a point of being so. Finally, they show the least shading shock of any of the four groups of research scientists. Considering their openness to experience, this finding seems to be directly relevant to their tolerance of ambiguity since shading shock, according to Roe (1952b: 221), may "indicate a basic anxiety, a readiness to be upset, a fear of what is unknown, and a consciousness of danger . . ." In sum, on the basis of their Rorschach performances, one might predict that these anthropologists would be able to tolerate the ambiguity, inconsistency, and unpredictable flux of the stranger's experience without resort to the perceptual distortions which more authoritarian types would find necessary. Of course there is the possibility that a person may be so "non-authoritarian" in his perceptual approach to the world (i.e., disorderly) as to fall beneath the minimum level for making enough sense out of it to survive. This does not appear to be so for these anthropologists. They are loose in their perceptual set, and this means that they could submit to the potentially disorganizing experience of the stranger's role and still maintain more than enough direction to survive and complete their mission.

Other data gathered by Roe tend to confirm the non-authoritarian character of her eight eminent anthropologists. Several studies have found authoritarians to be more concerned with religion (Adorno, Frenkel-Brunswik, Levinson, and Sanford, 1950: 208–21; Goldsen, Rosenberg, Williams, and Suchman, 1960: 169–95). The anthropologists are not religious. Authoritarians do not vent their aggression freely (Adorno, Frenkel-Brunswik, Levinson, and Sanford, 1950). The anthropologists tend to do so. One finding by Roe is equivocal as it stands. She (1952a: 25) notes that the anthropologists are "often troubled with conflicts over dominance and authority" and "over half of her psychologists and anthropologists (taken as a single group of social scientists) reacted (to their parents) with more rebelliousness than is generally usual . . ." How this syndrome is integrated (or not integrated) into the generally non-authoritarian picture of these scientists is not clear.

On the basis of Roe's data, then, we can conclude that her anthropologists possess personality traits which could contribute to success as a particular kind of social scientist, i.e., an ethnologist-stranger. They are intelligent and concerned with people and the exotic. They are normally detached, flexible, and tolerant of ambiguity. They look like Autonomous Men whose specialty is ethnology. They do not appear to be capable of the rigorously rational approach which characterizes the natural scientists, but it is doubtful that such an approach can be successful in a science which requires major adaptations to people by its practitioners.

We have worked with the advantage of hindsight (knowing that the subjects were successful anthropologists) to establish plausible connections between personality traits and adaptation to the role of ethnologist-stranger. The data at hand suggest that the ethnologists possess the personality traits which would not dictate serious perceptual distortions in the conditions of the stranger's role. But the procedure of working after the fact of success inevitably leads one to "strain for connections" and to ignore potentially dysfunctional or non-functional traits. How personality traits are related to the requirements of a specific role can only be ascertained after a series of progressively refined experiments utilizing the method of difference. In the ultimate experiment concerning our problem a group of ethnologists who attain a certain level of adaptation in the field would be compared with another group who do not in order to ascertain conclusively the functions of specific personality traits in such adaptation. The possibility of conducting such an experiment, however, is remote.

Though it has been suggested that some anthropologists *as individuals* possess traits which could lead to successful adaptation to the role of ethnologist-stranger, it would be a mistake to conclude that their personalities are the only means of adaptation available to them. Ethnologist teams (including those of husband and wife) have come into vogue, and they, while permitting more of the culture to be covered in depth, also can perform the adaptive functions of the enclave mentioned earlier. Technological advances have tended to reduce (and in other cases magnify) the size of some field problems. Machines for recording and observing, devices for maintaining health and comfort in the field, and improved means of transportation and communication are some of the developments which may affect the over-all problem of adaptation. Finally, the disappearance of primitive societies and the increasing concern with underdeveloped and civilized societies by anthropologists tend to narrow the gulf between home and host cultures and thus reduce the adaptive problem. However, these are for the most part recent adjuncts to the ethnologist's adaptive repertoire. In the Golden Age of ethnology field workers had to depend very much on their own resources for adaptation to their particular roles. The evidence suggests that at least some of them possessed the necessary potential for negotiating these roles with a minimum of perceptual distortion.

CONCLUSION

That some ethnologists probably have been able to carry on near-normal perceptual operations under the abnormal conditions of the stranger's role should not obscure the fact that field work involves hard work and considerable internal wear and tear. The anthropologist, Lévi-Strauss (1961 : 17), sums up the personal costs of existence in the field as follows:

Anthropology is a profession in which adventure plays no part; merely one of its bondages, it represents no more than a dead weight of weeks or months wasted en route; hours spent in idleness when one's informant has given one the slip; hunger, exhaustion, illness as like as not; and those thousand and one routine duties which eat up most of our days to no purpose and reduce our "perilous existence" in the virgin forest to a simulacrum of military service.

Yet despite the undoubted travail of the field situation, many anthropologists were eager to endure it. Indeed, from personal acquaintance we know anthropologists who come alive only when a field trip is in prospect for them. This knowledge suggests that such expeditions provide rewards or satisfactions which overbalance their costs to the individual. In psychological functional terms the cultural trait may be thought to survive and flourish in the anthropological community because its functions for the individual exceed non-functions and dysfunctions. What are some of these functions? First, Roe found that all of her research scientists derived great satisfaction from the research task itself. The ethnologist in the field is doing his job and, presumably, gaining the intrinsic satisfactions which it offers. Second, organisms appear to have a "level of need" for new or varied experience.[16] Where this level of need is high (as it may be in ethnologists) normal satisfaction can only be obtained in a rapidly changing life space. Field trips would be one way of providing such satisfaction. Third, ethnologists may take pride in "possessing" a specific society and derive long-term satisfaction from being identified with it. This may serve the same function (on a grander scale) as belonging to some particular group at home by the average citizen. Fourth, the freedom of coming and going and existence as a stranger is one way of satisfying the strong need for independence which Roe found in her subjects. Finally, the field trip provides a status increment to the ethnologist in whose reference group the custom is at or near the cultural focus.

This essay has concerned the field trip as a source of bias, but experience *in* the field is only one of the adaptive problems which the ethnologist encounters. The return home requires a new adaptation, which may be accomplished more or less successfully with greater or lesser influence on the writing of the ethnographic report. As Schütz (1944–45) has noted, the homecomer also faces a condition of anomie which results from the fact that both he and the people at home have changed at different rates and possibly in different directions. Again the average citizen would be threatened with personal disorganization and resort to approach or avoidance reactions to maintain his integrity. By determining whether "the magic fruit of strangeness has been sweet or bitter" one would take a long step toward predicting which response will occur.[17] For the average citizen, anomie will tend to exaggerate his bias (derived from other sources) toward, or away from, home and host societies. Even though the ethnologist probably can negotiate this new condition of anomie with comparative equanimity, the return home is likely to reinforce the bias with which he began his field trip. Initially, he probably was alienated at home and in favor of primitives. Now, having undergone his ordeal by field work, he returns identified with a specific primitive tribe. Like people in some societies after a rite of passage, the ethnologist has a new self after his field experience. Considering his emotional investment in this new self and the probability that "distance will lend enchantment," it may be that the return home reinforces both his alienation from the home society and the romantic pluralism which we have noted in the anthropological community. Whether his homecoming does in fact emphasize his bias in favor of the people he studies and his idealization of them might be tested by comparing the ethnologist's publications with his fieldnotes.

In sum, the custom of the field trip appears to feed upon itself and to strengthen the character of anthropologists as *Wandervögel*. The typical anthropologist, by socialization, training and the practice of his profession, becomes a stranger who can never go home, i.e., never find a point of rest in any society. If he has any home, it is in the anthropological community which emerges as a kind of halfway station between cultures filled with transients whose frame of reference, i.e., romantic cultural pluralism, appears to be appropriate to such a station. It may be that the most satisfactory way to obtain a sociological understanding of this modern anthropological viewpoint is to conceive the anthropological community as a place where strangers meet.[18]

NOTES

1 The term ethnologist will be used hereafter to refer to the cultural anthropologist in his data-gathering capacity as a field worker. Most of the generalizations concern American ethnologists working in the Boas tradition of field work.

2 The importance of one's group in constituting one's self is discussed in Hallowell, 1954. That different people may be more or less dependent upon their membership group for the control of organization of their personalities is suggested by Riesman's famous typology of Tradition-, Inner-, and Other-Directed types which appears in Riesman, Denney, and Glazer, 1950.

3 Some men delight in freedom; others flee from it. See, e.g., Fromm, 1941.

4 This does not mean that they necessarily will conceive themselves to be like the hosts but that they will tend to acquire the hosts' frame of reference and see themselves and the world in terms of it. See Simpson and Yinger, 1958: 183–228.

5 Maddi (1961: 273), for example, says that "some people are simply more interested in, and disposed toward, the occurrence of change, novelty, and the unexpected than are others."

Durkheim's discussion and application of the concept of anomie is to be found in Durkheim, 1951. Robert Merton (1957: 121–94) is one modern social scientist who has done a great deal to develop and apply the concept.

6 The functions of the enclave are discussed in Nash and Schaw, 1962–63.

7 The evidence concerning travelers' reactions is from personal observation abroad.

8 A number of experiments in perception point to such a conclusion. See, e.g., Bruner and Postman, 1947–48; Postman and Bruner, 1948; Postman, Bruner, and McGinnies, 1948.

9 The possibility also exists that this perceptual defense will break down and leave the individual in a state of psychological anomie which is isomorphic with the situation around him.

10 H. H. Kelley (1952), among others, has indicated that reference groups are of two types: the normative and the comparative or evaluative. In terms of perception and cognition this means that reference groups provide norms for perceiving and for evaluating what has been perceived.

11 The role of these factors is discussed in Nash and Schaw, 1962–63.

12 The intimate study of deviant behavior in our own society may present nearly as many adaptive difficulties as are faced by the ethnologist.

13 Two of the more adequate reports by modern ethnologists are: Berreman, 1962; Malinowski, 1961: 5–25.

How much of Eleanore Bowen's novel (1954) *Return to Laughter* is fact and how much is fiction is not clear, but it has a ring of reality about it.

An early, somewhat autobiographical account by a man who definitely does not share the modern tendency toward cultural relativism is to be found in Frobenius, 1913.

14 The early doctrine of social evolution and the positions of some of the *Kulturkreis* school illustrate this strain. The aforementioned Frobenius, who appears from his writings to be ethnocentric and authoritarian, did a great deal of field work, though he probably did not achieve the kind of rapport which is considered ideal in modern ethnology. See Frobenius, 1913.

15 This does not mean that this method cannot be used if a group is sufficiently homogeneous as to personality type. In this case we do not know how many different types

of personality are to be found in the anthropological community, and since a variety of types may espouse the same ideology we must resort to a direct study of the personalities themselves for the necessary information.

16 This is abundantly demonstrated in Fiske and Maddi (eds.), 1961.

17 The phrase is used by Schütz, 1944-45: 375.

18 Besides the published accounts, I have drawn on my own experience in the field (among Japanese and Cuban peasants in Cuba) and personal acquaintance with a number of anthropologists in developing the point of view of this essay. Paul Leser of the Hartford Seminary Foundation was of particular help regarding sources.

BIBLIOGRAPHY

ADORNO, T., FRENKEL-BRUNSWIK, E., LEVINSON, D., and SANFORD, R.
  1950. *The Authoritarian Personality*. New York: Harper & Bros.
BENNETT, J.
  1946. "The Interpretation of Pueblo Culture: A Question of Values." *Southwestern Journal of Anthropology*, II, 361-74.
BERREMAN, G.
  1962. *Behind Many Masks*. Ithaca, N.Y.: The Society for Applied Anthropology, Monograph 4.
BIDNEY, D.
  1953. "The Concept of Value in Modern Anthropology." *Anthropology Today*. Edited by A. L. Kroeber. Chicago: University of Chicago Press, pp. 687-92.
BOAS, F.
  1938. "Methods of Research." *General Anthropology*. Edited by F. Boas. New York: Heath, pp. 666-86.
BOWEN, E.
  1954. *Return to Laughter*. New York: Harper & Bros.
BRUNER, J., and POSTMAN, L.
  1947-48. "Emotional Selectivity in Perception and Reaction." *Journal of Personality*, XVI, 69-77.
  1949. "On the Perception of Incongruity: A Paradigm." *Perception and Personality*. Edited by J. Bruner and D. Krech. Durham, N. C.: Duke University Press, pp. 206-23.
CHAPPLE, E.
  1952. "The Training of the Professional Anthropologist: Social Anthropology and Applied Anthropology." *American Anthropologist*, LIV, 341-42.
CLEVELAND, H., MANGONE, G., and ADAMS, J.
  1960. *The Overseas Americans*. New York: McGraw-Hill Book Co.

DEVOS, G.

    1961. "Symbolic Analysis in the Cross-Cultural Study of Personality.' *Studying Personality Cross-Culturally*. Edited by B. Kaplan. Evanston, Ill.: Row, Peterson & Co., pp. 599–634.

DOZIER, E.

    1955. "The Concepts of 'Primitive' and 'Native' in Anthropology." *Current Anthropology*. Edited by W. Thomas, Jr. Chicago: University of Chicago Press, pp. 187–202.

DURKHEIM, É.

    1951. *Suicide*. Glencoe, Ill.: The Free Press.

FISKE, D., and MADDI, S. (Eds.).

    1961. *The Functions of Varied Experience*. Homewood, Ill.: The Dorsey Press.

FORSTER, E. M.

    1924. *Passage to India*. New York: Harcourt, Brace & Co.

FRENKEL-BRUNSWIK, E.

    1949. "Intolerance of Ambiguity as an Emotional and Perceptual Personality Variable." *Perception and Personality*. Edited by J. Bruner and D. Krecht. Durham, N.C.: Duke University Press, pp. 108–43.

FROBENIUS, L.

    1913. *The Voice of Africa*. London: Hutchinson.

FROMM, E.

    1941. *Escape from Freedom*. New York: Farrar and Rinehart.

GOLDSEN, R., ROSENBERG, M., WILLIAMS, R., JR., and SUCHMAN, E.

    1960. *What College Students Think*. Princeton: D. Van Nostrand Co.

HALLOWELL, A. I.

    1954. "The Self and Its Behavioral Environment." *Explorations*, II, 108–65.

    1960. "The Beginnings of Anthropology in America." *Selected Papers from the American Anthropologist: 1888–1920*. Edited by F. DeLaguna. Evanston, Ill.: Row, Peterson & Co., pp. 1–90.

HART, C.

    1957. "Cultural Anthropology and Sociology." *Modern Sociological Theory in Continuity and Change*. Edited by H. Becker and A. Boskoff. New York: Dryden Press, pp. 528–49.

KELLEY, H. H.

    1952. "Two Functions of Reference Groups." *Readings in Social Psychology*. Edited by G. Swanson, T. Newcomb, and E. Hartley. New York: Holt, pp. 410–14.

LEDERER, W., and BURDICK, E.

    1958. *The Ugly American*. New York: W. W. Norton Co.

LÉVI-STRAUSS, C.

    1961. *World on the Wane*. London: Hutchinson.

MADDI, S.

    1961. "Exploratory Behavior and Variation-Seeking in Man." *Functions of*

Varied Experience. Edited by D. Fiske and S. Maddi. Homewood, Ill.: The Dorsey Press, pp. 253–77.

MALINOWSKI, B.
1961. *Argonauts of the Western Pacific.* New York: E. P. Dutton.

MEAD, M.
1952. "The Training of the Cultural Anthropologists." *American Anthropologist,* LIV, 343–46.

MERTON, R.
1957. *Social Theory and Social Structure.* Revised ed. Glencoe, Ill.: The Free Press.

NADEL, S.
1951. *The Foundations of Social Anthropology.* Glencoe, Ill.: The Free Press.

NASH, D., and SCHAW, L.
1962–63. "Personality and Adaptation in an Overseas Enclave." *Human Organization,* XXI, 252–63.

NASH, D., and WOLFE, A.
1957. "The Stranger in Laboratory Culture." *American Sociological Review,* XXII, 400–405.

PAUL, B.
1953. "Interview Techniques and Field Relationships." *Anthropology Today.* Edited by A. L. Kroeber. Chicago: University of Chicago Press, pp. 430–51.

POSTMAN, L., and BRUNER, J.
1948. "Perception Under Stress." *Psychological Review,* LV, 314–23.

POSTMAN, L., BRUNER, J., and McGINNIES, E.
1948. "Personal Values as Selective Factors in Perception." *Journal of Abnormal and Social Psychology,* XLIII, 142–54.

RIESMAN, D., DENNEY, R., and GLAZER, N.
1950. *The Lonely Crowd.* New Haven: Yale University Press.

ROBERTS, A. H., and ROKEACH, M.
1956. "Anomie, Authoritarianism, and Prejudice: A Replication." *American Journal of Sociology,* LXI, 355–58.

ROE, A.
1952a. "A Psychological Study of Eminent Psychologists and Anthropologists, and a Comparison with Biological and Physical Scientists." *Psychological Monographs,* LXVII, 1–55.
1952b. "Analysis of Group Rorschachs of Psychologists and Anthropologists." *Journal of Projective Techniques,* XVI, 212–24.

SCHÜTZ, A.
1944. "The Stranger: An Essay in Social Psychology." *American Journal of Sociology,* XLIX, 499–507.
1944–45. "The Homecomer." *American Journal of Sociology,* L, 369–76.

SIMMEL, G.
  1950. *The Sociology of Georg Simmel.* Edited by K. Wolff. Glencoe, Ill.: The Free Press.
SIMPSON, G., and YINGER, J. M.
  1958. *Racial and Cultural Minorities.* Revised ed. New York: Harper & Bros.
SROLE, L.
  1956. "Social Integration and Certain Corollaries: An Exploratory Study." *American Sociological Review,* XXI, 709–16.
  1955. "The Integration of Anthropology." *Current Anthropology.* Edited by W. Thomas, Jr. Chicago: University of Chicago Press., pp. 313–28.

7

DIANA CRANE

---

*The Gatekeepers of Science: Some Factors Affecting the Selection of Articles for Scientific Journals**

THE NORMS OF scientific behavior as described by Merton[1] include the prescription that scientific achievements are to be judged without reference to scientists' social characteristics. This article will attempt to assess the extent to which this norm is followed with respect to the evaluation of articles by scientific journals.

Merton's discussion refers to the possibility that a scientist's "personal or social attributes," such as "race, nationality, religion, class and personal qualities," might interfere with the objective evaluation of his work. Recent studies suggest that it is more probable that a scientist's position in the social structure of science itself may affect the evaluation of his scientific work. One aspect of the social structure of basic science is the fact that basic scientists are located in institutions of varying prestige. The scientist's location in the academic stratification system affects his scientific career. For example, several studies have shown that productivity of scientists is related to the prestige of their university affiliations.[2] One study also found that highly productive scientists were more likely to receive recognition if they were located at major universities.[3]

Since scientific rewards are based on publications, the ease with which he can publish his work is of great importance to the scientist. If the academic

*I am grateful for the assistance of Mary Elizabeth Hintze and Savin Ungaro in collecting the data on which this article is based.

The American Sociologist, II (November, 1967), 195–201. Reprinted by permission of the American Sociological Association and the author.

stratification system controls opportunities for publication and distributes them differentially to scientists differently located in the system, the system is inhibiting some scientists from performing their scientific roles and possibly also the diffusion of scientific ideas. De Grazia has suggested that journal editors are the "gatekeepers" of science, screening the information which is permitted to circulate widely among members of the discipline.[4] He claims that they tend to support the currently orthodox views in their fields and that their receptivity to new ideas is variable. The possibility of an "establishment" in scientific disciplines has been suggested but never empirically confirmed.

There is some evidence from previous studies which suggests that the evaluation of scientific articles may not always be entirely objective. A number of studies have shown that a large proportion of the articles appearing in scientific journals are contributed by scientists from major universities.[5] There is also some indication that the selection of articles by journals may be influenced by knowledge of the academic affiliations of the authors. A study of the articles published by three economics journals found that journals edited at a particular university tended to publish a higher proportion of articles by authors at the same university.[6] A study done in 1945 found that articles by authors from minor universities were rejected more frequently by the *American Sociological Review* than articles by authors from major universities.[7] Finally, recent studies of citation practices have shown that articles by authors from departments which have been rated highly by members of a discipline are more frequently cited than articles by authors from other departments. This finding held even when ability (as measured by intelligence tests administered during adolescence) was held constant.[8]

It seems likely that knowledge of an author's academic affiliation has some effect on the evaluation of his work by referees. An author's academic affiliation may cast a kind of "halo" effect over his work which impedes objective evaluation.[9] Since a few scientific journals evaluate manuscripts anonymously, this article will attempt to assess the influence of editors' awareness of scientists' locations in the academic stratification system upon their selection of articles for publication. Characteristics of scientists whose articles were accepted for publication on the basis of anonymous evaluation will be compared with the characteristics of scientists whose articles were selected without such controls against bias.

Undoubtedly, however, a number of factors limit the effectiveness of anonymous evaluation. There are always referees who recognize the work of friends. The identity of well-known authors is often recognizable from their style or theoretical orientation. In some fields, the "invisible college" may be so effective that most scientists are aware of the research which their colleagues are doing.[10]

Since anonymity is seldom complete, it will be necessary to examine other variables which may be influencing the publication opportunities of scientists. It seems likely that the academic backgrounds of journal editors have an indirect effect upon their selection of articles for publication. First, doctoral training may influence editorial readers to respond favorably to certain aspects of methodology, theoretical orientation, and mode of expression in the writings of those who have received similar training. Secondly, both doctoral training and academic affiliations probably influence the personal ties which a scientist forms with other scientists and these in turn may affect his evaluation of scientific work. Since most scientific writing is terse, knowledge of details not usually included in journal presentations may influence the reader's response to an article. Thirdly, professional age (number of years past Ph.D.) may affect an editor's evaluation in both of these ways, by influencing the types of material to which he responds favorably and his personal ties with other scientists. In this article, academic backgrounds of editors will be examined in relation to the academic backgrounds of authors whose papers have been selected for publication.[11]

THE DATA

A survey of fifty journals published by national professional associations in seven disciplines[12] found nine journals (eight of them in sociology) which required that the authors' names and institutional affiliations be concealed from referees. One of the journals which evaluates articles anonymously is the *American Sociological Review*. The procedure was instituted in 1955.[13] In order to find out whether anonymous evaluation of articles has any noticeable effect on the distribution of academic characteristics of authors of articles selected for publication, university affiliations, doctoral origins, and professional ages (number of years since Ph.D.) were examined for 1,322 authors of articles published in the *American Sociological Review* during the ten years preceding and succeeding 1955. In addition, the characteristics of 294 contributors to the *American Economic Review* were compared with the contributors to the *American Sociological Review*.[14] The *American Economic Review* was chosen because it does not evaluate articles anonymously, it is the publication of the major professional association of another social science discipline, and its contributors do research under conditions approximately similar to those in sociology. Thus comparisons between the two publications are appropriate. Educational origins were examined, as well as academic affiliation at the time of publication, in order to see if anonymous evaluation has the indirect effect of diversifying educational backgrounds of contributors. Similarly, professional age was examined to see if younger (and probably less eminent) authors are more likely to be selected under a system of anonymous evaluation of articles. The same information was collected for the editorial boards of these journals during the same periods.

Institutional affiliations of authors and editors were coded using Berelson's categories of university prestige.[15] Berelson based his classification of American universities on the quality ratings obtained by Keniston in 1957.[16] The first category (here described as major universities) included the top ten universities in Keniston's study with two major technological schools added. The second category (here described as "high minor universities") included the next ten schools in the Keniston ratings. The remaining seventy universities are grouped together here as "low minor universities."[17]

The universities from which the authors and editors obtained their Ph.D.s were classified in the same way. Biographical information was obtained from *American Men of Science*, 1956 and 1962 editions, and from the *1964 Handbook of the American Economic Association*. Authors were coded as having no Ph.D. if at the time of publication of the article concerned they had not yet obtained a Ph.D.[18] It was not possible to locate biographies for authors of 9–22 per cent of the articles in any year (since this proportion is higher for the last three years, 1963 to 1965, these years are excluded from the analysis of doctoral origins). Since academic affiliation at time of publication is given in the journal articles, this information is complete for virtually the entire sample.

In order not to give undue weight to academic affiliations of authors of collaborative articles, collaborators' academic affiliations were given fractional credit and thus not permitted to total more than one for a single article. This procedure was used in classifying academic affiliations and the universities from which authors had obtained their Ph.D.s.

Professional age was obtained by calculating the number of years between the date of the author's Ph.D. and the date of publication of his article. In the case of an editor, his professional age was the number of years between his Ph.D. and the final year of his editorship. On both journals, most editors serve for three-year periods. Since the range of ages was quite large, the median was used to describe the distributions of professional ages. In this instance, collaborators were included as individuals rather than fractionally.

THE EFFECTS OF ANONYMOUS EVALUATION

When the academic affiliations of contributors to the *American Sociological Review* between 1956 and 1965 are compared with the academic affiliations of contributors to the *American Economic Review*. the principal difference is the higher representation of authors from the low minor universities in the *American Sociological Review*. Differences between the two journals in the proportions of authors with other types of affiliations were slight.

In order to assess the true influence of anonymous evaluation of articles, it is necessary to compare the contributors to the *American Sociological Review* after anonymous evaluation was begun with those who were selected under the previous system. When the total number of articles published during the two periods is examined, the proportion of articles by authors from both the major universities and the low minor universities have increased during the later period.

TABLE 1

PRESTIGE OF ACADEMIC AFFILIATIONS OF AUTHORS
SELECTED BY ANONYMOUS AND NON-ANONYMOUS
EVALUATION*

	Type of evaluation:		
	Not Anonymous	Anonymous	Not Anonymous
	American Sociological Review		*American Economic Review*
	1946–55	1956–65	1956–65
Percentage of authors at:			
Major universities	26	33	36
High minor universities	21	14	18
Low minor universities	26 } 57·5	34 } 55	20 } 45
Colleges	10·5	7	7
Non-academic positions	14	8	11
Foreign positions	2	4	7.66
Affiliation unknown	·5	0	·33
Total	101**	100	100
Total number of papers:	(712)	(610)	(294)

* Since the entire population of articles during relevant periods was selected for examination rather than a random sample, tests of significance are not applicable.
** Rounding error.

In both the *American Sociological Review* and the *American Economic Review* the proportion of authors with doctorates from minor universities is much lower than the proportion of authors with doctorates from major universities. However, the proportion of authors with doctorates from minor universities is higher in the *American Sociological Review*.[19] When the *American Sociological Review* during the period of anonymous evaluation of articles is compared to the earlier period, there is an increase in the proportions of authors with doctorates from major universities and from low minor universities. The number of authors without Ph.D.s decreases. The latter may simply reflect the fact that the Ph.D. has become a basic requirement for most university teaching positions.

TABLE 2

PRESTIGE OF DOCTORAL ORIGINS OF AUTHORS SELECTED
BY ANONYMOUS AND NON-ANONYMOUS EVALUATION

	Type of evaluation:		
	Not Anonymous	Anonymous	Not Anonymous American Economic Review
	American Sociological Review		
	1946–55	1956–62	1956–62
Percentage of authors with doctorates from:			
Major universities	40	45	60
High minor universities	17 } 28	18 } 32	8 } 11
Low minor universities	11	14	3
Foreign degrees	3	1	9
Graduate school unknown	15	16	13
No Ph.D.	14	6	7
Total	100	100	100
Total number of papers:	(712)	(446)	(202)

Does anonymous evaluation of articles tend to favor younger authors? The median professional age of authors of articles in the *American Sociological Review* between 1956 and 1962 is 5.3.[20] During the same period, the median professional age of authors of articles in the *American Economic Review* is 7.3.

The median professional age of authors is 9.1 for the *American Sociological Review* during the first six years of the earlier period. However, it drops to 4.0 during the four years prior to the commencement of anonymous evaluation of articles. Since the editorship of the *American Sociological Review* changed at the point when the decline begins, median age during those years may reflect editorial policy.

ACADEMIC CHARACTERISTICS OF EDITORS AND CONTRIBUTORS

While there do appear to be some differences in the characteristics of authors whose articles are selected by means of anonymous evaluation as compared to those whose articles are selected by the other system, it seems likely that other factors may be influencing the findings. An obvious possibility is the characteristics of the journal editors who are the most usual choice for referees. The *American Economic Review* had a small group of editors (eight in number) and its chief editorship changed only once during the period 1956 to 1965. The institutional location of the chief editorship did not change.

By contrast, during the same period, the *American Sociological Review* had a board of twelve editors from 1956 to 1958. The number was increased to fifteen from 1959 to 1962 and to twenty from 1963 to 1965. There were four chief editors and four different institutional locations of the journal during the period. Prior to 1956, the board of editors was somewhat smaller (between six and eight), although the chief editorship and institutional location of the chief editorship changed regularly. There were three chief editors and three institutional locations during the earlier period.

The institutional affiliations of the editors of the *American Sociological Review* were considerably more diverse than those of the editors of the *American Economic Review*. Editors from minor universities represented 65 per cent of the editorship of the *American Sociological Review* during the earlier period, 61 per cent of the editorship during the later period, and only 29 per cent of the editorship of the *American Economic Review*.

The doctoral origins of editors of both journals were less diverse than their academic affiliations. However, the editors of the *American Sociological Review* during both periods were more likely to have received their doctorates from minor universities than the editors of the *American Economic Review*.

These figures, juxtaposed with the previous findings regarding the academic affiliations and doctoral origins of contributors to these journals, suggest that diversity in the academic characteristics of journal editors may be an important factor contributing to the selection of articles by authors

TABLE 3

PRESTIGE OF ACADEMIC AFFILIATIONS OF EDITORS OF THE
AMERICAN SOCIOLOGICAL REVIEW, 1946–65, AND THE
AMERICAN ECONOMIC REVIEW, 1956–65

	American Sociological Review		American Economic Review
	1946–55	1956–65	1956–65
Percentage of editors at:			
Major universities	23	34	55
High minor universities	18 ⎫	19 ⎫	13 ⎫
Low minor universities	⎬ 65	⎬ 61	⎬ 29
and colleges	47 ⎭	42 ⎭	16 ⎭
Non-academic positions	0	0	16
Affiliation unknown	12	5	0
Total	100	100	100
Total number of editors:	(34)	(67)	(31)

from varied academic backgrounds. It is possible that bias in the selection of journal articles may be prevented in two ways: anonymous evaluation of articles and the use of staffs of editors with diverse academic backgrounds. During the period 1956 to 1965, the *American Sociological Review* had both types of controls while the *American Economic Review* had neither. From 1946 to 1955, the *American Sociological Review* had only one of the two— diverse editorship. This control by itself appears to have been effective.

Analysis of the academic affiliations of contributors to a journal which represents the fourth possibility, anonymous evaluation coupled with a staff of editors primarily from the major universities, is necessary to test the effectiveness of anonymous evaluation. *Sociometry* began to evaluate manuscripts anonymously in 1956 when it became an American Sociological Association publication.[21] From 1956 to 1958, 24 (59 per cent) of the editors were from major universities and 8 (20 per cent) from minor universities; 9 (22 per cent) were located in non-academic settings. From 1959 to 1961, the number of editors from major universities declined to 18 (45 per cent), while the number of editors from minor universities increased to 12 (31 per cent). Nine (23 per cent) were in non-academic settings. Finally, between

TABLE 4

PRESTIGE OF DOCTORAL ORIGINS OF EDITORS OF THE
AMERICAN SOCIOLOGICAL REVIEW, 1946–65, AND THE
AMERICAN ECONOMIC REVIEW, 1956–65

	American Sociological Review		American Economic Review
	1946–55	1956–65	1956–65
Percentage of editors with doctorates from:			
Major universities	56	66	71
High minor universities	20 } 29	24 } 28	6 } 9
Low minor universities	9	4	3
Foreign universities	3	0	16
Graduate school unknown	12	4	0
No Ph.D.	0	2	3
Total	100	100	99*
Total number of editors:	(34)	(67)	(31)

*Rounding error.

1962 and 1965, 13 (26 per cent) of the editors were from major universities and 24 (48 per cent) from minor universities; 11 (22 per cent) were in non-academic settings and information was unavailable for 2 (4 per cent).

If anonymous evaluation of manuscripts has an effect on the selection of articles, it ought to be noticeable if the institutional backgrounds of authors of articles in *Sociometry* between 1956 and 1958 (the period when the academic affiliations of the editors were least diverse) are compared with the institutional backgrounds of authors of articles appearing in the *American Economic Review*. Since the editorship of the *American Economic Review* was least diverse between 1956 and 1962, this period was chosen for comparison.[22] The institutional affiliations of authors of articles appearing in the two journals were different with corresponding effects upon the doctoral origins of the contributors.[23]

These findings suggest that anonymity does not produce the expected results. That diversity in the academic backgrounds of editors rather than anonymous evaluation of manuscripts is the more important factor

TABLE 5

PRESTIGE OF ACADEMIC AFFILIATIONS OF AUTHORS, BY
TYPE OF EVALUATION AND ACADEMIC AFFILIATIONS OF
EDITORS

	Type of evaluation:	
	Anonymous	Not Anonymous
	Percentage of editors at minor universities:	
	20%	26%
	Sociometry	*American Economic Review*
	1956–58	1956–62
Percentage of authors at:		
Major universities	37	38
High minor universities	13 ⎫	16 ⎫
Low minor universities	27 ⎬ 42	17 ⎬ 42
Colleges	2 ⎭	9 ⎭
Non-academic positions	21	11
Foreign positions	0	9
Total	100	100
Total number of papers:	(75)	(201)

influencing the selection of manuscripts can be seen in the fact that the proportion of articles by authors from minor universities increases in *Sociometry* as the proportion of editors from these institutions increases, although the manuscripts were evaluated anonymously during the entire period.[24]

A similar relationship between the academic affiliations of editors and the academic affiliations of contributors to the *American Economic Review* can also be seen although the differences are not as pronounced. Between 1963 and 1965, when the editorship became more diverse, there was an increase in the proportion of articles by economists from minor universities. It might be argued that these findings reflect the increase in the amount of research being conducted at minor universities during this period and hence in the number of articles being submitted from these institutions rather than changes in the academic affiliations of editors. However, the fact that a large proportion of the articles published by the *American Sociological Review* between 1946 and 1955 were by authors from minor universities contradicts this argument.[25]

TABLE 6

PRESTIGE OF DOCTORAL ORIGINS OF AUTHORS, BY TYPE OF
EVALUATION AND DOCTORAL ORIGINS OF EDITORS

	Type of evaluation:	
	Anonymous	Not Anonymous
	Percentage of editors with doctorates from minor universities:	
	24%	9%
	Sociometry	*American Economic Review*
	1956–58	1956–62
Percentage of authors with doctorates from:		
Major universities	56	60
High minor universities	21 ⎱ 29	8 ⎱ 11
Low minor universities	8 ⎰	3 ⎰
Foreign universities	0	9
Graduate school unknown	8	13
No Ph.D.	7	7
Total	100	100
Total number of papers:	(75)	(202)

It appears that the academic characteristics of authors of articles selected for publication by scientific journals are similar to the characteristics of the editors of the journals and that anonymity does not affect this relationship. This relationship is seen quite clearly when the findings from the several journals discussed here are juxtaposed. These tables show that diversity in the academic affiliations of editors is related to diversity in the academic affiliations of contributors; diversity in the doctoral origins of editors is related to diversity in the doctoral origins of contributors.

Another characteristic of editors which might also be reflected in their selection of articles is professional age. There is some indication that editors prefer the work of contributors who are closer to their own professional age.[26]

However, since the majority of authors tend to be relatively young (due partly to the steady increase in the numbers of scientists entering these fields

TABLE 7

PRESTIGE OF ACADEMIC AFFILIATIONS OF AUTHORS
(SELECTED BY ANONYMOUS EVALUATION), BY
PRESTIGE OF ACADEMIC AFFILIATIONS OF EDITORS

	Percentage of editors at minor universities:		
	20%	31% Sociometry	48%
	1956–58	1959–61	1962–65
Percentage of authors at:			
Major universities	37	30	26
High minor universities	13 ⎫	10 ⎫	12 ⎫
Low minor universities	27 ⎬ 42	38 ⎬ 49	47 ⎬ 62
Colleges	2 ⎭	1 ⎭	3 ⎭
Non-academic positions	21	18	9
Foreign positions	0	3	3
Total	100	100	100
Total number of papers:	(75)	(91)	(134)

TABLE 8

ACADEMIC AFFILIATIONS OF AUTHORS, BY ACADEMIC AFFILIATIONS OF EDITORS

	ASR 1946–55	ASR 1956–65	Sociometry 1962–65	AER 1963–65	Sociometry 1959–61	AER 1956–62	Sociometry 1956–58
Percentage at minor universities, colleges:							
Editors	65	61	48	38	31	26	20
N	(34)	(67)	(50)	(13)	(39)	(23)	(41)
Authors	57.5	55	62	52	49	42	42
N	(712)	(610)	(134)	(92)	(91)	(201)	(75)

TABLE 9

DOCTORAL ORIGINS OF AUTHORS, BY DOCTORAL ORIGINS OF EDITORS

	Sociometry 1959–65	ASR 1956–62	ASR 1946–55	Sociometry 1956–58	AER 1956–62
Percentage with doctorates from minor universities:					
Editors	30	31	29	24	9
N	(74)	(45)	(34)	(41)	(23)
Authors	35	32	28	29	11
N	(225)	(446)	(712)	(75)	(202)

TABLE 10

Median Professional Ages of Authors, by
Median Professional Ages of Editors

	AER 1956–62	ASR 1946–55	Sociometry 1956–62	ASR 1956–62
Median professional age:				
Editors	16·2	13·0	10·4	10·4
N	(20)	(30)	(63)	(43)
Authors	7·3	6·4	5·8	5·3
N	(178)	(594)	(251)	(481)

and partly to the decline in scientific productivity with increasing age), the effect is not as large as it might be otherwise. On the other hand, the finding does provide some insight into the ways in which generational styles and orientations toward scientific work are perpetuated.

SUMMARY AND CONCLUSION

Examination of the academic characteristics of contributors and editors of three scientific journals indicates that the distribution of characteristics such as academic affiliation, doctoral origin and professional age of contributors to scientific journals is similar to the distribution of these same characteristics among journal editors. Anonymous evaluation of articles does not change this relationship.

It appears that the evaluation of scientific articles is affected to some degree by non-scientific factors. At least two interpretations of the role of the latter are possible: (*1*) As a result of academic training, editorial readers respond to certain aspects of methodology, theoretical orientation, and mode of expression in the writings of those who have received similar training; (*2*) Doctoral training and academic affiliations influence personal ties between scientists, which in turn influence their evaluation of scientific work. Since most scientific writing is terse, knowledge of details not usually included in journal presentations may influence the reader's response to an article. Professional age affects the reader's evaluations in both of these ways.

The data presented here supports the first of these interpretations more strongly than the second. In all three journals, the majority of authors and editors have degrees from major universities. This suggests that editors and contributors share common viewpoints based on training, rather than on personal ties.[27] However, as the academic affiliations of editors become more diverse, the academic affiliations of authors become more diverse also. This suggests that personal ties may play a secondary role.

Any such interpretation must of course be tentative pending further investigation of these relationships. The analysis presented here suggests that disciplines vary in the extent to which articles by authors from diverse institutional backgrounds are selected for publication in their principal journals. Both the factors producing these differences and their consequences for the progress of the field are difficult to trace. It appears that during a decade when the amount of research and the number of doctrines being produced in low minor universities has been increasing, the *American Sociological Review*, due to the academic backgrounds of its editors, has been more receptive to the publications produced in these settings than the *American Economic Review*. It may not be entirely a coincidence that an economist, Martin Bronfenbrenner, in discussing "trends, cycles, and fads" in economic writing, described the history of economics, including the present period, in terms of its reigning orthodoxies which he saw as being capable of interfering for a time with the progress of the discipline.[28] These elusive problems comprise an important area for future investigation in the sociology of science.

NOTES

1 Robert K. Merton. "Science and Democratic Social Structure," in *Social Theory and Social Structure* (Glencoe, Ill.: The Free Press, 1957), p. 553.

2 Bernard Berelson, *Graduate Education in the United States* (New York: McGraw-Hill Book Co., 1960), p. 127; Paul F. Lazarsfeld and Wagner Thielens, Jr., *The Academic Mind* (Glencoe, Ill.: The Free Press, 1958), p. 30; Jerome G. Manis, "Some Academic Influences upon Publication Productivity," *Social Forces*, XXIX (1951), 267-72; Nicholas Babchuk and Alan P. Bates, "Professor or Producer: The Two Faces of Academic Man," *Social Forces*, XL (1962), 341-48.

3 Diana Crane, "Scientists at Major and Minor Universities: A Study of Productivity and Recognition," *American Sociological Review*, XXX (1965), 699-714.

4 Alfred de Grazia, "The Scientific Reception System and Dr. Velikovsky," *American Behavioral Scientist*, VII (1963), 38-56.

5 Berelson, *Graduate Education in the United States*, pp. 127, 273-74; Frank R. Cleary and Daniel J. Edwards, "The Origins of the Contributors to the A.E.R. During the Fifties," *American Economic Review*, L (1960), 1011-14; Charles A. Kraus, "The Present State of Academic Research," *Chemical and Engineering News*, XXVIII (1950), 3203-4. A recent article in the *American Sociologist* indicates that a high proportion of authors of articles appearing in the *American Sociological Review* had received their doctoral degrees from a

small group of universities. See Jules J. Wanderer, "Academic Origins of Contributors to the ASR, 1955–1965," *American Sociologist*, I (1966), 241–43.

6 Pan A. Yotopoulos, "Institutional Affiliation of the Contributors to Three Professional Journals," *American Economic Review*, LI (1961), 665–70.

7 Dorris West Goodrich, "An Analysis of Manuscripts Received by the Editors of the *American Sociological Review* from May 1, 1944, to September 1, 1945," *American Sociological Review*, X (1945), 716–25.

8 Alan E. Bayer and John Folger, "Some Correlates of a Citation Measure of Productivity in Science," *Sociology of Education*, XXXIX (1966), 381–90. See also Stephen Cole and Jonathan R. Cole, "Scientific Output and Recognition: A Study in the Operation of the Reward System in Science," *American Sociological Review*, XXXII (1967), 377–90.

9 An analogous phenomenon in another area is the well-known placebo effect which has led to the extensive use of "double-blind" tests in the scientific evaluation of new drugs. See Walter Modell, "Placebo Effects in the Therapeutic Encounter," in W. Richard Scott and Edmund H. Volkart (eds.), *Medical Care: Readings in the Sociology of Medical Institutions* (New York: John Wiley & Sons, 1966), pp. 368–80.

10 Derek Price, *Little Science, Big Science* (New York: Columbia University Press, 1963), pp. 62–91. Editors of some scientific journals, in replying to my queries about how articles were evaluated, stressed this point.

11 Although editors do not necessarily review all articles submitted, presumably they select referees whom they know and who are thus likely to have academic characteristics similar to their own.

12 The disciplines were biology, chemistry, economics, physics, psychology, sociology, and statistics.

13 According to a personal communication, November 9, 1966, from Leonard Broom, then editor of the *American Sociological Review*, the first articles were circulated anonymously in June, 1955, but it was not until April, 1956, that an entire issue of anonymously evaluated articles appeared. For this reason, the following issues of the *American Sociological Review* have been excluded from the analysis: August, October, and December, 1955, and February, 1956.

14 Only articles which could have been circulated anonymously were included in the analysis. For this reason, the following materials were excluded: presidential addresses, MacIver Award lectures, book reviews and review articles, official reports, memorials, and comments on articles previously published. Comments are not circulated anonymously, according to a personal communication from Norman B. Ryder, Editor, *American Sociological Review*, November 9, 1966.

15 Berelson, *Graduate Education in the United States*, pp. 126–27.

16 Hayward Keniston, *Graduate Education and Research in the Arts and Sciences at the University of Pennsylvania* (Philadelphia: University of Pennsylvania Press, 1959).

17 The ratings by Allan M. Cartter were not used since they are probably too recent to apply to the entire period under consideration. However, for both economics and sociology, there is considerable agreement between the Keniston ratings and the Cartter ratings. See Allan M. Cartter, *An Assessment of Quality in Graduate Education* (Washington, D.C.: American Council on Education, 1966), pp. 35, 43.

18 A few authors had advanced degrees other than the Ph.D., for example, doctorates of business administration, education, law, and medicine. These were treated as comparable to the Ph.D. for the purposes of the study.

19 The proportions of doctorates awarded by minor universities are very similar in the two disciplines. Between 1953 and 1962, 59 per cent of the doctorates in sociology were awarded by minor universities. During the same period, 57.5 per cent of the doctorates in economics were awarded by minor universities. These figures were computed from data contained in Allan M. Cartter (ed.), *American Universities and Colleges* (9th ed.; Washington, D.C.: American Council on Education, 1964).

20 Since the proportion of authors for whom the date of Ph.D is unknown increases substantially after 1962, these years were not included in this part of the analysis. Younger authors are less likely to be included in biographical directories and thus a high proportion of individuals for whom biographical information is unavailable is likely to raise the median professional age.

21 According to Leonard S. Cottrell, Jr. (personal communication, April 5, 1967), who was editor of *Sociometry* during that period, all articles which appeared in the journal, beginning with the March, 1956, issue, had been evaluated anonymously.

22 Between 1956 and 1962, 12 (52 per cent) of the editors of the *American Economic Review* were from major universities and 6 (26 per cent) from minor universities. Between 1963 and 1965, 6 (46 per cent) were from major universities and 5 (38 per cent) from minor universities. The remainder were in non-academic settings.

23 From 1956 to 1958, 29 (71 per cent) of the editors of *Sociometry* had doctorates from major universities; 10 (24 per cent) had degrees from minor universities; doctoral origins of 2 editors could not be ascertained. From 1959 to 1961, 27 (69 per cent) had degrees from major universities, 10 (26 per cent) from minor universities and the doctoral origins of 2 could not be ascertained. Between 1962 and 1965, 32 (64 per cent) had degrees from major universities, 16 (32 per cent) from minor universities and doctoral origins of 2 could not be identified. See Table 4 for the doctoral origins of the editors of the *American Economic Review*.

24 Doctoral origins of editors of *Sociometry* changed only slightly in the direction of increasing diversity between 1956 and 1965. Doctoral origins of contributors also changed very moderately in the same direction during the same period. However, although the doctoral origins of editors of the *American Economic Review* did not become more diverse during this period, the doctoral origins of authors did broaden to some extent. This shift in the doctoral origins of *American Economic Review* authors suggests the importance of personal ties based on academic affiliations, since the academic affiliations of editors did become more diverse during this period.

25 It is also possible that the number of articles submitted by scientists at minor universities is a function of the number of editors from minor universities, since personal ties with editors may increase the likelihood that an author will submit an article to a particular journal.

26 Since the percentage of authors whose doctoral origins could not be ascertained increases substantially after 1962, data for all contributors for the years 1963, 1964, and 1965 were not included in this part of the analysis.

27 Wanderer found that 41 per cent of the articles and reports in the *American Sociological Review* between 1955 and 1965 were written by authors with doctorates from four major universities. Fifty-eight per cent of the editors during that period had degrees from those same four universities.

28 Martin Bronfenbrenner, "Trends, Cycles, and Fads in Economic Writing," *American Economic Review*, LVI (1966), 538–52.

Part Four: The Sociology of Knowledge and Sociology

I

ROBERT K. MERTON

Social Conflict over Styles of Sociological Work

AFTER ENJOYING more than two generations of scholarly interest, the sociology of knowledge remains largely a subject for meditation rather than a field of sustained and methodical investigation. This has resulted in the curious condition that more monographs and papers are devoted to discussions of what the sociology of knowledge is and what it ought to be than to detailed inquiries into specific problems.

What is true of the sociology of knowledge at large is conspicuously true of the part concerned with the analysis of the course and character taken by sociology itself. This, at least, is the composite verdict of the jury of twelve who have reviewed for us the social contexts of sociology in countries all over the world. Almost without exception, the authors of these papers report (or intimate) that, for their own country, they could find only fragmentary evidence on which to draw for their account. They emphasize the tentative and hazardous nature of interpretations based on such slight foundations. It follows that my own paper, drawing upon the basic papers on national sociologies, must be even more tentative and conjectural.

In effect, these authors tell us that they have been forced to resort to loose generalities rather than being in a position to report firmly grounded generalizations. Generalities are vague and indeterminate statements that bring together particulars which are not really comparable; generalizations report definite though general regularities distilled from the methodical comparison of comparable data. We all know the kind of generalities found in the sociology of knowledge: that societies with sharp social cleavages, as

Transactions of the Fourth World Congress of Sociology, III (Louvain: International Sociological Association, 1959), 21–44. Reprinted by permission of the International Sociological Association and the author.

allegedly in France, are more apt to cultivate sociology intensively than societies with a long history of a more nearly uniform value-system, as allegedly in England; that a rising social class is constrained to see the social reality more authentically than a class long in power but now on the way out; that an upper class will focus on the static aspects of society and a lower one on its dynamic, changing aspects; that an upper class will be alert to the functions of existing social arrangements and a lower class to their dysfunctions; or, to take one last familiar generality, that socially conservative groups hold to multiple-factor doctrines of historical causation and socially radical groups to monistic doctrines. These and comparable statements may be true or not, but as the authors of the national reports remind us, we cannot say, for these are not typically the result of systematic investigations. They are, at best, impressions derived from a few particulars selected to make the point.

It will be granted that we sociologists cannot afford the dubious luxury of a double standard of scholarship; one requiring the systematic collection of comparable data when dealing with complex problems, say, of social stratification and another accepting the use of piecemeal illustrations when dealing with the no less complex problems of the sociology of knowledge. It might well be, therefore, that the chief outcome of this first session of the Congress will be to arrange for a comparative investigation of sociology in its social contexts similar to the investigation of social stratification that the Association has already launched. The problems formulated in the national papers and the substantial gaps in needed data uncovered by them would be a useful prelude to such an undertaking.

The growth of a field of intellectual inquiry can be examined under three aspects: as the historical filiation of ideas considered in their own right; as affected by the structure of the society in which it is being developed; and as affected by the social processes relating the men of knowledge themselves. Other sessions of the Congress will deal with the first when the substance and methods of contemporary sociology are examined. In his overview, Professor Aron considers the second by examining the impact on sociology of the changing social structure external to it: industrialization, the organization of universities, the role of distinctive cultural traditions, and the like. He goes on to summarize the central tendencies of certain national sociologies, principally those of the United States and the Soviet Union, and assesses their strengths and weaknesses. Rather than go over much the same ground to arrive at much the same observations, I shall limit myself to the third of these aspects. I shall say little about the social structure external to sociologists and focus instead on some social processes internal to the development of sociology and in particular on the role in that development played by social conflict between sociologists.

There is reason to believe that patterns of social interaction among sociologists, as among other men of science and learning, affect the changing contours of the discipline just as the cultural accumulation of knowledge manifestly does. Juxtaposing the national papers gives us an occasion to note the many substantial similarities if not identities in the development of sociology in each country that underlie the sometimes more conspicuous if not necessarily more thoroughgoing differences. These similarities are noteworthy if only because of the great variability and sometimes profound differences of social structure, cultural tradition, and contemporary values among the twelve nations whose sociology has been reviewed. These societies differ among themselves in the size of the underlying population, in the character of their systems of social stratification, in the number, organization and distribution of their institutions of higher learning, in their economic organization and the state of their technology, in their current and past political structure, in their religious and national traditions, in the social composition of their intellectuals, and so on through other relevant bases of comparison. In view of these diversities of social structure, it is striking that there are any similarities in the course sociology has taken in these societies. All this suggests that a focus on the social processes internal to sociology as a partly autonomous domain can help us to understand a little better the similarities of sociological work in differing societies. It may at the least help us identify some of the problems that could be profitably taken up in those monographs on the sociological history of sociology that have yet to be written.

One last introductory word: we have been put on notice that since the papers on national sociologies could not be circulated in advance, we should keep our general remarks to a minimum. I shall therefore omit much of the concrete material on which my paper is based.

PHASES OF SOCIOLOGICAL DEVELOPMENT

From the national reports, we can distinguish three broad phases in the development of sociology: first, the differentiation of sociology from antecedent disciplines with its attendant claim to intellectual legitimacy; second, the quest to establish its institutional legitimacy or academic autonomy; and third, when this effort has been moderately successful, a movement toward the re-consolidation of sociology with selected other social sciences. These well-known phases are of interest here insofar as they derive from processes of social interaction between sociologists and between them and scholars in related fields, processes that have left their distinctive mark on the kinds of work being done by sociologists.

Differentiation from Other Disciplines

The beginnings of sociology are of course found in the antecedent disciplines from which it split off. The differentiation differs in detail but has much the same general character in country after country. In England, we are told, sociology derived chiefly from political economy, social administration, and philosophy. In Germany, it shared some of these antecedents as well as an important one in comparative law. In France, its roots were in philosophy and, for a time, in the psychologies that were emerging. Its varied ancestry in the United States included a concern with practical reform, economics, and, in some degree, anthropology. Or, to turn to some countries which have been described by their reporters as "sociologically underdeveloped," in Jugoslavia, sociology became gradually differentiated from ethnology, the history of law and anthropogeography; in Spain, it was long an appendage of philosophy, especially the philosophy of history. The Latin American countries saw sociology differentiated from jurisprudence, traditionally bound up as it was with an interest in the social contexts of law and the formation of law that came with the creation, in these states, of governments of their own.

The process of differentiation had direct consequences for the early emphasis in sociology. Since the founding fathers were self-taught in sociology—the discipline was, after all, only what they declared it to be—they each found it incumbent to develop a classification of the sciences in order to locate the distinctive place of sociology in the intellectual scheme of things. Virtually every sociologist of any consequence throughout the nineteenth century and partly into the twentieth proposed his own answers to the socially induced question of the scope and nature of sociology and saw it as his task to evolve his own system of sociology.

Whether sociology is said to have truly begun with Vico (to say nothing of a more ancient lineage) or with St. Simon, Comte, Stein, or Marx is of no great moment here, though it may be symptomatic of current allegiances in sociology. What is in point is that the nineteenth century—to limit our reference—was the century of sociological systems not necessarily because the pioneering sociologists happened to be system-minded men but because it was their role, at that time, to seek intellectual legitimacy for this "new science of a very ancient subject." In the situation confronting them, when the very claim to legitimacy of a new discipline had to be presented, there was little place for a basic interest in detailed and delimited investigations of specific sociological problems. It was the framework of sociological thought itself that had to be built, and almost everyone of the pioneers tried to fashion one for himself.

The banal flippancy tempts us to conclude that there were as many sociological systems as there were sociologists in this early period. But of course this was not so. The very multiplicity of systems, each with its claim to being the genuine sociology, led naturally enough to the formation of schools, each with its masters, disciples, and epigoni. Sociology not only became differentiated from other disciplines but became internally differentiated. This was not in terms of specialization but in the form of rival claims to intellectual legitimacy, claims typically held to be mutually exclusive and at odds. This is one of the roots of the kinds of social conflict among sociologists today that we shall examine in a little detail.

Institutional Legitimacy of Sociology

If it was the founding fathers who initiated and defended the claim of sociology to intellectual legitimacy—as having a justifiable place in the culture—it was their successors, the founders of modern sociology—who pressed the claim to institutional legitimacy, by addressing themselves to those institutionalized status-judges of the intellect: the universities. Here again, the pattern in different nations differs only in detail. Whether ultimate control of the universities was lodged in the state or the church, it was their faculties that became the decisive audience for a Weber, Durkheim, or Simmel. Sociology was variously regarded by the faculties as an illegitimate upstart, lacking warrant for a recognized place in the collegial family, or sometimes as an institutional competitor. And this social situation repeatedly led to a limited number of responses by sociologists of the time.

They directed themselves, time and again (as some still do), to the questions that, satisfactorily answered, would presumably make the case for sociology as an autonomous academic discipline. They continued to deal with the question: is a science of society possible? And having satisfied themselves (and hopefully, others in the university) that it is, they turned above all to the further question, whose relevance was reinforced by the social condition of being on trial: what is sociology? that is to say, what is its distinctive scope, its distinctive problems, its distinctive functions; in short, its distinctive place in the academic world.

I do not try to enumerate the many answers to these questions, which we can all readily call to mind. What I do want to suggest is that the long-lasting focus on these questions seemed peculiarly pertinent, not only because of an immediate intellectual interest in them but because these were generations of sociologists seeking but not yet finding full academic legitimation. This sort of public search for an identity becomes widespread in a group rather than being idiosyncratic to a few of its members whenever a status or a way of life has yet to win acceptance or is under attack.

The socially induced search for an institutional identity led sociologists to identify a jurisdiction unshared by other disciplines. Simmel's notion of a geometry of social interaction and his enduring attention to the so-called molecular components of social relations is only one of the best-known efforts to center on elements of social life that were not systematically treated by other disciplines. It would be too facile to "derive" his interest in the distinctive sociology of everyday life from his experience of having been excluded, until four years before his death, from a professorship in a field that was still suspect. But this kind of individual experience may have reinforced an interest that had other sources. The early sociologists in the United States were responding to a comparable social situation in much the same way, locating such subjects of life in society as "corrections and charities" that had not yet been "pre-empted" for study.

A related consequence of the quest for academic legitimacy was the motivated separation of sociology from the other disciplines: the effort to achieve autonomy through self-isolation. We have only to remember, for example, Durkheim's taboo on the use of systematic psychology which, partly misunderstood, for so long left its stamp on the work stemming from this influential tradition in sociology.

The struggle for academic status may have reinforced the utilitarian emphasis found in sociology, whether in its positivistic or Marxist beginnings. However much the dominant schools disagreed in other respects, they all saw sociology as capable of being put to use for concerted objectives. The differences lay not in the repudiation or acceptance of utility as an important criterion of sociological knowledge but in the conception of what was useful.

As sociology achieved only limited recognition by the universities, it acquired peripheral status through the organizational device of research institutes. These have been of various kinds: as adjuncts to universities; as independent of universities but state-supported or -aided; and, in a few cases, as private enterprises. Socially, they tended to develop where the university system was felt to provide insufficient recognition. Just as in the seventeenth century, when no one arrived at the seemingly obvious thought of basing research laboratories for the physical sciences in the university, so we have witnessed a comparable difficulty, now overcome in many quarters, in arriving at the idea that the universities should house research organizations in the social sciences. They are now to be found in just about every country represented here. With their prevalently apprentice system of research training and, as the national papers report, with their greater readiness to try out new orientations in sociology, these institutes might well turn out to be a major force in the advancement of sociology. If so, they would represent an intellectual advance substantially responsive to the social situation of institutional exclusion or underrecognition.

Re-consolidation with Other Disciplines

As the institutional legitimacy of sociology becomes substantially acknowledged—which does not mean, of course, that it is entirely free from attack—the pressure for separatism from other disciplines declines. No longer challenged seriously as having a right to exist, sociology links up again with some of its siblings. But since new conceptions and new problems have meanwhile emerged, this does not necessarily mean re-consolidation with the same disciplines from which sociology drew its origins in a particular country.

Patterns of collaboration between the social sciences differ somewhat from country to country, and it would be a further task for the monographs on the sociology of sociology to try to account for these variations. Some of these patterns are found repeatedly. In France, we are told, the long-lasting connection between sociology and ethnology, which the Durkheim group had welded together, has now become more tenuous, with sociologists being increasingly associated with psychologists, political scientists, and geographers. In the United States, as another example, the major collaboration is with psychology—social psychology being the area of convergence—and with anthropology. Another cluster links sociology with political science and, to some extent, with economics. There are visible stirrings to renew the linkage, long attenuated in the United States, of sociology with history. The events long precede their widespread recognition. At the very time that American graduate students of sociology are learning to repeat the grievance that historical contexts have been lost to view by systematic sociology, the national organization of sociologists is devoting annual sessions to historical sociology and newer generations of sociologists, such as Bellah, Smelser, and Diamond, are removing the occasion for the grievance through their work and their program.

Each of the various patterns of interdisciplinary collaboration has its intellectual rationale. They are not merely the outcome of social forces. However, these rationales are apt to be more convincing, I suggest, to sociologists who find that their discipline is no longer on trial. It has become sufficiently legitimized that they no longer need maintain a defensive posture of isolation. Under these social circumstances, interdisciplinary work becomes a self-evident value and may even be exaggerated into a cultish requirement.

Summary

In concluding this sketch of three phases in the development of sociology, I should like to counter possible misunderstandings.

It is not being said that sociology in every society moves successively through these phases, with each promptly supplanted by the next. Concretely, these phases overlap and coexist. Nevertheless, it is possible to detect in the national reports a distinct tendency for each phase to be dominant for a time and to become so partly as a result of the social processes of opposition and collaboration that have been briefly examined.

It is not being said, also, that the social processes internal to sociology and related disciplines fully determine the course sociology has taken. But it is being said that together with *culturally* induced change in the contours of sociology, resulting from the interplay of ideas and cumulative knowledge, there is also *socially* induced change, such that particular preoccupations, orientations, and ideas that come to "make sense" to sociologists in one phase elicit little interest among them in another. The concrete development of sociology is of course not the product only of social processes immanent to the field. It is the resultant of social and intellectual forces internal to the discipline with both of these being influenced by the environing social structure, as the reports on national sociologies and the companion piece by Professor Aron have noted. The emphasis on social processes internal to sociology is needed primarily because the sociology of knowledge has for so long centered on the relations between social structures, external to intellectual life, and the course taken by one or another branch of knowledge.

Continuing with this same restriction of focus on social processes internal to the discipline, I turn now to some of the principal occasions for conflict between various styles of sociological work. In doing so, I am again mindful of the need for monographs on the sociological history of sociology emphasized in the papers presented to this session. If the linkages between sociology and social structure are to be seriously investigated, then it is necessary to decide which aspects of sociology might be so related. These would presumably include, as Professor Aron has indicated, the questions it asks, the concepts it employs, the objects it studies and the types of explanations it adopts. One way of identifying the alternative orientations, commitments, and functions ascribed to sociology is by examining, however briefly, the principal conflicts and polemics that have raged among sociologists. For these presumably exhibit the alternative paths that sociology might have taken in a particular society, but did not, as well as the paths it has taken. In reviewing some of these conflicts, I do not propose to consider the merits of one or another position. These are matters that will be examined in the other sessions of the Congress that deal with the various specialties and with the uses of sociology. I intend to consider them only as they exhibit alternative lines of development in sociology that are influenced by the larger social structure and by social processes internal to sociology itself.

SOME UNIFORMITIES IN THE CONFLICT OF SOCIOLOGICAL STYLES

A few general observations may provide a guide through the jungle of sociological controversy.

First, the reports on national sociologies naturally center on the dominant kinds of sociological work found in each country; on the modes rather than on the less frequent variants. But to judge from the reports, these sociologies differ not only in their central tendencies but also in the *extent of variation* around these tendencies. Each country provides for different degrees of heterodoxy in sociological thought, and these differences are probably socially patterned. In the Soviet Union, for example, there appears to be a marked concentration in the styles of sociological work with little variability: a heavy commitment to Marxist-Leninist theory with divergence from it only in minor details; a great concentration on the problem of the forces making for sequences of historical development of total societies; and a consequent emphasis, with little dispersion, upon historical evidence as the major source material. It would be instructive to compare the extent of dispersion around the dominant trends of sociological work in the United States, which are periodically subjected to violent attacks from within, as in the formidable book by Sorokin *Fads and Foibles in Modern Sociology* and in the recent little book by C. Wright Mills which, without the same comprehensive and detailed citation of seeming cases in point, follows much the same lines of argument as those advanced by Sorokin. As we compare the national sociologies, we should consider how the social organization of intellectual life affects the extent to which the central tendencies of each country's sociology are concentrated.

Much of the controversy among sociologists involves social conflict and not only intellectual criticism. Often, it is less a matter of contradictions between sociological ideas than of competing definitions of the role considered appropriate for the sociologist. Intellectual conflict of course occurs; an unremitting Marxist sociology and an unremitting Weberian or Parsonian sociology do make contradictory assumptions. But in considering the cleavages among a nation's sociologists, or among those of different nations, we should note whether the occasion for dispute is this kind of substantive or methodological contradiction or rather the claim that this or that sociological problem, this or that set of ideas, is not receiving the attention it allegedly deserves. I suggest that very often these polemics have more to do with the allocation of intellectual resources among different kinds of sociological work than with a closely formulated opposition of sociological ideas.

These controversies follow the classically identified course of social conflict. Attack is followed by counter-attack, with progressive alienation of each party to the conflict. Since the conflict is public, it becomes a status battle more nearly than a search for truth. (How many sociologists have publicly admitted to error as a result of these polemics?) The consequent polarization leads each group of sociologists to respond largely to stereotyped versions of what is being done by the other. As Professor Germani says, Latin American sociologists stereotype the North Americans as mere nose-counters or mere fact-finders or merely descriptive sociographers. Or others become stereotyped as inveterately speculative, entirely unconcerned with compelling evidence, or as committed to doctrines that are so formulated that they cannot be subjected to disproof.

Not that these stereotypes have no basis in reality at all, but only that, in the course of social conflict, they become self-confirming stereotypes as sociologists shut themselves off from the experience that might modify them. The sociologists of each camp develop selective perceptions of what is actually going on in the other. They see in the other's work primarily what the hostile stereotype has alerted them to see, and then promptly mistake the part for the whole. In this process, each group of sociologists become less and less motivated to study the work of the other, since there is manifestly little point in doing so. They scan the out-group's writings just enough to find ammunition for new fusillades.

The process of reciprocal alienation and stereotyping is probably reinforced by the great increase in the bulk of sociological publication. Like many other scholars, sociologists can no longer "keep up" with all that is being published in their field. They must become more and more selective in their reading. And this selectivity readily leads those who are hostile to a particular line of sociological work to give up studying the very publications that might possibly have led them to abandon their stereotype.

All this tends to move toward the emergence of an all-or-none doctrine. Sociological orientations that are not substantively contradictory are regarded as if they were. Sociological inquiry, it is said, must be statistical in character *or* historical; only the great issues of the time must be the objects of study *or* these refractory issues of freedom or compulsion must be avoided because they are not amenable to scientific investigation; and so on.

The process of social conflict would more often be halted in midcourse and instead turn into intellectual criticism if there were non-reciprocation of affect, if a stop were put to the reciprocity of contempt that typically marks these polemics. But we do not ordinarily find here the social setting that seems required for the non-reciprocation of affect to operate with regularity. This requires a differentiation of status between the parties, at least with respect to the occasion giving rise to the expression of hostility. When this status differentiation is present, as with the lawyer and his client or the psychiatrist and his patient, the non-reciprocity of expressed feeling is governed by a technical norm attached to the more authoritative status in the relationship. But in scientific controversies, which typically take place among a company of equals for the occasion (however much the status of the parties might otherwise differ) and, moreover, which take place in public, subject to the observation of peers, this structural basis for non-reciprocation of affect is usually absent. Instead, rhetoric is met with rhetoric, contempt with contempt, and the intellectual issues become subordinated to the battle for status.

In these polarized controversies, also, there is usually little room for the third, uncommitted party who might convert social conflict into intellectual criticism. True, some sociologists in every country will not adopt the all-or-none position that is expected in social conflict. They will not be drawn into what are essentially disputes over the definition of the role of the sociologist and over the allocation of intellectual resources though put forward as conflicts of sociological ideas. But typically, these would-be noncombatants are caught in the crossfire between the hostile camps. Depending on the partisan vocabulary of abuse that happens to prevail, they become tagged either as "mere eclectics," with the epithet, by convention, making it unnecessary to examine the question of what it asserts or how far it holds true; or, they are renegades, who have abandoned the sociological truth; or, perhaps worst of all, they are mere middle-of-the-roaders or fence-sitters who, through timidity or expediency, will not see that they are fleeing from the fundamental conflict between unalloyed sociological good and sociological evil.

We all know the proverb that "conflict is the gadfly of truth." Now, proverbs, that abiding source of social science for the millions, often express a part-truth just as they often obscure that truth by not referring to the conditions under which it holds. This seems to be such a case. As we have noted, in social conflict cognitive issues become warped and distorted as they are pressed into the service of "scoring off the other fellow." Nevertheless, when the conflict is regulated by the community of peers, it has its uses for the advancement of the discipline. With some regularity, it seems to come into marked effect whenever a particular line of investigation—say, of small groups—or a particular set of ideas—say, functional analysis—or a particular mode of inquiry—say, historical sociology or social surveys—has engrossed the attention and energies of a large and growing number of sociologists. Were it not for such conflict, the reign of orthodoxies in sociology would be even more marked than it sometimes is. Self-assertive claims that allegedly neglected problems, methods and theoretical orientation merit more concerted attention than they are receiving may serve to diversify the work that gets done. With more room for heterodoxy, there is more prospect of intellectually productive ventures, until these develop into new orthodoxies.

Even with their frequent intellectual distortions (and possibly, sometimes because of them), polemics may help redress accumulative imbalances in scientific inquiry. No one knows, I suppose, what an optimum distribution of resources in a field of inquiry would be, not least of all because of the ultimate disagreement over the criteria of the optimum. But progressive concentrations of effort seem to evoke counter-reactions, so that less popular but intellectually and socially relevant problems, ideas, and modes of inquiry do not fade out altogether. In social science as in other fields of human effort, a line of development that has caught on—perhaps because it has proved effective for dealing with certain problems—attracts a growing proportion of newcomers to the field who perpetuate and increase that concentration. With fewer recruits of high caliber, those engaged in the currently unpopular fields will have a diminished capacity to advance their work and with diminished accomplishments, they become even less attractive. The noisy claims to underrecognition of particular kinds of inquiry, even when accompanied by extravagantly rhetorical attacks on the work that is being prevalently done, may keep needed intellectual variants from drying up and may curb a growing concentration on a narrowly limited range of problems. At least, this possibility deserves study by the sociologist of knowledge.

These few observations on social conflict, as distinct from intellectual criticism, are commonplace enough, to begin with. It would be a pity if they were banalized as asserting that peace between sociologists should be sought at any price. When there is genuine opposition of ideas—when one set of ideas plainly contradicts another—then agreement for the sake of peaceful quiet would mean abandoning the sociological enterprise. I am suggesting only that when we consider the current disagreements among sociologists, we find that many of them are not so much cognitive oppositions as contrasting evaluations of the worth of one and another kind of sociological work. They are bids for support by the social system of sociologists. For the sociologist of knowledge, these conflicts afford clues to the alternatives from which the sociologists of each country are making their deliberate or unwitting selection.

TYPES OF POLEMICS IN SOCIOLOGY

These general remarks are intended as a guide to the several dozen foci of conflict between sociologists. Let me comfort you by saying that I shall not consider all of them here, nor is it necessary. Instead, I shall review two or three of them in a little detail and then merely identify some of the rest for possible discussion.

The Trivial and the Important in Sociology

Perhaps the most pervasive polemic, the one which, as I have implied underlies most of the rest stems from the charge by some sociologists that others are busily engaged in the study of trivia, while all about them the truly significant problems of human society go unexamined. After all, so this argument goes, while war and exploitation, poverty, injustice and insecurity plague the life of men in society or threaten their very existence, many sociologists are fiddling with subjects so remote from these catastrophic troubles as to be irresponsibly trivial.

This charge typically assumes that it is the topic, the particular objects under study, that fixes the importance or triviality of the investigation. This is an old error that refuses to stay downed, as a glance at the history of thought will remind us. To some of his contemporaries, Galileo and his successors were obviously engaged in a trivial pastime, as they watched balls rolling down inclined planes rather than attending to such really important topics as means of improving ship construction that would enlarge commerce and naval might. At about the same time, the Dutch microscopist Swammerdam was the butt of ridicule by those far-seeing critics who knew that sustained attention to his "tiny animals," the microorganisms, was an unimaginative focus on patently trivial minutiae. These critics often had authoritative social support. Charles II, for example, would join in the grand joke about the absurdity of trying to "weigh the ayre," as he learned of the fundamental work on atmospheric pressure which to his mind was nothing more than childish diversion and idle amusement when compared with the Big Topics to which natural philosophers should attend. The history of science provides a long if not endless list of instances of the easy confusion between the seemingly self-evident triviality of the object under scrutiny and the cognitive significance of the investigation.

Nevertheless, the same confusion periodically turns up anew in sociology. Consider the contributions of a Durkheim for a moment: his choice of the division of labor in society, of its sources and consequences, would no doubt pass muster as a significant subject, but what of the subject of suicide? Pathetic as suicide may be for the immediate survivors, it can seldom be included among the major troubles of a society. Yet we know that Durkheim's analysis of suicide proved more consequential for sociology than his analysis of social differentiation; that it advanced our understanding of the major problem of how social structures generate behavior that is at odds with the prescriptions of the culture, a problem that confronts every kind of social organization.

You can add at will, from the history of sociology and other sciences, instances which show that there is no *necessary* relation between the socially ascribed importance of the object under examination and the scope of its implications for an understanding of how society or nature works. The social and the scientific significance of a subject matter can be poles apart.

The reason for this is, of course, that ideally that empirical object is selected for study which enables one to investigate a scientific problem to particularly good advantage. Often, these intellectually strategic objects hold little intrinsic interest, either for the investigator or anyone else.

Again, there is nothing peculiar to sociology here. Nor is one borrowing the prestige of the better-established sciences by noting that all this is taken for granted there. It is not an intrinsic interest in the fruitfly or the bacteriophage that leads the geneticist to devote so much attention to them. It is only that they have been found to provide strategic materials for working out selected problems of genetic transmission. Comparing an advanced field with a retarded one, we find much the same thing in sociology. Sociologists centering on such subjects as the immigrant, the stranger, small groups, voting decisions or the social organization of industrial firms need not do so because of an intrinsic interest in them. They may be chosen, instead, because they strategically exhibit such problems as those of marginal men, reference group behavior, the social process of conformity, patterned sources of nonconformity, the social determination of aggregated individual decisions, and the like.

When the charge of triviality is based on a common-sense appraisal of the outer appearance of subject matter alone, it fails to recognize that a major part of the intellectual task is to find the materials that are strategic for getting to the heart of a problem. If we want to move toward a better understanding of the roots and kinds of social conformity and the socially induced sources of nonconformity, we must consider the types of concrete situations in which these can be investigated to best advantage. It does not mean a commitment to a particular object. It means answering questions such as these: which aspects of conformity as a social process can be observed most effectively in small, admittedly contrived and adventitious groups temporarily brought together in the laboratory but open to detailed observations? which aspects of conformity can be better investigated in established bureaucracies? and which require the comparative study of organizations in different societies? So with sociological problems of every kind: the forms of authority; the conditions under which power is converted into authority and authority into power; limits on the range of variability among social institutions within particular societies; processes of self-defeating and self-fulfilling cultural mandates; and so on.

If we ask, in turn, how we assess the significance of the sociological problem (rather than that of the object under scrutiny), then, it seems to me, sociologists have found no better answer than that advanced by Max Weber and others in the notion of *Wertbeziehung*. It is the relevance of the problem to men's values, the puzzles about the workings of social structure and its change that engage men's interests and loyalties. And the fact is that this rough-and-ready criterion is so loose that there is ample room for differing evaluations of the worth, as distinct from the validity and truth, of a sociological investigation even among those who ostensibly have the same general scheme of values. The case for the significance of problems of reference-group behavior, for example, stems from the cumulative recognition, intimated but not followed up by sociologists from at least the time of Marx, that the behavior, attitudes, and loyalties of men are not uniformly determined by their current social positions and affiliations. Puzzling inconsistencies in behavior are becoming less puzzling by systematically following up the simple idea that people's patterned selection of groups other than their own provide frames of normative reference which intervene between the influence of their current social position and their behavior.

In short, the attack on the alleged triviality of much sociological work, found apparently in all the national sociologies, is something less than the self-evident case it is made out to be. It often derives from a misconception of the connection between the selection of an object for study, the object having little intrinsic significance for people in the society, and the strategic value of that object for helping to clarify a significant sociological problem. In saying this, I assume that I will not be misunderstood. I am not saying that there is no genuinely trivial work in contemporary sociology any more than it can be said that there was no trivial work in the physical science of the seventeenth century. Quite otherwise: it may be that our sociological journals during their first fifty years have as large a complement of authentic trivia as the *Transactions* of the Royal Society contained during their first fifty years (to pursue the matter no further). But these are trivia in the strict sense rather than the rhetorical sense: they are publications which are both intellectually and socially inconsequential. But much of the attack on alleged trivia in today's sociology is directed against entire classes of investigation solely because the objects they examine do not enjoy widespread social interest.

This most pervasive of polemics sets problems for those prospective monographs on the sociological history of sociology. As I have repeatedly said, we are here not concerned with the substantive merit of the charges and rejoinders involved in any particular polemic of this kind. These can be and possibly will be discussed in the later sessions of this Congress. But for the sociological analysis of the history of sociology, there remains the task of finding out the social sources and consequences of assigning triviality or importance to particular lines of inquiry. It seems improbable that the angels of light are all on one side and the angels of darkness all on the other. If the division is not simply between the wise and the foolish, there must be other bases, some of them presumably social, for the various distributions of evaluation. The discussions that are to follow in this session might usefully be devoted to interpretations that might account for the opposed positions taken up in the assignment of merit to particular kinds of sociological work.

The Alleged Cleavage Between Substantive Sociology and Methodology

Another deep-seated and long-lasting conflict, requiring the same kind of interpretation, has developed between those sociologists who are primarily or exclusively concerned with inquiry into substantive problems of society and those who are primarily or exclusively concerned with solving the methodological problems entailed by such inquiry. Unlike the kind of intellectual criticism often developed within each of these camps, designed to clarify cognitive issues, this debate has the earmarks of social conflict, designed to best the opponent.

The main lines of attack on methodology and the replies to these are familiar enough to need only short summary.

Concern with methodology, it is said, succeeds only in diverting the attention of sociologists from the major substantive problems of society. It does so by turning from the study of society to the study of how to study society.

To this it is replied, in the words of one philosopher: "you cannot know too much of methods which you always employ." Responsible inquiry requires intellectual self-awareness. Whether they know it or not, the investigators speak methodological prose and some specialists must work out its grammar. To try to discover the rates of social mobility, and some of their consequences, for example, first requires solving the methodological problems of devising suitable classifications of classes, appropriate measures of rates, and the like, as some sociologists have learned, to their discomfiture.

Again, it is charged, that a concern with the logic of method quickly deteriorates into "mere technicism." These would-be precisionists strain at a gnat and swallow a camel: they are exacting in details and careless about their basic assumptions. For an interest in substantive questions they substitute an interest in seeming precision for its own sake. They try to use a razor blade to hack their way through forests. These technical virtuosos are committed to the use of meticulous means to frivolous ends.

The rebuttal holds that it is the methodologically naïve, those knowing little or nothing of the foundations of procedure, who are most apt to misuse precise measures on materials for which they are not suited. Further, that it is the assumptions underlying the quick and ready use of verbal constructs by investigators of substantive problems which need, and receive, critical scrutiny and clarification by the methodologist.

It is argued that the methodologist turns research technician, in spite of himself, and becomes an aimless itinerant, moving in whatever direction his research techniques summon him. He studies changing patterns of voting because these are readily accessible to his techniques rather than the workings of political institutions and organizations for which he has not evolved satisfying techniques of investigation.

The rejoinder holds that the selection of substantive problems is not the task of specialists in methodology. Once the problem is selected, however, the question ensues of how to design an inquiry so that it can contribute to a solution of the problem. The effort to answer such questions of design is part of the business of methodology.

During at least the last half-century, ideological significance has also been ascribed to methodological work. The methodologist is said to choose a politically "safe" focus of work rather than attending to substantive inquiries that might catch him up in criticism of the social institutions about him.

This allegation is treated by methodologists as not only untrue, but irrelevant. Practically all disciplines, even the strictly formal ones of logic and mathematics, have at one time or another been assigned political or ideological import. As we have been told here, even certain procedures of sociological research, such as "large-scale fieldwork" and the use of attitude scales, have been regarded as politically suspect in some nations. The irrelevance of the charge lies on its surface where the indefensible effort is made to merge intellectual and political criteria of scientific work.

The complaint is heard that the methodologist supposes knowledge to consist only of that which can be measured or at least counted. He is addicted to numbers. As a result, he retreats from historical inquiry and from all other forms of sociological inquiry where even crude measures have not been devised or where, in principle, they cannot be.

To the methodologist, this is a distorted image, fashioned by the uninformed who run as they read. He regards himself as no more committed to working out the logic of tests and measurements than the logic of historical and institutional analysis. This, he points out, has been understood by sociologists of consequence, at least from the time of Max Weber who, as Professor Adorno reminds us, "devoted a large part of his work to methodology, in the form of philosophical reflections on the nature and procedures of sociology," and who considered the methodology of historical inquiry, in particular, an important part of the sociological enterprise.

Since the opponents in this controversy show no trace of being either vanquished or converted, this raises anew the question of the grounds, other than intellectual, for maintaining their respective positions. Like the other persistent conflicts I shall now summarize far more briefly, this one sets a problem for the sociologist of knowledge.

The Lone Scholar and the Research Team

Until the last generation or so, the sociologist, like most other academic men, worked as an individual scholar (or, as the idiom has it, as a "lone scholar"). Since then, as the national reports inform us, institutes for sociological research have multiplied all over the world. This change in the social organization of sociological work has precipitated another conflict, with its own set of polarized issues.

The new forms of research are characterized, invidiously rather than descriptively or analytically, as the bureaucratization of the sociological mind. The research organization is said to stultify independent thought, to deny autonomy to members of the research staff, to suffer a displacement of motive such that researches are conducted in order to keep the research team or organization in operation rather than have the organization provide the facilities for significant research; and so on through the familiar calendar of indictments.

In return, it is pointed out that the individual scholar has not been as much alone as the description may imply. He was (and often is) at the apex of a group of research assistants and graduate students who follow his lead. Moreover, he has had to limit his problems for serious research to those for which the evidence lay close to hand, principally in libraries. He cannot deal with the many problems that require the systematic collection of large-scale data which are not provided for him by the bureaucracies that assemble census data and other materials of social bookkeeping. The research institute is said to extend and to deepen kinds of investigation that the individual scholar is foreclosed from tackling. Finally, it is suggested that close inspection of how these institutes actually work will find that many of them consist of individual scholars with associates and assistants, each group engaged in pursuing its own research bents.

This continuing debate affords another basis for inquiry, this time into the ways in which the social organization of sociological research in fact affects the character of the research. This would require the kind of systematic comparison of the work being done by individual scholars and by research teams, a methodical comparison which, so far as I know, has yet to be made. Not that the results of this inquiry will necessarily do away with the conflict but only that it will contribute to that as yet largely unwritten sociological history of sociology whose outlines all of us here aim to sketch out.

Cognitive Agreement and Value Disagreement

A particularly instructive type of case is provided by seeming intellectual conflict that divides sociologists of differing ideological persuasion. Upon inspection, this often (not, of course, always) turns out to involve cognitive agreements that are obscured by a basic opposition of values and interests.

To illustrate this type of conflict, we can draw upon a few observations by Marx and by so-called bourgeois sociologists. You will recall Marx's observation that in a capitalist society, social mobility "consolidates the rule of capital itself, enabling it to recruit ever new forces for itself out of the lower layers of society." This general proposition has won independent assent from all manner of non-Marxist sociologists, not least of all, from one such as Pareto. The lines of disputation are not therefore drawn about the supposed fact of these systematic consequences of social mobility. The conflict appears only in the evaluation of these consequences. For, as Marx went on to say, the "more a ruling class is able to assimilate the most prominent men of the dominated class the more stable and dangerous is its rule." A Pareto could agree with the stabilizing function of such mobility while rejecting the judgment of it as "dangerous." What empirical investigations by "bourgeois sociologists" can do, and are doing is to find out how far the cognitively identical assumption of a Marx and a Pareto holds true. To what extent do these mobile men identify themselves with their new-found class? Who among them retain loyalty to the old? When does it result in a consolidation of power and when, under conditions of retained values, does it modify the bases of cleavage between classes?

You can readily add other instances of agreement in sociological ideas being mistaken for disagreement, owing to an overriding conflict of values or interests between sociologists. When the functionalists examine religion as a social mechanism for reinforcing common sentiments that make for social integration, they do not differ significantly in their analytic framework from the Marxists, who, if the metaphor of the opium of the masses is converted into a neutral statement of alleged consequences, assert the same sort of thing, except that they evaluate these consequences differently. Religion is then seen as a device for social exploitation.

Again, it has often been noted that Marx, in his theory, underrated the social significance of his own moral ideas. The emphasis on Communist doctrine and ideology is perhaps the best pragmatic testimony that, whatever Marxist theory may say in general of the role of ideas in history, Marxists in practice ascribe great importance to ideas as movers, if not as prime movers, in history. If this were not so, the Communist emphasis on a proper ideological commitment would be merely expressive rather than instrumental behavior.

Or, to take one last instance, Marx repeatedly noted that the patterns of production—for example, in large-scale industry and among smallholding peasants—have each a distinctive social ecology. The spatial distribution of men on the job was held to affect the frequency and kind of social interaction between them and this, in turn, to affect their political outlook and the prospects of their collective organization. In these days, a large body of investigation by non-Marxists, both in industrial and in rural sociology, is centered on this same variable of the social ecology of the job, together with its systematic consequences. But again, this continuity of problem and of informing idea tends to be obscured by conflicts in political orientation. Detailed monographic study is needed to determine the extent to which lines of sociological development fail to converge and instead remain parallel because of ideological rather than theoretical conflict.

Formal (Abstract) and Concrete Sociology

Time and again, in the papers on national sociology, reference is made to the dangers of a "merely" formal sociology. This signals another familiar cleavage, that between concrete and abstract sociology. The first centers on interpreting particular historical constellations and developments. Sometimes these are society-wide in character; sometimes they are more limited social formations. The problem may be to explain the rise and transformation of Christianity or of capitalism, of particular class structures, family systems, or social institutions of science. The second, the formal orientation, is directed toward formulating general propositions and models of interpretation that cut across a variety of historically concrete events. Here the focus is on such abstract matters as role theory, social processes of legitimation, the effect of the size of a group on its characteristic patterns of social interaction, and so on.

To some, formal sociology is an invidious epithet. It is ascribed to "defenders of the established order" who expressly neglect social change and deny that there are discoverable uniformities of social change. For these critics, formal sociology is like a sieve that strains out all the awkward facts that fail to suit its theory. To others, concrete sociology is seen as having some utility but at the price of abdicating the search for those social regularities that presumably occur in cultures of most different kind.

It would serve little purpose to note the obvious at this point, for it is precisely the obvious that gets lost in this conflict between commitments to primarily concrete and primarily abstract sociologies. Little will be gained in repeating, therefore, that concrete sociological investigations of course make at least implicit use of abstract models—that, for example, in order even to depict social change, let alone account for it, one must identify the formally defined elements and patterns of social structure that are changing—and conversely, that these models often grow out of and are modified and judged by their applicability to selected aspects of concrete social events. With respect to this conflict, the sociology of knowledge confronts such problems as that of finding out whether, as is commonly said, formal sociology is linked with politically conservative orientations and concrete sociology with politically radical orientations. Furthermore, how this social cleavage affects the prospects of methodical interplay between the two types of sociology.

A Short Miscellany of Sociological Conflicts

There is time only to list and none at all to discuss a few more of the current conflicts in sociology.

The Microscopic and the Macroscopic. More than ever before conflict is focused on the social units singled out for investigation. This is often described by the catchwords of "microscopic" and "macroscopic" sociology. The industrial firm is said to be studied in isolation from the larger economic and social system or, even more, particular groups within the single plant are observed apart from their relations with the rest of the organization and the community. A microscopic focus is said to lead to "sociology without society." A counter-emphasis centers on the laws of evolution of "the total society." Here, the prevailing critique asserts that the hypotheses are put so loosely that no set of observations can be taken to negate them. They are invulnerable to disproof and so, rather a matter of faith than of knowledge.

Experiment and Natural History in Sociology. A parallel cleavage has developed between commitment to experimental sociology, typically though not invariably dealing with contrived or "artificial" small groups, and commitment to study of the natural history of groups or social systems. Perhaps the instructive analogue here is to be found in the well-known fact that Darwin and Wallace found certain problems forced upon their attentions when they reflected on what they saw in nature "on the large, on the outdoor scale" but that they failed to see other related problems that came into focus for the laboratory naturalists. Polarization into mutually exclusive alternatives served little purpose there and it remains to be seen whether it will prove any more effective in the advancement of sociology.

Reference-Groups of Sociologists. Conflict is found also in the sometimes implicit selection of reference-groups and audiences by sociologists. Some direct themselves primarily to the literati or to the "educated general public"; others, to the so-called "men of affairs" who manage economic or political organizations; while most are oriented primarily to their fellow academicians and professionals. The recurrent noise about jargon, cults of unintelligibility, the over-abundant use of statistics or of mathematical models is largely generated by the sociologists who have the general public as their major reference group. The work of these outer-oriented sociologists, in turn, is described by their academic critics as sociological journalism, useful more for arousing public interest in sociology than for advancing sociological knowledge. They are said to persuade by rhetoric rather than to instruct by responsible analysis—and so on. It would be instructive to study the actual roles and functions of these diversely oriented sociologists, rather than to remain content with offhand descriptions such as these, even though again we cannot expect that the results of such study would modify current alignments.

Sociology vs. Social Psychology. One last debate requires mention, at least. It is charged that many sociologists, especially in the United States, are converting sociology into social psychology, with the result that the study of social institutions is fading into obscurity. The trend toward social psychology is said to be bound up with an excessive emphasis on the subjective element in social action, with a focus on men's attitudes and sentiments at the expense of considering the institutional conditions for the emergence and the effective or ineffective expression of these attitudes. To this, the polarized response holds that social institutions comprise an idle construct until they are linked up empirically with the actual attitudes and values and the actual behavior of men, whether this is conceived as purposive or as also unwitting, as decisions or as responses. These sociologists consider the division between the two disciplines an unfortunate artifact of academic organization. And again, apart from the merits of one or the other position, we have much to learn about the social bases for their being maintained by some and rejected by others.

A CONCLUDING OBSERVATION

In a final remark on these and the many other lines of cleavage among sociologists, I should like to apply a formulation about the structure of social conflict in relation to the intensity of conflict that was clearly stated by Georg Simmel and Edward Ross. This is the hypothesis, in the words of Ross, that

> a society . . . which is riven by a dozen . . . [conflicts] along lines running in every direction, may actually be in less danger of being torn with violence or falling to pieces than one split along just one line. For each new cleavage contributes to narrow the cross clefts, so that one might say that society *is sewn together* by its inner conflicts.

It is an hypothesis borne out by its own history, for since it was set forth by Simmel and by Ross, it has been taken up or independently originated by some scores of sociologists, many of whom take diametrically opposed positions on some of the issues we have reviewed. (I mention only a few of these: Wiese and Becker, Hiller, Myrdal, Parsons, Berelson, Lazarsfeld and McPhee, Robin Williams, Coser, Dahrendorf, Coleman, Lipset, and Zelditch, and, among the great number of recent students of "status-discrepancy," Lenski, Adams, Stogdill, and Hemphill.)

Applied to our own society of sociologists, the Simmel-Ross hypothesis has this to say. If the sociologists of one nation take much the same position on each of these many issues while the sociologists of another nation consistently hold to the opposed position on them all, then the lines of cleavage will have become so consolidated along a single axis that any conversation between the sociologists of these different nations will be pointless. But if, as I believe is the case, there is not this uniformity of outlook among the sociologists of each nation; if individual sociologists have different combinations of position on these and kindred issues, then effective intellectual criticism can supplant social conflict.

That is why the extent of heterodoxies among the sociologists of each nation has an important bearing on the future development of world sociology. The heterodoxies in one nation provide intellectual linkages with orthodoxies in other nations. On the world-wide scale of sociology, this bridges lines of cleavage and makes for the advance of sociological science rather than of sociological ideologies.

2

JAMES B. McKEE

Some Observations on the Self-Consciousness of Sociologists

MOST OF US, as working sociologists, are deeply absorbed in our teaching and research, our writing and our professional activities, and like busy people in most academic fields, we have little time to ruminate upon just what it is we are doing. Only on occasion are we brought to some conscious inspection of ourselves, our lives, and the discipline to which we are committed. Sometimes, this may occur when a C. Wright Mills or another disenchanted or even alienated colleague publishes a severely critical piece, or when sociologists accuse other sociologists of being ideological or selling out to the establishment. Perhaps more than other disciplines, we make charges and counter-charges about our scientific status, our proper commitments to mankind, etc. Some even publish books that seek to put sociology on trial.

I am not here to make charges and certainly not to put my discipline on trial. I would like to try another stance. I would like to invite you to share with me this evening an effort to take a somewhat bemused and sympathetic view of our discipline as it engages from time to time in a self-consciousness of sociologists.

I would begin by asserting that sociology lives in an eternal tension between two polar thrusts: a concern for the relevance of sociology in providing an understanding of our society and our times, and a conscious determination to create a science of sociology. I am aware that many of you would argue that there is no necessary contradiction or incompatibility

Presidential Address to the Ohio Valley Sociological Society, 1967. Originally published in the *Ohio Valley Sociologist* (now *Sociological Focus*), XXXII (Summer, 1967), 1–16. Reprinted by permission of the Ohio Valley Sociological Society and the author.

between these two; but I am also aware that these two aims have produced discrepant views of the discipline in its past, and that the tension still exists.

As a teacher of sociology I have long had the impression that we have been little concerned with telling our students very much about our own social origins. It is as if we were like the second-generation children of immigrants or eager mobile aspirants for upper-middle class status: we are a little embarrassed, if not ashamed, of our humble origins. Our too long marginal status in the scientific community leads us to emphasize present accomplishments and future prospects over antecedents and genealogy.

But when we do say something to them, we often confuse *wish* with *fact*, because we describe our growth and development as if it followed the model of science-building according to the prescriptions of the philosophers of science. However, our discipline did not grow in that way (nor did any other science, for that matter, if we pay serious attention to the historians of science). We did not construct sociological theory in a cumulative fashion; we did not arrive at where we are now by steadily placing brick upon verified brick. Rather, our route was twisting and arduous, largely unmapped, and ever shifting in emphasis and interest with changes in the concerns of our society.

I have always felt that there is epistemological significance in the fact that sociology is itself involved in its own subject matter; it is inescapably a part of what it is analyzing. Thus, its consciousness of its universe of discourse is part of its self-consciousness. But its consciousness of the universe it studies have never been a cultural perspective unique to sociology. Rather, we have shared with most other men a view of the world that states at the outset what is valued and what is real.

The tension between social relevance and scientific sociology has often raised that consciousness to a more critical point, to a more intense awareness of ourselves as sociologists behaving in the context of the world we study. And the tension has pressed many sociologists to develop two distinct images of sociological consciousness and commitment.

One of these is a concerned and relevant sociology that probes into the meaning of private lives in the context of changing public institutions, a consciousness brilliantly expressed by C. Wright Mills in *The Sociological Imagination*. The other is that sober image of a rigorous science, inspiring in its rational aspirations, that strives toward methodological skill, careful theory construction, and a value-free position that would keep it from being caught up in the ever changing concerns and troubles of society.

Sociology has never been able to choose irrevocably between them, in the sense that a full commitment to one would exclude the other. We are now in a time in which we have strongly opted for scientific sociology, and the future seems assuredly to be that. Yet, many who welcome the scientific advance still cling to the more humanistic concerns of an earlier day. A large number of sociologists, I am sure, are ambiguous and would prefer not to choose in any final sense. Indeed, the argument that we do not have to do so is one protective stance on this issue.

But I am going to argue that we are not going to be able to make any such choice in the near future, anyway. And I am going to argue further that sociology is going to continue in one major way as it has in the past: its own development is so intricately involved in modern society that its major internal changes are going to be in response to changes in society, rather than the cumulative development of a science by the model set forth by the philosophers of science. Let me see if I can make myself clear by glancing quickly into our past and relating it to the present.

SOCIAL PROBLEMS AND SCIENTIFIC STATUS

We are all aware that American sociology began around the turn of the century with an intensive involvement in the then relevant social problems of American life. Immigration and urbanization seemed to produce a range of problems that centered largely upon social life under conditions of transiency and difficult social adjustment for large numbers of people recently arrived either from Europe or from the American farm or small town.

Nurtured by society's interest in turning social scientific scrutiny upon the troublesome and disturbing transition to a modern, urbanized society, sociology recruited students and faculty preponderantly around this concern. The result largely shaped the structure of the discipline for the first third of this century. The curriculum of a typical department offered courses in social problems (then first called social pathology, later social disorganization) and courses in criminology, juvenile delinquency, social work, race and ethnic relations, the family, social control, immigration, population, the city, and rural life. And the teaching to undergraduates was permeated by a preaching of a moral perspective, a professional ideology, as C. Wright Mills called it, that generated an anti-urban bias in sociology, while strongly reflecting the small-town, Protestant background of so many of those who were early recruits to the discipline. Even the urban sophistication of a Louis Wirth did not escape this influence, as the implicit value structure of his justly famous and influential essay, "Urbanism as a Way of Life," makes abundantly clear to any perceptive reader.

The concern for social problems, then, constituted the strongest link between sociology and society. It permeated sociology with a moral concern that reflected middle-class values, it strongly influenced recruitment, it shaped the sociological curriculum, it linked sociology closely to social work, and it even influenced sociological theory: witness the emphasis upon social control and the implicit typological distinction between rural and urban.

It was this social-problems orientation that came under attack when a growing desire for scientific status led to an emphasis upon methodology and to the use of natural science as a significant reference group. The implicit value judgment contained in the concept of social disorganization was replaced, at least partly, by the concept of social problems as defined by Fuller and Myers. Sociology departments increasingly divorced themselves from social work, emphasized their value neutrality, and more and more the social-problems emphasis was confined to the undergraduate program. Graduate work was increasingly concerned with the problems of methodology and research, and a new order of dominant research interests came to the fore during the 1940's: formal organization and industrial sociology, for example, and the experimental study of small groups.

Such a development, largely during the two decades from the mid-1930's to the mid-1950's, played down the middle-class reformist concerns which had so predominantly articulated sociology to society and replaced it with a new emphasis upon graduate training and research, a new set of research interests that were sociological problems but not usually social problems, and a greater concern for developing sociology as a science than for solving society's problems. The new points of articulation became that between the research scholar and the foundation and government agency. Increasingly, sociologists took a professionalized view of their discipline, giving primacy to the profession and its growth and development and secondary consideration to the university and its historic commitments.

Yet, the interest in social problems as a major way of relating sociology to society maintained itself; the formation in the early 1950's of the Society for the Study of Social Problems gave structure and visibility to those who held a definition of sociology different from the dominant one. But this resurgence of social problems has clearly been different from what it was in the early days of sociology. The specific substantive issues have changed considerably and the obvious moralizing tone has gone. Now the sociologists of social problems struggle with two difficult issues: the need for a theory of social problems and the issue of values and objectivity. The latter is of particular importance, but both exist only because the model of science defines largely what we want sociology to be.

Alvin Gouldner's now classic presidential address five years ago, "Anti-

Minotaur: The Myth of a Value-Free Sociology," with impressive scholarship made the case that the myth of objectivity had once served sociology positively by enhancing its autonomy, thus freeing it from an inhibiting involvement with meliorist and service institutions and rendering it freer to pursue what interested sociologists. Yet, as Gouldner noted, sociology paid a price for such autonomy, particularly, the muting of its criticism of society.

Gouldner's persuasive argument that a value-free sociology is a myth left many problem-oriented sociologists in a quandary. Thus, one of its most capable practitioners, Howard Becker, in his 1966 presidential address to SSSP, asked us, "Whose side are we on?" What I take to be most crucial was his apparent central assumption, shared, I believe, by many sociologists, that sociological research cannot avoid taking one ideological stance or the other: to conduct research that reflects the perspective of the superordinates, the dominants, management, the top elite, the responsible and respected one, the establishment, *or* to conduct research that leads us to sympathize with, and better understand, the underdogs, the lower class, the minorities, the employees, the subordinates, even the outcasts, and so to be critical of society in a way which the former research does not encourage. Since we idealize a pure science, such ideologically tinged research is incomplete and unsatisfactory to us. Becker seems to offer a long-run solution in that "each 'one-sided' study will provoke further studies that gradually enlarge our grasp of all the relevant facets of an institution's operation." The truth, apparently, is a sociological putting together into a single whole the several truths gained from divergent, conflicting and even incompatible perspectives. This is clearly a hope rather than a program, and an expressed hope that fails to examine the tough epistemological issues implied. Certainly it is not self-evident that one reaches some higher level of truth simply by conducting research from the perspectives of several participants different in status and power within a social structure.

Yet, Gouldner and Becker are correct in making it clear that sociological research does not proceed value-free. Perhaps it is most evident in research on social problems that a value commitment, even if unexplicit, underlies the theoretical perspective from which a research program emanates. Research begins with a stance toward the world, an existential assertion of what is valued and what is real.

Witness, for example, the study of race relations by American sociologists. In their first efforts to measure prejudice and social distance in the 1920's, American sociological research proceeded on the assumption that the basic problem was the prejudicial attitude and discriminatory behavior of whites toward Negroes in a society in which whites are dominant and have both power and social competency. Negroes, in turn, were seen as powerless and also largely incompetent by virtue of low status and limited educational experience. Thus, research sought to discover why whites were prejudiced, how they discriminated, and so became research on whites. Not until the late 1930's did sociological research turn its attention to the Negro, and much of that research, you may recall, was the study of Negro socialization in varying urban and rural, Southern and Northern, contexts: e.g., *Growing Up in the Black Belt*.

In short, the basic ideological assumptions of American sociologists until very recently were those of the middle-class liberal, in particular, his assumptions about power and organization. I would refer you specifically to an influential work of the 1950's, *A Manual of Intergroup Relations*, by John Dean and Alex Rosen, which quite explicitly assumed that the social power to alter the existing structure of discriminatory relations was held entirely by a small power elite of the community. This logically dictated a strategy based almost entirely upon inducing and manipulating in a behind-the-scenes manner key members of the elite; the authors made it quite clear that social change could come only in this way. Since I have more carefully argued the ideological nature of this position more fully elsewhere, I will cite it here only in passing as an example of what is most evident, perhaps, in research on controversial social problems, but certainly is true of all social research.

One could note in passing that the incident of the Moynihan Report only further adds to this issue. Though basing his study upon E. Franklin Frazier's classic analysis of the Negro family, Moynihan soon discovered that his report encountered the ideological opposition of the Negro revolt and the Civil Rights movement. It is not my intent here to explore the merits of this issue in detail, but only to suggest again that what could be a comfortable sociological position at one time may be ideologically controversial at another.

Or, again, witness the new concern for poverty. Social scientists, except for some economists, had little interest in this problem until the late fifties and early sixties. They seemed to share the common attitude that the welfare state had largely gained control of the problem and that the central issues of our time were those made problematic by affluence. So stated John Galbraith in *The Affluent Society*. But economic efforts to measure poverty quantitatively, and then Michael Harrington's widely influential *The Other America*, based partly on these studies, simply redefined the issue—and poverty became a significant aspect of the social reality of modern America. We saw clearly now what we had not seen for years. You are probably all familiar with the flood of books that have followed—if nothing else, sociologists and publishers have found a new, marketable commodity. It is not merely the rediscovery of poverty that invites explanation in terms of some sociology of knowledge, but a recognition on our part of what such a loss from our perspective and subsequent rediscovery tells us about the consciousness of sociologists.

Perhaps even more relevant is the fact that a government-sponsored war on poverty has underwritten a great deal of social research and has produced almost overnight a plethora of sociological experts on poverty. But note one thing pertaining to the ideological issue. Oscar Lewis' concept of the "culture of poverty" has been interpreted by some as defining the social psychological character of poor people, logically requiring certain types of remedial programs aimed particularly at education and the raising of levels of individual social competency. But other sociologists have opted for the organization of the poor and for their opportunity to participate in decisions concerning their own welfare, thus postulating the need for radical structural reform. Two major research centers, both at midwestern universities, have been organized for social research on poverty; one emphasizes education and training, and is supported generously by federal grants. The other operates from an ideologically different perspective and receives much less support. Their two journals are a remarkable contrast in how social scientists can so differently view the presumably same social world.

What does this short excursion into the area of social problems, ideology, and sociological research tell us? Certainly, among other things it provides no basis for dismissing Gouldner's strictures on the value-free mythology; instead, it provides data that must impress us about the pervasive power of ideology to shape sociological thinking, define problems, provide perspective and point of view, and state a culturally powerful definition of reality that undergirds, in assumptions, the sociological research we undertake. The sociological perspective is conscious that values deny full objectivity and it also recognizes the relativity of stances by which truth is perceived. But it is still too often unaware and unimaginative about the power of cultural assumptions to shape sociological definitions to the situation, in short, of how diffuse cultural perspectives provide sociological assumptions about what is real and what is valued, about what is taken for granted and what is open for definition—and this at the outset of social research. Methodological rigor can never erase these.

Our long experience with the study of social problems, then, continues to provide us with relevant experience about problems of ideology, definitions of reality, relativity, and bias toward and against superiors and inferiors, as these bear significantly upon the research we carry on. Yet, it seems that such experience has not taken us beyond the positions articulated by Gouldner and Becker: Gouldner, that a genuine value freedom is unattainable but that a belief in it by sociologists has functions and dysfunctions for the discipline; Becker, that research from different ideological perspectives may someday hopefully provide a sociological truth. Both recognize that sociology can and usually does get caught on opposing value positions with consequences for what it does and what it even purports to be. But we are left without any way to extricate ourselves—and without any full discussion of what this means for our conception of a relevant epistemology. Thus, for all their relevance and cogency, Gouldner and Becker are pre-Mannheim.

No amount of scientific improvement, no increase in our confidence in stating that we are constructing a science of sociology, has resolved a basic issue. Unlike the natural sciences, we have not created a scientific perspective that views the world in terms that are different from various non-sociological perspectives. Whether we can do so remains a moot point.

But I am primarily concerned with one simple point: that our sociological consciousness has been deficient in failing to appreciate how much what happens to sociology as it changes and develops is part and parcel of what is happening to the larger world into which we are inextricably interwoven. What *has* happened to us, what *is* happening to us, and what *will* happen to us, is part of a broader experience and change that is happening to the world. We can neither understand nor control our own development except as we become intensely conscious and critical of this basic process. Let me suggest what seem to be several major developments that now are changing sociology and will continue to do so in the years that lie ahead.

PROFESSIONALIZATION

Many of you share with me the experience of having been in sociology long enough to be sensitive to and appreciative of many changes that have occurred. Perhaps one of the most significant of these has been the thrust toward professionalization that has become a major aspect of the discipline in recent years—so much so that "discipline" has become a term less frequently heard. Certainly, much of our national reorganization has been to create a professional association, instead of a scholarly society. We have acted as if "professional" and "scientific" denoted the same or at least mutually reinforcing processes, even though our own specialists can tell us a great deal about the structure and perspective of professions that ought to be instructive to us. Yet, the sociology of professions and the professionalization of sociology have seemingly had little intellectual contact.

What is important for us, it seems to me, is to recognize that professionalization is a basic process in modern society, a fundamental transformation of the status of the middle class, with significant structural and ideological implications for industrial societies. It alters the relationships of social classes, redistributes social power, redefines the meaning of elite, creates professionalized experts and specialists, and enhances the value placed upon education. In short, it creates a new social reality, a new pattern of human society; it maximizes a new set of values and gives dominance to a professionalized perspective of the social world.

The professionalization of sociology is occurring in the context of this wider change. The newer breed of professional sociologists coming into being will view the world more and more from the detached and cool perspective of the professional. This clearly is functional for the promotion of scientific detachment and that kind of objectivity so highly desired by the methodologically conscious—an ability to remain emotionally uninvolved in order to perform expertly.

But any sociologist of the professions can also suggest the problems and dysfunctions that beset all professions: their concern for status relations to others, their sometimes constraining system of rewards and sanctions, their conception of social obligations, their need to define a professional code of ethics, their often closed and rigid structure, their ideological orthodoxy. If professions serve society expertly, they do so by converting the value-laden and ideological issues of one time into the technical problems of another. Witness the way in which the ideological conflicts of the 1930's between labor and management were reduced to technical problems of negotiation and arbitration between great and established bureaucracies, mediated by skilled professionals. The peace that society attained has not been without its price, the major one being the decline of a genuine labor movement. The charismatic labor leader has been replaced by the professional negotiator and arbitrator. Another example: since the 1940's we have built in America a new profession of intergroup relations experts, temporarily overshadowed and ideologically confused by the Negro revolt (some of it being a rejection of them and their professional functions) and we are also now building a new profession for negotiating with and for the poor. Each of these draws heavily upon the paralleling professional development of sociology. Though we have not yet succeeded in America, we are clearly intent on mastering and taming these ideological issues by establishing ground rules and basic rights that then permit negotiations and mediation, gradual change, and the keeping of the peace.

To point this out is not to criticize. Rather, it is to underscore the sweeping impact of professionalization in modern society and to suggest how important it is that we be aware of this. Our urge to professionalize needs to be tempered with a recognition of the consequences of professionalization, not all of which are conducive to the maintaining of a critical and inquiring perspective. Scientific and professional are only sometimes compatible.

MODERNIZATION

One of the great events of our time is the modernization of traditional societies; here is a radical transformation of the world, a change in the relationships among societies, and a revolutionary reorganizing of social structure. New ideologies and new elites have come into being, and the Western world seeks a new *rapprochement* with the non-Western.

The involvement of intellectuals, professionals, and technicians in this has provided new horizons and opportunities for social science, and American sociology in particular will never be the same. We have long told ourselves that we are too American, too parochial—and the process of modernization in Africa, in Asia, and in Latin America has created just the conditions for change.

But as yet we have not been self-conscious enough about just what this change in sociology, induced by its involvement in the study of modernization, has been. We have noted only the obvious benefit—the opportunity for comparative study. Let me suggest that these are the significant points:

(*1*) By becoming comparative, sociology has enriched the materials of analysis and broken through an American parochialism, but the implications of this for theory and methodology are yet to come.

(*2*) The once denounced and discredited evolutionary approach has returned to intellectual respectability. To be sure, contemporary neo-evolutionary theorizing is a restatement that carefully avoids all those aspects that once discredited it. But the return to an evolutionary perspective is a return to the same kind of problems that interested so many of the pioneer sociologists in the nineteenth century—the radical transformation of the structure of human societies from one basic type or form to another.

(*3*) There is the emergence of a dominant interest in processes of social change, rather than in more static versions of social structure—indeed, a return to an interest in process *and* structure. What this suggests to me is that a changed sociological perspective will simply no longer find the same dominating interest in the kind of structural-functional theorizing that reached its high-water mark in the late 1950's.

(*4*) There is a renewed interest in macrosociology, in the study of society and social institutions. During the last two decades, many sociologists simply ceased to employ "society" and "institution" in their sociological vocabulary, for they were in fact studying something else. Now sociologists are looking at whole societies, at large social structures, not merely at small pieces.

(5) The return to the study of society once more links us with so many of the seminal thinkers of the nineteenth century. But we are also twentieth-century social scientists, and we feel compelled to do our studying scientifically. Yet, it is just in the methodology of such study that we are most wanting. There has now emerged a pressure for methodological innovations in the study of large social structures.

More than anything else, I think, the study of modernization has broken the apparent unity of method and theory, the conceptual consensus, that so many sociologists, from Parsons on, thought they saw a decade ago. It has produced a consciousness of new directions of theoretical development, of breaking with seemingly solidly established sociological orthodoxies. There may today be more sociologies than there were ten, fifteen, or even twenty years ago.

NATIONAL POLICY AND RATIONAL KNOWLEDGE

But if the non-Western world is changing and forcing intellectual change upon us, so is our own society. One major change is the growth of a rational perspective toward social issues that converts them into scientifically solvable problems and then into social policies and programs of concerted action. First the sciences, and now the social sciences, have become nationally valued brain power. Science is an instrument of national policy.

This has led to the cultivation of scientific talent, to national support for graduate education, and to the underwriting of research. It has produced new, complex relationships between sociologists and government. Camelot is but one example of new kinds of experiences in mixing social research and government interests that is likely to occur more than once.

We would be naïve indeed if we did not recognize how we are changing as part of this process. Here are some of the conditions inducing our professionalization, here is the extensive support for research that has turned our major departments into primary centers for graduate training and research. We have, then, a professional stake in this change, and we have become relatively affluent because of it. But certainly we have lost some options, too. We have been coopted into the national skilled manpower pool, and sociologists are so dutifully listed. We have joined the nationally supported professions. Intellectually, our range of critical perspective has been narrowed, for we are more integrated into society, more committed to its basic policies and processes.

THE POST-MODERN WORLD AND FUTURE-MAKING

Let me extend this concern with the implications for sociology of an increasingly rationalized world. What needs to enter into the sociological consciousness is an appreciation of the change that so many different social scientists have come to call *post-modern* or some related term. It is a growing recognition that the world called modern has changed so much that today it is very unlike what it was even a few decades ago. The topological contrast between *Gemeinschaft* and *Gesellschaft*, or between modern and traditional in studying developing societies, or between rural and urban in the American experience, no longer suffice to define the contemporary world, or to give us any sensitivity to where we are going. We have been modern long enough to have absorbed the experience, and we are moving on.

The consequence of this has been an outbreak of some bold and exciting literature that seeks to compare modern, industrial, urban, as we have sociologically defined it, with something newer, a post-modern. It is not merely a world in which change occurs rapidly, but in which change and innovation is deliberately induced as a matter of rational policy, and in which the redesigning of social structure is a major intellectual task. It is a world in which men deliberately and consciously create new values, new life styles, new roles and structures, yes, even new traditions—it is, in short, a world in which men are aware of their capacity to create their own future.

Indeed, a new intellectual elite—the future-makers—are already upon us. I see their impact upon sociology as severalfold:

Their most devastating impact will be upon our conceptualizations, our images of reality. For they will make it clear that we can create new realities not even dreamed of before. The epistemological implications of man's capacity to creat culture, deliberately and rationally, may perhaps suggest more strongly than ever before that the social sciences are not indeed of the exact same order as the natural sciences.

Yet, the future-makers will have a positive effect upon methodology and research design. Their innovations will encourage the development of more refined techniques, all the way to computer simulation. Indeed, the new culture of change may prove that what will develop cumulatively in sociology will be methodology, but that theory will be unable to do so. Perhaps there can only be theories, each one adequate to the culturally created social world in which it emerges and with which it shares assumptions about reality, and for which it was designed as scientific analysis.

THE TWO CULTURES AND MASS SOCIETY

Several of the issues that I have mentioned—professionalization, national policy and rational knowledge, post-modern and future-making—converge in emphasizing one fundamental change in Western culture, the progressive rationalization of social life that Max Weber bequeathed to us as his greatest insight. And Weber, dedicated to reason as he was, nonetheless hesitated to embrace the conception of a totally rational and rationalized society. In large part, though not entirely, sociology stands with those who press for the development and use of rational knowledge, and thus for the shaping of a rational society. We are largely on the side of science, rationality, and technology.

But our sociological consciousness should be aware that this is not the only side to be on, the only stance toward the future to take. Those who are resistant to taking this side have brought into sociology the concept of mass society, and this diffuse, ill-defined term connotes a view of the world that is primarily romantic and existentialist. It harkens back to such nineteenth-century names as Nietzsche and Kierkegaard, Jacob Burckhardt and Dostoevsky, the young Marx and Max Weber, and in our time to Ortega y Gasset, Sartre and Camus, and many others. Its current flows from many sources and human experiences, but its basic position is clear: an unequivocal moral stand against the social world that the Industrial Revolution brought into being. From the nineteenth-century bohemian attack upon bourgeois values and life-style to beatnik and beat and hippie culture with its cult of personal freedom and autonomy and its uncommitted, cool world view, there has been an underground of opposition to a world increasingly rationalized. It is a struggle against a technologically dominated world defined as dehumanizing. It manifests itself in varied ways over time, and it loses ground when it becomes too popular and tolerated.

Some of this is manifested among the sociologists of deviant behavior, who present romantic descriptions of social deviants or of lower-class Negro males or uncommitted youth and make of them heroic anti-heroes of the modern world. The sensitive and perceptive writings of Goffman and Becker and Jules Henry are found here. Even much of pop culture is permeated with this perspective. Indeed, one reason that the old division between serious and popular art has lost its sharpness is because both share in the same world view.

C. P. Snow recognized that the world of science and the world of art were two worlds that did not communicate, but he totally failed to understand why. In the last analysis, his world view was the view of rational science and he simply could not grasp the other perspective. The commitment of science to rationality puts it clearly on one side; it has little problem. The commitment of humanism to man over science puts art and literature mostly on the other side. But social science simply cannot move entirely to one side or the other, though undoubtedly most sociologists opt for rationality.

The very effort of sociologists to understand the underground perspective opens the sociological consciousness to the integrity of another world view and to the significance of its definitions of reality. Once concepts like alienation and commitment and mass society have entered the sociological tent, we are back to the problem that Howard Becker worried over, whose side are we on?

But for now at least there is undoubtedly one significant, and I think positive, contribution of the division: we are prevented from a too early closure of our own world view by being forced both to understand and take theoretical account of underdog and deviant perspectives that define what is valued and what is real in ways remote from our other studies and our own experiences, for as professionals we are not of that other world.

It may be worth an additional note, too, to point out that sociology has always emphasized certain features of society and studiously neglected others. It has long neglected the sociology of ideology, of religion (in the sense of religious belief), of art and literature, and the sociology of knowledge. But our need to understand the revolt against a rationalized world requires that we probe these areas, that, in short, we develop a sociology of culture and thus press sensitive sociological inquiry into the conscious efforts of men to define themselves, to seek meaning for human existence, and to construct social worlds out of the meanings attributed to human experiences. Certainly, what makes the religious world so sociologically exciting today is the revolt of the theologically conscious and committed, a revolt manifested best in sensitive minds in seminaries and coffee-houses, college campuses and Negro slums, a revolt in search of religious meaning relevant to a secular and rational world which cannot provide its own context of meaning sufficient for most men to live by.

And so I come to the end of my humble message. I have tried to make three simple points: (1) that there is a persistent, troubling tension between sociologists' concern to be socially relevant and also to build a scientific sociology, and this tension is fruitful for the development of our sociological consciousness; (2) whatever grand aspirations we may otherwise have, we are so much a part of the processes we study that we change even as these processes do, and I have tried to delineate what seems to me to be several significant ones for the near future; and (3) from time to time, at least, we need to expose ourselves to an intense and critical self-consciousness, an awareness of what we have been, where we are, and what is happening to us. Only from such painful effort can we know what we can be.

3

KURT H. WOLFF

*The Sociology of Knowledge and Sociological Theory**

In memory of Karl Mannheim

I. SCIENTIFIC VS. EXISTENTIAL TRUTH

It is important to realize that methodological problems, including those of testing methodological premises, on the one hand, and volitional and metaphysical problems, with the corresponding inclusion, on the other, have different criteria of confirmation or truth. For methodological problems, the criterion of truth is pragmatic in relation to a given inquiry or type of inquiry; in this sense, it is a "means" criterion. For volitional and metaphysical problems, the criterion is agreement with the result of the most rigorously imaginable intrasubjective "dialectical" examination of one's most important experiences: it is an "end" criterion.[1]

The truth sought in the solution of methodological problems may be called *stipulative*, in the sense that the predicate "true" is stipulated as suitable to the investigatory purpose in hand (or to the class of investigatory purposes of which the one in hand is an instance). It may also be called *hypothetical*, in the sense that it is contingent on the validation of a given hypothesis which is being examined in respect to its truth; or in the more compelling

* I am deeply indebted particularly to John W. Bennett and Llewellyn Gross, but also to Aron Gurwitsch, Paul Kecskemeti, Anthony Nemetz, Talcott Parsons, Alfred Schütz, and Melvin Seeman for critical readings of earlier drafts of this paper and for pertinent comments. Unfortunately, I have not been able to act on all of them.

sense that even if validated, hypotheses remain hypotheses, namely propositions which can be validated only within the hypothetical methodological, pragmatic, scientific attitude—that attitude for which metaphysical propositions (concerning the nature of reality) are irrelevant. Finally, this truth may be called *propositional*, in the sense that it is predicated only (or predominantly)[2] of propositions. It is clear that this stipulative, hypothetical, propositional truth, which is the truth sought in the solution of methodological problems, also is the truth sought in the solution of scientific problems. This is widely, if not generally, recognized by philosophers of science and of value. It implies that science makes no claims about the nature of (ultimate) reality; it is not concerned with this reality. We shall refer to this stipulative, hypothetical, propositional truth as "*scientific* truth."

The truth sought in the solution of volitional and metaphysical problems may, in accordance with the definition given above, be called experiential or *existential*. From a sociological standpoint, the seeker after scientific truth who commits an error risks his technical well-being, including, if he is a scientist, his professional reputation. By contrast, the seeker after existential truth risks his life and the world. Concerning both he may die in greater error than he would if he had "surrendered"[3] more fully, consciously, and intelligently to them.

Paul Kecskemeti has illuminated the nature of Mannheim's sociology of knowledge by arguing that Mannheim in effect distinguished between two kinds of truth, which are closely related to scientific and existential truth, respectively. These are the "Aristotelian concept of truth as 'speaking the truth,'" or "the truth of propositions . . ."; and truth as "one's response to reality," "the existential concept of truth as 'being in truth.'" We should remember, Kecskemeti writes, that truth has been conceived in these two ways throughout the history of philosophy. For the first, "truth" is predicative of sentences; it "has nothing to do with the things of the world as they exist in themselves. According to the other definition, 'truth' is first and foremost an attibute of *existence*, and only secondarily of *discourse*. One *is* or *is not* in the Truth; and one's possession of Truth depends on being in communion with a reality which 'is' or embodies truth."[4]

II. SOCIAL NOMINALISM VS. SOCIAL REALISM

This reality, for Mannheim (for the early Mannheim, as we shall see later in this section), was history. The positing of history, or of anything else, as "real," is not for the scientist to do. He pursues scientific truth, and in so doing ignores metaphysical questions. In other words, the scientific attitude "brackets"—to use the language of phenomenology—the ontological quest.

To the extent, however, that a given science or scientist deviates from the type, there may be metaphysical premises which have their influence on the selection and formulation of problems, on the interpretation of findings, etc. Mannheim is by no means alone, or even an exception, in such deviation. Thus, it has been said of American sociology as a whole that it is characterized by "voluntaristic nominalism," that is, by "the assumption that the structure of all social groups is the consequence of the aggregate of its separate component individuals and that social phenomena ultimately derive from the motivations of these knowing, feeling, and willing individuals." American sociology, therefore, is unsympathetic to any social determinism.

> A sociology of knowledge, for instance, which maintains a strict causal relationship between a specific form of social existence of class position and knowledge is unlikely to gain many adherents among American sociologists . . . neither Durkheim's notion of society as an entity *sui generis* nor Marx's interpretation of social stratification in terms of economic relations and consequent class consciousness has been accepted in American sociology in spite of widespread familiarity with these ideas.[5]

Not being pure, that is, self-conscious, self-critical, self-correcting, neither American nor European sociology wholly rejects its own metaphysical inclinations. As sciences, they should withhold an "accent of reality," whereas, in fact, they bestow it, although each of them bestows it on a different sphere. American sociology places it on the individual, withdrawing it from society. We may refer to this by saying that American sociology represents individual realism (and social nominalism, to paraphrase the term "voluntaristic nominalism"). European sociology places it on society or history withdrawing it from the individual. It represents social realism (individual nominalism).

Social realism is related to historical realism. This relation has been shown by Ernest Manheim in respect to Karl Mannheim's career. The later stages of this career, Manheim observes, show increasing interest in psychology, which "is inherent in Mannheim's adoption of the nominalist theory of groups, the view that groups have no reality of their own beyond the existence of their individual members." (This is, of course, the characteristically American conception of sociology.) And this turning toward "social nominalism" also explains Mannheim's *"abandonment of the doctrine which asserts the primacy of the historical frame of reference."* As Ernest Manheim points out, it is only in what has been called "individual realism," that is, "when the individual becomes the ultimate term of reference of sociological constructs (as is typically the case in American sociology) that questions of motivation can have meaning for the analysis of social action. Sociological concepts formed on the level of the group are impervious to psychology."[6] Thus we can formulate a further contrast: American sociology is characterized by psychological realism (social nominalism); European sociology, by social realism (psychological nominalism).

It is perhaps unnecessary to point out that these are no more than broad characterizations. For a fuller description (surely not to be undertaken here), qualifications must be entered. Also, there are exceptions. For instance, much recent American work in bureaucracy and social stratification leans more toward social realism; and on the other hand, there is a strong interest in psychology, verging on psychological realism, in as different European writers as Tarde, LeBon, and some of Simmel. It is also possible to make relevant distinctions on the American scene according to individual and typical sociologists, institutions, and levels (textbook vs. monograph, for instance). On the whole, nevertheless, American sociology has from almost the beginning been more deeply involved with ("social") psychology ("interests" "social forces," "instincts," "needs," "attitudes," etc.) than with society or history, whereas the opposite tends to describe European sociology.

Ernst Grünwald's distinction of the "psychological theory" and the "historical theory" as the "roots" or forerunners of the sociology of knowledge suggests the pertinence of this discussion for the sociology of knowledge itself. The "psychological theory," including its conceptions of truth and falsehood, is based on a theory of human nature; the "historical theory," with the same inclusion, on a theory of history.[7] Without detailing names, tendencies, and movements, it is clear that the sociology of knowledge, although the German variant more than the French, is in the "historical" rather than the "psychological" tradition. Along with much European sociology—to add a last generalization—the sociology of knowledge operates with a concept of existential truth, sometimes at the cost of inadequate attention to the concept of scientific truth. This last contrast gives credence to the often heard derogatory designation of European sociology generally as "philosophical," "metaphysical," "speculative," "armchair," etc., and, on the other hand, to the European comments that in American sociology "reliability has been won by surrendering theoretic relevance."[8]

A summary presentation of the characteristics of American and European sociology that have been suggested may be useful:

TABLE 1

METAPHYSICAL TENDENCIES OF AMERICAN AND EUROPEAN
SOCIOLOGY

American Sociology	European Sociology (and Sociology of Knowledge)
Scientific Truth	Existential Truth
Individual-Psychological Realism	Social-Historical Realism
Social-Historical Nominalism	Individual-Psychological Nominalism

III. CONNECTIONS BETWEEN THE SOCIOLOGY OF KNOWLEDGE AND OUR TIME

In this section we would like to discuss the nature of the connection between the sociology of knowledge and our time. For this purpose it may be helpful to recall the cause of a previous argument that we have made.[9]

We began by asking, "What is the sociology of knowledge?"—a question raised and answered by an outsider requesting and receiving scientific knowledge. The central concern of the insider, who then was introduced, emerged as the concern to recognize himself and his fellow men in their common time and place in order to know what to do. This—our—time and place appeared to us as characterized by the administered nature of our lives by "the world as underdeveloped," and by "one-world-and-cultural-relativism" with understanding as the hope of transcending this time, and dualism—and, as we saw later, naturalism—as the metaphysical premises of such understanding. These also were seen as the metaphysical premises, related to its methodological and volitional premises, of the sociology of knowledge. We may now make explicit those implications of the subsequent steps of our inquiry that are relevant to the task of showing that the connection between the sociology of knowledge and our time can be analyzed and can be argued to be of a determinable kind and importance.

These steps dealt with the distinction between scientific and existential truth and with the preponderant association of the former with individual-psychological realism (social nominalism) and of the latter with social-historical realism (individual nominalism). Social-historical realism and existential truth, we suggested, characterize the sociology of knowledge, and one indication of this is its notion of historical consciousness. We had earlier remarked on the absence of this notion from the American preoccupation with the sociology of knowledge and had illustrated this absence by Wirth's and Merton's observations on the time in which the sociology of knowledge arose.

The connection between the sociology of knowledge and our time thus appears as follows. (*1*) To speak of such a connection makes sense only if the concept "our time" itself makes sense. And it does this only on a historical (social-historical-realist) view, rather than a psychological (individual-psychological-realist) one. (*2*) Once such a view is adopted, the sociology of knowledge can be seen as one of several articulations[10] of the consciousness of our time, an articulation which, as it becomes conscious of being such, contributes to the transcendence of this consciousness. The sociology of knowledge thus emerges as the reaffirmation or, better, reinvention of the Socratic position, on the occasion of its insight into its own time and place. (*3*) In becoming conscious of being an articulation of the consciousness of our time—in becoming conscious of its methodological, volitional and metaphysical premises in their historical relevance—the sociology of knowledge appears.

> as a revision of our way of . . . looking at ourselves and the world, of our attitude toward the world, of our interpretation of it. It "defines" a new "situation" . . . and prior to this self-realization of the sociology of knowledge the situation was merely new, profoundly fascinating and profoundly threatening. The sociology of knowledge, therefore, may be called an elucidation of a new experience man has had and is still having. Through it, man adapts himself to living in one world, and through it he transcends cultural relativism toward the view of himself as dual and inexhaustibly challenging his own exploration.[11]

In other words, the sociology of knowledge transforms a new and shattering experience into a problem.

IV. NINETEENTH- AND TWENTIETH-CENTURY CIVILIZATIONAL-HISTORICAL DICHOTOMIES, MODERN AMERICAN SOCIOLOGY, AND THE SOCIOLOGY OF KNOWLEDGE

In the exploration of our time and place, "the world as underdeveloped" appeared as a correction of the notion of "underdeveloped countries," that is, of the tendency to project our own underdevelopment on non-Western peoples. In that connection, we commented on some civilizational-historical dichotomies as attempts at coming to terms with the emerging one world. We now wish to apply our subsequent distinction between scientific and existential truth to a reinterpretation of these dichotomies so that differences and relations between the sociology of knowledge and American sociology may be brought out further.

Henry Maine's contrast between societies based on status and societies based on contract; Herbert Spencer's military and industrial societies; Ferdinand Tonnies' *Gemeinschaft* and *Gesellschaft*; Émile Durkheim's societies characterized by mechanical and those characterized by organic solidarity; Max Weber's distinction between traditionalism and rationalism; Howard Becker's sacred and secular societies; Ralph Linton's ascribed and achieved status (and "universals" and "alternatives"); Robert Redfield's folk and urban societies; and Godfrey and Monica Wilson's primitive and civilized,[12] to mention only some of the dichotomies articulated during the last hundred years, are not only what they were predominantly intended by their authors to be, namely scientific hypotheses submitted for confirmation or falsification by subsequent research. They also claim existential truth:

> For decades, the pictures of primitive character brought back by anthropologists, no matter how well intended, were used by the denizens of Western industrialized civilization, either to preen themselves on their progress or to damn their cities, machines, or customs by reference to a constructed preliterate Eden—all, of course, under the guidance of such supposedly scientific terms as "folk society," "*Gemeinschaft*," "sacred society," and other such phrases.[13]

In our words, the existential element in these dichotomies is the mixture of faith and doubt that liberalism, increasing rationalization, reasonableness, progress are indeed true. The faith probably is more plausible than the doubt, but we must recall that some of the dichotomies did express their worries. Thus, Durkheim was disturbed by anomie, Weber by bureaucratization, Mannheim by the preponderance of functional over substantial rationality— and Durkheim looked to social reorganization through professional groups; Weber expressed his belief in prophecy; Mannheim, in ecstasy.[14] The appearance of these dichotomies and their authors' attitudes toward them thus tell the later story of liberalism (more spontaneously or, one might say, in a more clinical sense than do Nietzsche, Spengler, or Toynbee) as the doubt concerning the existential truth of the liberal historical interpretation and the scientific truth of its historical account.[15] The dichotomies (or other Westerners) have not succeeded either in writing a scientifically more accurate history or in revising liberalism toward greater historical adequacy. Instead, we have been overwhelmed by totalitarianism—among other things an alternative, antiliberal interpretation of the historical moment—and have experienced and witnessed the helplessness of liberalism confronted with it.[16]

Reinhard Bendix has shown that certain trends in the development of the Western image of man from Bacon through the Enlightenment to Marx, Nietzsche, and Freud represent an increasing "distrust of reason."[17] The last four centuries, especially the last hundred years, have thrown man ever more back on himself, unmasking ideas, beliefs, customs, and traditions as unreliable and unworthy crutches, as ideologies (Marx) or sublimations (Freud).

There arose, therefore, the question, "What, then, is man?" It was being asked by the same analysts who had stripped man to the necessity of (again) asking it, as well as by many others, from Descartes through Kierkegaard to the contemporary existentialists, phenomenologists, and various theologians. But this question intruded during the same period in which science and technology developed and (especially in its later phases) the standard of living rose to levels never reached before. These developments themselves thus appeared tempting as the very answers. The question, "What is man?" therefore, had to be asked in a whisper, in an embarrassed whisper—as a lover asks his beloved in the din of a factory, a cafeteria, a movie house, and (particularly in the twentieth century) the roar of world wars, an atom-bomb explosion, a concentration camp. Science, technology, prosperity, and disaster seem to have kept our self-inspection in a balance between the desire for it and its postponement as long as the automobile and the screen were there for us to escape with; and as long as the war, which had to be fought, urged us to tell who we are by asking science and ignoring history, ourselves. Witness scientism, infatuation with methodology in general, and more particularly such phenomena as formal literary criticism, philosophical analysis, structural linguistics, and the strong ritualistic element in social relations.[18]

These are some historical problems to which modern sociology specifically might address itself. Instead, it appears to be preoccupied, in America possibly more than elsewhere, with rather ahistorical formal "structural" relations and processes and with improving itself as a specialty in such preoccupation. To say this is not to suggest that sociology should not be a generalizing science. Rather it is to argue that sociology would facilitate its task of being a generalizing science if it recognized its need for a historical theory of society, no matter how crude it might be to begin with.[19] If sociology wants to be historically relevant, it cannot reject its commitment to historical realism and abide its psychological realism which no longer is historically adequate. For even a generalizing science, *if it is a social science*, starts with the historical situation; it may deny it but it cannot escape it. In this respect, social science cannot be entirely true to the pure type of science which "brackets" the ontological quest.[20]

The sociology of knowledge escapes this difficulty of modern American sociology by its historical realism and its much more openly recognized connection with the quest for existential truth. It is alien to the formalism of our time and in this sense, and by contrast, substantive;[21] it is "applied" theory in the service of changing the world, whether in the sense of Marx (specifically the *Theses on Feuerbach*) or Durkheim. Both Marx and Durkheim preceded the modern bifurcation of the world into Is and Ought, a bifurcation which has been shared and pushed by contemporary social science. Marx, much more than Durkheim, was one of the "strippers" of modern man, but his historical focus kept the Is and Ought together. Durkheim, like Max Weber, is a figure of transition in the sense that in their actual researches both keep Is and Ought together while in their explicit methodological writings they separate them (Weber more pointedly and passionately than Durkheim).[22] In the United States, the form secularization took in Marx (by way of Hegel and Feuerbach) appears to be an unmanageable alternative to American liberalism.[23] The other, the separation of Is and Ought, is intimately connected with the phenomena discussed in the next to the last paragraph above. In American sociology, this separation is of recent date, probably the 1920's. It had not yet appeared in Cooley's *Social Process* (1918); Lundberg-Anderson-Bain's *Trends in American Sociology* (1929) was a milestone in its articulation and acceptance. Already ten years later, Robert S. Lynd manifested discontent with it in *Knowledge for What?*

NOTES

1 Kurt H. Wolff, "A Preliminary Inquiry into the Sociology of Knowledge from the Standpoint of the Study of Man," in *Scritti di sociologia e politica in onore di Luigi Sturzo* (Bologna: Nicola Zanichelli, 1953), III, 612 [Henceforth cited as "Inquiry"].

2 Predominantly if (in addition to propositions) truth is also considered predictable of definitions. It can be so considered if a cognitive function of the operational character of definitions is emphasized: in this case, "definition" borders on hypothesis. It cannot be, if a definition is considered to be an analytical proposition and nothing else: in this case, it has no truth dimension, while of course the *use* of the definition (in methodology or research) does, namely that of stipulative (hypothetical, propositional) truth.

3 On the concept of "surrender," see my "Before and After Sociology," *Transactions of the Third World Congress of Sociology*, VII, 151–52, and more fully, "Introduction," *Loma Culture Change: An Introduction to the Study of Man* (Columbus:, Ohio: Ohio State University, 1952), pp. 22 ff. (Mimeographed.) It is a not irrelevant, further characterization of our time that one should be led to ask, in a footnote, whether the concern here

exhibited with existential truth won't alienate professional colleagues; or, hyperbolically, whether, in trying to save my life and the world, I am not risking the loss of my profession.

4 Paul Kecskemeti, "Introduction," Chap. I in Karl Mannheim, *Essays on the Sociology of Knowledge* (London: Routledge & Kegan Paul, 1952), pp. 15, 31. The difference between scientific and existential truth corresponds, in a way that cannot be discussed here, to that between mathematical and "inner" time (*durée*); on the latter, see, e.g., Alfred Schütz, "On Multiple Realities," *Philosophy and Phenomenological Research*, V (June, 1945), 538–42; Pitirim A. Sorokin, *Sociocultural Causality, Space, Time* (Durham, N.C.: Duke University Press, 1943), Chap. IV; Igor Stravinsky, *Poetics of Music in the Form of Six Lessons* (1939–40) (New York: Vintage Books, 1956), pp. 31–34.

5 Roscoe C. Hinkle, Jr., and Gisela J. Hinkle, *The Development of Modern Sociology: Its Nature and Growth in the United States* (Garden City, N.Y.: Doubleday & Company, 1954), pp. vii, 73, 74.

6 Ernest Manheim, "Introduction" to Karl Mannheim, *Essays on the Sociology of Culture* (New York: Oxford University Press, 1956), p. 5.

7 Cf. Ernst Grünwald, *Das Problem der Soziologie des Wissens* (Wien-Leipzig: Wilhelm Braümuller, 1934), Chap. I. (This important work has not been adequately appreciated in this country. Aside from a few citations there is only as far as I know, Arthur Child's analysis of Grünwald's own position [in several of his papers on the sociology of knowledge] and a very brief exposition of parts of it in Franz Adler, "The Range of Sociology of Knowledge," in Howard Becker and Alvin Boskoff [eds.], *Modern Sociological Theory in Continuity and Change* [New York: Dryden Press, 1957], pp. 412–13). A more detailed presentation and critique of Grünwald's discussion of the "psychological" and "historical" theories, while relevant and highly interesting, exceeds the scope of this paper. The central significance of his own position on the sociology of knowledge, however, must be registered. This position is what might be called "interpretational relativism": according to Grünwald, the sociology of knowledge is only one among many equally valid or invalid interpretations of intellectual phenomena. (It has also, and rightly, been designated as "postulational skepticism": Arthur Child, "The Theoretical Possibility of the Sociology of Knowledge," *Ethics*, LI [July, 1941], 404; Wolff, "Inquiry", pp. 592–93, esp. n. 21.) If we ask how it is possible that a number of interpretations can be entertained, that is, if we inquire into the basis of interpretational relativism, we find that interpreter and interpretandum emerge as relatively unanalyzable presuppositions or "givens," that is, we find the dualism of reality as relative and absolute—the same dualism we came upon as a metaphysical premise of the sociology of knowledge. If this dualism is in turn posited as, in some sense, optional, the burden of proof rests on the exploration of this positing, wherewith the continuity of analysis is made both possible and mandatory: this consideration vindicates the continuity of analysis (naturalism), the second metaphysical premise of the sociology of knowledge.

8 Robert K. Merton, *Social Theory and Social Structure* (rev. ed.; Glencoe, Ill.: The Free Press, 1952), p. 449.

9 The following summary refers to part of Wolff's essay not included here; see Kurt H. Wolff, "The Sociology of Knowledge and Sociological Theory," in *Symposium of Sociological Theory*, ed. by Llewellyn Gross (Evanston, Ill.: Row, Peterson & Co., 1959), pp. 579–87.—Ed.

10 Many examples of such articulations are given and analyzed in Erich Kahler, *The Tower and the Abyss: An Inquiry into the Transformation of the Individual* (New York: George Braziller, 1957), Chaps. IV–V.

11 Wolff, "Inquiry," p. 618.

12 Godfrey and Monica Wilson, *The Analysis of Social Change on the Basis of Observations in Central Africa* (Cambridge, Eng.: University Press, 1945). For a convenient conspectus of many such dichotomies (and trichotomies), see Howard Becker, *Through Values to Social Interpretation* (Durham, N.C.: Duke University Press, 1950), pp. 258–61.

13 David Riesman, "Some Observations on the Study of American Character," *Psychiatry*, XV (August, 1952), 333.

14 Émile Durkheim, *The Division of Labor in Society* (1893), trans. by George Simpson (Glencoe, Ill.: The Free Press, 1947), Preface to the second edition (1902), "Some Notes on Occupational Groups," and, particularly, *Professional Ethics and Civic Morals (1890's)* trans. by Cornelia Brookfield (London: Routledge & Kegan Paul, 1957), esp. Chaps. I–III; Max Weber, "Science As a Vocation" (1918), in *From Max Weber*, trans. and ed. by H. H. Gerth and C. Wright Mills (New York: Oxford University Press, 1946), esp. p. 153. ". . . the decisive state of affairs: the prophet . . . simply does not exist"— Mannheim, "The Problem of Ecstasy" (in "The Democratization of Culture" [1933]), in *Essays on the Sociology of Culture*, the argument of which the translator, Paul Kecskemeti, characterizes (p. 239, n. 1) as the "necessity to transcend the purely pragmatist and positivist approach."; Mannheim himself writes: "We inherited from our past another need: that of severing from time to time *all* connection with life and with the contingencies of our existence. We shall designate this ideal by the term 'ecstasy' " (p. 240).

15 Related to these civilizational-historical dichotomies is that between "culture" and "civilization," independently formulated by Alfred Weber and Robert M. MacIver. (Cf. Alfred Weber, "Der soziologische Kulturbegriff" [1912], *Ideen zur Staatsund Kultursoziologie* [Karlsruhe: G. Braun, 1927], pp. 31–47; *Kulturgeschichte als Kultursoziologie* [Leiden: Sijthoff, 1935], pp. 9–10, 421. MacIver has discussed the distinction in numerous places, from *Community* [London: The Macmillan Co., 1917], pp. 179–80, to MacIver and Charles H. Page, *Society* [New York: Rinehart & Co., 1949], pp. 446, 486–87, 498–506. Also cf. Robert K. Merton, "Civilization and Culture," *Sociology and Social Research*, XXI [November–December, 1936], 103–13, and Howard Becker, *Through Values to Sociological Interpretation*, pp. 165–68). In reference to the concerns of the present paper, this distinction has a twofold significance. (*1*) It is a formulation of a dualism which parallels, within culture itself, that between what here has been called "transcultural human nature" and "human culture." (*2*) It is an attempt at preserving historical continuity (through "culture") and, at the same time, independence from it ("civilization")—at preserving, that is, both the absolute and the relative in man (cf. the last quotation in Part III above).

16 Its most dramatic expression probably is the confusion of Soviet Communism with a historically more adequate version of liberalism and the shock, if not despair, on the realization of this confusion. Cf. such works as Arthur Koestler, Ignazio Silone, Richard Wright, André Gide, Louis Fischer, and Stephen Spender, *The God That Failed* (New York: Bantam Books, 1952).

17 Reinhard Bendix, *Social Science and the Distrust of Reason* (Berkeley and Los Angeles: University of California Press, 1951). Cf. also Institüt für Sozialforschung, *Soziologische*

Exkurse, nach Vorträgen und Diskussionen (Frankfurt am Main: Europäische Verlags-anstalt, 1956), chap. xii, "Ideologie." Both this chapter and Bendix draw heavily on Hans Barth, *Wahrheit und Ideologie* (Zurich: Manesse Verlag, 1945). Chapter I of the Frankfurt volume ("Begriff der Soziologie") is an impressive description of the fate of social thought, beginning with Plato, in its shift toward sociology (Comte), and of the development of sociology itself to the present time. Among the various but rare critiques of modern sociology, this and Bendix's are important. In this context, special attention should also be called to C. Wright Mills, "'The Power Elite'; Comment on Criticism," *Dissent*, IV (Winter, 1957), 22–34.

18 Portrayed more in fiction than in social science; but see C. Wright Mills, *White Collar: The American Middle Classes* (New York: Oxford University Press, 1951), esp. Part III, and William H. Whyte, Jr., *The Organization Man* (New York: Simon & Schuster, 1956), esp. Parts VI and VII.

19 Cf. my "Before and After Sociology," p. 153, and "Sociology and History; Theory and Practice" (presented at the 1958 meetings of the American Sociological Society); and John W. Bennett and Kurt H. Wolff, "Toward Communication Between Sociology and Anthropology," in William L. Thomas, Jr. (ed.), *Yearbook of Anthropology—1955* (New York: Wenner-Gren Foundation, Anthropological Research, 1955), p. 330 (reprinted in William L. Thomas, Jr. [ed.], *Current Anthropology: A Supplement to Anthropology Today* [Chicago: University of Chicago Press, 1956], p. 330).

20 This, on the surface of it, would appear to contradict Alfred Schütz's characterization of "the world of scientific theory" (in his "On Multiple Realities," pp. 563–75) but actually seems a consequence of affirming his proposition "that sociality and communication can [only] be realized within . . . the world of everyday life which is the paramount reality" (p. 575). Space limitations make it impossible to enter into a discussion of this important, if not crucial, question of the philosophy of science.

21 This meaning of "substantive," in contrast to "formalistic," is obviously different from H. Otto Dahlke's ("The Sociology of Knowledge," in Harry Elmer Barnes, Howard Becker, and Francis Bennett Becker [eds.], *Contemporary Social Theory* [New York and London: Appleton Century, 1940], *passim*, e.g., p. 86) or from Karl Mannheim's "empirical" (*Ideology and Utopia*, trans. by Louis Wirth and Edward Shils [New York: Harcourt, Brace & Co., 1936], pp. 239 ff.), both of which contrast with "epistemological."

22 Cf., e.g., Durkheim's *Rules of Sociological Method* (1895) or "The Determination of Moral Facts" (1906), in *Sociology and Philosophy*, trans. by D. F. Pocock (Glencoe, Ill.: The Free Press, 1953), chap. ii, with his worry about anomie (cf. n. 17, above); or Max Weber's *Methodology of the Social Sciences*, trans. and ed. by Edward A. Shils and Henry A. Finch (Glencoe, Ill.: The Free Press, 1949), with, e.g., his *The Protestant Ethic and the Spirit of Capitalism*, trans. by Talcott Parsons (New York: Charles Scribner's Sons, 1958), and on the discrepancy between Weber's methodological prescriptions for practice and his practice itself, Leo Strauss, *Natural Right and History* (Chicago: University of Chicago Press, 1953). I am not acquainted with a corresponding analysis of Durkheim's work. Cf., however, some relevant observations in my "The Challenge of Durkheim and Simmel," *The American Journal of Sociology*, LXIII (May, 1958), 590–93.

23 In respect to American sociology, cf. the Hinkles' remark quoted above (p. 547). On the unrivaled position of liberalism in American political and social thought, cf. Louis Hartz, *The Liberal Tradition in America: An Interpretation of American Political Thought Since the Revolution* (New York: Harcourt, Brace & Co., 1955).

4

EMIL BEND AND MARTIN VOGELFANGER

A New Look at Mills' Critique

THE STUDY OF social problems was one of the original areas of inquiry of American sociology, and an important impetus to its development. Today it is among the most frequently offered courses in the sociology curriculum.[1] One might guess that such a traditional and popular subject would be completely accepted within the field, and fairly well integrated with the theory it has produced. On the face of it, one might not expect much controversy over such a "veteran crowd-pleaser"[2] as social problems. Yet controversy there is, for over the study of social problems, disorganization, pathology, hover some of the persistent dilemmas of sociology. Published criticism of this area either explicitly or implicitly, but invariably, touches upon such basic issues as the boundaries and goals of sociology, the professional roles of sociologists, and public images of sociology. Behind every critique of the sociology of social problems reside questions in the sociology of knowledge. In some cases, these questions remain half-hidden; in others, they are prominently displayed. The latter is true of C. Wright Mills' widely quoted article, "The Professional Ideology of Social Pathologists."[3] Mills, whose paper is summarized below, wrote: "Because of its persistent importance in the development of American sociology, and its supposed proximity to the social scene, 'social pathology' seems an appropriate point of entry for the examination of the style of reflection and the social historical basis of American sociology."[4]

The criticism of social problems that has found its way into articles and book reviews in the professional journals falls into several classes. One contains the descriptions and/or denunciations of social problems as too distant from the mainstreams of contemporary sociology. One should examine the problems of society as one would any other sociologically relevant phenomena, as a means to the end of more and better facts and theories of social behavior. The foci of interest, modes of analysis, and underlying values in the field of social problems prevent its serving the above purpose. So runs this type of argument.

A second class of criticisms emphasizes the inability of the sociologists of social problems to solve, or perhaps even to perceive, the important problems of society. The field of social problems should apply the available resources of sociology toward the goal of understanding and ameliorating the conditions that trouble mankind. The foci of interest, and so on, of social problems prevent the achievement of that goal.

The origins of such a classification can be traced to the very early days of American sociology, to Ward's distinction between "pure" and "applied" sociology, and to the many early references to societal or scientific problems versus social or ameliorative ones.

C. Wright Mills' critique, mentioned above, contains elements of both types of criticism. Mills examined a number of social problems books of the 1920's and 1930's, and discovered great uniformities in the "typical perceptives and key concepts" of the field. He examined the life histories of the pathologists, and attributed the textbook uniformities to the overwhelming homogeneity in the social extraction, class, and career patterns of the authors. They were middle-class, rural-oriented individuals who interacted within academic and reform movement environments. The similarity in background, argued Mills, tended to lead to common unchallenged values which entered into the literature and were perpetuated.

The uniformities that Mills uncovered clustered about three points: (1) the nature of society, as seen by the pathologists; (2) the nature of social problems, as seen by the pathologists; and (3) the criteria for the selection and organization of problems in textbooks utilized by the pathologists.

(1) The model of social organization that the pathologists tended to adopt was that of the small town, blown up in scale. "The good society" was one where the intimacy and homogeneity of primary groups prevailed; where proper social change occurred in a slow and orderly fashion. The "good citizen" was one who joins and helps and is adjusted. Mills pointed to Cooley as one of the original architects of this model, through his emphasis on the "organic" (a harmonious balance of elements) and "processual" (continuous through time) nature of society.

(*2*) Mills suggested that the concept of disorganization utilized by the pathologists quite often meant merely the absence of that type of organization described above. Social problems were often defined in terms of deviations by aggregates of individuals from the existing norms. They arise when numbers of individuals are unwilling or unable to conform to the status quo standards, as a result of encroaching urbanization, immigration, and so on. Norm violations were sometimes seen simply as biological impulses breaking through societal restrictions. This analysis was supported, in Mills' remembered phrase, by "a paste-pot eclectic psychology."

In addition to the "deviation from norms" approach, another popular orientation to social problems centered about the concept of social change. The assumption in this type of analysis was that stability of any social pattern inevitably results in an adjustment to it, whereas change, except for the slow, orderly variety, invariably unlocks the Pandora's box of social problems. A frequent variant of the social change approach was that of culture lag, where social problems emerge out of the unequal rates of change of the different aspects of the culture.

The solutions to social problems served up by pathologists had as their major ingredient more and better socialization. In this way, individuals with problems could be adjusted or readjusted, and the repercussions of social change could be controlled more effectively.

(*3*) The value uniformities which led to typical notions of social organization and disorganization also determined the principles for selecting and organizing problems in texts. For example, the method of presenting social problems was greatly influenced by the case-study approach of the social worker, in that problems selected leaned to the "practical problems of everyday life," problems of individuals in specific situations. The "situational approach" of W. I. Thomas contributed greatly to this mode of problems perception. The case-study approach plus the lack of any theory resulted in books that were "fragmentary collections of scattered problems and facts" selected in a non-random fashion, and characterized by an extremely low level of abstraction.

It has already been mentioned that Mills attributed the value patterns underlying pathology books primarily to the class origins and experiences of the authors. A second determining factor, present but less fully developed in Mills' analysis, is worth mentioning because of its relevance to our analysis of the contemporary social problems literature which comprises the major portion of this paper. This deals with the various academic pressures that have shaped the development of the social problems field. Almost everything written by sociologists about social problems has been in the form of textbooks, intended for student audiences. Mills commented on some results in the student-centered orientation: "[Textbook] systematization occurs in a context of presentation and justification rather than within a context of discovery."[5] And "Since one test of [textbook] success is wide adoption, the very spread of the public for which they are written tends to insure a textbook tolerance of the commonplace."[6]

What, according to Mills, have been the consequences of the middle-class, rural-oriented value uniformities shared by social pathologists?

First, they have been responsible for the lack of any sociological orientation in social problems writing. Mills' sample of pathologists exhibited an inability to focus upon the structural bases of society, to perceive the structural origins and interrelations of the individual conditions that have been described as social problems. This lack of theory has had the effect of supporting the acceptance of the existing norms as given and therefore good, and of portraying deviation as undesirable. Pathologists could not recognize that problems can emerge not only from deviation, but from conformity as well—conformity to conflicting or changing norms. Similarly, almost all stratificational aspects of social problems have been obscured by the lack of theory.

Second, the common values have prevented pathologists from attaining their avowed goal, the amelioration of problems, the reformation of the status quo. Mills insisted that the ways problems have been perceived and analyzed, giving tacit and often open support to the status quo, made collective action oriented to their solution virtually impossible.

The above rough sketch does not do justice to the fullness and vigor of Mills' argument. With all its shortcomings, several of which Mills acknowledges in footnotes, we feel that it adequately describes a major portion of the output of American social pathologists of the post-World War I and pre-World War II period.

We would like to comment on a major problem inherent in the non-empirical type of analysis of which Mills' and the present paper are both examples. Mills does caution his readers that "the aim is to grasp typical perspectives and key concepts. Hence no one of the texts . . . exemplifies *all* the concepts analyzed; certain elements are not so visible in given texts as in others, and some elements are not evidenced in certain texts at all."[7] After reading his article, one still imagines a fraternity of pathologists, befriending each other socially, and supporting each other ideologically. While it is beyond doubt that there existed a common core of values underlying the social problems literature, it must be noted that many pathologists were aware of the situation, and themselves critical of the consequences of such homogeneity. One can see this clearly in pathologists' book reviews of their "brethren's" works, or in the introductory remarks in a textbook, justifying the need for it to be published. Elliott and Merrill, whose very popular text is included in Mills' sample, wrote in 1933: "Courses in 'Social Problems' or 'Social Pathology' have been among the most popular offerings of academic sociology, yet there has seldom been any attempt to integrate the subject matter within a scheme of systematic sociology. For the most part, the approach to the conglomerate topics listed under these headings has been on a strictly common-sense level."[8]

It is interesting to see that Elliott and Merrill have, in turn, been found guilty of quite similar "textbook crimes."

The acceptance of Mills' description of the social problems literature does not commit us to accept his orientation to social pathology and pathologists. It is not difficult to see that the concepts and perspectives that Mills offers as replacements for the existing rural, middle-class oriented ones are themselves bound up in an ideology. Martindale, for example, in his excellent outline of past and present developments in the study of social problems in America, notes that "the one thing . . . all the critics—from Mills to Lemert, and many others in addition—are agreed upon is the presence of valuations in the theory of social disorganization. There is no question whatsoever about the fact that they are correct." Still, "the criticism is frequently marred . . . by the fact that the critic objects to *particular* evaluations rather than to the confusion of facts with values."[9]

The present analysis focuses upon certain aspects of the modern body of writing of social pathologists. In common with Mills' article, it is not a systematic study. The content of the volumes in our sample has not been categorized or counted by formal techniques. The attempt has been to establish ideal types, which some existing works closely resemble, others, less so.

Let us stress that we are not interested in describing and evaluating the various approaches to social problems. This material can be found in the introductory chapters of a number of social problems textbooks. We are concerned with the present position and prospects of the field, much as Mills was fifteen years ago. He asked the question, "What has the field of social problems to do with society?" The question underlying this paper is, "What has the field of social problems to do with sociology?" The values underlying that question are those of academic sociology.

We are interested in social pathology only because it has been generally recognized to be a subdivision of sociology,[10] because most such courses have been offered in sociology departments, and because much of the literature of the field has been produced by people with sociology degrees.

We make explicit the belief that the valuation of any substantive segment or movement in sociology should be based on the answers to the following questions:

(*1*) To what extent does segment or movement X utilize any of the theoretical schemes that are representative of modern sociological analysis?

(*2*) To what extent does X contribute to the existing bodies of sociological facts and theories or point to possibly fruitful new directions in sociology?

About half a dozen different approaches to the study of the ills of society have been identified in the contemporary problems literature. As mentioned above, they are described in many pathology texts, as well as in the Martindale article.[11] We are interested in the ways the various approaches have been organized and presented to their readers. Three major organizational types can be distinguished. Beside differing in their structure, the types appear to differ in their authors' intentions, and in their attractiveness to various kinds of audiences. Although certain problems approaches have had an affinity for certain organizational types, the relationship is far from a consistent one.

The first type is the one most distant from the sociological center. As a matter of fact there is often not even the pretense of a sociological approach. This type has been called the "omnium gatherum," the collection of myriad, miscellaneous problems from Abortion to Zooerasty, with little or no attempt to relate them to a sociological framework, or, for that matter, to any framework. The problems in this collection are held together by tradition and expectation alone. There is usually some minimal preliminary material, where mention may be made of several approaches to social problems. However, such material is decidedly prefatory to the major business at hand—the description of the many, many problems of society.

This type is often the third or fourth edition of a "best-seller," originally published in the 1920's or 1930's. There are a very few books that have changed little since then. Only the dates on charts and tables give them away as "modern" texts. It is common for this organizational type to have a "social problems" as opposed to a "disorganization" or "pathology" orientation. The various problems "readers," collections of articles and fragments of articles, fit neatly into this category.[12] Books of this type are produced simply to escort many college and junior college students along social problems paths well-traveled by "satisfied" student generations of the past.[13]

The second organizational type deserves more attention, because it attempts to do more, sociologically. In this volume one finds two sections: (*1*) a theoretical outline, which is intended to provide a basis for analyzing, (*2*) the assortment of problems, comprising the major portion of the book. The theoretical material often bears resemblance to modern sociological theory; structural concepts are identified, the terminology is up to date, and so on. Invariably, however, the "analysis" of the problems in the second section turns out to be the standard descriptions of the standard problems. The theory rarely reaches the problems. Where it does reach, it appears to have been squeezed in, as a concession or an afterthought.

In this type of volume are reflected some of the "cross-pressures" experienced by present-day pathologists. Problems texts are no longer written by ex-social workers or ex-ministers located in sociology departments comprised of ex-ministers and ex-social workers. Contemporary pathologists have been trained as sociologists. One's professional self-image and relations within the academic department and within the profession are undoubtedly influences in determining what kind of book one should write. On the other horn of the dilemma are the other influences involved in the writing and selling of textbooks. It is known that in all but a few colleges and universities, pre-social work, pre-education, pre-nursing, and pre-domesticity students occupy most of the seats in sociology classes. It is also known that courses in social problems and in applied sociology have always been stellar attractions for these students. It is difficult for an author to remain unmoved by this information. If unimpressed he does remain, there is always his publisher to remind him. We know of no study of the influence of publishers on the ultimate content and form of texts. We feel that the odds in favor of rejection of the hypothesis of no association are great. The image of the "good book" held by those who purchase, print, design, and market manuscripts seem to be that of a text, similar to those that are known to have done well, with a new wrinkle or two to justify publication, and to provide copy for advertising.[14]

The type of book under discussion represents a way out of the pathologist's dilemma, containing as it does the little island of theory (the sociological imprimatur) separated from the vast archipelago of problems (for students and sales).

The last major organizational category contains the more serious efforts to present theories of disorganization, deviation, and others. In this type, the theoretical material is elaborately developed, sometimes taking up as much as half the volume. Problems are generally selected with a greater care for consistency than in the other types. This is achieved by narrowing the range of problems selected for analysis, because the specific theory can only handle certain kinds of problems.

Although attempts at theory-building are to be applauded and encouraged whenever they occur in the social problems area, we find that the actual theories leave much to be desired. They contain, at best, selected sociological elements. Some are theories of psychological more than sociological disorganization. Not one can be said to be a structural theory. One is disappointed by this lack more in this type of work than in the others. The others are completely devoid of *any* theory, but, when a sociologist works hard to present a theoretical system in a sociological work (thereby probably sacrificing junior college and schools of nursing adoptions), it is to be regretted that the result isn't sociology.

One did not have to read much between the lines of the above paragraphs to discover that, although writing of differences in the literature, we were implying that in a most important way the organizational types were more or less similar. The common feature of the sociology of social problems literature of today is its non-sociological, sometimes even anti-sociological, character.

This is not to suggest that the extreme simplifications, the unabashed moralizing, the exhortations to reform that characterized Mills' samples are to be found in the literature of today. A quarter of a century has elapsed since most of the volumes that Mills examined were published. Writings in pathology have not remained unaffected by the advances in sociology in those twenty-five years.

The important question is what lies behind the shiny, new exterior of up-to-date terminology, attempts at theories, and professed value neutrality that many modern works in social problems display. Have the old values been expunged, or do they still remain, in less extreme, less explicit form, but nonetheless present? The answer is "yes" and "no." Some of the standard concepts and usages of the 1920's and 1930's have gone completely out of sociological fashion and do not appear in modern problems literature. Other uniformities noted by Mills are still quite in evidence.

Two such examples are (1) the analysis of social problems as individual problems and (2) the non-random selection of social problems.

(1) Many of the modern pathology primers contain a subdivision titled "personal or individual problems, crises, disorganizations." In this category fall the illnesses, addictions, vices, crimes, and the like.

The first critical question concerns the relevance of many of the individual problems to a sociological analysis. To be sure, such conditions as accidents, blindness, and mental deficiency affect many individuals in the population. But there are literally hundreds of potentially threatening conditions in man's environment, to which he attempts adjustment. The study of most of these conditions neither requires sociological theory nor contributes to it. Although members of the society may acknowledge the infirmities and handicaps and modify expectations in certain statuses; and deny participation in others. These are not sociological problems, for neither their causes nor the reasons for their persistence can be located within the structure of relationships that make up a human society.

Quite often the conditions singled out for consideration as social problems are simply those which affect the largest numbers of individuals. As one pathologist wrote: "One question often raised in the effort to locate and define problems is, what is the number of people who are affected by them? . . . The assumption is that any problem is of major or minor significance in accordance with its incidence. Financial costs are used for the same purpose. The implication in the use of either implement is sound."[15]

A more serious deficiency in the literature revolves about those problems that could be structurally significant, and the ways in which they are treated. Variously labeled "group," "institutional," "family," "community," and so forth, they are with few exceptions analyzed as problems of individuals. One can illustrate this by considering the limited and unrewarding way "institution" might be used in the problems literature. An "institutional problem" is a condition that affects aggregates of individuals as they participate in an area of group life known to sociologists as an institution. The label serves only to indicate where in the society the problem is visible. Therefore divorce is a family problem, corruption and graft a political problem, unemployment an economic one. How is the "institutional problem" "analyzed" in the literature? Pathologists generally describe how many people are affected, how these rates have changed, and in what ways the problem is experienced by those affected and by others in the society. What brought the problem about (either "lags," "disorganization," or "value conflicts," or any combination of the three), and perhaps, what can be done about it. In other words, the problems that are located in areas of the group life upon which modern sociological theory has been focused are "analyzed" in the same manner as the myriad ailments of mankind (physical, geographical, economic) with which the sociologist does not even pretend to be involved.

The simple message of this paper is that the state of present-day sociological knowledge permits so much more than this to be done.

(2) Almost every author will inform his readers that there are many social problems, both big and small. Of the large number of recognized problems, a handful can be thought of as the "GOP" (Grand Old Problems). Veritable universals are problems of physical and mental health, crime and delinquency, marriage and family problems, and problems of some kinds of minority groups. Also quite popular are some conditions that can be located in the economic institution—poverty, unemployment, and industrial relations, as well as population problems. Political and stratification problems (beside

poverty) are two examples of those less frequently offered in the works of the pathologists.

There are several reasons why some problems are textbook universals, and others are rarely discussed. One is apparent from the following statement: "... Certain social problems have been central in the concept from the very beginning. A discussion of them is expected in books and courses on social problems, and this expectation has been respected."[16]

Another can be related to the criteria pathologists utilize in their definition of a social problem. We mentioned above that pathologists often define problems as conditions that affect aggregates of individuals. A very popular method of ascertaining which are the important problems of a society involves scrutinizing the population for the things that worry them, the conditions they would like to change. There are all sorts of evidence to support the position that Americans are generally not concerned with world or national issues. They worry about what is closest to them, what they experience most frequently—health, family, job. These, then, become the "universals," plus a few conditions which represent clear-cut and widely censured deviations from American norms and values.

Not only are certain problems rarely included in the literature, but one also finds that certain dimensions of the "acceptable" problems are ignored or barely noted. For example, the chapters on religion or religious minorities stress the discrimination against certain religions, the contributions of religious organizations toward amelioration of social problems, and so on. Rarely are the divisive consequences of religion in America discussed. The progess of the Negro is a popular theme in the chapters on minorities, but the consequences of progress, ranging up to mixed marriages, are hastily skipped over. In the ubiquitous chapter on health, syphilis, or whatever other interesting disease, is mentioned much more frequently than the AMA, although several recent texts have criticized developments in medical practice.

We have tried to point out, in the language of the pathologists, that there exists a great "lag" between the developments in sociological theory and those in that branch of the field known as social problems, pathology, disorganization, deviation.

Let us review some of the factors that have contributed to this situation:

(*1*) Most students who are enrolled in undergraduate courses in sociology are not especially interested in careers in sociology, nor in courses in sociological theory.

(*2*) Since the size of the staff and the prestige of the department in many colleges are tied to the number of students enrolled, there are pressures to make available to students courses that will attract and satisfy. It is difficult to think of any other academic department that appears as concerned with what the student wants as is sociology. Perhaps the comparatively recent origins of sociology on the campus, and the widespread ignorance of it beyond the campus, help explain this.

(*3*) Since it is not uncommon for authors to aspire to write books that sell, the literature geared to undergraduates tends to be lean on theory and rather overweight on the uncomplicated descriptive material that has been known to sell books.

(*4*) The question of the role of the publisher in determining the content of the pathologists' literary output was raised in the body of the paper.

(*5*) Since the study of social problems is so overwhelmingly an undergraduate proposition, the compulsion and the opportunity to do creative work, by either faculty or student body, are not very strong.

(*6*) In many of the smaller colleges there are no conflicts between academic and applied sociology, as the former is barely to be seen. Social awareness and adjustment are the major educational aims of the social science program.

To criticize the field of social problems as we have done is neither novel nor difficult. What is harder to do, and therefore rarer, is to suggest how to infuse the problems field with significant theoretical content. Although the works of several important modern sociologists contain theories and theory fragments relating to disorganization and deviation, it remained for a recent article by A. K. Cohen[17] to provide a first step toward a *rapprochement* between theory and social pathology. It is also to be noted as a hopeful sign that a recent issue of the *American Sociological Review* devoted most of its pages to theoretical papers in the sociology of deviation and of disorganization.

In spite of these first steps, it will be a long time before social problems offerings to undergraduates are reconstituted as truly sociological courses. A less distant goal would be for some of the theoretical material to filter down into social pathology syllabi, and for some of the more blatantly non-sociological approaches to be transferred out of sociology departments and into some interdisciplinary artifact, such as "Problems of American Civilization" or "Problems of the Twentieth Century."

Ultimately, if we survive the "social problems" of the atomic era, we can look forward in this area to subdisciplines that are sociological, not through tradition and student expectations, but because of their ties to sociological theory and research. A sociology of deviation and one of disorganization would not only contribute to our scientific knowledge of the social behavior of man, but would also place powerful tools in the hands of those who by training and inclination are dedicated to the betterment of man's life.

NOTES

1 The terminological smog is very heavy in this region. The field has been titled "social problems," "social disorganization," "social pathology," "social deviation," and still more. Although the different approaches vary in emphasis, they essentially cover the same ground, and fit into the same niches within sociology curricula. Since this paper is concerned with this whole sector of sociology, the terms shall be used interchangeably, except when otherwise noted.

2 Podell, Vogelfanger, and Rogers, "Sociology in American Colleges: 15 Years Later," *American Sociological Review* (February, 1959). Of the 3,763 undergraduate courses in the sample of 263 college catalogues, 13.9 per cent were categorized as "social problems" courses. It was noted that a number of courses dealing with social problems were placed in other categories for various reasons.

3 C. Wright Mills, "The Professional Ideology of Social Pathologists," *American Journal of Sociology*, XLIX (September, 1943), 165–80.

4 *Ibid.*, p. 165.

5 *Ibid.*, p. 167.

6 *Ibid.*, p. 168.

7 *Ibid.*

8 Mabel A. Elliott and Francis E. Merrill, *Social Disorganization* (4th ed.; New York: Harper & Row, 1961), p. ix.

9 Don Martindale, "Social Disorganization . . . ," in Howard Becker and Alvin C. Boskoff (eds.), *Modern Sociological Theory* (New York: Random House, 1961), p. 348.

10 This, of course, refers to our "professional interest." In our other statuses, we can be interested or disinterested in the problems of society for a variety of different reasons.

11 See, for example, Abbott P. Herman, *An Approach to Social Problems* (New York: Harper & Bros., 1949); Martin H. Neumeyer, *Social Problems and the Changing Society* (Princeton: D. Van Nostrand Co., 1953); and Edwin H. Lemert, *Social Pathology* (New York: McGraw-Hill Book Co., 1951). Martindale noted the various approaches to social problems found in a number of the more important pathology textbooks.

12 Alfred McClung Lee and E. B. Lee (eds.), *Social Problems in America: A Source Book* (New York: Holt, 1949). Lee and Lee, in their reader, combine excerpts from the works of famous sociological theorists, with those of journalists, clergymen, lawyers, government officials, and so on. The representatives of the other professions contribute little to the sociology of social problems.

13 William W. Weaver, *Social Problems* (New York: Sloan Associates, 1951). As Weaver writes, "This book is submitted with few pretensions to erudition but with the earnest hope that it may be a useful guide for undergraduate students in their study of social problems."

14 We do not wish to suggest that all publishers are anti-intellectual, or that all textbooks contain only pap. We are dealing with types, rather than with individuals.

15 Harold A. Phelps and David Henderson, *Contemporary Social Problems* (4th ed.; Englewood Cliffs, N.J.: Prentice-Hall, 1952).

16 Jessie Bernard, *Social Problems at Mid-Century* (New York: Holt, Rinehart, & Winston, 1957), p. 114.

17 A. K. Cohen, "The Study of Social Disorganization and Deviant Behavior," in Merton, Broom, and Cottrell (eds.), *Sociology Today* (New York: Basic Books, 1959).

5

LEONARD LIEBERMAN

The Debate over Race

THE SOCIOLOGY OF knowledge invites us to discover how reason is shaped by social factors.[1] The sociological imagination suggests that the social function of reason is "to formulate choices, to enlarge the scope of human decision in the making of history."[2] The concept of race provides a case study in the growth of distorted reason and the formulation of choices within changing social structures.

In the seventeenth century, following the era of worldwide exploration, Europeans awoke to renewed awareness of the fact that there were many other peoples and cultures. The concept of race emerged in the effort to assimilate this new information. "Race" was introduced into common usage and scientific taxonomies. In common usage it became racist ideology, and in scientific circles it was first debated whether the races had separate origins; then in the nineteenth century the debate shifted to emphasize the issue of equality. Scientific and popular ideas influenced each other and both served the cause of justifying ideologically European colonialism, slavery, nationalism, and imperialism.

In the first decades of the twentieth century, anthropology, sociology and psychology took up the issue of inequality, debated it, and with the aid of a changing social structure succeeded in shifting the majority opinion of scientists and educated persons from racism to equalitarianism. Having helped persuade many that races are not unequal, many anthropologists began to argue that races do not exist. They argued that race is a fiction or a myth which must be exorcized like ghosts, the humors, instincts, and phlogiston.

The debate has been underway among physical anthropologists for three

Phylon, XXIX (Summer, 1968), 127–41. Reprinted by permission of *Phylon* and the author.

decades. The affirmative states that races exist, the negative claims that race
is a myth. Their discussion was the most recent in a tournament lasting over
two centuries. In this work, this debate will be analyzed from the perspective of the sociology of knowledge, which leads to the question of how ideas
have been shaped by existing ideology, social structure, social problems, and
the debating process itself.

THE CURRENT DEBATE: LUMPERS VS. SPLITTERS

The splitters, adherent of the position that races exist, include Dobzhansky,
Garn, Laughlin, Mayr, Newman, and others. The lumpers, who argue that
races do not exist, include Livingstone, Montagu, Brace, Hiernaux, Hogben,
and Fried.

The splitters claim that:

(1) Races are the taxonomic unit below the species level, and if such units
are not called race, "it still has exactly the same taxonomic meaning."[3]

(2) Races vary from populations "differing only in the frequencies of a few
genes to those groupings that have been totally isolated for tens of thousands
of years and are at least incipient species."[4]

(3) Clines (gradations) exist but it is necessary to distinguish clines between subspecific populations and clines within subspecific populations.
Interracial clines are found in intermediate populations between subspecific
populations or races.[5]

The no-race position of the lumpers holds that:

(1) Biological variability exists but "this variability does not conform to
the discrete packages labeled races."[6]

(2) So called racial characteristics are not transmitted as complexes.[7]

(3) Human differentiation is the result of natural selection forces that
operate in ecological zones, and such forces and their zones do not coincide
with population boundaries. Furthermore, different selective forces may
operate in overlapping ecological zones.[8] Thus geographic distributions of
more than one trait have no necessary correlation.[9]

(4) Races do not exist because isolation of groups has been infrequent;
populations have always interbred.[10]

(5) "Boundaries between what have been called 'races' are completely
arbitrary, depending primarily upon the wishes of the classifier."[11]

The debate over an issue helps clarify it by generating finer distinctions.
Thus among the lumpers and splitters it is possible to distinguish polar
positions and moderate views about the number of races and their existence:

(1) No races exist now or ever did.[12]

(2) Very few races have existed.[13]

(*3*) In its anthropological sense, the word "race" should be reserved for groups of mankind possessing well-developed and primarily inheritable physical differences from other groups. Many populations can be so classified but, because of the complexity of human history, there are also many populations which cannot easily be fitted into a racial classification.[14]

(*4*) The number of races varies with the size of the unit studied and or the scope of the definition.[15]

(*5*) A race is a breeding population, hence there are thousands of races.[16]

The first thought that occurs to an observer of this debate has to do with the arbitrary nature of definitions. Similar problems have been discussed by distinguishing realism and nominalism, absolutism or arbitrariness, reality and ideal types. But in this debate both sides accept essentially the same definition. The common meaning of their definitions is a population which can be distinguished from other populations on the basis of inherent physical characteristics. There must be some identifiable boundary, therefore, where one population ends and another begins. The general acceptance of boundary lines in fact or as arbitrary necessity leaves the two sides contending over the issue of whether or not one can locate boundaries and thereby prove that races exist. One of the problems discussed later in this paper considers why the contending sides do not resolve the issue by simply calling it a matter of definition.

The debate sketched above is not an argument in which a minority is opposed to a majority or in which experts oppose non-experts. Both debate teams include widely recognized specialists in physical anthropology. Briefly, the argument hinges on the significance of the gradation of genetically based physical characteristics. The race-exists supporters argue that these genetic gradations are intergradations between races; the no-race position holds the gradations are not intergradations but are overlapping gradients which are not confined to the boundaries of particular populations.

Although the early physical anthropologists were aware of the conflict between their taxonomy and the question of validity, the issue lay dormant until the 1950's. The eruption of the debate has been stimulated by the availability of new data. The dispute has been concentrated in the pages of *Current Anthropology*, where in three issues in 1962–64, some twenty-four 8″ × 11″ triple-column pages in small print were given over to the topic. Paradoxically, while the new data are better and more abundant, they have intensified the issue rather than resolved it.

Race as a concept appeared before there were techniques for measuring physical attributes. For some time the major source of information on race characteristics depended upon whatever struck the fancy of explorers and travelers, and often this was skin color and hair texture. Several biometric techniques were developed before Darwin's publication of the *Origin of Species* in 1859. Camper (1722–89) developed the facial angle, "the interior angle the face makes with the horizontal."[17] In 1842 Retzius introduced the cephalic index, the ratio of head length to width. By 1900 A. Von Torok found enough techniques available to take 5,000 measurements on a single skull.[18]

The old data were external phenotypical traits; the new data are genetic in character. Examples of genes which have been identified and used in studying taxonomy and variations in man include: the Rh series of alleles, the ABO system, the sickle cell trait, the gene of M blood type in the MNS series, and frequency of tasting phenylthiocarbamide by females.[19]

Examples of the uses of this kind of data will indicate how they can be used to support either the lumpers or splitters position. Glass and Li compared blood types of Negroes in the United States with those of African Negroes and concluded that North American Negroes have about 30 per cent genes from white populations. The authors estimated that at the same rate of gene flow Negro North Americans will be indistinguishable from white Americans in about 1,000 years.[20] In this way the authors use the new genetic viewpoint to investigate change but do so with the old taxonomy of races.

The most ambitious taxonomic undertaking so far attempted is that of Edmondson, who used 124 populations from all over the world and classified twenty-four genetic traits to construct a measure of population distance.[21] The lumpers argue that he ignores clines and that the twenty-four genes are not a random representation of the assumed 10,000 to 40,000 genes.

The studies relating to the no-race position include the classic study on sickle cell anemia in which one sickling gene gives resistance to malaria and inheritance of two sickling genes causes anemia and early death. The West African populations studies revealed a series of clines ranging from a population where 29 per cent of the genes are of the sickling type to a population without any sickling genes.[22] Livingstone interprets these clines as indicating that boundaries between races are non-existent, hence races are non-existent.

Another study in Africa by Hiernaux questions the general validity of race taxonomies. Hiernaux asks if "human populations . . . form clusters within which the distances are less than the inter-cluster distances?" Hiernaux answers the questions with research on fifteen populations in central Africa. He finds "one cluster of two closely related populations (the Tutsi of Rwanda and those of Burundi) is clearly apart, but the remaining thirteen populations allow no further clustering . . ." Hiernaux believes a similar situation would apply to published data on Asia or America.[23] The splitters would argue that Hiernaux has identified at least two races, perhaps three, and thus races do exist and better techniques might reveal the existence of still more.

The reponse of the splitters and lumpers to the improvement in data is not unlike that of debaters. The splitters are on the defensive and argue that more data and methods are needed to identify races properly. "There are valid races but biology is only beginning to properly discern and define them."[24] New mathematical models are needed better "fitting the human condition."[25]

The lumpers, on the offensive, find that present data provide sufficient ammunition to argue that mankind cannot be split into races. "The theoretical analysis of clines has barely begun, but there seems to be no need for the concept of race in this analysis."[26] From their strategically superior position the lumpers generally do not concede that further data are needed to clarify the taxonomic question of the existence of races. Instead, they view further data as necessary to study current processes of evolution. On this point the lumpers seem to have the splitters on the defensive, since more data tends to show more overlapping clines, to which the splitters can only reply that new methods and data are needed.

One possible position which neither side seems to use is that there are not yet sufficient data to determine whether races do exist or do not exist. Not enough data are available because too few groups have been studied, and too few genetic traits have been measured. These are all traits controlled by one allele; and, since most traits are controlled by interaction of multiple alleles, then the present collection of data is based on a biased sample.

If science were a self-correcting inquiry, then checking concept against better data in time should clarify the question of race. But science is not free of social influences and, while a theory is pulled toward validity by data, it may be pulled back by ideology, social structure, and social problems. Even the best of data must be interpreted, and the interpretation itself must be interpreted by inquiring into the social process in which ideas are formulated.

THE SOCIOLOGY OF KNOWLEDGE

The formation of ideas is a process influenced by many social factors. For analytical purposes it is possible to group these factors into five classes:

(1) Ideas may emerge from existing ideology, philosophy, science, or common sense.

(2) Ideas are shaped by existing social structure. The range of theoretical

influences includes the position of scientists or intellectuals in the social stratification system of their society, the nature of systems of social stratification established between nations or societies in contact, and the nature of their economic and political relationships.

(3) Ideas are also shaped in answer to social problems.

(4) Scientists and intellectuals, working independently or in cliques, debate with each other and from their dialectic emerge differing views. They also debate the popular conceptions held by non-scientists and this debate influences their position.

(5) New techniques of measurement and new data shift the bases of argument.[27]

The perspective of the sociology of knowledge is not intended to mean that a statement cannot be examined for its logical and empirical value. A statement is not proven false if one points out that its author was expressing his group perspective, vested interests, or personality characteristics. Yet it is useful to examine how thought is distorted in order to improve reason and its effectiveness. The race concept illustrates how reason may shift and change in relation to changing social structure.

CHANGING SOCIAL STRUCTURE AND CHANGES IN CONCEPT AND IDEOLOGY: THE EMERGENCE OF "RACE"

The idea of inherited differences is ancient, but men have not always been classified into races. The notion of race is a comparatively recent development which has existed according to historians only since the sixteenth century.[28] The emergence of the idea of "race" occurred in the seventeenth century following upon the explorations of the preceding two centuries, in which Europeans ranged the globe, established themselves as conquerors and colonizers, and brought back reports of aborigines and sometimes the aborigines themselves. The effect was to create vivid awareness of physical and cultural differences between man.

The first known use of the word was in 1606 by Tant in *Thresor de la langue française*. The seventeenth century was a period in which race was not yet a concept in wide use. Montagu claims that during the whole of the seventeenth century only five discussions relating to the varieties of mankind were published.[29] In the eighteenth century the idea of race was introduced into the scientific literature by Linnaeus in his *Systema Naturae* (1735). He saw the human species as a fixed and unchanging entity made up of four varieties of races identified primarily by color. His contribution to the race concept was primarily to place man in the animal kingdom and thereby make a scientific problem of racial classifications.

EUROPEAN EXPLOITATION AND THE GROWTH OF RACISM

During the two centuries from 1700 to 1900 Europe completed its worldwide colonization. By the year 1900 European nations and the offshoots of Western civilization controlled 85 per cent of the earth's land surface. During this period of time the awareness of race was converted into an ideology of racism.

"Racism" is defined here as the emotional conviction that race and behavior are linked in heredity and that some races are superior to others. An "ideology" is defined as a cluster of ideas that is widely shared and emotionally defended by the members of a society as a justification for their activities.

The ideology of racism took a mild form in the course of the eighteenth century and became particularly intense in the second half of the nineteenth century.[30] Other major phenomena in Western civilization which intensified the existing racism were the slavery issue and the emergence of nationalism, both in the nineteenth century. These forces later in the century received the assistance of Europe's last adventure in imperialism, and, in the United States from 1890 to 1920, a pattern of events known as nativism.

During this period of time the race concept held by scientists went through two debates which helped influence the growth of the ideology of racism and was in turn influenced by it. The polygenic-monogenic debate occurred in eighteenth-century scientific circles and helped support and develop racist ideology. The polygenic view held that races had separate origins and were possibly separate species. Having looked at the world through taxonomic glasses, the debaters explained taxonomy in terms of existing cosmology, and so in the eighteenth century they asked if God had created these races all at once or if he had created them separately.

The monogenic view had been held earlier by Linnaeus and came to be the position of the leading naturalists and intellectuals of the eighteenth century and into the early nineteenth century, including Buffon, Blumenbach, Kant, Cuvier, Camper, and Heider. They were in agreement that there was one common source for the races, and most of them held that race differences intergraded.[31] Blumenbach described the intergradation in 1793: "No variety of mankind exists, whether of color, countenance, or stature, etc., so singular as not to be connected with others of the same kind by such an imperceptible transition, that it is very clear they are all related, or only differ from each other in degree."[32]

Today Blumenbach would be classified as a splitter, but in his time he was a lumper. The splitters of that day held the polygenic view. Usually they were non-scientists such as Voltaire or lesser scientists such as Nott, Gliddon,

Morton, and others[33] who held that the different races were products of creation and that changes occurred by hybridization.[34] Gliddon, Morton and Nott, in the first half of the nineteenth century, expressed the polygenic position dominant in the United States among scientists and laymen. It fitted their reading of Genesis and helped justify their view of themselves as children of God among the barbaric Canaanites—the Canaanites being any Indians occupying desirable land. But many Southerners found the polygenic view too much at odds with their fundamentalist interpretation of Genesis and so they took the monogenic stance. Their virtue was rewarded by the discovery that one of Noah's sons had seen his father's nude body and had been cursed for it, and that his descendants had turned black and become the servants of man.

The debate over the inequality of man grew out of the monogenic-polygenic debate. During the latter portion of the nineteenth century it was hardly a debate at all, since inequality of races was the predominant view of scientists and intellectuals. American thought from 1880 to 1920 "generally lacks any perception of the Negro as a human being with potentialities for improvement. Most of the people who wrote about Negroes were firmly in the grip of the idea that intelligence and temperament are racially determined and unalterable."[35] In 1925 Sorokin wrote that: "perfect agreement of all these tests: the historico-cultural, the mental, the absence of geniuses . . . seems to indicate strongly . . . that the cause of such a difference in the Negro is due not only, and possibly not so much to environment, as to heredity."[36]

The scientific racism extended also to psychologists. G. Stanley Hall, a pioneer psychologist, held that primitive races were at earlier evolutionary stages,[37] and by 1916 the Binet intelligence test was regarded as perfected and "a powerful school of psychologists appeared which took up the old argument that intelligence is largely hereditary and little affected by environment."[38] Racists found support in the idea that some persons could not benefit from education as much as others.[39]

In literary circles the list of those believing in the inequality of races included James Fenimore Cooper, Henry Adams, Frank Norris, Jack London, Owen Wister, and Henry James.[40] In Europe a comparable group of writers included Kipling and Sir Walter Scott, whose *Ivanhoe* converted a feudal class struggle into an affair of "self-conscious racial conflict" between Saxon and Norman.[41]

The majority of intellectuals and scientists had ideas which helped give racism respectable veneer. But there were some intellectuals and scientists who were not racists. Most of the opponents of racism were humanitarians and intellectuals such as George Washington Cable, Winslow Homer, Mark Twain, Stephen Crane, and J. S. Mill. Among the scientists there were a few men who were not racist in their thinking. The list includes Adolf Bastian, Rudolph Virchow, William Ripley, Theodore Waitz, Friedrich Ratzel, Henry Rowe Schoolcraft, Lewis Henry Morgan, and John Wesley Powell.[42] They were not active anti-racists. They were forerunners of a reformed view of race who generally held that races differed only in minor respects.

The debate over the inequality of races was largely one-sided until the 1920's. The historian Gossett writes that the stemming of the tide was the work of "one man, Franz Boas, who was an authority on several fields which had been the strongest sources of racism." He asked for proof that race determines mentality and temperament. From then on "it would be the racists who were increasingly on the defensive . . . it was clearly Boas who led the attack."[43]

The techniques used by Boas were based on research he carried out or stimulated in physical and cultural anthropology. In 1912 he published work in physical anthropology demonstrating changes in head shape in children of immigrants. It weakened the older concept of the fixity of race[44] and the implication that mentality was also racially determined.

But Boas' influence on racism was even more significant through his leadership in cultural anthropology. According to Gossett, the ethnographic work his students began "had the utmost importance for race theory because the close and detailed knowledge of . . . primitive peoples showed how directly ideas and customs are interrelated and how fallacious is the idea that any society can be meaningfully interpreted in terms of its racial inheritance."[45] Gossett holds that what was needed to break through the dominant misconception was a way to explain character as an outcome of institutions, history, and environment. Boas and his students did that by building on the foundation left by Tylor, by their development of the relativisitic approach to cultural differences, and by the insistence on the masses of evidence. Gossett believes "it is possible that Boas did more to combat race prejudice than any other person in history."[46]

A broader explanation is needed in terms of how Boas' ideas came to be part of anti-racist theory in the social sciences and then how they gained wide popular acceptance. Boas' influence on his students explains the spread of his views into anthropology. One of Boas' most prominent students was Kroeber, whose 1917 article, "The Superorganic," was one of the influential statements calling for a social rather than an organic interpretation of human behavior.[47]

Psychologists began to shift their position. Otto Klineberg[48] was one psychologist who had contact with Boas and his students. He later gathered experimental support for the culture concept through his work in the changing IQ of Negro children as they moved from South to North. "In sociology the same trend occurred but under differing influences: 'Racial explanation disappears from serious sociology with the great generation of the early twentieth century: Pareto, Durkheim, Hobhouse and Max Weber made the issue of race irrelevant by the introduction of new canons of analysis and by their attempt to explain the social by the social . . ."[49]

What the social sciences had done was to respond to racism with a scientific rebuttal. Scientific anti-racism came to be the accepted position in the social sciences and among intellectuals. The idea was soon to spread and become a new popular ideology partly replacing racism and engaged in competing with it.

But a set of ideas does not become an active ideology simply because it is scientific. It spreads when cultural conditions are appropriate. The earlier ideas ran against the tide of conditions causing racism. But in the 1940's a social base was emerging for anti-racism.

Gossett lists several of these conditions and comments that: "We owe something to impersonal forces in the decline of racism, but the trouble with impersonal forces is that they can as easily work one way as another. We owe far more to the people and the organizations motivated by a concern for equality of all."[50]

Gossett's position seems to be that of the historian and humanist: men and ideas make history. The view that must be added concerns the influence of cultural conditions. Boas' ideas could only spread when the social structure was ready. Man may make history, but they do not do so unilaterally.

In the early decades of the century the forces for equality began to develop in the United States in the emergence of the social sciences as organized disciplines and in the advanced growth of urbanism and industrialism. To these must be added the transcendent influence of World War II. The propaganda developed during the war was based on the fact that Nazi Germany was totalitarian and racist. Since the enemy was racist, America had to become anti-racist. The massive anti-racist propaganda and the racist enemy undermined the strength of the racist groups in the United States that were so vocal in the 1930's. Racism began to recede on the surface and to be replaced by an appearance of genteel tolerance as a public policy, a trend aided by the shift in the American social classes in which the middle class increased in size and in its level of living.

THE CURRENT DEBATE AND ITS RELATIONSHIP TO PAST AND PRESENT IDEOLOGY

The major debates of the past two centuries were over the issues of separate or common origins for races and the equality or inequality of races. Both of these issues still persist within the current debate over the existence of races. The three debates all pivot on one common problem: equality. Each emphasized a different aspect of that equality: equality of origins, equality of intelligence, and taxonomic equality, but in each debate the same issue of equality or rights has been present.

The influence of ideology in the current debate can be discovered in the statements of the two men who take opposite positions as lumpers and splitters. Consider the position of Montagu who for decades has held that race is a myth:

> . . . How many times will it have to be reiterated that human beings are not "races" or for the simple principle that all men, by virtue of their humanity, have a right . . . to fulfill themselves. None of the findings of physical or cultural anthropology . . . can in any way affect this principle, this is an ethical one—an ethical principle which happens in every way to be supported by the findings of science.[51]

Montagu's statement is one that expresses values with which the author fully agrees, but they are nonetheless values which influence his particular interpretation of the available data. The fact remains that the data do not adequately support his position. Too few hereditary characteristics have been studied for too small a segment of world populations for one to be able to conclude that races do not exist.

Carleton Coon, who is a willing splitter, takes a position opposite to Montagu. Coon's thesis is that 500,000 years ago man was one species, Homo erectus, which perhaps already was divided into five geographic races or subspecies. Homo erectus then evolved into Homo sapiens five times as each subspecies or race living in different territories passed a threshold from erectus to sapiens state. In this parallel evolution the races passed over the threshold from erectus to sapiens species at different times: Caucasoid was first at 250,000 years ago; then Mongoloid, 150,000 years ago; Australoid, 40,000 years ago; Congoloid (Negroes and Pygmies), 40,000 years ago; and then the Capoid (Bushmen, Hottentots).[52]

Coon's values may be inferred from several scattered statements in *The Origin of Races*.

... it is a fair inference that fossil men now extinct were less gifted than their descendants who have larger brains, that the subspecies that crossed the evolutionary threshold into the category of *Homo sapiens* the earliest have evolved the most, and that the obvious correlation between the length of time a subspecies has been in the *sapiens* state and the levels of civilization attained by some of its populations may be related phenomena.[53]

... the Australian aborigines "come closest, of any living peoples, to the erectus sapiens threshold.[54]

If Africa was the cradle of mankind, "it was only an indifferent kindergarten. Europe and Asia were our principal schools."[55]

As far as we know now, the Congoid line started on the same evolutionary level as the Eurasiatic ones in the Early Middle Pleistocene and then stood still for half a million years, after which Negroes and Pygmies appeared as if out of nowhere.[56]

Genes in a population are in equilibrium if the population is living a healthy life as a corporate entity. Racial intermixture can upset the genetic as well as the social equilibrium of a group, and so, newly introduced genes tend to disappear or to be reduced to a minimum percentage unless they possess a selective advantage over their local counterparts.[57]

It is a common observation among anthropologists who have worked in many parts of the world in intimate contact with people of different races that racial differences in temperament also exist and can be predicted.[58]

The polar positions of Montagu and Coon on the question of the existence of races involve opposite views on the *equality* of populations or races. But most anthropologists who take a position on this matter are equalitarians. A racist can only be a splitter, a lumper can only be an equalitarian, but an equalitarian has the choice of being a lumper or a splitter. Since lumpers can logically only be equalitarian it is worth noting that the debate over the existence of races can be kept active only by the lumpers. There would be no issue if the lumpers as challengers of the status quo did not contend that races do not exist. These lumpers, represented by Ashley Montagu, express the values of equalitarianism.

The division of anthropologists into lumpers and splitters when most of them are equalitarian requires further explanation. The general liberal orientation of most anthropologists may relate to their selection of anthropology as a career. It is also supported by group definition and pressure in the social organization of the profession. A related condition might be the change in social climate about race since World War II; an atmosphere of tolerance means that the battle to fight racism is not so pressing to some intellectuals. It is no longer necessary to minimize race by arguing there are only three or only a few very similar races, and then, too, arguing there are many races is a way of quietly saying that race is not important. Thus equalitarians can comfortably be either lumpers or splitters. Their equalitarian values are shown in their opposition to racism. Lumpers generally oppose splitting as invalid and playing into the hands of bigotry, and splitters generally oppose lumping as unrealistic and playing into those same hands. Dobzhansky takes this latter view:

> Nowadays, a scientist cannot ignore the uses and misuses of his findings by politicians and special pleaders. He certainly cannot and should not refrain from recording the facts which he discovers, but he had better see to it that the language he uses to describe the facts does not invite misrepresentation. To say that we have discovered that races of man do not exist is such an invitation. It is far better to find out, and to explain to others, the real nature of the observable phenomenon which is, and will continue to be, called "race."[59]

Can racism be fought by persuasion, semantics, and data? Freed, Montagu, and others think so. Race is an evil concept, says Montagu, and therefore should be fought. It is too ambiguous to be redefined, and so he proposes to substitute the concept of ethnic group. He claims that "ethnic group," being noncommittal and of uncertain meaning, would raise questions about meaning.[60] Unfortunately, Montagu's semantic magic is likely to raise evil spirits already thought dead, since the term ethnic group is given cultural meaning by sociologists to clarify that many groups are unified by non-biological characteristics. If not semantics, then perhaps data will solve this problem, but the concept of race may be one that is so sensitive to social pressures that mere data will never resolve the issue.

THE FUTURE OF RACE AND RACISM

Men can most easily change ideas in directions which express their social structures. If social structure can facilitate the idea that race exists, then it can also facilitate the disappearance of the idea. If the idea of race was invented and transformed under the influence of social structure, it can be asked whether current changes support the lumpers or the splitters or neither.

The notion that mankind consists of populations with different hereditary taxonomic positions may disappear during the next century if certain trends in world social structure continue. The European notion that mankind consisted of races developed as Europeans became aware of the great variety of human differences. It became an ideology of racism to justify colonialism, slavery, imperialism, nationalism, wars, and genocide. Currently the leaders of many new nations of the world desire to move their nation from subordinate status as underdeveloped former colonies into the status of industrialized nation-status where their members will be the equal of any man, especially the white man of Western civilization. At present nationalistic ideology in new nations is intense in its insistence upon equality, but insistence is not enough. If they succeed in adopting and developing the new technology, their nations become important beyond their present role as allies or votes in the United Nations; they then become power centers, and their economics become interdependent with those of other nations. This kind of structural equality puts direct pressure upon the concept and ideology of race.

Within nations that value equality and are able to reach a stage of industrialization and high mass consumption, it is possible that segregated stratification systems will break down and racism will be reduced. During that future, if racism dissipates, the race concept will either become as forgotten as phlogiston or will be used without its present undesirable connotation. If these events occur it should not be viewed as the unfolding of the law of progress so much as indicating that old problems are replaced by new ones.

During these changes the role of the intellectual will be to transform the clash of power groups and vested interests into intellectual issues. They can carry out their role in such a way as to hasten a change and perhaps avoid some of the pitfalls in the change. The present debate between lumpers and splitters offers two alternative ways of expressing a future social structure of interdependence and coordinate status: the lumpers say there are no races, the splitters say there are thousands. The author takes the position that the data and the assumed future world social structure are better formulated in terms of the lumpers' position. If pressed to explain, the answer is that by using the splitters' definition of race, races can exist, but they are no more typical of the human species than hermits are of human societies.

CONCLUSIONS

Several generalizations are suggested by the above review of the debate over race.

(1) The race concept developed in a dialectic that has been controlled

largely by the same structural forces that generated the growth of racist and equalitarian ideology.

(2) The specific issue debated has shifted with changing social structure.

(3) Whatever the specific issue under discussion, the underlying theme has been the equality or inequality of different populations.

(4) With one exception it is possible to take any side of the issue and debate for or against equality. The exception is that of the non-existence of races, which makes all men equal.

(5) Improvement in data has not helped bring consensus about the nature of race, because the concept is polarized between two groups influenced by the ideology of equality: Splitters believe that equality of man is a matter of values and that the idea of the existence of many overlapping races will erode racism faster than the idea of the non-existence of races. The lumpers accept the unity of man and argue against race as man's most dangerous myth.

(6) The existence or non-existence of races remains a problem to be explored empirically as better data are gathered and better techniques devised. A crisp answer to the question may be obtained if adequate data are available for longitudinal as well as contemporaneous comparisons. Gathering data of this kind over a century may also answer a far more important question than the taxonomic; it may answer the question of how the species is changing.

(7) Although the data push toward greater similarity of taxonomic groups, it is argued here that the short-run fate of race as a concept and racism as an ideology will depend upon the range of possibilities created by changes in social structure.

(8) The role of scientific data in past disputes over race and the present dispute over the existence of races has been largely controlled or made possible by changes in social structure. The role of science in this view is that of a catalytic agent that can speed and channel the change by developing one or another of the possible alternative formulations for conceptualizing biological differences. It is the hope of action-oriented intellectuals that adopting one formulation rather than another will lead to changes in man's future which transcend the limits of the social structure that made the formulation possible.

NOTES

1 Lewis A. Coser and Bernard Rosenberg, "Sociology of Knowledge," in *Sociological Theory* (New York: The Macmillan Co., 1964), pp. 667–84.

2 C. Wright Mills, *The Sociological Imagination* (New York: Grove Press, 1959), p. 174.

3 Stanley Garn, "Comment," *Current Anthropology*, V (October, 1964), 316.

4 *Ibid.*

5 Carleton Coon, "Comment," *Current Anthropology*, V (October, 1964), 314.

6 Frank B. Livingstone, "On the Non-existence of Human Races," *Current Anthropology*, III, (June, 1962), 279.

7 Ashley Montagu, *Man's Most Dangerous Myth: The Fallacy of Race* (New York: Columbia University Press, 1942), p. 33.

8 C. Loring Brace, "On the Race Concept," *Current Anthropology*, V (October, 1964), 320.

9 *Ibid.*, 313.

10 Morton H. Fried, "A Four Letter Word That Hurts," *Saturday Review*, XLVIII (October 2, 1965), 22.

11 Brace, "On the Race Concept," p. 313.

12 Fried, "A Four Letter Word That Hurts."

13 Jean Hiernaux, "The Concept of Race and the Taxonomy of Mankind," in Ashley Montagu (ed.), *The Concept of Race* (New York: The Free Press of Glencoe, 1964), 42–43.

14 "Statement on the Nature of Race and Race Differences by Physical Anthropologists and Geneticists" (June, 1951); reprinted in *Current Anthropology*, II (October, 1961), 304–6.

15 Stanley Garn and Carleton Coon, "On the Number of Races of Mankind," in Stanley Garn (ed.), *Readings on Race* (Springfield, Ill.: C. C. Thomas, Publisher, 1960), p. 9.

16 *Ibid.*, pp. 9, 13–14.

17 W. Stanton, *The Leopard's Spots, Scientific Attitudes Toward Race in America, 1815–59* (Chicago: University of Chicago Press, 1960), p. 25.

18 Jacques Barzun, *Race, A Study in Modern Superstition* (London: Methuen and Company, 1938), p. 117.

19 A list of genetic traits is presented by Munro S. Edmondson, "A Measurement of Relative Racial Differences," *Current Anthropology*, VI (April, 1965), pp. 167–98.

20 Bentley Glass and C. C. Li, "The Dynamics of Racial Intermixture—An Analysis Based on the American Negro," *American Journal of Human Genetics*, V (March, 1953), 1–20.

21 Edmondson, "A Measurement of Relative Racial Differences."

22 Frank B. Livingstone, "Anthropological Implications of Sickle Cell Gene Distributions in West Africa," *American Anthropologist*, LX, 553–62.

23 Hiernaux, "The Concept of Race and the Taxonomy of Mankind," pp. 36–37.

24 M. T. Newman, "Geographic and Microgeographic Races," *Current Anthropology*, II (April, 1963), 189.

25 Stanley Garn, "Comment," *Current Anthropology*, IV (April, 1963), 197.

26 Frank B. Livingstone, in *Current Anthropology*, III (June, 1962), 279.

27 One example of how the existence of more data has shifted interpretations is seen in the lumping trend in classification of fossil hominids. Paranthropus robustus is increasingly being classified as an Australopithecus, Pithecanthropus erectus has been raised to the status of Homo, and Neanderthal is being considered for promotion to sapiens. This trend is partly the result of increased data which changes taxonomies by presenting a fossil series ranging over 1.75 million years and thereby reducing the relative time span and physical differences between fossils.

28 Louis L. Snyder, *The Idea of Racialism* (Princeton: D. Van Nostrand Co., 1962), p. 25.

29 Ashley Montagu, *The Idea of Race* (Lincoln, Neb., 1935), pp. 9–10.

30 Interpreters of the development disagree as to the starting point for racism, and suggestions range from the age of exploration to the slavery controversy, the French Revolution, and nationalism late in the nineteenth century. The basis for disagreement seems to be the fact that the intensity of racism increased during the period in question.

31 John C. Greene, *The Death of Adam* (New York: Mentor Books, 1959), pp. 222 4.

32 Johann Blumenbach, as cited in Montagu, *Man's Most Dangerous Myth*, p. 15.

33 John C. Greene, "Some Early Speculations on the Origins of Human Races," *American Anthropologist*, LVI (February, 1954), 22.

34 Stanton, *The Leopard's Spots*, p. 195.

35 Thomas F. Gosset, *Race: The History of an Idea in America* (Dallas, Texas: Southern Methodist University Press, 1964), p. 286.

36 Pitirim Sorokin, *Contemporary Sociological Theories* (New York: Harper & Bros., 1928), pp. 297–98.

37 Gosset, *Race*, p. 154.

38 *Ibid.*, p. 363.

39 *Ibid.*, p. 368.

40 *Ibid.*, p. 198.

41 Donald G. MacRae, "Race and Sociology in History and Theory,' in Philip Mason (ed.), *Man, Race and Darwin* (London: Oxford University Press, 1960), p. 80.

42 Gosset, *Race*, p. 245.

43 *Ibid.*, pp. 429–30.

44 H. L. Shapiro, "The History and Development of Physical Anthropology," *American Anthropologist*, LXI, (June, 1959), 376.

45 Gosset, *Race*, p. 416.

46 *Ibid.*, p. 418.

47 A. L. Kroeber, "The Superorganic," *American Anthropologist*, XIX (April–June, 1917), 163–213.

48 Otto Klineberg, *Negro Intelligence and Selective Migration* (New York: Columbia University Press, 1935).

49 MacRae, "Race and Sociology in History and Theory," p. 84.

50 Gosset, *Race*, p. 445.

51 Ashley Montagu, *Race, Science and Humanity* (Princeton: D. Van Nostrand Co., 1963), pp. 144–45.

52 Carleton Coon, *The Origin of Races* (New York: Alfred A. Knopf, 1962). Coon's argument can be questioned on the basis of incomplete evidence, the difficulty of distinguishing race in fossils, and the flow of genes between populations.

53 *Ibid.*, pp. ix–x.

54 *Ibid.*, p. 427.

55 *Ibid.*, p. 656.

56 *Ibid.*, p. 658.

57 *Ibid.*, p. 661.

58 *Ibid.*, p. 116.

59 Theodosius Dobzhansky, "Comment," *Current Anthropology*, IV (April, 1963), 197.

60 Ashley Montagu, "The Concept of Race," *American Anthropologist*, LXIV (1962), 919–28.

6

JOHN HORTON

The Dehumanization of Anomie and Alienation

SUMMARY

CONTEMPORARY DEFINITIONS of anomie and alienation have confused, obscured, and changed the classical meanings of these concepts. Alienation for Marx and anomie for Durkheim were metaphors for a radical attack on the dominant institutions and values of industrial society. They attacked similar behavior, but from opposing perspectives. Marx assumed an immanent conception of the relationship between man and society and the value of freedom from constraint; Durkheim, a transcendental conception and the value of moral constraint. Marx was interested in problems of power and change, Durkheim in problems of the maintenance of order. Paradoxically, contemporary definitions accept what was most problematic for these classical theorists—the dominant institutions of society. I raise the question: are contemporary definitions of alienation and anomie actually value-free, or are we witnessing a transformation from radical to conformist definitions and values under the guise of value-free sociology?

One of the mysteries of contemporary American sociology is the disappearance of the sociologist. His respondents speak, the social system functions loudly, but he who gave respondents language and the social system life is obscured beneath a fog of editorial "we," "they," or "it." His magic rests not only on the clever use of language but also on the ideology of the end of ideology and on an elaborate mythology starring Max Weber as sociological hero. Incanting an Americanized version of Max Weber's logic—there is, after all, a real distinction between fact and value—the

British Journal of Sociology, XV (December, 1964), 283–300. Reprinted by permission of Routledge & Kegan Paul, Ltd., and the author.

sociological magician accepts and justifies as a universal tenet of scientific objectivity his division into professional scientist and political animal. Perhaps I would be unsociological to suggest that he could do otherwise; this is not a conscious and intended self-deception. He is only affirming in theory what he does in practice; divided and alienated in his work, he is alienated in his thinking about his work.

Alienated thinking is especially apparent when the sociologist thinks about alienation. In the works of Marx and Durkheim, alienation and anomie critically and negatively describe states of social disorder from utopian standards of societal or human health. Today dehumanization has set in, the concepts have been transmogrified into things instead of evaluations about things, and it is no longer clear what alienated men are alienated from.[1] The intellectual problem of dehumanization is how to make an evaluation of a discontent pass for an objective description, or at least for another's evaluation.

Some would argue that values have indeed been done away with, and in the name of objective sociology. I would argue that such a position is the epitome of alienated and unsociological thinking. In sociological fact, time and sociologists have changed or obscured the classical meanings and values of alienation and anomie, and have added new ones. Under the banner of progress toward a more objective science, there has been a movement from radical to conformist values (or perhaps a movement toward value relativism), from anti-middle-class to middle-class values.

The sociological transformation of alienation and anomie would make a lively chapter in the much avoided sociology of sociology, for the differences in classical and contemporary definitions show how such sociological thought is affected by the particular historical position of the sociologist. But the chapter is only begun here: In this paper I shall attempt first to clarify the radically different values which gave the classical definitions of Marx and Durkheim their significance for social research and social action. Secondly, I shall outline differences between these and the contemporary definitions of Melvin Seeman and Robert K. Merton.

The task of defining and comparing definitions and values is not purely ideological. Sociological clues to the history of transformation can be found in the changing social position and organization of sociology—in the middle position of the modern sociologist, in the increasingly specialized nature of his occupational roles, and in his language, which expresses his occupational and class position.

Finally, throughout the discussion, I shall raise more general and disputable questions for sociological thinking about sociology. If our concepts have changed, and if these changes reflect changes in the questions we ask (ideology) as well as changes in how well we ask them (methodology), then we must rethink the implications of what should be most obvious to the sociologist—his knowledge is propositional, perspectivistic, and relational. Karl Mannheim has stated it much better: "Reality is discovered in the way in which it appears to the subject in the course of his self-extension."[2] The social history of alienation and anomie is a history of different ideologies, different types of self-extension, different and socially conditioned approaches to the problem of social discontent.

ALIENATION AND ANOMIE AS RADICAL CONCEPTS: THE TRADITION OF MARX AND DURKHEIM

A first step in the ideological analysis of anomie and alienation is an examination of their classical meanings in the works of Marx and Durkheim. The discussion will be organized around several contentions:

(*1*) Classical definitions of anomie and alienation contain radical ethical and political directives. The concepts are ethically grounded metaphors for an attack on the economic and political organization of the European industrial middle classes. Paradoxically, alienation and anomie are used today by the successors of the very classes that the classical concepts attacked.

(*2*) Classical definitions of anomie and alienation contain different ideologies; they are counter-concepts with different directives for action; they describe essentially the same behavior and discontents, but from polar opposite perspectives, which look for different causes and call for different remedies.

(*3*) These opposed perspectives follow from different interests in the social process, values, and assumptions about the relation between man and society.

Considered outside of any particular historical context, anomie refers to the problems of social control in a social system. Cultural constraints are ineffective: values are conflicting or absent, goals are not adjusted to opportunity structures or vice versa, or individuals are not adequately socialized to cultural directives. Whatever the particular meanings, anomie is a social state of normlessness or anarchy; the concept always focuses on the relationship between individuals and the constraining forces of social control. Durkheim used rates of deviation and the state of law and punishment as behavioral indices of anomie. Although he avoids psychological definitions, he implies that egotism, insatiable striving, meaninglessness, and aimlessness would be the probable reactions to living in an anomic society.

Alienation represents less a problem of the adequacy of social control than the legitimacy of social control; it is a problem of power defined as domination, a concept conspicuously absent from the anomie perspective. Anomie concentrates on culture or culture transmitted in social organization; alienation on the hierarchy of control in the organization itself. The critical focus of alienation is on whatever social conditions separate the individual from society as an extension of self through self-activity, rather than as an abstract entity independent of individual selves. For Marx, alienation from society is a priori alienation from self. Anomie concentrates on barriers to the orderly functioning of society; alienation on barriers to the productive growth of individuals, and by extension, barriers to the adaptive change of the social system. The non-alienated condition is not necessarily social harmony as social control, but social harmony as the spontaneous result of individuals being free to realize their historical potentialities. Free means autonomous and self-determining, not controlled by external forces. Alienated persons are powerless and estranged from the reified creations of their own self (social) activity.

In the works of Marx and Durkheim, there are no simple operational definitions of alienation or anomie on either a purely psychological or sociological level. The concepts imply complete social theories explaining relationships between a social condition and behavior. Critical concepts, they also imply the judgment of society in terms of ideal, or at least future and unrealized standards.

When alienation and anomie are returned to the concrete historical conditions which gave them their significance for social action, it becomes apparent that they represent radical criticisms of specific historical situations. Neither Durkheim nor Marx was interested in abstract historical and psychological definitions of anomie and alienation. This observation cannot be over-emphasized because it is precisely the original radical, historical, and sociological content which has been removed or altered by contemporary definitions.

The classical definitions have in common their condemnation of economic individualism and its rationalization in the middle-class doctrines of economic and political liberalism. These were interpreted as expressions of thinking under anomic and alienating conditions. Marx and Durkheim critically describe societies in which economic self-interest has been reified and raised to the level of a collective end. The consequences, they agreed, were that economic activities and values had become separated from and commanding over all other spheres of collective life. The most intense social activity in modern industrial societies, economic activity, was the least social.

In *Suicide*, Durkheim writes that anomie is endemic in modern economic life. By this he means that the economy, traditionally restrained by the moral codes of church, state, or guild, now dominates as the realm of un-restrained self-interest, or even class interest. Formerly a means to, and a means limited by other ends, economic activity had become an end in itself. In other words, anomie has become institutionalized.

> These dispositions (self-interested striving toward indefinite goals) are so inbred that society has grown to accept them and is accustomed to think them normal. It is everlastingly repeated that it is man's nature to be eternally dissatisfied, constantly to advance, without relief or rest, toward an indefinite goal. The longing for infinity is daily represented as a mark of moral distinction, whereas it can only appear within unregulated consciences which elevate to a rule the lack of rule from which they suffer.[3]

From a differing perspective, Marx makes a similar observation in his *Economic and Philosophical Manuscripts*. Here he argues that self-interest appears to be the motivating force of society because man has been alienated from his human and social activity, labor. The doctrine of self-interest is an example of alienated thinking.

> Since alienated labor: (1) alienates nature from man; and (2) alienates man from himself, from his own active function, his life activity; so it alienates him from the species. It makes *species-life* into a means of individual life. In the first place it alienates species-life and individual life, and secondly, it turns the latter, as an abstraction, into the purpose of the former, also in its abstract and alienated form.[4]

THE SOCIOLOGICAL FOUNDATIONS OF RADICALISM

A radical criticism cannot be derived from descriptions of facts alone; it rests on standards which transcend them. In nineteenth-century Europe, where the middle-class ethic of self-interest was justified by an essentially psychological and atomistic interpretation of man and society, one source of radicalism was sociology itself. Marx and Durkheim made their criticism of the self-interest ethic and the contractual interpretation of society in the name of history and sociology. The radicalism of their concepts comes in part from a sociological and collectivistic definition of man. This is their counter to the psychological and individualistic images of man and society, which they saw as expressions of alienated and anomic life conditions. By definition their respective social images of man mean that history could not be explained with reference to what individuals think and that events are not necessarily, and certainly not ideally, the result of a universal self-interest drive. Even Durkheim has acknowledged his agreement with Marxists on this point.

> We believe fruitful this idea that social life should be explained not by the conception which the participants have of it, but by the fundamental causes which escape their consciousness; and we think also that these causes ought to be sought principally in the way in which associated individuals are grouped. It is only on this condition that history can become a science and sociology, consequently, exist.[5]

Durkheim never tires of telling his reader that sociological facts must be explained sociologically. As Parsons suggests, his argument is both formal and empirical.[6] The formal, logical argument rests on the assumption that society, being qualitatively different from its parts, cannot be explained only with reference to the characteristics of its parts. The empirical and sociological argument emerges in Durkheim's explanation of order and anomie, and in his attack on all who would explain and reform society with a psychological and atomistic definition of man.

In *The Division of Labor*, Durkheim questions Spencer's psychological concept of man and society when he asks essentially how can we explain order and cooperation, if man, whose dispositions are not universally the same, acted only out of their different and opposing definitions of self-interest.[7] He also makes a sociological and collectivistic criticism of what he understood to be socialism. Socialism, he argued, was basically as anarchistic in result as classical liberalism. Both fail to recognize the need for social control over individual and economic activities.

> Because riches will not be transmitted any longer as they are today does not mean that the state of anarchy will disappear, for it is not a question as to the regulations of activity to which these riches give rise. It will not regulate itself by magic, as soon as it is useful, if the necessary forces for the constitution of this regulation have not been aroused and organized.[8]

Thus, Durkheim believed that the reification of self-interest was a contradiction of man's social nature, which required constraint through social control. Marx, on the other hand, contended that any reification of man's activity and products contradicted human nature, which developed fully only in the absence of reification and constraint. Far from being the natural disposition of man, whose dispositions are historically relative, the doctrine of the pursuit of self-interest was the propaganda of the capitalist ruling class, the ideological expression of class society and the alienating division of labor.

The critical content of alienation and anomie is sociological in the sense that Marx and Durkheim examined relationships between individuals and the collectivities which are products of their activity rather than psychological characteristics of individuals. Neither sociologist studied man outside of the subject-object (man-society) relationship; both condemned any attempt to do so. As sociologists they agreed that any doctrine which conceives of society as a congeries of contractual relationships between self-seeking individuals is false in its denial of the social nature of man. At the very most, such doctrines universalize the particular and transitory conditions of nine-teenth-century industrial society.

THE PHILOSOPHICAL SOURCES OF RADICALISM: ANOMIE AND ALIENATION AS TRANSCENDENT AND IMMANENT INTERPRETATIONS OF THE RELATIONSHIP BETWEEN MAN AND SOCIETY

If Marx and Durkheim distinguish themselves as sociologists by interpreting man as a social relationship, they nevertheless are in complete disagreement on the precise nature of this relationship. Indeed, alienation and anomie are founded on opposite conceptions of man and society. The opposed conceptions parallel those used in theology to describe the relationship between man and God. God is transcendent if he is exalted above man and the world by his moral perfection. God is immanent when he dwells in the world, when he is the essence of the world and the world the essence of him. Similarly, society can be interpreted transcendentally and extrinsically as an entity different from and morally superior to individual men; or it can be interpreted immanently as the extension of men, the indwelling of men. Alienation assumes an immanent interpretation of man and society; anomie a transcendent one. Both interpretations provide an ethical basis for a radical criticism of society.

Anomie is basically a utopian concept of the political right; it criticizes traditional economic liberalism of the middle classes from a philosophical position which could be called naturalistic transcendentalism. It carries radical rightist implications as it derives from the philosophical positivism of Comte, who founded his critique of the social organization of the rising middle classes on an analysis of the form of social control in the *ancien régime.*[9]

Alienation is a utopian concept of the radical left; it attacks economic liberalism from the futuristic perspective of the deprived classes and not from the backward glances of a declining class. The concept is formulated within a tradition of naturalistic and historical immanence; it represents an attempt to put the ideas of German idealism and the Enlightenment within a tradition of scientific and historical research.

Marx stressed the human and the active side of the man-society relationship and ultimately denied the dualism of man-society. Man's human and social activity is labor, and the products of labor, including society, are the extensions of man's own nature. Thus, man is his activity, his objects, man *is* society. Any reification of men's objects, any transcendence of men's products over men so that they do not see their interests, powers, and abilities affirmed and expressed therein, is evidence of the alienation of man from his self-activity, his objects, and himself. The whole notion of social alienation presupposes this immanent conception of human nature. Alienation is an historical state which will ultimately be overcome as man approaches freedom. Freedom for Marx, as well as for Hegel, meant autonomous and self-contained existence. Men will be free when the world has become so humanized and free of exploitation that man and society are one in theory and in practice. Marx's work could be interpreted as an empirical analysis of the historical process wherein man becomes separated from and reunited with society as self.

Preoccupied with the nature of order rather than change, Durkheim emphasized the passive side of the man-society relationship, how society makes and constrains men. His definition of anomie with its focus on the problems of social control and morality presupposes an absolute and eternal distinction between man and society and a dualistic conception of human nature. Marx's man is *homo laborans*, an historical variable developing through his own self-activity. But Durkheim's man is *homo duplex*, part egoistic, anarchistic, and self seeking, part moral in so far as he is regulated and constrained by society, which is the source of all logic and morality.[10] The object of men's orientation, society, being collective and outliving the life of individual men, is transcendent, qualitatively different from the parts which compose it. Durkheim's transcendence is in part a logical extension of his sociological and relativistic interpretation of man. If man's nature is plastic and therefore without a system of inner direction and control, then the needed control system must be external. Society is the source of order and control since it is analytically, and, Durkheim apparently believed, actually independent of individual man. The transcendence like the immanence argument, with its value of freedom as a condition of growth, is also an ethical argument. Influenced by Kant, Durkheim contended that morality is motivated not by self-interest, but by *dis*interest; men conform to rule out of a feeling of obligation and duty in the face of a superior entity. Anomie is thus a state of amorality and anarchy which can be overcome only by establishing societal rules. Freedom for Durkheim does not end with constraint; freedom begins with constraint over the conflicting passions of man. Alienation, as the transcendence of society over particular men, is the condition of morality.

The immanence ideology of alienation and the transcendence ideology of anomie reveal themselves also in Marx's and Durkheim's respective criticisms of the self-interest ethic and in their programs for social change. The concepts describe similar historical phenomena, but in sharply contrasting ways with radically different implications for action. For Marx, the doctrine of self-interest is one indication of alienation, self-estrangement and powerlessness in a class society. For the transcendentalist Durkheim, the same thing indicates anomie, a problem of inadequate rather than illegitimate social control. An immanent and materialist reform requires that alienation be overcome through revolutionary practice to end class society and to establish the material base for freedom in productive activities. But: "It is above all necessary to avoid postulating "society" once more as an abstraction confronting man."[11]

Marx wanted to humanize society, to organize the actual world so that man could experience himself as man (free and autonomous in his human or productive activity). Durkheim proposed to humanize Hobbesian man through the extension of social control. He called for the re-establishment of morality in a way that would take into account, not abolish, the specialized division of labor in society. Durkheim's specific proposal was the establishment of occupation communities which would be the modern carriers of moral discipline and social control. "For anomie to end, there must exist, or be formed, a group which can constitute the system of rules actually needed.[12] The problem must be put this way: to discover through science the moral restraint which can regulate economic life, and by its regulation control selfishness and thus gratify needs."[13]

THE CONTINUATION OF IMMANENT AND TRANSCENDENT SOCIOLOGY

Immanent and transcendent interpretations of social problems are of more than historical interest; they continue to oppose each other in contemporary American sociology. The opposition also continues to parallel different interests in the social process. Contemporary functionalists, interested in order and society as the unit of analysis, favor the transcendent (Durkheimian) interpretation of society. Those interested in process, change, and major social reform naturally emphasize the immanent nature of society. Talcott Parsons probably comes closest to Durkheim in asserting the functional need for transcendent social control. His position is nowhere clearer than when he

is criticizing C. W. Mills, who has approached a self-styled immanent interpretation of man and society. In a review of Mills' *The Power Elite*, Parsons
shows himself less critical of Mills' facts about power than of his interpretation of facts, his immanent ideology. As a transcendentalist, Parsons charges
Mills with holding to a utopian ideology which conceived of the possibility
of a society without constraint:

> Back of all this lies, I am sure, an only partially manifest "metaphysical"
> position, which Mills shares with Veblen and a long line of indicters of
> modern industrial society in which power does not play a part at all.
>
> This is a philosophical and ethical background which is common both
> to utopian liberalism and socialism in our society and to a good deal of
> "capitalist" ideology. They have in common an underlying "individual-
> ism" of a certain type. This is not primarily individualism in the sense that
> the welfare and rights of the individual constitute fundamental moral
> values, but rather that both individual and collective rights are alleged to
> be promoted only by minimizing the positive organization of social
> groups. The question of the deeper and longer-run dependence of the
> goals and capacities of individuals themselves on social organization is
> simply shoved into the background. It seems to me that he is clearly and,
> in the degree to which he pushes this position, unjustifiably anti-
> capitalist.[14]

The analogy could be pushed further. As a transcendentalist Parsons tends
to view stratification and power in terms of their contribution to system
order; Mills is interested not in legitimate, but in illegitimate stratification
and power and its negative effect on individuals within a society. The preoccupation of immanentists with problems of freedom and transcendentalists
with problems of authority and constraint is even more succinctly demonstrated in the opposition of Erich Fromm and John Schaar. Schaar significantly titles his attack on Fromm *Escape from Authority*, authority being the
concept conspicuously absent from the works of Fromm.[15]

CONTEMPORARY DEFINITIONS OF ANOMIE AND ALIENATION: THE QUEST FOR OBJECTIVITY AND THE TRANSFORMATION OF SUBJECTIVITY

Although immanentist and transcendental traditions continue, the existing
trend is to deny ideological influences in the firm belief that value and science,
social practice and theory, are and should be, separated in the name of scientific objectivity. This trend is well illustrated by most contemporary definitions
of anomie and alienation. As a private humanist the sociologist may be

seduced by the radical ethical overtones of alienation or anomie; as a scientific sociologist he denies, in the name of objectivity, the very object of his attraction. With the exception of a few vocal mavericks from R. S. Lynd to C. W. Mills,[16] men who did not distinguish absolutely in action or in theory between value and science, American sociologists have made a concerted effort to cleanse alienation and anomie of the messy conditions of their birth in the polemical writings of Marx and Durkheim. Ideologically, they proclaim the "end of ideology."

There are at least three standard formulas for the rite of purification; all three involve begging the question of values. In each, the ethical content of the concepts and the historically grounded perspective of the sociological observer are overlooked. The necessary relationship between occupational structure of the sociologist, his perspective, and his concepts are obscured. Not only is the role of values overlooked, but, under the guise of value-free sociology, the values are generally changed in a conservative direction.

The question of value and the perspective of the sociologist is begged by shifting the source and responsibility for evaluation away from the observer to (1) the persons being observed (the psychological approach), (2) the values of the dominant groups that set the boundaries of the social system being observed (the middle-range approach), and/or (3) the supra-individual standards of the community of sociologists (the professional ideology approach). The techniques are characteristic of occupational specialties in the contemporary social structure of sociology: the survey research man, the middle-range theoretician, and professional ideologist. I shall discuss these approaches in turn as they relate to the dehumanization of anomie and alienation.

THE PSYCHOLOGICAL APPROACH TO ANOMIE AND ALIENATION

The first approach, shifting the source of meaning to the persons observed, that is, from a sociological to a social-psychological level of analysis, is typical of survey research. The sociologist who specializes in finding correlations usually defines anomie and alienation in terms of feelings individuals have about themselves, other people, or goals and means to goals. By this formula, he transforms alienation and anomie into broad metaphorical terms for a vast range of personal, psychological discontents, which can be operationalized for survey research. For example, alienation defined as powerlessness, or anomie psychologized into anomia, is measured by agree-disagree questions. Then these measures are related to levels of socio-economic status, to prejudice, political extremism, or some other form of non-conforming behavior.[17] If the resulting constellation of correlations suggests social disorder, the narrowly empirical sociologist can argue that it is because his respondents, not he, have defined it as such. The question of the observer's perspective is thus circumvented by fragmenting the concepts and making them psychological; thereby appearing to divest them of their values.

The social psychological approach is exemplified in some of the work of Melvin Seeman.[18] Seeman calls his six measures alienation. However, he includes probable reactions to anomie as well as to alienation. His "self-estrangement" and "powerlessness" come very close to the feelings of one who might be alienated in the Marxist sense. "Normlessness" and "meaninglessness" might be reactions to unstructured situations or anomie. "Isolation" could be included under either of the classical definitions. Of course, neither Marx nor Durkheim would have tested their cases by measuring attitudes. One can be falsely conscious (not conscious of *de facto* alienation); there are also Freudians, religionists, and hip existentialists who see egoism and anarchy as the human condition (accepting of anomie).

In spite of the inclusiveness of Seeman's measure, it does leave out one meaning crucial to the original radical concepts of alienation and anomie—egoism and self-interest. Perhaps this is because self-interest is so widely accepted as a value in the American system, and, therefore, is not usually thought of as a reason for discontent and deviant behavior.

However, the question remains, in what sense are the psychological definitions value-free? By combining some of the classical meanings, operationally separating them from their theoretical contexts, and by reducing them to psychological measures, only the appearance of value-free objectivity is gained. One must still be alienated from something, anomic in terms of some standards of health. Presumably, it is the job of the respondents to tell us that they are alienated, and that this is the source of their problems. But are not Seeman and others in fact building in a theory of order and disorder by relating operationalized measures to non-conforming behavior, and, incidentally, assuring the nature of their findings? Are they not merely hiding their own conviction, projected on the "objective" facts, that alienation and anomie are important causes of social disorder and deviance? If this be error, it is error which cannot be eliminated by controlling bias or dreaming of better value-free concepts. Seeman is justifiably testing his own perspective, not that of his respondents. The error lies in not admitting it, not discussing the question of alienation from what knowledge for what purpose.

THE MIDDLE-RANGE APPROACH

In the occupational structure of sociology, the "value-free" theoretician behind value-free survey research is the "middle-range" sociologist. He repackages classical theories into workable hypotheses which can be used by any number of non-theoretically inclined specialists in the many substantive areas of sociology. The "middle-range" market alters old theories;[19] in the process of simplification, they are fragmented and divested of their original ethical, historical, and often radical significance. The problem of the perspective of the observer and of the community of sociologists is avoided by interpreting values not as political and utopian ideals, but as neutral objects of the social system being observed. The question of whose values, and why, goes unanswered. The technique of middle-range value-free sociology is unsuccessful, for the neutral attitude toward social phenomena is by conviction or default identification with the cultural order of the middle classes.

The middle-range approach to the concept of anomie is exemplified in the works of R. K. Merton and others who have used variations of this concept in their analysis of deviant behavior.[20] Merton's value-free concept rests on acceptance of the success and self-interest ethic of the American middle classes. I understand Merton to mean that a given society is anomic where there is a disjunction between the legitimate goals (culture) and opportunity structures (social structure). Specifically, American society is anomic in so far as there are socially structured barriers to the achievement of the culturally legitimate goal of success and status.

The political and essentially conservative content of his definition is apparent when it is compared with that of Durkheim. Anomie, defined as a disjunction between the success goal and legitimate opportunities to achieve success, may very well be a socially structured discontent in American society, yet Merton's anomie differs from that of Durkheim's in one crucial respect—in its identification with the very groups and values that Durkheim saw as the prime source of anomie in industrial societies. For Durkheim, anomie was endemic in such societies not only because of inequality in the conditions of competition, but, more importantly, because self-interested striving (the status and success goals) had been raised to social ends. The institutionalization of self-interest meant the legitimization of anarchy and amorality. Morality requires, according to Durkheim's modification of Kantian views, social goals obeyed out of disinterest and altruism, not self-interest and egoism. To maximize opportunities for achieving success would in no way end anomie. Durkheim questioned the very values which Merton holds constant.

The essential difference between classical and most contemporary definitions of anomie and alienation is not that the former are value-laden and the latter value-free. Both contain values, but different values. Classical concepts are radical and utopian: their values refer to ideal social conditions. Contemporary concepts are ideological in their identification with existing social conditions. Marx and Durkheim described and condemned. They condemned modern Western societies as alienated and anomic in terms of standards that transcended their institutions. For many American sociologists the referent for anomie and alienation is the present; but if they condemn existing conditions, it is in terms of the values of the dominant groups reified into the values of the social system. Paradoxically, from either a Marxian or a Durkheimian perspective, contemporary uses of the concepts of anomie and alienation would be examples of alienation and anomie. To define a concept in terms of the success goal or to attempt to make concepts value-free might be the expected response of sociologists working in an alienating division of labor and pursuing the self-interest ethic of the middle classes. Such sociologists need not question that which was most problematic for Marx and Durkheim.

THE IDEOLOGY OF OBJECTIVITY

A third formula for value-free sociology locates objectivity in the standards of the scientific community. This is the solution of the professional ideologist, and it provides a rationale for both the middle-range and survey research sociologists. It has been Karl Popper's answer to the threatening subjectivism of the sociology of knowledge.[21] He rightly asserts that objectivity need not be influenced by the prejudices of the individual scientists. Whatever his prejudices, they can be corrected by the collective, constraining standards of the community of scientists, the standards of intersubjective testability and criticism. No one can doubt this important source of social control. However, the Popper solution is no solution because it begs the question of value by confusing consensus with objectivity; there is also collective as well as individual bias. For example, our functional models and our methods of testability may reflect our agreement on a way and method of looking at reality, and not reality itself. There are as many alternatives as there are alternatives for social action. If the perspective of the American sociologists is to be located in the social organization of sociology, then the standards of that organization must also be located in the changing context of social history, and objectivity as verification and predictability will be seen to operate within the changing context of collective subjectivity.

THE SOCIAL CONDITIONS OF VALUE EVASION

These tactics of evasion are in no sense unique to contemporary American sociology; what is unique are the social conditions which have made them so convincing. Marx and Durkheim also begged the question of values by shifting the focus of value to the things being observed. Durkheim invested former patterns of social control with moral qualities and interpreted the world as a natural order. Marx projected humanist values into the evolving pattern of history seen as a political order.[22] Unlike contemporary sociologists, they have less successfully escaped the charge of value-laden sociology. Their escape was barred by the radical values which they asserted and by the unspecialized character of their practical sociological activity; they were personally responsible for the now separated functions of sociology—theory, method, and use of findings. In modern sociology values are officially overlooked and actually changed. The sociological question is, importantly, why is this so?

One obvious explanation for a lack of awareness of values is that values in contemporary sociology often are descriptions of crucial values in the existing social order. (Values are invisible unless looked for—or challenged.) The definitions of Marx and Durkheim are readily exposed as value-laden, not because they contain values, but because they contain radical values, opposed to and not realized in the status quo. Radical values are likely to be identified for what they are. In the present atmosphere of consensus and lack of debate in the social sciences, conservative values will pass for natural and objective descriptions of things.

More profound sociological reasons could be found in the changing social organization of sociology and in the social origins of sociologists. The present specialization and division of labor in sociology could account for the habit of denying the role of value and social structure in obtaining objective and socially significant knowledge; the position of the sociologist in sociology and in the broader community could account for the kind of values expressed.

Concepts can appear to be value-free as long as the sociologist does not question his values and as long as he does not see their influence because in practice he is able to separate his role of scientist from his role as private citizen. Values and action may be united in one person, as was the case with Marx and Durkheim, or dispersed in a system of specialized roles. It is only in the latter situation that the theoretically inclined sociologist can appear to escape the charge of value-laden sociology. Being specialized in his activity and isolated from the total sociological enterprise, he may not personally experience or have control over the connections which exist between occupational structure, perspective and value, and directions of research. Identified with the dominant institutions and values in his sector of society, these values become unproblematic and irrelevant for his problem of prediction within the accepted boundaries of his social system.

In other words, the doctrine of value-free sociology might be most strongly asserted under the social conditions of value consensus and occupational division of theoretical and practical aspects of sociology. The occupational division of labor in sociology complicates and clouds the relationship between values and research for individual, specialized sociologists. Consensus, by turning values into things, hides the subjective basis of consensus; it transforms subjectivity into the objective and natural boundaries of social action. Thus, the province of social research and concept formation falls within the invisible, subjective boundaries of consensus. The sociologist talks more about means and methods than goals. The radical concept of anomie, which questioned the goal of individual success, is redefined conservatively as a problem of inadequate means of achieving success. Nothing in the environment of Marx and Durkheim gave support for the ideology of objectivity. They were opposed to the dominant values; they combined theory and practice in their own activities—in them were fused those roles which later have been differentiated.

CONCLUSIONS AND IMPLICATIONS

I have argued first that the classical definitions of anomie and alienation rested on opposed utopian descriptions of essentially the same social discontent. Secondly, I asserted that the history of these concepts since then has been a history not of the emergence of value-free concepts but of the transformation of values. Thirdly, and in less detail, I have suggested that these ideological changes might be explained sociologically in terms of the changing class position of the sociologist and the organization of sociology. Finally the paper raises a more general question of the relationship between value and research in sociology. By locating the practice and ideology of value-free sociology in time, historical research throws doubt on any theoretical position which defines science and objectivity ahistorically through the reification of what is practiced in one historical period. If the sociologist should practice sociology on himself, he is obliged to recognize the possibility that the doctrine of value-free concepts of alienation and anomie and value-free sociology reflect a generalized awareness of a particular historical situation of value consensus and division of sociology into practical and theoretical activities. Being a sociologist, the sociologist must ask, is the doctrine of value-free sociology the only way, and necessarily the only desirable way, of perceiving the relationship between value and knowledge? Is he perhaps accepting uncritically and finding ideological justification for his own historical situation?

The conclusion doubtless requires a footnote of clarification. Since any discussion of the sociology of sociology may be taken as a direct attack on science by those behavioristically and positivistically inclined sociologists who do not accept the premise that a social fact is behavior seen from a perspective, I should be more precise about what I am and am not attacking. I am not pro-irrationality, pro-subjectivity, and anti-science. Science operates within a changing context of subjectivity. There is no necessary conflict between the sociologist of knowledge and the methodologist, because one prefers to study the social determination of thought, and the other to test the accuracy of propositions within a given universe of value. I think the proponents of the sociology of knowledge are not denying external reality, but affirming the human connection with that reality. They argue that knowledge is relational to man. They do not deny objectivity, but contend that men are objective about quite different things: What things is a practical question of what perspective and what values for what purpose. The accuracy of what is found out certainly depends on predictability and the old trial and error methods of science. I am not suggesting that Marx and Durkheim were better sociologists, and that we should return to their radical definitions of anomie and alienation and to their ways of handling the problem of values. I am not systematically attacking sociologists for being conservative. However important that attack may be, it is a political and polemical issue which would necessitate a political criticism of the social organization of sociology.

I am arguing that alienation and anomie, however dehumanized, contain values, and that these values have changed rather than disappeared in the practice of objectivity. With this statement, which can and should be more systematically verified, I do attack that abstract and hopefully mythical sociologist who cannot think sociologically about himself and his work. The subject of attack is ideological thinking in sociology, and particularly alienated thinking about anomie and alienation.[23] The ideologist represents socially determined knowledge as not socially determined, claims that his perspectives have nothing to do with his concepts. It may be a personal misfortune not to know one's own values; it is uncomfortable to attack and be attacked from value positions; but it is simply unsociological to deny the influence of values—whatever one's values or value confusion—and to represent one's work as objective in the highly ambiguous sense of value-free.

NOTES

1 In selecting the word "dehumanization" I was thinking of Ortega y Gasset's essay, "The Dehumanization of Art." By this association, I am suggesting that objectification and reification in the social sciences may be part of a more general social trend.

2 Karl Mannheim, *Ideology and Utopia* (New York: Harvest Books, 1936), p. 49.

3 Émile Durkheim, *Suicide* (Glencoe, Ill.: The Free Press, 1951), p. 257.

4 Karl Marx, "Economic and Philosophical Manuscripts," in Erich Fromm, *Marx's Concept of Man* (New York: Frederick Unger Publishing Co., 1961), p. 101.

5 Émile Durkheim, book review of Antonio Labriola's *Essais sur la conception materialiste de l'histoire, Revue Philosophique*, XLIV (1897), 648.

6 Talcott Parsons, *The Structure of Social Action* (Glencoe, Ill.: The Free Press, 1949), pp. 308–24.

7 Émile Durkheim, *The Division of Labor in Society* (Glencoe, Ill.: The Free Press, 1960), pp. 200–206.

8 *Ibid.*, p. 30. For an elaboration of this argument, see Émile Durkheim, *Socialism* (New York: Collier Books, 1962).

9 For a discussion of the relationship between Comte and Durkheim, see Alvin W. Gouldner, "Introduction," in Durkheim, *Socialism*, pp. 7–36. Gouldner argues that Durkheim was, in fact, a critic of Comte; much less conservative than Comte, he envisaged not a return to a Comtean mechanical solidarity. However, I believe that Gouldner goes too far in stressing Durkheim's reformism. Durkheim, like other utopian conservatives, wanted the re-establishment of social control and constraining moral forces. He held to a fixed and a historical conception of social control and a historical and relativistic conception of its expression. Whether the division of labor was simple or complex, social control still rested on supra-individual standards. Durkheim is essentially conservative in his Hobbesian conception of man and his transcendent conception of society.

10 Durkheim clearly annunciated his doctrine of the dualism of man and the transcendence of society. This he contrasted with what he called monistic (immanent?) definitions of man and society. He argued that socialism and utilitarianism as monistic doctrines were false because they could not explain altruistic behavior or the existence of general concepts. They failed to explain social phenomena that do not have their origin in self-interested and utilitarian motives of individuals. See Émile Durkheim, "The Dualism of Human Nature and Its Social Conditions," in Kurt A. Wolff (ed.), *Émile Durkheim, 1858–1917* (Columbus, Ohio: Ohio State University Press, 1960), pp. 325–39.

11 Marx, "Economic and Philosophical Manuscripts," p. 77.

12 Durkheim, *The Division of Labor in Society*, p. 5.

13 Durkheim, *Socialism*, p. 285.

14 Talcott Parsons, "The Distribution of Power in American Society," *World Politics*, X (October, 1957), 140–41.

15 John H. Schaar, *Escape from Authority, The Perspectives of Erich Fromm* (New York: Basic Books, 1961).

16 Robert S. Lynd, *Knowledge for What?* (Princeton: Princeton University Press, 1948); C. Wright Mills, *The Sociological Imagination* (New York: Oxford University Press, 1959).

17 For psychological definitions of anomie and alienation, see, among many others, Melvin Seeman, "On the Meaning of Alienation," *American Sociological Review*, XXIV

(December, 1959), 783–91. See also Gwynn Nettler, "A Measure of Alienation," *American Sociological Review*, XXII (December, 1957), 670–77; Leo Srole, "Social Integration and Certain Corollaries: An Exploratory Study," *American Sociological Review*, XXI (December, 1956), 706–16; Dwight Dean, "Meaning and Measurement of Alienation," *American Sociological Review*, XXVI (October, 1961), 753–58.

18 Seeman, "On the Meaning of Alienation."

19 For a discussion of the relationship of middle-range to classical theories, see Maurice R. Stein, "Psychoanalytic Thought and Sociological Inquiry," *Psychoanalysis and the Psychoanalytic Review*, XLIX (Summer, 1962), 22–23.

20 Robert K. Merton, "Social Structure and Anomie" and "Continuities in the Theory of Social Structure and Anomie," in *Social Theory and Social Structure* (Glencoe, Ill.: The Free Press, 1957), pp. 161–94.

21 Karl Popper, *The Open Society and Its Enemies* (Princeton: Princeton University Press, 1956), esp. chaps. xxiii and xxiv; *The Poverty of Historicism* (Boston: Beacon Press, 1957), sec. 32; *Logic of Scientific Discovery* (New York: Basic Books, 1959), pp. 44–48.

22 For a discussion of the uses of concepts of natural order and natural law in sociology, see Leon Bramson, *The Political Context of Sociology* (Princeton: Princeton University Press, 1961), pp. 18–26.

23 For lack of more precise words, I have employed ideology in three different senses: (1) ideology as any socially determined perspective; (2) ideology as thought identified with existing social conditions—in this Mannheimian meaning it is opposed to utopian thinking or thought identified with ideal or at least non-existing social conditions; (3) finally, ideology in the Marxist sense of false-thinking, representing socially determined thought as free of social determination.

7

JOHN HORTON

Order and Conflict Theories of Social Problems as Competing Ideologies

A RECENT BEST SELLER, *The One Hundred Dollar Misunderstanding*,[1] should be required reading for every student of social problems and deviant behavior. The novel makes clear what is often dimly understood and rarely applied in sociology—the fundamentally social and symbolic character of existing theories of behavior. In the novel a square, white college boy and a Lolita-esque Negro prostitute recount their shared weekend experience. But what they have shared in action, they do not share in words. Each tells a different story. Their clashing tales express different vocabularies and different experiences. The author, Robert Glover, stereotypically dramatizes a now hackneyed theme in the modern theater and novel—the misunderstandings generated by a conflict of viewpoints, a conflict between subjective representations of "objective" reality.

Paradoxically, this familiar literary insight has escaped many social scientists. The escape is most baffling and least legitimate for the sociologists of deviant behavior and social problems. Social values define their phenomena; their social values color their interpretations. Whatever the possibilities of developing empirical theory in the social sciences, only normative theory is appropriate in the sociology of social problems. I would accept Don Martindale's definitions of empirical and normative theory:

> The ultimate materials of empirical theory are facts; the ultimate materials of normative theory are value-imperatives . . . empirical theory is formed out of a system of laws. Normative theory converts facts and laws into

American Journal of Sociology, LXXI (May, 1966), 701–13. Reprinted by permission of The University of Chicago Press and the author.

requisite means and conditions and is unique in being addressed to a system of objectives desired by the formulator or by those in whose service he stands.[2]

The problem for the sociologist is not that normative theories contain values, but that these values may go unnoticed so that normative theories pass for empirical theories. When his own values are unnoticed, the sociologist who studies the situation of the American Negro, for example, is a little like the middle-class white boy in Glover's novel, except that only one story is told, and it is represented as *the* story. The result could be a rather costly misunderstanding: the Negro may not recognize himself in the sociological story; worse, he may not even learn to accept it.

One of the tasks of the sociologist is to recognize his own perspective and to locate this and competing perspectives in time and social structure. In this he can use Weber, Mills, and the sociology of knowledge as guides. Following Weber's work, he might argue that in so far as we are able to theorize about the social world, we must use the vocabularies of explanation actually current in social life.[3] This insight has been expanded by C. W. Mills and applied to theorizing in general and to the character of American theorizing in particular. The key words in Mills' approach to theorizing are "situated actions" and "vocabularies of motive." His position is that theories of social behavior can be understood sociologically as typical symbolic explanations associated with historically situated actions.[4] Thus, Mill argues that the Freudian terminology of motives is that of an upper-bourgeois patriarchal group with a strong sexual and individualistic orientation. Likewise explanations current in American sociology reflect the social experience and social motives of the American sociologist. Mills contends that for a period before 1940, a single vocabulary of explanation was current in the American sociologist's analysis of social problems and that these motives expressed a small town (and essentially rural) bias.[5] He interpreted the contemporary sociological vocabulary as a symbolic expression of a bureaucratic and administrative experience in life and work.[6]

Continuing in the tradition of Weber and Mills, I attempt to do the following: (1) propose a method of classifying current normative theories of deviant behavior and social problems; (2) discuss liberal and sociological approaches to the race question as an example of one of these theories; and (3) point out the implications of the normative character of theory for sociology. My general discussion of competing theories will be an elaboration of several assumptions:

(1) All definitions and theories of deviation and social problems are

normative. They define and explain behavior from socially situated value positions.

(2) Existing normative theories can be classified into a limited number of typical vocabularies of explanation. Contemporary sociological theories of deviation are adaptations of two fundamental models of analysis rooted in nineteenth-century history and social thought. These are *order* and *conflict* models of society. Order models imply an *anomie* theory of societal discontent and an *adjustment* definition of social deviation. Conflict models imply an *alienation* theory of discontent and a *growth* definition of deviation.

(3) In general, a liberalized version of order theory pervades the American sociological approach to racial conflict, juvenile delinquency, and other social problems. I use the term "liberal" because the sociological and the political liberal vocabularies are essentially the same. Both employ an order model of society; both are conservative in their commitment to the existing social order.

(4) Alternatives to the liberal order approach exist both within the context of sociological theory and in the contemporary social and political fabric of American society. More radical versions of order models have been used by European sociologists such as Émile Durkheim; radical versions of order models are presently being used in American society by political rightists. The conflict vocabulary has been most clearly identified with Karl Marx and continues today in the social analysis of socialists and Communists, while an anarchistic version of conflict theory pervades the politics of the so-called new left.

(5) Current vocabularies for the explanation of social problems can be located within the social organization of sociology and the broader society. As a generalization, groups or individuals committed to the maintenance of the social status quo employ order models of society and equate deviation with non-conformity to institutionalized norms. Dissident groups, striving to institutionalize new claims, favor a conflict analysis of society and an alienation theory of their own discontents. For example, this social basis of preference for one model is clear in even the most superficial analysis of stands taken on civil-rights demonstrations by civil-rights activists and members of the Southern establishment. For Governor Wallace of Alabama, the 1965 Selma-Montgomery march was a negative expression of anomie; for Martin Luther King it was a positive and legitimate response to alienation. King argues that the Southern system is maladaptive to certain human demands; Wallace that the demands of the demonstrators are dysfunctional to the South. However, if one considers their perspectives in relationship to the more powerful Northern establishment, King and not Wallace is the order theorist.

In sociology, order analysis of society is most often expressed by the professional establishment and its organs of publication. Alienation analysis is associated with the "humanitarian" and "political" mavericks outside of, opposed to, or in some way marginal to the established profession of sociology.

ORDER AND CONFLICT THEORIES: ANOMIE AND ALIENATION ANALYSIS OF SOCIAL PROBLEMS AS IDEAL TYPES

The terms "alienation" and "anomie" current in the analysis of social problems derive historically from two opposing models of society—order and conflict models.[7] A comparison of the works of Marx and Mills (classical and contemporary conflict models) and Durkheim and Merton or Parsons (classical and contemporary order models) highlights the differences between the two social vocabularies. These competing vocabularies can be abstracted into ideal types of explanation, that is, exaggerated and ideologically consistent models which are only approximated in social reality.

The Order Vocabulary

Order theories have in common an image of society as a system of action unified at the most general level by shared culture, by agreement on values (or at least on modes) of communication and political organization. System analysis is synonymous with structural-functional analysis. System analysis consists of *statics*—the classification of structural regularities in social relations (dominant role and status clusters, institutions, etc.)—and *dynamics*—the study of the intrasystem processes: strategies of goal definition, socialization, and other functions which maintain system balance. A key concept in the analysis of system problems (social problems, deviation, conflict) is anomie. Social problems both result from and promote anomie. Anomie means system imbalance or social disorganization—a lack of or breakdown in social organization reflected in weakened social control, inadequate institutionalization of goals, inadequate means to achieve system goals, inadequate socialization, etc. At a social psychological level of analysis, anomie results in the failure of individuals to meet the maintenance needs of the social system.

Order theories imply consensual and adjustment definitions of social health and pathology, of conformity and deviation. The standards for defining health are the legitimate values of the social system and its requisites for goal attainment and maintenance. Deviation is the opposite of social conformity and means the failure of individuals to perform their legitimate social roles; deviants are out of adjustment.

A contemporary example of an order approach to society and an adjustment interpretation of health and pathology has been clearly stated in Talcott Parsons' definition of mental health and pathology:

> Health may be defined as the state of optimum *capacity* of an individual for the effective performance of the roles and tasks for which he has been socialized. It is thus defined with reference to the individual's participation in the social system. It is also defined as *relative* to his "status" in the society, i.e., to differentiated type of role and corresponding task structure, e.g., by sex or age, and by level of education which he has attained and the like.[8]

The Conflict Vocabulary

Conflict theorists are alike in their rejection of the order model of contemporary society. They interpret order analysis as the strategy of a ruling group, a reification of their values and motivations, a rationalization for more effective social control. Society is a natural system for the order analyst; for the conflict theorist it is a continually contested political struggle between groups with opposing goals and world views. As an anarchist, the conflict theorist may oppose any notion of stable order and authority. As a committed Marxist, he may project the notion of order into the future. Order is won, not through the extension of social control, but through the radical reorganization of social life; order follows from the condition of social organization and not from the state of cultural integration.

Conflict analysis is synonymous with historical analysis: the interpretation of intersystem processes bringing about the transformation of social relations. A key concept in the analysis of historical and social change (as new behavior rather than deviant behavior) is alienation—separation, not from the social system as defined by dominant groups, but separation from man's universal nature or a desired state of affairs. Change is the progressive response to alienation; concepts of disorganization and deviation have no real meaning within the conflict vocabulary; they are properly part of the vocabulary of order theory, where they have negative connotations as the opposites of the supreme values of order and stability. Within the conflict framework, the question of normality and health is ultimately a practical one resolved in the struggle to overcome alienation.

Conflict theory, nevertheless, implies a particular definition of health, but the values underlying this definition refer to what is required to grow and change, rather than to adjust to existing practices and hypothesized requirements for the maintenance of the social system. Health and pathology are defined in terms of postulated requirements for individual or social growth and adaptation. Social problems and social change arise from the exploitive and alienating practices of dominant groups; they are responses to the discrepancy between what is and what is in the process of becoming. Social problems, therefore, reflect, not the administrative problems of the social system, nor the failure of individuals to perform their system roles as in the order explanation, but the adaptive failure of society to meet changing individual needs.

A growth definition of health based on a conflict interpretation of society is implicit in Paul Goodman's appraisal of the causes of delinquency in American society. Unlike Parsons, he does not define pathology as that which does not conform to system values; he argues that delinquency is not the reaction to exclusion from these values, nor is it a problem of faulty socialization. Existing values and practices are absurd standards because they do not provide youth with what they need to grow and mature:

> As was predictable, most of the authorities and all of the public spokesmen explain it [delinquency] by saying there has been a failure of socialization. They say that background conditions have interrupted socialization and must be improved. And, not enough effort has been made to guarantee belonging, there must be better bait or punishment.
>
> But perhaps there has *not* been a failure of communication. Perhaps the social message has been communicated clearly to the young men and is unacceptable.
>
> In this book I shall, therefore, take the opposite tack and ask, "Socialization to what? to what dominant society and available culture?" And if this question is asked, we must at once ask the other question, "Is the harmonious organization to which the young are inadequately socialized perhaps against human nature, or not worthy of human nature, and *therefore* there is difficulty in growing up?"[9]

The conflict theorist invariably questions the legitimacy of existing practices and values; the order theorist accepts them as the standard of health.

PARADIGM FOR THE ANALYSIS OF CONFLICT AND ORDER APPROACHES TO SOCIAL PROBLEMS

In order more sharply to compare order and conflict models in terms of their implications for explanations of deviation and social problems, essential differences can be summarized along a number of parallel dimensions. These dimensions are dichotomized into order and conflict categories. The resulting paradigm can be used as a preliminary guide for the content analysis of contemporary as well as classical studies of social problems.

ORDER PERSPECTIVE

CONFLICT PERSPECTIVE

(1) UNDERLYING SOCIAL PERSPECTIVE AND VALUE POSITIONS (IDEAL)

(a) *Image of man and society*

Society as a natural boundary-maintaining system of action

Society as a contested struggle between groups with opposed aims and perspectives

Transcendent nature of society, an entity *sui generis*, greater than and different from the sum of its parts; lack of transcendence as lack of social control means anomie

Immanent conception of society and the social relationship; men are society; society is the extension of man, the indwelling of man; the transcendence of society is tantamount to the alienation of man from his own social nature

Positive attitude toward the maintenance of social institutions

Positive attitude toward change

(b) *Human nature*

Homo duplex, man half egoistic (self-nature), half altruistic (socialized nature), ever in need of restraints for the collective good

Homo laborans existential man, the active creator of himself and society through practical and autonomous social action

or

Tabula rasa, man equated with the socialization process

or

Homo damnatus, the division into morally superior and morally inferior men

(c) *Values*

The social good: balance, stability, authority, order, quantitative growth ("moving equilibrium")

Freedom as autonomy, change, action, qualitative growth

ORDER PERSPECTIVE   CONFLICT PERSPECTIVE

(2) MODES OF "SCIENTIFIC" ANALYSIS

Order Perspective	Conflict Perspective
Natural science model: quest for general and universal laws and repeated patterns gleaned through empirical research Structural-functional analysis	Historical model: quest for understanding (*Verstehen*) through historical analysis of unique and changing events; possible use of ideal type of generalization based on historically specific patterns
Multiple causality; theory characterized by high level of abstraction, but empirical studies marked by low level of generalization (separation of theory from application)	Unicausality; high or low level of theoretical generalization; union of theory and practice in social research and social action
Conditions of objectivity: accurate correspondence of concepts to facts; rigid separation of observer and facts observed —passive, receptive theory of knowledge	Utility in terms of observer's interests; objectivity discussed in the context of subjectivity— activistic theory of knowledge
Analysis begins with culture as major determinant of order and structure and proceeds to personality and social organization	Analysis begins with organization of social activities or with growth and maintenance needs of man and proceeds to culture
Dominant concepts: ahistorical; high level of generality; holistic; supra-individual concepts; ultimate referent for concepts—system needs considered universally (i.e., the functional prerequisites of any social system) or relativistically (i.e., present maintenance requirements of a particular social system)	Historical, dynamic; low level of generality and high level of historical specificity; ultimate referent for concepts— human needs considered universally (i.e., man's species nature) or relativistically (demands of particular contenders for power); referent often the future or an unrealized state of affairs

ORDER PERSPECTIVE	CONFLICT PERSPECTIVE

(3) ORDER AND CONFLICT THEORIES OF SOCIAL PROBLEMS AND DEVIATION

(a) Standards for the definition of health and pathology

Health equated with existing values of a postulated society (or a dominant group in the society), ideological definition	Health equated with unrealized standards (the aspirations of subordinate but rising groups), utopian definition

(b) Evaluation of deviant behavior

Pathological to the functioning of the social system	Possibly progressive to the necessary transformation of existing relationships

(c) Explanation of deviation or a social problem

A problem of anomie in adequate control over competing groups in the social system; disequilibrium in the existing society	A problem of self-alienation, being thwarted in the realization of individual and group goals; a problem of illegitimate social control and exploitation

(d) Implied ameliorative action

Extension of social control (further and more efficient institutionalization of social system values); adjustment of individuals to system needs; working within the system; the administrative solution	Rupture of social control; radical transformation of existing patterns of interaction; revolutionary change of the social system

(4) ORDER AND CONFLICT THEORIES AS SOCIALLY SITUATED VOCABULARIES

Dominant groups: the establishment and administrators of the establishment	Subordinate groups aspiring for greater power
Contemporary representatives: Parsonian and Mertonian approach to social problems as a liberal variant of order models; politically conservative approaches	C. W. Mills, new left (SNCC, SDS, etc.) approaches and old left (socialistic and Communistic)

The order and conflict models as outlined represent polar ideal types which are not consistently found in the inconsistent ideologies of actual social research and political practice. If the models have any utility to social scientists, it will be in making more explicit and systematic the usually implicit value assumptions which underlie their categories of thinking. In this study as an exercise in the use of conflict-order models, I examine some of the normative assumptions which can be found in the approach of the sociologist and the political liberal to the Negro question. My thinking is intentionally speculative. I am not trying to summarize the vast literature on race relations, but merely showing the existence of an order pattern.

LIBERALS AND SOCIOLOGISTS ON THE AMERICAN NEGRO: A CONTEMPORARY ADAPTATION OF ORDER THEORY

Contemporary liberalism has been popularly associated with a conflict model of society; actually it is a variant of conservative order theory. Within the model, conflict is translated to mean institutionalized (reconciled) conflict or competition for similar goals within the same system. Conflict as confrontation of opposed groups and values, conflict as a movement toward basic change of goals and social structures is anathema.

The liberal tendency of American sociology and the essentially conservative character of contemporary liberalism are particularly marked in the sociological analysis of the Negro question. In the field of race relations, an order model can be detected in (1) consensual assumptions about man and society: the "oversocialized" man and the plural society; (2) a selective pattern of interpretation which follows from these assumptions: (a) the explanation of the problem as a moral dilemma and its solution as one requiring adjustment through socialization and social control; (b) the explanation of the minority group as a reaction-formation to exclusion from middle-class life; (c) an emphasis on concepts useful in the explanation of order (shared values as opposed to economic and political differences); an emphasis on concepts useful in the explanation of disorder or anomie within an accepted order (status competition rather than class conflict, problems of inadequate means rather than conflicting goals).

THE LIBERAL VIEW OF MAN: EGALITARIAN WITHIN AN ELITIST, CONSENSUAL FRAMEWORK: ALL MEN ARE SOCIALIZABLE TO THE AMERICAN CREED

No one can see an ideological assumption as clearly as a political opponent. Rightist and leftist alike have attacked the liberal concept of man implicit in the analysis of the Negro question: conservatives because it is egalitarian, radicals because it is elitist and equated with a dominant ideology. The rightist believes in natural inequality; the leftist in positive, historical differences between men; the liberal believes in the power of socialization and conversion.

A certain egalitarianism is indeed implied in at least two liberal assertions: (1) Negroes along with other men share a common human nature socializable to the conditions of society; (2) their low position and general inability to compete reflect unequal opportunity and inadequate socialization to whatever is required to succeed within the American system. These assertions are, in a sense, basically opposed to the elitist-conservative argument that the Negro has failed to compete because he is naturally different or has voluntarily failed to take full advantage of existing opportunities.[10]

The conservative, however, exaggerates liberal egalitarianism; it is tempered with elitism. Equality is won by conformity to a dominant set of values and behavior. Equality means equal opportunity to achieve the same American values; in other words, equality is gained by losing one identity and conforming at some level to another demanded by a dominant group. As a leftist, J.-P. Sartre has summarized this liberal view of man, both egalitarian and elitist. What he has termed the "democratic" attitude toward the Jew applies well to the American "liberal" view of the Negro.

> The Democrat, like the scientist, fails to see the particular case; to him the individual is only an ensemble of universal traits. It follows that his defense of the Jew saves the latter as a man and annihilates him as a Jew . . . he fears that the Jew will acquire a consciousness of Jewish collectivity. . . . "There are no Jews," he says, "there is no Jewish question." This means that he wants to separate the Jew from his religion, from his family, from his ethnic community, in order to plunge him into the democratic crucible whence he will emerge naked and alone, an individual and solitary particle like all other particles.[11]

The conservative would preserve a Negro identity by pronouncing the Negro different (inferior), the radical by proclaiming him part of the superior vanguard of the future society; but the liberal would transform him altogether by turning him into another American, another individual competing in an orderly fashion for cars, television sets, and identification with the American Creed. In their attack on the liberal definition of man, the conservative and leftist agree on one thing: the liberal seems to deny basic differences between groups. At least differences are reconcilable within a consensual society.

THE LIBERAL SOCIETY: STRUCTURAL PLURALISM
WITHIN A CONSENSUAL FRAMEWORK

Thus, the liberal fate of minorities, including Negroes, is basically containment through socialization to dominant values. Supposedly this occurs in a plural society where some differences are maintained. But liberal pluralism like liberal egalitarianism allows differences only within a consensual framework. This applies both to the liberal ideal and the sociological description: the plural-democratic society *is* the present society.

This consensual pluralism should be carefully distinguished from the conflict variety. J. S. Furnivall has called the once colonially dominated societies of tropical Asia plural in the latter sense:

> In Burma, as in Java, probably the first thing that strikes the uisitor is the medley of peoples—European, Chinese, Indian, native. It is in the strictest sense a medley, for they mix but do not combine. Each group holds to its own religion, its own culture and language, its own ideas and ways. As individuals they meet, but only in the marketplace, in buying and selling. There is a plural society, with different sections of the community living side by side, but separately within the same political unit. Even in the economic sphere there is a division along racial lines.[12]

For Furnivall, a plural society has no common will, no common culture. Order rests on political force and economic expediency. For liberals and sociologists, American society has a common social will (the American Creed). Order rests on legitimate authority and consensus. The whole analysis of the Negro question has generally been predicated on this belief that American society, however plural, is united by consensus on certain values. Gunner Myrdal's influential interpretation of the Negro question has epitomized the social-will thesis:

> Americans of all national origins, classes, regions, creeds, and colors have something in common: a social ethos, a political creed. . . . When the American Creed is once detected the cacophony becomes a melody . . . as principles which ought to rule, the Creed has been made conscious to everyone in American society. . . . America is continuously struggling for its soul. The cultural unity of the nation is sharing of both the consciousness of sin and the devotion to high ideals.[13]

In what sense can a consensual society be plural? It cannot tolerate the existence of separate cultural segments. Robin M. Williams in a recent book on race relations writes: "The United States is a plural society which cannot settle for a mosaic of separate cultural segments, nor for a caste system."[14] Norman Podhoretz, a political liberal who has written often on the Negro question, has stated the issue more bluntly. In his review of Ralph Ellison's *Shadow and the Act*, a series of essays which poses a threat of conflict pluralism by asserting the positive and different "cultural" characteristics of Negroes, Podhoretz states his consensual realism:

> The vision of a world in which many different groups live together on a footing of legal and social equality, each partaking of a broad general culture and yet maintaining its own distinctive identity: this is one of the noble dreams of the liberal tradition. Yet the hard truth is that very little evidence exists to suggest that such a pluralistic order is possible. Most societies throughout history have simply been unable to suffer the presence of distinctive minority groups among them; and the fate of minorities has generally been to disappear, either through being assimilated into the majority, or through being expelled, or through being murdered.[15]

The liberal and the sociologist operating with an order ideology positively fear the conflict type of pluralism. As Sartre rightly observed, the liberal who is himself identified with the establishment, although avowedly the friend of the minority, suspects any sign of militant minority consciousness. He wants the minority to share in American human nature and compete like an individual along with other individuals for the same values.

As Podhoretz has observed, pluralism never really meant the coexistence of quite different groups: "For the traditional liberal mentality conceives of society as being made up not of competing economic classes and ethnic groups, but rather of competing *individuals* who confront a neutral body of law and a neutral institutional complex."[16]

How then can ethnic groups be discussed within the plural but consensual framework? They must be seen as separate but assimilated (contained) social structures. Among sociologists Milton Gordon has been most precise about this pluralism as a description of ethnic groups in American society.

> Behavioral assimilation or acculturation has taken place in America to a considerable degree. . . . Structural assimilation, then, has turned out to be the rock on which the ships of Anglo-conformity and the melting pot have foundered. To understand the behavioral assimilation (or acculturation) without massive structural intermingling in primary relationships has been the dominant motif in the American experience of creating and developing a nation out of diverse peoples is to comprehend the most essential sociological fact of that experience. It is against the background

of "structural pluralism" that strategies of strengthening inter-group harmony, reducing ethnic discrimination and prejudice, and maintaining the rights of both those who stay within and those who venture beyond their ethnic boundaries must be thoughtfully devised.[17]

Clearly then the liberal vocabulary of race relations is predicated on consensual assumptions about the nature of man and society. The order explanation of the Negro problem and its solution may be summarized as follows.

(*1*) *An order or consensual model of society.* American society is interpreted as a social system unified at its most general level by acceptance of certain central political, social, and economic values. Thus, the Negro population is said to have been acculturated to a somewhat vaguely defined American tradition; at the most, Negro society is a variant or a reaction to that primary tradition.

(*2*) *Social problems as moral problems of anomie or social disorganization within the American system.* Social problems and deviant behavior arise from an imbalance between goals and means. The problems of the Negro are created by unethical exclusion from equal competition for American goals.

(*3*) *The response to anomie: social amelioration as adjustment and extension of social control.* Liberal solutions imply further institutionalization of the American Creed in the opportunity structure of society and, therefore, the adjustment of the deviant to legitimate social roles.

THE RACE QUESTION AS A MORAL DILEMMA

A familiar expression of liberal-consensualism is Gunnar Myrdal's interpretation of the American race question as a moral dilemma. According to this thesis, racial discrimination and its varied effects on the Negro—the development of plural social structures, high rates of social deviation, etc.—reflect a kind of anomie in the relationship between the American Creed and social structure. Anomie means a moral crisis arising from an incongruity between legitimate and ethical social goals (for example, success and equality of opportunity) and socially available opportunities to achieve these goals. American society is good and ethical, but anomic because the American Creed of equality has not been fully institutionalized; the ethic is widely accepted in theory but not in practice.

Sidney Hook as a political liberal has likewise insisted that American society is essentially ethical and that the Negro problem should be discussed in these ethical terms:

> Of course, no society has historically been organized on the basis of ethical principles, but I don't think we can understand how any society functions

without observing the operation of the ethical principles within it. And if we examine the development of American society, we certainly can say that we have made *some* progress, to be sure, but progress nevertheless—by virtue of the extension of our ethical principles to institutional life. If we want to explain the progress that has been made in the last twenty years by minority groups in this country—not only the Negroes, but other groups as well—I believe we have to take into account the effect of our commitment to democacy, imperfect though it may be.[18]

THE SOLUTION: WORKING WITHIN THE SYSTEM

The liberal solution to the racial question follows from the American-dilemma thesis: the belief in the ethical nature and basic legitimacy of American institutions. Amelioration, therefore, becomes exclusively a question of adjustment within the system; it calls for administrative action: how to attack anomie as the imbalance of goals and means. The administrator accepts the goals of his organization and treats all problems as errors in administration, errors which can be rectified without changing the basic framework of the organization. Karl Mannheim has aptly characterized the bureaucratic and administrative approach to social problems. What he says about the perspective of the Prussian bureaucrat applies only too well to his counterpart in American society:

> The attempt to hide all problems of politics under the cover of administration may be explained by the fact that the sphere of activity of the official exists only within the limits of laws already formulated. Hence the genesis or the development of law falls outside the scope of his activity. As a result of his socially limited horizon, the functionary fails to see that behind every law that has been made there lie the socially fashioned interests and the *Weltanschauungen* of a specific social group. He takes it for granted that the specific order prescribed by the concrete law is equivalent to order in general. He does not understand that every rationalized order is only one of many forms in which socially conflicting irrational forces are reconciled.[19]

The liberal administrator's solution to the Negro question entails the expansion of opportunities for mobility within the society and socialization of the deviant (the Negro and the anti-Negro) to expanding opportunities. Hence, the importance of education and job training; they are prime means to success and higher status. Given the assumption that the American Creed is formally embodied in the political structure, the liberal also looks to legislation as an important and perhaps sole means of re-enforcing the Creed by legitimizing changes in the American opportunity structure.

NEGRO LIFE AS A REACTION FORMATION

Another important deduction has followed from the assumption of the political and cultural assimilation of the American Negro: whatever is different or distinct in his life style represents a kind of negative reaction to exclusion from the white society. The Negro is the creation of the white. Like the criminal, he is a pathology, a reaction formation to the problem of inadequate opportunities to achieve and to compete in the American system.

Myrdal states: "The Negro's entire life and, consequently, also his opinion on the Negro problem are, in the main, to be considered as secondary reactions to more primary pressures from the side of the dominant white majority."[20]

More recently Leonard Broom has echoed the same opinion:

Negro life was dominated by the need to adjust to white men and to take them into account at every turn. . . . Taken as a whole, the two cultures have more common than distinctive elements. Over the long run, their convergence would seem inevitable. . . . Because Negro life is so much affected by poverty and subservience, it is hard to find distinctive characteristics that can be positively evaluated. In the stereotype, whatever is admirable in Negro life is assumed to have been adopted from the white man, while whatever is reprehensible is assumed to be inherently Negro.[21]

CONFLICT THEORIST LOOKS AT ORDER THEORIST
LOOKING AT THE NEGRO

A liberal order model—consensual pluralism, with its corollary approach to the race question as moral dilemma and reaction formation—colors the sociological analysis of the race question. It is interesting that the fundamental assumption about consensus on the American Creed has rarely been subjected to adequate empirical test.[22] Lacking any convincing evidence for the order thesis, I can only wonder whom the sociologist is speaking for. He may be speaking for himself in that his paradigm answers the question of how to solve the Negro problem without changing basic economic and political institutions. He probably speaks least of all for the Negro. The liberal sociologists will have some difficulty describing the world from the viewpoint of Negro "rioters" in Los Angeles and other cities. In any case, he will not agree with anyone who believes (in fact or in ideology) that the

Negro may have a separate and self-determining identity. Such a view suggests conflict and would throw doubt on the fixations of consensus, anomie, and reaction formation.

Conflict interpretations are minority interpretations by definition. They are rarely expressed either by sociologists or by ethnic minorities. However, a few such interpretations can be mentioned to imply that the end of ideology and, therefore, the agreement on total ideology has not yet arrived.

Ralph Ellison, speaking from a conflict and nationalistic perspective, has made several salient criticisms of the liberal American-dilemma thesis. He has argued that Myrdal's long discussion of American values and conclusion of multiple causality have conveniently avoided the inconvenient question of power and control in American society.

> All this, of course, avoids the question of power *and* the question of who manipulates that power. Which to us seems more of a stylistic maneuver than a scientific judgment. . . . Myrdal's stylistic method is admirable. In presenting his findings he uses the American ethos brilliantly to disarm all American social groupings, by appealing to their stake in the American Creed, and to locate the psychological barriers between them. But he also uses it to deny the existence of an American class struggle, and with facile economy it allows him to avoid admitting that actually there exist two American moralities, kept in balance by social science.[23]

Doubting the thesis of consensus, Ellison is also in a position to attack Myrdal's interpretation of the American Negro as a reaction formation, and assimilation to the superior white society as his only solution.

> But can a people (its faith in an idealized American Creed notwithstanding) live and develop for over three hundred years simply by reacting? Are American Negroes simply the creation of white men, or have they at least helped to create themselves out of what they found around them? Men have made a way of life in caves and upon cliffs, why cannot Negroes have made a life upon the horns of the white men's dilemma?
> Myrdal sees Negro culture and personality simply as the product of a "social pathology." Thus he assumes that "it is to the advantage of American Negroes as individuals and as a group to become assimilated into American culture, to acquire the traits held in esteem by the dominant white American." This, he admits, contains the value premise that "*here in America*, American culture is 'highest' in the pragmatic sense. . . ." Which aside from implying that Negro culture is not also American, assumes that Negroes should desire nothing better than what whites

consider highest. But in the "pragmatic" sense lynching and Hollywood, faddism and radio advertising are products of "higher" culture, and the Negro might ask, "Why, if my culture is pathological, must I exchange it for these?" . . . What is needed in our country is not an exchange of pathologies, but a change of the basis of society.[24]

CONCLUSION

The hostile action of Negro masses destroying white property is perhaps a more convincing demonstration of conflict theory than the hopes of Negro intellectuals. But as a sociologist I am not really interested in raising the question of whether a conflict definition of the race question is more correct than the more familiar order model. Each view is correct in a normative and practical sense in so far as it conforms to a viable political and social experience. What indeed is a correct interpretation of the Negro problem or any social problem? The answer has as much to do with consensus as with correspondence to the facts. Normative theories are not necessarily affected by empirical evidence because they seek to change or to maintain the world, not describe it.

Whenever there is genuine conflict between groups and interpretations, correctness clearly becomes a practical matter of power and political persuasion. This seems to be the situation today, and one can expect more heated debate. If conflict continues to increase between whites and Negroes in the United States, the liberal sociologist studying the "Negro problem" had better arm himself with more than his questionnaire. A militant Negro respondent may take him for the social problem, the sociologist as an agent of white society and the scientific purveyor of order theory and containment policy.

This clash of perspectives would be an illustration of my general argument; explanations of the Negro question or any other social problem invariably involve normative theory, values, ideologies, or whatever one may care to call the subjective categories of our thinking about society. Concepts of deviation and social problems can be discussed only in the context of some social (and therefore contestable) standard of health, conformity, and the good society. Terms like "moral dilemma," "pluralism," "assimilation," "integration" describe motives for desirable action: they are definitions placed on human action, not the action itself independent of social values.

The error of the sociologist is not that he thinks politically and liberally about his society, but that he is not aware of it. Awareness may help him avoid some of the gross errors of myopia: (1) mistaking his own normative categories for "objective" fact; thus, the liberal sociologist may mistake his

belief in the consensual society for actual consensus; (2) projecting a normative theory appropriate to the experience of one group onto another group;
this is what Ellison means when he says that the liberal sociologist is not
necessarily speaking for the Negro. Indeed, the errors of myopia are perhaps
greatest whenever the middle-class sociologist presumes to describe the
world and motivation of persons in lower status. Seeing the lower-class
Negro within a white liberal vocabulary may be very realistic politics, but
it is not very accurate sociology.

Once the sociologist is involved in the study of anything that matters, he
has the unavoidable obligation of at least distinguishing his vocabulary from
that of the groups he is supposedly observing rather than converting. As a
scientist, he must find out what perspectives are being employed, where they
are operating in the society, and with what effect. Perhaps this awareness of
competing perspectives occurs only in the actual process of conflict and
debate. Unfortunately, this is not always the situation within an increasingly
professionalized sociology. The more professionalized the field, the more
standardized the thinking of sociologists and the greater the danger of internal myopia passing for objectivity. But outside sociology debate is far from
closed; conflict and order perspectives are simultaneously active on every
controversial social issue. The liberal order model may not long enjoy
uncontested supremacy.

NOTES

1 Robert Glover, *The One Hundred Dollar Misunderstanding* (New York: Ballantine Books, 1961).

2 Don Martindale, "Social Disorganization: The Conflict of Normative and Enpirical Approaches," in Howard Becker and Alvin Boskoff (eds.), *Modern Sociological Theory* (New York: Dryden Press, 1959), p. 341.

3 For Weber's discussion of explanation in the social sciences, see *Max Weber: The Theory of Social and Economic Organization*, trans. by A. M. Henderson and Talcott Parsons (Glencoe, Ill.: The Free Press, 1947), pp. 87–114.

4 C. Wright Mills, "Situated Actions and Vocabularies of Motive," *American Sociological Review*, V (December, 1940), 904–13.

5 C. Wright Mills, "The Professional Ideology of the Social Pathologists," *American Journal of Sociology*, XLIX (September, 1942), 165–80.

6 C. Wright Mills, *The Sociological Imagination* (New York: Oxford University Press, 1959).

7 In contemporary sociology, the concepts of alienation and anomie are often used syn-
onymously. In practice, this usually means that alienation, a key term in conflict analysis,
has been translated into a more conservative order vocabulary; for a discussion of

differences between past and present uses of these concepts, see John Horton, pp. 586–604, above.

8 Talcott Parsons, "Definitions of Health and Illness in the Light of American Values and Social Structure," in E. Gartley Jaco (ed.), *Patients, Physicians and Illness* (New York: The Free Press of Glencoe, 1963), p. 176.

9 Paul Goodman, *Growing Up Absurd* (New York: Random House, 1960), p. 11.

10 For a conservative argument see, among many others, Carleton Putnam, *Race and Reason* (Washington, D.C.: Public Affairs Press, 1961).

11 Jean-Paul Sartre, *Anti-Semite and Jew*, trans. by George J. Becker (New York: Grove Press, 1962), pp. 56–57.

12 J. S. Furnivall, *Colonial Policy and Practice* (London: Cambridge University Press, 1948), p. 304.

13 Gunnar Myrdal, *An American Dilemma* (New York: Harper & Bros., 1944), pp. 3–4.

14 Robin M. Williams, Jr., *Strangers Next Door* (Englewood Cliffs, N.J.: Prentice-Hall, 1964), p. 386.

15 Norman Podhoretz, "The Melting-Pot Blues," *Washington Post*, October 25, 1964.

16 Norman Podhoretz, as quoted in "Liberalism and the American Negro—a Round-Table Discussion," with James Baldwin, Nathan Glazer, Sidney Hook, Gunnar Myrdal, and Norman Podhoretz (moderator), *Commentary*, XXXVII (March, 1964), 25–26.

17 Milton Gordon, "Assimilation in America: Theory and Reality," *Daedalus*, XC (Spring, 1961), 280, 283.

18 Sidney Hook, "Liberalism and the American Negro—a Round-Table Discussion," *Commentary*, XXXVII (March, 1964), 31.

19 Karl Mannheim, *Ideology and Utopia* (New York: Harcourt, Brace & Co., 1936), p. 118.

20 Gunnar Myrdal as quoted by Ralph Ellison, "An American Dilemma: A Review," in *Shadow and the Act* (New York: Random House, 1964), p. 315.

21 Leonard Broom, *The Transformation of the American Negro* (New York: Harper & Row, 1965), pp. 22–23.

22 For a recent attempt to test the American-dilemma thesis, see Frank R. Westie, "The American Dilemma: An Empirical Test," *American Sociological Review*, XXX (August, 1965), 527–38.

23 Ellison, *Shadow and the Act*, p. 315.

24 *Ibid.*, pp. 316–17.

8

BERT N. ADAMS

Coercion and Consensus Theories: Some Unresolved Issues

DOWN THROUGH THE centuries social theorists have been divided concerning the basis of societal integration. Many have asserted that it is consensus, or common interest and need, that links human beings in institutional or societal structures. Others have claimed that coercion, or the oppression of some by others, is the cement of social organization. While it would be of interest to trace the history of these two theoretical viewpoints, such is not the purpose of the following brief commentary. Instead, we begin by noting that the coercion-consensus debate, while still largely unresolved, has in recent years been productive of important synthesizing attempts, some of the more important being those of Ralf Dahrendorf, Max Gluckman, Lewis Coser, and Pierre van den Berghe.[1] However, in the course of these efforts certain ambiguities have been allowed to persist which, in the opinion of the present author, require explication.

FUNCTIONALISM AND DIALECTICS

In his recent article in the *American Sociological Review*, van den Berghe has taken steps toward a synthesis of functional and dialectic theories. He points out that, as Coser and Gluckman observe, conflict may be functional, and, on the other hand, consensus may be upon competition or conflict as a societal value.[2] Furthermore, both functionalism and dialectics tend to be evolutionary, and both are based on an equilibrium model of society.[3] While these similarities between functionalism and dialectics may be granted,

American Journal of Sociology, LXXI (May, 1966), 714–17. Reprinted by permission of The University of Chicago Press and the author.

the difficulty lies in the tacit assumption that functionalism is virtually synonymous with the consensus theory of social integration, as is dialectics with the coercion theory. A more adequate statement of the relations between these four conceptualizations would seem to be that dialectics is a *species* of the coercion theory *genus*, and functionalism is an overarching "family" principle of which coercion and consensus theories of integration are *genera*. Let us further develop this thesis.

Coercion theory, as a basic understanding of the manner in which groups and societies cohere, has been well expressed in Dahrendorf's treatise on class conflict. Coherence and order in society, Dahrendorf affirms, are "founded on force and constraint, on the domination of some and the subjection of others."[4] However, he admits, society actually has two faces, that is, integration, or consensus, and coercion.[5] The idea of authority reveals these two faces, for it is not only productive of and the product of conflict, as C. Wright Mills suggests; neither is it only a facility for the performance of function in and on behalf of the society as a system, as Talcott Parsons indicates.[6] Yet, says Dahrendorf, underlying the various allegiances of men in society is always coercion; this is in fact the pervasive characteristic of social organization.

Dahrendorf is considerably indebted to and appreciative of Marx's treatment of class conflict, but he rejects two key tenets of the Marxist position, or of the Hegelian dialectic in general. In the first place, Dahrendorf's conceptualization is non-evolutionary; there is no logical progression within the system. Second, stability or equilibrium is foreign to his thinking. It is conflict, disintegration, and change which are ever present in social groups and societies. Van den Berghe's interpretation of the thesis-antithesis-synthesis scheme of the dialectician makes certain assumptions which are not common to coercion theory in general: the assumptions of stability with each new synthesis and of progress from stage to stage. Therefore, the finding of a common ground between coercion and consensus theories is a more formidable task than van den Berghe would have us believe. The dialectic, as he interprets it, is simply the species of coercion theory which most closely resembles consensus theory in its basic presuppositions.

At times social theorists have been wont to label the polar theoretical positions regarding social cohesion "functional" and "conflict" theory, or, in van den Berghe's case, functional and dialectic theory. To propose that functionalism is the antithesis of coercion theory requires an acceptance of an extremely narrow definition of functionalism, in which each part of a system is contributing willingly to the ongoing of the whole. However, in recent years Robert Merton, Kingsley Davis, and others have sought to redefine functionalism more broadly in terms of the proposition that the elements of any society or social group are interdependent. On the basis of such a definition, Davis has asserted that functionalism is in fact sociology parading under another label.[7] Whether or not we accept Davis' dictum that the time has come to abandon the term "functionalism," it is noteworthy that two decades ago Robert Merton pointed to the inclusive nature of functionalism as social theory. Functional analysis, we were reminded, does not require acceptance of the viewpoint that all cultural items are indispensable for the entire society.[8] More important, functionalism is neither conservative nor inherently radical. It can be either in the hands of the user.[9] Coser and Gluckman have made quite apparent the functional character of conflict at various societal levels. By this they mean that conflict frequently serves to perpetuate, or even establish, the boundary lines of groups and societies.[10] This, however, does not signify that in these writings the authors have espoused either the coercion or the consensus position regarding societal integration. What it means is that conflict is not necessarily disruptive on any given level of social organization.[11] It is therefore misleading to claim that functionalism is the antithesis of coercion theory: to the point is the introductory comment in an article on "The Functional Prerequisites of a Society," that "functional prerequisites refer broadly to the things that must get done in any society if it is to continue as a going concern."[12] The continuation, or "functioning," of the society may be by means of mutual cooperation and consensus, or it may be a result of the coercion of some by others. A functional approach does not necessarily presuppose either generic theoretical base.

THOUGHTS ON CONSENSUS AND COERCION

Perhaps we should have granted at the outset that in many ways the dilemma of consensus and coercion theories resembles that concerning free will and determinism: both problems may be approached from so many vantage points as to lead many to consider them inherently insoluble. Yet theoretical discussions and syntheses are valid as attempts to provide better keys with which to unlock social reality; that is, they are valid in so far as deductions derived from them make possible the more adequate interpretation of empirical social relationships.

The results of the current synthesizing attempts are primarily effected by assimilating one viewpoint in the other. That is, in one form of synthesis the focus is upon the social system as a mechanism for meeting the mutual needs of its constituents. Conflict is seen as a temporary upset requiring system adjustment. Coercion may, therefore, be viewed as a necessary deviation from consensus in order to control the non-cooperative. On the other hand, it is argued by some that consensus is a tool for the entrenchment of the elite, a creation for the purpose of legitimating the coercion which is already in progress.[13] In the former view consensus is ubiquitous, in the latter coercion. Each viewpoint grants that consensus and coercion are both present in society; disagreement arises concerning which is more fundamental, or which is the basis of societal integration.

At this point we have sociological presuppositions which are not being utilized to the full in this theoretical controversy. These presuppositions or understandings may be helpful in our synthesizing, and they also present us with an interesting problem in the sociology of knowledge. Above it was noted that there is some similarity between the coercion-consensus argument and that regarding free will and determinism. However, most sociologists are agreed that determinism predominates over free will; they have, in fact, decided this issue. The socialization process produces social men, imbued with their culture, and not merely individual personalities. This quasi-deterministic position in sociology has been so prevalent that Dennis Wrong, Melford Spiro, and others have felt it necessary to caution us not to be led to extremes in describing social man.[14] Yet even critics of the "oversocialized" conception of man generally accept the proposition that socialization is the primary means for the perpetuation of social forms. This process itself is one of coercion: we learn to curb our aggression and other impulses deemed "antisocial" to keep our behavior within the range of the socially permissible, and in so doing we learn to cooperate. Any sort of organic analogy breaks down when we consider the basis of societal integration, for the members of an *organism* do not have to be taught to work for the good of the whole. It may be granted that there are many organized manifestations, such as voluntary associations, of human beings arriving at a consensus and cooperating in the meeting of needs or the furthering of common interests. These appear, however, to be epiphenomena grounded in socialization and control processes.

Social control, we have said, whether through socialization or through differing access to society's rewards, is basic to any level of societal integration. Conflict thus becomes a rebellion against coercion, and viewed this way consensus becomes more a group-imposed phenomenon than the basic aspect of social existence. In other words, consensus is derived from coercion. From toilet-training to taxes and take-home pay, it is coercion which maintains society and its subdivisions, and it is conflict which changes them.

It is perplexing, albeit somewhat tangential, that many of those who place great emphasis upon socialization and boundary maintenance in the social system also find it possible to argue that society is held together primarily by an inherent consensus of the constituent parts. How did American social theorists fail to link the conception of social man with a coercion theory of social integration? At this point the problem becomes one in the sociology of knowledge; the social history of the theorists is involved. The accusation has been made that in consensus theories we are actually viewing social organization in terms of American idealism, rather than social realism. Be that as it may, our major concern in this brief commentary has been to point out some difficulties in current synthesizing attempts and to introduce to the discussion of consensus and coercion the sociological understanding of socialization and control. To the present author it appears that coercion theory comes closer to accounting for social organization in its various manifestations. Coercion, conflict, and change do seem, on balance, to be more basic societal attributes than consensus and equilibrium.

NOTES

1 Ralf Dahrendorf, *Class and Class Conflict in Industrial Society* (Stanford, Calif.: Stanford University Press, 1959); Max Gluckman, *Custom and Conflict in Africa* (Oxford: Blackwell Press, 1955); Lewis A. Coser, *The Functions of Social Conflict* (Glencoe, Ill.: The Free Press, 1956); Pierre van den Berghe, "Dialectic and Functionalism: Toward a Theoretical Synthesis," *American Sociological Review*, XXVIII (October, 1963), 695–705.
2 Van den Berghe, "Dialectic and Functionalism," pp. 702–3.
3 *Ibid.*, pp. 703–4.
4 Dahrendorf, *Class and Class Conflict in Industrial Society*, p. 157.
5 *Ibid.*, p. 159.
6 *Ibid.*, p. 170.
7 Kingsley Davis, "The Myth of Functional Analysis as a Special Method in Sociology and Anthropology," *American Sociological Review*, XXIV (December, 1959), 771.
8 Robert K. Merton, *Social Theory and Social Structure* (Glencoe, Ill.: The Free Press, 1949), p. 25.
9 *Ibid.*, p. 39.
10 See especially Coser, *The Functions of Social Conflict*, p. 38.
11 Although not essential to the discussion of the basis of societal integration, a further clarification of the issues involved in conflict would be of considerable value. As a corrective upon Coser's and Gluckman's emphases, stress is needed upon the dysfunctionality of conflict on levels of organization other than the one at which it is acting as an integrative agent. A public official may, for example, espouse a viewpoint which results in conflict and the disintegration of relations with his constituents, but which furthers integration on a higher societal level. Examples of this are plentiful in John F. Kennedy's popular little book, *Profiles in Courage*. Or the same conflict which binds together the

members of a nation may be extremely dysfunctional or disintegrative on the international level. Furthermore, on the personal and familial level, a man may permit internal conflict between his ideal and actual family identity, even though it is dysfunctional for his mental health, for the sake of familial integration. While these problems deserve much attention, we mention them but in passing.

12 D. F. Aberle, A. K. Cohen, A. K. David, M. J. Levy, F. X. Sutton, "The Functional Prerequisites of a Society," *Ethics*, LX (January, 1950), 100.

13 Gerhard Lenski has recently done a monumental task in spelling out this synthetic position in his book *Power and Privilege* (New York: McGraw-Hill Book Co., 1966).

14 Dennis Wrong, "The Oversocialized Conception of Man," *American Sociological Review*, XXVI (April, 1961), 183–93; Melford E. Spiro, "An Overview and a Suggested Reorientation," in Francis L. K. Hsu (ed.), *Physical Anthropology* (Homewood, Ill.: The Dorsey Press, 1961), pp. 459–92, in which the author asserts that the study of culture and personality has been overly concerned with the role of culture and not concerned enough with the active role of personality.

9

ROBIN M. WILLIAMS, Jr.

*Some Further Comments on Chronic Controversies**

EACH INTELLECTUAL generation in certain of the social sciences seems to return, again and again, to a list of basic questions that repeatedly arouse interest, challenge imagination, and generate debate. Included are the issues of free will and determinism, the nature of human nature, heredity and environment, reality of society, subjective versus objective factors and rationality and non-rationality in social behavior, and others too numerous and familiar to catalogue here.

In American sociology only a few years ago the hope was sometimes expressed that many of the old "schools" of thought—with all their rigidity and distortion—might be dissolving in favor of an emerging pluralistic consensus in methodology and concepts that would mark initial scientific maturity. After all, many sociologists did use a wide range of concepts and research techniques; they no longer argued so fiercely about "attitudes versus actions," or the four wishes, or the number of instincts involved in stamp-collecting; nor did the new experimentalists stone the participant observer off the golf links. In some sociologists' offices it was not a matter of special comment to find classical and modern books peaceably coexisting— with the works of order theorists, conflict theorists, statisticians, social psychologists, anthropologists, demographers, and just ordinary sociologists contributing greatly to new ideas and approaches.

But this amiable disorder could not be expected to last. New lines of battle

*Williams is commenting on the previous two selections by John Horton and Bert N. Adams.—Eds.

American Journal of Sociology, LXXI (May, 1966), 717–21. Reprinted by permission of The University of Chicago Press and the author.

were being drawn. Some persons who earlier had warned of the dissolution of social order through anomie now saw hope in the reorganization of alienation to shatter this "sorry state of things entire" in the interests of a new social order. First, fresh significance gradually came to be attached to the older distinctions between "action-oriented" and "knowledge-oriented" approaches.[1] Second, sociology was once more charged with being too empirical, provincial, and value-laden, on the one hand and being socially trivial and timidly captive to the power structure on the other.

A second line of cleavage appeared in the numerous debates over the meaning and significance of "functional" theories of various kinds, ranging from totalistic functionalism applied to whole societies over to causal-functional analysis of specified variables in exactly delimited small-group experiments. Although recent analyses by A. Kaplan, E. Nagel, T. Parsons, R. Brown, K. Davis, R. Merton, and others might seem to have provided adequate basis for resolving misunderstandings, clarifying issues, and getting on with the work, argument has continued unabated. Meanwhile, the proposal that we agree to regard functional analysis as one special class of causal analysis seems to have been mislaid in the fray. Adams' article helps to clarify these disputes.

The debates over functional theory have overlapped with the "consensus versus conflict" (or, more narrowly, "coercion") dichotomy to which Adams directs attention. Throughout these controversies, running references abound to "equilibrium," "social change," and "evolutionary" notions. In turn, the distinction between "order" models and "conflict models" is a variant on the same central theme.

I have been asked to comment on this confused and turbulent intellectual scene. Let me first try to clear the ground a little. It seems clear that many of the debates have consisted of the demolition of strawmen. Indeed, what sociologist in his right mind ever regarded any empirical society as *only* "consensus" or *only* conflict? Certainly not Simmel, or Marx, or Weber, or Durkheim, or Parsons. (Strange as it may seem, I have found no difficulty personally in understanding Coser and Parsons, Merton and Horowitz, Dahrendorf and Moore, or van den Berghe and Davis.)

For purpose of clarity in discussion, we propose the following empirical propositions:

(*1*) All interacting human populations exhibit many social conflicts.

(*2*) All interacting human populations that remain in interaction over a period of time develop normative regularities.

(*3*) All interacting human populations manifest some continuity of social patterns.

(*4*) All interacting human populations manifest change in social patterns, over time.

(*5*) All interacting human populations show both coerced and voluntary conformity.

If intercommunicating actors remain in interaction long enough, some of them will develop some agreements concerning beliefs, norms, and values. They do not *all have* to develop shared norms; some may continue to fight to the death, to be followed by others who do the same. The question is merely, under what specific conditions does order or chaos ensue, does conflict or agreement emerge? This is not, in any usual sense, an "ideological" question; its answer is one of fact.

Second, many "order" theories contain a great deal of conflict, and many "conflict" theories manage to find a great deal of order. Awareness of conflict did not begin with Hobbes nor end with Marx. Have modern sociologists really neglected social conflict and social change? Who, then, are these negligent students of society—do they include Coser, Mills, Dahrendorf, Lynd, Park? Can they encompass such students of racial, ethnic, and religious groups as Hughes, Myrdal, Rose, Thompson, or Frazier? Do they include such political sociologists as Barrington Moore, Jr., Selznick, Lipset, Janowitz? Why is it in the twentieth century—which Sorokin has called the bloodiest of all centuries—that every few years we have to persuade ourselves that we should rediscover social conflict, violence, revolution, and social change? How can we suppose that any sophisticated social theorist could be *un*aware of these massive events?

Certainly Adams is correct in holding that there is *no* insuperable theoretical barrier to a synthesis of "conflict" and "consensus" approaches. Our real task is to build workable models that depict social systems in which both conflict and consensus are *continuous processes* in *differentiated structures*. All empirical systems of this kind will include some exercise of sheer power as well as of legitimate authority, some power will be *zero-sum* (power *over*); some will be *non-zero-sum* (power *with*—facilitating or mobilizing power). Some "power" will be coercive; other power will not. It is bootless to discuss whether these social phenomena exist; they do. It is fruitless to argue which is more important; it depends on the problem and the facts of the case.

Likewise, there are always norms, socialization, and social control; there is always violation of norms, resistance to socialization and social control, deviance, anomie, alienation, conflict, innovation, and drastic organized breaches of established orders. Is not all this obvious?

But consensus is not *merely* an epiphenomenon "derived from coercion" (Adams, pp. 628–29, above). In their turn socialization and social control derive in part from prior culture, for example, accepted resolutions of past conflicts. These processes are inherently mutually causal in overlapping series through time. The "disorder" of a jungle becomes a scientific order to the properly equipped biologist. The obvious concrete "normative" disorder of many social events may be similarly lawful in terms of basic initial conditions and processes.

With reference to the global judgment as to whether "coercion, conflict, and change" are "more basic" as societal attributes than "consensus and equilibrium," I shall have to plead lack of omniscience as well as the lack of existence of a single, unidimensional tested scale of basicness. Most sociologists, at least, surely have encountered *all* these aspects of reality in their research as well as in their personal lives.

Dr. Horton's paper raises still other facets in his review of "normative" versus "existential" theories. Now, all theories (or propositions and explanations) that describe and explain aspects of reality are existential to the extent that they rest upon cognitively certified procedures and data concerning what *is*. Of course, all science is *at the same time* methodologically "normative" in the sense that it represents agreement on the criteria of fact, evidence, proof, honesty, communicability, and so on. But within such limits, it surely is not merely "evaluative." In this sense, I must disagree that "only normative theory is appropriate in the sociology of social problems" (Horton, pp. 605–6, above). Somebody's values identify some characteristics of "social problems," but these do not have to be my values. Of course, if a sociologist is competent to ply his profession he surely must not allow implicit values to go unnoticed "so that normative theories pass for empirical theories." However, one would think that after decades of saturation in Marx, Freud, Pareto, Weber, *Wissenssoziologie*, semantics, analytical philosophy, C. Wright Mills, Talcott Parsons, and modern methodology, the profession has some rather high level of sophistication in these matters. Obviously, all sociology (like all physics) is located in time and space, and it changes through history. But this does not in any important sense negate objectivity or explanatory capacity.

It is possible to argue endlessly as to whether sociological analyses of social problems are "conservative" or "radical." The characterization depends upon the point of reference. But if the facts are facts and the reasoning correct, the descriptions and explanations should be clear to any properly detached, qualified observer, whether in South Africa, U.S.S.R., Viet-Nam, Los Angeles, Chicago, or Jackson (Mississippi) or Jackson Heights (New York).

I do not question that ideological and even temperamental preferences help to generate preferences for one rather than another vocabulary or for one or another problematical hypothesis or conceptual scheme. What I do deny is that the findings of a *Wissenssoziologie* of sociology demonstrate inherent unreliability in the scientifically controlled investigations of sociological research.

Some caveats:

(*1*) I do not see why "conflict analysis is synonymous with historical analysis"; it would seem that much historical analysis has been profoundly alienated from a "conflict" perspective.

(*2*) Let us not denigrate sociological accomplishments. I do not believe that Everett Hughes—contrary to the tone of his own presidential address—lacked "imagination" in his understanding of racial and ethnic relations during the 1940's and 1950's. The record shows that some sociologists understood quite well many of the conditions necessary for intergroup violence, at least as early as the close of World War II. Not everyone was surprised by the Negro revolution, and some white sociologists said what was coming nearly twenty years before Watts. The trouble was that very few people were listening. (To counter *One Hundred Dollar Misunderstanding*, I recommend Albert Camus, *The Rebel.*)

This is not a protest against Horton's rich, subtle and stimulating polemic; his article serves some very valuable purposes and the explicited insights into types of ideologies could become the starting point of numerous excellent researches. I do find it difficult to understand why names are seldom named when broad characterizations are offered of "liberals," "sociologists," and the like; thus the first paragraph on page 614 is either true by definition or *someone* should be cited as an empirical case.

(*3*) Finally, I fail to see why "systems analysis is synonymous with structural-functional analysis" (p. 608). Are there not examples of good structural-functional analyses that pretty well avoid the notion of systems? Are there not systems-analysts who just work with descriptive simulations?

As valuable as these two commentaries are in focusing issues and encouraging professional self-awareness, have we not now reached a stage at which our (highly necessary) theoretical and methodological debates can put aside the global issues that are here at the center of attention? Aside from the present papers, furthermore, much of the discussion of structural-functional "theory," conflict "theory," and consensus "theory"[2] seems to have been marked by failure to read, or at least to comprehend, the alleged opponents; this is notably true of some critics of Parsons.

Let us end these remarks as briefly as possible. Some conceptions of society would have it exist purely as an outgrowth of consensus—that is, of agreement upon basic values and beliefs shared within any human population aggregate. This is "Consensus Doctrine."

Some conceptions hold that society is an interlocking web of advantaged interdependence, either as a mutual-reward system or a system of stabilized exchanges of scarce divisible and transferable values. There are the doctrines of "Economic Man," of "bribed interdependence," of the "invisible hand," of organic solidarity, and so on.

Some theorists have seen society as a network of cathexes of positive interpersonal sentiments, or of natural social affinity, "gregariousness," and the like. The result is a "Community of Personal Attractions." This is "Sociability Doctrine."

Some theorists—often regarded as tough-minded or pessimistic—have regarded society as primarily the outcome of conflict and resulting relationships of domination and subordination. This is Conflict Theory, so called.

As we have seen, much controversy has raged over the question, which of these doctrines is correct? My own answer is quite direct: all are correct in part, all are partly wrong, none is wholly adequate. Actual societies are held together by consensus, by interdependence, by sociability, and by coercion. This has always been the case, and there is no reason to expect it to be otherwise in any foreseeable future. The real job is to show how actual social structures and processes operating in these ways can be predicted and explained. That task will require our best efforts for a long time to come.

NOTES

1 See my comments in "Continuity and Change in Sociological Study," *American Sociological Review*, XXIII, No. 6 (December, 1958), 622–23.

2 The quotation marks signify my doubts that these are genuine scientific theories; they are more nearly conceptual schemes, perspectives, or simply points of view.

IO

JOHN WALTON

---

*Discipline, Method, and Community Power**

THE PRINCIPAL THESIS of the sociology of knowledge—"that there are modes of thought which cannot be adequately understood as long as their social origins are obscured"[1]—has been widely accepted and employed by social scientists in research on various social groups, classes, and cultures. Seldom, however, have social scientists examined their own knowledge in this light, the assumption being that scientific rigor tends to eliminate the influence of group-determined perspectives. We will be concerned with an investigation of the credibility of this assumption.

Important differences exist between the intellectual worlds of the political scientist and the sociologist. The former is socialized in the tradition of Locke, Jefferson, Bentley, Dahl, and Easton, while the latter is more apt to encounter Durkheim, Weber, Pareto, Parsons, and C. Wright Mills. A cursory glance at the professional journals of the two disciplines reveals divergent perspectives. Sociologists tend to be concerned with theoretical and methodological considerations, political scientists with descriptive studies. Evidence is also available pointing to differences in political attitudes, with sociologists tending to be somewhat more liberal.[2]

In recent years, a distinct interdisciplinary field has developed that provides a setting for a systematic comparison between the findings of the two disciplines. The study of community power structure has been actively undertaken by both sociologists and political scientists. Their investigations have led to disparate conclusions, and ensuing debate has concerned the relative

* I would like to thank David Gold, Thomas Scheff, and John Shiflett for their helpful advice on the preparation of this paper.

American Sociological Review, XXXI (October, 1966), 684–89. Reprinted by permission of The American Sociological Association and the author.

merits of an elitist[3] versus a pluralist[4] interpretation of local politics, as well as appropriate research methods. Political scientists have stressed the analysis of participation in actual community decisions[5] while certain sociologists have opted for the virtues of the reputational method.[6]

In a recent analysis of community power research, thirty-three studies dealing with fifty-five communities were classified with respect to a number of variables.[7] It was demonstrated that there are certain correlates of power structure types and possible biases associated with particular research methods. An extension of this analysis, introducing the disciplinary background of the investigator as a variable, provides an opportunity to examine the relevance of the sociology of knowledge to social research.

PROCEDURE

Attention is focused on three variables: the disciplinary background of the researcher, the research method used, and the type of power structure identified.

The selection of studies was intended to be exhaustive of the published literature in social science devoted to the study of community power structure. Thus, the thirty-three studies are regarded as a universe rather than a sample.[8] The universe was defined by three criteria. First, by dealing with the published literature some unpublished studies were excluded, especially dissertations. Second, confining the analysis to the social science literature excluded journalistic reports.[9] Third, the criterion that the research be specifically concerned with community power excluded a number of community studies dealing with stratification, local government, and related aspects of social and political life.[10] These criteria were employed in a screening of the literature, and the resulting list of studies was checked against several lengthy bibliographies to ensure its inclusiveness.[11]

Research methods used in identifying leadership groups have been classified by various schemes.[12] In the area of community power, four types of method adequately encompass the variety of procedures encountered in the literature.[13]

(1) *The Reputational Method:* Informants are asked to identify the most influential people in the community. Leaders may be nominated directly, in a one-step procedure, or nominees of informants may be interviewed and leaders designated by this second panel.

(2) *The Decision-Making Method:* Historical reconstructions of community decisions are made using documents; active participants are defined as leaders.

(3) *The Case Study Method:* Includes less explicit approaches based on general observation.

TABLE 1
LIST OF COMMUNITY POWER STUDIES, BY DISCIPLINE OF INVESTIGATOR, RESEARCH METHOD, AND TYPE OF POWER STRUCTURE IDENTIFIED

Discipline and Investigator	Method	Type of Power	Discipline and Investigator	Method	Type of Power
Sociologists			Political Scientists		
1. Hunter	R	P	21. Scoble	RD	F
2. McKee	CS	F	22. Gore, Peabody	CS	C
3. Olmstead	R	F	23. Dahl	D	C
4. Pellegrin, Coates	CS	A	24. Sofen, Wood*	CS	A
5. Belknap, Smuckler	R	P	25. Martin, *et al.*	D	C
6. Fanelli	R	P	26. McClain, Highsaw*	D	C
7. Miller	R	P	27. Booth, Adrian	R	F
	R	C	28. Kammerer*	CS	P
8. Schulze	R	F		CS	F
9. Vidich, Bensman	CS	P		CS	F
10. Form, D'Antonio	R	C		CS	P
	R	F		CS	P
11. Klapp, Padgett	R	A		CS	F
12. Smith	R	P		CS	F
13. Barth	R	P		CS	F
	R	P	29. Presthus	RD	C
	R	F		RD	F
	R	F	30. Kimbrough*	RD	F
	R	A		R	C
	R	A		R	P
14. Stone	CS	C		R	P
15. Freeman, *et al.*	RD	C	31. Jennings	RD	C
16. Miller	R	C	32. Agger, *et al.*	RD	P
17. Bonjean	R	P		RD	C
18. Belknap, Steinle	R	P		RD	C
	R	P		RD	P
19. Thometz	R	P	33. Wildavsky	D	C
20. Clelland, Form	R	F			

* These researchers are not political scientists; see note 16.

NOTE: Labels are as follows. Research Method: R—reputational, D—decision-making, CS—case study, and RD—combined. Type of power structure: P—pyramidal, F—factional, C—coalition, and A—amorphous.

(4) *Combined Methods:* Simultaneous use of (1) and (2).

The studies provide considerable variation with regard to the types of power structure identified. The terms "elitism" and "pluralism" did not adequately distinguish a number of cases and the following scheme was adopted to accomplish that end.[14]

(1) *Pyramidal:* A monolithic, monopolistic, or single cohesive leadership group.

(2) *Factional:* At least two durable factions that compete for advantage.

(3) *Coalitional:* Leadership varies with issues and is made up of fluid coalitions of interested persons and groups.

(4) *Amorphous:* The absence of any persistent pattern of leadership or power exercised on the local level.

Employing these classifications, a coding guide was developed and applied to each of the studies.

TABLE 2

CLASSIFICATION OF COMMUNITY POWER STUDIES BY DISCIPLINE OF INVESTIGATOR AND RESEARCH METHOD USED

| Research Method Used | DISCIPLINE OF INVESTIGATOR | | |
	Sociology	Political Science	Total
Reputational	23	4	27
Other	5	23	28
Total	28	27	55

NOTE: $Q = +0.93$; chi-square $= 24.91$, $p < .0005$ (one-tailed).

RESULTS

Table 1[15] summarizes the thirty-three studies dealing with fifty-five communities in terms of the three variables.[16] Tables 2, 3, and 4 indicate the zero-order association between each of these variables.[17] Inspection of the tables[18] demonstrates that (1) sociologists have more frequently employed the reputational technique while political scientists tend to prefer the decision-making and closely related methods; (2) political scientists compared to sociologists tend to find less monolithic power structures, and (3) use of the reputational method tends to be associated with identification of a monolithic power structure.

TABLE 3

CLASSIFICATION OF COMMUNITY POWER STUDIES BY DISCIPLINE OF INVESTIGATOR AND TYPE OF POWER STRUCTURE IDENTIFIED

Type of Power Structure Found	DISCIPLINE OF INVESTIGATOR		
	Sociology	Political Science	Total
Pyramidal	12	7	19
Other	16	20	36
Total	28	27	55

NOTE: $Q = +0.36$; chi-square $= 1.75$; $p < .10$ (one-tailed).

Given the fact that the time-order of the variables is clear [discipline→ method (independent variables)→power structure (dependent variables)], one of three interpretations is possible: (*1*) the association between method and results is spurious and can be accounted for by the antecedent variable, discipline of the investigator; (*2*) the associations represent a developmental or causal sequence[19] (an "interpretation" in Hyman's terms);[20] or (*3*) there is interaction among the three.

Controlling for academic discipline, shown in Table 5, rules out the first possibility, for the association between method employed and results

TABLE 4

CLASSIFICATION OF COMMUNITY POWER STUDIES BY RESEARCH METHOD USED AND TYPE OF POWER STRUCTURE FOUND

Type of Power Structure Found	RESEARCH METHOD USED		
	Reputational	Other	Total
Pyramidal	13	6	19
Other	14	22	36
Total	27	28	55

NOTE: $Q = +0.55$; chi-square $= 4.33$, $p < .025$ (one-tailed).

obtained remains substantially unchanged.[21] Table 6 indicates no association between academic discipline and type of power structure identified after controlling for type of method used. Since "in general, the association

TABLE 5

CLASSIFICATION OF COMMUNITY POWER STUDIES BY
RESEARCH METHOD USED AND TYPE OF POWER
STRUCTURE FOUND, FOR SOCIOLOGISTS AND POLITICAL
SCIENTISTS

Discipline and Type of Power Structure Found	RESEARCH METHOD USED		
	Reputational	Other	Total
Sociologists			
Pyramidal	11	1	12
Other	12	4	16
Total	23	5	28
Political Scientists			
Pyramidal	2	5	7
Other	2	18	20
Total	4	23	27

NOTE: For sociologists, $Q = +0.57$; for political scientists, $Q = +0.57$.

between two variables in a developmental or causal sequence will tend to disappear when an intervening variable is held constant,"[22] the existence of a developmental sequence has been demonstrated: the disciplinary background of the investigator tends to determine the method of investigation he will adopt which, in turn, tends to determine the image of the power structure that results from the investigation.

DISCUSSION

These results illustrate the influence of ideological perspectives within one area of social research. This finding, however, has implications for a wide variety of social research. If it can be shown that similar perspectives operate in other areas,[23] social scientists will have to begin a reappraisal of their knowledge. In so doing, however, it is essential that the import of these applications of the sociology of knowledge be recognized. Commenting on a paper which parallels the present discussion in many respects,[24] one soci-

TABLE 6

CLASSIFICATION OF COMMUNITY POWER STUDIES BY
TYPE OF POWER STRUCTURE IDENTIFIED AND DISCIPLINE OF
INVESTIGATOR, FOR REPUTATIONAL AND ALL OTHER
RESEARCH METHODS

Research Method Used and Type of Power Structure Found	DISCIPLINE OF INVESTIGATOR		
	Sociology	Political Science	Total
Reputational			
Pyramidal	11	2	13
Other	12	2	14
Total	23	4	27
Other Methods			
Pyramidal	1	5	6
Other	4	18	22
Total	5	23	28

NOTE: For the reputational method, $Q = -0.04$; for the other methods combined, $Q = -0.05$.

ologist observed: "What I do deny is that the findings of a *Wissenssoziologie* of sociology demonstrate inherent unreliability in the scientifically controlled investigations of sociological research."[25]

The point is that to demonstrate the influence of ideological perspectives is *not* to demonstrate "inherent unreliability."[26] Mannheim was most explicit about this: "We cannot emphasize too much that the social equation does not always constitute a source of error but more frequently than not brings into view certain interrelations which would otherwise not be apparent. . . . In every situation, it is, therefore, indispensable to have a total perspective which embraces all points of view."[27] Once we recognize the influence of our own perspectives on the research process we are in a position to control them and, perhaps, move a bit closer to Mannheim's "total perspective."

CONCLUSION

Studies of local power structure will benefit from use of a combination of research methods as protection against this source of bias.

Comparative studies provide another avenue for the elimination of bias and the development of generalizations about community power. As one writer has put it: "So long as community power studies remain on the level of case studies of individual communities, the constraint of data upon interpretation will be minimal."[28] The development of comparative research methods is one of the principal tasks facing students of community power. Progress in this direction will not only serve to temper biases, but should also lead to a better understanding of the exercise of power on the local level.

In more general terms, this analysis documents the significance of the sociology of knowledge as a perspective for interpreting social research. Mannheim has commented on the significance in the following way: "Perhaps it is precisely when the hitherto concealed dependence of thought on group existence and its rootedness in action becomes visible that it really becomes possible for the first time, through becoming aware of them, to attain a new mode of control over previously uncontrolled factors in thought."[29]

NOTES

1 Karl Mannheim, *Ideology and Utopia: An Introduction to the Sociology of Knowledge* (New York: Harvest Books, 1936), p. 2.

2 Henry A. Turner, Charles B. Spaulding, and Charles G. McClintock, "Political Orientations of Academically Affiliated Sociologists," *Sociology and Social Research*, XLVII (April, 1963), 273–89, and "The Political Party Affiliation of American Political Scientists," *Western Political Quarterly*, XVI (September, 1963), 650–65.

3 Floyd Hunter, *Community Power Structure: A Study of Decision Makers* (Chapel Hill, N.C.: University of North Carolina Press, 1953), and Hunter's review of Dahl's *Who Governs?*, *Administrative Science Quarterly*, VI (March, 1962), 517–19.

4 Robert A. Dahl, *Who Governs?: Power and Democracy in an American City* (New Haven: Yale University Press, 1961); Nelson W. Polsby, *Community Power and Political Theory* (New Haven: Yale University Press, 1963).

5 Robert A. Dahl, "A Critique of the Ruling Elite Model," *American Political Science Review*, LII (June, 1958), 463–69; Nelson W. Polsby, "How to Study Power: The Pluralist Alternative," *Journal of Politics*, XXII (August, 1960), 474–84; Raymond E. Wolfinger, "Reputation and Reality in the Study of Community Power," *American Sociological Review*, XXV (October, 1960), 636–44.

6 William V. D'Antonio and Eugene Erickson, "The Reputational Technique as a Measure of Community Power: An Evaluation Based on Comparative and Longitudinal Studies," *American Sociological Review*, XXVII (June, 1962), 362–76; Howard J. Ehrlich, "The Reputational Approach to the Study of Community Power," *American Sociological Review*, XXVI (December, 1961), 926–27; Baha Abu-Laban, "The Reputational Approach in the Study of Community Power: A Critical Evaluation," *Pacific Sociological Review*, VIII (Spring, 1965), 35–42. In recent studies, these methods have

been combined by representatives of both fields. See, for example, Robert Presthus, *Men at the Top: A Study in Community Power* (New York: Oxford University Press, 1964); William V. D'Antonio and William H. Form, *Influentials in Two Border Cities: A Study in Community Decision-Making* (Notre Dame, Ind.: University of Notre Dame Press, 1965).

7　John Walton, "Substance and Artifact: The Current Status of Research on Community Power Structure," *American Journal of Sociology*, LXXI (January, 1966), 430–38.

8　Any claim to exhaustiveness is, of course, impossible to support. While an effort was made to accomplish this, it was subject to limitations of knowledge and the accuracy of decisions made with respect to the criteria defining the universe. Following the completion of this paper, the literature was re-surveyed and six additional studies were found that met the criteria. A replication of this analysis, using the larger universe, produced nearly identical results. The studies added include: Floyd Hunter, Ruth C. Schaffer, and Cecil G. Sheps, *Community Organization: Action and Inaction* (Chapel Hill, N.C.: University of North Carolina Press, 1956): Edward C. Banfield, *Political Influence: A New Theory of Urban Politics* (New York: The Free Press of Glencoe, 1961); Benjamin Walter, "Political Decision Making in Arcadia," in F. Stuart Chaplin, Jr., and Shirley F. Weiss (eds.), *Urban Growth Dynamics* (New York: John Wiley & Sons, 1962), pp. 141–86; Floyd Hunter, "Housing Discrimination in Oakland, California" (study prepared for the Mayor's Committee on Full Employment and the Council of Social Planning of Alameda County, 1964), and *The Big Rich and the Little Rich* (Garden City, N.Y.: Doubleday & Co., 1965); Francis M. Carney, "The Decentralized Politics of Los Angeles," *The Annals*, CCCLIII (May, 1964), 107–21; Ritchie P. Lowrey, *Who's Running This Town?* (New York: Harper & Row, 1965).

9　No implication of the inferiority of these reports is intended; the criterion was adopted for the sake of practicality.

10　It was in connection with this criterion that the most difficult decisions arose. Several excellent studies were excluded from consideration because they dealt primarily with the more formal workings of local government. See, for example, Wallace Sayre and Herbert Kaufman, *Governing New York City* (New York: Russell Sage Foundation, 1960); and Oliver P. Williams and Charles Adrian, *Four Cities* (Philadelphia: University of Pennsylvania Press, 1963).

11　For their assistance in providing bibliographies I am indebted to Michael T. Aiken, Terry N. Clark, and Claire W. Gilbert. Other sources employed include Wendell Bell, Richard J. Hill, and Charles R. Wright, *Public Leadership* (San Francisco: Chandler Publishing Co., 1961); and Charles Press, *Main Street Politics: Policy-Making at the Local Level* (East Lansing, Mich.: Michigan State University, 1962).

12　Bell, Hill, and Wright, *Public Leadership*; Peter H. Rossi, "Community Decision Making," *Administrative Science Quarterly*, I (March, 1957), 415–43; Charles M. Bonjean and David M. Olsen, "Community Leadership: Directions of Research," *Administrative Science Quarterly*, IX (December, 1964), 278–300.

13　The "positional" method, in which leaders are taken to be those persons occupying important positions in formal and/or informal organizations, is frequently used in these studies but always in conjunction with one of the four listed.

14　Except for some differences in emphasis in types (2) and (3), this typology closely resembles one proposed by Peter H. Rossi, "Power and Community Structure," *Midwest Journal of Political Science*, IV (November, 1960), 390–401.

15 The identification of each study can be found in Walton, "Substance and Artifact," note 5.

16 No difficulty was encountered in classifying sociologists. In the case of political scientists; however, several researchers did not fit precisely into that category. These are indicated by stars in Table 1. In the order of their appearance, the first group of investigators belongs to the field of government, the next two are from public administration, and finally, education. In the first three instances, I had no hesitancy in grouping them with the political scientists. The educator was included with the political scientists in order to provide a contrast between sociologists and others. If the four communities listed under No. 30 are dropped from the analysis, the Q measures in Tables 5 and 6 are somewhat altered (due to the small N's) but the patterns within the tables remain the same.

17 The rationale for the dichotomies employed on the method and power structure variables is provided in *ibid.*, notes 15 and 16. Following the procedure outlined there, the case study and combined methods are grouped with the decision-making category in order to contrast the reputational method with others.

18 It should be noted that the cell frequencies represent communities, not studies. The chi-square test is employed in Tables 2, 3, and 4 with the recognition that the assumption of independent cell frequencies is not fully met, since over half of the communities were studied in conjunction with at least one other. With respect to the Q measures, this assumption does not apply.

19 David Gold, "Independent Causation in Multivariate Analysis: The Case of Political Alienation and Attitude Toward a School Bond Issue," *American Sociological Review,* XXVII (February, 1962), 85–87.

20 Herbert Hyman, *Survey Design and Analysis* (Glencoe, Ill.: The Free Press, 1955), chap. vii.

21 Table 5 is presented to make this point explicit, though obviously Table 6 implies that the association in Table 5 will not change, i.e., "within a system of three variables, all of which are related at the zero-order level, if the association between any two disappears with the third held constant, then the association between any other two will not change with the third constant and, in particular, cannot become zero"—Gold, "Independent Causation in Multivariate Analysis," note 5.

22 *Ibid.*, p. 85.

23 For a suggestive discussion of that possibility, see John Horton, pp. 605–24 and pp. 586–604, above.

24 Horton, pp. 605–24, above.

25 Robin M. Williams, Jr., pp. 634–35, above.

26 Mannheim recognized two usages of the "theory of ideology," the first referring to intentional falsifications or incorrect observations (Marx's meaning) and the second referring to "total mental structure." Realizing the need for a distinction, he termed the first type "particular" conceptions and the second "total" conceptions or perspectives. It is this second type that interested Mannheim and was the subject of his sociology of knowledge or *Wissenssoziologie*. See Mannheim, pp. 110–11, above.

27 Mannheim, *Ideology and Utopia*, p. 172.

28 Peter H. Rossi, in a review of M. Kent Jennings, *Community Influentials: The Elites of Atlanta, American Journal of Sociology,* LXXI (May, 1966), 725.

29 Mannheim, *Ideology and Utopia*, p. 5.

Part Five: Criticisms and Problems

I

KARL POPPER

*The Sociology of Knowledge**

Rationality, in the sense of an appeal to a universal and impersonal standard of truth, is of supreme importance . . . not only in ages in which it easily prevails, but also, and even more, in those less fortunate times in which it is despised and rejected as the vain dream of men who lack the virility to kill where they cannot agree.—BERTRAND RUSSELL

IT CAN HARDLY be doubted that Hegel's and Marx's historicist philosophies are characteristic products of their time—a time of social change. Like the philosophies of Heraclitus and Plato, and like those of Comte and Mill, Lamarck and Darwin, they are philosophies of change, and they witness to the tremendous and undoubtedly somewhat terrifying impression made by a changing social environment on the minds of those who live in this environment. The more modern social philosophers appear to react very differently, since they accept, and even welcome, change; yet this love of change seems to me a little ambivalent. For even though they have given up any hope of arresting change, as historicists they try to predict it, and thus to bring it under rational control; and this certainly looks like an attempt to tame it. Thus it seems that, to the historicist, change has not entirely lost its terrors.

In our own time of still more rapid change, we even find the desire not only to predict change, but to control it by centralized large-scale planning.

---

* A brief complementary treatment of problems of the sociology of knowledge is contained in K. R. Popper, *The Poverty of Historicism* (London: Routledge & Kegan Paul, 1957), pp. 155–56.

From *The Open Society and Its Enemies* (2 vols.; 4th rev. ed.; Princeton University Press, 1963, and 5th ed.; Routledge & Kegan Paul, 1966). Reprinted by permission of the Princeton University Press, Routledge & Kegan Paul, Ltd., and the author.

These holistic views (which I have criticized in *The Poverty of Historicism*) represent a compromise, as it were, between Platonic and Marxian theories. Plato's will to arrest change, combined with Marx's doctrine of its inevitability, yield, as a kind of Hegelian "synthesis," the demand that since it cannot be entirely arrested, change should at least be "planned," and controlled by the state, whose power is to be vastly extended.

An attitude like this may seem, at first sight, to be a kind of rationalism; it is closely related to Marx's dream of the "realm of freedom" in which man is for the first time master of his own fate. But as a matter of fact, it occurs in closest alliance with a doctrine which is definitely opposed to rationalism (and especially to the doctrine of the rational unity of mankind . . .), one which is well in keeping with the irrationalist and mystical tendencies of our time. I have in mind the Marxist doctrine that our opinions, including our moral and scientific opinions, are determined by class interest, and more generally by the social and historical situation of our time. Under the name of "sociology of knowledge" or "sociologism," this doctrine has been developed recently (especially by M. Scheler and K. Mannheim)[1] as a theory of the social determination of scientific knowledge.

The sociology of knowledge argues that scientific thought, and especially thought on social and political matters, does not proceed in a vacuum, but in a socially conditioned atmosphere. It is influenced largely by unconscious or subconscious elements. These elements remain hidden from the thinker's observing eye because they form, as it were, the very place which he inhabits, his *social habitat*. The social habitat of the thinker determines a whole system of opinions and theories which appear to him as unquestionably true or self-evident. They appear to him as if they were logically and trivially true, such as, for example, the sentence "all tables are tables." This is why he is not even aware of having made any assumptions at all. But that he has made assumptions can be seen if we compare him with a thinker who lives in a very different social habitat; for he too will proceed from a system of apparently unquestionable assumptions, but from a very different one; and it may be so different that no intellectual bridge may exist and no compromise be possible between these two systems. Each of these different socially determined systems of assumptions is called by the sociologists of knowledge a *total ideology*.

The sociology of knowledge can be considered as a Hegelian version of Kant's theory of knowledge. For it continues on the lines of Kant's criticism of what we may term the "passivist" theory of knowledge. I mean by this the theory of the empiricists down to and including Hume, a theory which may be described, roughly, as holding that knowledge streams into us through our senses, and that error is due to our interference with the sense-given material, or to the associations which have developed within it; the best way of avoiding error is to remain entirely passive and receptive. Against this receptacle theory of knowledge (I usually call it the "bucket theory of the mind"), Kant[2] argued that knowledge is not a collection of gifts received by our senses and stored in the mind as if it were a museum, but that it is very largely the result of our own mental activity; that we must most actively engage ourselves in searching, comparing, unifying, generalizing, if we wish to attain knowledge. We may call this theory the "activist" theory of knowledge. In connection with it, Kant gave up the untenable ideal of a science which is free from any kind of presuppositions. . . . He made it quite clear that we cannot start from nothing, and that we have to approach our task equipped with a system of presuppositions which we hold without having tested them by the empirical methods of science; such a system may be called a "categorical apparatus."[3] Kant believed that it was possible to discover the one true and unchanging categorical apparatus, which represents, as it were, the necessarily unchanging framework of our intellectual outfit, i.e., human "reason." This part of Kant's theory was given up by Hegel, who, as opposed to Kant, did not believe in the unity of mankind. He taught that man's intellectual outfit was constantly changing, and that it was part of his social heritage; accordingly the development of man's reason must coincide with the historical development of his society, i.e., of the nation to which he belongs. This theory of Hegel's, and especially his doctrine that all knowledge and all truth is "relative" in the sense of being determined by history, is sometimes called "historism" (in contradistinction to "historicism . . .). The sociology of knowledge or "sociologism" is obviously very closely related to or nearly identical with it, the only difference being that, under the influence of Marx, it emphasizes that the historical development does not produce one uniform "national spirit," as Hegel held, but rather several and sometimes opposed "total ideologies" within one nation, according to the class, the social stratum, or the social habitat, of those who hold them.

But the likeness to Hegel goes further. I have said above that according to the sociology of knowledge, no intellectual bridge or compromise between different total ideologies is possible. But this radical skepticism is not really meant quite as seriously as it sounds. There is a way out of it, and the way is analogous to the Hegelian method of superseding the conflicts which preceded him in the history of philosophy. Hegel, a spirit freely poised above the whirlpool of the dissenting philosophies, reduced them all to mere components of the highest of syntheses, of his own system. Similarly, the sociologists of knowledge hold that the "freely poised intelligence" of an intelligentsia which is only loosely anchored in social traditions may be able to avoid the pitfalls of the total ideologies; that it may even be able to see through, and to unveil, the various total ideologies and the hidden motives and other determinants which inspire them. Thus the sociology of knowledge believes that the highest degree of objectivity can be reached by the freely poised intelligence analyzing the various hidden ideologies and their anchorage in the unconscious. The way to true knowledge appears to be the unveiling of unconscious assumptions, a kind of psychotherapy, as it were, or if I may say so, a *sociotherapy*. Only he who has been socioanalyzed or who has socioanalyzed himself, and who is freed from this social complex, i.e., from his social ideology, can attain to the highest synthesis of objective knowledge.

[Previously] when dealing with "Vulgar Marxism" I mentioned a tendency which can be observed in a group of modern philosophies, the tendency to unveil the hidden motives behind our actions. The sociology of knowledge belongs to this group, together with psychoanalysis and certain philosophies which unveil the "meaninglessness" of the tenets of their opponents.[4] The popularity of these views lies, I believe, in the ease with which they can be applied, and in the satisfaction which they confer on those who see through things, and through the follies of the unenlightened. This pleasure would be harmless, were it not that all these ideas are liable to destroy the intellectual basis of any discussion, by establishing what I have called[5] a "reinforced dogmatism." (Indeed, this is something rather similar to a "total ideology.") Hegelianism does it by declaring the admissibility and even fertility of contradictions. But if contradictions need not be avoided, then any criticism and any discussion becomes impossible, since criticism always consists in pointing out contradictions either within the theory to be criticized, or between it and some facts of experience. The situation with psychoanalysis is similar: the psychoanalyst can always explain away any objections by showing that they are due to the repressions of the critic. And the philosophers of meaning, again, need only point out that what their opponents hold is meaningless, which will always be true, since "meaninglessness" can be so defined that any discussion about it is by definition without meaning.[6] Marxists, in a like manner, are accustomed to explain the disagreement of an opponent by his class bias, and the sociologists of knowledge by his total ideology. Such methods are both easy to handle and good fun for those who handle them. But they clearly destroy the basis of rational discussion, and they must lead, ultimately, to anti-rationalism and mysticism.

In spite of these dangers, I do not see why I should entirely forgo the fun of handling these methods. For just like the psychoanalysts, the people to whom psychoanalysis applies best,[7] the socioanalysts invite the application of their own methods to themselves with an almost irresistible hospitality. For is not their description of an intelligentsia which is only loosely anchored in tradition a very neat description of their own social group? And is it not also clear that, assuming the theory of total ideologies to be correct, it would be part of every total ideology to believe that one's own group was free from bias, and was indeed that body of the elect which alone was capable of objectivity? Is it not, therefore, to be expected, always assuming the truth of this theory, that those who hold it will unconsciously deceive themselves by producing an amendment to the theory in order to establish the objectivity of their own views? Can we, then, take seriously their claim that by their sociological self-analysis they have reached a higher degree of objectivity; and their claim that socioanalysis can cast out a total ideology? But we could even ask whether the whole theory is not simply the expression of the class interest of this particular group; of an intelligentsia only loosely anchored in tradition, though just firmly enough to speak Hegelian as their mother tongue.

How little the sociologists of knowledge have succeeded in sociotherapy, that is to say, in eradicating their own total ideology, will be particularly obvious if we consider their relation to Hegel. For they have no idea that they are just repeating him; on the contrary, they believe not only that they have outgrown him, but also that they have successfully seen through him, socioanalyzed him; and that they can now look at him, not from any particular social habitat, but objectively, from a superior elevation. This palpable failure in self-analysis tells us enough.

But, all joking apart, there are more serious objections. The sociology of knowledge is not only self-destructive, not only a rather gratifying object of socioanalysis, it also shows an astounding failure to understand precisely its main subject, the *social aspects of knowledge*, or rather, of scientific method. It looks upon science or knowledge as a process in the mind or "consciousness" of the individual scientist, or perhaps as the product of such a process. If considered in this way, what we call scientific objectivity must indeed become completely ununderstandable, or even impossible; and not only in the social or political sciences, where class interests and similar hidden motives may play a part, but just as much in the natural sciences. Everyone who has an inkling of the history of the natural sciences is aware of the passionate tenacity which characterizes many of its quarrels. No amount of political partiality can influence political theories more strongly than the partiality shown by some natural scientists in favor of their intellectual offspring. If scientific objectivity were founded, as the sociologistic theory of knowledge naïvely assumes, upon the individual scientist's impartiality or objectivity, then we should have to say goodby to it. Indeed, we must be in a way more radically skeptical than the sociology of knowledge; for there is no doubt that we are all suffering under our own system of prejudices (or "total ideologies," if this term is preferred); that we all take many things as self-evident, that we accept them uncritically and even with the naïve and cocksure belief that criticism is quite unnecessary; and scientists are no exception to this rule, even though they may have superficially purged themselves from some of their prejudices in their particular field. But they have not purged themselves by socioanalysis or any similar method; they have not attempted to climb to a higher plane from which they can understand, socioanalyze, and expurgate their ideological follies. For by making their minds more "objective" they could not possibly attain to what we call "scientific objectivity." No, what we usually mean by this term rests on different grounds.[8] It is a matter of scientific method. And, ironically enough, objectivity is closely bound up with the *social aspect of scientific method*, with the fact that science and scientific objectivity do not (and cannot) result from the attempts of an individual scientist to be "objective," but from the cooperation of many scientists. Scientific objectivity can be described as the intersubjectivity of scientific method. But this social aspect of science is almost entirely neglected by those who call themselves sociologists of knowledge.

Two aspects of the method of the natural sciences are of importance in this connection. Together they constitute what I may term the "public character of scientific method." First, there is something approaching *free criticism*. A scientist may offer his theory with the full conviction that it is unassailable. But this will not impress his fellow-scientists and competitors; rather it challenges them: they know that the scientific attitude means criticizing everything, and they are little deterred even by authorities. Secondly, scientists try to avoid talking at cross-purposes. (I may remind the reader that I am speaking of the natural sciences, but a part of modern economics may be included.) They try very seriously to speak one and the same language, even if they use different mother tongues. In the natural sciences this is achieved by recognizing experience as the impartial arbiter of their controversies. When speaking of "experience" I have in mind experience of a "public" character, like observations, and experiments, as opposed to experience in the sense of more "private" æsthetic or religious experience; and an experience is "public" if everybody who takes the trouble can repeat it. In order to avoid speaking at cross-purposes, scientists try to express their theories in such a form that they can be tested, i.e., refuted (or else corroborated) by such experience.

This is what constitutes scientific objectivity. Everyone who has learned the technique of understanding and testing scientific theories can repeat the experiment and judge for himself. In spite of this, there will always be some who come to judgments which are partial, or even cranky. This cannot be helped, and it does not seriously disturb the working of the various *social institutions* which have been designed to further scientific objectivity and criticism; for instance the laboratories, the scientific periodicals, the congresses. This aspect of scientific method shows what can be achieved by institutions designed to make public control possible, and by the open expression of public opinion, even if this is limited to a circle of specialists. Only political power, when it is used to suppress free criticism, or when it fails to protect it, can impair the functioning of these institutions, on which all progress, scientific, technological, and political, ultimately depends.

In order to elucidate further still this sadly neglected aspect of scientific method, we may consider the idea that it is advisable to characterize science by its methods rather than by its results.

Let us first assume that a clairvoyant produces a book by dreaming it, or perhaps by automatic writing. Let us assume, further, that years later as a result of recent and revolutionary scientific discoveries, a great scientist (who has never seen that book) produces one precisely the same. Or to put it differently, we assume that the clairvoyant "saw" a scientific book which could not then have been produced by a scientist owing to the fact that many relevant discoveries were still unknown at that date. We now ask: is it advisable to say that the clairvoyant produced a scientific book? We may assume that, if submitted at the time to the judgment of competent scientists, it would have been described as partly ununderstandable, and partly fantastic; thus we shall have to say that the clairvoyant's book was not when written a scientific work, since it was not the result of scientific method. I shall call such a result, which, though in agreement with some scientific results, is not the product of scientific method, a piece of "revealed science."

In order to apply these considerations to the problem of the publicity of scientific method, let us assume that Robinson Crusoe succeeded in building on his island physical and chemical laboratories, astronomical observatories, etc., and in writing a great number of papers, based throughout on observation and experiment. Let us even assume that he had unlimited time at his disposal, and that he succeeded in constructing and in describing scientific systems which actually coincide with the results accepted at present by our own scientists. Considering the character of this Crusonian science, some people will be inclined, at first sight, to assert that it is real science and not "revealed science." And, no doubt, it is very much more like science than the scientific book which was revealed to the clairvoyant, for Robinson Crusoe applied a good deal of scientific method. And yet, I assert that this Crusonian science is still of the "revealed" kind; that there is an element of scientific method missing, and consequently, that the fact that Crusoe arrived at our results is nearly as accidental and miraculous as it was in the case of the clairvoyant. For there is nobody but himself to check his results; nobody but himself to correct those prejudices which are the unavoidable consequence of his peculiar mental history; nobody to help him to get rid of that strange blindness concerning the inherent possibilities of our own results which is a consequence of the fact that most of them are reached through comparatively irrelevant approaches. And concerning his scientific papers, it is only in attempts to explain his work to *somebody who has not done it* that he can acquire the discipline of clear and reasoned communication which too is part of scientific method. In one point—a comparatively unimportant one —is the "revealed" character of the Crusonian science particularly obvious; I mean Crusoe's discovery of his "personal equation" (for we must assume that he made this discovery), of the characteristic personal reaction time affecting his astronomical observations. Of course it is conceivable that he discovered, say, changes in his reaction time, and that he was led, in this way, to make allowances for it. But if we compare this way of finding out about reaction time with the way in which it was discovered in "public" science— through the contradiction between the results of various observers—then the "revealed" character of Robinson Crusoe's science becomes manifest.

To sum up these considerations, it may be said that what we call "scientific objectivity" is not a product of the individual scientist's impartiality, but a product of the social or public character of scientific method; and the individual scientist's impartiality is, so far as it exists, not the source but rather the result of this socially or institutionally organized objectivity of science.

Both[9] Kantians and Hegelians make the same mistake of assuming that our presuppositions (since they are, to start with, undoubtedly indispensable instruments which we need in our active "making" of experiences) can neither be changed by decision nor refuted by experience; that they are above and beyond the scientific methods of testing theories, constituting as they do the basic presuppositions of all thought. But this is an exaggeration, based on a misunderstanding of the relations between theory and experience in science. It was one of the greatest achievements of our time when Einstein showed that, in the light of experience, we may question and revise our presuppositions regarding even space and time, ideas which had been held to be necessary presuppositions of all science, and to belong to its "categorical apparatus." Thus the skeptical attack upon science launched by the sociology of knowledge breaks down in the light of scientific method. The empirical method has proved to be quite capable of taking care of itself.

But it does so not by eradicating our prejudices all at once; it can eliminate them only one by one. The classical case in point is again Einstein's discovery of our prejudices regarding time. Einstein did not set out to discover prejudices; he did not even set out to criticize our conceptions of space and time. His problem was a concrete problem of physics, the redrafting of a theory that had broken down because of various experiments which in the light of the theory seemed to contradict one another. Einstein together with most physicists realized that this meant that the theory was false. And he found that if we alter it in a point which had so far been held by everybody to be self-evident and which had therefore escaped notice, then the difficulty could be removed. In other words, he just applied the methods of scientific criticism and of the invention and elimination of theories, of trial and error. But this method does not lead to the abandonment of all our prejudices; rather, we can discover the fact that we had a prejudice only after having got rid of it.

But it certainly has to be admitted that, at any given moment, our scientific theories will depend not only on the experiments, etc., made up to that moment, but also upon prejudices which are taken for granted, so that we have not become aware of them (although the application of certain logical methods may help us to detect them). At any rate, we can say in regard to this incrustation that science is capable of learning, of breaking down some of its crusts. The process may never be perfected, but there is no fixed barrier before which it must stop short. Any assumption can, in principle, be criticized. And that anybody may criticize constitutes scientific objectivity.

Scientific results are "relative" (if this term is to be used at all) only in so far as they are the results of a certain stage of scientific development and liable to be superseded in the course of scientific progress. But this does not mean that *truth* is "relative." If an assertion is true, it is true forever.[10] It only means that most scientific results have the character of hypotheses, i.e., sentences for which the evidence is inconclusive, and which are therefore liable to revision at any time. These considerations (with which I have dealt more fully elsewhere[11]), though not necessary for a criticism of the sociologists, may perhaps help to further the understanding of their theories. They also throw some light, to come back to my main criticism, on the important role which cooperation, intersubjectivity, and the publicity of method play in scientific criticism and scientific progress.

It is true that the social sciences have not yet fully attained this publicity of method. This is due partly to the intelligence-destroying influence of Aristotle and Hegel, partly perhaps also to their failure to make use of the social instruments of scientific objectivity. Thus they are really "total ideologies," or putting it differently, some social scientists are unable, and even unwilling, to speak a common language. But the reason is not class interest, and the cure is not a Hegelian dialectical synthesis, nor self-analysis. The only course open to the social sciences is to forget all about the verbal fireworks and to tackle the practical problems of our time with the help of the theoretical methods which are fundamentally the same in *all* sciences. I mean the methods of trial and error, of inventing hypotheses which can be practically tested, and of submitting them to practical tests. *A social technology is needed whose results can be tested by piecemeal social engineering.*

The cure here suggested for the social sciences is diametrically opposed to the one suggested by the sociology of knowledge. Sociologism believes that it is not their unpractical character, but rather the fact that practical and theoretical problems are too much intertwined in the field of social and political knowledge, that creates the methodological difficulties of these sciences. Thus we can read in a leading work on the sociology of knowledge:[12] "The peculiarity of political knowledge, as opposed to "exact" knowledge, lies in the fact that knowledge and will, or the rational element and the range of the irrational, are inseparably and essentially intertwined." To this we can reply that "knowledge" and "will" are, in a certain sense, always inseparable; and that this fact need not lead to any dangerous entanglement. No scientist can know without making an effort, without taking an interest; and in his effort there is usually even a certain amount of self-interest involved. The engineer studies things mainly from a practical point of view. So does the farmer. Practice is not the enemy of theoretical knowledge but the most valuable incentive to it. Though a certain amount of aloofness may be becoming to the scientist, there are many examples to show that it is not always important for a scientist to be thus disinterested. But it *is* important for him to remain in touch with reality, with practice, for those who overlook it have to pay by lapsing into scholasticism. Practical application of our findings is thus the means by which we may eliminate irrationalism from social science, and not any attempt to separate knowledge from "will."

As opposed to this, the sociology of knowledge hopes to reform the social sciences by making the social scientists aware of the social forces and ideologies which unconsciously beset them. But the main trouble about prejudices is that there is no such direct way of getting rid of them. For how shall we ever know that we have made any progress in our attempt to rid ourselves from prejudice? Is it not a common experience that those who are most convinced of having got rid of their prejudices are most prejudiced? The idea that a sociological or a psychological or an anthropological or any other study of prejudices may help us to rid ourselves of them is quite mistaken; for many who pursue these studies are full of prejudice; and not only does self-analysis not help us to overcome the unconscious determination of our views, it often leads to even more subtle self-deception. Thus we can read in the same work on the sociology of knowledge[13] the following references to its own activities: "There is an increasing tendency toward making conscious the factors by which we have so far been unconsciously ruled. . . . Those who fear that our increasing knowledge of determining factors may paralyze our decisions and threaten 'freedom' should put their minds at rest. For only he is truly determined who does not know the most essential determining factors but acts immediately under the pressure of determinants unknown to him." Now this is clearly just a repetition of a pet idea of Hegel's which Engels naïvely repeated when he said:[14] "Freedom is the appreciation of necessity." And it is a reactionary prejudice. For are those who act under the pressure of well-known determinants, for example, of a political tyranny, made free by their knowledge? Only Hegel could tell us such tales. But that the sociology of knowledge preserves this particular prejudice shows clearly enough that there is no possible short-cut to rid us of our ideologies. (Once a Hegelian, always a Hegelian.) Self-analysis is no substitute for those practical actions which are necessary for establishing the democratic institutions which alone can guarantee the freedom of critical thought, and the progress of science.

NOTES

1 Concerning Mannheim, see especially *Ideology and Utopia* (quoted here from the German editions, 1929). The terms "social habitat" and "total ideology" are both due to Mannheim; the terms "sociologism" and "historicism" are dealt with in my *The Open Society and Its Enemies* (Princeton: Princeton University Press, 1963), chap. xxii. The idea of a "social habitat" is Platonic.

    For a criticism of Mannheim's *Man And Society in an Age of Reconstruction* (1941), which combines historicist tendencies with a romantic and even mystical Utopianism or holism, see my *The Poverty of Historicism, II, Economica* (1944).

2 Cf. my interpretation in "What Is Dialectic?," *Mind*, XLIX, esp. 414.

3 This is Mannheim's term (cf. *Ideology and Utopia*, p. 35). For the "freely poised intelligence," see *op. cit.*, p. 123, where this term is attributed to Alfred Weber. For the theory

of an intelligentsia loosely anchored in tradition, see *op. cit.*, pp. 121–34, and esp. p. 122.

4 For the latter theory, or, rather, practice, cf. notes 51 to 52 to chapter 11 of *The Open Society and Its Enemies.*

5 Cf. "What Is Dialectic?," p. 417. Cf. note 33 to chapter 12 of *The Open Society and Its Enemies.*

6 The analogy between the psychoanalytic method and that of Wittgenstein is mentioned by Wisdom, "Other Minds," *Mind,* XLIX, 370 *n.*: "A doubt such as 'I can never really know what another person is feeling' may arise from more than one of these sources. This overdetermination of skeptical symptoms complicates their cure. The treatment is like psychoanalytic treatment (to enlarge Wittgenstein's analogy) in that the treatment is the diagnosis and the diagnosis is the description, the very full description, of the symptoms." And so on. (I may remark that, using the word "know" in the ordinary sense, we can, of course, never know what another person is feeling. We can only make hypotheses about it. This solves the so-called problem. It is a mistake to speak here of doubt, and a still worse mistake to attempt to remove the doubt by a semiotico-analytic treatment.)

7 The psychoanalysts seem to hold the same of the individual psychologists, and they are probably right. Cf. S. Freud's *History of the Psychoanalytic Movement* (1916), p. 42, where Freud records that Adler made the following remark (which fits well within Adler's individual-psychological scheme, according to which feelings of inferiority are predominantly important): "Do you believe that it is such a pleasure for me to stand in your shadow my whole life?" This suggests that Adler had not successfully applied his theories to himself, at that time at least. But the same seems to be true of Freud: None of the founders of psychoanalysis were psychoanalyzed. To this objection, they usually replied that they had psychoanalyzed themselves. But they would never have accepted such an excuse from anybody else; and, indeed, rightly so.

8 For the following analysis of scientific objectivity, cf. my *Logik der Forschung,* sec. 8, pp. 16 ff.

9 I wish to apologize to the Kantians for mentioning them in the same breath as the Hegelians.

10 Cf. *The Open Society and Its Enemies,* note 23 to chapter 8 and note 39 (second paragraph) to chapter 11.

11 Cf. *ibid.,* notes 34 ff., to chapter 11.

12 Cf. Mannheim, *Ideology and Utopia,* p. 167.

13 For the first of these two quotations, cf. *op. cit.,* 167. (For simplicity's sake, I translate "conscious" for "reflexive.") For the second, cf. *op. cit.,* p. 166.

14 Cf. *Handbook of Marxism,* p. 255 (*GA,* Special Volume, pp. 117–18): "Hegel was the first to state correctly the relation between freedom and necessity. To him, freedom is the appreciation of necessity." For Hegel's own formulation of his pet idea, cf. *Hegel Selections,* p. 213 (*Werke* [1832–87], VI, 310): "The truth of necessity, therefore, is freedom." 361 (*WW,* XI, 46): ". . . the *Christian* principle of self-consciousness—Freedom." 362 (*WW,* XI, 47): "The essential nature of freedom, which involves in it absolute necessity, is to be displayed as the attainment of a consciousness of itself (for it is in its very nature, self-consciousness) and it thereby realizes its existence." And so on.

2

GERARD DE GRÉ

The Sociology of Knowledge and the Problem of Truth

IN THE OPENING article by Professor Lovejoy in the first issue of *The Journal of the History of Ideas*[1] the question has again been raised concerning the epistemological consequences of the "sociology of knowledge." In bringing this question to our attention, Mr. Lovejoy has indirectly reminded us of the necessity of distinguishing between the *sociology* of knowledge and what may be called the sociological *theory of knowledge*, a distinction which, as Mr. Lovejoy has indicated in his article, is unfortunately often overlooked by both the sociologists of knowledge themselves and their critics.

Inasmuch as the history of ideas may find a useful ally in the sociology of knowledge for the analysis of their common data, it may be advisable to devote a few pages to the consideration of the epistemological status of what are here termed *gnosio-sociological*[2] propositions, in order to clear up this question of the bearing of gnosio-sociological research on the general problem of the validity of ideas.

In order to answer this question it will be necessary to consider briefly the nature of gnosio-sociological research: the focus of interest from which it approaches its data, the conceptual tools which it may find useful, and, especially, what aspect of ideas it is with which it is primarily concerned.

As in all sociological inquiry on the interpretative level, gnosio-sociology must make some basic analytical distinctions in approaching its problems. There are first the social facts that are to be explained. For gnosio-sociology

The Journal of the History of Ideas, II (1941), 110–15. Reprinted by permission of *The Journal of the History of Ideas* and the author.

these facts are to be found in the thoughts or ideas that are explicit or implicit in communication between individuals. "Thought which is meaningful but non-sensory is communicated or expressed by language or some other symbolism; the symbolism in its turn being sensory but having in itself no meaning."[3] Consequently, although we are primarily concerned with the thoughts and ideas that play a role in the communicative process, we nevertheless have to approach these ideas indirectly, that is, through their concrete manifestations in language or some other symbolism. This problem, however, could well furnish a topic for a separate paper, and for the purposes of this inquiry it must suffice to have merely raised it. It must be mentioned that gnosio-sociology is not concerned with the thought of a theoretically isolated individual existing in a social vacuum, but with the knowledge of concrete persons who are members of social groups, and who orient their thinking to other persons by attempting to communicate or express their ideas in some overt manner by either embodying them in language or expressing them in gesture, ritual, or art.

The second level of interpretation concerns itself primarily with the meaningful and understandable aspects of the social facts to be explained. We attempt to relate the concrete particular thoughts expressed by individuals to their more basic underlying world-conception (*Weltanschauung*), ultimate values, interests, beliefs, and sentiments. We endeavor to penetrate through the individual's external behavior and isolated concrete statements in order to discover the basic complex of ideas and the motivations involved in his action. It is only in so far as we succeed in doing this that we can *understand* the *subjective meaning*, that is, the meaning of the propositions *for the individual who states them*.

The subjective content, and the *acts* of judgment through which individuals arrive at their ideas, must be distinguished from the *truth-value* of a proposition, that is, its correspondence with actual facts or its formal logical validity. Gnosio-sociology is not concerned with this latter aspect of the ideas with which it deals. It is not concerned with what a proposition says about something, only with what a proposition may tell us about someone. It is not the function of gnosio-sociology to pass value judgments as to the intrinsic truth, worth, beauty, or comparative value or validity of the thought-products with which it deals; but merely to establish on a purely sociological level the functional, causal, structural or meaningful relationships that it may find amongst its data.

The gnosio-sociologist, however, is not merely concerned with understanding the meaningful elements in knowledge, he must also, as a sociologist, attempt to relate these meaningful complexes to the sociohistorical conditions within which they occur. For example, it is not enough to demonstrate that a particular literary work is the product of a deeply rooted resentment that the author has for certain social strata; we must go further and discover the sociological genesis of this resentment within the system of social stratification with which the author found himself confronted, the prestige and privileges of the group of which he was a member, the accepted currents of thought which were pervasive in his society, and the clash of ultimate values characteristic of his group as opposed to that of some other group.[4]

All three of these elements are necessary to arrive at an adequate sociological explanation: the social actions which provide us with our data, the interpretation of the social actions in order to make them understandable and meaningful, and the causal, functional and structural investigation of the sociohistorical situations in which social actions occur and the subjective orientations of the individuals arise. These elements, however, are characteristic of all sociological interpretation that attempts to do justice both to the causal and meaningful aspects of social action, and not of the sociology of knowledge alone. We shall now turn, therefore, to the consideration of their application to the problems that are the particular concern of the sociology of knowledge.

There is first the problem why in certain social situations specific aspects of experience are stressed more than others. This is not a semantic problem, that is, we do not ask what is the relationship between thought-products and the external facts to which they may refer, but rather what are the societal factors that influence the *selection* of a particular subject matter by those who make statements about their experience. For example, we may ask: "How did the sociohistorical situation of the Middle Ages condition the widespread preoccupation with the problems of the Kingdom of God and the salvation of the soul?"

Secondly, we are interested in discovering the social roots of the manner in which experience is interpreted. We must search for the concrete ideas that give us an insight into the ultimate values, sentiments, interests, beliefs, and attitudes that influence the perspective or meaningful orientation of persons to their experience. These factors must then be related to the sociological factors existing in the historical situations in which they are found. Karl Mannheim's discussion of what he calls the ideological and utopian mentalities may illustrate this focus of interest. These constructs are heuristically constructed generalizations and are not restricted to any particular sociohistorical situation. By an "ideological" mentality is meant, in Mannheim's perhaps unfortunate terminology, a social perspective that is so

much concerned with preserving the existing social and political arrangements that it is blind to any factors that might tend to disrupt or invalidate
them. In contrast, the "utopian" mentality is so obsessed with the idea of
destroying the existing social order that it cannot see any of the valid or
useful aspects that inhere in it.[5] These two constructs represent two differing
perspectives through which experience may be interpreted, and toward
which divergent social groups may respectively gravitate. The gnosio-
sociological problem would concern itself both with the social conditions
that influence groups to gravitate toward one or the other of these mentalities, and with demonstrating how particular concrete thoughts may be
functions of these more general perspectives.

A third problem lies in the investigation of the societal factors influencing
the most general concepts of knowledge, particularly what are called the
categories: space, time, number, causality, relation, being, etc., as well as
the general concepts of science, philosophy, theology, law, art and literary
criticisms, and morals. For example, it may be asked: "Why did the Chinese
at a certain period of their history develop *that kind* of conception of number?"
The "why" in this question refers to the social context of an occurrence.
The answer to this question would be couched in sociological-meaningful
terms, i.e., with reference to certain social relationships, institutions, currents
of thought, common attitudes, etc., which exercise a specific influence on
the members of certain strata of Chinese society. This is what Marcel Granet
attempts to do when he analyses the social factors which condition the
qualitative conception of hierarchical essences pertaining to numbers that
was characteristic of Chinese mathematical theory.[6] On a somewhat more
mundane level we may investigate the role played in societies by highly
charged concepts such as Communism, Democracy, Fascism, Freedom,
Equality, Aryan Supremacy, International Finance, etc., when used as
hypostatized entities and associated with deeply rooted emotions, prejudices,
ideals, or interests. Two problems may be raised in regard to these concepts:
(1) How is the genesis, meaning, or acceptability of these concepts conditioned by the social situations in which they operate? and (2) How do these
concepts influence social adjustments and condition men's mutual orientation
to one another?

Finally, gnosio-sociology is interested in discovering the reciprocal influence of sociohistorical conditions and the most general structure of thinking on the logical and formal level. Certain rules are set up during the course
of time by social groups as to how valid knowledge is to be acquired, and
how propositions are to be logically operated with. Gnosio-sociology is interested in the social situations in which these rules were developed and in

the influence of these rules on social action. We may ask, for example: "What were the social and intellectual conditions existing in Germany that account for the reception of Roman jurisprudence and its displacement of the old German folk-law, starting with the sixteenth century onward?"[7] or "What were the conditions in the later Middle Ages that made the synthesis of medieval and Aristotelian thinking so successful for the social and intellectual purposes of that period?"

It will be observed that in all of these procedures gnosio-sociology never raises the question of the material truth or logical validity of the ideas or of the thought systems that provide its subject matter. Ideas and idea-complexes may be treated as symbolic adjustments[8] made to the world of experience by individuals within and conditioned by social situations. The sociology of knowledge regards these thought products as different possible ways through which thinking beings interpret, know, or attempt to control reality, and adjust their existence to the flux of phenomena in which they participate. All of these thought patterns are symbolic: some poetic and imaginative; others dogmatic, normative, regulative, or philosophic; still others empirical and logico-experimental. Some have their value in the world of action and politics, others in so far as they reflect the structure of reality. The type of reality about which the ideas attempt to enlighten us does not concern the gnosio-sociologist on an epistemological or ontological level of analysis. It may be real or illusory, material or spiritual, sacred or profane, empirical or transcendental; with regard to these distinctions gnosio-sociology strives to be non-evaluative, and makes every effort to avoid passing value judgments as to the intrinsic superiority of science over mythology, or the "higher" truth of religion as compared to the "mere" experimental truth of science. "Knowledge" in the context of gnosio-sociology is a non-evaluative term and carries with it no implications as to the truth or falsity of that knowledge.

At all stages of gnosio-sociological research we are concerned only with establishing a relationship between ideas and men, and not between statements and reality (material truth), nor between statements and other statements on a strictly logical level (formal truth). That is, we are not concerned with establishing the material or formal validity of the ideas and thought systems with which we deal as our subject matter, but only in discovering their *subjective meaning* for the human agents involved, and in relating the acts of judgment through which these subjective meanings arise to certain more pervasive currents of thought, affective complexes, and the social situations which condition them.

The gnosio-sociologist is interested in how the problems that knowledge attempts to solve reflect the problems with which a social group is faced. He may describe how the structure of men's societies influences the structure of their thought. He may show why certain parts of men's experience become more vital to them at some times rather than others. And he may even attempt to demonstrate that certain of their thought structures have lost their utility for purposes of certain practical adjustments, or operate to inhibit the most efficient solution of specific problems; but even in this last case the gnosio-sociologist is relating ideas to persons, and not ideas to the objects to which they may refer. Any epistemological implications that may be found in these observations may be of concern to the philosopher, but not to the sociologist. The utmost that gnosio-sociology may contribute to the general theory of knowledge is to demonstrate the sociological limits within which a conceptual position can hope to attain acceptance. That is, it may demonstrate within a sociological frame of reference, and in terms of the human agents who do the thinking, who are limited by their social heritage and the structure of the society in which they exist, why specific ideas are not likely to attain complete acceptability by all men at all times and under all social conditions; and why no particular individual can possibly attain a total picture of reality which would include all possible human points of view. The laity expresses this fact in its adage: "A man is a product of his times."

However, the demonstration of the limiting factors in the perspectives of thinkers and the multiplicity of possible thought styles does not have any bearing on the problem of the ultimate epistemological validity of what these thinkers *do say* about that limited part of the total reality with which they *are concerned.*

The sociological *theory of knowledge*, as contrasted with the *sociology* of knowledge, however, is an epistemological position which attempts to infer from the findings of gnosio-sociology certain hypotheses concerning the relationship between propositions and *that which* the propositions are about. Of such a nature are the statements of Durkheim about the social locus of the referents of the categories and other ideas. If this position is pushed far enough it results in a kind of *social idealism* which posits that, although the "world" is not the "idea" of any specific individual, as some of the subjective idealists have maintained, it is a kind of "collective idea" and exists only in the "collective consciousness." When Durkheim or other sociologists make statements of this kind they are no longer speaking *qua* sociologists, but *qua* epistemologists. Such epistemological statements must be carefully distinguished from the preliminary gnosio-sociological analysis that Durkheim makes of the social factors, such as religious festivals, kin and clan groups, the spatial arrangements of villages, etc., that influence the primitive conceptions of the categories of time, space, causality, etc.[9]

If this distinction between the sociological theory of knowledge and the sociology of knowledge is carefully maintained, and the exclusive reference of gnosio-sociological propositions to the relationships between thoughts and thinkers, and *not* thoughts and facts, is kept in mind, this confusion—which is always cropping up with reference to gnosio-sociological research and its supposed trespassing on the precincts of epistemology—will be finally cleared up, to the mutual benefit of both the sociologists of knowledge and those other thinkers who are concerned with the analysis, interpretation, or history of ideas.

NOTES

1 Arthur O. Lovejoy, "Reflections on the History of Ideas," *Journal of the History of Ideas*, I (1940), 17–18.

2 "Gnosio-sociology," a direct translation of the German "*Wissenssoziologie*," is suggested in this paper in preference to the somewhat cumbersome "sociology of knowledge." It is especially useful in that it provides an adjectival form.

3 Ernst Grünwald, *Das Problem der Soziologie des Wissens* (Wien-Leipzig: Wilhelm Braumüller, 1934), quoted by A. H. Child in "The Problems of the Sociology of Knowledge" (unpublished Ph.D. dissertation, University of California, Los Angeles, 1939), p. 70.

4 Cf. Max Scheler, *L'Homme du ressentiment* (Paris: Librairie Gallimard, 1933).

5 Cf. Karl Mannheim, *Ideology and Utopia* (New York: Harcourt Brace & Co., 1936), esp. p. 36.

6 Cf. Marcel Granet, *La Pensée chinoise* (Paris: La Renaissance du Livre, 1934), especially Book II, chap. iii.

7 Cf. Eugen Ehrlich, *Fundamental Principles of the Sociology of Law* (Cambridge, Mass.: Harvard University Press, 1936), esp. chap. iii.

8 Symbolic in so far as thinking, particularly that type of thought usually associated with knowledge, takes place mainly through the mediation of language, and consequently, through the symbols of language.

9 Émile Durkheim, *Elementary Forms of Religious Life* (New York: The Macmillan Co., 1915), especially pp. 1–28, 200–22, 268–92, 518–28, and 609–38.

3

ARTHUR CHILD

The Problem of Imputation Resolved

THE PROBLEM OF imputation arises for theory when one considers reflectively the significance of the ascription or "imputation" of some ideology or ideological idea to some particular social group. In a previous article we examined certain unsuccessful attempts at solving this problem.[1] We pointed out the naïveté of the economic-interest theory, according to which an ideology pertains to that social class whose economic interests it happens to serve. Of the postulation of an ideal class consciousness, as proposed by Georg Lukács, we showed not only that it provides an insubstantial basis for ideological imputation in general but that, if employed merely as a basis for the imputation of proletarian ideology, it leads straightway to a vicious circle. We showed, further, that, because the theory developed by Karl Mannheim around the notion of an ideal totality of the class ideology contains serious internal inconsistencies, this latter theory, too, must stand convicted of inadequacy to the problem. Finally, we showed that Ernst Grünwald's elaborately contrived theory of imputation to a metaphysical class entity suffers from internal contradiction and, in any case, that it does not supply a criterion for imputation. Here, however, resuming our study of the problem of imputation, we propose to treat it independently in its character as, simply, a problem to be solved.

The failure of Lukács, Mannheim, and Grünwald suggests that, while undoubtedly these theorists were attacking a real problem, perhaps they did not attack it on a level sufficiently fundamental. Now, their theories all presuppose the validity of the attribution of ideas to socio-economic classes. Precisely this unexamined primary presupposition, however, as unexamined,

Ethics, LIV (January, 1944), 96–109. Reprinted by permission of The University of Chicago Press and the author.

in our opinion makes inevitable the failure of any theory that builds thereon. We might indeed discover, in the end, that this assumption is not altogether incorrect, that in some sense it is true. But by that time the assumption would have become an examined assumption, and the sense in which and the extent to which it is true would have been specified. After a few precedent clarifications we must investigate, then, the sense in which ideas can be imputed, the nature of that which they can be imputed to, and, thus, the justification for the practice of imputation. Such a study, we should think, would necessarily disclose the conditions and limitations of the imputation of ideas to socio-economic classes.

I

While Lukács would attribute ideas to an ideal class consciousness (escaping, in this way, certain difficulties of outright imputation to a socio-economic class), we find it necessary to restrict the theory of imputation to matters of fact. Admittedly, Lukács himself insisted that the ideal class consciousness is fact rather than fiction, that it is ideal in the sense of a mathematical limit rather than in the sense of an object of desire. But, after all, within any class there are tendencies in different directions, any of which directions one might declare, in accordance with one's own ideals, to constitute the direction of the ideal class consciousness. Hence, if the ideal class consciousness is ideal in the sense of a mathematical limit, it is also ideal in the sense of an end of personal or group desire; and there is no point in speaking of an ideal class consciousness, therefore, except in intercourse with those who share the same relevant presuppositions. This is not to assert that no such presuppositions can be correct; it is not to deny the possibility of some objective norm; but it is, indeed, to cast grave doubt on the possibility of establishing any such norm except for those who may share the same hypothetically correct presuppositions.[2] On these grounds, then, we must insist that the proper inquiry has to do with the ascription of ideas to groups as they are rather than with an ascription to an ideal—or, more exactly, idealized—class consciousness.

Imputation, again, though perhaps more commonly associated with ideas, actually concerns modes of thinking no less than it concerns thoughts. Since thoughts may function as modes of thinking and since modes of thinking may become explicit in consciousness as thoughts, there would appear, indeed, to be no strict line between thoughts and modes of thinking. But a functional distinction certainly exists. And if one imputes a whole system of thought, one does so, we should say, because of the basic modes of thinking which categorially organize it and not because of some additive character of the separate ideas involved. The basic convictions of any system of thought, that is, as convictions rather than mere verbalized propositions, are themselves categorizing predispositions. Thus we believe that, even if the categorial imputation does not become explicit, it is nevertheless presupposed as the primary imputation in any imputation of mere ideas.

To be sure, one does discover modes of thinking through a study of thoughts. Then, once the modes of thinking have been articulated, one can turn back to the actual thoughts and regard them, in greater detail and with deeper understanding, with respect to the working-out of the modes of thinking into the expressed thoughts. This, apparently, is the process Mannheim referred to in his projection of an inquiry into the extent to which the ideal styles of thought are actually realized. We cannot see, however, that the notion of articulated modes of thinking or the notion of an ideal style of thought could constitute, at bottom, anything more than the notion of a hypothesis as to the way in which various categories are in fact organized in relation to one another. The study of actual thoughts with reference to the modes of thinking constitutes, then, an investigation of the hypothesis that these are the modes of thinking genuinely operative in the origin, development, and term of those thoughts. Thus to speak of studying the extent to which an ideal style of thought is actually "realized" is to express in distorted form the notion of the testing of a hypothesis. And if one does not find that, in so far as one can reasonably judge, the hypothesized style of thought actually did nor actually does function as the thought-norm of the group, then the hypothesis is simply shown to be, in so far as one can judge, a false hypothesis. The hypothesis may be an "ideal" in the mind of the investigator, but it is an ideal in no other sense, and it cannot lay claim to any reality superior to the reality of the real.

As we have observed, however, between modes of thinking and actual thoughts there is no strict line of division. Thoughts, as we said, may become functionalized into modes of thinking, and modes of thinking may become explicit in consciousness as thoughts. Or, at all events, this transformability of the one into the other holds on the theoretical level. In the nature of the case it could not obtain to the same extent on the level of perception. For modes of thinking, while operating in perception, could first become conscious as thoughts only on the level of explicit judgment. But these qualifications hardly affect our further point—namely, that as regards the practice of imputation there is no essential difference between thoughts and modes of thinking and that, therefore, except in so far as the modes of thinking are more basic and the actual thoughts more easily discoverable, one may speak indifferently of the imputation of thoughts or of the imputation of modes of thinking.

It is important to note that, after all, the problem of imputation arises mainly on the level of systematic interpretation. While perception admittedly reveals the influence of social categories, the fact that perceptions do in general agree for practical purposes creates a strong doubt, for us at least, that the social imputability of perception could become the subject for any extensive series of significant studies. And in respect to the level of simple explicit judgment, the process of imputation would consist merely in the formation and verification of a hypothesis as to the implicit systematic relationship between simple judgments; the end-in-view would consist merely in the discovery of the extent to which these simple judgments represent fragments of some integral mode of interpretation. The primary concern of imputation quite evidently lies, therefore, with the level of systematic theory; and its concern with the other levels derives from, and refers back to, the more complex and more comprehensive—and, in this context, the more fundamental—level.

It must finally be pointed out that imputation relates, by and large, rather to the constitutive than to the selective function of the categories. The selection of certain aspects of the world for interpretation involves a denial, not of the existence, but only of the importance (at least in the given connection), of the neglected aspects of the world; and any selection from these neglected aspects may become the central subject of some other interpretation. Hence little conflict of interpretation can arise as a result of the selective function; for, while the consequent interpretations do differ, they refer to different objects. On the other hand, the constitutive structure of an interpretation of any given aspects of the world involves the claim that certain other interpretations—those, namely, which refer to the same or to approximately the same facts—lie in error. Here, then, a grave conflict of interpretation must arise; for not merely do the interpretations differ, but they refer competitively to the same object. In other words, the constitutive function of the categories entails a far more stringent peculiarity than does the selective function and thus a far more thorough and radical incompatibility between the divergent interpretations. It is the constitutive function of the categories, therefore, which chiefly provides the material for imputation and upon which, in any case, the practice of imputation must chiefly direct what power of social clarification it may possess.

II

The three questions—"In what sense can one impute ideas?" "What can one impute them to?" and "What is the justification of such imputation?" —will, we believe, obtain a simultaneous answer in the analyses that follow.

The ideas imputable to a group are those ideas which derive from categories that are either peculiar to or primary to the given group. It is obvious that ideas which no one would impute to a given group might nevertheless qualify that group because of propaganda, permeation, tradition, etc. But ideas will not uniquely qualify a group, in such a sense that one would attribute certain ideas to that particular group out of all groups, unless those ideas do proceed from categories which are either peculiar to or primary to that group. The question of which categories are peculiar to or primary to some certain group is precisely the question that we proclaim a question of fact rather than a question of speculation, idealization, projection, or fiat. For an idea to be imputable to any given social class, subclass, or stratum, it must so prevail among the members of that group, therefore, as recognizably to constitute the norm. The thought of any member of the group who does not have as his own that particular idea (or, more exactly, who does not think in such fashion that he has, or in principle could have, that particular idea as his own when the appropriate occasion arises) must, on the other hand, be recognizable as a deviation from the norm.

To us it seems doubtful that any class but a ruling class would possess, under normal conditions, any considerable body of ideas—any more or less systematically articulated set of convictions, principles, beliefs, and opinions —of the nature which one terms "ideological." A ruling class definitely can possess an ideology, because it is the ruling class which, as dominant materially, dominates spiritually as well. Inasmuch as the thoughts peculiar to the ruling class have the greatest prestige, it is these thoughts that receive the greatest measure of theoretical development: thinking is in general oriented toward, and proceeds in general in terms of, the ruling-class ideas. What sort of criteria can one find, then, for imputation to a class which is a ruling class? We should say that, if the members of a ruling class reward the person who thinks in certain ways, if, that is, they encourage such thinking; if they themselves, in so far as they are themselves ideologically fertile, produce ideology of the type in question; if such ideology, by whomever produced, appears acceptable to, and vital in the lives of, the normal members of that class—then the imputation of the ideological tendency in question to the particular class in question seems quite justified. The fact that the ideology in question may also prevail among the members of the subordinate classes within the society in question does not seem a legitimate ground for withholding an imputation from the class which rules that society; for it is precisely one of the tasks of a ruling class, in order to establish and preserve its power, so to spread its ideology among the members of the society as a whole that spiritual as well as material circumstances can constitute a bulwark of its power. Primarily, therefore, however far the ideology may have spread, it belongs to the ruling class if such criteria as we have given above are met.[3]

But non-ruling classes do not seem, in general, to possess any dominant ideological trend such as one might discover to characterize a ruling class. We should say that the subordinate classes would *have* ideologies, properly speaking, only at times of revolutionary crisis or under the influence of some special group, some deliberate grouping, marked by ideological as well as material organization—and such influence can obtain to any considerable extent, after all, only in the presence of social crisis. Besides the rather definite ideas that compose ideologies, there are also, of course, the categories or modes of thinking. And common conditions of life, even with ideologically subordinate classes, will sometimes generate peculiar vague modes of thought which prefigure some possible systematic ideology. Such ways of thinking may justifiably be imputed if they can be established; but, because of the relative inarticulateness of ideologically subordinate classes, the evidence for the normal character of these modes of thought might well prove, in general, difficult of discovery. At all events, since as a problem imputation concerns mainly the non-ruling classes, it is to the non-ruling classes that our further analysis must, in the main, refer.

With respect to a non-ruling class, we have indicated, the first condition for a norm of specific attitudes is the presence of some great social crisis. But if in a crisis a specific categorial structure can appear as a norm, then, one might ask, must it not in some form have existed previously? Might not one justifiably insist, with Lukács, that this structure existed previously in the form of an ideal which was actually realized to an extent varying between different members of the class? This suggestion does have a certain plausibility. For at times, as we said, one can detect a general tendency of thought even within a non-ruling class; even, that is, though the literary expressions of the proletariat or the peasantry might prove limited in scope and number, one will still find it possible, at times, to infer certain ways of thinking from certain ways of acting. However, while the possibility of such inferences would constitute a necessary condition for the validity of the theory of ideal existence, it would not constitute a sufficient condition: other theories might succeed in explaining more satisfactorily the significance of these vague tendencies of thought. What, in any case, could justify the claim that the ways of thinking in question are the ideal ways of thinking? Even the concept of the ideal as a limit cannot be used except in reference to some specification of the ideal. Does the specification derive, then, from conformity to class interests? Hardly. On other occasions, at some length, we have expounded various crippling difficulties of the class-interest theory.[4] And we believe that, if the concept of "ideal" is to have any real use in the present context, it must be taken in the sense of that which is consciously held as ideal. The "ideal" ways of thinking, in consequence, can derive their ideality only from an assimilation to the group aims of the class in question. However, the existence of group aims among non-ruling classes during non-critical periods is itself a highly debatable matter; and to the theory of ideal modes of thought, therefore, attaches all the dubiety of the notion of such class aims.

The honorific of ideality dispensed with, one might still try to achieve the same theoretical desideratum in this manner: Taking as point of reference the mode of thinking that exists in a time of revolutionary crisis, one would proceed to impute thoughts by the criterion of revolutionary categories. That is, ascertaining (as, in principle, one could) the modes in which a non-ruling class thinks in a revolutionary crisis, one would then investigate the extent to which the earlier or the later thought of members of that class is informed by these categories. And we could not deny an investigator the right to make such investigations if he should so choose. But even if we accept the legitimacy, in some sense, of such investigations, we must still raise a number of objections from the standpoint of the requirements for an adequate theory of imputation.

Following the procedure we have sketched, one can work far more surely in retrospect than in prospect. One cannot work with such surety in prospect because one cannot know for certain that a class will behave in a future crisis, even a future revolutionary crisis, in the same manner in which it has behaved in the past. For the future does offer novelty. The assumption that a class will behave in the same way and think in the same way in future crises as it may have behaved and thought in past crises is, therefore, no more than a prediction. And, being only a prediction, it might prove false equally as well and often as true. Any assumption, outspoken or (more probably) tacit, that a class *ought* to behave in the future as it has in the past is purely *ad hoc*. Such an assumption is irrelevant to a scientific imputational procedure, because the assumption itself presupposes an ideal personal to the assumptor, and ideal with reference to his peculiar personal ends—and the fact that he may share these ends with persons of a similar political tendency makes no difference in the objective difficulty.

Again, while it might prove interesting to ascertain the extent to which the previous thought of the members of a class does accord with the dominant class tendency in a revolutionary period, the situation offers an antagonistic possibility as well. Quite plausibly one might contend that during non-critical periods a non-ruling class is characterized by modes of thinking which differ notably from those characterizing it in periods of crisis. And, if such should be the case, the proposed method we are considering would possess only a very limited value as a method of imputation. With reference to certain ends, certain ideals, certain purposes, a transcendent importance would indeed attach to the discovery, in the past of a group, of the pre-figuration of certain characteristics dominant at a later period. But that is not what we understand imputation to mean. Imputation, as we understand it, concerns primarily the discovery of the modes of thinking actually character-istic of a class during some given period. And the proposal objected to here rests, therefore, upon a tendentious magnification of small beginnings.

Common activities and interests, we should indeed agree, might fixate, influence the development of, or even congenerate certain vague categories which, in a manner peculiar to the given class, would in some measure in-form the thinking of most members of that class at the given time. However, these categories would not be systematically elaborated, in the case of a non-ruling class, into an integrated ideological structure; for the ideology actually prevalent in that class during a normal period would be the ideology of the dominant social class. Furthermore, we should not deny that the categories of critical or revolutionary periods may exist implicitly in, and develop from, earlier vague tendencies of thought. We do insist, however, that the proposition must not be prejudged; that it is by no means easy to settle; that, above all, it cannot be settled by fiat in accordance with the requirements of some particular theoretical system; and, in any case, that it forms a subject of investigation for the history of a particular ideology rather than constituting a foundation for a theory of imputation.

Moreover, while a common mode of living and common tasks and activities will lead to certain vague categories, there is no guarantee that the members of the class to which those categories belong will acknowledge those categories as at all appropriate to their socio-economic group. Nor can we see that (whether logically or in virtue of interests or in any other sense apart from reference to the ideals of the person or persons advancing the claim) it could be said that the members of the class *ought* to acknowledge such categories. By various methods individuals may be brought to—or for various reasons or from various causes they may come to—recognize the appropriateness of these vague categories; but to say this is by no means to grant either that they certainly will or that they, in any event, ought to. Furthermore, such recognitions have nothing essentially to do with the question of whether the categories actually are appropriate in any sense other than the sense that a certain number of members of the class might, by the bare fact of acknowledgment, have constituted these particular categories as somehow appropriate.

Mere vague attitudes, again, hardly provide a very promising subject for imputation. It is organized convictions, sets of ideas, ideological systems—or, from the subjective side, categorial structures—which one really wishes to impute. And the existence of such complex constellations presupposes a positive expansion, as well as an explication and integration, of the original value attitudes. During the process as a whole, in any case, elements foreign to the original attitudes will doubtless enter; for any conceptual organization must proceed in terms of a vast body of already existing material that belongs not to any one class alone but rather to the entire society. Personal additions, too, will occur; for the development of thought is an activity not of any folk spirit or of any "class spirit" or even of the class consciousness, but, on the contrary, of specific individuals who possess their own peculiar originality. And here we might recall what Goethe said of the Time-Spirit:

> *Was ihr den Geist der Zeiten heisst,*
> *Das ist im Grund den Herren eigner Geist,*
> *In dem die Zeiten sich bespiegeln.*[5]

With the necessary changes, the same could be said of the consciousness of a class.

Thus, even if an ideology develops from, or embraces, certain categorial predispositions characteristic, by and large, of some certain non-ruling class, one might not be justified in imputing it to that class. First, because of its necessarily critical, expanded, additive, and organized nature, one could hardly attribute it to the class, as distinguished from particular individuals within the class, under normal or relatively stabilized conditions. Second, since likewise in a revolutionary period it would stand beyond the grasp of the vast majority of the members of the class in virtue of its complex and systematic nature, neither could one attribute it to the class in a revolutionary period except in the sense (which we shall revert to below) that it is in line with, or in accordance with the tendency of, the comparatively simple modes of thought available to the majority of the class under the difficult conditions of social chaos. However, such an attribution (unless the criterion of imputation is to be defined, somehow, as a matter of coherence with the more elementary of the socialized predispositions) could constitute no more, obviously, than an attribution of just those simple modes of thought. Fourth, while there is indeed another possibility—namely, that the whole complex ideology should be attributed to the class as a whole on the ground that it is rationally adhered to by the leaders or the representatives of the class—this contention would actually, we believe, require the abandonment of the notion of *class* imputation.

For, fifth, leadership or representation is, after all, the function of affiliational groups of a particular kind—the function, that is, of deliberately and self-consciously organized ideological groups. These affiliational groups may not always be as disciplined as the Communist Party or as completely equipped ideologically. Still, we should say that in any revolutionary movement, as distinguished from a mere uprising, the leadership must come from some organization which is distinct from the class or the classes it leads both in virtue of its special organization and in virtue of the fact that its ideology, however vague and confused, is nevertheless more coherent, more explicit, more complete, more "advanced," than the fragmentary thought of the masses which follow its lead. Our claim that the ability to lead a social movement presupposes an organizational and ideological superiority finds validation in the histories of the English, the American, the French, the Spanish-American, the Mexican, and the Chinese, no less than the Russian, revolutions. Reverting to our recent discussion, we must here observe that, in so far as the categories of a revolutionary period occur in a non-revolutionary period, they do occur chiefly within a particular organization which, while usually composed in the main of members of the class in question, is, nonetheless, an organization quite distinct from the class itself. And, moreover, even in so far as in a revolutionary period the ideology in question characterizes the class as a whole, that general characterization may (and, we believe, does) depend to a high degree on the activity of the distinct revolutionary organization. Of course, the period must be in itself somehow favorable to the spread of the ideology of that organization; and in the measure possible, as a means to victory if for no other reason, the organization will purposefully spread both its organization and its ideology over the wide scope of the masses it strives to lead; and victory does bear a close relation to the breadth and depth of ideological and organizational diffusion. However, these facts, it seems to us, hardly affect our contention that the categories of an affiliational group are primarily its own categories and purely by extension the categories of the non-ruling socio-economic class and that, therefore, in a full and primary sense, the imputation of an integrated, systematically elaborated ideology can be made only to a group which is organized deliberately and ideologically. It cannot be made to the class or classes which that specialized group attempts to lead.

With the realization that such a systematic way of thinking, as distinguished from rudimentary tendencies, can be imputed with total legitimacy only to a particular kind of affiliational group, the problems of the sense in which ideologies can be imputed to non-ruling classes begin to disappear. For these problems arise in large part from the ignoring (or, possibly, the ignorance) of the fact that in general an ideology is possessed in relative completeness—an ideology, at all events, which one might speciously attribute to a non-ruling class—only by a few ideologically organized members of the class and by those further few individuals who have fallen under the plenary influence of the ideologically organized group. But the concept of imputation must also be examined in its new form of an imputation to an affiliational, rather than a sociostructural, group; and to this examination, then, we now turn.

III

What does, or what can, imputation mean as imputation to a deliberately organized ideological group? Not even all the members of such an organized group (at any rate, when it has become large enough to acquire an important social efficacy) can "possess" the entire ideology of that group. And this statement seems rather obviously true in consideration of the inevitable differences in education, culture, intelligence, etc., among the members of any such group.

Nonetheless, the group is, precisely, organized. And, as an ideologically organized group, it attempts to inculcate within its own membership at least the principles of its organizing and dynamizing ideology. Beyond these principles, moreover, it demands a faith in their consequences even when not understood or known, and it demands a rational assent to the whole system in so far as the whole system does come to be rationally apprehended.[6] Thus an ideologically organized group possesses an appropriate ideology in the sense, in any case, of a group demand. The group as organized expects, requires, demands, that its members shall accept certain principles of belief and action rather than others, that they shall acknowledge one body of thought rather than another as the fitting or the correct or the true set of propositions about the world and man and society (and perhaps the supernatural) and their interrelationships. And, indeed, since membership in such an affiliational group is almost altogether a matter of voluntary choice (because the obligatory member would tend more frequently to disrupt than to consolidate and sustain the necessary discipline) and since, in no small measure, this choice is a rational choice,[7] many of the members deliberately set out to acquire, and actually do acquire, a considerable proportion of the ideology of the group.[8] In any event, accepting the basic principles, the members of the group regard a mastery of the whole ideological system as an ideal. They feel that their knowledge ought to be thorough and complete, for in that way lies the salvation both of the individual and of society. Even if they do not understand the farther reaches of their ideology, they will defend their ideology, they will fight for it, and they will die for it. Thus an ideology characterizes an ideologically organized group not merely as a demand on the group, not merely as a body of doctrine actually understood, to a greater or lesser extent, by most of the group, but also as an ideal of the members of the group. The members of the group feel their ideology as perhaps their most precious group possession. And, when this feeling exists, there should be no doubt at all either of the fact of imputability or of the objective consent to a specific imputation.

The imputation of ideologies to socio-economic classes and the imputation of ideologies to affiliational groups of a particular kind may be contrasted, as we now see, in the following way: In the case of a socio-economic class, an ideology can legitimately be imputed only in the sense of prevailing among what appears to be the majority of the members of the class. However, at least with non-ruling classes, such imputations must prove rather difficult to make and scanty in number. In the case of ideologically organized groups, on the other hand, imputation proceeds on the basis of the acknowledged ideal of the members as organized. On the ground, then, that adherence to a specific ideology is one of the defining marks of an ideologically organized group, it might be objected that imputation here becomes so easy as to lose significance: a given ideology does indeed characterize some certain affiliational group, but the characterization is obvious. With this important objection, we must agree; and we shall presently return to it in our concluding observations.

First, however, we must consider the problem presented by the frequent origination of ideologies in the mind of some particular individual. The definition of ideology would presumably include the notion of a group, rather than an individual, reference; and, definitions quite aside, it would patently be inadequate, in many cases, to attribute ideas merely to the individual in whose mind they originate or from whom they receive new form and meaning. But for ideas which are not taken as somehow or other ideological, one rests content with a purely individual reference. What is it, therefore, that necessitates a group attribution for certain ideas, termed ideological, even when these ideas possess a distinguishable origin in the mind of some individual?

One might seek an easy answer in the fact that the mind of the individual himself and hence his ideas originate in the processes of group interaction. But in this sense, obviously, a group origin must be affirmed of all ideas. Obviously, too, ideological ideas possess a group relevance of a further and more special kind than the group relevance possessed by ideas in general. Thus the easy answer will scarcely do.

Now, it must be emphasized that we are here discussing not the expression but the origin of ideological ideas. An ideology may be expressed with perfect unconsciousness of any group relevance—both, that is, in innocence of any ulterior purport and in ignorance of any extrinsic import. In so far, however, as an ideology originates in a single mind rather than developing, all but imperceptibly, in the slow culture of the mass mind, it seems true to say that there exists, at the origin of the ideology, a more or less explicit and more or less conscious reference to a particular group. Of course, the originative genius might occasionally err as to the group which he represents, and the fact of group reference might itself be partially obscured by ideological factors. The chief exception, perhaps, would occur when the ideologist claims to defend the interests of a whole society or even of those individuals or groups against whose true interests his theories actually militate. One might take as an example those infant labor apologists of the early nineteenth century who claimed that infant labor was pre-eminently beneficial to the infants themselves. However, we feel that in such instances the group relevance is generally too palpable to require demonstration. And in the main, in any case—above all, in the more sophisticated recent centuries—the individual origination of ideologies does seem to involve a quite explicit and conscious group reference.

Early in our study of the problem of imputation we touched on the difficulties involved in the concept of "belonging to" a group: in various respects, such as birth, education, and socio-economic status, a single individual may belong to different and even antagonistic groups.[9] But in the context of the conscious origination of ideology the concept of "belonging to" becomes rather irrelevant. The important consideration is the group which the individual "represents"—and representation is, after all, by no means as automatic and unconscious a function as many who employ the concept appear to assume; representation is, on the contrary, an active function, and it is also a reciprocal function. To be sure, the groups to which a thinker belongs in various of the many senses of "belonging to" will tend to retain an influence over his thinking; but he will adapt these influences, in so far as possible, to his current representational function. And the group which a thinker "represents" is the group which he actively identifies himself with, whose interests, whose aims, whose desires, whose ideals, perhaps even whose mode of life—in that form, at all events, which he conceives them to have—he attempts to make his own. For an ideology to be an ideology, however; for the ideas of an individual to be attributable to the group which he has identified himself with, for him truly to represent that group, still more is required: his leadership must be recognized by the group. For representation is, as we have said, reciprocal. And such group recognition provides the only decisive confirmation of the group relevance of the individual's ideas.[10]

But here we must note again the distinction between, on the one hand, the sociostructural group and, on the other hand, that affiliational group that is ideologically and organizationally constituted into an independent social force. It is through a confusion of these two distinct types of groups that an ideologist and his interpreters most easily mistake the group which that ideologist represents. That is, an ideologist, with the assent of his interpreters, may claim and believe that he represents some sociostructural group when actually, in any intelligible and non-disputable sense, he represents only that self-consciously organized ideological group with which he has a deliberate affiliation. We do not mean to deny that at one and the same time an ideologist can represent both such an affiliational group and a sociostructural group; for the greater part of a social class may, and sometimes does, recognize some affiliational group (and even some particular individual within that group) as the ideological leader of that class. But in all such cases—and in any case—the final test as to who is representing whom must lie in the recognition of the presumed leadership. And in most cases, we should say, however broad the representation claimed, it is actually the ideologically organized group and its periphery alone (among, at all events, non-ruling classes) which recognizes the leadership of the ideologist; it is therefore the ideologically organized group alone of which the ideologist can be a "representative"; and it is only such an affiliational group, in final consequence, to which in general the ideas of the ideologist can legitimately be imputed.

This, then, is our solution to the problem of imputation. It will hardly prove satisfactory, as we realize, to those who most diligently make imputations. And the reason therefore will be clear, if it is not obvious already, upon a brief summation of the bearing of our solution on the significance of the concept of imputation.

The problem of imputation is a problem not of fact, but of knowledge of fact. It is, hence, only from the standpoint of knowledge of fact that we restrict the validity of imputation, by and large, to the ideologically organized group. And in so far as one can discover facts justifying an imputation to a social class (except, of course, in the case of a ruling class or at a moment of deep social crisis), the imputation will be more an imputation of very broad and rather vague tendencies of response than an imputation of a coherent ideological system. These tendencies, moreover, can hardly be excogitated in the pure light of pure reason, as Max Scheler seems to have attempted to excogitate the categorial forms which he imputed to the bourgeoisie and the proletariat;[11] it is only, on the contrary, by a concrete sociopsychological investigation that one can discover those divergent general categories which arise in different groups of men in consequence of their peculiar and proper activities, traditions, modes of living, etc. But, while admitting the probable validity of such broad categorial imputations, we must deny the validity of the imputation of a whole system of ideology to a particular social class as distinguished from an ideologically organized group or an entire culture except, first, to a ruling class, whose very position of command allows of the inculcation of an ideology among its proper membership (as, indeed, throughout its whole society), and, second, to a non-ruling class in certain extraordinary situations of social crisis in which the majority of the class will accept the leadership, ideological as well as practical, of some affiliational group within that class. For otherwise we have not been able to find a defensible meaning, with reference to knowledge of fact, for the imputation of an entire ideological system to an entire social class.

Our theory, as we have suggested, makes imputation somewhat less meaningful than it has usually appeared to thinkers who emphasize the social derivation of thought. For our theory grants the legitimacy of imputation mainly in reference to ideologically organized groups—and in reference to such groups, which possess self-conscious ideologists and which acknowledge the leadership of these ideologists, there would exist very little disagreement on the score of imputation; for their ideologies are, precisely, the ideologies of their own ideologists. And as to the imputation of vague attitudes, the imputation which, we have conceded, can legitimately be made to broad social classes—the sociological student of thought has not been chiefly concerned with such imputations. It might be argued that imputation to ideologically organized groups or imputation of indefinitely determined predispositions is not at all what one means by imputation or that it does not at all accomplish what one wishes to accomplish through the practice of imputation. But in regard to the theoretical contention, to state our position once again, the scientific issue is not the issue of what one does mean by imputation: it is the issue of what, with reference to the known facts, one *can* mean. And if one insists on meaning something disallowed by knowledge of fact, then one's meaning is subjective and is, therefore, theoretically illegitimate. As to the second and pragmatic contention, it may indeed be relevant to the technology of propaganda, but it is not relevant to a scientific examination of the facts involved; if imputation will not accomplish what one desires to accomplish, so much the worse for one's desires.

But we need not conclude pessimistically. For the relationship of ideologically organized groups to the larger and more amorphous groups in which they arise, in which they have their being, and on which they exert their influence—this relationship remains an important subject for investigation. And especially important to cultural history is a study of the extent to which ideologies do partly arise from the vaguer and simpler categories of broadly specified minds and the study, also, of the reaction of developed ideologies upon the thinking of the masses. But all this constitutes a far more comprehensive and far more complex matter than "imputation." The notion of imputation, indeed, perhaps obscures considerably more than it illuminates. For, by its peculiar emphasis, it substitutes a rather superficial problem of specious simplicity for the immensely more complicated problems which the work of criticism reveals.

NOTES

1 Arthur Child, "The Problem of Imputation in the Sociology of Knowledge," *Ethics*, LI, No. 2 (January, 1941), 200–19.
2 Precisely because the imputations of Marxism derive from presuppositions guaranteed elsewhere in the Marxian system of thought and for the Marxists, therefore, subject to no doubt, the Marxists can maintain their imputational opinions in the face both of adverse criticism and of the difficulties internal to the process of imputation itself.
3 Ultimately, indeed, one might have to grant to the interest theory that the members of a ruling class persistently cling to their ideology—if even but with a dim, dull, vague persistence—because their ideology does, in some sense, uniquely serve what they deem —or, at least, feel as—their interests. However, because of the difficulties involved in the interest theory, proof of service to class interests (granted their specification) cannot constitute the criterion of imputation; it could only, at best, provide an occasional auxiliary confirmation. The actual criteria must be criteria which can consistently be used in investigation; and we believe that the criteria we have proposed are, in fact, just such criteria.
4 Child, "The Problem of Imputation in the Sociology of Knowledge," pp. 202–3; "The Existential Determination of Thought," *Ethics*, LII, No. 2 (January, 1942), 178–84.
5 *Faust*, Part I, ll. 224–26.
6 Cf. the remarks of Florian Znaniecki on the advantage of "knowledge" as a weapon for gaining adherence or sympathetic neutrality in social struggles and on the need of "sages" to theorize for the ordinary people, who "are apt to commit silly 'errors' of judgment which, instead of supporting their own side in the controversy, furnish arguments for the other side. Some intellectually superior and widely informed person must do the thinking for them, and their duty is then simply to imitate his thinking and assimilate its results as well as they can." (*The Social Role of the Man of Knowledge* [New

York: Columbia University Press, 1940], p. 71; the succeeding pages are also highly
relevant to the present discussion.)

7 Fascism, because of its obscurantism, might appear to furnish an exception. Nevertheless, it does not provide any real exception, for our discussion concerns ideologies rather
than systems of lies. Ideologies, in a strict sense, are sincere and serious attempts at
explaining the world. Hoaxes, therefore, however gigantic, are not ideologies. It might
be argued that even the fascist swindles become ideological in so far as they are truly
believed; but we should have to question, in regard to such an argument, whether, after
all, one can truly believe a fascist "ideology" or whether, on the contrary, one does not
merely reiterate it under certain emotional stimuli and with a greater or lesser volume
of noise.

8 Membership in an ideologically organized group—and, particularly, in the Communist
Party—has affinities with both the concept of participative submission and the concept
of purposive submission as developed by Florian Znaniecki (in *Social Actions* [New
York: Farrar & Rinehart, 1936], pp. 312–79). On the one hand, the "agent" generally
pursues a purpose of his own that he finds also pursued by the "social object," and this
mutuality of purpose is generally a precondition for his submission; but, on the other
hand, the agent generally expects of—or certainly, at all events, receives from—the
social object both a more perfect determination of the situation (see n. 6, above) and an
assignment of his own proper function in the activity in which he participates. We
might, perhaps, describe the phenomenon as a purposive submission to a participative
collectivity. The applicability of this description to an obscurantist movement we tend
to doubt; here, to be sure, both participative and purposive submission exist, but they
would seem to exist separately and in the pure forms analyzed by Znaniecki rather than
in the integrated form which we find in an ideologically organized group.

9 Child, "The Problem of Imputation in the Sociology of Knowledge," *op. cit.*, pp.
201–2.

10 On the relationship between the individual and the social context to which the individual belongs, C. Wright Mills has made an excellent statement from a point of view
very close to that of the present writer. We venture, therefore, to quote at some
length: "The thinker does not often play an immediate active role in large social strata
or institutional frames, and hence, does not build through direct action a generic
pattern of habit and value which would constitute a selective detector of 'problems,'
a background of mind. Nevertheless, there are two other modes by which he may come
to be influenced by such residues. He may intentionally identify himself with an ethos
rooted in a structure of social habits, thus vicariously participating in and articulating a
particular social segment's interests; or, if his thought is appreciatively diffused, members of his audience will possess mental characteristics built by direct social action. It is
often through such audiences that a thinker is culturally claimed, because, when his
doctrine and his *further* thought gravitate toward a responsive audience it means that he
has responded (whether he is at first aware of it or not) to 'problems' defined by the
activities and values of his audience. A reflective response to a social environment,
assimilated by its members, is always related to the 'needs' of that particular environment. Defined operationally (externally and behaviorally) that environment is the
largely unreflective behavior patterns of a specific set of groups, e.g., a class, or a set of
institutions. Viewed internally, as a function or field of mind, we have contended for
this environment's influence on thought, because such specific fields of social behavior

develop and sustain organized sets of attitudes; when internalized, these constitute a thinker's generalized other which functions as that with and against which he carries on his internal conversation. It is by virtue of this essentially social structure of mind that sociological factors influence the fixation not only of the evaluative but also of the intellectual" (in "Language, Logic, and Culture," *American Sociological Review*, IV, No. 5 [1939], 675–76).

11 Here, at all events, is a sample of Scheler's excogitations: the thinking of the lower classes, he says, is mechanistic, realistic, materialistic, pragmatic, inductive, empirical and oriented toward the future; while the thinking of the upper classes is, in precise antithesis, teleological, idealistic, spiritualistic, intellectualistic, aprioristic, rationalistic, and oriented toward the past (in *Die Wissensformen und die Gesellschaft* [Leipzig: Der Neue Geist Verlag, 1926], pp. 204–5).

4

FRANK E. HARTUNG

Problems of the Sociology of Knowledge

I

THE SOCIOLOGY OF knowledge can most generally be defined as the discipline devoted to the social origins of thought. It is an analysis concerned with specifying the existential basis of thought, and with establishing the relationship obtained between mental structures, or thought, and that existential basis. Some very interesting and difficult problems arise from this conception of the sociology of knowledge. Perhaps the most obvious of these is whether or not a sociology of knowledge, as here conceived, is theoretically possible. This is a problem I do not intend to deal with at present because limitations of time prevent me from doing even partial justice to it.

There are perhaps two other major problems of this discipline. First, there is the problem of specifying the locus of the existential basis of thought. This involves at least three subsidiary problems, namely, an analysis of (*a*) the concept "existential basis of thought"; (*b*) of the structure and dynamics of society; (*c*) and of the concept "thought." Secondly, there is the problem of specifying the way in which thought is related to its alleged existential basis. This problem divides into (*a*) the imputation of interests or motives to social classes and to individual members of these classes; and (*b*) the possibility of achieving valid knowledge.

This paper is devoted for the most part to a discussion of Karl Mannheim's sociology of knowledge. Any kind of complete discussion of the sub-

Paper presented to the meeting sponsored jointly by the American Association for the Advancement of Science, the Philosophy of Science Association, and the American Philosophical Association, New York, December 29, 1949. First published in *Philosophy Of Science*, XIX (January, 1952), 17–32. Copyright © 1952, The Williams and Wilkins Co., Baltimore, Md., 21202, U.S.A. Reprinted with permission.

ject would also have to include an analysis of the works of Marx and Engels. Max Scheler, Pitirim Sorokin, George Lukács, Émile Durkheim, Leslie A. White, Friedrich Nietzsche, and Vilfredo Pareto. Of these, only Mannheim, Scheler, and Lukács have published under the specific heading of the sociology of knowledge. Mannheim's work is by far the best known in English and has had the most influence among American social scientists, perhaps because his *Ideology and Utopia* has been translated into English. Furthermore, this paper will be concerned with an aspect of Mannheim's work that has been largely neglected in the literature up to this time. Primary emphasis is laid upon the irrationalism of his position and upon one of his fundamental concepts, that of the collective unconscious. It has seemed necessary to stress these in order to correct what appears to be the usual estimate of Mannheim, namely, that his work constitutes a genuine sociological analysis of the relationship obtaining between thought and society. It is to this extent an admittedly partial, but nevertheless accurate, interpretation of *Ideology and Utopia*.

II

The existential basis of thought and mental structures appears to be ubiquitous in the social structure and in the stimuli to which people respond. It is important to note that the concern is with "people's" thought, and not simply "scientists'" thought. Mannheim, for instance, alleges that what can be learned by analyzing philosophical, mathematical, and scientific types of thought is not directly transferable to other spheres of life. He is concerned with the presumably broader problem of "how men actually think." [2, p. 1]*

The existential basis of thought has been held to include the impulsive and societal factors that influence thought, the private purposes that motivate the individual in his thought, and the role and status of the person in the social structure. An inventory of these irrational and non-rational aspects of thought would include the "real" factors of *race* and kinship, the conditions of political *power*, geographical and *geopolitical* conditions, the quantity and *quality* of the population, and the *economy* or the "economic factors" of a society. Also included would be affective or emotional items such as sentiments and feelings, and impulses both conscious and unconscious. It would also include all those institutional influences that exercise a constraint on the person's thinking, as well as the relations between such institutions as science, religion, the state, and economic enterprise, that could affect the development of knowledge. The inventory of private purposes would include all

* Numbers in brackets refer to References at the end of this chapter.—Eds.

the wishes or drives that motivate a person; classifications of them abound in psychology. The role and status of the person include all the parts he plays in different groups and the position he holds in these groups. For the sociology of knowledge, *class* is the most important of the groups to which one belongs or with which one identifies oneself.

The existential basis of thought, then, appears to include all stimuli to thought that are not referable to the logical or immanent development of thought. Mannheim claims that he has, in his theory of ideology, greatly improved upon Marx. But he still bases his analysis of the structure and dynamics of society on the Marxian notion that ideas and institutions arise upon the "real" foundations of the "modes" and "relations" of production. He still holds to the statement that

> In the social production which men carry on they enter into definite relations that are indispensable and independent of their will; these relations of production correspond to a definite stage of development of their material powers of production. The sum total of these relations of production constitutes the economic structure of society—the real foundation on which rise legal and political superstructures and to which correspond definite forms of social consciousness. The mode of production in material life determines the general character of the social, political and spiritual processes of life. It is not the consciousness of men that determines their existence, but, on the contrary, their social existence determines their consciousness ... [3, p. 11]

The sociology of knowledge analysis of the structure and dynamics of society raises the problem as to how the existential determination of thought is to be demonstrated. There is some vagueness in *Ideology and Utopia* as to just what Mannheim means by the concept of the existential determination of knowledge. Sometimes he appears to be concerned with what has been sociologically commonplace for about fifty years—at least in this country. At other times he goes to the opposite extreme and claims that even the principles of epistemology must be revised in light of the situational determination of thought. The claim for the existential determination of thought thus asserts either too little or too much. As an example of the sociological commonplace, Mannheim asserts that the "significant element" in the sociology of knowledge "is the discovery that political thought is integrally related to social life." [2, p. 112] Or, "According to this view human thought arises, and operates, not in a social vacuum but in a definite social milieu." [2, p. 71] It is unlikely that many people would question these assertions, and others of a like nature, which frequently appear in *Ideology and Utopia*.

Such observations are insufficient warrant to claim that sociology of knowledge is a "key" discipline capable of reforming science and epistemology. Mannheim claims a greater mission for his system, however, than this restatement of the obvious. He says, for instance, that its "problem is to show how, in the whole history of thought, certain intellectual standpoints are connected with certain forms of experience, and to trace the intimate interrelation between the two in the course of social and intellectual change." [2, p. 72]

Near the end of his work, Mannheim says that as a theory the sociology of knowledge attempts to analyze the relationship between knowledge and existence, and that as a historical-sociological method of research it seeks to trace the forms that this relationship has taken in the intellectual history of man. He tries to establish his position inductively and empirically, as follows:

> The existential determination of thought may be regarded as a demonstrated fact in those realms of thought in which we can show (*a*) that the process of knowing does not actually develop historically in accordance with immanent laws, that it does not follow only from the "nature of things" or from "pure logical possibilities" . . . [but] On the contrary . . . is influenced in many decisive points by extra-theoretical factors of the most diverse sort . . . called . . . existential factors. This existential determination of thought will also have to be regarded as a fact (*b*) if the influence of these existential factors on the concrete content of knowledge is of more than mere peripheral importance, if they are relevant not only to the genesis of ideas, but penetrate into their forms and content and if, furthermore, they decisively determine the scope and intensity of our experience and observation, i.e., . . . the perspective of the subject. [2, pp. 239–40].

A second glance at this statement of the empirical test of existential determination shows that the test raises more problems than it answers. We are left wholly in the dark as to what a "decisive point" is in the history of knowledge. Then, too, we are not told how to recognize those existential factors of "more than peripheral significance" from those of less. And, how are we to know if these existential factors *are* relevant to the genesis of an idea, and if they do in fact penetrate into both the form and content of an idea and the thought "perspective" of the observer?

How does Mannheim develop his first condition, namely, that social processes influence the process of knowledge? He devotes a large part of three pages [2, pp. 240–43] to the sociologically obvious proposition that every problem involves some previous experience, that the observer selects from among the "multiplicity of data," and that previous trends are significant in the treatment of the problem. Pleading that it is impossible to list "all the manifold social processes" that shape and condition our theories, he gives a few illustrations and says that even in the case of these examples he "shall have to leave the detailed proof to the instances cited in the index and bibliography"! [2, p. 241]

Mannheim makes it fairly clear that in his position the "living forces and actual attitudes" which underlie and determine ideas and knowledge are believed to be irrational. In his second condition of the existential determination of thought Mannheim takes an *ad hominem* position in reference to the validity of a proposition. In answering the question, do existential factors merely condition the factual development of ideas or do they penetrate into the "perspective" of concrete assertions, he says that "The historical and social genesis of an idea would only be irrelevant to its ultimate validity if the temporal and social conditions of its emergence had no effect on its content and form." [2, p. 243]

Mannheim is saying here that it is relevant and necessary to establish *who* asserts a proposition if we wish to judge if that proposition is true or false. The implication of his sociology seems at this point to be a chaotic kind of relativism, in which there are as many truths as there are perspectives of observers.

Perhaps it would be well at this point to define Mannheim's concept of "perspective." According to him, the sociology of knowledge does not criticize thought on the level of the propositions themselves. Rather, it judges them according to the "perspective" of the thinker, a term which means the subject's whole mode of conceiving things as determined by his historical and social setting. [2, p. 239] Perspective thus has reference to qualitative elements in the structure of thought that necessarily must be overlooked by a formal logic, and that are elements responsible for the fact that two people, applying the same formal-logical rules to the same object, may arrive at different judgments about that object. [2, p. 244] A person's perspective, then consists of the irrational "living forces and actual attitudes" that underlie and determine ideas. These arise out of the collective unconscious purposes of the group, purposes which underlie the thought of the person, and in the prescribed outlook of which he merely participates. [2, p. 241]

Even if Mannheim's formulation of the irrational determination of knowledge be granted, there is a twofold rational aspect to this existential basis. First, some particular group needs or wants or uses the knowledge that the intellectual obtains on the basis of his collective unconscious motivations (i.e., his existential basis). This application of knowledge would certainly seem to entail some rational behavior. Secondly, every piece of research requires persons motivated by the desire to know and psychologically able to inhibit "drives" or "needs" which are irrelevant to scientific thinking. [5, pp. 266–67]

Mannheim adduces seven criteria by means of which one may attempt to ascertain empirically the extent to which a given theoretical position has been conditioned by existential influences. If his epistemological speculations are ignored, I think it will be found that this particular aspect of his position would be very fruitful in research. The criteria for the determination of extra-theoretical influences are (*1*) analysis of the meaning of the concepts used; (*2*) the phenomenon of the counter-concept; (*3*) the absence of certain concepts; (*4*) the structure of the categorial apparatus; (*5*) dominant models of thought; (*6*) level of abstraction; and (*7*) the ontology that is presupposed. [2, pp. 244–50]

Mannheim's position can reasonably be described, I think, as one which leads to the apotheosis of the unconscious and the devaluation of reason. In his discussion of "The Political and Social Determinants of Knowledge" he maintains that "impulsive, irrational factors . . . furnish the real basis for the further development of state and society." [2, p. 106] He devalues reason in his argument that in the development of philosophy and mathematics, contemplation was "taken over" from the seer, as being the prophet's ideal of the "mystic vision." [2, p. 265] Research occurs, he maintains, in a context colored by "collective-unconscious, volitional impulses." [2, p. 4] He asserts that thought requires an "emotional-unconscious undercurrent to assure the continuous orientations for knowledge in group life." Knowing "presupposes a community of knowing which grows primarily out of a community of experiencing prepared for in the subconscious." [2, p. 28] He devotes eighteen pages to a discussion of the topic, "Control of the Collective Unconscious as a Problem of Our Age." [2, pp. 20–48]

In addition to the problems raised in the orthodox psychoanalytic concept of the unconscious, Mannheim raises others for himself by his concept of the collective unconscious, which is attributed to groups. The collective unconscious of a group "obscures the real condition of society both to itself and to others and thereby stabilizes it." This notion of the collective unconscious is implicit, he says, in his concepts of ideology and utopia: the collective unconscious makes it impossible for either the conservative or the progressive to analyze society. "Their thought," he says, "is never a diagnosis of the situation." [2, p. 36] In the political conflicts of the modern historical period, each party has succeeded in "unmasking," in "laying bare" the collective unconscious of its opponent. Today this unmasking has proceeded to such an extent that it has "destroyed . . . man's confidence in thought in general. . . . There is nothing of the accidental but rather more of the inevitable in the fact that more and more people took flight into skepticism and irrationalism." [2, p. 37] In reference to this collective unconscious, Mannheim offers another definition of the sociology of knowledge: it is the systematization of the doubt which is to be found in social life as a vague insecurity and uncertainty. It has three main concerns: First, the further unmasking of the collective unconscious motivations that determine thought; secondly, the rewriting of intellectual history in terms of the collective unconscious; and thirdly, the revision of epistemology, which up to the present has not taken into account this influence on thought.

Mannheim seems to be restating Hume's proposition that reason is and ought only to be the slave of the passions. Behavior—and Mannheim is greatly concerned with social class behavior—has as its objective a selfish shift in security, and reason has a function only in reference in the unconsciously motivated security needs of a given class. In his analysis of the relation between ideas and social reality, reason simply cannot advance any claims to universal or even interclass validity, because such a claim would merely serve the political function of helping to maintain a given class in power, and of helping to prevent a lower class from attaining power. A direct implication of his position seems to be that there are only class reason, class reasoning, and class truth. [2, pp. 240–41; 248]

Mannheim has attempted to sociologize psychoanalysis and has encountered in an insuperable form all the difficulties involved in a literal translation of individualistic psychological terms into the collective terms of sociology. In his survey of the history of the sociology of knowledge, Mannheim is emphatic in stressing that its emergence as a separate discipline is due to the work of men who are notorious for their insistence upon irrationalism in thought and action: Karl Marx, Friedrich Nietzsche, Vilfredo Pareto, and Sigmund Freud. Mannheim says that "From Nietzsche the lines of development led to the Freudian and Paretian theories of human impulses and to the methods developed by them for viewing human thought as distortions and as products of instinctive mechanisms." [2, p. 279] I would like now to consider the content of the thought that Mannheim insists is the collective-unconscious expression of class needs and insecurity.

Considerable attention is devoted by Mannheim to discussing the prospects of a scientific politics, to social movements and the philosophy of history, to political parties and class conflict. These discussions and examples raise a fundamental question about the sociology of knowledge, namely, the extent to which the proposition of the collective unconscious determination of thought is to be applied to thought. When he talks about the sociology of knowledge, is *all* knowledge to be included? Mannheim does not attempt any definition of thought and knowledge. His references to mathematics and physical science, and his insistence upon reforming epistemology indicate, I think, that he is constantly troubled with the meaning of "knowledge" in his system. Sometimes he uses "knowledge" so broadly as to seem to mean the total sum of information conserved by man, from the prehistorical or prescientific prophet to the present-day mathematical physicist. Then he qualifies his position so as to include only "most of the domains of knowledge." [2, p. 243] But he believes that the "categories" of thought (time and space?) have their origin below consciousness. [2, p. 246] Whereas in one place he seems to exempt mathematics from collective unconscious determination [2, p. 243], in another place he takes issue with the exponents of classical logic and philosophy who, he complains, are accustomed to maintain that the genesis of an idea is immaterial so far as its validity is concerned. [2, p. 22]

Enough has been said of Mannheim's conception of "thought" and "knowledge" to indicate a considerable confusion on his part in relation to these concepts. I think that if Mannheim had excluded folklore, and ethical, religious, and political beliefs and rationalizations from his category of knowledge, his entire analysis of the relation of thought to social reality should have been quite different. For one thing, he would not have been so likely to assume that the physical and social sciences are different in kind, in that the latter are throughout subject to collective unconscious determinations, while the former are free from them. This assumption of a difference of this kind too often turns out to be an apology and an excuse for faulty logic, indifferent research, and lack of status on the part of social science.

If I may turn Mannheim's analysis upon himself, I would say that he was logically precluded from making an analysis of scientific thought, because he was actually making a plea for the employment of the intellectual, who had but little place in strife-torn Germany between the wars except as he attached himself to some action group. [See: "The Contemporary Predicament of Thought," "The Origin of the Modern . . . Points of View," and "Control of the Collective Unconscious as a Problem of Our Age" (2, pp. 5–48).] Could *Ideology and Utopia* have been written anywhere save in Germany between 1919 and 1933?

III

We may now consider a second major problem of the sociology of knowledge. This is the problem of specifying the way in which thought or knowledge is causally related to its alleged existential basis. It seems to me that the relation of thought to its collective unconscious basis is the very core of Mannheim's sociology of knowledge. In his proposition that it is the impulsive, irrational factors which furnish the *real* basis for the further development of state and society [2, p. 106], Mannheim certainly implies a theory of social causation. And yet he never grapples with this problem or with his implied theory in a direct and systematic fashion. I want to consider two aspects of this problem: first, the imputation of interests or motives to social classes and to individual members of these classes; and secondly, the possibility of valid knowledge in relation to the collective unconscious basis of knowledge.

It may be recalled that Leslie A. White has asserted that every technology has a philosophy or ideology proper to it. [6, pp. 363–93] The problem of knowing when a philosophy or ideology is a proper one would be simplified if it could be assumed that propriety is directly and invariably associated with the class position of a spokesman. It is ridiculously easy to show that such an assumption cannot logically be made, even though it is held in the sociology of knowledge that social class is the primary determinant of a philosophy or ideology. The problem of imputing motives and class position to a person, and interests and philosophy to a class, has harassed every student whose position on this matter is derived from Marxism. It is held in the sociology of knowledge that a philosophy or ideology "corresponds" to a class position, even though uttered by a person not a member of that class. Marx and Engels struggled with the problem of imputation many times. The imputation of motives and interests on a class basis is troublesome because of the lack of a consistent relationship between the class membership of the spokesman of a given position, and the social class whose interests are allegedly expressed by that given position. Mannheim follows Marx in imputing interests to a class and motives to the individual.

Marx's analysis raises very specifically the question of what the criteria are, on the basis of which any imputation is to be made. A man does not always remain in the class into which he was born; if he leaves this class, his allegiance may remain with his former class; if he remains in the class, he may identify himself with another class. The trade-union and socialist movements themselves are notorious in this respect. I suppose everyone knows that Marx was a bourgeois intellectual, while Friedrich Engels, his co-worker of decades, was a capitalist, and Lenin, perhaps the greatest revolutionist, was by birth a member of the Russian minor nobility. Still, there is general agreement, I suppose, that the writings of these men comprise a systematic statement of the proletarian ideology or philosophy. And anyone who has tried to organize a trade union—especially among the white-collar and professional workers, who presumably would be more enlightened and aware of their interests than manual workers—knows how stubbornly backward these people can be in continuing to identify with their employer instead of with their fellow workers. And no light is shed on this problem when the members of a certain political party describe themselves as "the advanced section of the working class." We still want to know how they came to be "advanced" while the overwhelming majority of workers are still "backward." And it is a notorious fact that periodically some members of this "advanced section" mistake their class interests and are more or less politely purged. Who is to judge in such a case who was right in the estimate of class interest, the purged or the purgers? It is of no assistance in solving the problem of imputation to say, as Marx did in his *Eighteenth Brumaire* [4, pp. 58–59], that the lower classes failed to transcend their limitations; or as he said in the *Communist Manifesto*, that some upper class members do transcend their material limitations. We want to know why some do and some don't, and what the conditions are that are related to these successes and failures. If some bourgeois have a proletarian philosophy or ideology, and some proletarians have a bourgeois philosophy or ideology, what becomes of the imputation of interests and motives?

Mannheim in several places deals partially with the problem of imputation. He has the notion of an ideal-type class ideology. It is a theory which holds that the total ideology of a class is implicit in the single judgments of the individual members of a given class. The ideology of class could not come into being except through the thought of individuals because, he says, every psychic phenomenon is basically individual. But the "inner structure" of a class ideology, he says,

> is not to be found in a mere integration of these individual experiences . . . Every individual participates only in certain fragments of this thought-system, the totality of which is not in the least a mere sum of these fragmentary individual experiences. As a totality the thought-system is integrated systematically, and is no mere casual jumble of fragmentary experiences of discrete members of the group. . . . As soon as the total conception of ideology is used, we attempt to reconstruct the whole outlook of a social group, and neither the concrete individuals nor the abstract sum of them can legitimately be considered as bearers of this ideological thought system as a whole. The aim of the analysis on this level is the reconstruction of the systematic theoretical basis underlying the single judgments of the individual. [2, p. 52]

In a later discussion of the problem of imputation, Mannheim speaks of two "levels" of imputation. His first level (*Sinngemässe Zurechnung*) "deals with general problems of interpretation. It reconstructs integral styles of thought and perspectives, tracing single expressions and records of thought which appear to be related back to a central *Weltanschauung* which they express." This does not completely solve the problem of imputation, because he says that there is the further question as to "whether this explicit reference to a central outlook which proceeds purely on an intellectual level actually corresponds to the facts." [2, p. 276] The second level of imputation (*Faktizitatszurechnung*) operates with the ideal types constructed on the first level, and attempts to ascertain the extent to which the given groups have in fact thought as they are alleged to have thought, and also, "in what measure, in individual cases, these ideal-types were actually realized in their thinking." [2, p. 277] Mannheim then claims that this method offers the "maximum reliability" in the reconstruction of intellectual history because the ideal-type method "analyzes into its elements what at first was merely a summary impression of the course of intellectual history, and by reducing this impression to explicit criteria makes possible a reconstruction of reality." [2, p. 277]

When the "structure and tendencies" of a style of thought have thus been specified there arises "the task of their sociological imputation." This task involves the attempt to explain the "forms and variations" of a given thought system by seeking

> to derive them firstly from the composition of the groups and strata which express themselves in that mode of thought. And, secondly, we seek to explain the impulse and the direction of development (of a given thought-system) through the structural situation and the changes it undergoes within a larger, historically conditioned whole . . . and through the constantly varying problems raised by the changing structure. [2, pp. 277–78]

Mannheim's position on imputation at once raises a number of questions. First, he asserts the existence of an integrated thought system which, as a totality, is carried neither by concrete individuals nor by the group of which these individuals are members! But one asks, then, how could and where does such a thought system exist? Secondly, Mannheim says that "every" individual participates only in "certain fragments of this thought system." Not only do we again ask, where does this thought system exist in such fashion that it can be partially participated in; we also raise a further question about Mannheim's conception of the ideal type. On the one hand he makes it quite clear that the ideal type exists as a construction of the researcher, and makes no claim to its existence beyond this. And on the other hand, he wants to use this intellectual fiction to reconstruct reality. Thirdly, there is the question as to how this ideology is related to "the single judgments of the individual" if it has no existence save in the mind of the investigator. It can hardly be said to "underlie" the single judgments of every individual if it exists neither in the mind of the individual nor in the mind of the group. And fourth, these critical remarks apply to one of Mannheim's most important concepts—the collective unconscious, because this unconscious is an integral aspect of a total ideology or thought system. Is not Mannheim saying that the collective unconscious, which is regarded by him as the real factor behind further social development, is his own creation and does not exist in either the mind of the individual or in the mind of his group?

Mannheim is apparently aware of his failure to demonstrate his fundamental proposition of the "existential determination of knowledge" (*Seinsverbundhenhit des Wissens*), because he says that: "Here we do not mean by 'determination' a mechanical cause-and-effect sequence: we leave the meaning of 'determination' open, and only empirical investigation will show us how strict is the correlation between life-situation and thought-process, or what scope exists for variations in the correlation." [2, p. 239, n. 1]

In addition to leaving open the meaning of one of his fundamental propositions, he admits the obscurity of his position in two other ways. First, instead of developing criteria by means of which the existential determination of knowledge can be ascertained, he says that this existential determination is immediately apprehended, through understanding: "by use of the technique of understanding, the reciprocal functional interpenetration of psychic experiences and social situations becomes immediately intelligible." [2, p. 40]

Mannheim's term "understanding" is used in a context which makes it just about the equivalent of sympathy or intuition in American usage. The second (implied) admission of the nebulous character of his demonstration of the existential determination of thought is his substitution of an annoying phrase for an empirical or experimental attempt at demonstration. He uses variations of the phrases "it was no accident" and "it was in accord with" just at those places in which some evidence of a causal relation between thought and existential determination is needed. Here are examples from *Ideology and Utopia* of these "no accident" and "in accord with" phrases:

> It is by no means an accident that the problem of the social and activitistic roots of thinking has emerged in our generation. [p. 5]

. . . it is obviously no accident that the sociological standpoint was added to the others only at a relatively advanced date. Nor is it by chance that . . . [p. 29]

It was in accord with the needs of an industrial society and of [certain] intellectual strata for them to base their collective action . . . on a rationally justifiable system of ideas. [p. 33]

It is never an accident when a certain theory, wholly or in part, fails to develop beyond a given stage of relative abstractness and offers resistance to further tendencies toward becoming more concrete . . . [p. 248]

It is no accident that Romanticism was the first to take up those tendencies in thought which showed a renewed emphasis on the specific cognitive value of qualitative knowledge of the whole. [p. 148]

. . . it is no accident that today the *Gestalt* theory of perception, and the theories of morphology and characterology, etc., which constitute a scientific and methodological counterattack against positivistic methodology, are coming to the fore in an atmosphere which derives its *Weltanschauung* and political outlook from neo-romanticism. [p. 148]

I counted twenty-one of these "accidental" passages, and this is by no means an exhaustive count. It is no accident that Mannheim's discussions of his fundamental proposition concerning the existential determination of thought are so vague, because he has developed no criteria by means of which a causal relation between thought and its existential basis can be recognized.

In spite of the fact that Mannheim has failed to establish his postulated relation between thought and the collective unconscious, he frequently offers ideological interpretations of thought. In addition, he insists a number of times that epistemology must be reformed in such a way that *who* asserts a proposition will be considered relevant to the validity of the proposition. In expounding this position he both makes and defends *ad hominem* attacks. His concept of the collective unconscious raises the question as to whether any group is able to achieve valid knowledge in the sense of achieving objective analysis. This question he attempts to answer by means of his conception of the intelligentsia. I am going to consider briefly his commitment to the genetic fallacy, his program for the revision of epistemology, and his conception of the intellectual. His treatment of the problem of the possibility of valid knowledge implies, I think, a basic self-contradiction in his system: if Mannheim's analysis is correct, then it is incorrect!

The genetic fallacy, of course, occurs when the truth or falsity of a proposition is made dependent on its source. In his "Preliminary Approach to the Problem of Sociology of Knowledge," written especially for the American edition of his work, Mannheim discusses Socrates' intellectual development and argues that it is necessary to investigate the person who asserts a proposition, if we want to understand what he is saying. Later [2, p. 41–42], he asserts that the "principal propositions of the social sciences," being "closely connected with the evaluations and unconscious strivings of the observer," require knowledge of those who assert them if the propositions are to be understood. He emphasizes an *ad hominem* approach in his definition of "particular" and "total" ideology. In his ideological approach, he says, there is no reliance "solely on what is actually said by the opponent in order to reach an understanding of his real meaning and intention." Ideological analysis, he continues, "falls back on the subject, whether individual or group, proceeding to an understanding of what is said by the indirect method of analyzing the social conditions of the individual or his group." [2. p. 50] Some contemporary historians, he says, use this approach, and adds that "This mode of thought will always strive . . . to cast doubt upon the integrity of the adversary and to deprecate his motives." [2, p. 56] Despite this admission, Mannheim still defends the method of attacking the opponent's person in order to achieve "genuine meaning":

> This procedure, nevertheless, has positive value as long as in a given case we are interested in discovering the genuine meaning of a statement that lies concealed behind a camouflage of words. This "debunking" tendency in the thought of our time has become very marked. And even though in wide circles this trait is considered undignified and disrespectful . . . this intellectual position is forced upon us in an era of transition like our own . . . [2, p. 56–57]

Mannheim is guilty of the genetic fallacy in his approach to the problem of validity. He contends that the historical and social genesis of an idea would only be irrelevant to its validity if these had no effect on its content and form. [2, p. 243] Ideological analysis is relevant in determining the truth of a statement. He then develops an ideological attack upon those who insist on retaining the viewpoint that *who* asserts a proposition is irrelevant to its validity or truth content. He hurls epithets at the latter position, calling it "this theory of self-sufficiency, this theory of self-preservation" [2, p. 258], and then continues with an *ad hominem* attack by saying that it:

> serves no other purpose than that of a bulwark for a certain type of academic epistemology which, in its last stages, is attempting to preserve

itself from a collapse which might result from a more developed empiricism. The holders of this older view overlook the fact that they are thereby perpetuating not epistemology as such and preserving it from revision at the hands of the individual sciences, but rather merely one specific kind of epistemology . . . [2, p. 258]

Considering Mannheim's insistence on the necessity of making personal attacks upon one's opponents, it is quite easy to predict what his position on epistemology is likely to be. It will be sufficient, I think, to show briefly that he insists throughout his work that epistemology must be revised so that it will be in accordance with his type of the sociology of knowledge. Near the beginning of his book he disagrees with those logicians and philosophers who insist that who said what, and under what social conditions, are matters immaterial to the validity of propositions. [2, p. 22]

Mannheim contends, also, that an investigator using the sociology of knowledge approach has an advantage over others, in that the sociologist of knowledge "will no longer be inclined to raise the question as to which of the contending parties has truth on its side." He then continues, saying that: "The modern investigator can answer, if he is accused of evading the problem of what is truth, that the indirect approach to truth through social history will in the end be more fruitful than a direct logical attack." [2, p. 75]

It is not only a more or less gratuitous assumption upon his part that his approach will "in the end" be more fruitful, but it also sounds suspiciously like a rationalization for "the profound skepticism toward science and especially cultural sciences" which he says his sociology of knowledge approach engenders. [2, p. 123]

In the latter part of *Ideology and Utopia*, Mannheim has an extended discussion of what he regards as the "Epistemological Consequences of the Sociology of Knowledge." [pp. 256–78] He is concerned with the question of what the sociology of knowledge can tell us about the validity of an assertion that we would not know if we had not been able to relate it to the standpoint of the assertor. Have we, in other words, said anything about the truth or falsity of a statement when we have shown that it is to be imputed to a Democrat, a Republican, a capitalist, a Communist, a unionist, a Protestant, or a Romanist? His position can perhaps best be summarized by indicating his choice of three possible answers to this question.

Mannheim rejects the first answer, which is to the effect that the validity of an assertion is denied completely when its structural relationship to a given social situation has been shown. This answer, he says, would annihilate the validity of all assertions.

The second possible answer is also rejected: the imputations which the sociology of knowledge establishes between a statement and its assertor tell us nothing concerning the truth value of the assertion, because the manner in which a proposition originates does not affect its validity. Whether a statement, for example, is made by a liberal or by a conservative in and of itself gives no indication of its correctness [2, p. 254]

Mannheim accepts a third possible way of judging the truth value of assertions, an alternative that he claims represents some kind of middle position between the first two. Every complete sociological analysis of knowledge delimits, he says, in both content and structure, the view to be analyzed. This analysis attempts not only to establish the influence of an existential determination of knowledge, but at the same time it tries to particularize the scope and the extent of the validity of this knowledge. [2, p. 255] The existential determination of knowledge "to say the least, furnishes an obstacle to the construction of a sphere of validity in which the criteria of truth are independent of origins." [2, p. 258] He also says that: "The function of the findings of the sociology of knowledge lies somewhere in a fashion hitherto not clearly understood, between irrelevance to the establishment of truth on the one hand, and entire adequacy for determining truth on the other." [2, p. 256]

I can only comment that the relevance of the existential determination of knowledge to truth or truth value is still not clearly understood, if for no other reason than that Mannheim has completely failed to show how the validity of a proposition is even partially dependent upon the social situation of the one who asserted it.

Although the sociology of knowledge derogates the intellect, Mannheim accords the intellectual a major position in his system. He defines the intelligentsia as being those social groups in every society "whose special task it is to provide an interpretation of the world for that society." [2, p. 9] He maintains that only the free-floating intellectual (*freischwebende Intelligenz*) is able to overcome the handicap of ideology. He discusses this proposition under the heading of "The Sociological Problem of the 'Intelligentsia.'" [2, pp. 136–46] The intellectuals, according to him, are an unanchored, relatively classless stratum of society. Thus they stand above the interests and objectives of the other, conflicting strata. Because intellectuals are in competition with each other, they adopted in an every-increasing fashion the most various modes of thought available in society, "and played them off against one another." [2, p. 11] They did this because they had to compete for the favor of the public; in this competitive situation the intellectual's illusion that there is only one way of thinking disappeared. Although individual intellectuals are characterized by "endless wavering" and the "lack of conviction," as a group intellectuals are distinguished by the ability to attach themselves to any class to which they originally did not belong, because they can adapt themselves to any situation. [2, p. 141]

Incidentally, it may be remarked that Mannheim's proposition that the intellectual has no fixed convictions and can hire himself out to anyone seems to contradict another fundamental proposition of his, namely, that a given position in the social structure carries with it a definite probability that he who occupies it will think in a certain way.

It is because of their free-floating quality that intellectuals can uncover the collective-unconscious and other hidden motivations that stimulate other groups and persons enmeshed in their respective class positions. The free-floating intellectual is, in this view, therefore the only one who can achieve objectivity in analysis, and consequently the only one to whom valid knowledge is possible. The free-floating intellectual thus performs a kind of social analysis and social therapy, it is alleged.

This view undoubtedly enjoys a certain prestige today. One reason for this may be the ease with which it allows one to destroy his opponent through *ad hominem* and *ad captandum* attack. If one assumes the validity of the concept of the free-floating intellectual, it is only necessary to unmask the historical, or economic, or class, or religious, or the like "roots" of the other's argument in order to destroy its validity and render it practically meaningless. There could be no great objection to this if it were confined to passing the time on rainy Sunday afternoons. The basic objection to it is that it destroys any possible rational basis for discussion of an issue, making it resolvable ultimately only through the use of physical force.

Mannheim has an ideological explanation to account for logical objections to his sociology of knowledge. He asserts that the social position of the thinker is "significant" in explaining his "resistance" to the sociology of knowledge. The resistance is due "to a subconscious reluctance to think out the implications of a concretely formulated insight to a point where the theoretical formulations latent in it would be clear enough to have a disquieting effect on one's own position." [2, p. 249]

Mannheim does not wish in any way, he says, to question the legitimacy of formal (general?) sociology as a possible type of sociology. But he also says that formal sociology

is unconsciously guided by motives similar to those which prevented its historical forerunner, the bourgeois-liberal mode of thought, from ever getting beyond an abstract and generalizing mode of observation in its theory. It shies away from dealing historically, concretely, and individually with the problems of society for fear that its own inner antagonisms, for instance the antagonisms of capitalism itself, might become visible. [2, pp. 249-50]

I will not comment on Mannheim's reification of sociology; it may be simply a function of language. But it should be indicated that in this ideological destruction of an opponent's position, he is showing how thoroughly he has studied one of his mentors, Sigmund Freud. There is a remarkable similarity between the way in which both Mannheim and Freud meet the problem of logical objections to their positions. In discussing "One of the Difficulties of Psychoanalysis," Freud begins by saying that:

it is not an intellectual difficulty that I am thinking of, not anything that makes psychoanalysis hard for the hearer or reader to understand, but an affective one—something that alienates the feelings of those who come into contact with it, so that they become less inclined to believe in it or take an interest in it. As may be observed, the two kinds of difficulty amount to the same thing. [1, p. 347]

Clyde Kluckhohn, following Freud, has offered the same kind of *ad hominem* explanation in accounting for the resistance of anthropologists to psychoanalysis that Mannheim gave in accounting for the resistance of sociologists to the sociology of knowledge. Kluckhohn says that:

The conventional American anthropologist dismissed Freud's anthropology as bad and his conclusions as worthless. With regrettable but familiar illogic, psychoanalytic method and theory were therewith rejected. To some degree, this may be merely the rationalization covering a deeper psychological factor. Perhaps the tendency to ignore or to be resistive to psychiatry springs from a temperamental selectivity of the anthropological occupation. Anthropology as it was conceived (and still is) by many in this country was a refuge for those who were impelled by inner, largely unconscious, needs to escape from the personal or "to crawl back into the womb of the cultural past." [7, p. 594]

Kluckhohn asks of A. L. Kroeber, an anthropologist who has continued to be an anthropologist, the following question: "The question can be fairly put: was Kroeber's relentless pursuit of 'objective' and 'historical' enquiries and his avoidance of research into the genesis and functioning of personalities . . . based upon deep-seated, unconscious factors, or was it primarily the submission to an occupational psychosis of his profession?" [7, pp. 596-97]

In a discussion concerning the validity of a psychoanalytic interpretation, the psychoanalyst can destroy his opponent's position by indicating that the objections are due to some personality need which causes him to reject psychoanalysis. However, in so arguing, he destroys the validity of his own psychoanalytic position. Because, if one man's objection to psychoanalysis is due to some unconscious motivation that determines his *rejection* of it, then it must be concluded that the *acceptance* of psychoanalysis is likewise determined by an unconscious motivation beyond the control of the psychoanalytic devotee. Such an approach to psychoanalysis precludes the establishing of a scientific basis for it. This is also true of the sociology of knowledge. Let us for the moment assume the correctness of Mannheim's theory of ideology and of the existential determination of thought. This theory asserts it to be a part of every total ideology that those who hold it believe their viewpoint to be free of bias, and that only they as individuals are capable of objectivity. A necessary conclusion from this is that every group holding an ideology must be biased in its viewpoint, and its individual members unconsciously deceived by their ideology into holding themselves to be objective and their analyses to be correct.

Indeed, if Mannheim's theory of total ideology is correct, then it must be concluded that his analysis of the intellectual, as well as his theory of the existential determination of thought, are incorrect. This conclusion must be reached because the theory of total ideology is simply the ideological expression of the interests of the class of free-floating intellectuals. This is a class whose ideology has unconsciously deceived it into "the quest for the fulfillment of their mission as the predestined advocate of the intellectual interests of the whole." [2, p. 140]

Mannheim is caught in the self-contradiction inherent in every form of anti-intellectualism, such as racialism, instinctivism, and psychoanalysis. As the conclusion of highly rational behavior—the analysis of society and thought as he sees it—he claims that man is primarily irrational!

REFERENCES

1 FREUD, SIGMUND. "One of the Difficulties of Psychoanalysis." *Collected Papers*. London: The Hogarth Press, 1948 printing. IV, 347–56.

2 MANNHEIM, KARL. *Ideology and Utopia: An Introduction to the Sociology of Knowledge.* With a preface by Louis Wirth. Translated by Louis Wirth and Edward Shils. New York: Harcourt, Brace & Co., 1936.

3 MARX, KARL. *A Contribution to the Critique of Political Economy*. Translated by N. I. Stone. Chicago: C. H. Kerr and Co., 1904.

4 MARX, KARL. *The Eighteenth Brumaire of Louis Bonaparte*. Translated by Eden and Cedar Paul. New York, International Publishers, 1926.

5 SPEIER, HANS. "The Social Determination of Ideas," pp. 263–81, above.

6 WHITE, LESLIE A. *The Science of Culture*. New York: Farrar, Straus & Co., 1949.

7 American Psychiatric Association. *One Hundred Years of American Psychiatry*. New York: Columbia University Press, 1949.

THE CONTRIBUTORS

BERT N. ADAMS is Assistant Professor of Sociology at the University of Wisconsin.

FRANCIS BACON (1561–1626), the English philosopher, was one of the earliest publicists for modern science. In *Novum Organum* he urged that scientists become aware of their prejudices and the "idols" that controlled their minds.

EMIL BEND is a Research Scientist with American Institutes for Research, Pittsburgh, Pennsylvania.

PETER L. BERGER is Professor of Sociology at the New School for Social Research and Editor of the journal *Social Research*.

ARTHUR CHILD is Professor of Philosophy at the University of California, Davis.

DIANA CRANE is Assistant Professor of Sociology at Johns Hopkins University,

IAN D. CURRIE is Lecturer in Sociology at the University of Toronto.

GERARD DE GRÉ is Professor of Sociology at the University of Waterloo, Canada.

JOHN DEWEY (1859–1952) was best known for his work in education and social philosophy. He was one of the earliest American exponents of an interactionist theory of behavior.

VERNON K. DIBBLE is Associate Professor of Sociology at Columbia University.

ÉMILE DURKHEIM (1858–1917), a French sociologist, was one of the most important influences on modern sociology. His direct contributions to the sociology of knowledge are a relatively small part of his total works on such topics as methodology in the social sciences, religious institutions, and factors related to suicide.

FRIEDRICH ENGELS (1820–95) was a German socialist and manufacturer who collaborated with Karl Marx on several major works on economics and ideology.

ERNST GRÜNWALD (1912–33) was a German student of humanities and social sciences. He died at the age of twenty-one.

707

FRANK E. HARTUNG is Professor of Sociology at Wayne State University.

JOHN HORTON is Associate Professor of Sociology at the University of California, Los Angeles.

LEONARD LIEBERMAN is Assistant Professor of Sociology at Central Michigan University.

JAMES McKEE is Professor of Sociology at Michigan State University.

KARL MANNHEIM (1893–1947), a distinguished German sociologist, was best known for his work on the sociology of knowledge, especially *Ideology and Utopia*.

KARL MARX (1818–93), a German economist and social philosopher, was best known for his writings on ideology, economic institutions, and stratification. The Marxian tradition was one of the major influences on early European variants of the sociology of knowledge.

GEORGE HERBERT MEAD (1863–1931) was an American philosopher and social psychologist whose works provided the foundation for social behaviorism and symbolic-interaction theory.

ROBERT K. MERTON is Professor of Sociology and Associate Director of the Bureau of Applied Research at Columbia University.

DENNISON NASH is Associate Professor of Sociology at the University of Connecticut.

VILFREDO PARETO (1848–1923) was an Italian economist and sociologist, best known for his four-volume work on the distribution of power in society, *Mind and Society*.

TALCOTT PARSONS is Professor of Sociology at Harvard University.

SIR KARL POPPER is Professor at the London School of Economics and Political Science.

MAX SCHELER (1874–1928) was a German social and political philosopher widely regarded as the founder of the sociology of knowledge. Although several of his works are available in English, his major writings in the sociology of knowledge have not been translated previously.

MELVIN SEEMAN is Professor of Sociology at the University of California, Los Angeles.

HANS SPEIER is a member of the Rand Corporation Research Council.

MARTIN VOGELFANGER is a Vice-President of Lieberman Research, Inc.

JOHN WALTON is Assistant Professor of Sociology at Northwestern University.

JULES J. WANDERER is Assistant Professor of Sociology at the University of Colorado.

MAX WEBER (1864–1920), a German economist and sociologist, was perhaps the greatest single influence on modern sociology. He dealt systematically with problems in the sociology of knowledge in his works on methodology, authority, social class, bureaucracy, economic organization, and religion.

ROBIN M. WILLIAMS, JR, is Professor of Social Science at Cornell University.

KURT H. WOLFF is Professor of Sociology at Brandeis University.

FLORIAN ZNANIECKI (1882–1957) was a Polish-born sociologist and philosopher who taught at Columbia University and the University of Illinois. He is best known for his theoretical analyses of the structure and process of social action and for his study (with W. I. Thomas) of *The Polish Peasant in Europe and America*.

INDEX

(Page numbers in italics indicate authorship of article.)